D0409194

Also by Gregg Herken

The Winning Weapon:
The Atomic Bomb in the Cold War, 1945–1950

Counsels of War

Cardinal Choices: Presidential Science Advising
from the Atomic Bomb to SDI

BROTHERHOOD OF THE BOMB

Brotherhood of the Bomb

THE TANGLED LIVES AND LOYALTIES OF ROBERT OPPENHEIMER, ERNEST LAWRENCE, AND EDWARD TELLER

GREGG HERKEN

A JOHN MACRAE BOOK

HENRY HOLT AND COMPANY · NEW YORK

Henry Holt and Company, LLC
Publishers since 1866
115 West 18th Street
New York, New York 10011

Distributed in Canada by H. B. Fenn and Company Ltd.

Library of Congress Cataloging-in-Publication Data

Herken, Gregg, 1947–
Brotherhood of the bomb the tangled lives and loyalties of Robert Oppenheimer, Ernest Lawrence, and Edward Teller / Gregg Herken.—1st ed.
p. cm.
Includes bibliographical references and index.
ISBN 0-8050-6588-1 (hb)
1. Oppenheimer, J. Robert, 1904–1967. 2. Lawrence, Ernest Orlando, 1901–1958. 3. Teller, Edward 1908– 4. Physicists—United States—Biography. 5. Atomic bomb—United States—History—20th century. 6. Nuclear physics—United States—History—20th century. I. Title

QC16.O62 H47 2002
539.7'092'273—dc21
[B] 2002017219

Henry Holt books are available for special promotions
and premiums. For details contact: Director, Special Markets.

First Edition 2002

Designed by Victoria Hartman

Printed in the United States of America

1 3 5 7 9 10 8 6 4 2

For Ben

Who can be wise, amaz'd, temperate and furious,
Loyal and neutral, in a moment? No man

—*Macbeth,* Act II, Scene III

It takes an error to father a sin.

—Letter, Robert Oppenheimer to his brother, Frank,
March 12, 1930

CONTENTS

Part Four: Sorcerer's Apprentice

Part Five: All the Evil of the Times

PROLOGUE: DEAD FILES

"THE GREAT DAY when the F.B.I. gives up its dead file is worth looking forward to. We shall then learn . . . what bastards everybody used to be," wrote Nuell Pharr Davis in *Lawrence and Oppenheimer*, a 1968 book on the two physicists and their times. What Davis could not have known—or imagined—is that, some thirty years later, the sources available to historians would include not only the Bureau's "dead files," with its verbatim transcripts of wiretapped conversations, but thousands of pages of declassified U.S. government documents, the intercepted and decrypted secret cables sent between Moscow and its spies in wartime, and even official Communist Party records, released from Moscow's archives following the collapse of the Soviet Union in 1991.

Supplemented by private papers and numerous personal interviews, the historical record now available makes it possible to piece together and to tell, for the first time in detail and with some authority, the story of that turbulent time. The record does indeed reveal "bastards," but it also shows more than a smattering of real heros.

The physicists who are the subject of this book—Robert Oppenheimer, Ernest Lawrence, and Edward Teller—were among the most influential scientists of the twentieth century. Theirs is a story that encompasses not only the making of the atomic bomb and its far more destructive successor, the thermonuclear "Super," but allegations of treason and the political trials that resulted in a Cold War at home.

Much that has happened since—from the nuclear arms race, to the relationship between scientists and their government—has its roots in those days.

Although Oppenheimer's loyalty hearing took place at the same time as the televised army-McCarthy hearings that brought down the Wisconsin senator, it was Oppenheimer's trial behind closed doors that had perhaps the greater and more lasting effect: forty years later, Teller would blame his difficulties in recruiting scientists for "Star Wars," Ronald Reagan's missile defense campaign, upon the outcome in the Oppenheimer case.

It is also, and no less, a human story. For the three who are its focus, putting their science in the service of the state brought great power but, with it, wrenching choices—forcing each to decide, for example between the interests of his nation, his patron, or his friend. It is, among other things, a tale of overweening ambition and the surprising love and loyalty of a brother; one which shows that there can be nobility even in the making of bombs.

Not surprisingly, it is the kind of story that dramatists as well as historians have been drawn to. Yet is it not *Faust* but another of Goethe's works that the plot perhaps most closely resembles. Like *The Sorcerer's Apprentice,* it is a cautionary tale of arrogance, betrayal, and unforeseen consequences; of what comes from invoking forces—both political and physical—that one neither fully understands nor controls.

PART ONE

TEMPLES OF THE FUTURE

Take interest, I implore you, in those sacred dwellings which one designates by the expressive term "laboratories." . . . These are the temples of the future—temples of well-being and happiness.

—Ernest Lawrence,
commencement address, 1938

1

THE CYCLOTRON REPUBLIC

EARLY IN 1939, Ernest Orlando Lawrence, the Berkeley physicist and inventor of the cyclotron, was planning a machine to change the world. It would be the largest and most expensive instrument thus far dedicated to scientific research. Requiring enough steel to build a good-sized freighter and electric current sufficient to light the city of Berkeley, Lawrence's latest "atom-smasher" would, in theory, accelerate elementary particles to an energy of 100 million electron volts, enough to break the bonds of the atom and penetrate to its heart, the nucleus.

Almost a year after German scientists had first observed the fissioning of uranium, the atomic nucleus remained the unexplored ultima Thule of twentieth-century physics. Striking to its heart required giant machines capable of generating energies close to that of cosmic rays traveling from space. At such energies, charged particles, or neutrons, colliding with an atom broke it apart, laying bare its inner workings. The cyclotron was, in effect, a means of replicating the elemental forces of Nature.

Lawrence's first atom-smasher had been an unimpressive glass contraption barely 4 inches across, covered with red sealing wax against vacuum leaks. By 1939, that original cyclotron hung, like a trophy, above the entrance to one of the new laboratories on the Berkeley campus. Unprepossessing, it was yet the stuff of which the dreams of alchemy were made: a twentieth-century philosopher's stone, promising its possessor the ability to transform the elements of matter, once thought immutable.

But, beyond smashing atoms, exactly what the new machine would do remained mysterious even to Lawrence. The prospect he held up to Robert Gordon Sproul, the patrician president of the University of California, was worthy of a pre-Columbian explorer both for its sweeping vision and its lack of specificity: "Until we cross the frontier of a hundred million volts, we will not know what riches lie ahead, but that there are great riches there can be no doubt."[1]

Like Paracelsus, Lawrence promised to turn lead into gold—but in infinitesimal amounts, and at prodigious cost. Mindful of the recent discovery of fission, Ernest chose to emphasize to Sproul another long-held hope of humanity that most scientists, he among them, had until now dismissed as illusory: "we may be able to *tap the unlimited store of energy in the atom.*"

Lawrence's moment of discovery had come a decade earlier, in early 1929. Then an unmarried twenty-eight-year-old associate professor of physics newly arrived from Yale, he was living at Berkeley's Faculty Club and working late nights at the university library. It was on one such lonely evening, while struggling through a recent article by a Norwegian engineer, Rolf Wideröe, in a German journal, the *Archiv für Elektrotechnik,* that Ernest had his epiphany.

Wideröe's article was about a new way of speeding particles to high energies by repeated applications of a lower voltage. Resonance acceleration was an electromagnetic phenomenon without obvious practical application, in which positively charged particles are accelerated sequentially by electrical impulses as they pass through a succession of vacuum tubes. The acceleration ceased only when the experimenter ran out of tubes, or the particles fell out of step with the electrical impulses and spread out, shotgun-like, hitting the tube walls. A diagram in the article showed the vacuum tubes arranged in a straight line, end to end. Since his German was weak, Lawrence was drawn to the diagram rather than the text.

With the intuitive understanding that was always his greatest strength, Lawrence instantly recognized that if the particles could be confined to a circle rather than a straight line, and kept focused by a magnet while electrical impulses accelerated them—alternately pulling and pushing—there might be no limit to the energies obtained. The following day, Ernest excitedly described his idea for a "proton merry-go-round" to Berkeley colleagues.[2]

For $25, Ernest built a tabletop model of his machine, debuting it a few months later before the American Physical Society. Lawrence reported on its promise to a September 1930 meeting of the National

Academy of Sciences.[3] Attached to a kitchen chair by a clothes hanger, it was a sensation among the scientists assembled. The first lilliputian device never achieved the energies that Lawrence promised the National Academy, but proved the principle sound. A twenty-five-year-old graduate student from Dartmouth, Stanley Livingston, helped Lawrence fashion his next machine of durable brass.

Progress thereafter was rapid, for both Lawrence and his machines. In 1930, at the age of twenty-nine, Ernest became the youngest full professor in the history of the University of California. *Magnetic resonance accelerator*—Livingston's term for the proton merry-go-round—gradually gave way to *cyclotron,* a word inspired by the particles' path and the Radiotron vacuum-tube oscillators that propelled them. *Cyclotron* had the additional bonus of sounding futuristic to prospective funders.[4]

An enthusiast by nature, Lawrence began planning larger cyclotrons even before the capabilities of the existing one had been explored. A little more than a year after his first success, Lawrence and Livingston had built a machine capable in theory of accelerating protons to energies of 1 million electron volts. Measured by the diameter of the magnet's pole face, the 11–inch cyclotron was nearly three times the size of their first effort and cost disproportionately more to build: $800. Lawrence installed it, without fanfare, next to his office on the second floor of Berkeley's physics building, LeConte Hall.

That summer, Lawrence and Livingston discovered the principle of magnetic focusing, using soft iron shims between the poles and the vacuum tank to compensate for variations in the magnetic field. Voltages obtained by the 11-inch were doubled, and then doubled again—approaching the energy believed necessary to penetrate the invisible barrier that surrounds the atomic nucleus. Moving gradually up the slope, Lawrence and Livingston crossed the milestone million volts in August 1931. On a visit to New Haven to see his fiancée, Molly Blumer, Lawrence received the good news in a telegram from his secretary: "Dr. Livingston has asked me to advise you that he has obtained 1,100,000 volt protons. He also suggested that I add 'Whoopee!'"[5]

Ernest wed his longtime sweetheart in May 1932. Molly was a tall, statuesque Vassar honors graduate whose father was dean of Yale's medical school. Enrolled in bacteriology courses at Radcliffe, Molly gave up her own promising scientific career to marry Lawrence. While still on their honeymoon, the newlyweds had just returned from a sail on Long Island Sound when Ernest learned in a radio broadcast that British scientists had been first to disintegrate an atom, using a simple voltage multiplier and a few hundred thousand volts. In a properly designed experiment, the 11-inch could have accomplished the same feat a year earlier. Quickly returning to California, Ernest made sure that he and his colleagues got credit for achieving the first atomic disintegration outside Europe. He promised Molly a longer honeymoon later.

The British discovery highlighted the fact that Lawrence's enthusiasm sometimes overcame the discipline necessary to do science. Since he was often more interested in building grand new machines than in doing the hard work necessary to interpret experimental results, Ernest had paid less attention to having sensitive detection instruments.

To remedy that weakness, Ernest imported a friend from his Yale days, Donald Cooksey, a journeyman physicist who specialized in designing detectors. The son of a Yale professor and scion of an old California family, Cooksey had never bothered to finish the language requirement for his graduate degree. Nine years older than Lawrence, Cooksey was more cosmopolitan by far. Ernest's first view of the New York City skyline had come from the roof of the Yale Club, where he was staying as Cooksey's guest.[6] "DC," as he was known, soon became Ernest's factotum, troubleshooter, and confidant at the lab.[7]

Following his embarrassment at the hands of the British, Lawrence proposed an order-of-magnitude increase in the power of his next cyclotron. Early in 1932, he and Livingston had begun sketching plans for a 27-inch machine capable of accelerating particles to energies in excess of 20 million volts.

There would be no more trophies to hang on the wall. In the otherwise relativistic world of cyclotron physics, one linear relationship ruled: an almost direct correlation between input and output. Higher energies required proportionately larger and more powerful vacuum pumps and electromagnets. The magnet for the 11-inch cyclotron had weighed 2 tons. For the 27-inch, Lawrence already had his eye on an 80-ton magnet, originally built for a Bay Area firm, the Federal Telegraph Company, but now obsolete and rusting away in a Palo Alto junkyard.[8]

Bigger machines and an expanding empire also required more room. Lawrence installed the 27-inch in an old wooden building on campus known as the Civil Engineering Testing Laboratory; the forestry and linguistic departments still maintained offices upstairs. He christened the structure, somewhat grandiosely, the "Penetrating Radiations Laboratory," a title later shortened to "Radiation Laboratory." For the growing number of grad students gathering around him, however, it was simply the "Rad Lab," just as their remarkable young phenom of a professor was "EOL."[9]

By sheer force of personality more than by any power of intellect, Lawrence was a commanding presence at Berkeley by the early 1930s.

Although tall and good-looking—he was over six feet, with startlingly blue eyes and a shock of blond hair combed straight back—Lawrence spoke in a tenor rather than a baritone and was never comfortable addressing large groups.

Ernest was born of Norwegian immigrants at the start of the new century. His father, Carl, was school superintendent and later president of a teachers college in Canton, South Dakota. Ernest's mother, Gunda, recalled an early childhood spent in a sod hut on the prairie. Educated at St. Olaf College and the University of South Dakota, Ernest developed values that were decidedly, even determinedly, midwestern.

Yet Lawrence's plebeian background had not yielded egalitarian beliefs. *Primus inter pares* would never be a familiar concept at the Rad Lab. To the cyclotroneers, EOL was "the Maestro" or simply "Boss." Visitors to the lab noticed a single gleaming china teacup and saucer amid the workers' grimy porcelain mugs. Following the morning coffee break, Cooksey locked the cup and saucer as well as a silver-plated spoon in a drawer conspicuously marked "Reserved for the Director."[10]

Like a medieval lord, Lawrence presided over weekly meetings of the physics department's Journal Club—convened promptly at 7:30 every Monday evening in LeConte's library—from a massive red leather chair reserved for him alone. It was the one time that the cyclotron was turned off. Ernest introduced the presenter, usually asked the first question, and brought the proceedings to an abrupt close exactly ninety minutes later with the first ring of the campanile's chimes, even if it meant interrupting the speaker in midsentence.[11]

Colleagues from eastern schools found Lawrence's informal manner popular with students, if somewhat disconcerting. Physicist Henry DeWolf Smyth, visiting from Princeton, was dismayed by one of Ernest's typically boisterous pep talks: "This seemed to me a rather inappropriate talk to a group of graduate students presumably of some sophistication. I found, however, not only that this was the tone of the talk which depressed me somewhat but it seemed to work, which depressed me even more."[12]

Ernest's strict Lutheran upbringing meant that frustrations and setbacks at the cyclotron seldom provoked expletives stronger than "Fudge!" or "Oh, Sugar!" But Lawrence, for all his Scandinavian stolidness, had a quick and livid temper. When it flared, a vein stood out above his left temple—a kind of weather gauge and warning to students and colleagues alike.

Disdainful of most human frailties, Lawrence had a particular intolerance for lying. Once, after berating Molly for not listening to an interview he had given on the radio, Lawrence was brought up short by her reply: "Ernest, would you rather I lied?"[13]

The anodyne to Lawrence's withering temper was his charm, equally celebrated and just as quick to surface. When Northwestern University had tried to lure him from Berkeley, Sproul joined with the head of the physics department, Raymond Birge, to thwart the attempt. As ammunition to persuade the regents to promote Lawrence to full professor, Birge and Ernest's colleagues wrote a long letter to Sproul. In it, Lawrence's affability and winning personality were given almost as much prominence as his research.[14]

Possessed of energy and enthusiasm in seemingly equal measure, Lawrence terrorized the Rad Lab's cyclotroneers—whom he affectionately called "the boys"—when at the controls of the machine. In those early days, starting the cyclotron involved closing a knife-switch. This simple act, noted one of the boys, was sometimes accompanied by an "ensuing sparking, crash, and blowing out of lights," plunging the campus and even adjacent neighborhoods into sudden darkness.[15]

Once the cyclotron was running, Lawrence always tried to coax the maximum voltage out of the machine. A penciled mark next to a slide-switch in the control room indicated the pinnacle reached on the last attempt. Success was measured by the intensity and focus of the ionized particle beam, which emerged into the target chamber as a thin line of bright blue light. These sessions, usually brief, ended when an oscillator tube burned out or the cyclotron's vacuum chamber sprung a leak—whereupon Ernest cheerfully promised to return when the boys had the problem fixed.

Hazards abounded. The popular method of locating vacuum leaks—by playing a jet of natural gas over the sealing wax—was likened by the boys to a race between explosion and asphyxiation. The cyclotron bathed its operators in so much radio frequency energy that it inspired a favorite trick: standing next to the machine, a cyclotroneer could get a lightbulb to flicker in one hand by holding onto a grounded piece of metal with the other.

Frequent electrical faults caused heavy hooks to fall from overhead cages, shorting out the cyclotron with a resounding bang and an overpowering smell of ozone. Water spraying from the cooling system that Cooksey installed—common garden hose, for the most part—sparked fires as often as two or three times a day. The boys then ran around the machine with handheld extinguishers, desperately trying to put out the flames before they spread to the wooden floor, which was soaked with highly flammable transformer oil. (One cyclotroneer, puzzled that strangers at campus parties were always able to guess where he worked, finally realized that the sickly sweet smell of the oil on his clothes was the giveaway.)

Seemingly oblivious to the smoke, water, and stench of burned insulation, Lawrence remained resolutely hunched over the controls, pressing on to higher voltages and more tightly focused beams for as long as the current flowed.[16]

Ernest's obsession was legendary at Berkeley. Late at night or even in the early morning hours, Lawrence—sometimes still in formal wear, having just arrived from a dinner party at Sproul's house—would appear without notice in the control room and demand a report on the current experiment from the cyclotron's stunned operator. These impromptu nocturnal visits came to be known, not always affectionately, as the "bed check."[17] Canny graduate students learned to leave the lights burning, their coats on a hook behind the door, while they stole away for dinner. Cyclotroneers grew used to the sight of Molly sprawled asleep in the red leather chair, following what Ernest had promised would be only a brief detour to the lab before dinner or a movie. Two-year-old Eric, the couple's first child, learned to salute his father's colleagues with a cheery, "How's the vacuum?"[18]

On those occasions when illness kept him at home, Lawrence remained in touch by means of a bedside radio tuned off station to the cyclotron's operating frequency. When the telltale hum ceased, Ernest was instantly on the telephone to inquire whether the machine was down or the boys simply malingering.[19]

By the time he and Livingston broke the million-volt barrier, Lawrence was already an internationally recognized figure among physicists. Notoriety, of course, came with a price. In the company of such august figures as Lord Rutherford and James Chadwick, members of Britain's famed Cavendish Laboratory, and even among young contemporaries like German physicist Werner Heisenberg, Lawrence had the reputation of a headstrong American upstart in a field long dominated by Europeans.[20]

Among the remarkable discoveries of 1932—the *annus mirabilis* of particle physics—was a revelation from the Rad Lab.[21] Experimenting that spring with deuterons (an isotope of hydrogen consisting of a proton and a neutron), Lawrence noticed that atoms struck by the heavy particles not only disintegrated readily but in the process seemed to release more energy than it took to break them apart. For Ernest, this unexpected outcome opened up a sudden vista of cheap, reliable, and virtually limitless energy from cyclotrons.

That June, Lawrence promoted just such a vision in a radio broadcast from the Chicago World's Fair, at the Century of Progress Exposition, where the boys had put a scale-model cyclotron on display.[22] In October, he was the only American invited to the annual Solvay Congress, a prestigious international meeting of physicists in Brussels.

Lawrence's so-called disintegration hypothesis was greeted with skepticism just short of ridicule by the doyens of physics gathered in Belgium. Just weeks earlier, Lord Rutherford had indignantly dismissed as infeasible for many generations the kind of practical application of atomic energy that Lawrence already claimed for his cyclotron. In a much-publicized speech before the British Association for the Advancement of Science, Rutherford had asserted that "anyone who looked for a source of power in the transformation of the atoms was talking moonshine."[23]

Reluctant to contradict the "lion of the Cavendish," Ernest conceded the difficulty of penetrating the atomic nucleus—a feat he had once compared to hitting a fly in a cathedral—but nonetheless defended his new-age cannon, claiming that it all came down to a "matter of marksmanship."[24]

At Solvay, Rutherford maintained a studied silence while younger representatives of Britain's scientific establishment quietly savaged the brash American. John Cockcroft noted, ominously, that other laboratories had been unable to reproduce Berkeley's results. "Inconclusive," sniffed Chadwick. Heisenberg, author of the uncertainty principle, intimated that Lawrence either had not witnessed what he claimed or had misinterpreted the results. Lawrence made matters worse by innocently suggesting that the Europeans were simply handicapped by antiquated and obsolete equipment.[25]

Returning to Berkeley, Ernest set the boys to settling the question of whether he or his critics were right. Within weeks it became evident that his startling "discovery" was actually the result of contamination of the target in the 27-inch cyclotron. The vista of limitless energy evaporated, like a mirage, as quickly as it had appeared. In its wake, Lawrence and his laboratory seemed guilty of slapdash science and a premature rush to the publicist.

For someone less self-assured, the error and subsequent rebuff by his peers might have been devastating. Instead, Ernest's humiliation at Solvay became a valuable object lesson. Notoriously impatient with long-winded mathematics, Lawrence had achieved success to date largely owing to a combination of remarkable intuition and dogged empiricism.[26] "Brawn prevailed over brain," summed up an Italian physicist visiting the Rad Lab.[27] For so long as Lawrence and the boys lacked a theoretical foundation in physics, their experiments would continue to be ill conceived and the results likely to be misinterpreted.

After Solvay, Lawrence the experimentalist resolved to work more closely with his opposite number in the world of physics: the theorists.

One was readily at hand. Robert Oppenheimer had been hired by Birge almost a month before Lawrence but delayed his arrival on campus so that he could finish postdoctoral studies in Europe. Thin and gangly rather than tall, "Oppie" walked with the peculiarly rolling gait of the chronically flat-footed.*[28] Three years younger than Lawrence, he had similarly striking blue eyes. (His face was that of an "overgrown choirboy . . . both subtly wise and terribly innocent," remembered a friend, who compared Oppenheimer's visage to that of the apostles in Renaissance paintings.)[29]

Oppie was another physics phenom much in demand; he had already been successfully courted by Caltech. Oppenheimer ultimately signed contracts with both schools, teaching quantum mechanics at the University of California in the fall and winter, then driving south to teach the same class at Pasadena when Berkeley's term ended in early spring.

It was shortly after he arrived at Berkeley, in August 1929, that Oppenheimer met Lawrence, who was still living at the Faculty Club.

Their personalities were more complementary than similar. On the surface, the two seemed to have little in common. In contrast to Lawrence's solidly midwestern and Lutheran upbringing, Oppenheimer was a Jew and a graduate of Manhattan's elite Ethical Culture School. Oppie had gone on to study at Harvard, Cambridge, and Göttingen, where he received his Ph.D. in physics at the age of twenty-three.

Possessed of famously bohemian tastes, Oppenheimer favored exotic cuisines: a spicy Indonesian dish often served to guests, Nasi Goreng, was rendered as "nasty gory" by Lawrence, who knew to avoid it. Oppie was also an accomplished linguist. (While a postdoc in Leiden, he had given his seminars in Dutch.) But Oppenheimer's fondness for classical allusions and obscure, convoluted metaphors was sometimes irritatingly evident, even in casual conversations with friends.[30] His nervous mannerisms—including the constant flicking of his fingers, stained with nicotine from chain-smoking, when he performed calculations at the chalkboard—stood in contrast to Lawrence's usually detached Olympian calm.

Like Lawrence the son of first-generation immigrants, Oppenheimer was far better off financially. Carl Lawrence had earned $3,000 a year as

* Oppenheimer's nickname varied according to time, place, and associates. It was "Opje" while he was a postdoc in Holland, later becoming "Oppy" or "Oppie" when he moved to California. The *J* at the beginning of his name was given to him at birth by his father, Julius. The initial did not stand for anything, and Oppenheimer rarely used it as an adult. His wife, Kitty, tried—but failed—to get friends to address him as "Robert."

head of the Northern Normal and Industrial School in Aberdeen, South Dakota, and died without a pension. Julius Oppenheimer owned a successful textile-importing firm in New York City. The Oppenheimer family lived in a spacious Riverside Drive apartment overlooking the Hudson River and spent vacations at a rambling white summer home on Long Island Sound. Ernest had sold aluminum cookware door-to-door to help pay for college. At the same age, Oppie had his own twenty-eight-foot sloop, which he christened with an appropriately esoteric name: *Trimethy,* the abbreviation of a particular chemical compound.[31]

Despite having between them what Oppenheimer called "the distance of different temperaments," the two men quickly became close friends. While still bachelors living at the Faculty Club, Lawrence and Oppenheimer double-dated together, spending Thanksgivings at Yosemite and going horseback riding on weekends around the Berkeley hills. Oppie originally thought Ernest's jodhpurs and English saddle a curious affectation—until he realized that, growing up in South Dakota, Lawrence looked upon horses as draft animals. For Ernest, it was a way of distancing himself from his roots.[32]

Oppenheimer introduced Lawrence to impressionism; Oppie's mother, Ella, was a Paris-trained painter who maintained a studio in Manhattan. The art on the walls at the Riverside Drive apartment included a Renoir, drawings by Picasso and Vuillard, a Rembrandt etching, and van Gogh's *Landscape with Plowed Fields.*[33] Oppie likewise broadened Ernest's horizons in classical music. Tellingly, Lawrence favored Beethoven's popular symphonies—the Fifth and the Pastoral—while Oppie preferred the composer's more complex and moodier later work. The String Quartet No. 14 in C-sharp Minor was a particular favorite.

Oppenheimer—who, as an adolescent, had seen a succession of psychiatrists for "dementia praecox" and had at least once contemplated suicide—found Ernest's "unbelievable vitality and love of life" his friend's most endearing trait: "His interest was so primarily active, instrumental and mine just the opposite."[34]

Lawrence's practical nature, simple tastes, and driving ambition served as an antidote to Oppie's whimsical otherworldliness.[35] ("The kind of person I admire most would be one who becomes extraordinarily good at doing a lot of things but still maintains a tear-stained countenance," Oppenheimer once confided to college friends.)[36] Oppie later claimed to have learned of the 1929 stock market crash some six months after it happened, while on a walk with Lawrence.[37]

The differences between them were evident in their attitudes toward material possessions. Lawrence drove a 1927 Reo Flying Cloud, a flashy red coupe with rumble seats which he bought while at Yale in eager anticipation of the move to California. Ernest treated the car lovingly and kept it regularly tuned, washed, and waxed.[38] Oppenheimer arrived in Berkeley driving a battered tan Chrysler roadster that he and his younger brother, Frank, had nearly flipped and later run up the steps of a courthouse on the route west. By the time they reached California, Oppie's right arm was in a sling, and his clothes showed holes from the battery acid that had spilled when the car almost turned over. (It is unclear who was the worse driver. "That he was worried was evident by the fact that when I drove up to the edge of the Grand Canyon he yelled 'STOP!'" Frank later wrote of his brother and the trip.)[39]

Despite their disparate natures, a bond based on mutual affection and respect gradually formed between Oppenheimer and Lawrence. For Ernest, an inveterate tinkerer, Oppie seemed the perfect counterpart. "His type of mind is analytical, rather than physical, and he is not at home in the manipulations of the laboratory," Oppenheimer's adviser at Harvard had warned Cambridge.[40] But to friends at other universities, Oppie quietly boasted that Berkeley, which Lawrence had described as a "Mecca" of physics, was actually a "desert" where a young theorist like himself could make a mark.[41]

When Oppenheimer had to return to New York in 1931 to care for his ailing mother, he asked Lawrence to look after his "fatherless theoretical children." Ernest sent roses to the dying woman's bedside.[42] Later, when Oppie was visiting Harvard, Lawrence sent him frequent updates on the progress being made with the cyclotrons. "I know you are having a good time, but hurry back," Ernest implored.[43]

Settling into Berkeley, Oppenheimer rented the bottom floor of a rambling Craftsman-style house set amid redwoods in the hills above campus. His rooms afforded "a view of the cities and of the most beautiful harbor in the world," he wrote Frank, who was then studying at the Cavendish.[44] Oppie's simple flat on Shasta Road soon became the scene of riotous parties, fueled by the host's trademark 4:1 frozen martinis, served in glasses whose rims were dipped in lime juice and honey. Latecomers were amused to find those who would become the top physicists of their generation, drunk and crouched on all fours, playing a version of tiddlywinks on the geometric patterns of Oppenheimer's Navajo rug.[45] On special occasions, like a dissertation defense, Oppie would take a handpicked group of students to Jack's, a favorite restaurant across the Bay; he ordered the food and always picked up the bill.

During winter vacations, Oppenheimer and Lawrence went on high-speed trips to Death Valley in "Garuda"—the new Chrysler roadster which Robert's father had bought for him and that he named for the flying mount of the Hindu god Vishnu.[46] It was on one such jaunt that

Oppie confided to Ernest that physics and the desert were his two enduring loves.

In summer, a rough-hewn log cabin on six acres in the mountains east of Santa Fe became a sanctuary. Years earlier, Oppie and Frank had come across the cabin while horseback riding in the Jemez range near Cowles. The older brother had first come to the area as a sickly teenager, staying at a nearby dude ranch while he recovered from a bout with colitis. Oppie named the ranch "Perro Caliente" (*hot dog* in Spanish) upon learning that the land was available on a long-term lease from the Forest Service. Between the end of Caltech's term and the start of classes at Berkeley in mid-August, the Oppenheimers and a select band of their friends, which often included Lawrence, spent idyllic days at the ranch.[47]

When Lawrence married, Oppie simply became part of Ernest's extended family. Robert presented the couple with a silver coffee service as a wedding gift. Since Oppenheimer's flat was only around the corner and up the hill from the Lawrences' house, the man the children knew as "Uncle Robert" was a frequent and welcome dinner guest, always bringing flowers—usually orchids—for Molly.[48]

The bond between Oppenheimer and Lawrence was further strengthened by their work together at a time of great ferment in high-energy physics. He and Ernest were "busy studying nuclei and neutrons and disintegrations; trying to make some peace between the inadequate theory and the absurd revolutionary experiments," Oppie wrote Frank in fall 1932.[49]

While Oppenheimer, as a theorist, likely viewed Lawrence's focusing of the cyclotron beam with iron shims as akin to tuning a concert piano with matchbooks, he was surprisingly solicitous of his friend's feelings—in contrast to his attitude toward the rest of Berkeley's physics faculty. Slow colleagues and dim-witted students alike came to be familiar with Oppie's notorious "'blue glare' treatment."[50] Despite his misstep at Solvay, Lawrence was the exception. "For all his sketchiness, and the highly questionable character of what he reports, Lawrence is a marvelous physicist," Oppenheimer confided to his brother in early 1934, adding, "But I think that he is probably wrong about the disintegration of the [deuteron]."[51]

Lawrence, for his part, freely acknowledged his own intellectual debt to Oppie.[52] In a confidential letter to university administrators urging his friend's promotion to full professor, Ernest wrote of Oppenheimer: "He has all along been a valued partner at the Radiation Laboratory, providing on many occasions important interpretations of puzzling experimental facts brought to light in an almost virgin field of investigation."[53]

A growing mutual dependence caused the two men to ignore not only disparate temperaments but other, more significant differences between them. Whereas Ernest was constitutionally unable to feign laughter at an uncomprehended joke, Oppie's sly, enigmatic smile became a distinguishing trait at Berkeley seminars. It was Oppenheimer's fanatically loyal graduate students, not Oppie himself, who made legend the story of how their mentor had read Marx's entire *Das Kapital*—in German—during a cross-country train trip and was learning Sanskrit at Berkeley in order to read the Hindu classics in the original. Yet, in the eyes of more detached observers, like Molly Lawrence, Oppenheimer was, at heart, a poseur.[54]

His values had been influenced, if not shaped, by years spent at the Ethical Culture School, where a pedagogical philosophy known as "American Pragmatism" held sway. As interpreted by the school's German-immigrant founder, Felix Adler, pragmatic ethics taught that there were few ideal, unchanging moral laws, but that values instead evolved over time to fit the needs of society.[55] The result was a kind of high-minded ethical relativism that put the greatest emphasis upon the selfless act—what was known at the school as doing "the noble thing."[56]

The impact of Adler's teachings upon Oppenheimer in later life was evident in the ironic comment of a Dutch physicist who had befriended Oppie at Leiden. "Robert, the reason you know so much about ethics," he observed cheerily, "is that you have no character."[57]

Almost all who knew Oppenheimer at Berkeley agreed that one incident—Oppie's date with Melba Phillips, his first graduate student—was emblematic of the riddle that was his personality. When Phillips had fallen asleep during a drive with Oppie up into the Berkeley hills, Oppenheimer had simply parked the car and left the girl stranded while he walked home. To Oppie's defenders, the episode was an example of their professor's endearing absent-mindedness. To his detractors, including many he had snubbed or humiliated on the Berkeley faculty, it was proof of his casual cruelty.[58]

"I can only think that perhaps when they were such really good friends, maybe they'd never really understood each other yet," noted one of the boys who came to know both Oppenheimer and Lawrence well.[59]

One difference between them had to do less with temperament than with the times. As an experimentalist rather than a theorist, Lawrence was aware that a serpent lived in the garden of high-energy physics. The advent of the 27-inch cyclotron had flushed it out of the grass.

With the increasing scale of his machines came a corresponding rise in cost and a subsequent need to find practical applications. While an experimental apparatus on a laboratory bench provided its own justification, finding funds for an 80-ton behemoth that required constant attention and consumed an enormous amount of electrical power needed a firmer anchor on utility; even if, as Lawrence firmly believed, the ultimate benefit to humanity—knowledge—was real and indisputable. The depression had imposed further parsimony upon science.

Lawrence's stint as a teenage cookware salesman had shown his early talent for raising the funds necessary to do his work. The economy with which Lawrence ran the Rad Lab was likewise notorious among colleagues. Scientists were routinely reminded to pick solder off the floor and reuse it. Lawrence once fired a fellow physicist—a subsequent group leader at Los Alamos—for ruining a pair of pliers.[60]

Lawrence's kitchen-chair cyclotron had given him the necessary foot in the door: a $500 bequest from the National Research Council toward a bigger machine that would reach energies of interest to physics. The expense of each successive cyclotron had increased by almost an order of magnitude, as had the energies achieved. The 11-inch cost less than $1,000. The 27-inch was nearly ten times that amount. In order to pay for getting its huge magnet trucked across the Bay to Berkeley, Lawrence persuaded a scientist-entrepreneur and philanthropist, Frederick Cottrell, that the work going on at the Rad Lab might bear looking into.[61]

But luck, timing, and serendipity also contributed importantly to Lawrence's success. Cyclotrons would probably have remained a theoretical curiosity were it not for the nearly simultaneous progress of vacuum tube technology, itself the result of the phenomenal growth of commercial radio in the early 1930s. Lawrence's introduction to science had come as an amateur radio buff in high school.[62] Merle Tuve, another early experimenter with wireless—and Ernest's boyhood friend on the prairie—later became a department head at Washington's Carnegie Institution.

In another happy coincidence, the oscillator vacuum tubes used in the cyclotron operated near the same part of the radio-frequency spectrum as x-ray tubes made for the diagnosis and treatment of disease. This overlap fortuitously pushed the boys early on into building machines for medical research.

One of Lawrence's graduate students, David Sloan, had already built a 1-million-volt x-ray tube three times more powerful than existing hospital equipment. Sloan's invention interested Cottrell as well as Lawrence's colleagues across the Bay, at the University of California's medical school and hospital in San Francisco. By 1933, radiologists at University Hospital were using Sloan's x-ray tube for the treatment of cancer patients.[63] But Ernest hoped that the cyclotron itself might someday become a weapon in the physician's armamentarium against disease. As he was quick to recognize, the ability of neutrons to penetrate tissue promised to make them useful in the treatment of cancer: a tightly focused cyclotron beam might conceivably destroy malignant tumors while leaving nearby healthy organs untouched. Cottrell's support left Lawrence optimistic about invoking the muse of medicine to pay the bills for his cyclotroneers.

Ironically, Ernest's interest in the biological effects of radiation also stemmed from a concern with how the cyclotron might be affecting the health of the boys.[64] He soon found that there was good reason to worry.

Early in 1934, a husband-and-wife team of physicists in Paris, Frédéric and Irène Joliot-Curie, discovered the phenomenon of induced, or "artificial," radioactivity. Two months later, in Italy, physicist Enrico Fermi proved that radioactivity could also be induced by neutrons, a feat that earned him the Nobel prize.[65]

Both discoveries could and should have been made at the Rad Lab, since neutrons were something that the 27-inch at Berkeley was already producing in prodigious quantities. The tale would later be told that Lawrence had missed discovering artificial radioactivity because the cyclotron and the Rad Lab's Geiger counter were both wired to the same switch—a tale that reflected upon Lawrence's frugality as well as his impatience. But the truth was more damning, if less poetic.

Two years after the Cavendish had stolen a march on the Rad Lab, Lawrence and the boys were still so preoccupied with where they might go that they had neglected to notice where they had been. The strong but variable background radiation that accompanied the operation of the 27-inch had long been attributed to an equipment problem. Evidently, no one had thought to look at a Geiger counter after the cyclotron stopped running.[66] His laboratory's headlong rush toward bigger machines, higher energies, and future funding had caused Ernest, once again, to ignore those more modest instruments that recorded the results of cyclotron experiments.

Maddeningly, Lawrence and the boys were able to reproduce the Curies' results within a half hour of reading about them in *Nature*. The steady clicking of the Geiger counter in the silent control room made it suddenly obvious to the cyclotroneers that they had been creating radiation artificially, and unknowingly, for more than a year.

The Curies' discovery brought changes both big and small to the Rad Lab. On the bright side, the 27-inch promised an unending supply of new radioisotopes, with different properties and as-yet-undreamed-of applications.[67] But whereas it had once been common for tired experimenters to lean against the cyclotron when it was not operating, crude hand-lettered signs went up overnight warning against such behavior. Water-filled metal cans were hastily stacked around the machine to absorb stray neutrons. Whereas the boys had once only to fashion hats from newspaper to protect themselves against the machine's best-known hazard—oil spraying from the vacuum pumps—they now had a more serious concern. "We realized we were wading through a sea of neutrons much more intense than existed anywhere else, and the lab itself was alive with radioactivity induced by cyclotron radiations," one later wrote.[68] Not only the coins in their pockets but even the silver and gold fillings in their teeth were made radioactive by the machine.

Gruesome stories of carelessness around radiation were plentiful and well-known at the lab. All were aware of the tragic fate that had befallen the radium dial painters of the previous decade, who had inadvertently ingested the deadly element by licking the tips of their brushes to get a better point. The bones of the young girls had gradually grown brittle and melted away. Closer to home, the telltale black glove that covered the radiation-scarred hand of one of Ernest's wedding guests still haunted Molly's sleep.

Nonetheless, a kind of disdaining bravado persisted among the cyclotroneers, many of whom viewed overexposure to radiation as a kind of occupational hazard. The attitude of one researcher at the Rad Lab—Joseph Hamilton, a physician from University Hospital—was not so much brave as reckless, or even bizarre.[*69]

Lawrence, tending toward the other extreme, declined even routine chest and dental x-rays. "I'm deathly afraid of cancer," he once confided to a family member.[70]

But Lawrence's caution was sometimes overridden by enthusiasm, or thoughtlessness. Robert Stone, the chief radiologist at University Hospital, recalled how shivers had run down his spine when Ernest first showed him the poorly shielded Sloan x-ray tube in operation at Berkeley. Stone was further astonished to learn that Lawrence had forgotten to budget any funds for shielding the 1-million-volt tube when it was about to be installed in the hospital clinic.[71]

For all that, the only radiation casualty thus far at the Rad Lab had been the tube's inventor, Sloan—who damaged his spine carrying 200-pound pieces of lead battery plate, scrounged from the dump and belatedly seized upon by Lawrence as the answer to the shielding problem.[72]

In summer 1935, Ernest enlisted the aid of John, his physician brother, then teaching at Yale, to deal with radiation concerns at the lab. An early experiment by John provided what seemed at the time a suitable cautionary tale: the boys were left silent and chastened when a laboratory rat placed in the target chamber of the 27-inch was found dead following a bombardment—until the gleeful cyclotroneers discovered that it was asphyxiation, not radiation, that killed the rat.

* Hamilton later achieved notoriety as the physician who oversaw secret human radiation experiments at University Hospital, where three patients were injected with plutonium between 1945 and 1947. Although these experiments were funded by the wartime Manhattan Project and its successor, the U.S. Atomic Energy Commission, Hamilton's apparent intent was to identify so-called magic bullets—radioisotopes that would concentrate selectively in different organs—for eventual therapeutic use.

His brother's visit convinced Ernest that the future of the cyclotron, and perhaps of the Rad Lab, lay in medical research. Both the Macy and the Rockefeller foundations, searching for cancer cures, had meanwhile joined Cottrell's Research Corporation as major backers of Lawrence's laboratory. With showmanship worthy of Barnum, Ernest and John used graduate students, colleagues, and themselves to demonstrate how radiosodium coursed through the body, promising a faster and safer tracer than radium. Moments after volunteers drank a solution of the isotope in water, Ernest or John would follow its path with a clicking Geiger counter.[73]

John eagerly returned to Berkeley the following year, driving cross-country from Yale with a car full of cancer-ridden mice to be used in cyclotron experiments.

The spreading fame of Lawrence and his laboratory was making Berkeley a beacon that attracted physicists from around the world. In 1936, shortly after beating back an attempt by Harvard to lure Ernest east, Sproul agreed to make the Radiation Laboratory an autonomous part of Berkeley's physics department, with Lawrence as its director.[74] Birge, who paid the most for this concession, pronounced himself satisfied with the bargain. But even the physics chairman, who supposedly had jurisdiction over Ernest's growing empire, admitted that he did not really know what went on at the Rad Lab. As Birge wearily remarked to a professor at another school, Berkeley had become less "a university with a cyclotron than a cyclotron with a university attached."[75]

A year later, the 27-inch was transformed into a 37-inch cyclotron; durable rubber gaskets replaced the ubiquitous red sealing wax. Cooksey's prized yellow Packard Phaeton—"The Creamliner"—was used to anchor the hoist that brought the huge vacuum chamber into the lab.[76] In September 1937, the machine reached a record 8 million electron volts. A few weeks later, Lawrence appeared on the cover of *Time* magazine after winning the National Academy of Sciences' prestigious Comstock award. Lawrence used the prize money to buy a cabin cruiser for impromptu overnight trips up the Sacramento River. Although the vessel slept four, Lawrence routinely invited ten of the boys. Molly claimed her husband kept navigation charts onboard just to identify the sandbars they became stuck on.[77]

By late that year, the new cyclotron was being run around the clock to meet the demand for medical radioisotopes, which Ernest and John distributed without charge to hospitals and research laboratories around the world. Tiring of the commute from New Haven, John had finally decided to join his brother permanently on the West Coast.[78] He, Stone, and Hamilton had been the first physicians to put cyclotron-produced radioisotopes to medical use.

Experiments by physics graduate students were suspended for one day a week so that cancer patients could be treated with neutrons from the cyclotron. White hospital screens temporarily hid the oil-covered machinery and the boys grudgingly agreed to don hospital gowns for the day. Cyclotroneers who complained that the medical research tail had begun to wag the physics dog were not-so-gently reminded by Ernest which end it was that brought in the necessary grants.[79]

The Lawrence brothers put their faith in the new medical technology to the test at the end of 1937, when Gunda was diagnosed with incurable uterine cancer. Doctors at the Mayo Clinic had given the sixty-five-year-old woman only months to live. Once a week, John accompanied Gunda on the ferry across the Bay to Stone's clinic, where she received several times the usual radiation dose from Sloan's x-ray tube. The treatments were both painful and debilitating; Gunda often vomited out the car window from radiation sickness on the drive back from the hospital. But the tumor gradually shrank. By that spring, John predicted the eventual full recovery.[80]

The boys had meanwhile been joined by new recruits, drawn to Berkeley like a flame by Ernest's self-proclaimed "paradise of physics." Already a veteran was Edwin McMillan, a shy, soft-spoken physicist who had arrived from Princeton in the winter of 1932. An experimentalist like Lawrence, the two men shared another, more personal bond: Ed was dating and would soon marry Molly's younger sister, Elsie.

Luis Alvarez was still a student at the University of Chicago when he met Lawrence at the Century of Progress Exposition. Despite his Spanish surname, "Luie" was the grandson of Irish-born missionaries and looked Scandinavian. Brilliant, arrogant, and ambitious, Alvarez was recruited to Berkeley by Birge in 1936 but soon concluded that Ernest and the Rad Lab offered more of a career open to talent.[81] While Lawrence would later speak admiringly of "the Alvarez style—something out of the ordinary," for the interim his new star was obliged to share quarters with John's laboratory animals in a smelly building known on campus as the "Rat House."[82]

The most recent new arrival at the Rad Lab was an émigré from fascist Italy. A small, outspoken, and volatile man, Emilio Segrè was a former student of Fermi's. Segrè had been teaching at the University of Palermo when he received a letter from Lawrence that contained a piece of the 37-inch's deflector. From that radioactive metal fragment, Segrè and a colleague had isolated the first man-made element, which they dubbed "technetium."[83] Segrè was visiting Berkeley in 1938 when he learned that Mussolini's anti-Jewish decrees made it impossible for him to return to Italy.[84]

Although Lawrence would later claim to have rescued Segrè from the fascists, some at the Rad Lab—Segrè included—felt that Ernest actually took advantage of the Italian's plight, paying him barely more than a graduate assistant. Behind Ernest's back, the touchy Italian returned the affront—spreading the story that John Lawrence had never really recovered from a blow to the head received in a near-fatal car accident. Segrè also found Oppenheimer's continental pretensions "slightly ridiculous."[85] While resolved to be a good citizen of what he called "the Cyclotron Republic," Segrè nonetheless discreetly sounded Birge out about finding a permanent job in the physics department.[86]

Martin Kamen, a slight and somewhat disheveled-looking chemist from Chicago, was put to work making radiophosphorus for John's medical experiments. The late-night antics and bohemian lifestyle of the twenty-three-year-old Kamen drew pursed lips and disapproving looks from Lawrence but favor from the boys. (In one celebrated contest, initiated by Kamen, inebriated cyclotroneers vied to see who could do the greatest number of pull-ups on the suspension cables of the new Golden Gate Bridge; Kamen won.)[87]

Years later, Kamen would learn about the price of empire the hard way, when he and a colleague in the chemistry department, Sam Ruben, used Lawrence's cyclotron to synthesize the first long-lasting radioisotope of carbon. Like radiosodium, carbon-14 held promise as a biological tracer. When Kamen went to Ernest's home one rainy night to announce the discovery, Lawrence, suffering from a bad head cold, sprang from his sickbed to embrace the young man.

But Lawrence's joy turned to "ill-concealed anger" just days later, Kamen recalled, when the scientific paper announcing the discovery gave Ruben and the chemistry department precedence over the Rad Lab.[88] Lawrence had turned on his heel and wordlessly walked away when Kamen offered him the paper. To the young chemist, the incident showed that not even Ernest was immune to chauvinistic pride, and that there was a dark side to Lawrence's ambition.

Even before the 37-inch cyclotron had reached its theoretical limits, Ernest was looking for new worlds to conquer. Indeed, he already had a bigger machine in mind. At Chicago's Century of Progress Exposition, he had talked about a future "atomic gun which in comparison with the present one will be like a 16-inch rifle alongside a mere one-pounder."[89] At the time there had been no interest in building such a machine, but that changed with the discovery of artificial radioactivity less than a year later.

The next cyclotron would be specifically designed to produce radioisotopes and treat cancer patients. Since it was no longer as a supplicant physicist but as a freshly minted hero of medicine that Lawrence made his appeal, this time he planned to custom build the machine rather than assemble it from scrounged parts. Ernest asked Alvarez to calculate the optimum size of the magnet and McMillan to build the power supply. Edward Lofgren, a young grad student from southern California, was assigned to help McMillan and William Brobeck, the Rad Lab's only engineer.[90]

Lawrence had decided that his "medical cyclotron" should operate in the neighborhood of 20 million electron volts—an energy which, not coincidentally, was also of interest to physics. The pole faces of the new cyclotron would be 60 inches across; its magnet weighed 200 tons. A wealthy University of California regent, William Crocker, offered $75,000 toward construction of a new building on campus to house the machine.[91]

The 60-inch was still under construction in January 1939 when word came of the discovery of nuclear fission in Germany. This time Lawrence and his colleagues learned of the development from the newspapers rather than academic journals. Once again for the boys, surprise and elation rapidly gave way to the frustrating realization that another major find had narrowly escaped them.

On Telegraph Avenue, Luis Alvarez leaped from a barber's chair and ran to the lab upon seeing the headline in the *San Francisco Chronicle*. A graduate student of his, Philip Abelson, had been puzzled for weeks by x-rays emanating from uranium following neutron bombardment. ("I have something terribly important to tell you," Alvarez told Abelson. When the student proceeded to sit down, Luie suggested that Abelson lie down instead.) It was immediately clear to both men that fission was the solution to the mystery.[92]

Within hours of receiving the news, Oppenheimer had given a seminar on atom-splitting at LeConte, and McMillan had fashioned a simple but elegant experiment to demonstrate the phenomenon.[93] Chemist Glenn Seaborg, a Berkeley graduate whom Lawrence had recruited to help with the radioisotope work, walked the streets of the city that evening, incredulous that he and his colleagues had failed to see what was right before their eyes.

But the disappointment that Lawrence felt was soon overcome by the dawning realization of fission's possibilities. "This uranium business is certainly exciting," he wrote Fermi that winter.[94] Ernest had been thinking about building a new and more powerful accelerator since the previous year.[95] This latest discovery gave that project new impetus.

There was, moreover, a certain cold logic behind Lawrence's warm enthusiasm this time. The Germans at Berlin's Kaiser Wilhelm Institute had split the uranium atom using neutrons from a natural radiation source, a small lump of radium. Ernest reasoned that the cyclotron—a much more powerful source of *directed* radiation, able to penetrate to the atom's very core—would yield proportionately more interesting results.

As he had observed in his riposte to Rutherford, atom-smashing was just a matter of marksmanship.

The goal this time would be 100 million electron volts, the threshold of energy believed to hold atomic nuclei together. For the boys, Lawrence's new machine held out not only the promise of exciting discoveries in science but something more personal: a chance at redemption.

That spring, during a nationally broadcast radio lecture, Lawrence spoke for the first time publicly of his plans for a gargantuan supercyclotron. Fully two months before the 60-inch began operating at the brand-new Crocker Laboratory—its pencil-thin blue beam of light reminding the assembled journalists of a science-fiction death ray—Ernest had already moved well beyond the medical cyclotron in his mind.

Lawrence calculated that the next machine would require a 2,000-ton magnet. Artist's drawings commissioned for a lecture tour showed a beam 140 feet long, compared to the 60-inch's 4-foot beam. There was, as yet, no structure on the Berkeley campus big enough to house the mammoth machine, nor any charitable foundation willing to bear its projected million-dollar cost.

But Ernest's hope was that his new machine might yield answers to some of the fundamental questions that the experiment in Germany had raised. Among them, whether other elements could be made to fission, and whether the number and energy of neutrons released by splitting uranium atoms would be sufficient to sustain a chain reaction. On the resolution of that last question, physicists realized, lay the answer to whether atomic energy could be used to propel ships and power industry—or to build a bomb.[96]

True to type, Lawrence chose to focus on the brighter prospect. "We are trying to find out whether neutrons are generally given off in the splitting of uranium; and, if so, prospects for useful nuclear energy become very real!" he enthused in a February 1940 letter to scientists at the Cavendish. Although it went unmentioned, between the lines was Ernest's hope that the vindication of his long-deferred dream at Solvay might be at hand. "It may be that the day of useful nuclear energy is not so far distant after all," he mused.[97]

By contrast, Oppenheimer remained wary and pessimistic. Writing to friends at the University of Michigan, he professed to find uranium and fission more worrisome than exciting, and the potential consequences ominous indeed: "So I think it really not too improbable that a ten [centimeter] cube of uranium deuteride . . . might very well blow itself to hell."[98]

2

A PRACTICAL PHILOSOPHER'S STONE

LAWRENCE'S OPTIMISM EXTENDED to politics. "I still think war is going to be avoided. All this discussion certainly must mean that Hitler is backing down," he wrote to his parents on August 29, 1939, three days before the Germans invaded Poland, sparking the Second World War.[1]

A few weeks earlier, other physicists—European born and hence preternaturally more inclined toward pessimism—had sent a warning letter to President Franklin Roosevelt that proved far closer to the mark.

Leo Szilard was a Hungarian theorist who had fled Germany in 1933, only days before the border was closed to Jews, and found a sinecure at Columbia University. Eugene Wigner, a friend of Szilard's from Budapest, joined Princeton's physics faculty in 1930. Another fellow countryman and theoretician, Edward Teller, had come to the United States in 1935. A professor at George Washington University, Teller in summer 1939 was teaching at Columbia during the day and discussing fission with Szilard at night.[2] Albert Einstein, the German-born physics theorist, was the oldest and by far the best known of their number.

While their leader was Szilard—the letter was his idea—the driving force was Teller, literally.[3] Since Szilard lacked an operator's license, he relied upon Teller and the latter's temperamental 1935 Plymouth to get him to Einstein.

At thirty-one, Teller already had a dark and somewhat moody visage, famously prominent eyebrows, and a noticeable limp, the result of a streetcar accident years earlier in Munich, where he had lost part of his right foot. He possessed an agile, self-deprecating wit, but his easy and high-pitched laugh hid a large and surprisingly fragile ego. (Overprotected by his mother, he "reached adolescence still a serious child with no sense of humor," Teller later wrote. He found the taunts of his schoolmates "intolerable.") Once, in 1934, while Teller was a student at Niels Bohr's famous physics salon in Copenhagen, he had been casually reprimanded by the master for a careless comment. The rebuke was not intended as an insult, and the moment quickly passed. But Bohr's students were surprised to see Teller left pale and shaken by the incident.[4]

Teller's colleagues then, and later, would remark upon his restless, seemingly driven energy. (Teller himself described his personality type as neither "melancholic" nor "sanguine" but "choleric," or quick to anger. Fermi thought Teller the only monomaniac he knew who had several manias.) This peculiar intensity was evident not only in Teller's work but even in his piano playing: friends observed that he played all of Mozart's pieces fortissimo.

Late one evening in March 1939, Teller and a violin accompanist had been in the middle of a Mozart sonata at Edward's home when they were interrupted by an urgent telephone call from Szilard. "I have found the neutrons," Szilard announced melodramatically, in Hungarian—their secret code—before hanging up. Since Teller knew that his colleague's most recent experiments concerned chain reactions in uranium, he had reason to suspect, with Szilard, that the world was headed for grief.[5]

At the end of July, Szilard asked Teller to drive him to Einstein. Despite Edward's car breaking down and another stop along the way to ask directions of a child, the pair finally made it to the famous physicist's summer house on the north fork of Long Island. While Einstein served tea, Szilard persuaded the author of the relativity theory to sign the letter he had drafted, which warned FDR that since "the element uranium may be turned into a new and important source of energy in the immediate future," . . . "it is conceivable . . . extremely powerful bombs of a new type may thus be constructed."[6]

The letter was forwarded to a contact of Szilard's at the White House. The Hungarians sat and waited impatiently for an answer while, in Europe, Hitler's armies began their advance.[7]

Although the outbreak of war briefly brought work at the Rad Lab to a halt, Lawrence insisted that the march of science continue. On September 2, 1939, the day after the war began, the conflict came suddenly closer to home. Ernest received word that John, returning from a European vacation onboard the *Athenia*, was listed as missing after that liner was torpedoed and sunk by a German submarine. For several anxious days, Molly and Ernest sat by the radio awaiting news, until a telegram confirmed that John was among the survivors.

Life at the Rad Lab quickly returned to routine. On only one occasion in those early days had Lawrence been heard to express an opinion on the war. ("That man must be stopped," McMillan heard him mutter while the two listened to one of Hitler's speeches on the radio.) Oppenheimer told friends that Lawrence's aversion to politics stemmed from the fact that Ernest's father had lost his job teaching German during the First World War. Like the rest of the boys, McMillan believed that Ernest did not start taking the war seriously until his brother had almost been killed.[8]

Lawrence's focus since the preceding spring had been upon raising money for what he called the "great cyclotron." During the summer, Ernest had approached the Rockefeller Foundation with a request that $750,000 be devoted to building the machine. That fall, Lawrence appealed to Vannevar Bush—the newly installed president of Washington's Carnegie Institution—and also promoted the giant cyclotron at the annual meeting of the National Academy of Sciences in Providence, Rhode Island.[9]

A flinty New Englander who traced his seafaring ancestry to Provincetown whalers, Bush was dean of the American scientific establishment and a crucial ally for Lawrence. (Trained as an electrical engineer, Bush had a pragmatic approach to life, which was revealed in his choice of hobbies. He took up archery during the war because it required neither expensive equipment nor rationed gasoline.)[10] Ernest was already certain of his standing with Sproul, who had instructed the university's comptroller to "do your best to keep [Lawrence] happy."[11]

On November 9, Lawrence wrote again to Bush, noting that his hopes of getting money from a previous benefactor, dying of cancer, had begun to look dim.[12] Later that afternoon, in the midst of a game at the Berkeley Tennis Club, Lawrence learned that Sweden's Nobel committee had voted him the 1939 prize in physics. The Nobel prize came in recognition of his invention of the cyclotron and the machine's role in producing radioisotopes. Lawrence was the first professor at a state-funded American university to receive one.

It took Cooksey and the boys a week to organize the celebration at DiBiasi's, a cheap Italian restaurant in nearby Albany that was a favorite hangout for Berkeley's cyclotroneers. The centerpiece of the party was a giant cake in the shape of a cyclotron. Since no one was yet certain what the great cyclotron would look like, the 60-inch provided the model. Inscribed on it was a boast that exceeded even Lawrence's lofty ambitions: "Eight Billion volts or Bust!"[13]

For Lawrence, the significance of the Nobel prize was evident soon enough. Confident at last that the machine would be built, he was convinced that it could also begin to grow. Just two weeks earlier, he had spoken of a 120-inch cyclotron with a 2,000-ton magnet. Responding to a congratulatory telegram from Niels Bohr in mid-November, Ernest described a machine with a magnet weighing 3,000 tons.[14] The new cyclotron was still "growing progressively and has now attained the size of four thousand tons—correction four thousand five hundred—the four thousand was yesterday," a visiting alumnus of the lab wrote in mid-December.[15]

By Christmas, the giant cyclotron had swelled to 5,000 tons, with pole faces 184 inches across—the largest diameter of commercially available steel plate. (Until that barrier, Lawrence had reportedly flirted with the idea of submitting plans for a 210-inch machine to Rockefeller. His cyclotron would then outdo the 200-inch-diameter Palomar telescope, also Rockefeller funded.) The cost of the great cyclotron had likewise soared, to $1.5 million.[16]

At that far shore, the supercyclotron finally came to rest. As the maximum obtainable, it had become the minimum acceptable to Lawrence.[17]

Yet for all his grandiose designs, and his success in achieving them, Lawrence still had no clear idea of what his mammoth machine might actually achieve. In a memorandum to Rockefeller trustees that December, he raised the possibility that 100 million volts was the threshold at which nuclear chain reactions could be initiated: "Should this prove to be true we will have a discovery of great immediate practical importance. On the one hand, we will have a practical philosopher's stone transmuting elements on a large scale; and, as a corollary thereto, we will have tapped, on a practical scale, a vast store of nuclear energy."[18] Thus was Lawrence's vision at Solvay boldly resurrected.

But another, competing view of the future lay buried among the telegrams and well-wishes of the previous month. It came from Johns Hopkins physicist R. W. Wood, whose letter showed that Wood saw further and understood even better than its own inventor the destiny of the new machine: "As you are laying the foundations for the cataclysmic explosion of uranium (if anyone accomplishes the chain reaction)," he wrote Lawrence, "I'm sure old Nobel would approve."[19]

On the morning of March 29, 1940, the cream of the country's scientific establishment crowded into a cramped corner office on the second floor of Berkeley's Durant Hall to decide the fate of Lawrence's great cyclotron. The gathering showed not only the concentration of power in the world of American science but also how small and closely knit that world really was.

Two of the six men present were brothers. Arthur Holly Compton was a Nobel prize–winning physicist at the University of Chicago who had gotten to know Lawrence in 1923, when the latter was a graduate student. Arthur's younger brother, Karl, also a physicist, was president of MIT. Vannevar Bush and James Conant, a chemist who was president of Harvard, would soon be made as close as brothers by the war.[20] Lawrence attended long enough to sketch his plans for the big machine on the blackboard and to answer questions before discreetly withdrawing. The outcome was never really in doubt.[21]

Cooksey—it was his office—stopped by long enough to take a photograph of the group laughing at a joke. A figure at the edge of the picture, partly cut out of the scene, was Alfred Loomis, the man who had summoned the great and powerful for the occasion yet remained virtually unknown outside the room.[22]

Loomis was a former Wall Street financier and eccentric whose real advocation was physics, which he indulged at a well-equipped private laboratory on his Tuxedo Park estate some thirty-five miles north of New York City. The Loomis Institute for Scientific Research was located in a Tudor-style stone mansion, complete with turrets and battlements, to which the world's eminent physicists were invited annually to carry out research at their host's expense.[23] Loomis was so taken with Lawrence's project that he promised not only to help raise foundation money but to supplement the budget with his own funds if necessary.

Karl Compton left immediately after the Berkeley meeting to carry the group's endorsement to Rockefeller trustees in New York. Lawrence and Cooksey drove those remaining down the coast to Carmel, where they spent the weekend at Del Monte Lodge, a posh resort overlooking Monterey Bay, at Loomis's expense. Between passing rain squalls, Lawrence and Loomis led picnic excursions to view the sea lions at nearby Point Lobos.[24]

But this seaside idyll was soon spoiled by talk of the war. Arthur Compton was surprised to find Lawrence moody and distracted by events in Europe. Conant and Bush, both recently returned from a tour of England's laboratories, spoke of rumors among British scientists that the Germans were working to harness the energy of fission for a revolutionary new kind of weapon.[25]

Although Oppenheimer had seen the Nazis in action while a student at Heidelberg, the war in Europe initially seemed an abstraction. It only became real when a favorite aunt escaped from Germany in 1937 and moved to nearby Oakland with her son and his family.[26]

Like many on the political left, Oppenheimer remained resolutely opposed to U.S. intervention in the struggle—particularly after the signing of the Hitler-Stalin nonaggression pact in August 1939. "I know Charlie [Lauritsen] will say a melancholy I told you so over the Nazisoviet pact, but I am not paying any bets yet on any aspect of the hocuspocus except maybe that the Germans are pretty well into Poland. *Quel* stink," Oppie wrote to a Caltech colleague that fall.[27]

Oppenheimer's political awakening had occurred only a few years earlier, the result of his association with two individuals.[28]

Jean Tatlock was an attractive green-eyed brunette whom Oppenheimer had met in spring 1936 at a benefit for the Spanish Loyalists organized by his landlady, Mary Ellen Washburn. Tatlock was working on a graduate degree in psychology at Stanford University; her father was a professor of English literature at Berkeley, an expert on Chaucer.

Oppenheimer's students believed that Jean Tatlock had a humanizing influence upon their mentor. ("I need physics more than friends," Robert once wrote to Frank during his bachelor days.)[29] Jean introduced Oppie to the romantic poetry of John Donne.[30]

Theirs was a tempestuous, on-again, off-again relationship. Twice Oppie had come close to proposing marriage, but Jean had drawn away. Finally, after graduation, she had gone back east to medical school, and their passion had cooled with distance. Given to frequent and prolonged bouts of depression, Tatlock wanted to become a psychiatrist.[31]

Intense about politics as well as poetry, Jean had belonged to several organizations on campus and felt a particular affinity for the Loyalist cause. At one point she joined the local branch of the Communist Party. That first fall, when they had begun dating regularly, Tatlock introduced Oppie to Rudy Lambert, a party functionary in nearby Alameda County, and also to Dr. Thomas Addis, a physician at Stanford Medical School who was a recruiter for the party.[32]

Another among Tatlock's circle of radical friends was Haakon Chevalier, a thirty-five-year-old assistant professor of French literature at Berkeley when Oppenheimer first met him in early 1937.[33] Born in Lakewood, New Jersey, of French and Norwegian parents, Chevalier was a big man who combined continental manners with Viking good looks. ("6 ft. 1 in.; 175 lbs.; slender; left cheek twitch, large hands" is how the FBI would later describe Chevalier.) He had led a picaresque life—including a stint as a deckhand on a four-masted schooner during an around-the-world voyage in 1921—before returning to the United States and entering academe.[34]

Following visits in 1932–33 to New York and Paris—the site of what he later described as his own political awakening—Chevalier began attending Communist Party meetings shortly after he came home to Berkeley.[35] Having literary ambitions of his own, Chevalier dreamed of one day writing a semiautobiographical novel describing his private intellectual journey to radicalism. ("A gradual disintegration, disgust with the contemporary world, modern America, various escapes, until at the end he finds a hope in Communism" is how he outlined the protagonist's role in notes taken on the steamer back from Europe.)*[36]

For the interim, however, Chevalier's heroic deeds, like his novel, remained the stuff of fantasy. In 1931, he had married a former student, Barbara Lansburgh, an heiress whose grandfather had built San Francisco's first department store during the Gold Rush. By 1939, the couple had rented a ten-room, Tudor mansion high in the Berkeley hills. The house became the venue for political benefits which the Chevaliers hosted. Money raised from the sale of drinks and orchid corsages went to the Spanish Loyalists, California's farmworkers, and other progressive causes of the day.[37]

Despite surrounding himself with the trappings of affluence, Chevalier remained a zealous defender of the party line throughout the Stalinist purges. When Berkeley radicals, protesting the expulsion of a Communist student from a nearby junior college, were followed back to campus and hounded by the school's football team, Chevalier offered the terrorized students shelter in his faculty office.[38] A week before the Nazi-Soviet pact was announced, he joined a handful of Californians in signing an open letter, later published in *Soviet Russia Today,* attributing to "fascists" and "reactionaries" the "fantastic falsehood that the USSR and the totalitarian states are basically alike."[39]

Oppenheimer had met Chevalier, like Tatlock, at a rally for the Spanish Loyalists; the two men and Oppie's girlfriend subsequently helped organize an East Bay fund-raiser that purchased an ambulance which was sent to Spain.[40] Shortly thereafter, Oppenheimer and Chevalier founded a campus branch of the American Federation of Teachers following a union organizing meeting at Berkeley's Faculty Club. Local 349 apparently spent more time taking controversial stands on international issues than lobbying for higher salaries—a rally at Oakland High School, where Oppie was the featured speaker, attracted only a few members—but the two men remained dedicated to the union nonetheless. Chevalier briefly served as its president; Oppenheimer was elected to the role of recording secretary, where, improbably, he licked stamps and addressed envelopes.[41]

By the late 1930s, Oppenheimer's flat on Shasta Road had become a political as well as a physics salon, attracting "those who desired respite

---

* Wrote Chevalier in a subsequent, fictional account of his friendship with Oppenheimer: "No amount of casuistry, however, could eradicate the fact that in joining the Communist Party, as in taking holy orders or in committing murder, one entered a world that separated one from all those who did not belong to the brotherhood. . . . [i]t was a world of passion, of dedication and sacrifice, and it bore the future darkly in its womb."

from the halls of academe—professors, graduate students, the Berkeley intellectual Left," observed one habitué.[42] The frozen martinis remained, but Bach fugues had been replaced by Mozart's Concerto No. 24 in C Minor on Oppenheimer's custom-built record player. Oppie and Chevalier thought the Allegretto perfect for a revolutionary anthem.

Trips continued across the Bay to Jack's, with the coterie of favored students in tow. Yet dinner now typically followed not a dissertation defense but a political rally.[43] From one of his graduate students, Oppie bought a subscription to *People's World*.[44]

Coincident with the founding of the teachers union local, Oppenheimer and Chevalier also began meeting regularly with a group of like-minded colleagues to discuss the issues of the day. The group usually met evenings, once or twice a month, alternating between members' homes during the school term. Besides Oppie, Chevalier, and Thomas Addis, the regular attendees included Arthur Brodeur, chairman of the Scandinavian languages department at Berkeley; Paul Radin, an anthropology professor on campus; Robert Muir, an employee of the California Labor Bureau, and Lou Goldblatt, a union organizer from San Francisco.[45]

Oppenheimer would later characterize the group as an innocent and rather naive political coffee klatch. To Chevalier, however, it was something much more: "a 'closed unit' of the Communist Party"—in effect, a secret Communist "cell" whose members, part of the CP's so-called professional section, were discouraged from holding open membership in the party.[46]

After Oppenheimer helped Chevalier edit a broadside for a political rally, the two got the idea of publishing a periodic newsletter. Titled *Report to Our Colleagues,* on February 20, 1940, the first edition was sent to faculty members at Berkeley as well as to colleges and universities up and down the West Coast. According to Chevalier, Oppie wrote most of the four-page pamphlet, paid for the printing, and even chose the epigram: "But curs'd is he who is their instrument."*

A second report, bearing a quotation from W. H. Auden, one of Oppenheimer's favorite poets, followed on April 6.[47] Like the first, it closely followed the party line, which at the time strongly opposed intervention:

> Europe is in the throes of a war. It is a common thought, and a likely one, that when the war is over Europe will be socialist, and the British Empire gone. We think that Roosevelt is assuming the

* "For, on lustful kings, / Unlook'd-for, sudden deaths from heaven are sent, / But curs'd is he who is their instrument."

The quotation was from the finale of *The Maid's Tragedy,* a play written in 1622 by Francis Beaumont and John Fletcher, English poets who were contemporaries of Donne. It was vintage Oppie.

> role of preserving the old order in Europe and that he plans, if need be, to use the wealth and the lives of this country to carry it out. We think, that is, that Roosevelt is not only a "war-monger" but a counter-revolutionary war-monger. We think it is this that has turned him from something of a progressive to very much of a reactionary.[48]

"There has never been a clearer issue," April's *Report* noted in conclusion, "than that of keeping this country out of the war in Europe." The second *Report,* like the first, was signed "College Faculties Committee, Communist Party of California."

Oppenheimer's emotional isolation from the war was shaken by the fall of France in summer 1940. Driving back to Berkeley from the American Physical Society's annual meeting in Seattle, Washington, late that June, colleagues were struck by the eloquence and passion with which Oppenheimer denounced fascism as a threat to civilization.[49]

But Oppie evidently remained ambivalent about what he called the "hocuspocus" going on in Europe. As much as a year later, only six months before the attack on Pearl Harbor, he wrote to friends that his "own views could . . . hardly be gloomier, either for what will happen locally & nationally, or in the world."[50]

Thus far, Lawrence had observed Oppenheimer's political activism from afar, with a combination of concern and bemusement.[51] But a telling incident that occurred at this time sparked a blowup between the two friends. When Ernest came across a notice that Oppie had written on the Rad Lab blackboard, announcing an upcoming benefit for the Spanish Loyalists, the boys saw him silently clench and unclench his jaw in rage before wiping the notice off the board. Later that day, Ernest angrily admonished Oppie to never again bring politics into the laboratory. Alvarez, seated nearby at the controls of the cyclotron, was shocked; it was the first time he could remember seeing the two men argue.[52]

By the late spring of 1940, Edward Teller was still waiting for a response to the letter by Einstein and Szilard. Roosevelt had put the matter in the hands of the director of the National Bureau of Standards, Lyman Briggs—a slow-moving, pipe-smoking physicist who was an expert in pedology, the science of soils. Briggs seemed more agitated about the possibility of a security leak than with the prospect of a German atomic bomb. After Briggs excluded Fermi—technically still an enemy alien—from meetings of his Uranium Committee, Teller agreed to go in the Italian's place. While Edward succeeded in getting $6,000 to pay for the graphite needed for the first large-scale fission experiment, he, like Wigner and Szilard, was becoming daily more frustrated at the seemingly glacial pace with which atomic research seemed to be proceeding in his adopted country.[53]

Like Lawrence, Teller had hitherto shown little interest in politics. Although a resident of Washington, D.C., Edward had yet to visit the Capitol or even listen to one of Roosevelt's famous fireside chats. But Germany's invasion of the Low Countries on May 10, 1940, brought a sudden end to Teller's personal isolationism. He canceled previous plans in order to attend the annual Pan American Scientific Conference a few days later, where FDR was the keynote speaker.

Roosevelt appealed to the nation's scientists to "act together to protect and defend, by every means at our command, our science, our culture, our American freedom and our civilization," Teller remembered. For Edward, the moment was one of epiphany: "I had the strange impression that he was talking to me." Indeed, FDR's call to arms was the president's *real* answer to the letter from Einstein and the Hungarians, Teller felt. Roosevelt's twenty-minute speech "resolved my dilemma," Edward later wrote.[54]

That summer, after Teller and a friend, Cornell physicist Hans Bethe, had finished a teaching stint at Stanford, the pair drove down to Pasadena to ask Caltech's famed aerodynamicist, Theodore Von Kármán, how they might contribute to the war effort. Bethe and Teller spent two days at Caltech and several more on the drive back east, discussing the behavior of air behind a shock wave—a subject of great importance to ballistics, Von Kármán had told them. A month later, Bethe mailed their paper to Caltech. Although it was unclassified—neither Bethe nor Teller was yet a citizen—the U.S. Army kept the document behind locked doors.[55]

At Berkeley, meanwhile, the war had brought about changes both subtle and large. Since travel across the Atlantic was deemed too hazardous, Ernest received his Nobel prize at a ceremony in Berkeley's Wheeler Hall. Sweden's consul general stood in for the king.

But the bad news from Europe could do nothing to dim the luster of Lawrence and his laboratory. In February 1940, *Life* magazine featured a two-page color photograph of the new medical cyclotron at the Crocker lab.[56] "There are no insurmountable technical difficulties in the way of producing greater cyclotrons," Ernest told a reporter from the campus newspaper, adding that only "financial" obstacles remained. "This problem has now been handed over to the University president," he observed imperiously.[57]

Because of the Nobel prize, Lawrence had also begun to receive recognition from the world outside science and medicine. That March, he was invited to a "Young Men of the Year" banquet at the Waldorf-Astoria organized by Minnesota governor Harold Stassen. Lawrence was thrilled to be the only physicist in a constellation of ten notables that included Spencer Tracy and Lou Gehrig.[58]

In early April, the news that Lawrence had been anxiously awaiting finally arrived in a telephone call from Rockefeller's Warren Weaver, who confirmed the foundation's grant of $1.15 million for the great cyclotron. Ernest told Weaver that he expected completion of the big machine by late June 1944—presuming no "unforeseen difficulties" intervened.[59]

Ebullient, Lawrence telegraphed his thanks to Bush. Lawrence showed his gratitude to Alfred Loomis in more tangible fashion: he and Karl Compton sponsored Loomis for membership in the National Academy of Sciences. Recognition by his peers in academe was one of the few things that had eluded Loomis in his life, but there was perhaps nothing he valued more.[60]

Operating behind the scenes, Alfred continued to make the big wheels turn for Ernest. While Lawrence was in New York for the Waldorf-Astoria dinner, Loomis introduced him to Edward Stettinius, president of U.S. Steel, who promised to set aside enough metal from the current mobilization to build the big accelerator. Following Loomis's similar appeal to the Guggenheims, the Phelps Dodge Corporation agreed to supply 400 tons of copper at a bargain rate for the machine's magnetic coils.[61]

In addition, Loomis continued to support Lawrence in his traditional way. With Sproul's approval, the wealthy entrepreneur established a $30,000 unrestricted bequest at the university for Lawrence's personal use. Because of the Loomis fund, Molly could henceforth accompany Ernest on his increasingly frequent trips back east.[62]

Lawrence had meanwhile located another prospective donor for the giant machine while on a visit with out-of-town guests to the Golden Gate International Exposition on Treasure Island. As others in his entourage watched the Folies Bergère, Lawrence mentally sized up the portable steel-frame structure that had been custom-built for the show.[63]

With his appeal to the Folies pending, Lawrence eyed a prospective building site on campus, in Strawberry Canyon, where a stream meandered through tall redwoods. Current occupants included the university's poultry husbandry department. But Sproul soon offered Ernest a better and far more prominent location: the summit of Charter Hill, where a big white *C* stood out against the green grass.[64] Lawrence no doubt thought it appropriate that the Rad Lab would henceforth occupy the heights above campus, next to the university's symbol.

⚛

Gradually, however, despite Lawrence's efforts, the overseas conflict began to impinge upon his Mecca.[65] He felt the possibility of an atomic bomb "in his bones," Ernest told Arthur Compton that spring.[66]

Still, Lawrence was too busy fixing teething problems with the 60-inch and promoting the great cyclotron to carry out the work that might have settled the question of whether a uranium bomb was feasible. Not enough of the element's scarce fissionable isotope, U-235, had yet been separated from natural uranium, U-238, to conduct the necessary experiments in any case. The physicist whom Briggs asked to carry out that task, Minnesota's Alfred Nier, had run into difficulties trying to "soup up" the apparatus he was using to separate the isotopes.[67]

Others in Berkeley and at the Rad Lab had already begun to respond to the clarion call. At the army's request, Alvarez designed a Geiger counter that could be concealed in a book and smuggled into Germany, in an effort to determine if the Nazis were already at work on a fission weapon.[68]

McMillan and Segrè were engaged in a search for as-yet-undiscovered fissionable elements, farther up the periodic chart than uranium. Abelson, now at Washington's Carnegie Institution, returned to Berkeley that spring for a brief working vacation to help out. By bombarding uranium with neutrons in the 60-inch, Abelson and McMillan created a previously unknown and unstable transuranic with an atomic weight of 93. It decayed after two days to a stable new element with an atomic weight of 94. Following the convention, McMillan named element 93 "neptunium," for the planet next in line after Uranus. Abelson's vacation ended before he and McMillan could prove the existence of element 94, so it remained unnamed. Since neptunium had many of the same properties as uranium, however, both it and the mysterious 94 seemed logical candidates for fission.[69]

On the same day in June 1940 that Abelson and McMillan announced their discovery in the *Physical Review,* the Germans entered Paris.

The Hungarians were not the only ones frustrated at the somnolent pace of Briggs's Uranium Committee. Bush, Conant, and Karl Compton joined with National Academy of Sciences's president Frank Jewett later that month to lobby for an organization that would mobilize America's scientific manpower. Headed by Bush, the National Defense Research Committee would become the dynamo behind technical ideas aimed at helping win the war, if and when America entered the conflict.

Bush moved quickly to have the NDRC assume oversight of Briggs and the Uranium Committee.[70] Although it was too late to keep Berkeley's discovery of neptunium under wraps, Bush suggested a voluntary moratorium upon the publication of scientific papers dealing with uranium and fission. By informal agreement among the scientists themselves rather than by government fiat, the age of discovery in high-energy physics had come to an end, at least for the duration.

Lawrence returned to the Rad Lab from vacation in August, disappointed that so little progress had been made in atomic research during his absence. Nonetheless, he remained unwilling to take a more direct role in preparing the nation for war.[71] Ernest also brushed off an appeal from Columbia University chemist Harold Urey that he join in endorsing the interventionist cause.[72]

A few days later, Bush tried another approach: flattery.[73] He hoped to recruit him to head "a sort of fire department," Bush wrote Lawrence, emphasizing that he would not have to abandon his work at the Rad Lab.[74] The kind of organization that Bush had in mind would have started fires under recalcitrant research problems, not put them out. But, while Lawrence agreed on the need for such an effort, Bush himself abandoned the idea when Ernest pointed out that senior scientists would surely object to reporting to a younger man.[75]

On October 2, 1940, Bush telegraphed Lawrence again, this time with a single urgent question: "When could you come for conferences important matter?"[76]

The meeting to which Lawrence was summoned dealt not with the atomic bomb but with a new British invention: microwave radar. It took place over the weekend of October 12–13 at Alfred Loomis's mansion-laboratory. Bush, Karl Compton, and the Cavendish's John Cockcroft also attended. Loomis was the logical host, since his institute had done some of the earliest work in the country on radar detection. (Loomis's colleagues had invented the world's first portable radar gun, successfully testing it the previous summer on unsuspecting motorists traveling a nearby highway. "For the Lord's sake, don't let the cops know about this," one researcher reportedly warned.)[77]

Of immediate interest to the British, of course, was using radar to detect and intercept the German bombers that were then attacking London in the Blitz. While the key invention, the cavity magnetron, came from a laboratory in England, the British wisely realized that their wealthy American cousins had a better chance of improving radar in time for it to make a difference in the war.

The group chose a site at MIT for the radar work, giving it the deliberately misleading title "Radiation Laboratory" in hopes of deceiving Nazi spies. Lawrence resisted Loomis's appeal that he head the enterprise.

Instead, Ernest picked its director, Rochester University physicist Lee DuBridge, a Lawrence protégé, and further demonstrated his commitment to the cause by volunteering two of his best scientists, McMillan and Alvarez, for the East Coast Rad Lab. By November, the duo was already on their way to Cambridge. Oppenheimer gave each a bottle of whiskey as a going-away gift; Cooksey arranged for the university's brass band to serenade the departing heroes on the train platform.[78]

The reason for Lawrence's reluctance to personally take part in the scientific mobilization for which he had become a willing recruiter was already beginning to take shape on the land above campus. In August, construction had begun of the steep road that would wind up Charter Hill to the site of the 184-inch. Early that October, the 1,000-ton concrete base for the cyclotron was poured. The first shipment of steel was trucked up to the construction site at the end of the month. By November, the metal skeleton of the distinctive twenty-four-sided building that would house the machine had begun to go up.[79]

Following McMillan's departure, the job of identifying the properties of element 94 had been taken over by Seaborg and Segrè. In December, while at Columbia University on a recruiting drive for MIT's radar lab, Lawrence volunteered use of the 60-inch to create enough of the element for experiments.

Because of the war, funding at least had ceased to be a problem for Berkeley's Rad Lab. No longer was Lawrence's enterprise dependent upon the largesse of foundations and grants from philanthropists. By underwriting the investigation into elements 93 and 94, the NDRC supplemented the Rad Lab's budget with monies from another and most welcome source: the federal government.

The change was both sudden and apparent. "This war is achieving alterations we would never have seen under other circumstances, Kamen wrote to McMillan at MIT.[80] Depression-era parsimony had ended. Given free rein to purchase equipment from a scientific catalog, Kamen ordered one of everything in the book—including "a 'Podbielniak fractional distillation apparatus' with gold-plated seals and ground joints, which cost in the neighborhood of a thousand dollars and which I included mostly out of curiosity to see what such an apparatus looked like." Cooksey took one quick look at Kamen's request and suggested he triple it.[81]

Taking the place of the boys was an unfamiliar army of young engineers and technicians who were put to work building the 184-inch. Strapped for personnel because of the draft, the Rad Lab's personnel manager turned to Hollywood. The man he put in charge of fabricating sheet metal for the new cyclotron had previously made fake armor for the movies' medieval knights.[82] For the first time, the magnet yoke of the 60-inch was no longer large enough to accommodate the lab's research staff in the annual holiday party photograph. "The esprit has perked up considerably with everybody conscious of the necessity to work like the devil," wrote Kamen to his homesick compatriots in snowy Boston.[83]

Early in 1941, as the war news worsened, Lawrence resolved to focus attention upon what seemed the most stubborn roadblocks on the way to a bomb. Separating uranium was highest on his list. Three different methods were then being investigated under NDRC sponsorship: a high-speed centrifuge, diffusion through a permeable membrane, and electromagnetic means. All three relied upon the slight difference in mass between natural uranium, U-238, and its lighter, more fissionable isotope, U-235.

The centrifuge and gaseous diffusion, deemed most promising, were being studied at the University of Virginia and Columbia, respectively. The third method, electromagnetic separation, was the means that Minnesota's Nier had used to obtain the tiny amount of U-235 available. But the difficulties had been so great that Nier himself dismissed the electromagnetic method as simply not feasible on an industrial scale.[84]

Lawrence was not so easily discouraged. The apparatus that Nier had used, a mass spectrograph, was mechanically similar to a cyclotron; both required a powerful magnet, a vacuum chamber, and a high-voltage power supply. Lawrence ordered the boys to investigate the feasibility of converting the idled 37-inch into a mass spectrograph for separating uranium.

In early March, Lawrence used the occasion of a Charter Day dinner to urge Conant to "light a fire under" Briggs.[85] Visiting MIT in mid-month, Lawrence repeated his concern with the pace of the Uranium Committee to Karl Compton and Alfred Loomis. Lawrence also told of his own plans to convert the 37-inch and to carry out uranium experiments at the Rad Lab. In relaying Lawrence's message, Compton went so far as to suggest that Bush appoint Lawrence his deputy until the uranium project was as well launched as MIT's radar lab.

Initially fearful that Lawrence might decide to sit out the war, Bush now worried about Ernest usurping his authority. While insisting that he was "running the show," Bush named Lawrence to a recently appointed scientific panel, headed by Arthur Compton, which was meant to take things out of Briggs's hands and bypass the Uranium Committee.[86]

On May 17, 1941, Compton's panel submitted its first report. Listed under the category of things that it said fission might make possible were radiological poisons and a new form of propulsion for ships and submarines. But the atomic bomb was a distant third on the list, and nowhere, Bush felt, was there a sense of urgency. Unsatisfied with this first effort, Bush and Conant urged Compton to take another look, adding two engineers to the panel for the purpose.

In the interim, Lawrence had received information that seemed to move the atomic bomb closer to realization. Seaborg and Segrè, having completed their experiments with the mysterious element 94, pronounced it not only fissionable but nearly twice as likely as U-235 to sustain an atomic chain reaction. Ernest immediately telephoned the news to Compton, who passed the word to Bush.

Due to the illness of his daughter, Margaret, Ernest missed the meeting that drafted the second report, which Compton sent to Bush in mid-July. In it, the news about element 94 received curiously little prominence. Indeed, the second report remained substantially unchanged from the first and expressed "primarily the engineers' point of view," Compton sniffed.[87] Hoping in vain to drum up some enthusiasm for a bomb, Lawrence had appended his own memorandum announcing the fissionability of element 94.[88]

Before Bush sent the panel back for a third try, he decided to reorganize the government apparatus that was preparing the country for war. The NDRC was superseded in June 1941 by a larger umbrella organization, the Office of Scientific Research and Development, which reported directly to Roosevelt. Bush took control of OSRD, leaving the NDRC to Conant.[89]

While he was certainly patriotic, Lawrence's reasons for belatedly rallying to the colors were not wholly altruistic. The slowly accelerating mobilization had opened his eyes to what could be done in science with government support. Alvarez remembered Ernest returning from meetings at MIT's Rad Lab with Loomis, bubbling over about the possibilities if one had the money, the resources, and the motivation.[90]

With German tanks rolling across Russia by July, motivation was soon in abundance. But Bush cannily declined to give construction of the 184-inch a wartime priority as a way of keeping a rein upon Lawrence.[91]

It was a visitor from overseas that fall who finally spurred Ernest to action. An Australian-born physicist working at the Cavendish, Marc Oliphant had been one of those to challenge Lawrence's disintegration hypothesis at the Solvay Congress.[92] By mid-1941, Oliphant shared the worry of his British colleagues that their American counterparts, Lawrence included, were too sanguine about fission's peaceful potential and too naive about its prospects for a bomb.[93]

Weeks earlier, England's scientists had come to their own conclusions about the feasibility of a uranium weapon. Their top-secret M.A.U.D. report speculated that as little as 22 pounds of U-235 might be required for a bomb. The British also estimated that building the device would take approximately two years and cost $25 million. As with radar's cavity magnetron, they had deliberately leaked the secrets of the M.A.U.D. report to the Americans. But Briggs, in another fit of security-inspired paranoia, locked the document in his safe, leaving his Uranium Committee colleagues in the dark.[94]

Oliphant had come to Washington in late August to find out why there had been no reaction to the M.A.U.D. report and was "amazed and distressed" to discover the reason. He flew to California to brief Lawrence, the only person Oliphant trusted to salvage the situation.[95]

On Sunday, September 21, 1941, Lawrence drove Oliphant up the twisting dirt road of what was already called "Cyclotron Hill" for the obligatory tour. Cooksey took a picture of the two men standing next to the magnet frame for the 184-inch—which sat, like the magnet itself, out in the open, surrounded by a green sward of grass and weeds. Returning to Lawrence's office, the two were joined by Oppenheimer. As Oliphant proceeded to tell the Americans about the M.A.U.D. report, he realized, from Oppenheimer's expression, that it was the first Oppie had heard of plans to build an atomic bomb.[96]

Oliphant's visit made Lawrence more confident than ever that a fission bomb could be made to work. Ernest set out with his characteristic energy to spread the word and was soon dismayed at the response. At Lawrence's urging, Bush and Conant agreed to see Oliphant, but were unwilling at that meeting even to acknowledge the existence of the M.A.U.D. report, since it had not yet been officially transmitted to the U.S. government. ("Oliphant's behavior does not help the cause of secrecy!" Conant wrote in a peeved note to Bush afterward.)[97]

Lawrence had also contacted Arthur Compton and relayed Oliphant's news, coloring it with his own opinion that such a weapon "might well determine the outcome of the war."[98] Compton told Lawrence that he should make his case to Conant personally. The Harvard president and Lawrence were scheduled to be Compton's guests the following week, at a celebration honoring the fiftieth anniversary of the founding of the University of Chicago.

On a chill evening in late September, following a lecture by Ernest at Chicago's Museum of Science and Industry on the medical uses of the cyclotron, Lawrence and Conant stood huddled before Compton's fireplace with their host.[99] Over coffee, Lawrence gave a brief account of the recent research in Britain, summarized the work he was planning to undertake at Berkeley, and spoke with some passion—he was "very vigorous in his expression of dissatisfaction," Compton recalled—of Washington's complacency in the face of mounting evidence of German interest in an atomic bomb.[100] Compton, content to remain in the background, chimed in occasionally to echo Lawrence's message.

Lawrence had gone to Chicago merely intending to play the role of cheerleader for the bomb project.[101] Just three days earlier, he had written to Cottrell's Research Corporation with assurances that the Rad Lab intended to continue its basic research into high-energy physics, despite the war.[102] Construction of the giant cyclotron had resumed earlier that month, after Bush finally granted the 184-inch a defense priority. Lawrence hoped to carry out the first trials of the machine sometime in 1943, a full year ahead of schedule.[103]

Moreover, the concrete foundation for a major addition to the Crocker lab had just been poured the previous May. Ground-breaking for another new edifice, the Donner Laboratory, where John would carry out biomedical experiments, followed in June. He was overseeing "at least a three-ring circus," Ernest recently wrote a friend.[104]

To Lawrence's surprise, it was Conant who seized the initiative in the meeting at Compton's house, bringing Ernest up short with what amounted to an ultimatum.[105] Claiming that he was considering putting the uranium project "in wraps," Conant asked Lawrence if he were willing to devote the next several years of his life to building the bomb that he saw as so important. Caught unawares by Conant's question, Ernest hesitated for a moment, openmouthed, before responding. "If you tell me this is my job, I'll do it," he said finally.[106]

Lawrence and Conant asked Compton to convey the new, now-collective sense of urgency to Vice President Henry Wallace, an amateur expert in plant genetics and thus the closest thing to a scientist in Roosevelt's high circle.[107] Compton left by train the following day on a *tour d'horizon* that ultimately took him not only to Washington but also to see Fermi and Urey at Columbia and Wigner at Princeton. All affirmed Lawrence's view that a bomb could be made and would work.[108]

But, for Bush, still a nagging concern was Lawrence's cavalier attitude toward security in the project. On more than one occasion, the head of OSRD had told Conant that Ernest could not be trusted to keep a secret. For the past year, Lawrence had been complaining to various scientists about Briggs, when even the existence of the Uranium Committee was still a secret. More recently, as they gathered in Compton's living room, Conant had reprimanded Ernest for telling Oppenheimer about the bomb without authorization.[109]

On October 9, 1941, Roosevelt authorized Bush to speed up the preparatory work in any way possible. The president also decided that he would look to a small group of senior advisers—the so-called Top Policy Group—to make recommendations on whether to proceed with building the weapon and subsequent steps he should take.[110] Later that day, Bush asked Compton's review panel to take a third and final look at how the project might be organized.[111]

On his own, Bush put together a short list of scientists to advise OSRD on the bomb. Bush sent the list to the National Academy's Frank Jewett, along with a self-justifying apologia for earlier delays: "Much of the difficulty in the past has been due to the fact that Ernest Lawrence in particular had strong ideas in regard to policy, and talked about them generally."[112] Bush had already decided who he did *not* want to head the group. Since the project "would have to be handled under the strictest sort of secrecy," he wrote Jewett, "I hesitate at the name of Ernest Lawrence."[113]

Alarmed by Lawrence's volubility, Bush and Conant were torn over who else to initiate into the secret bomb project. It was already obvious that Berkeley's top theorist was aware of what was afoot. Moreover, the next report by Compton's panel would necessarily need to come to some conclusions about the internal workings of an atomic bomb—conclusions based upon complex calculations involving hitherto unimaginable pressures and temperatures, which only a theoretical physicist could provide.

Compton had been having trouble getting answers to such questions from the Uranium Committee's head theorist, Wisconsin's Gregory Breit. Physical chemists W. K. Lewis from MIT and George Kistiakowsky from Harvard, as well as Robert Mulliken, a physicist at Chicago, had been hurriedly added to the review panel to fill in the gap. Recognizing the urgency of the task, Compton scheduled a meeting of the expanded group for Tuesday, October 21, at General Electric's research laboratory in Schenectady, New York.[114]

A week before the meeting, Lawrence cabled Compton with a request that he be allowed to add another name to the roster: "Oppenheimer has important new ideas. Think it desirable he meet with us Tuesday. Can you arrange invitation?"

Compton telegraphed back that Lawrence was welcome to bring Oppenheimer, but suggested instead that Ernest simply relay Oppie's ideas—"to avoid duplication travel cost." Lawrence countered that, if necessary, he would use the Loomis fund to pay for his friend's travel. "I have a great deal of confidence in Oppenheimer," Ernest added, "and, when I see you, I will tell you why I am anxious to have the benefit of his judgment in our deliberations."[115]

3

A USEFUL ADVISER

By mid-1941, Oppenheimer probably welcomed the opportunity to become involved in the bomb project—if only out of simple loneliness and boredom. "The situation in Berkeley & here in Pasadena is in some ways very gloomy . . . almost all the men active in physics have been taken away for war work," he wrote to friends that May.[1] Oppie predicted "that physics in our sense will just about stop by next year."

But Oppenheimer may also have begun to feel guilty about sitting out the war. The German invasion of the Soviet Union in June had caused a sudden turnabout in the Communist Party's position on intervention.[2] There would not be a third *Report to Our Colleagues*. In October, Lawrence and Oppenheimer—his ticket paid by the Loomis fund—boarded the eastbound streamliner *City of San Francisco* for the final meeting of Compton's panel.

Ernest opened the Schenectady meeting by reading aloud Oliphant's summary of the M.A.U.D. report. The discussion ranged widely, with various techniques for separating uranium being debated. But the group agreed that the electromagnetic method—Lawrence's approach—deserved "especially urgent attention."[3]

Oppenheimer's contribution included an all-important estimate of how much uranium would be necessary for a bomb. Oppie had calculated that a critical mass of U-235 might weigh more than 200 pounds. This estimate accorded closely with a guess made earlier by Fermi, but was nearly ten times the figure cited in the M.A.U.D. report. The difference depended upon assumptions made about the bomb's efficiency, one of the most difficult things to calculate.[4]

Compton confronted the group with other frustrating unknowns: how long would it take to build a weapon, and what would it cost? Unable to prod the engineers on his panel even to speculate, Compton hazarded his own guesses: three to five years to build the bomb, at a cost of "some hundreds of millions of dollars."[5] He decided against including a cost estimate—"lest the government should be frightened off."

Disappointed and vexed by such indecision, Lawrence and Oppenheimer left for California the following day, October 22. On the streamliner, Lawrence drafted an angry letter to Compton, decrying the panel's timidity and hinting darkly that any failure would be on Compton's head.

> It will not be a calamity if, when we get the answers to the uranium problem, they turn out negative from the military point of view, but if the answers are fantastically positive and we fail to get them first, the results for our country may well be a tragic disaster. . . . I feel strongly, therefore, that anyone who hesitates on a vigorous, all-out effort on uranium assumes a grave responsibility.[6]

What Lawrence did not tell Compton was that he had already decided to proceed on his own in the bomb project—with Oppenheimer's help.[7]

Thus far, Nier's spectrograph had produced only minute traces of U-235. At the current rate, it would take some 25 million years to produce the amount of uranium that Oppenheimer thought necessary for an atomic bomb.

In early November, Lawrence went to see Nier in Minnesota, "to see if he could not 'steam up' his output and produce the needed quantities in a hurry."[8] His visit convinced Ernest that Nier was not up to the task, and that the "only immediate recourse was to undertake the job ourselves at home." Indeed, Nier himself arrived at the Rad Lab soon afterward to help with the conversion of the 37-inch. The boys began dismantling the cyclotron under Brobeck's direction later that month.

Originally content to wait for the British to determine the fissionability of U-235, Ernest was no longer willing to let others set the pace.[9] Since his return from Schenectady, the cyclotroneers had begun working late into the night and on weekends.

On November 27, 1941, Lawrence received a further push from the final report of Compton's panel, whose conclusion this time was brief and unequivocal: "A fission bomb of superlative destructive power will result from bringing quickly together a sufficient mass of element U-235."[10] The chief uncertainty remaining was how much uranium would be necessary for a bomb. Here Compton had hedged his bets, citing a range of estimates—from less than 5 to more than 220 pounds—an answer which reflected the persisting ignorance about the properties of U-235.

While Compton's brief summary noted that both the centrifuge and gaseous diffusion were approaching practical tests, there was only a vague allusion to "other methods . . . which may ultimately prove superior, but are now farther from the engineering stage."[11] No specific mention was made of the electromagnetic method on which Lawrence had begun to pin his hopes.

Sick in bed with a bad cold on November 27, Lawrence dictated a congratulatory letter to Compton. But, in Ernest's eyes, the panel's final report hardly mattered. "The boys here already have their 37-inch mass spectrograph between the poles of the magnet," he exulted.[12]

While Lawrence understood that transforming a cyclotron into a working uranium separator was not a simple matter, the concept behind the mass spectrograph, at least, was straightforward enough—relying upon the slight but unvarying difference in mass between isotopes to carry out the separation, atom by atom.[13]

In principle, it was not unlike pitching rocks into buckets. In the spectrograph, an electrically charged beam of ionized uranium atoms bent by a magnet would split into two, carrying U-238 farther from the source than the lighter isotope, U-235, because of the heavier isotope's greater mass. When the uranium hit the metal collector "bucket," the ions gave up their charge and the vapor condensed as microscopic flakes of metal. By repeating the process—putting the contents of the closer bucket back into the beam—further concentration, or "enrichment," of the U-235 would result.[14]

While the theory was simple, the practical difficulties were many. Since the difference in mass between U-238 and U-235 was barely 1 percent, this translated—even under ideal circumstances—into a separation of 3/10 inch between collectors for a beam with a 4-foot arc. In reality, this distance was almost vanishingly small.

Yet even before the practical problems of separating uranium by this method had been given serious consideration, a seemingly insurmountable theoretical barrier threatened to put an end to the work. The prevailing wisdom was that a powerful, narrowly focused beam would be impossible in a mass spectrograph because of an elemental fact of physics: electrostatic repulsion would force any stream of ions bearing the same charge to spread out, defocusing the beam and making the process unworkable.[15]

The "space charge" problem had persuaded Nier and Britain's M.A.U.D. committee that gaseous diffusion remained the most promising method of separating uranium. The Uranium Committee told Princeton physicist Henry Smyth early in 1941 that electromagnetic separation on an industrial scale "had been investigated and was considered impossible."[16] Among physicists, only Lawrence persisted in believing that intuition and an empirical approach could, once again, defeat the pessimism of the theorists.

That faith was to be tested in the coming days and weeks, as Ernest and the boys working on the 37-inch cyclotron oscillated between hope and despair.

But in the early morning hours of Monday, December 1, the rebuilt cyclotron produced the first beam in its incarnation as a mass spectrograph. "Got ions in the 37-inch," Cooksey laconically recorded in his diary. Berkeley's beam was already ten times more powerful than that of Nier's machine.[17]

On Saturday, December 6, 1941, Ernest was back in Washington, summoned to OSRD headquarters by Bush to discuss reorganization of what was being called the "S-1 Project." That morning in Berkeley the new spectrograph had defied the theorists by separating uranium, albeit an almost-infinitesimal amount. Receiving the news by telephone from Cooksey, Lawrence boasted to the new S-1 Committee that the Rad Lab spectrograph was producing a microgram of enriched uranium every hour.[18]

In truth, the tiny green speck of U-235 left in the near bucket was almost too small to see. Most of the uranium had been smeared around the inside of the machine by the beam. But with the future at stake, Lawrence touted even this meager success as a triumph.

Largely on the strength of Lawrence's claim, Bush and Conant assigned to him the responsibility for providing the first samples of enriched uranium for later experiments.[19]

When the meeting broke up at noon, Bush, Conant, and Compton went around the corner for lunch to the Cosmos Club. Realizing that he now had to make good on his commitment, Ernest promptly left for the airport and the next flight west.

By Sunday morning, he was back at the 37-inch. Lawrence and the boys learned of the Japanese attack on Pearl Harbor from the radio that was always left on at the lab. Elsewhere on campus, word spread quickly. Kamen was startled when the normally unflappable Seaborg burst into the Faculty Club reading room in an agitated state. Cooksey, enjoying a weekend sail on the Bay, did not hear of the attack until he returned to the marina. Oppenheimer received the news at home, where he was sleeping late after attending a benefit for Spanish civil war veterans the night before.[20]

At the Rad Lab that evening, the first visible traces of shiny uranium metal began accumulating in the spectrograph's collectors. The uranium in the near bucket was five times richer in U-235 than the far collector. That night, after most of the cyclotroneers had gone home to be with their families, Lawrence stayed behind, filled with what he later described as a mixture of hope and foreboding, walking the perimeter fence until nearly dawn.[21]

Bleary-eyed, he called the boys together on Monday morning to announce that henceforth any work not directly related to defense would be immediately suspended.[22] Later, he sent telegrams and worked the phones, pleading with Rad Lab alumni at colleges and universities across the country to return to Berkeley. A great many not only answered the call but brought their own acolytes with them. Ernest persuaded the campus representative of Realsilk Hosiery, a company that hired student salesmen, to become the lab's recruiter for nonscientific personnel. For the first time, a guard—a young law student—was stationed at the bottom of the road up to Cyclotron Hill, armed with a .410 shotgun borrowed from Cooksey.[23]

Back in Washington by mid-December, Lawrence asked for $400,000 to explore electromagnetic separation for the next six months. His request was the first made to the S-1 Committee in wartime. In a measure of how much things had changed since Pearl Harbor, it was approved promptly and virtually without discussion.[24]

The funds would be used to build the prototype of a production mass spectrograph five times the 37-inch in size. Even as he returned, discouraged, from Nier's lab the previous month, Lawrence had already mentally resolved to take the next logical step: converting the still-uncompleted 184-inch to separate uranium. Not yet born as an instrument of science, the great cyclotron was to be transformed while still in the womb into a weapon of the war.[25]

As Lawrence was aware, the race was no longer only with the Axis. Berkeley's immediate rival was not Germany but Princeton; his challenger the former student he had fired twice from the Rad Lab.

Robert Wilson was a twenty-one-year-old experimentalist from Frontier, Wyoming, whom Ernest had dismissed the first time for losing a rubber seal in the 37-inch. Since the seal prevented the machine from running on the very day that John had scheduled a demonstration of his neutron-ray therapy to a prospective funder, both brothers had flown into a rage.[26] Rehired at Alvarez's instigation, Wilson had later been fired a second time for melting a pair of pliers while welding a probe onto the cyclotron vacuum tank.[27] Offered his job back again, Wilson not surprisingly decided instead to accept an offer from Princeton, where Henry Smyth was exploring a different approach to electromagnetic separation.

Smyth's project, subsequently taken over by Wilson, had by early 1941 produced a device dubbed the "Isotron," which used an electrical rather than a magnetic field to separate uranium.[28] Wilson began to suspect that the reason why Lawrence stopped by Princeton on his way home from Washington was not only to check on his rival's progress but to lure workers away to the Rad Lab.[29]

Once the decision to proceed with the bomb had been made, a location for the project had to be found. The leading candidates were Columbia, Princeton, Chicago, and Berkeley. Ernest, of course, remained a strong advocate for the Rad Lab. Operation of the 37-inch spectrograph was steadily improving, and the 60-inch was still the world's only source of element 94. Moreover, one practical consideration dominated all: there was no possibility of moving the massive machines.[30]

Another compelling argument for Berkeley was Oppenheimer. Shortly after Pearl Harbor, Compton had asked Oppie to take over the theoretical calculations on bomb physics from Gregory Breit.[31]

Despite Ernest's earlier promise to Bush and Conant, approaching year's end the Rad Lab had produced a mere 25 micrograms of uranium metal, enriched to barely 3 percent U-235.[32] Lawrence was nonetheless in a triumphant mood by Christmas Eve, when the regents approved his plan to convert the 184-inch into a uranium separator.[33] His race with Princeton remained neck and neck. That day, when Smyth cabled Lawrence with the latest results from the Isotron, Ernest's competitive spirit overruled the holiday mood in his reply: "Three cheers. How about lower temperatures? Merry Christmas."[34] On New Year's Day, Lawrence wrote to Smyth suggesting that he and Wilson consider shifting their workers to Berkeley—"since you are having difficulties recruiting there."[35]

A week later, Lawrence was once again on his way east by train, this time in the company of Alvarez and Alfred Loomis. Compton had declared the project's deadlines: January 1943 to achieve the first self-sustaining atomic chain reaction; January 1944 to extract the first samples of element 94 from an atomic reactor; January 1945 for a bomb.[36]

From New York, Lawrence and Alvarez took the train to Chicago, where they found Compton at home, sick with the flu. Sitting on the edge of the bed, Ernest presented the case for moving the entire bomb project to Berkeley. Compton had recently decided upon Chicago as the most practical site.[37]

Lawrence challenged the decision, declaring that, compared to Berkeley, the "tempo of the University of Chicago" was too slow.[38] Bristling, Compton countered that he would have an atomic chain reaction going by the end of the year. "I'll bet you a thousand dollars you won't," replied Lawrence with some heat.

When tempers cooled, Ernest dropped the stakes to a nickel cigar.[39] His wager aside, Lawrence remained unwilling to accept that Berkeley had lost out to Chicago. In a telegram, he notified Conant that Compton's choice was "acceptable only as temporary arrangement."[40]

Within six weeks, however, there was an entirely new enterprise on the Chicago campus, the Metallurgical Laboratory, which would oversee research into the atomic chain reaction. Work already under way at Columbia, where Fermi had been designing a so-called atomic pile to produce element 94, was unceremoniously moved to the Windy City. Lawrence consented, reluctantly, to lend Seaborg and Segrè to the new "Met Lab." Seaborg, a codiscoverer of the mysterious element, had meanwhile decided to call it plutonium.[41] If Ernest's uranium enrichment plans failed, plutonium still offered a promising candidate for the bomb. But wartime secrecy would keep it off the periodic chart.[42]

At Berkeley, the war had brought a halt to normal academic routine. Called upon to carry out chemical warfare experiments for the army, Martin Kamen and Sam Ruben released small quantities of isotope-tagged gas on Marin County beaches late at night. Ruben's adviser, chemist Kenneth Pitzer, had already left for Washington, where he led an OSRD-funded project—headquartered at the Congressional Country Club—to develop secret weapons for Allied spies and saboteurs.[43]

At the Donner Laboratory, the exigencies of war had literally crowded out the healing arts.[44] The brand-new third floor, added to the lab to accommodate John's radiophosphorous clinic, was commandeered by Ernest for the bomb project before the first patient arrived.[45]

By mid-January 1942, the winding of the upper core of the magnet for the 184-inch was completed. A week later, the final shipment of copper arrived. Lawrence's latest plan—approved by Sproul—was to fit a number of individual mass spectrographs between the poles of the giant magnet. Originally, the magnet was not expected to be finished until November.

After Lawrence obtained emergency funds from the Rockefeller Foundation, however, work was begun around the clock; the completion date was moved up to spring.

Yet even as conversion of the 184-inch proceeded at a breakneck pace, the feasibility of electromagnetic separation remained unproven on an industrial scale. One recent arrival at the Rad Lab was surprised to hear Lawrence shout with joy after a particular run on the converted 37-inch. The fact that a Geiger counter showed the uranium in the bucket to be only very slightly enriched did not seem to dull Lawrence's enthusiasm.[46]

But things were steadily improving. By February, the "stockpile" of uranium metal at the Rad Lab exceeded 200 micrograms, enriched to an average 35 percent U-235.[47] The converted 37-inch had begun producing 2 micrograms an hour.

During a quick visit to Berkeley that month to check on progress, Bush found the upbeat mood at the Rad Lab not only "refreshing" but contagious.[48] Bush wrote Roosevelt a few days later that the electromagnetic method could conceivably provide a shortcut to the bomb, delivering enough material for a weapon by the summer of 1943. A finished bomb might then be ready as early as 1944.

In other encouraging news, Oppenheimer's latest calculations indicated that the amount of U-235 needed for a weapon was at the low end of the original estimates: closer to 2 kilograms than 100.[49] Still, even that goal—a mere 4 to 5 pounds of silvery metal, 80 to 90 percent pure—lay far in the future.

Lawrence remained enough of a realist to want to hedge his bets. Unlike Conant, who was now willing to stake everything on the electromagnetic method, Lawrence urged that the government also back the other "horsemen" in the race: the centrifuge, gaseous diffusion, and Fermi's plutonium-producing atomic pile.[50]

In letters to Conant that winter, Lawrence's mood seesawed between jubilation and despair.[51] But in the spring, when the output of the 37-inch hit a new peak, Ernest's confidence returned.

While designing the spectrographs to go between the poles of the big magnet, Brobeck had invented a C-shaped vacuum chamber and increased the power of the beam by another factor of ten. The Rad Lab's personnel director proposed a name for the new machine that would forever link it to the University of California: the "Calutron."[52]

Two weeks after the first new vacuum tank was installed between the poles of the 37-inch magnet, the prototype Calutron was already exceeding expectations. "It, therefore, seems clear that we should proceed immediately with the design and construction of a multiple mass spectrograph using the giant cyclotron magnet," Lawrence wrote to Conant—requesting an additional $200,000 for the purpose.[53] "We are rapidly learning the art, and things look better all the while," Ernest boasted at the end of March.[54]

Since the magnet of the 184-inch was due to be finished in another week, Lawrence also judged the time propitious to bring Berkeley's foremost theoretical physicist closer to the project.

Whereas iron shims had been adequate for focusing the beam of the 37-inch, separating enough uranium for a bomb required a more fundamental understanding of the physics behind the spectrograph. Mindful that he had been scolded before for prematurely revealing secrets, Lawrence this time approached Conant cautiously:

> One other matter I should like to bring to your attention is the desirability of asking Oppenheimer to serve as a member of S-1. I think he would be a tremendous asset in every way. He combines a penetrating insight of the theoretical aspects of the whole program with solid common sense, which sometimes in certain directions seems to be lacking, and I am sure that you and Dr. Bush would find him a useful adviser.[55]

Oppenheimer, of course, had already been introduced to the bomb project, as Conant had rueful reason to know. What Lawrence proposed to do was make Oppie a full-time consultant to the S-1 Committee, laying bare all of its secrets. Unmentioned by Lawrence in his letter was a concern that had already given Conant pause, and that remained a worry even with Ernest: Oppenheimer's politics.

Lawrence had continued to show a grudging tolerance, mixed perhaps with some degree of envy, toward Oppenheimer's bohemian lifestyle. The memory of their earlier blowup over the benefit for Spanish Loyalists had long since faded. When his second son was born that January, Ernest named the boy Robert Donald Lawrence in honor of his two closest friends, Oppenheimer and Cooksey.[56] Still, Ernest was no less disapproving of Oppie's devotion to "left-wing" causes.

It was not only Oppie's politics but those of the people closest to him that prompted concern. Oppenheimer's long and tempestuous relationship with Jean Tatlock had finally ended late in 1939.[57] A year later, on November 1, 1940, Oppie married Kathryn Puening, the twenty-nine-year-old daughter of a Pittsburgh mining engineer.[58]

"Kitty" was the widow of Joe Dallet, a Communist organizer from Youngstown, Ohio, and a member of the Abraham Lincoln Brigade who had been killed in battle at Saragossa, Spain, in 1937.[59] Kitty herself had joined the Communist Party sometime after marrying Dallet in 1934 but was separated from both the party and her husband by mid-1936. Enrolled shortly after Dallet's death at the University of Pennsylvania, she had been on a vacation in England, visiting her parents, when she became romantically involved with a former acquaintance, a young British doctor named Richard Stewart Harrison.[60] The couple returned to America and were married two months later, in November 1938.[61]

Oppenheimer met Kitty the following August during a party at the home of a Caltech physicist, Richard Tolman, and his wife, Ruth.[62] Kitty and Harrison had meanwhile moved to Pasadena, where he was interning at a nearby hospital. Oppie invited Kitty to Perro Caliente that next summer.[63] After spending six weeks at a dude ranch near Reno to establish Nevada residency, Kitty divorced Harrison and wed Oppie on the same day at a civil ceremony in Virginia City. A county clerk and the courthouse janitor served as witnesses. The Lawrences were the first to congratulate the newlyweds upon their return to Berkeley; Molly was mildly shocked to see the bride already wearing a maternity dress.[64]

In a sudden burst of domesticity, Oppenheimer abandoned his rented bachelor quarters on Shasta Road and sublet a modern, rambling house on Kenilworth Court in nearby Kensington from an art department colleague on sabbatical.[65] Oppie also sold his beloved "Garuda" and bought Kitty a pearl-gray Cadillac, dubbed "Bombsight." Their baby—whom Oppie nicknamed "Pronto"—was expected in May.

Perhaps even more troubling than Kitty's background, from the standpoint of security, was the political worldview of Oppenheimer's brother. Eight years younger and far more shy and introverted than Robert, Frank shared with his sibling an early interest in science. As a child, Frank understood that he was supposed to treasure the extensive rock and mineral collection he inherited from Robert, but he sometimes felt overwhelmed by the gift. Although Frank dutifully acquired and cataloged his own samples, his collection paled in comparison with his brother's. As an adolescent, Frank developed an interest in biology after using the microscope he was given as a birthday present to view the wiggly motion of his own sperm.[66]

Frank also lacked both the ambition and the direction of his older brother. Until Robert kindled his interest in physics, Frank had been thinking about becoming a professional flutist.[67]

Mirroring the relationship between Ernest and John Lawrence, Oppie grew unusually protective of his younger brother—"in some ways perhaps part of a father to him," as Robert would later observe.[68] When Frank went away to study in England, the brothers corresponded regularly, Robert proffering advice from "the fruit and outcome of his erotic labors."[69]

Robert's letters also waxed philosophical. When Frank complained of a failed romance, Oppie volunteered a perspective that would later seem hauntingly apt to his own situation: "The reason why a bad philosophy leads to such hell is that it is what you think and want and treasure and foster in the times of preparation that determines what you do in the pinch, and that it takes an error to father a sin."[70]

Forever conscious of laboring in the shadow of his famous brother, Frank, not surprisingly, showed occasional flashes of a rebellious nature. ("Poor laddie, the mark is on you," Oppie once wrote to Frank in commiseration.)[71] Robert attributed his brother's halting progress toward a physics doctorate at Caltech to the influence of Frank's fiancée, Jacquenette Quann, an economics major at Berkeley who was active in the campus Young Communist League. Until he met "Jackie," Frank had only skirted the edge of involvement in politics. As an undergraduate at Johns Hopkins, he remembered attending a Carnegie Hall concert where the orchestra played without a conductor. ("It was a kind of 'down with the bosses' movement," Frank explained.)[72]

Robert urged his brother to break off the engagement. Frank, defiant, married Jackie late in 1936, while he was still a graduate student.[73] The couple joined the Communist Party together early in 1937, once again in defiance of Oppie's wishes.[74]

As was customary for party members, Frank picked a fictitious last name—Folsom—under which he paid dues to the Pasadena chapter. He and Jackie also socialized and briefly shared a house with several other Communists likewise affiliated with Caltech.[75] But Frank's commitment to communism was apparently neither particularly passionate nor deep. While at Caltech, he and Ruth Tolman organized and performed at a benefit concert for Spain. Frank and Jackie joined the Pasadena chapter's crusade to racially integrate the municipal swimming pool. Robert, visiting from Berkeley, attended the demonstration and professed to find it "pathetic."[76]

In June 1941, a teaching job that Frank held at Stanford abruptly ended. Oppie told friends that his brother had been fired for radical talk and unionizing. (A Stanford colleague complained to the FBI that Frank had called him "a hopeless bourgeois not in sympathy with the proletariat.")[77] Robert thought Frank's subsequent, brief period of unemployment "very, very salutary."[78]

At Oppie's urging, Lawrence agreed to hire Frank at the Rad Lab. To get the job, Frank assured Robert that he was no longer an active Communist, having withdrawn from the party that spring. Robert cautioned his brother that Ernest would fire him "if he was not a good boy."[79]

While Oppie evidently told Lawrence something of Frank's involvement with politics, he did not disclose his brother's Communist past.[80] As a condition of his employment at the lab, Frank promised Lawrence not to become involved in political causes.[81] Ernest assigned him to the team of cyclotroneers converting the 37-inch with the thought that working fourteen- to sixteen-hour days would leave him no time for mischief. Shortly after Pearl Harbor, Lawrence put Frank in charge of the night shift building the 184-inch. The boys remembered him nervously chain-smoking, pacing back and forth on the wooden latticework that rose above the big magnet.

It was no coincidence that Frank's new job also made it easier for Oppie to keep a watch on his younger brother. Yet Robert's intervention on Frank's behalf was a reflection not only of his concern as the older sibling but of true affection. Years later, under much different circumstances, Oppie would say of Frank: "He is a much finer person than I am."[82]

By spring 1941, Oppie's own political dalliances were coming back to haunt him. Jack Tenney, the new chairman of the California legislature's Committee on Un-American Activities, had recently announced an investigation of hiring practices at the university.[83] Tenney was incensed that a teaching assistant in Berkeley's math department, Kenneth May, was being kept on the university payroll after admitting to being a Communist.[84] (May was ultimately not only expelled but disinherited by his father, a Berkeley dean.)[85] An earlier investigation by the same committee had focused attention upon the AFT's Local 349 in Berkeley, with which Oppenheimer and Chevalier were associated.[86]

The threat of being hauled before the Tenney Committee passed, and the scare seemed to have little effect upon Oppenheimer's behavior. That fall, he attended a house-warming party at May's new home in neighboring Albany.[87]

Oppenheimer's near run-in with Tenney also did not discourage him from further behind-the-scenes unionizing. When Paul Pinsky, a Berkeley alumnus turned organizer for the Federation of Architects, Engineers, Chemists, and Technicians, encountered difficulty in organizing a chapter of the radical union at the Shell Development Corporation in nearby Emeryville, Oppenheimer brought Pinksy and Shell's scientists together at his home.[88] Pinsky would credit Oppenheimer for the creation of FAECT's Local 25 at Shell.[89]

Later, when Berkeley's teachers union split over factional differences, Oppenheimer sponsored another union meeting at his house. He hoped this time to organize the Rad Lab.[90] Oppie invited two chemical engineers from Shell's FAECT Local—George Eltenton and Jerome Vinograd—to make the case for joining the union to Berkeley's physicists and cyclotroneers.[91]

The gathering took place at the new home on Eagle Hill that Robert and Kitty had bought that August.[92] The modern, Spanish-style house was close by Kenilworth Court and had a sweeping vista of Berkeley and the Bay. The meeting had just begun, Kamen remembered, when it "broke up in some disarray" after Oppenheimer admitted, in response to Kamen's question, that he had failed to notify Lawrence of his plans.[93]

Predictably, Lawrence was enraged to learn of the incident the following day. Before Kamen, Ernest unburdened himself that "Oppie had given him much trouble in the past with his fuzzy-minded efforts to do good."[94] As a result, Lawrence said, he was having difficulties getting Oppenheimer a security clearance.

Lawrence took Oppie aside a few days later to warn him against any further political activity. Ernest was surprised when his friend turned angry and defiant.[95] Oppenheimer defended his actions on the grounds that "underdogs" should be helped by the more fortunate. Lawrence replied with equal heat that the best way to help humanity was by subordinating all political activities, unionizing included, to defeating the Nazis, and the best way to achieve that goal was by attending to the scientific work of the lab. Since he had brought Oppenheimer into the S-1 Project in the first place, Lawrence none-too-subtly reminded him, he was the one who bore the responsibility for getting him access to its secrets. Ernest insisted that Oppie's "leftwandering" must stop.[96]

The confrontation ended on a bitter note. In the coming weeks, its memory rankled with both men.

Robert Oppenheimer officially came to the attention of the Federal Bureau of Investigation in late March 1941, the date that the FBI opened its file on him. Oppie entered the bureau's penumbra of suspicion by accident, when he attended a special meeting of his discussion group at Chevalier's home the previous December.[97] Agents had written down the license plate number of Oppie's Chrysler parked on the street outside. Ironically, it was not Oppenheimer but others at the meeting—specifically, Issac Folkoff and William Schneiderman—who were the real target of the bureau's surveillance.[98]

Schneiderman, a longtime Communist, was the party's secretary in California.[99] "Pops" Folkoff was a sixty-year-old Latvian émigré who owned a clothing repair shop, the Model Embroidery and Pleating Company, in downtown San Francisco.[100] Although Folkoff had been in the United States since 1904, he still spoke with a thick guttural accent; a burn he received from a steam press in his youth had left him with a maimed right hand. Folkoff was best known to the FBI as a dogmatic

Marxist and the party's local "bag man," who collected monthly dues in the Bay Area.

For almost a year, the bureau had been surreptitiously listening to the telephone calls of both Folkoff and Schneiderman, from wiretaps secretly installed in their homes and at Communist Party headquarters on Market Street. The wiretaps were part of a clandestine FBI program targeted against the Soviet Union's so-called Comintern Apparatus, and hence known by the shorthand label "COMRAP."[101]

For round-the-clock surveillance, a hidden third wire would be added to the telephone mouthpiece, converting it into an open microphone.[102] Conversations picked up either by wiretap or by such "bugs" were recorded on large cellulose-covered metal platters—known as Presto disks—at the bureau's listening post in Oakland. Because the early taps were not only secret but of questionable legality, information gained from them was puckishly identified in FBI reports as coming from "Informant T-1" or "an informant of known reliability who is not available to testify."[103]

The man in charge of the COMRAP program in San Francisco was Robert King, a young lawyer who had joined the bureau early in 1940, shortly after receiving a law degree from Georgetown University. Following months of fruitlessly driving up and down the West Coast, looking for saboteurs and smugglers, King was reassigned in midyear to the task of identifying political subversives. King boasted that he was the office's "one-man commie squad."[104]

In the case of the December 1940 meeting at Chevalier's house, King's interest had been piqued by Folkoff's comment, intercepted by the bureau's bug, that the gathering was to be of "the big boys."[105] Through its technical surveillance—*tesur* in FBI parlance—the bureau learned of subsequent meetings and conversations that took place between Oppenheimer, Addis, and Folkoff.[106]

On Sunday, October 5, 1941, the FBI bug picked up plans for a meeting later that day between Oppenheimer and Steve Nelson, the Bay Area's top Communist. The rendezvous had been arranged by Folkoff, whom Oppenheimer had promised a donation of $100 for striking California farmworkers. However, at the last minute Folkoff had begged off and telephoned Oppenheimer, asking that he meet with Nelson instead. Nine days later, shortly before leaving for the Schenectady meeting, Oppie had phoned Folkoff and asked that Steve contact him.[107]

A mysterious figure to the FBI, Nelson had only recently become a focus of the bureau's attention in San Francisco. Born Stefan Mesarosh in Croatia in 1903, "Nelson" had entered the United States with fraudulent immigration papers at the age of seventeen and became a naturalized American citizen five years later.[108] He joined the Communist Party in

1923, at Pittsburgh. During the early 1930s, Nelson was trained in espionage techniques at Moscow's Lenin Institute and, in 1933, served as an active agent for the Soviet Comintern in Europe and China. Later volunteering for Spain, Nelson became a political officer, or commissar, in the Abraham Lincoln Brigade, rising to the rank of lieutenant colonel.[109] Returning to the United States, he traveled around the country raising money and recruits for the Loyalist cause.

More than politics had brought Oppenheimer and Nelson together; the two also shared a personal bond. Nelson had been a friend of Kitty's late husband in Spain and was the one to tell her of Joe Dallet's death. After Dallet was killed, Kitty had briefly stayed with Nelson at his apartment in Paris, and then later with Nelson and his wife in New York.[110]

Oppenheimer first met Nelson at a Spanish war relief party in fall 1939, and the two men and their families had subsequently gone on social outings together. Nelson spent much of 1940 "on the shelf"—hiding out at a cabin in Redwood City under an assumed name, at a time when it appeared that the government was about to declare the Communist Party illegal. He had emerged shortly after America's entry into the war to become chairman of the San Francisco branch of the Communist Party. He moved the party's base of operations to a storefront office in Oakland when the big shipyards in the East Bay began recruiting new workers.[111]

What was said between Nelson and Oppenheimer in the meetings arranged by Folkoff remained outside the range of the bureau's microphones. But Oppenheimer's continuing involvement in progressive causes showed that he had decided to ignore Lawrence's admonition against left-wandering.

Since the Schenectady meeting, however, Oppie had apparently begun rethinking his activist role. In mid-November, after failing to catch Lawrence before the latter left for a meeting in New York, Oppenheimer wrote a letter to him, apologizing for the blowup over the union and offering assurance that "there will be no further difficulties."[112]

Still, it was soon evident that Oppie had not completely forsworn political causes. Three weeks later, on December 6, he attended a benefit for veterans of the Spanish war's Abraham Lincoln Brigade. As late as April 1942, Oppenheimer was still giving $150 monthly to Folkoff.[113]

Acting on King's recommendation, on January 26, 1942, the agent in charge of the San Francisco FBI office—N. J. L. "Nat" Pieper—asked bureau director J. Edgar Hoover for permission to extend COMRAP's technical surveillance to Oppenheimer, Chevalier, and Addis. "This group of individuals is on such a plane that it is unlikely that any confidential Party informant now available to this office will be able to reach them and determine their actual position in the Party," Pieper wrote Hoover.[114]

Ignorant of the S-1 Project and of Oppenheimer's role in it, Hoover approved only the wiretap on Chevalier—which was subsequently denied by the attorney general. Pieper renewed his appeal to Hoover in March, citing further evidence from existing wiretaps that Addis remained an active party recruiter. On April 15, the FBI director turned down this request as well, chiding Pieper in the process for putting mention of the secret COMRAP program in writing.[115]

Just two weeks later, Oppenheimer filled out OSRD's personnel security questionnaire, his first step in getting a clearance to work on the bomb project. Although Oppie, listing organizations to which he belonged, included the American Federation of Teachers and the left-wing American Association of Scientific Workers, there was no mention either of FAECT or of the "discussion group" that he and Chevalier had organized.*[116]

Lawrence's was the first name that Oppie listed as a reference. While McMillan and Birge would also write glowing letters of recommendation to go in Oppenheimer's file, Ernest's was by far the strongest endorsement:

> I have known Professor J. Robert Oppenheimer for fourteen years as a faculty colleague and close personal friend. I am glad to recommend him in highest terms as a man of great intellectual caliber and of fine character and personality. There can be no question of his integrity.[117]

Although Conant had grudgingly agreed to approve a temporary clearance for Oppenheimer, he had not ceased to worry about project security at Berkeley. In February 1942, Conant summoned John Lansdale, a newly promoted captain in the U.S. Army's Military Intelligence Service, to OSRD headquarters. A Harvard law graduate, Lansdale before the war had defended the Cleveland Railway Company against personal injury suits resulting from trolley accidents. Since being recalled to active duty, he had been assigned to G-2's Counter-Intelligence Group in Washington.[118]

Conant ordered Lansdale to Berkeley in civilian clothes to test security procedures at the Rad Lab. Lansdale was given a temporary membership card for the Faculty Club, obtained by Conant from Sproul, and a copy of a recent Stanford commencement speech by Lawrence describing the operation of the cyclotron.[119]

---

* In pencil at the bottom, Oppenheimer added this partial disclaimer: "I have endeavored to make this list complete. It includes all organizations to which I now belong. It does not include so-called sponsorships. It includes all past memberships I can remember. I believe it to be accurate."

By chance, Lansdale encountered a Berkeley professor on the train en route to California who wrote him a letter of introduction to the dean of the law school, Max Radin.[120] Max's brother, Paul, was an anthropology professor on campus and a member of the political discussion group to which Oppenheimer and Chevalier belonged.

Renting a room at International House, Lansdale bought a notebook on Telegraph Avenue to serve as a diary and on Friday morning, February 20, strolled up Cyclotron Hill—through a pair of open gates posted with "No Visitors" signs, he noted—to the site of the unfinished 184-inch. After spending a leisurely two hours studying blueprints laid out on a bench and talking with the construction superintendent, Lansdale joined Max Radin for lunch at the Faculty Club. Radin pointed out Lawrence, who, he explained, was a frequent traveler to Washington on a government project seeking "an explosion from the sudden expansion of the atom."

Later that afternoon, Lansdale returned to the 184-inch and was considering stealing some of the blueprints when he was noticed by Alvarez and asked to leave. During dinner at the Faculty Club, Lansdale brought up the subject of the cyclotron's possible military use with Cooksey, who warily skirted the subject, speaking instead of the machine's application to cancer research.[121]

Lansdale spent a total of two weeks in Berkeley getting to know many of those he identified in his diary as "Lawrence's Brain Trust." At breakfast one day, chemist Joseph Kennedy boasted that since a pound of U-235 contained enough energy to lift all the buildings in San Francisco half a mile into the air, whichever country separated enough uranium to make a bomb would win the war. But Kennedy told Lansdale that he doubted a way could be found to separate that much uranium before the fighting ended.

Lansdale returned to Washington in early March to brief Conant. ("Oh, dear . . . oh, dear," the Harvard president muttered as Lansdale read from his diary.) Conant promptly ordered Lansdale back to Berkeley, this time in his army uniform.

Asking Cooksey to assemble the boys, Lansdale read them the same diary entries that had so shocked Conant.[122] Subsequently upbraided a second time by Conant, Lawrence promised to tighten security measures at the Rad Lab. Lansdale, with Conant's blessing, left on a similar mission to Compton's Met Lab in mid-May.

By that spring, the separation of uranium was progressing well enough on the 37-inch, Lawrence wrote Bush, that the OSRD chairman might have to make good on an earlier wager.[123] There was now under way a friendly race between the Calutron and Fermi's atomic pile as to which would produce the first material for a bomb.[124] On May 23, 1942, Lawrence, determinedly upbeat, wrote to Conant that work was "proceeding somewhat faster than anticipated." He asked for, and got, another $25,000 to make it to the end of June.[125]

Later that day, Ernest met in Washington with Conant and the S-1 section leaders to discuss construction of a pilot plant. An NDRC study had recently concluded that electromagnetic separation seemed the most promising method of enriching uranium; results from both gaseous diffusion and the centrifuge looked to be at least a year away. But Conant worried aloud that separating uranium by all known techniques would cost $500 million—and result in "quite a mess of machinery."[126]

Ernest told the S-1 managers that a full-scale electromagnetic separation plant could be producing 100 grams of U-235 a day within a year. Reluctantly, Conant agreed to continue backing all four "horsemen." But he recommended to Bush that $12 million be spent on an electromagnetic production plant, to be completed by September 1943.[127] When the meeting adjourned that afternoon, Lawrence promptly flew back west with the good news.

On Tuesday evening, May 26, current flowed to the 184-inch for the first time. A few days later, the first C-shaped vacuum chamber was installed between the pole pieces of the giant magnet.[128] Lawrence wrote to Bush in mid-June that the results justified a decision for a full-scale factory.[129] Ernest wanted both the Calutron pilot plant and the scaled-up production facility to remain on the West Coast, under his direction. He had located a possible site for the production plant in the far northern corner of the state, near Shasta Dam, and was looking into having the university lease to the army a parcel of land in the hills back of the Rad Lab for the pilot plant.[130]

By the time he forwarded his own recommendations to Roosevelt on June 17, Bush agreed with Lawrence on the necessity to proceed promptly on all fronts. But he and Conant had already decided to put the army in charge of building the factories that would separate the uranium for the bomb. The president, too, acted with unusual dispatch, approving Bush's plan on the same day by scrawling "OK. FDR" in blue pencil at the top of the page.

To keep electromagnetic separation in the race and meet OSRD deadlines, Lawrence and Oppenheimer had begun recruiting young physics graduate students on campus for the S-1 Project. One of Oppie's earlier acolytes, still in his midtwenties, was shocked upon returning to Berkeley that spring to find a "bunch of kids" doing war work at the Rad Lab.[131]

Competition for the jobs was brisk. The position of research physicist paid $150 a month—compared to the $65 a teaching assistant received—and included a draft deferment.

With the 184-inch already up and running, the greatest need was for theoretical physicists to perform calculations aimed at improving the efficiency of the Calutron. Not surprisingly, the best of the young theorists at Berkeley worked for Oppenheimer. Many shared not only their mentor's passion for physics but likewise his affinity for progressive causes.[132]

One such student was Giovanni Rossi Lomanitz, who arrived in Berkeley from Oklahoma in the late summer of 1940, a month before his nineteenth birthday. Big, extroverted, and cheerful, Lomanitz had been immediately swept up in the radical politics and bohemian culture of the place.[133] He attended rallies opposing the deportation of labor leader Harry Bridges and joined the Student Workers Federation on campus. Moving into Barrington Hall, a dormitory on campus that attracted students with similarly left-wing views, Lomanitz met other kindred spirits. From Arthur Rosen, Rossi bought a 1927 Nash, biblically nicknamed "Hepzibaa," for $25. Rosen's brother, Alfred, was leader of Berkeley's Young Communist League.[134]

Another physics grad student whom Lomanitz befriended was Joseph Weinberg, a New Yorker from the Lower East Side who came to Berkeley via the University of Wisconsin. Only three years older but far more worldly wise than Lomanitz, Weinberg was a graduate of City College, where he had also been a student activist. Like Rossi's, Weinberg's parents were Jews who had emigrated from Poland. Joe arrived on campus in spring 1939 with reportedly only the clothes on his back and a spare pair of shoes in a paper sack. By 1941, he was a teaching assistant in Oppenheimer's undergraduate physics class.[135]

A friend to both men was David Bohm, who had graduated from Penn State in 1939 and shortly thereafter came west to work with Oppenheimer. After a frustrating year spent at Caltech, Bohm had followed Oppie north to Berkeley and, at his mentor's instigation, joined the youthful group working at the lab.[136]

Unlike his fellows, Max Friedman arrived in Berkeley as a young man with means. Friedman had grown up in Los Angeles and graduated from UCLA. He drove a shiny new 1942 Pontiac dubbed "Lady Godiva," one of the last made before the war shut down the production line. Despite his relative affluence, Friedman shared the political views of his peers. He subscribed to the *Daily Worker* and for a time was Lomanitz's roommate at Barrington Hall. Like the other three, Friedman was a TA in the physics department when he was recruited to the Rab Lab by Oppenheimer in early 1942.[137]

Brought together by their common interest in physics and politics, the foursome—Lomanitz, Weinberg, Bohm, and Friedman—taught classes during the day and attended rallies and protest meetings on weekends. Like many on campus, they and their friends were active in organizations like the Young Communist League, the Campus Committee to Fight Conscription, and the Committee for Peace Mobilization, all branded communist fronts by the Tenney Committee and FBI.[138]

The four were also neighbors. By spring 1942, Bohm and Lomanitz had moved into a duplex in a working-class neighborhood just south of campus. Joe and Merle Weinberg rented a one-bedroom apartment on Blake Street, just around the corner. Joined by Friedman, the group gathered often for dinner at the Weinbergs' home, where they listened to Joe's coveted collection of classical records and discussed politics and philosophy late into the night.[139]

That May, Oppenheimer asked Lomanitz to look over a theoretical paper that two other graduate students, Stanley Frankel and Eldred Nelson, had written on how to improve the focusing of the Calutron beam.[140] While uranium was never specifically mentioned, the purpose of the "experiment" was clear.[141] Offered full-time employment at the lab by Oppie, Lomanitz understood all too well where such work was headed and balked. Subsequently invited to his mentor's home on Eagle Hill, Rossi admitted to having ethical qualms about participating in the creation of such a terrible weapon. But Lomanitz, like his professor, had also begun to feel guilty about sitting out the war. He was thinking about quitting school and going to work in the East Bay shipyards or even enlisting, Rossi told Oppenheimer.[142]

Two days later, running into Oppie on campus, Lomanitz accepted his offer. As he had done with his brother, Frank, Oppenheimer made Lomanitz and all those working on the project pledge to give up political activity. Oppie had evidently decided against recruiting Weinberg because of Joe's previous reputation as a campus radical.[143]

By that summer, three of the four—Lomanitz, Bohm, and Friedman—were engaged in some form of classified work related to the bomb. Oppenheimer assigned Lomanitz to refining calculations dealing with the Calutron's magnetic field. Bohm and Friedman supported the efforts of Eldred Nelson and Frankel to better focus the beam. Despite Lawrence's promise to Conant, the urgent need for results had pushed concerns with security into the background. All three were given interim clearances, pending a more complete background investigation. Until they could be put on the government payroll, Lawrence agreed to pay the salary for Oppie's students out of the Loomis fund.

Rossi used his sudden windfall to purchase two blue suits, a phonograph, and a collection of jazz and classical records that he hoped would one day rival Weinberg's. With gas rationing in effect, Lomanitz used the last of the money to buy a bicycle to commute to his new job at the lab.

4

AN ADVENTUROUS TIME

By summer 1942, Oppenheimer had become all but indispensable to building the atomic bomb, even as OSRD officials dithered about whether to grant him a security clearance. In May, Gregory Breit had suddenly quit the project—citing, ironically, lax security as the reason in his letter to Bush.[1] Arthur Compton promptly assigned Oppie the task of calculating fast-neutron reactions, crucial to the design of the weapon.

By mid-June, Oppenheimer was at Chicago's Met Lab to be briefed on the work inherited from Breit. Even Berkeley's wunderkind found the job and its deadlines daunting. Oppenheimer decided on the spot to invite the country's top theoretical physicists to Berkeley for an impromptu seminar on bomb physics. It was the start of what Oppie would later describe as "an adventurous time."[2]

First to arrive on campus was Robert Serber, a slight, soft-spoken former student of Oppenheimer's from the University of Illinois. In 1934, Serber had been on his way to a postdoctoral fellowship at Princeton with his wife, Charlotte, when the couple stopped off at Ann Arbor, Michigan, where Oppie was teaching quantum physics during the summer. Quickly falling under the master's spell, Serber had followed Oppenheimer back to Berkeley instead.[3]

Every spring since, Serber and Charlotte had crowded their possessions into a battered Nash roadster and joined the gypsy caravan of young physicists who migrated south to Caltech with their mentor. In Pasadena, they shared a garden apartment with Frank and Jackie Oppenheimer for $25 a month.

Like Oppie and Frank, Serber, too, married into radical politics: Charlotte was the daughter of Morris Leof, a Russian émigré and prominent Philadelphia physician who supported a variety of progressive causes in the city. Leof headed the local chapter of a medical aid committee for the Spanish Loyalists. Together with Jean Tatlock and Mary Ellen Washburn, Oppie's former landlady, Charlotte organized a similar chapter in Berkeley. (Robert Serber evidently inherited his wife's views. Teller claimed to have been shocked by Serber's summer 1940 description of the war in Europe as "a clash between capitalist interests.")[4]

Having both physics and politics in common, the Serbers soon became close friends of Oppie and Kitty and were frequent summer guests at Perro Caliente.[5] Even after Serber left Berkeley for Urbana, Illinois, in 1938, he and Oppenheimer stayed in touch with weekly letters.

Anticipating the need for additional theorists, Oppie recruited Serber to the bomb project during a walk in a cornfield near the Illinois campus just before Christmas 1941. Arriving in Berkeley the following spring, the Serbers moved into the apartment above the garage at the Oppenheimers' house on Eagle Hill. Charlotte found a job as a statistician at the Kaiser shipyards in nearby Richmond.[6]

Oppenheimer assigned Serber to oversee the work being done by Nelson and Frankel, who had, in turn, enlisted the assistance of Oppie's grad students. The latest task was to calculate, using data from the M.A.U.D. report, the critical mass and efficiency of an atomic explosion.[7] Distrusting Breit's estimates, Nelson and Frankel decided to do the laborious neutron diffusion calculations from first principles. Oppenheimer worried that their paper would not be ready in time for his seminar.

From campuses around the country came those whom Oppie called the "luminaries," including Harvard's John Van Vleck and University of Indiana physicist Emil Konopinski, then at Chicago's Met Lab. Physicist Felix Bloch drove up from nearby Stanford.

The two brightest stars arrived together on a train from the east. Hans Bethe was working at MIT's radar lab when Oppenheimer's summons reached him. Believing the atomic bomb an unlikely prospect anytime soon, Bethe had to be persuaded by Van Vleck to attend; Hans brought his wife, Rose, along for a California vacation. Joining them in Chicago, Edward Teller and his wife, Mici, shared a compartment on the streamliner with the Bethes. Since writing his paper with Bethe on ballistics, Teller had left Columbia to go to Chicago and work with Fermi, but he had not yet been given an assignment at the Met Lab.[8]

Although Bethe and Teller had first met as graduate students in Germany during the late 1920s, the two did not get to know each other until 1937, when they spent a summer driving through the western United

States, camping and discussing physics.[9] They discovered they had much in common.

Born in Alsace of a Jewish mother, Bethe had been fired from his position at the University of Tübingen in 1933—the victim of Hitler's racial purity laws—about the same time that Teller was forced from his teaching post at Göttingen's Institute of Physical Chemistry. Following a brief respite in Copenhagen to study under Bohr, and then England, both men found refuge in professorships at American universities. In 1938, Teller had persuaded Bethe to attend a conference on stellar evolution, a topic on which Bethe would become the world's expert. Bethe picked Teller as his replacement the following summer at Columbia.[10]

But in other respects—including temperament—Bethe and Teller were strikingly different. In contrast to Teller's often gloomy persona, Bethe seemed unfailingly affable and outgoing, with twinkling eyes and a cherubic face.

Teller had also met Lawrence and Oppenheimer in the vagabond summer of 1937, when he came to Berkeley at Oppie's invitation to give a seminar. Edward's lasting memory of Oppenheimer—whose personality he reportedly found "overpowering"—would always be associated with the spicy meal they shared before the seminar at a Mexican restaurant. The hot food caused the guest lecturer to temporarily lose his voice. It was perhaps the only time that Edward would be speechless in Oppie's presence.[11]

Ernest, too, left an indelible impression by taking Teller out on the Bay in his new boat, on a cruise memorable for strong winds and high seas. ("I withstood the choppy waters with a little less than complete equanimity," Edward later wrote. "Californians seemed to be more than I could handle comfortably.")

Arriving in Berkeley in early July 1942, Bethe and Teller looked forward to a pleasant interlude and a welcome break from the war. The two families shared with Konopinski a large house overlooking the Bay on the north side of campus. Teller found it amusing that Konopinski—a big, burly man—wound up with the frilly pink bedroom that had formerly been occupied by the landlord's daughter. "We have rented, with the Bethes, a palace and enjoy life very greatly," Teller wrote to Fermi at Chicago.[12]

The Berkeley seminar began at the start of the second week of July in a seminar room adjacent to Oppie's office at LeConte. The site had been made secure for the purpose by stretching wire netting over the balcony and posting a campus policeman downstairs. Serber began the first session by describing the current state of knowledge regarding the atomic bomb—how it might work and what it would look like. Oppenheimer relieved the tension that evening by taking his guests to dinner at Spengers, a seafood restaurant near the train tracks in Berkeley.[13]

The figures derived by Nelson and Frankel indicated that a 6-inch-diameter sphere of U-235, weighing about 33 pounds, would be needed for a fission weapon. They calculated that the core of a plutonium bomb would be just over 2 inches across and would weigh about 9 pounds. Breit's estimates of critical mass had been too high by a factor of eight.[14]

Near the end of the seminar's second day, Teller sidetracked the discussion onto an idea that he and Fermi had talked about at Columbia the previous winter. Over lunch, Fermi had made the simple observation that an atomic bomb might release enough energy to start the thermonuclear reaction that fueled the Sun and other stars. Powerful as a fission bomb might be, it would then be only an initiator for a very much larger bomb of a different sort—fusing hydrogen into helium. A so-called hydrogen bomb could theoretically be of virtually unlimited power.

Teller had discussed this possibility with Konopinski at Chicago and during the train trip west with Bethe.[15] The prospective thermonuclear fuel that Teller and Konopinski had looked at was liquid deuterium, which was easier to separate from heavy water than U-235 was from U-238. They calculated that a cubic meter of deuterium, heated to a temperature of 400 million degrees by an atomic bomb, would release the explosive energy of 1 million tons of TNT.

Teller had already made it plain at the Berkeley seminar that he regarded the atomic bomb as essentially an engineering problem. His enthusiasm was reserved for the deuterium superbomb, which, he argued, would guarantee victory to the first country that possessed it. The physicists in Oppie's office began to refer to Edward's hypothetical weapon as the "Super."[16] When Teller had left Chicago, he and Konopinski had tentatively concluded that the Super would not work. By the time Teller arrived in Berkeley, he was no longer so sure.

Serber recalled that the effect of Teller's revelation concerning the Super was electric: "Everybody forgot about the A-bomb as if it were old hat."[17] Yet, horrific as the theoretical Super might be, there was still another, even grimmer specter that haunted the theorists: the possibility that an exploding superbomb might release enough energy to ignite the nitrogen in the atmosphere, incinerating the planet. Bethe dismissed that possibility instinctively and later claimed to have disproved it with a few quick calculations.

Oppenheimer, however, remained so taken with the notion of the Super and the possibility of atmospheric ignition that he decided to contact Arthur Compton, vacationing at his lakeside summer cottage in upper Michigan. Finally reaching Compton by telephone at a country store nearby, Oppie set out by train to brief him on a matter too sensitive to be discussed on the telephone.[18]

Walking side by side along a deserted beach three days later, Oppenheimer and Compton briefly considered recommending that scientists go no further down the road that might lead to the superbomb.[19]

But the case for standing still did not win out. Compton and Oppie agreed that those at Berkeley should proceed with their calculations. They set a date of late September for a conference at the Met Lab to further investigate thermonuclear reactions.[20]

Back in Berkeley, meanwhile, the physicists at LeConte had gotten over whatever initial angst they felt about the Super.[21] Bethe discovered that Teller's earlier calculations had underestimated the effects of a fundamental process in physics—the manner in which the energy of a nuclear explosion is dissipated through radiation.[22] Not only did radiative cooling keep the planet safe from incineration by hydrogen bombs, Bethe pointed out, but it probably made the hypothetical Super itself unworkable. Konopinski briefly rescued Teller's thesis by proposing to light the deuterium with tritium, which has a lower ignition temperature. But Bethe seemingly knocked that theory flat, too.

By the time Oppenheimer returned from his meeting with Compton, the excitement over atmospheric ignition and the hydrogen superbomb had, in Serber's words, "fizzled out." For reasons of haste as well as secrecy, seminar participants did not bother drafting a final report.

Fatefully, what was left behind were two very different impressions of the conclusions that had been reached about the Super. Teller believed that his colleagues shared his optimism about the prospects for the weapon. For Bethe, Serber, and Oppenheimer, on the other hand, the Super was at best an interesting possibility—one worthy of further study, but only after the atomic bomb was already in hand.*

Oppenheimer informed Conant and the S-1 Committee of the prospective Super in late August. Conant passed the word along to Bush, who in turn alerted Secretary of War Henry Stimson.[23] In his report to Conant, Oppenheimer described a superbomb even more fearsome than that imagined by Teller at Berkeley. Oppie wrote that igniting 2 to 3 tons of liquid deuterium would produce an explosion equal to 100 million tons of TNT, laying waste some 360 square miles and contaminating the area with lethal radioactivity for several days.

* Perhaps anticipating that he would have trouble with the temperamental Hungarian, Oppie invited Edward and his wife, Mici, to Eagle Hill near the seminar's end. Nearly sixty years later, Teller remembered that Oppenheimer found his house gift—a recording of Mozart's Piano Concerto in E-flat Major, one of Edward's favorites—"uninteresting," and that Oppie predicted only the atomic bomb would be able to dislodge Hitler from Europe.

So startling and gruesome was this vision that his audience either was disbelieving or may have felt some obligation to tone it down. The Super that Conant described to Bush—a half ton of deuterium, equivalent to 100,000 tons of TNT, devastating some 100 square miles—was terrible enough, but less world shattering.[24]

The good news, if it could be called that, was that a very much larger and more powerful atomic bomb—"6 times the previous size," Conant wrote—was thought necessary to ignite a thermonuclear explosion. While the focus remained upon building the fission weapon, Conant and the S-1 Committee agreed to give new priority to a heavy water plant under construction in British Columbia. Originally designed to provide the moderator for Fermi's reactor, the facility would be used instead to produce deuterium for experiments connected with the Super.[25]

At the same time that he was reporting to Conant on the hydrogen bomb, Oppenheimer learned from Compton that the army had balked at granting him a security clearance.[26] The OSRD appealed the case to the army provost marshal's office, which overruled the earlier decision and granted Oppie another temporary clearance, pending "a further investigation of this individual." From Chicago, Compton assured Oppie that his radical past "would not prove a bar to . . . further work on the program."[27]

Lawrence, too, was having his own trouble with security officials. On September 1, 1942, an aide to Bush informed Ernest that the list he had given of people "who know of the new Oppenheimer work"—Berkeley's summer seminar—appeared incomplete. Bush was particularly upset that a construction engineer working for the army had somehow learned of the superbomb. Pointedly, Bush instructed the aide to "again remind [Lawrence] that this subject is to be discussed with no additional people at this time."[28]

In response, Lawrence asked Oppenheimer to put together a new list.[29] Oppie divided the names into three categories and sent the list to Conant on October 12. Group A knew "the whole story," Oppenheimer wrote. Group B had been involved in "technical calculations which do in fact concern the military applications." Group C had only done computations "and have essentially no knowledge of what it is all about."

Rossi Lomanitz's name was in Group B.

Security was being tightened in part because the army was about to take over the bomb project. Bush and Conant had agreed that the Corps of Engineers would assume oversight for building the mammoth industrial complex necessary to produce the weapon. Early in the summer, the corps had selected a Boston-based construction firm, Stone and Webster, as primary contractor.

The army also scouted out "Site X," some 56,000 acres of hardpan, woods, and scrub in a remote area near Oak Ridge, Tennessee. The Tennessee Valley Authority would provide electrical power and the Clinch River cooling water for the secret factories. In mid-June 1942, the army authorized creation of a new district in the corps, specifically to carry out the work of building the bomb. Two months later, the Manhattan Engineer District (MED) was officially established by the corps in New York.[30]

Although he welcomed the army's involvement, Lawrence still hoped to keep electromagnetic separation under his control. As late as mid-August, he was urging Sproul to approve the purchase of a privately owned parcel of land above the Rad Lab for a pilot plant.[31] But the recent shelling of an oil refinery in the Pacific Northwest by a Japanese submarine had persuaded military authorities that the West Coast was too vulnerable.[32]

Meeting in Berkeley on Sunday, September 13, the S-1 Committee approved $30 million for construction of both a pilot plant and a production facility. The latter would theoretically churn out 100 grams of U-235 a day at Site X.[33]

What had started out less than a year before as an experiment with the 37-inch was about to be scaled-up to an installation the size of several football fields in rural eastern Tennessee. Lawrence's latest plan called for ganging a series of ninety-six 4-foot-square vacuum tanks together between the poles of individual electromagnets arranged in an oval "racetrack." There would be two racetracks per building, each one consuming 100 times the electrical power used by the 184-inch. A total of twenty racetracks were thought necessary to reach the target 100-grams-a-day of enriched uranium. Lawrence called his machine the "Alpha Calutron," hinting that he was thinking ahead to more efficient and even bigger versions. In fact, he was already at work on a modification dubbed "Alpha II."[34]

When the Berkeley meeting wound up that afternoon, Lawrence and Oppenheimer drove the S-1 Committee and army representatives to the Bohemian Grove, the exclusive men's club located on the Russian River some 60 miles north of San Francisco. (Ernest had become a member through a social friend, Rowan Gaither, a wealthy attorney and financier in the city.)[35] In discussions held at the rustic lodge nestled among giant redwoods, Ernest conceded that the Calutrons would eventually be surpassed by other separation methods that were less laborious and less costly. But, for the present, his electromagnetic process offered the only means of obtaining the uranium necessary for a bomb.[36]

A few days later, Army Lieutenant General Brehon Somervell picked a rotund forty-six-year-old colonel—the army's deputy chief of construction—to head the newly created Manhattan Project.[37] Having recently overseen construction of the Pentagon, Leslie Groves had been looking forward to an overseas billet when he was handed the post. As a consolation, Somervell granted Groves's single request, promoting him to the rank of brigadier general.

Groves's aide-de-camp was Kenneth Nichols, a lieutenant colonel in the corps with a Ph.D. in hydraulic engineering from the University of Iowa. Both men were West Point graduates; Nichols had been assigned to the bomb project in the spring. Twelve years earlier, Nichols had served under Groves in the same battalion in Nicaragua, where the corps was surveying sites for a new inter-ocean canal.[38]

In a meeting at OSRD headquarters near the end of the month, Bush warned Groves that security in the S-1 Project was lax, and that the University of California was a particular concern.[39] He suggested that Groves get the details from John Lansdale. (Bush subsequently discovered that Groves had an agent following *him* around. "You take steps to see that it doesn't happen again," he scolded the general.)[40]

Hoping to limit knowledge of the bomb project to as few people as possible, Groves instructed Conant's traveling gumshoe to create a special counterintelligence organization—what Lansdale later called "a box within a box"—that would operate outside G-2 and the army's chain of command. For the purpose, Groves gave Lansdale a letter authorizing him to pick a single officer at each of the army's defense commands throughout the country. That individual would report only to Lansdale, while Lansdale would report only to Groves.[41] Armed with the letter, the new head of security for the Manhattan Project packed for another trip to the West Coast.

In the job barely two weeks, Groves was already a man in a hurry. He left his first meeting with the newly appointed Military Policy Committee to catch a southbound train for an inspection tour of Oak Ridge and other project sites.[42]

On October 8, 1942, Lawrence picked up Groves at the Naval Air Station in Alameda and drove him to the Rad Lab for a personal tour of the prototype Calutron, still under construction.[43] In his own office at LeConte, Oppie briefed the general on the theoretical work done thus far on the Super.[44] Oppenheimer also told Groves that the project needed a dedicated laboratory, located apart from the MED's production facilities, for the scientists who would build the bomb.[45]

Groves had recently come to the same conclusion. In fact, he had already picked a name for the place: Site Y. Groves had come to Berkeley with the thought of asking Lawrence to head the new lab. But he now changed his mind.[46] Ernest urged Groves to pick Ed McMillan for director. (Lawrence may even have told his brother-in-law that he had the job.)[47] Groves had met the quiet, somewhat diffident McMillan the previous month at the Met Lab.[48] Whatever impression McMillan had made then, Groves by the end of his Berkeley visit was considering Oppenheimer for the role.

A week later, Groves telephoned Oppie, asking that he join him in Chicago. On October 15, Oppenheimer crowded into a small compartment on the *Twentieth Century Limited* with Groves, Nichols, and a third army officer to discuss the new laboratory. As the train traveled east between Chicago and Detroit, Groves asked Oppenheimer to be the new lab's director.

Lansdale had already alerted the general to the earlier problems in clearing Oppie, and Groves would later claim to have personally read Oppenheimer's FBI file. Nothing he saw in the bureau's dossier caused him to change his mind. To Groves, moreover, Oppenheimer's difficulties with security probably seemed safely in the past.

Less than a month earlier, on September 20, the Investigations Division at the Presidio had closed its file on Oppenheimer after one of its agents interviewed Birge, who praised his colleague as "one of the two greatest World's physicist-mathematicians."[49] As before, no final decision was made on Oppenheimer's clearance, but the army recommended that he be kept under surveillance.

Before settling on Oppie, Groves had also asked others for their views. Ernest was reportedly amazed and upset that the army would choose a theoretician rather than an experimentalist for the job. "He couldn't run a hamburger stand" was the summary assessment of another of Oppenheimer's Berkeley colleagues.[50] Compton, too, expressed reservations about Oppie's administrative ability. "No one with whom I talked showed any great enthusiasm about Oppenheimer as a possible director," Groves later wrote, with admirable understatement.

But the general was confident that he himself could handle the administrative aspect of the job, if necessary.[51] Compton and Lawrence finally agreed to accept Oppenheimer on one condition: if Oppie did not work out, Groves would ask them to take over the laboratory.[52] McMillan was assigned a supporting role; his office at LeConte would be used as a temporary headquarters to plan the lab.

Just five days before Groves picked Oppenheimer, the FBI had obtained new and disturbing evidence of the physicist's "leftwandering."

On October 10, 1942, the FBI bug in Steve Nelson's office picked up a conversation between Nelson, Lloyd Lehmann—a Bay Area labor organizer affiliated with the Young Communist League—and another, unidentified member of the YCL.[53] According to bureau notes of the conversation:

> Lloyd told Steve about an important weapon that was being developed and indicated that he was on the research of it. Steve asked if "he" suspects you to be a YCLer. Steve then talked about a man, saying he was too jittery: he used to be active, but was inactive; was considered a "Red" and mentioned that the reason the Government lets him remain was because he was good in the scientific field. Steve indicated this man had worked in the Teachers' Committee and the Spanish Committee; and could not cover up his past.

The men in Nelson's office then went on to discuss someone else they knew in the project at Berkeley:

> Lloyd said [this individual] was in favor of coming out in the open more; said he had a three month deferment on the basis of war work; was 21; and had graduated. The unknown man then said Rossi was trained to do theoretical physics and should stay with that. Nelson said the project was extremely important and the third party said he would have to be an undercover Party member as if he quit his work they did not know what political work he could do as he might be drafted.

Further discussion revealed that "Rossi" was considering quitting the Berkeley project in order to organize workers at the Richmond shipyards. Nelson urged his visitors to persuade Rossi to remain at his current job as an undercover member of the party, since it was important "to have knowledge of such discoveries and research developments."[54]

Portions of the intercepted conversation were indistinct or garbled. The agents listening in did not recognize "Rossi" and knew nothing of the project at the Rad Lab. At the time, no one in the FBI had yet been made privy to that secret. In the army, Lansdale was still assembling his nameless box-within-a-box.

On October 19, Oppenheimer was back in Washington to see Groves. That morning, the general took the physicist along for a meeting with Bush at OSRD headquarters. When the Military Policy Committee had expressed objections to Oppie, Groves challenged its members to come up with a better candidate. He had yet to hear back from the committee. Getting Bush to approve Oppenheimer was likely the last hurdle to having the physicist appointed director. If Bush raised any objection, there is no record of it.

Oppenheimer, indeed, had already begun some discreet recruiting on his own—asking Bethe and Teller for the names of other scientists who might be brought into the fold. Immediately after the meeting with Bush, Oppie broke the news in a letter to Bethe:

> It is about time that I wrote to you and explained some of my wires and actions. I came east this time to get our future straight. It is turning out to be a very big order and I am not at liberty to tell you all that is going on. We are going to have a laboratory for the military applications, probably in a remote spot and ready for use, I hope, within the next few months.[55]

On a walk together along the shores of Lake Michigan, Oppenheimer sought Teller's advice about how best to organize the new lab. Later, sharing a berth on a train to Washington, Oppie was unusually solicitous of Edward—even rebandaging an infected wound on the latter's finger.

But Teller professed to find an ominous undertone in an innocuous remark that Oppenheimer uttered during the trip. Complaining, good-naturedly, about the restrictions that Groves was already imposing upon the project in the name of secrecy, Oppie predicted that the time would come "when we will have to do things differently and resist the military."

Teller, taken aback, voiced his objections. Privately, he wondered whether Oppie's comment did not foreshadow some future, unspecified act of civil disobedience, or worse. Oppenheimer, he noted, abruptly changed the subject. But the distance between them, Teller felt, had begun to grow.[56]

Three weeks after receiving Bush's wary benediction, Oppenheimer gave the army a list of personnel to be recruited for the new laboratory. The list contained forty-four names—McMillan, Segrè, Serber, Teller, and Bethe were prominent among them. Fermi would remain behind in Chicago, at least initially, to continue work on the atomic pile. Alvarez, originally suggested by Bethe, was stricken from the list by Oppenheimer and Teller. Luie was already busy with the radar project at MIT in any case, and his oversized ego may also have been a factor against him.[57]

On November 16, Oppenheimer and McMillan met up with John Dudley, an army colonel from the corps's Manhattan District, at the Hilton hotel in Albuquerque. From there the trio proceeded through a light snowstorm in an unmarked army sedan to the remote spot that Dudley had picked for the lab.[58]

The site, Jemez Springs, was a deep and heavily wooded canyon an hour's drive northwest of Santa Fe. Oppenheimer and McMillan found the location depressing—too dark, too confining. Groves, joining the group, worried about flash floods and the difficulty of building housing for the 265 people he told Dudley he thought the lab would employ.[59] Another headache was the close proximity of an Indian reservation, which Groves feared might require him to divulge the greatest secret of the war to Harold Ickes, FDR's garrulous secretary of interior.[60]

At Oppenheimer's suggestion, the group drove out of the canyon and up a mesa on the other side of the Jemez Mountains to the site of a private boys' school. Oppie knew of the school from summers spent at nearby Perro Caliente. The Los Alamos Ranch School took its name from the thick stands of trees growing on the two-mile-long mesa: *Los Alamos* was Spanish for "the cottonwoods."

At an elevation of 7,200 feet, the mesa had a commanding vista of the Sangre de Cristo Mountains to the east and was sufficiently isolated to satisfy Groves's concern with security. Although Indian reservations surrounded the land, they were at a far enough remove to avoid inference from Ickes.

The army began negotiations to purchase the land less than a week later; the Ranch School had never fully recovered from the depression, and the owners were eager to sell. A headquarters office for the project was rented on East Palace Avenue in Santa Fe, thirty miles to the southeast. A week later, Oppenheimer and McMillan returned with Lawrence to show him the proposed location of the new laboratory. "Lawrence was pleased by the site, and so, again, were we," Oppenheimer reported to Groves.[61]

Lawrence and McMillan also accompanied Oppenheimer on a cross-country recruiting drive for the new lab a few days later. In Washington, the three pressed Bush and Conant to release scientists from the government-funded laboratories at MIT and San Diego so that they could go to New Mexico.[62]

The remoteness of the site and Groves's strict security restrictions imposed unique burdens upon the recruiters. Because the army wanted to protect the identity of scientists working at the lab, there would be neither banks nor a post office at Los Alamos. Except for occasional forays to Santa Fe and the nearby Indian ruins, residents remained essentially prisoners behind the wire. (Los Alamos, Teller would observe, "gave one a new appreciation of grass and strangers.") But Oppenheimer found potential recruits worried less about the isolation and secrecy than about the army's domination of the project.

Initially, Oppie had not questioned Groves's decision to make the laboratory a military installation. Groves justified the move on the grounds that work at the lab would be inherently dangerous. (Unmentioned was the fact that such an arrangement also promised to make discipline easier—and would allow the general to court-martial anyone who violated his edicts.)

Early in 1943, Oppenheimer would even report to the Presidio for a physical examination, the first step toward receiving an army commission as a lieutenant colonel, the highest rank that Groves could obtain for a laboratory director. Groves instructed the officer who accompanied Oppie to advise the doctors that they were not to flunk the subject because of any physical or psychological infirmity. The examiners declared Oppenheimer eleven pounds underweight but otherwise fit for duty. Afterward, Oppie was measured for a uniform.[63]

However, avuncular advice from two senior physicists—Isidor Rabi, then at MIT's Rad Lab, and Caltech's Robert Bacher—persuaded Oppenheimer that he should insist upon "scientific autonomy" for Los Alamos. Reluctantly, Groves backed down.[64] With the army willing to cede at least some authority to civilians, the pace of recruiting picked up.[65]

Oppie surprised all by submitting a detailed organization chart in mid-December 1942. The lab was to have four main components: Bethe would head the Theoretical, or "T," Division. Bacher was in charge of Experimental Physics. Chemistry and Metallurgy would be in the hands of two men: Cyril Smith, a metallurgist then working for the NDRC in Washington, and Joseph Kennedy, the young Berkeley chemist who had predicted to Lansdale that no nation would have enough uranium to build a bomb during the war. The Ordnance Division, which would actually assemble the bomb, was to be headed by a navy captain, William "Deke" Parsons.[66]

John Manley, a University of Washington physicist originally assigned to help Oppenheimer at Chicago, became Oppie's right-hand man for planning and staffing the New Mexico lab. Asked to calculate the total number of buildings that would be required, Manley had simply added up the space committed thus far to atomic research at universities around the country; he estimated that about two dozen scientists would need offices.[67] Oppenheimer, looking ahead, ordered the buildings enlarged to allow for expansion and added a cryogenics laboratory to the blueprints, for research on the Super.[68]

As late as the end of 1942, exactly who or what would administer Los Alamos for the army had yet to be decided. But Chicago's Met Lab and the Rad Lab at MIT had established the precedent of university-run, federally funded laboratories for defense work in the wartime emergency. Oppenheimer suggested Caltech or Harvard as possible candidates to run the new lab in the desert.[69]

Groves, too, recognized, albeit grudgingly, that an affiliation with academe offered the best chance of attracting the "prima donnas" that he hoped would join the project. But New Mexico contained no university of a size or stature equal to the job, and Oppenheimer—nursing his own unspoken grievances—refused to make the case for his adopted alma mater.

Lawrence showed no such reticence. As Berkeley's biggest booster, he had already begun urging Sproul and the university's comptroller to bid on the army contract.[70]

The university's representatives in these negotiations was Robert Underhill, a short, stocky, determined man with a salt-and-pepper crew-cut. Underhill would later describe his charter from Sproul as "to see to it that the University didn't lose any money."[71] A 1915 graduate of Berkeley's College of Commerce, Underhill had been an accountant at a paint company before joining the university. By 1933 he was secretary-treasurer to the regents. As deputy chairman of a university committee created on the eve of the war to handle secret defense contracts, Underhill knew better than to ask questions.

Even so, he hit a brick wall with Oppenheimer and Groves, who refused even to divulge the name of the state that the secret laboratory would be located in—saying only that it was in "the Rocky Mountain area." (The general relented after Underhill explained that the university's insurance carrier would refuse to write an indemnification policy without such information.)

Underhill found Oppenheimer similarly tight-lipped when he visited Eagle Hill on a Sunday afternoon. Oppie at one point stopped speaking entirely, resuming only when Underhill threatened to walk out of both the meeting and the contract unless he were told more. Still, Oppie spoke "very guardedly and I learned very little," Underhill subsequently recalled.[72]

Remarkably, neither Sproul nor Underhill had been told the purpose of the secret enterprise that they were being asked to run in the far-off desert.*[73] When Berkeley's business manager complained to Groves in January that he had yet to see "the scratch of a pen—one written word" on the subject, Groves asked Stimson to personally reassure Sproul as to the project's importance.[74] (Sproul drolly assured Conant, in reply, that he had "no doubt as to which project is first and foremost, even if I were not reminded frequently by its distinguished director." But he was, Sproul protested, already doing everything he could for Ernest Lawrence: "Indeed, I have done enough so that there is some conflict in the minds of the faculty in general as to whether I am administering a University or a Radiation Laboratory.")[75]

* Underhill was not told the secret for another year; Sproul probably learned sometime after that. One evening in November 1943, Underhill was summoned to LeConte by Lawrence, who made a show of locking the door and drawing the blinds. "We practically crawled under the desk," Underhill later remembered. "Do you know what they're doing down there?" Lawrence asked. Underhill confessed his ignorance and became an initiate. The regents' representative was also told that he was never to divulge the secret to Sproul, who had appalled Groves by speculating in a commencement address that the Rad Lab was developing a secret "death ray."

Spurred on by Lawrence, Sproul and Underhill agreed to take the leap into the void. On February 1, 1943, Sproul initialed a $150,000, six-month contract between the university and the government "for certain investigations to be directed by Dr. J. R. Oppenheimer."[76] The single-page document specified that details of the contract would be worked out later.[77]

With plans for Oppenheimer's desert laboratory in place, the other crucial part of the Manhattan Project—obtaining the fissionable material for the bomb—had hit a major snag near the end of 1942.

In November, a British scientist casually mentioned to Conant over lunch that naturally occurring impurities in plutonium might cause it to fission spontaneously, making it unusable in a weapon. Seaborg had, in fact, pointed out this very problem to Oppenheimer weeks earlier. But it came as sudden and unexpected news to Conant and Groves.

Most worrisome of all was the fact that the warning had come from a British scientist. Groves feared that Lawrence's optimism might have subtly infected the entire U.S. project, causing other potentially fatal flaws to be overlooked. The fact that Fermi was building the world's first nuclear reactor in a heavily populated part of Chicago undoubtedly added to this concern.[78]

Lingering doubts and a pessimistic report by DuPont—the contractor chosen to build the plutonium production reactors at Hanford, in Washington State—prompted Groves to order a reappraisal of the entire S-1 Project that fall. He and Conant picked a five-man committee, chaired by MIT chemical engineer Warren Lewis, to review the status of Urey's gaseous diffusion project at Columbia, Lawrence's Calutrons, and Fermi's atomic pile. Lewis's committee arrived in Berkeley for an inspection visit on November 28.

Lawrence worried most about the reaction of DuPont's representative on the panel, engineer Crawford Greenewalt. Since "Greenie" was the man responsible for the negative report on Hanford, Ernest was eager to make a good impression.[79]

Lawrence had long since abandoned taking lab visitors to DiBiasi's, the cheap Italian eatery in Albany, in favor of Trader Vic's, an ersatz-Polynesian restaurant in downtown Oakland whose owner had become a friend.[80] "Vics" was famous for its Mai Tais—potent rum drinks served in tall glasses topped by paper umbrellas. Ernest's favorite table was on a raised platform near the bar, underneath a painting of a hula dancer. Dinner that night for the Lewis Committee followed a full-day tour of the Rad Lab and its one-sixteenth-scale model of a production Alpha Calutron. But Lawrence's hospitality failed to make a dent with Greenewalt, who showed a flinty indifference to Ernest's trademark bonhomie.

What bothered Greenewalt most was Lawrence's incessant talk about future plans for even bigger machines. Greenewalt glimpsed in the prototype Calutron the "mess of machinery" that Conant feared, but without results. Oppenheimer, tagging along on the tour, had tried at one point to rein-in Lawrence's jaunty enthusiasm. "So as a result of Oppenheimer holding Lawrence down, we finally got a view of what they had actually done," Greenewalt wrote in his diary that night.[81] The poker-faced engineer and the rest of Lewis's committee returned to Chicago in time to witness the successful start-up of Fermi's atomic pile.

Lewis submitted his report to the Military Policy Committee in early December. He recommended giving priority to gaseous diffusion and Fermi's plutonium-producing reactor. But the report cast a baleful eye upon electromagnetic separation, and Lewis dismissed Lawrence's Calutrons as unlikely to produce enough U-235 in time to be useful in the war.[82]

Conant and Groves simply ignored Lewis's advice. On December 10, 1942, the Military Policy Committee approved plans to build Lawrence's proposed 100-gram-a-day separation facility.

At Berkeley, the atomic bomb project had meanwhile outgrown Donner Laboratory, so Lawrence and his Rad Lab colleagues moved into the New Classroom Building nearby.[83] A campus policeman was stationed at the door, and Ernest's red leather chair was ceremoniously transferred from LeConte library to his new office on the second floor. Two days before Christmas, Lawrence presided over a first meeting with Groves and contractor representatives concerning construction of a planned 500-tank Alpha Calutron at Y-12, the army's code name for the electromagnetic separation plant in Tennessee's Bear Creek Valley.[84]

The Alpha Calutron design was frozen at year's end. Groves notified Stone and Webster that he expected the inaugural racetrack to be operating by the summer. The army had recently picked Tennessee Eastman Corporation to run the production plant, and employees of the company were already beginning to arrive in Bear Valley. Wallace Reynolds, the Rad Lab's business manager, opened one office at Oak Ridge and another near the contractor's headquarters in Boston to coordinate work on the Calutrons. In mid-February 1943, Stone and Webster broke ground for the first racetrack before the construction drawings had even been approved.[85]

On March 16, Robert and Kitty Oppenheimer left Berkeley for Santa Fe by train, bound for Los Alamos. Their son, Peter, a toddler not yet two, would follow with his nurse a few days later. In the weeks before, Oppenheimer had been saying his good-byes. He and Steve Nelson had met for lunch at a restaurant on University Avenue. Oppie, Nelson later wrote, was "excited to the point of nervousness. He couldn't discuss where he was going, but would only say that it had to do with the war effort."[86] They talked instead of other things: Spain and the war.

A last-minute call from Jean Tatlock—who continued to lean upon Oppie at moments of psychological distress—went unanswered.[87]

Another friend to whom Oppie bid adieux was Haakon Chevalier, who would subsequently describe their leave-taking elegiacally, as evoking "a 'Cherry Orchard' mood."[88] Chevalier remembered Oppenheimer expressing the fear that the Germans might win the war. "But perhaps we can think up a few tricks," Oppie added, brightening.[89] Barbara Chevalier had figured out that the couple must be headed for the mountains, since Kitty was buying woolen clothes for Peter. Oppie would later recall only that he had complained to Chevalier about his security clearance being held up.[90]

Their political coffee klatch had held its final meeting the previous spring, before disbanding on account of the war; Oppenheimer had missed this last gathering, having been summoned to Chicago by Compton.[91]

Chevalier, too, was adjusting to changes brought about by the war. He had long been aware that his fortunes at the university were on the wane. His department chairman had informed him that he should look for a teaching job elsewhere. But Chevalier, like Oppenheimer, was also feeling guilty to be sitting out the war. A week before he bid farewell to Oppie, Haakon had written to his son, Jacques, an undergraduate at Yale:

> We are such a small part of this big, world-shaking revolution that we may well feel discouraged. But the world does move, however slowly, and perhaps, even in our small way, we shall be able to play an effective role. It is ironic for me to feel how little I am doing for this war while I imagine the possibility of doing so much. I certainly don't intend to resign myself to remaining a bystander, but as yet I am not reconciled to becoming a small cog in the monster machine, where my hands would be tied and where, though I would be an integral part of the "war effort" I might have fewer possibilities of doing some [sic] effective within my feeble competence than if I retain, for the time being, some freedom of action.[*92]

* Haakon had recently received a letter from the dean, warning that his son was spending too much time on campus promoting political causes. Yet the admonitory letter that Haakon sent to Jacques may have said more about the father than the son: "There is nothing more pitiful than a left-wing campus intellectual who can't make the grade. He carries no authority and inspires nothing but contempt."

PART TWO

INSIDE THE WIRE

We shall all be one large family doing work inside the wire.

—Robert Oppenheimer,
Los Alamos, 1943

5

ENORMOZ

OPPENHEIMER HAD BARELY unpacked at Los Alamos when Underhill arrived by train on his first inspection trip. The regents' representative was still hoping to learn what he and Sproul had committed the university to do. Oppie, however, did his best to frustrate Underhill's investigation. Wedged in the backseat of an army sedan between Oppenheimer and Priscilla Duffield, Oppie's secretary at the lab, Underhill was driven quickly up the rough and dusty road that led to the mesa before being taken back to Santa Fe. The lab's director volunteered no useful information about the project during the drive.

Undeterred, Underhill would make monthly visits to Los Alamos for the duration of the war. As ever, the regents' representative remained the soul of discretion. To discourage questions from curious strangers, Underhill told everyone he met on the east-bound train that he was a farmer from Manhattan, Kansas—a town the railroad bypassed. On the return trip, Underhill introduced himself as a California olive farmer, knowing that there were only a few places in the state where olives were grown. He memorized the market price of oats and alfalfa and read a book on olive tree diseases so that his cover would be all the more believable.[1]

With a university attorney in tow, Underhill headed east again the following month to work out final arrangements with the army. On April 20, 1943, he signed Contract 36 on behalf of the regents, for administrating Los Alamos. Six weeks later, Underhill was back in Groves's suite at the Biltmore to sign Contract 48, for expenses related to the Calutrons and other army projects at the Rad Lab. Both agreements were dated January 1, 1943, to account for the work already done by the university.[2]

At Los Alamos, work on the bomb was already under way. Oppenheimer assigned Serber the job of briefing the dozens of scientists arriving from colleges and universities around the country. In early April, the recruits assembled in the uncompleted library of T Building, future offices for the theoretical physicists. In a series of five lectures given over the next two weeks, Serber laid out the current state of knowledge about the atomic bomb, including what had been learned since the Berkeley summer seminar.

Eager to dispel any illusions about the nature of the task, Serber emphasized at the outset that the "object of the project is to produce a *practical military weapon.*"[3] Cautioned about using the word *bomb* while uncleared construction workers were still crawling around in the ceiling above his head, Serber began calling it the "gadget" instead. Taking the last digit of the atomic number, 94, and the last digit of the atomic weight, 239, he referred to plutonium as "49"; uranium was simply "U" or "the material."

The first gadget discussed by Serber was the so-called gun, the earliest image of the bomb going as far back as the M.A.U.D. report. In a gun-type bomb, two subcritical pieces of U-235 or plutonium would be "assembled" by being fired into each other by a cannon. Theoretically, the 3,000-foot-a-second acceleration would drive the pieces together into a supercritical mass before stray neutrons could predetonate it. Serber named the long, skinny device the "Thin Man," after the character in the popular film starring William Powell and Myrna Loy.[4]

An alternative design, more complex but more efficient—if it worked—had been dubbed the "Introvert" by Caltech's Richard Tolman, whom Groves had sent to Los Alamos as a kind of inspector general.[5] The weapon that Tolman and Serber imagined would surround a hollow sphere of fissionable material with ordinary high explosives. When detonated, the explosives would collapse the shell of uranium or plutonium into a compact ball of supercritical density. Tolman talked of assembling the bomb by "imploding" it.[6] Serber eventually called the device "Fat Man," in honor of the figure played by Sidney Greenstreet in *The Maltese Falcon.*[7]

Using the latest critical mass figures derived by Eldred Nelson and Stanley Frankel, Serber announced that 33 pounds of enriched uranium or about 11 pounds of plutonium would be required for a single bomb.[8]

Before work could start on either design, however, cross-section measurements and neutron densities had to be obtained. For the purpose, huge scientific apparatuses were acquired and transported in secret to the remote site. Scouring the country, McMillan located a suitable cyclotron at Harvard and arranged to have it trucked up the treacherous road to the top of the mesa. (The army instructed McMillan to tell Harvard physicists that the machine was destined for a medical facility in St. Louis. No one believed him.)[9] By mid-April, the cyclotron was safely in place, along with a team to run it.

Wilson and his graduate students had meanwhile decamped Princeton en masse and were housed in Fuller Lodge, the Lincoln log–like assembly hall of the former Ranch School that was being used as a bachelor dormitory. Conant and the OSRD had decided to abandon the Isotron and put the money saved into Lawrence's Calutrons. On weekends, Serber tried, with varied degrees of success, to teach the Princetonians horsemanship.

Late in April, Groves sent another review committee to Los Alamos, headed by the ubiquitous Warren Lewis. Although irked by the interruption, Oppenheimer prepared three days of presentations on the lab's experimental program, aided by Serber and Teller.[10]

Edward was irritated that Oppie had passed him over and picked Bethe to head the Theoretical Division. (Teller privately considered Bethe a "brick maker" among physicists—thorough, meticulous, but unimaginative and even a bit pompous. In Oppenheimer, on the other hand, Edward recognized a kindred spirit—a "bricklayer," or synthesizer, who understood the underlying structure. "I was not happy about having him as my boss," Teller freely admitted of Bethe.)

Despite earlier defending Groves to Oppenheimer, moreover, Teller was already objecting to the strictures that secrecy imposed upon science at the lab. Reprimanded for discussing classified subjects outside the Tech Area, Edward had replied, sarcastically, "Aren't we all a big happy family here?"

But Teller's real difficulty at Los Alamos was more fundamental and concerned his reaction to something that most at the lab saw not only as indispensable but as a positive advantage: teamwork. He was uncomfortable with the fact that, at Los Alamos, "almost constant collaboration was necessary, all the work was done at a feverish pace, and one's new idea, once hatched, could be taken away and given to others to develop." It was, he later protested, "a little like giving one's child to someone else to raise."[11]

Oppie had assigned Edward to study unorthodox approaches to the fission bomb. These included "autocatalytic" weapons—bombs where the efficiency would increase as the chain reaction proceeded. The danger of a dud and instability were the major problems with this approach.[12]

One concept favored by Teller was a bomb whose active material was a compressed white powder containing uranium and hydrogen. Teller had raised the possibility of a so-called hydride bomb at the Berkeley seminar the previous summer. Its theoretical advantage was that the critical mass might be as little as one-twentieth that of metallic uranium. But the hydrogen in the mixture absorbed neutrons and thus slowed the chain reaction, reducing the power of the explosion and even running the risk of a fizzle. "Some bright ideas are needed," Serber concluded in his lecture on the subject. None had yet been forthcoming.[13]

On April 28, 1943, Teller, Fermi, and Bethe joined Earl Long, a University of Missouri chemist, in a presentation on the status of the Super. Long was an expert on cryogenics and in charge of the deuterium experiments that were being conducted at a shed on the mesa's south rim.[14] By way of introduction, Oppenheimer described the likelihood of sparking a thermonuclear reaction with a fission explosion as "highly probable . . . in principle." Development of the Super should "follow immediately the completion of the gadget," he felt.[15]

As at Berkeley, Teller described how the shock wave from an exploding atomic bomb might be used to ignite a cubic meter of liquid deuterium. But he conceded that his latest calculations showed that the fission trigger for such a superbomb would require more than 160 pounds of uranium, or nearly 60 pounds of plutonium. As all were aware, tiny flecks of uranium metal had only begun accumulating in the collectors of the prototype Calutron, and none had yet left Berkeley. It still took more than a week of bombardments on the Rad Lab's 60-inch to make enough plutonium to be visible to the unaided eye.

Thus, when Oppenheimer told the Lewis Committee that it might take only three years to build the Super—eighteen months for experimental measurements, and another eighteen months to design the actual weapon—his assumption was that the materials for the bomb would be already in hand.[16] Given the daunting task of building the first fission bomb, Oppie left no doubt that he put the Super far behind the gadget in terms of priority. Indeed, requirements for the Super, he reported to Groves that summer, were "sufficiently remote in time so that we would prefer to postpone listing them."[17]

Nonetheless, Oppenheimer's decision to subordinate work on the Super to the fission gadget further riled Teller.[18] After Edward, in a fit of pique, walked out of a meeting of section leaders, Oppie agreed to meet with the temperamental Hungarian every week in private. At these meetings, the Super was a recurrent theme that, Bolero-like, increased in both intensity and tempo, until it came to dominate the sessions.[19]

Teller's final presentation to the Lewis Committee, also at Oppenheimer's request, concerned not the Super but a prospect that none of those at the lab was eager to contemplate: the possibility of abject failure. Vannevar Bush had raised the thought—the hope, really—that some as-yet-undiscovered quirk of Nature might make a fission weapon impossible. Edward's lecture concerned an inelegant alternative to the bomb: the use of radioactive poisons. Even if the atomic bomb did not work, Teller noted, the waste from Hanford's reactors could still be used to contaminate up to 100 square miles of enemy territory with persisting and near-lethal levels of radioactivity. Fission products from the atomic piles could either deny an area to the enemy or be dumped on his soldiers to kill them outright.

Oppenheimer's decision to entertain this macabre alternative to the bomb was arguably simple prudence, a hedge against the unpredictable. Two years earlier, Compton's review panel had given radiological warfare precedence, ahead of the fission bomb, among the possible military applications of atomic energy. The figures that Teller cited in his lecture came from a December 1941 report by Princeton physicists Smyth and Wigner, who had likened the use of radiation as a weapon to "a particularly vicious form of poison gas." Wigner found the subject so distasteful that he subsequently tried to disassociate himself from the report.[20]

But eighteen months of war had changed the old way of thinking.[21] Fermi had already broached the subject of radiological weapons with Oppenheimer and was surprised at the reaction. Oppie wrote Fermi, in reply, of plans to poison "food sufficient to kill a half a million men, since there is no doubt that the actual number affected will . . . be much smaller than this."[22]

Visiting from Chicago that spring, Fermi found Oppenheimer's callous bravado indicative of a different mood among the scientists. He was surprised to discover, Fermi told Oppie, that his friends at Los Alamos now sounded like they actually *wanted* the bomb to work.[23]

By spring 1943, the Manhattan Project was also a priority of the Soviet Union's. Two years earlier, the NKVD—the People's Commissariat of Internal Affairs—had ordered its intelligence officers serving under diplomatic cover in Soviet embassies and consulates to begin collecting information on the status of technical research in the West. The NKVD's spies were supplemented by a parallel espionage network run by the Soviet army's Intelligence Directorate, the GRU.

Thirty-five-year-old Pavel Fitin, head of the NKVD's First Directorate (Foreign Intelligence), had been instructed to focus his efforts upon answering some technical questions of particular interest.[24] One of these concerned American progress toward a fission weapon. In preparations to steal U.S. secrets, Fitin had given his enterprise a code name appropriate to the Manhattan Project: *Enormous (Enormoz)*.[25] The cryptonyms that Fitin assigned to vital intelligence targets within the United States were borrowed from history. But they also reflected an ideological slant and, in some cases, a sense of humor: Washington, D.C., was *Carthage;* New York City was *Tyre;* San Francisco became *Babylon.*[26]

Nearly a generation's experience of running spies in the United States had given the Soviets a base of operations that was both broad and deep. In the capital alone, the Russians had two active espionage rings stealing secrets from the U.S. government. The larger ring, headed by a Berkeley-trained economist, Nathan Gregory Silvermaster (code name *Robert*), had twenty-seven members working in six different federal agencies.[27] The spies in *Robert*'s ring included the assistant secretary of the treasury, Harry Dexter White *(Richard)*, and Lauchlin Currie *(Page)*, a senior aide to President Roosevelt.[28] Others recruited by the Soviets to spy included a congressman from New York *(Crook)*, the daughter of the U.S. ambassador to prewar Berlin *(Liza)*, and at least three State Department officials *(Ernst, Frank,* and *Ales.)*[29]

With the outbreak of war, American intelligence, too, became a target of particular interest to Fitin. The Office of Strategic Services *(Cabin)* was compromised from its mid-1942 birth by more than a dozen agents, who reported on its activities to Moscow; as was the Office of War Information *(Wireless)*, which split off from the OSS that same year.[30] Not surprisingly, also of special interest to the Soviets were the U.S. government agencies responsible for spy hunting, the FBI *(Shack)* and army G-2 *(Salt)*.[31]

To pass stolen secrets to Russia, Fitin established a *residentura*, a base for espionage operations, at the four-story townhouse on East Sixty-first Street that served as the Soviets' New York consulate. He put an NKVD agent with a background in engineering—Leonid Kvasnikov, code-named *Anton*—in charge of spying on the bomb.[32]

Like agents at other Soviet diplomatic posts, Kvasnikov used Amtorg, the Soviet Union's import-export agency, as a cover for espionage activities. As the clearinghouse for the wartime Lend-Lease program, Amtorg had offices in major cities on both coasts. Soviet couriers sent purloined documents by diplomatic pouch on Russian-bound ships, as well as via a special air connection operating from an Army Air Corps field in Great Falls, Montana.[33]

Shorter messages were encrypted and sent between Moscow and the Soviets' diplomatic posts by regular commercial telegraphy.*[34] When the volume of cable traffic, including secrets, threatened to become overwhelming, the Soviets clandestinely installed illegal short-wave radio transmitters at their consulates in New York and San Francisco.[35]

But since research on a fission weapon had its true origins in England, it was through the NKVD's British spies, rather than Fitin's American network, that Moscow Center first learned about the bomb.[36]

* Copies of the cables were, of course, passed to U.S. Army cryptanalysts, who, beginning in late 1946, were able to partially decipher them in a secret code-breaking project named *Venona*. The *Venona* decrypts were subsequently used to identify Soviet agents operating in the United States. They are the primary source for the code names and cables cited in this section.

On the same day in July 1941 that British scientists completed the M.A.U.D. report, the NKVD *rezident* in London, Anatoli Gorski *(Vadim)*, had informed Moscow of its contents.[37] The reliability of *Vadim*'s information was confirmed by another spy, code-named *Rest.*

Rest was Klaus Fuchs, a German-born physicist and Communist who had fled to England in 1933. By 1941, Fuchs was working with M.A.U.D. Committee physicist Rudolf Peierls on gaseous diffusion and bomb physics at Birmingham University.[38] Shortly after Germany's invasion of Russia, Fuchs had begun passing information on British atomic research to Moscow through the Soviets' military attaché in London.[39]

With the enemy at the gates, the Russians did not react to the news from Gorski and Fuchs until March 1942, when Lavrentii Beria, head of the NKVD, informed Stalin and the State Defense Committee of the secrets received from British spies. Beria recommended that the Soviet Union set up its own scientific panel to carry out research on the atomic bomb—which he had previously feared might be a plot by the West to trick the Soviet Union into wasting its talent and resources on a technological dead end.[40]

It was not until September 1942 that Vyacheslav Molotov, Stalin's foreign minister and a member of the State Defense Committee, sent Mikhail Pervukhin, people's commissar of the chemical industry, the NKVD reports along with a request for advice on how to interpret them. Pervukhin, too, urged an independent assessment. The Soviet Academy of Sciences recommended thirty-nine-year-old Igor Kurchatov—a tall, barrel-chested physicist born in the Urals—to lead the review.

Energetic as well as tenacious, Kurchatov had been nicknamed "the General" by his academy colleagues. In the early 1930s, after he and another scientist at Leningrad's Institute for Physics and Technology had drawn up plans for a cyclotron, Kurchatov was invited to Berkeley's Radiation Laboratory by Lawrence. Kurchatov did not make the trip, but the Leningrad cyclotron was built in any event.[41]

Shortly after the Nazi invasion, Kurchatov, adopting the custom of Roman emperors in time of war, announced that he would refuse to shave until the enemy was vanquished. Predictably, "the General" became "the Beard."[42]

In the work he was assigned, Kurchatov benefited from the scientific publications that had appeared in the West prior to the secrecy embargo. These included the June 1940 *Physical Review* article by McMillan and Abelson, which the British had feared would tip the Germans off to the discovery of neptunium.[43] Kurchatov learned about neutron cross sections from a "Letter to the Editor," written by Alvarez, appearing in a 1941 issue of the *Review.* Like other Soviet physicists, Kurchatov correctly surmised that his American counterparts had gone underground when they abruptly stopped publishing their research.[44]

Kurchatov began by putting information from the pre-embargo journals together with the fragments of intelligence gathered by the NKVD. The result was a comprehensive report on atomic research in the West, which Kurchatov submitted to Pervukhin in two handwritten memos during early March 1943.[45] "The Beard" underlined in blue pencil information he considered of special interest "that it would be desirable to obtain from abroad."[46]

As in the West, the Russians' initial focus was upon isotope separation. Kurchatov's summary reflected considerable interest in gaseous diffusion—the method favored in the M.A.U.D. report, and the one that Fuchs was most familiar with. The summary likewise showed that the Soviet Union had learned of the success of Fermi's Chicago pile within six weeks of the event.[47]

But Kurchatov's report also revealed some surprising gaps in the Russians' knowledge. Among these was his conclusion that "the mass spectrography method . . . is . . . considered inapplicable to uranium." His report to Pervukhin showed, too, that the Soviets were still ignorant of, and thus eager to learn, the critical mass of U-235.[48]

Kurchatov was most excited about the realization, arrived at through espionage, of "a new direction in tackling the entire uranium problem"—the fact that plutonium could also be used for a bomb—and stressed in his report that *"prospects of this direction are unusually captivating. . . . In this connection I am asking you to instruct Intelligence Bodies to find out about what has been done in America in regard to the direction in question."*[49]

To help in identifying the next targets for Russia's spies, Kurchatov listed for Pervukhin a number of laboratories in the United States where work on plutonium might be taking place. Berkeley's Rad Lab was at the top of his list.

Fortunately for the Soviets, Kurchatov's seed fell upon fertile soil. The FBI considered the San Francisco Bay area, and particularly Berkeley, a recruiting ground for subversives going back to the West Coast waterfront strike of 1934.[50]

In November 1941, Fitin had established a secret *residentura* at the Soviets' consulate in San Francisco, a beaux-arts mansion overlooking the Bay on Divisidero Street. The NKVD *rezident* was the forty-two-year-old vice consul, Gregori Kheifets. Before his posting in California, Kheifets had reportedly served as secretary to Lenin's wife, later becoming a high-ranking official in the Moscow offices of the Comintern. The small, dark, and rather sinister-looking Russian had also served as an "illegal"—a spy without diplomatic cover—while a student in Italy and Germany. Returning to Moscow, Kheifets beat the odds and survived Stalin's notorious "blood" purges.[51] To Americans, Kheifets introduced himself as "Mr. Brown."[52] But to Fitin at Moscow Center, he was known as *Kharon (Charon),* after the boatman who ferried damned souls across the River Styx into Hell.[53]

Joined by the consulate's third secretary, Pyotr Ivanov, Kheifets set out almost immediately to recruit so-called talent spotters: sympathetic Americans, usually Communists, who agreed to identify prospective candidates for the Soviets' espionage effort.[54] One of *Kharon*'s early recruits was FAECT organizer George Eltenton, the Shell employee who had spoken for the union at Oppie's house.[55]

Eltenton was a British-born chemical engineer who had first visited Russia in summer 1931, with a group of fellow scientists, on a three-week tour. When he returned to England at the start of the depression, the only job the Cambridge-educated Eltenton could find was at the British Cotton Industry Research Association in grimy Manchester. Not surprisingly, George and his wife, Dorothea, eagerly accepted, in 1937, an invitation to Leningrad's prestigious Institute of Chemical Physics from Soviet physicist Yuri Khariton, whom Eltenton had met on his Russian tour. In Leningrad, George worked with another famed physicist, Nicholai Semenov, while "Dolly" served as personal secretary to a visiting American geneticist at the nearby Vavilov Institute.[56]

Despite the Stalinist purges already under way, the Eltentons became fervent believers in the Communist cause, as Dolly documented in a private journal. (Iconographic of her faith is Dolly's description of the December 1937 "election" of people's deputies: "The enthusiasm of the people was very genuine. To those of us there at the time the results were no surprise. There was not a candidate who received less than ninety per cent of the votes. In some cases almost one hundred per cent was recorded.")[57]

When foreigners' work permits were revoked in spring 1938—more fallout from Stalin's terror—the Eltentons showed little enthusiasm for returning to Manchester. Instead, they elected to move to California.

In 1946, George Eltenton would tell the FBI that he and his wife first met Kheifets and Ivanov on Berkeley's College Avenue one evening in November 1941, following a Cal football game, when they overheard the two diplomats speaking Russian. George said that he and Dolly ran into the two men again a few weeks later, at a cocktail party held in the home of a Berkeley professor, and shortly thereafter, during a benefit for Russian war relief held at the Chevaliers' house.[58]

The Eltentons invited Kheifets and Ivanov to their holiday party in 1941, as well as to subsequent social gatherings during the following year.[59] It was on one such occasion, in late spring 1942, that Kheifets asked Eltenton for the names of prominent American scientists who might be favorably disposed toward the USSR, and thus candidates for honorary membership in the Soviet Academy of Sciences. The NKVD had traditionally used such awards and prizes as a first step in the recruitment of prospective agents. (A week or two earlier, on May 8, 1942, Ernest Lawrence and Berkeley chemist Gilbert Lewis had been elected to honorary membership in the Soviet Academy. The following year, the two men and Walter Cannon, a Harvard physiologist, would be guests of honor at the Soviet embassy in Washington; Russian chargé d'affaires Andrei Gromyko personally presented the men with the little red-bound book that certified membership in the academy.)[60]

Eltenton told the FBI that he had raised Kheifets's question with Robert Oppenheimer. Oppie's suggested candidates included Vannevar Bush and the Compton brothers. Eltenton—who said he subsequently passed this information along to Kheifets—told the FBI that his contact with Mr. Brown had ended there.

Late in 1942, however, when the tide of battle had begun to turn at Stalingrad, it was Ivanov rather than Kheifets who came to the Eltentons' home. After dinner, Ivanov confided that he knew the work going on at the Radiation Laboratory was of military value and that it was connected with atomic energy. "Do you know any of the guys or any others connected with it?" Ivanov asked Eltenton.[61]

Ivanov's particular interest was with how well Eltenton knew Robert Oppenheimer, Ernest Lawrence, and a third scientist at Berkeley. (Eltenton subsequently said that he thought the individual was Alvarez, but he could not be sure.) Eltenton informed Ivanov that Lawrence was a most unlikely candidate for passing military secrets to the Soviet Union. Regarding Oppenheimer, Eltenton proposed that a mutual friend—Chevalier—act as an intermediary and approach the physicist. But Eltenton said that Chevalier had come back almost immediately afterward with the news "that there was no chance whatsoever of obtaining any data and Dr. Oppenheimer did not approve."[62]

How, Eltenton had asked Ivanov, would the information be given to the Russians? The Soviet diplomat had assured him, Eltenton subsequently told bureau agents, that the transfer would be "by very safe methods" and that the information could even be back in the informant's hands the same evening. Eltenton distinctly remembered Ivanov's description of the process by which secrets would be passed: it "went 'click, click, click.'"[63]

A friend of both Eltenton's and Kheifets's at this time was a thirty-three-year-old San Francisco socialite, Louise Bransten. Born Louise Rosenberg, the granddaughter of Gold Rush pioneers, she had inherited a fortune from her parents' dried fruit importing business.[64] Dubbed the "apricot heiress" by the local press, Bransten was also well-known in the city as an advocate of progressive causes. In 1929, Louise had married Richard Bransten, the scion of another prominent San Francisco family who went on to embrace communism.[65] During 1933, the two had traveled extensively in the Soviet Union.

Although Louise later divorced Bransten, she kept her former husband's name, and the couple remained on good terms. When San Francisco dockworkers were blocked from organizing a protest meeting during the waterfront strike, the two used their own money to hire the city's Scottish Rite Hall. Earlier, Louise and Richard had taken a course—"The Economics of Capitalism"—from Nathan Gregory Silvermaster, then a young professor at St. Mary's College in San Francisco.[66]

By 1941, Louise was assistant to the director of San Francisco's American-Russian Institute.[67] Dolly Eltenton and Thomas Addis served on the institute's board.[68] Like Haakon Chevalier, Bransten volunteered her home for parties benefiting political and humanitarian causes like the Spanish Loyalists and Russian war relief.[69]

Bransten's association with Kheifets had also made her an early target of the FBI's COMRAP investigation.[70] Bureau agents planted two bugs in her elegant home at 2626 Green Street, just around the corner from the Soviet consulate. The microphones—installed in an archway outside the library and in a light fixture in her bedroom—recorded dinnertime conversations and Bransten's romantic assignations with several individuals, including Kheifets, but yielded little of intelligence value.[71]

It was probably at Bransten's house that Kheifets first met Robert Oppenheimer, possibly at the benefit for veterans of the Abraham Lincoln Brigade that Oppie attended the night before the attack on Pearl Harbor.[*72] Like Eltenton and Bransten, Chevalier was another social contact whom the Russian diplomat had been careful to cultivate.[73] Frustrated

* According to *Sacred Secrets*, a book by Jerrold Schecter and Leona Schecter, and based in part upon Soviet sources, Kheifets first met Oppenheimer during this reception at Bransten's house, and thereafter had lunch with the physicist. The book claims that Oppenheimer ultimately informed Kheifets of the Einstein-Szilard letter and of Oppie's own concern that the United States was moving too slowly on the atomic project—information that Kheifets passed along in a coded telegram to Moscow. Reproduced in the book's appendix is a top-secret cable that the head of the wartime NKVD reportedly sent to Beria in October 1944, which includes this passage: "In 1942 one of the leaders of the scientific work on uranium in the USA, professor Oppenheimer (unlisted member of the *apparat* of Comrade Browder) informed us about the beginning of work. At the request of Comrade Kheifets, confirmed by Comrade Browder, he provided cooperation in access to the research for several of our tested sources including a relative of Comrade Browder."

Lacking additional documentation from former Soviet archives, it is difficult to know whether this cable is evidence of Oppenheimer's complicity in espionage or reflects the (understandable) desire of Kheifets and other NKVD operatives to curry favor with their boss.

about his stalemated career and stuck in an unhappy marriage, Chevalier had persuaded his department chairman to grant him a sabbatical for the coming academic year. Haakon decided to go to New York, where he hoped to get a literary job; he already had a contract with Dial Press to translate a novel by Salvador Dali.[74] But Chevalier also entertained notions of a more glamorous and exciting role. "I have filed application for some kind of work in one of the War services," he wrote to Jacques at Yale. "I am trying to wangle something through people who might remember me, but this is all very uncertain."[75] Bransten, also New York bound, was one of those helping Chevalier make connections on the East Coast.

In early April 1943, a few weeks after he had bid farewell to Oppie, Haakon sent a job application, including a completed personnel security questionnaire, to the Washington headquarters of the Office of War Information and the Office of Strategic Services.[76] Chevalier's application contained a letter of introduction written by Owen Lattimore, head of OWI's Pacific operations, addressed to White House aide Lauchlin Currie.[77]

At the FBI's San Francisco field office late in 1942, Robert King, the bureau's "one-man commie squad," was puzzled by Oppenheimer's suddenly frenetic travel schedule. Since the conversation intercepted in Steve Nelson's office that October, Oppie had become a subject of renewed interest to the bureau. Forbidden by Roosevelt's attorney general from tapping Oppenheimer's telephone, King and Special Agent-in-Charge Pieper were reduced to vicariously following the physicist around the country through the telephone company's log of his collect calls home to Kitty.[78] The only information gleaned thus far was that Oppenheimer seemed conscientious about keeping in touch.

Early in 1943, Pieper sent two of his agents across the Bay to talk with Harold Fidler, the army's area engineer in Berkeley. Fidler confirmed that there was indeed a secret military project going on at the Radiation Laboratory, and that Oppenheimer was involved, but he was unwilling or unable to say more.[79] (Conspicuous in their raincoats and fedoras, the two agents sat on the porch of the Faculty Club until Fidler pointed out Oppenheimer walking by.)

Frustrated at the army's lack of cooperation, King next called Lieutenant Colonel Boris Pash, the head of counterintelligence at the Presidio. Pash, as it turns out, was also Lansdale's handpicked man on the West Coast.

An intense and pugnacious bantamweight, Pash for the past two years had headed G-2, military intelligence, for the Western Defense Command and was the Fourth Army's foremost Soviet expert. Although born in San Francisco, he had fought the Bolsheviks in Russia's civil war; his father was the senior bishop of the Russian Orthodox Church in America. When the White armies were defeated, Boris returned to the United States with little job experience beyond coaching volleyball for a church youth camp in Sebastopol. For sixteen years, Pash headed the athletic department at Hollywood High School.[80]

Called to active duty following Pearl Harbor, Pash was assigned to running a network of army undercover agents sent into Mexico's Baja Peninsula to intercept saboteurs landed by Japanese submarines.[81] Although he encountered neither submarines nor saboteurs, Pash realized he had found his calling. Embracing the role of spycatcher, he assembled a personal collection of wigs, voice-altering devices, and disguises that he always carried with him on his travels.[82]

Pash abruptly told King that he had "no cognizance" of any military project across the Bay.[83] Disgusted, King asked the agent he had assigned to shadow Oppenheimer to draft a report on the physicist. Pieper sent the eighteen-page report to Hoover on February 10, 1943, and also had a copy hand-delivered to Pash at the Presidio.

The FBI director promptly forwarded Oppenheimer's file and an accompanying report on FAECT to G-2 headquarters in Washington.[84] Hoover warned the army that a major effort was under way by the radical union to recruit "'progressive' applicants" to spy upon an unknown secret project at the Rad Lab.[85]

Hoover's report arrived just as the army was setting up its own security and counterintelligence apparatus for the Manhattan Project. Early in February, Major General George Strong, the head of G-2, had appointed Captain Horace Calvert to run the project's Intelligence Section.[86] Calvert in turn picked an ex-FBI agent, Lieutenant Lyall Johnson, to be G-2's man in the Bay Area.

Johnson moved into an office on the first floor of Berkeley's New Classroom Building. To disguise its connection with the army's war effort, a campus policeman was stationed at the door. The room used by Oppie's grad students who were working on the project was just down the hall. Calvert had instructed Johnson to work closely with Pash and his shadow organization across the Bay. Johnson bought a supply of 3-by-5-inch cards from a stationery store on Telegraph Avenue and began keeping a file on Rad Lab employees who the army believed to be of questionable loyalty.

Ironically, the sudden interest in Oppenheimer had set off a turf war between the army and the bureau. General Strong's response to Hoover's warning had been to ask the FBI to cease its surveillance of the physicist—who, as Strong pointed out, was now the army's, not the bureau's, responsibility.[87] Believing that the bug in Steve Nelson's office had shown Oppenheimer complicit in espionage, however, the FBI director was reluctant to abandon his quarry. Thus, while Hoover dutifully instructed Pieper to close the file on Oppenheimer, he simultaneously approved the agent's plan for a new offensive aimed at uncovering Soviet spies in Berkeley. Titled "Communist Infiltration of the Radiation Laboratory," the FBI's latest file would become known at the bureau by its shorthand moniker, "CINRAD."[88]

A scant two weeks later, on March 29, 1943, the bureau's bug in Steve Nelson's home yielded the first hard evidence of espionage against the Manhattan Project. William Branigan was the FBI agent whom King had assigned to the wiretap.

Late that evening, Branigan monitored a conversation between Nelson's wife, Margaret, and a man who identified himself only as "Joe."[89] Told that Steve would not return from a union meeting until early morning, Joe agreed to come to the house to wait, since he said he had urgent and important information to convey.

When Nelson finally arrived, it was clear from his conversation with Joe that this was not their first encounter. The two had met a few days earlier with Bernadette Doyle, Nelson's assistant at Communist Party headquarters.[90] Steve apologized for not being able to speak more freely with Joe on that occasion, but "he would not discuss such matters even with the most trusted of Comrades."

Alone at the FBI listening post, Branigan alerted King, who dispatched Branigan's partner, Mike Cassidy, to Nelson's home in hopes of taking a photograph of Joe. Branigan frantically scribbled notes while he listened to the dialogue that took place in Nelson's living room: "Steve said that he was looking for a Comrade who was absolutely trustworthy. Joe insisted that he was and that he was willing to cooperate with the Party because he believed in it and the fact that it was right."

In Branigan's notes, Joe explained that the reason he needed to see Nelson on such short notice was because those working on the project would soon be relocated to a remote site, and he had been recently selected as one of those to go. The two discussed "the professor," who Nelson complained was "very much worried now and we make him feel uncomfortable."

"You won't hardly believe the change that has taken place," Joe agreed.

"To my sorrow, his wife is influencing him in the wrong direction," Steve said.

The discussion then shifted back to "the project." "Do you happen to know about what kind of materials they are working on?" Steve asked his guest. Joe hesitated before replying that most of the things he knew were already a matter of common knowledge among physicists around the world. Much of that early work had already been published, he said.

Branigan's notes recorded Nelson's delicate effort to coax more information from Joe:

> STEVE: "Joe, I'd like to ask you, would it be possible for you to give this elementary thing that's already been published, you know?"
> JOE: "Uh, huh." Long pause.
> STEVE: "Could I get a copy of that?"
> JOE: "The one that's published you mean?"
> STEVE: "Yeah. Is that possible?
> JOE: Long pause. "Now, wait just a second. Pauses. "It's natural I'm a little bit scared, because . . ." (trails off)

Joe worried that his Communist background—he had been a member of the party since 1938, he told Steve—would cause him to come under scrutiny by the project's investigators. Steve said that he had already been told something about the project by the professor: "What the nature of it is—as much as that." But his informant had been reluctant to discuss the subject, and Nelson had decided not to pressure him.

Finally, Joe gave in. Lowering his voice, he dictated in whispers while Nelson—and Branigan—took notes. The FBI agent strained to hear but was only able to catch and write down snippets: "Separation method is preferably that of the magnetic spectrograph with electrical and magnetic focusing, or less preferably, that of the velocity selector. . . . sphere 5 centimeters in diameter with material . . . deuterium. . . . this design is tentative and is being experimented upon."[91]

Joe also told Steve that there was already a separation plant under construction in Tennessee that was expected to employ from 2,000 to 3,000 workers.

Before he left, Joe and Steve discussed the logistics of future meetings. He had a sister in New York, Joe said, and her travels could be used as a cover for subsequent contacts, where he could pass additional information to Steve. Nelson advised Joe that comrades sent to Tennessee and other remote locations should work in teams of two and burn their party books as a precaution. As with Communists serving overseas in the army or navy, the names of those involved in the project would be kept in a secret list, which Steve said he would memorize and then destroy. In parting, Nelson again cautioned Joe not to put anything in writing.[92] Cassidy arrived outside Nelson's house in time only to catch a glimpse of Joe walking out the door.

Within hours of the meeting between Nelson and Joe, King had couriered a transcript of the conversation to G-2 at the Presidio, where the news hit

Pash like a thunderclap. Flying to Washington the following day to personally brief Groves and Lansdale on the incident, Pash believed that the FBI bug provided proof of Oppenheimer's involvement in an espionage plot.[93]

Pash assigned Lyall Johnson the task of discovering the identity of Joe. The conversation with Nelson had yielded several valuable clues: Joe had moved to California in 1939, and his wife was from Wisconsin; he had two sisters living in New York City, one of them a teacher.

At the San Francisco FBI office, King asked Branigan and Cassidy to begin immediate round-the-clock physical surveillance of Nelson.[94] Aware that the FBI director had been trying since the 1930s to outlaw the Communist Party in the United States as a haven for spies, Pieper wrote Hoover: "I believe a definite possibility exists of developing an espionage case against the CP, USA and the Bureau's advice is requested."[95]

The stakeout of Nelson's house on Grove Street yielded results the very next morning, April 1, when Nelson walked to a corner drugstore and telephoned the Soviets' San Francisco consulate from a pay phone. Nelson was overheard using the name "Hugo" and asking to speak with Ivanov; the two agreed to meet at "the usual place" a few days hence.

On the evening of April 6, Branigan and Cassidy followed Nelson to the grounds of St. Joseph Hospital in San Francisco, where Nelson met Ivanov in an open area surrounded by trees.[96]

Four days later, Cassidy captured another visitor to Nelson's house on film—a burly figure in an ill-fitting suit whom the FBI later identified as Vassili Zubilin, the recently appointed third secretary of the Soviet embassy in Washington. Despite his lowly title, the bureau suspected Zubilin—who in the United States went by the name "Mr. Cooper"—of being the new NKVD *rezident* at the embassy.[97]

The bug in Nelson's house picked up the Russian counting out bills or bundles of currency, and Branigan recorded this exchange:

NELSON: "Jesus, you count money like a banker."
UNKNOWN MAN: "Well, after all, I told (deleted), I used to pay out at Russia."[98]

For more than an hour, Nelson and Zubilin talked about the Soviet espionage apparatus in America. Nelson said that he had been recruited at the end of 1942 by "a man from Moscow" and that Earl Browder, the head of the Communist Party in the United States, was aware of and supported his mission. He was miffed, Nelson said, that Soviet officials had begun short-circuiting the established apparatus by recruiting rank-and-file members of the party to spy, and instructing them not to inform party superiors of their assignments. Nelson suggested that the Soviets instead choose a trustworthy comrade in every important city or state and allow that person to handle contacts with the local spies. He proposed himself as the contact in the Bay Area.[99]

Several current and prospective agents were also mentioned by their code names during the conversation. Nelson complained bitterly about the incompetence of two of the couriers who were responsible for liaison between the West Coast espionage apparatus and Browder. Bill Schneiderman, state secretary of the party, was said to be reluctant to involve Communists in such "special work." But Nelson told Zubilin that he nonetheless had a new recruit, one that "you can add to your company—her name is Bernstein."[100]

The conversations intercepted by the FBI put a prompt end to the battle between the army and the bureau. On April 5, 1943, G-2's Strong acknowledged to Hoover that the military was engaged in a secret "experimental program."[101] The following morning, Hoover's personal assistant, D. Milton "Mickey" Ladd, and the FBI's foremost Soviet expert, Lish Whitson, met with Lansdale and Groves in the general's office at the New War Department Building. Without disclosing its goal—he spoke only of producing an unidentified "material"—Groves outlined the scope, cost, and significance of the Manhattan Project, adding, in notes taken by Ladd: "General Groves advised that which ever country got the material first would win the war and could dictate the terms of the peace. He further said that if Switzerland could make only so much of the material as would fill a small room, Switzerland could rule the world."[102]

Groves's speech was the first that Hoover would hear of the Manhattan Project—and the fact that it was already the target of Soviet spies. Following the meeting, the FBI director sent a bulletin to the bureau's field offices, instructing them to report any instances of Communists soliciting information "re scientific experiments."[103] On May 7, Hoover sent FDR aide Harry Hopkins a memo outlining the Nelson-Zubilin conversation. ("I thought the president and you would be interested . . .")[104]

The FBI intercepts also galvanized the army into action. The day before his meeting with the bureau, Lansdale had submitted detailed plans for a major counterintelligence effort in the Bay Area; Strong now approved it immediately.[105]

With the cooperation of the Rad Lab's personnel director, Lyall Johnson placed army undercover agents on the research staff. One, an engineer, joined the local chapter of FAECT. Another secret informant, a secretary at the lab, reported to the army on particular people and events up on the hill.

Across the Bay in San Francisco, Pash set up a dummy business office—the "Universal Subscription Company"—in a building just off Market as a staging area for his undercover agents. An army lieutenant, James Murray, headed the plainclothes operation under the nom de guerre of Paul Sheridan.[106]

Two enlisted men, former telephone repairmen, installed wiretaps and bugs for the army in cooperation with the local telephone company. Under the arrangement agreed to between Hoover and Strong, the army focused upon university employees under contract to the Manhattan Project, while the bureau concentrated upon known or suspected Communists with connections to the Rad Lab.[107]

As its surveillance effort grew, the army rented a two-story house on Forest Avenue, a few blocks south of the Berkeley campus, to serve as a listening post. An undercover agent and his family lived downstairs; upstairs, in a back room, officers assigned to the Military Intelligence Division's Counter-Intelligence Corps (CIC) recorded the telephone calls of selected Rad Lab employees.[108] (On an early inspection visit, Groves nearly compromised the operation by arriving at the house in full uniform. Belatedly realizing that the neighbors might wonder what an army general was doing there, he wrapped himself in the diminutive Pash's raincoat and dashed back to his car.)[109]

Lansdale ordered Pash to launch his own investigations at Berkeley—not realizing that the eager counterspy already had one under way.

Pash did not have to be persuaded that Oppenheimer was a security threat. Under the pretext of protecting Oppenheimer against Axis assassins, he had earlier assigned the physicist a pair of bodyguards, who reported regularly on Oppie's activities. (Oppenheimer, however, foiled the eavesdroppers by keeping the back windows of the car open and by speaking in whispers.)[110] A few weeks before, Pash had ordered a young MID lieutenant assigned to the Presidio, Peer de Silva, to begin a personal investigation of Oppenheimer. De Silva, just two years out of West Point, quickly came to share Pash's suspicion that Oppie was a Soviet agent.[111]

Despite the army's efforts, it would be another two months before "Joe" was identified.[112] The break in the case came about purely by chance. Early in June, a commercial photographer stationed near Sather Gate snapped a picture of Rossi Lomanitz arm-in-arm with David Bohm, Max Friedman, and Joe Weinberg. After the group left, an army undercover agent standing nearby purchased the negative.[113]

Several days later, CIC agents followed Lomanitz, Friedman, and Weinberg home to Berkeley from San Francisco, where the trio and a woman friend had attended a celebration in honor of Soviet writer

Maxim Gorki. The address on Blake Street was passed along to Johnson, whose check of personnel records at the lab showed an exact match between Weinberg's background and that of "Joe."[114] Army investigators also located a handwritten note that Weinberg had written to Oppenheimer on April 12—two weeks after Joe's meeting with Nelson, and only two days before Weinberg filled out the required security questionnaire at the Rad Lab—indicating that he was already involved in the bomb project and eager to do more.[115]

Oppie had put Weinberg to work on magnetic field calculations—making a science out of what, for Lawrence, had been the art of focusing the cyclotron beam with iron shims.[116] Despite Oppenheimer's earlier reservations about hiring Weinberg, the urgent need to get the Calutrons running had short-circuited caution and the lab's rudimentary security procedures.[117]

Army agents began following not only Weinberg but the other three in the photograph as well. Since Joe had indicated in his talk with Nelson that future secrets might be passed through his family in New York, the FBI also wiretapped Weinberg's parents and his two sisters.[118]

In Pash's view, Oppenheimer's role in hiring Weinberg helped seal the case against the man Groves had chosen to lead Los Alamos.[119] But the identification of Joe was overshadowed by the news—received that same day, via a wiretap on Oppie's telephone—that the Los Alamos director was planning a surprise visit to Berkeley. Pash excitedly cabled Lansdale that he was preparing a reception: "Oppenheimer will be covered on arrival. Details by airmail. This office setting out all leads."[120]

Oppenheimer arrived in Berkeley on Saturday, June 12, ostensibly to recruit a personal assistant.[121] But his real purpose was to visit Jean Tatlock, whom he had avoided seeing before he left Berkeley.[122] Tatlock was being treated for depression at Mt. Zion Hospital in San Francisco and had recently sent word to Los Alamos via Oppie's former landlady that she wanted to see him.

For his assistant, Oppie chose David Hawkins, a young philosophy professor from Berkeley whom his brother, Frank, had known at Stanford. Army CIC agents followed Oppenheimer to Hawkins's apartment in the Sunset district of San Francisco and later put a tap on Hawkins's telephone.[123]

On Sunday evening, Oppenheimer had dinner with Lawrence, who was, as usual, cheerily optimistic about the progress of his Calutrons. Army agents in an adjoining booth at the restaurant overheard Ernest report that the lab was within sight of another milestone: 1 gram of U-235 per day.

On Monday morning, Oppie took the Key System train across the bridge to Jean Tatlock's apartment on Montgomery Street, with Pash's agents in tow. The couple had dinner at the Xochinilco Café on Broadway before returning to her apartment, where Oppenheimer spent the night. Army agents waited in a car parked on the street below.

Tuesday morning, Oppenheimer took the train back to Berkeley. He and Tatlock met again that evening for dinner, and afterward she drove him to the airport. Since Oppie had originally planned to be back in Los Alamos by Monday night, his tardiness required him to break Groves's rule that grounded laboratory directors.

Oppenheimer's rendezvous with Tatlock and his hiring of Hawkins—another suspected Communist—added further fuel to G-2's suspicions.[124] Pash warned Washington that the Los Alamos director was deliberately luring left-wing associates to the lab. Pash even hinted to Lansdale that Oppie might have agreed to work on the bomb just so he could give it to the Russians.[125] The army asked the FBI to investigate Hawkins and to plant a bug in Tatlock's apartment.[126] Pieper—protesting that Pash was asking the bureau to "run errands"—initially refused both requests but later relented.[127]

Aware that Groves seemed committed to Oppenheimer, Pash broached with Lansdale the possibility of gradually easing Oppie out of his job at Los Alamos and replacing him with another scientist.[128] The FBI's Whitson also raised the question of firing Oppenheimer. Groves, however, would have none of it, as Pash and the bureau learned from the project's head of security: "Lansdale stated that General Groves claims flatly that Oppenheimer is irreplaceable and that if anything happened to Oppenheimer, the project would be set back at least six months."[129] Moreover, Groves had argued, such a delay could be catastrophic—since recent intelligence showed that the Germans were laying new high-tension wires, leading the army to conclude that the Nazis might be building their own Calutrons.

A few weeks later, on July 20, 1943, Groves put a quick and decisive end to the long agonizing over Oppenheimer by summarily ordering the district engineer to issue a security clearance for Oppie "without delay, irrespective of the information which you have concerning Mr. Oppenheimer. He is absolutely essential to the project."[130]

6

A QUESTION OF DIVIDED LOYALTIES

Lansdale decided upon a quick visit to the desert mesa later that summer, to take his own measure of Oppenheimer. Without alluding to the FBI's wiretaps, Groves's security man told Oppie that Lomanitz had remained active in FAECT and other radical causes. Oppenheimer expressed anger at the graduate student, saying that he wanted no Communists working on the project, for "one always had a question of divided loyalties."[1] Lansdale was just about to ask Oppenheimer for the names of party members at Los Alamos—he had told Whitson that he intended to fire them all—when the conversation was interrupted. The question remained unasked.

Lansdale came away from his visit convinced that Oppenheimer's ego and Kitty's vicarious ambition for her husband were the two best reasons for believing that neither would endanger the success of the project by allowing its secrets to be passed to the Russians. When the head of MED security shared this view with Groves, the general agreed.[2]

At Los Alamos, de Silva had already alienated the scientists by imposing new restrictions on travel to Santa Fe and by confiscating their cameras—measures for which Groves, as usual, got the blame.[3]

The bad news had come to Berkeley early in 1943, when Oppie had informed Lawrence that calculations indicated the fissionable material for the bomb had to be more than 90 percent pure U-235. Using uranium of any lower enrichment would mean a weapon too big and too heavy for a bomber to carry.[4] Accordingly, the metal produced by the Alpha Calutrons would have to undergo a second, more careful separation. Lawrence and the boys had already designed a new machine for the purpose.[5]

Groves, looking ahead, also wanted to use the so-called Beta Calutrons to further enrich uranium that had been separated by other methods like gaseous diffusion. Work was begun on two Beta racetracks alongside the five Alpha Calutron racetracks already under construction on the 825-acre plot of land southeast of Oak Ridge. Lawrence's cyclotroneers had meanwhile given Y-12 their own, more affectionate appellation: "Dogpatch."[6]

By any scale, the operation there was mammoth. Plans called for installing a pair of 500-tank Calutron racetracks end-to-end in twin two-story buildings, each measuring more than four football fields long. The racetracks were on the second story; pumps and plumbing for the vacuum system occupied the first floor.[7] A third building would hold the fifth and last Alpha Calutron. The army purchased 85,000 electronic vacuum tubes for the Calutrons—commandeering the nation's entire annual production of one type.

Logistic and personnel requirements were in proportion. Every pair of vacuum tanks required an individual operator seated at a console, continually adjusting the current to focus the beam. An army of technicians was needed to monitor the orange uranium-oxide "feed" material for the beam and later scrape the errant green "gunk"—uranium salts dissolved in carbon tetrachloride—from the insides of each tank. An army of chemists would separate out the silvery powder containing U-235 that was left in the receivers following each weeklong run.

Initial guesses were that 2,500 people would be necessary to operate the production plant; by spring 1943 that estimate had already swelled to 13,500.[8] (A year hence it would exceed 25,000.) But the shortage of technicians turned out not to be the problem that Lawrence had anticipated: unskilled workers—mostly young women, recruited from the Tennessee hills—proved at least as adept at running the Calutrons as degree-bearing physicists, and posed less of a security concern for the army.[9]

Meanwhile, the output of Berkeley's scale-model Calutron was still meager at best. By mid-April, following its first full week's run, the machine had produced just under 4 grams of uranium metal, enriched to an average of 20 percent U-235. The "great optimism" that the boys had heard Lawrence express hardly seemed warranted. The beam had actually been too intense, eating its way through the receivers, and many vacuum tubes had burned out. "We've got to get the wrinkles out as soon as possible," Ernest needlessly admonished the boys.

But the results two weeks later seemed more dismal than ever. One vacuum tank had worked for only three days, whereas shorts and leaks had prevented a second tank from operating at all. Nonetheless, Ernest assured Groves—as he had Oppie—that the goal of 1 gram of U-235 per day was now in sight. "The thing that interests me," the general replied gruffly, "is where do we go from here."[10]

Groves had already decided that the fifth racetrack, still under construction, would be modified to become the first Alpha II Calutron. After Oppenheimer reported from Los Alamos that the gun-type bomb might require three times the amount of uranium originally estimated, Lawrence launched a campaign to double the number of Calutrons. Consideration was given to tearing down all the Alpha I racetracks and converting them to the new, four-beam Alpha II design.

Groves also authorized the building of two additional Beta units to process the expected additional output from the Alpha IIs—even though, as Lawrence pointed out, the design of the Betas remained unproven; not even a prototype had yet been tested.[11] The first full-scale Calutron was scheduled to go into operation that fall. On November 4, 1943, Lawrence reminded the Coordinating Committee that the "zero hour is approaching."[12]

Following the alert sounded by Hoover, bureau agents had fanned out from FBI field offices that summer, looking for instances of Communists contacting scientists about a vital but unspecified secret project. Except for San Francisco, the dragnet yielded few suspects. FBI agents at the El Paso, Texas, office reported that efforts to " 'shake down' " scientists arriving at Los Alamos had been frustrated by the wartime housing shortage: Oppenheimer was quartering new arrivals in guest ranches dispersed throughout the area.[13] A mail cover on letters going into and out of the lab was begun instead.

Agents in Santa Fe, shadowing a Russian-born man and wife who had recently moved to the city, described the couple as "a trifle Bohemian in their outlook" and reported that "their principle [sic] activity seemed to be drinking."[14] Other FBI agents tailed a Russian-born illustrator of children's books traveling by train from New York all the way to his home in New Mexico. A search of his luggage turned up playing cards, an address book, and *The Tall Book of Mother Goose.*

In San Francisco, Pieper was becoming increasingly exasperated both with his assignment and with Pash. The FBI man wrote Hoover complaining that his agents would be able to do a better job if they knew what they were looking for. But the army still stubbornly refused to publicly acknowledge its involvement in the project at Berkeley, although it was hardly a secret on campus. Pieper was also distraught about security at the Rad Lab—where "rejected material" was simply thrown into garbage cans in a public area, he noted—and contemptuous of the tradecraft practiced by his allies in the battle, the G-2 agents that the bureau knew as "creeps."[15]

In late July, Pieper informed Hoover of the latest idea hatched by his nemesis:

> Pash has been negotiating for authority from Washington to obtain a boat for the purpose of Shanghaiing various Communists employed in the Laboratory and taking them all out to sea where they would be thoroughly questioned "after the Russian manner." (Blank) stated that he realized any statements so obtained could not be used in prosecution but apparently Pash did not intend to have anyone available for prosecution after questioning.[16]

Pieper dissuaded Pash from carrying out this or his backup plan, which was to take Weinberg to a San Francisco hotel and interrogate him with the idea of "turning" the physicist into a double agent.[17] Fearful that the army's actions might have already tipped the spy suspects off to COMRAP's wiretaps, Pieper advised his boss: "Pressure was brought to bear to discourage this particular activity."[18]

Groves considered Soviet espionage at the Radiation Laboratory a serious enough matter to bring it before the Top Policy Group at a meeting in Washington on August 17, 1943. Following a progress report on the bomb project, Groves summarized the status of the army's investigation into what he called the "California trouble," including the Nelson-Joe conversation and Nelson's subsequent meetings with Ivanov and Zubilin.[19]

That same day, Groves had Lansdale hand-deliver a note to Secretary of War Stimson with an attached draft memorandum for the president. "It is essential that action be taken to remove the influence of FAECT from the Radiation Laboratory," the memo informed Roosevelt.[20] Groves urged FDR to order CIO president Philip Murray "in the strongest terms to issue directions to FAECT that all organizational activity regarding the Radiation Laboratory be stopped." When Stimson passed Groves's memo along to the president two weeks later, he appended his own handwritten warning: "Unless this can be at once stopped, I think the situation very alarming."[21]

By late October, when no action had been taken against Berkeley's FAECT, Stimson wrote a reminder to Roosevelt.[22] The president had, in fact, already brought the matter up with Murray, who promised FDR that "this would end at once."[23] But it took the intervention of the regional director of the War Manpower Commission before the CIO leader finally issued the necessary orders.[24] FBI agents were listening in when disbelieving officials of FAECT's Local 25 were informed that their union was out of business for the duration.[25]

On August 23, 1943, less than a week after Groves's briefing on Russian spying, Oppenheimer returned to Berkeley for what was ostensibly another recruiting drive. Following Lansdale's visit to Los Alamos, Oppie had become curious about the activities of his former graduate students. Dropping by the New Classroom Building, Oppenheimer asked Lyall Johnson if the army had any objection to his talking to Lomanitz in Lawrence's vacant office.

Following a testy exchange with Lomanitz—Oppenheimer urged Rossi to "get straight" with the security people, to which the latter retorted that he was being persecuted for his union organizing—the two continued their discussion on the street outside.[26] When Oppie returned, Weinberg and Bohm were waiting. They, too, complained that Lomanitz was being "framed" for his politics and expressed fears that they might be tarred by the same brush.[27] Oppenheimer reassured them they had nothing to fear so long as they stayed away from politics.[28] When Lawrence briefly appeared, Oppie requested that he be a witness to this promise. Asked by Weinberg if this meant he would still go to Los Alamos, Oppenheimer denied that it had ever been his intention to send Joe to the desert lab.[29]

During dinner that night, Oppie told Robert Bacher—and army undercover agents eavesdropping nearby—that he "gave EOL hell" about the security mess at the Rad Lab.

Earlier, when stopping by Johnson's office, Oppenheimer had casually mentioned that if the army was concerned about security, George Eltenton was someone who might also bear watching.[30] Johnson had immediately telephoned Pash, who arranged a meeting with Oppenheimer for the following day. On the morning of August 26, Pash interrogated Oppenheimer while a technician in the adjoining teletype room recorded the conversation.[31]

When Oppie brought up the subject of Lomanitz, Pash interrupted to say that it was not Rossi but Eltenton and "other groups" that interested the army.[32] Oppenheimer then surprised Pash with a lengthy and complicated story.

Several months earlier, Oppenheimer said, he had been contacted by "intermediaries" who were in touch with an unidentified official at the Soviet consulate. One of these individuals had talked about passing along information regarding the project at Berkeley. Oppenheimer told Pash his response had been that, while he had no objection to the president telling the Soviets about the bomb, he thought it inappropriate to do so by "having it moved out the back door."

Oppie admitted to knowing of subsequent approaches—which "were always to other people, who were troubled by them, and sometimes came and discussed them with me." Because he felt that those contacted had been picked by chance, he was reluctant to divulge names. However, two of the three men he knew to have been approached were now at Los Alamos, Oppie said, and the third was scheduled to be sent to Oak Ridge in the near future. All three had been approached independently, the first two within a week of one another, Oppenheimer claimed.

Under prodding by Pash, Oppenheimer identified Eltenton as one of the intermediaries. However, it was not Eltenton but another man who had approached his colleagues on behalf of Eltenton and the consular official, Oppie explained. Since this particular go-between was a friend of his as well as a member of the faculty at Berkeley—and, moreover, had acted in good faith, Oppie said—he saw no point in revealing his identity.

As diplomatically as he could, Pash pressed Oppenheimer for the names of the intermediary and his three contacts, but without success. Hinting that the unidentified professor had since left town, Oppenheimer told Pash that there was scant danger of any future such incidents.[33]

The interview lasted some forty-five minutes. That evening, while Oppenheimer returned to Los Alamos by train, Pash had an army stenographer transcribe the recording. After hurriedly adding his own last-minute corrections by hand, Pash couriered the transcript to Groves and Pieper, asking that the FBI also put Eltenton under surveillance.[34]

This time the bureau had no trouble complying with the army's request. Three weeks before, an anonymous letter, written in Russian, had been sent to Hoover by a disgruntled Soviet intelligence officer. The FBI determined that the missive had been mailed from a post office near the Soviet embassy in Washington, D.C. The letter identified Zubilin, Kvasnikov, and Kheifets as three of Russia's top spies in the United States.[35] Shortly thereafter, King's "one-man Commie squad" had ballooned to a force of 125 agents, or nearly half the complement working at the bureau's San Francisco office.[36]

The extended dragnet was eager for evidence that the spy ring was still active in Berkeley. On the morning of September 3, an army agent followed Weinberg on foot to a French laundry on Telegraph Avenue and then to a candy shop. Weinberg's next stop was the post office at Sather Gate, where he mailed a thick, business-sized envelope.[37]

Three days later, Pash received a photostat of the letter's contents from

CIC agent Jim Murray. In addition to a thirteen-page typewritten manuscript—"The Communist Party and the Professions"—the package contained a brief, unsigned note:

> Dear A., Please do not communicate with me during this period, nor discuss with others my reasons for this request. I should like you to pass on this message to S. or B., however, without mentioning my name. Thanks a lot. We'll take that walking trip when this is all over. Till then . . .

From previous surveillance, the army knew that the recipient, Al Flanigan, was a Berkeley graduate student and suspected party member who lived down the street from Chevalier and was a friend of Steve Nelson's. Pash interpreted the "S." and "B." of the note to stand for Nelson and Bernadette Doyle. Suspecting that the note had originated with Oppenheimer, Pash asked de Silva to compare it with letters written on the typewriter in Oppie's office at Los Alamos.[38] Pash was also convinced that the note cast new light upon the purpose of Oppenheimer's latest visit. As Murray wrote in his report to G-2: "The latent possibility that J. R. Oppenheimer tipped Weinberg off lies dormant."[39]

Army wiretaps revealed that Oppie's other grad students on the project continued to violate their promise to stay out of politics.[40] Agents followed David Bohm to meetings of the Communist Party, which he had joined late the previous year.[41] Until it was dissolved, Max Friedman had served as chairman of the Rad Lab's FAECT Local, while Lomanitz was on its organizing committee and had been an active recruiter.[42] (During one FAECT gathering, Lomanitz naively proposed organizing the campus police department. The idea was hooted down. The union had enough trouble "without inviting the FBI into the meetings," grumbled one member, according to an agent's report.)[43]

Having decided to keep Weinberg on campus in hopes that he might lead them to other spies, Groves and Lansdale resolved to rid the project of the other three.[44] Friedman was summarily fired only a week after he had been hired by the university to teach physics to army recruits on campus.[45] ("Promised jobs kept disappearing at the last moment," Friedman wrote plaintively to Oppenheimer.)[46] Bohm presented more of a problem, since Oppenheimer had recently asked him to come to Los Alamos. In a telephone call, Groves told Oppie that he could not approve the transfer since Bohm had relatives in Germany—an explanation that Oppenheimer found incredible but did not challenge.[47] Weinberg and Bohm stayed on as teaching assistants in the physics department, where the two took over Oppenheimer's course on quantum theory.[48]

Others at the Rad Lab who had been picked to go to Y-12—including Arthur Rosen, David Fox, and Bernard Peters—received similar notice that their assignments had been suddenly canceled, without explanation.[49]

Groves and Lansdale had already agreed that the simplest solution to the problem of what to do about Lomanitz was to draft him, since Rossi's deferment was about to come up for renewal.[50] On the same day that Lomanitz received a letter from his draft board, informing him that his deferment was canceled, he was ordered to report for a physical.[51] Less than a week before, Lawrence had picked Rossi to supervise the operation of the Calutrons at Oak Ridge. At age twenty-one, he was the youngest group leader at the Rad Lab.[52]

More than six months of army and FBI surveillance had uncovered a wealth of intimate details about the four subjects under investigation, but no further incidents of espionage. ("There was a discussion of music, Russian Army songs, Paul Robeson, and bacteriology," wrote the army agent monitoring Weinberg's apartment of a typical evening that fall.)[53]

What the wiretaps and bugs *did* reveal was that Lomanitz and Friedman believed they had been fired from the Rad Lab for their left-wing views and union activity.[54] It was their "firm conviction," the two wrote Oppenheimer, "that union discrimination is the cause of all that has occurred."[55] Army agents overheard Lomanitz and Friedman drafting the letter to Oppie in Weinberg's apartment, while Joe, in the background, offered advice.

That Weinberg's friends remained ignorant of the real reason behind the army's actions was evident even at the farewell party that Joe hosted for Rossi on the eve of his induction, where the conversation was *in vino veritas:*

> Weinberg was heard to remark that people who live quietly never get their names in history books or in the newspapers. . . . Further discussion indicated that Weinberg was enjoying Lomanitz' predicament. Lomanitz said "Both Joe and Dave have their necks out. Dave was my roommate and Joe has written three letters of recommendation for me." Weinberg said he didn't believe Max was in his present predicament because of his Union affiliations but because of something else.[56]

It was perhaps the closest that Weinberg would come to informing his friends that he was the source of all their troubles.[57]

The next morning, Joe drove Rossi to the induction center. The following week, Friedman, after borrowing a few road maps from Weinberg, left Berkeley at the wheel of his 1942 Pontiac on his way to Denver, Colorado, where he began the search for a new job.

Oppenheimer believed, mistakenly, that his confession to Pash had satisfied the G-2 man of his patriotism, or at least had drawn the bloodhounds off his trail. Pash, however, took Oppie's smug evasions and refusal to name names as a provocation. He wired Groves that it was "essential that name of professor be made available in order that investigation can continue properly."[58] Pash asked Groves to find out exactly who had been contacted, and whether anyone else—"the professor, Eltenton, or some other party"—had approached Oppenheimer for information.[59]

Groves and Lansdale found an occasion to interrogate Oppenheimer further in early September, when the three shared a compartment on an eastbound streamliner. Between Cheyenne, Wyoming, and Chicago, they discussed Oppenheimer's interview with Pash as well as his meeting in Berkeley with Lomanitz, Weinberg, and Bohm. Oppie said he was confident that no further approaches had been made and no secrets lost. He offered to identify the professor who had been Eltenton's intermediary if ordered to do so by Groves, but Groves demurred.[60]

Lansdale tried again to coax the story out of Oppenheimer when the physicist visited Washington later that month. Picking up Oppie at Union Station, Lansdale took him to Groves's office, where another hidden microphone lay waiting. Oppenheimer was apologetic but adamant in refusing to name either the intermediary or those contacted.[61] Stymied, Lansdale took up where he had been forced to leave off at Los Alamos—asking Oppenheimer to name those in the project he knew to be Communists.

Oppie said that he had only learned for certain that Weinberg and Lomanitz were party members during his last trip to Berkeley. When Lansdale mentioned the name Haakon Chevalier, Oppenheimer responded that he would not be surprised if Chevalier were a member of the party, since he was "quite a Red."

After two hours, the only additional names that Oppenheimer had offered Lansdale were those of Charlotte Serber—whom Oppie had previously identified as probably a Communist during the train ride with Groves—and Hannah Peters, a friend of Jean Tatlock's and the wife of Bernard Peters, a Rad Lab physicist who had served on FAECT's executive committee. Both women were already on Lansdale's list.

There the investigation languished for almost two months. Lansdale told the FBI in late October that he believed Oppenheimer was telling the truth when he denied ever being a member of the Communist Party. He also thought Oppie sincere in his claim that he would not permit Communists to interfere with the bomb project.[62] In private, however, Lansdale continued to pore over transcripts of Oppenheimer's telephone calls between Berkeley and Los Alamos, hoping that the intermediary and his contacts might thereby be revealed.[63]

On his own, Pash began assembling a list of candidates for the unnamed professor.[64] When one of the suspects on Pash's list slipped his army shadow and boarded the Southern Pacific's *Daylight* unescorted, Pash ordered the train stopped between San Francisco and Los Angeles, so that the agent—borrowing an army airplane—could catch up with his quarry. The outraged railroad lodged a formal protest with the Presidio.

On Thanksgiving Day 1943, Groves gave Pash a new assignment overseas, thereby removing the man who had been a persistent thorn in his side concerning Oppenheimer.[65] Groves made Pash head of Project *Alsos*, a plan to gather scientific intelligence on the German bomb in countries occupied by the Nazis.[66]

On Saturday, November 13, 1943, current flowed to the Alpha racetrack for the first time. Although tests had hinted that some problems remained with the Calutrons, Lawrence and Groves were nonplussed when multiple failures forced the shutdown of the machine almost immediately.[67] The magnetic field had been so unexpectedly strong that it pulled vacuum tanks from their fittings and pipes from the walls. No sooner were the vacuum tanks secured than magnet coils shorted out because of water in the oil used to cool them. Not a single source produced a beam; not a speck of U-235 arrived at the receivers.

Groves's reaction was surprisingly stoic. Believing that part of the problem with the Calutrons lay in incessant design changes, he ordered Rad Lab engineers to abandon any improvements that could not be put into effect before the end of 1944.[68] Lawrence was characteristically optimistic, predicting that the technical problems would be solved quickly and the Calutrons soon producing U-235 at maximum capacity.

Ten days later, however, the Tennessee Eastman representative in Oak Ridge telephoned Berkeley with more bad news: the electrical, vacuum, and cooling systems for the Alpha racetracks had all developed problems.[69] Work on the Calutrons came to a virtual halt, pending Lawrence's visit at the end of the month.

Ernest arrived to discover that mere enthusiasm could do little to salvage the situation at Y-12—where the racetracks had been shut down by faulty welds, electrical shorts, and incompetent technicians.[70] Unable to suggest a quick remedy, he left by train for a meeting of laboratory directors in Chicago.

Suffering painful muscle spasms in his back and a lingering sinus infection, Lawrence checked into the city's Stevens Hotel. After first attending the lab directors' meeting—he was carried into the room seated in a chair, rigid and grimacing—he telegraphed his brother for medical advice. A former Harvard classmate of John's arranged for him to be admitted to the University of Chicago's Billings Hospital.[71]

Stopping by the hospital on his way to Los Alamos from Boston, Luis Alvarez was shocked to find Lawrence prostrate and in poor spirits. Alvarez thought exhaustion and depression, not physical pain, the real cause of Ernest's condition.[72] Oppenheimer and Arthur Compton, also hoping to see Lawrence, were turned away by worried doctors. When treatments at the hospital failed to provide the expected relief, Ernest decided to go home to Berkeley rather than return to Tennessee.[73]

By mid-December, Lawrence was once again running the Coordinating Committee meetings, his back as well as his spirits recovered. Gradually, the problems with the Calutrons began to be solved. Stone and Webster installed filters to take moisture out of the transformer oil. Westinghouse announced that it had ironed out the kinks in the vacuum system. Allis-Chalmers agreed to remanufacture magnet coils that had shorted out because of insufficient space between the windings. Groves brought in a former civilian contractor to replace the army officer in charge of construction at the site.[74]

It was, nonetheless, clear to all that Eastman's original plan to run Y-12 without help from the Rad Lab was no longer realistic. Lawrence launched a frenetic effort to recruit workers from the lab to go to Oak Ridge. Old-time cyclotroneers as well as new arrivals came to dread Ernest's cheerful query, "How would you like to go to Tennessee?"[75]

On New Year's Eve, Lawrence telephoned Oak Ridge. "All the boys that you would like to have are coming," he promised the Eastman representative.[76] The first contingent of nearly 100 recruits would begin arriving in a few days. Ernest delayed his own departure until mid-January, to coincide with the scheduled start-up of the second Alpha racetrack. After chairing one final meeting of the Coordinating Committee in Berkeley, Ernest announced that the group was being disbanded. It would be reorganized and hold its next meeting in Tennessee.

Even with Pash gone, the case of the mysterious professor and of his three still-anonymous contacts continued to prey on Groves, who had been recently reminded by Lansdale of Oppenheimer's promise from the summer.

In early December 1943, Groves flew to Los Alamos. Meeting alone with Oppenheimer in the office that he kept at the lab, Groves ordered Oppie to divulge the identity of the go-between who had contacted the scientists. Oppenheimer promptly named Haakon Chevalier, the man he had told Lansdale was "quite a Red."

However, when Groves asked Oppenheimer to identify the three men whom Chevalier had approached, Oppie agreed to do so only on one condition: that Groves promise not to divulge the names to the FBI. Believing that the three were undoubtedly among Oppie's four graduate students, whom the army already had under surveillance, Groves agreed.

But what he heard next surprised him. There had been only one person contacted by Chevalier, Oppenheimer said: his brother, Frank.

Filling out the story, Oppenheimer told Groves that several months earlier Chevalier had approached Frank about the possibility of either passing secrets on the bomb project to the Russians or persuading his brother to. Uncertain how to respond, Frank had come to Oppie for advice. His recommendation, Oppenheimer told Groves, was that his brother should have nothing further to do with the scheme—and he had later given Chevalier his "comeuppance" for trying to recruit Frank as a spy.[77]

On the flight back to Washington, Groves wondered whether Oppenheimer was telling him the truth—or whether Oppie had simply introduced Frank into the story as a way to justify his own earlier failure to notify the army of Chevalier's overture. More important, Groves realized that by promising not to divulge Frank's name to the FBI, he, too, was now unwittingly a party not only to a lie but to a felony—namely, withholding the truth about an espionage conspiracy from federal authorities in wartime.

Back at the New War Department Building, Groves called Lansdale and Army Major William Consodine, his chief troubleshooter and lawyer, into his office. Putting a yellow legal pad in front of them, Groves asked each man to write down his guesses as to the names that Oppenheimer had given. Lansdale wrote down three names, all presumably from Pash's list. Consodine put down only one—Frank's.[78]

When Groves revealed what Oppie had told him, the trio discussed whether the general should consider himself bound by his promise to Oppenheimer. As Groves's lawyer, Consodine argued that the security of the nation represented a higher and overriding obligation.[79] But Groves felt that the bomb project itself might be fatally compromised if he lost Oppenheimer's trust by violating his pledge. When Groves raised the possibility of a secret prosecution of Chevalier and Eltenton, Consodine warned that not even the wartime emergency allowed the suspension of due process.[80]

Either on his own—or with Groves's willing connivance—Lansdale decided that he would verbally inform the FBI of the information received from Oppenheimer, but without putting anything down in writing.[81]

Remarkably, Groves chose not to let his own former deputy, the MED district engineer, Kenneth Nichols, in on the secret.

On December 13, Nichols wired Lyall Johnson at Berkeley that Oppenheimer's intermediary was Chevalier. But Nichols's cable unknowingly perpetuated the earlier fiction that Oppie had told Pash: "Oppenheimer states in his opinion Chevalier engaged in no further activity other than three original attempts."[82] Nichols sent similar telegrams that same day to de Silva at Los Alamos and Calvert at Oak Ridge. Pash, who was already in Italy, working for Alsos, remained unaware of the latest developments.[83]

That same evening, Lansdale went to FBI headquarters to personally inform Hoover aides Lish Whitson and Frank Tamm that Haakon Chevalier had tried to recruit Robert Oppenheimer's brother to spy for the Soviet Union.[84]

The first contingent of cyclotroneers arrived at "Dogpatch" in the early days of 1944 to find things in utter disarray.[85] Delayed by another bad cold, Lawrence, with Cooksey in tow, detrained at Oak Ridge on January 20 to take control of the operation. Ernest was assigned a comparatively luxurious E-unit apartment on Tennessee Avenue, near the camp store and movie theater.[86] With the help of a little long-distance troubleshooting by Brobeck, some of the teething problems with the Alpha racetrack had already been worked out by the time that Ernest appeared.[87]

Martin Kamen arrived in the second wave of Berkeley recruits, to supervise the process of chemically separating uranium, only to discover that he had left the package containing the necessary floats and filters behind on the train.[88] Kamen subsequently found that even when the racetracks were working properly, only about 10 percent of the orange uranium oxide—the "feed" material—was converted by the Calutron beam into a focused, ionized arc. Of that, only a few percent emerged in the receivers at the other end. Most of the "gunk" was spewed by the beam around the innards of the Calutron. The vacuum tanks had to be dismantled at the end of each run and their contents laboriously scraped, dissolved, and precipitated out to be fed into the machine once more.[89]

Lawrence proposed ingenuous ways to work around the remaining problems. When the Calutrons began to overheat, he had the Oak Ridge fire department play their hoses upon the cooling towers until temperatures dropped to a safe level. The design flaw was found and corrected. At Lawrence's request, Frank Oppenheimer flew out to Y-12 late in the month to deal with a corrosion problem, caused when chlorine used in the chemical process reacted with nickel in the stainless steel pipe.[90] Copper liners proved the solution and Frank returned to Berkeley.

At the end of January 1944, Alpha Calutron 2 became the first racetrack to begin continuous operation. The mistakes and problems that surfaced in the initial start-up meant that the original Alpha track would not be back on-line till March. Recently imposed security strictures added another headache. Henceforth, all personnel assigned to Y-12 from Berkeley had to be cleared first by the army.[91]

With the confidence born of experience, however, the pace began to quicken that spring. In March, the first U-235 was shipped to Los Alamos—a few dozen grams. It found immediate use in experiments at the lab.[92] By the end of April, all four of the original Alpha racetracks had been upgraded to the four-beam design and were in round-the-clock operation. In May, the first Beta track ran successfully, boosting the enrichment of the uranium received from the Alpha tracks.[93]

Barring discovery of any new and unforeseen technological impedimenta, Lawrence was beginning to be optimistic that Dogpatch could provide the uranium to meet Compton's revised schedule—a bomb by mid-1945. The chief uncertainty remaining was the design of the weapon.

Many of Lawrence's boys who had not been sent to Oak Ridge began to show up at Los Alamos early in the year. By February 1944, Emilio Segrè was a group leader in the Physics Division.[94] Luis Alvarez finally got to the desert lab from MIT in late spring, following a detour to the Met Lab at Oppenheimer's request. Alvarez was assigned to work with George Kistiakowsky, another recent arrival, on electrical detonators for the implosion bomb.[95] After helping to find equipment and recruit other scientists for Los Alamos, Ed McMillan worked on early implosion experiments and, later, on design of the gun.[96]

The main effort at the lab was now focused upon the gun and the implosion gadget, although work was stalemated on the latter, Tolman reported to Groves in March. The "prime objective" for the remainder of the year, Oppenheimer wrote Groves, was "to bring to a successful conclusion the development of the implosion unit with (U-235)."[97]

Alternative concepts for the atomic bomb had been gradually discarded, one by one. An imaginative proposal put forward by Bohr was studied by Bethe and Teller and found to be "a quite useless military weapon," Oppenheimer informed Groves.[98] Work on the hydride bomb, the weapon that Teller had championed early on at the lab, was finally, and reluctantly, abandoned by him in the winter of 1943–44. Studies showed that uranium hydride could not be easily compressed in a gun, and that any explosion that resulted would be far less efficient than a weapon using metallic uranium or plutonium.[99] The yield of Teller's hydride would be "negligible or less," concluded Princeton's Richard Feynman.[100]

But a far more serious problem would soon comc to light, in an experiment by Segrè. When the first significant sample of reactor-produced plutonium arrived in early summer, Segrè's group was surprised to find it had a rate of spontaneous fission five times that of the plutonium produced on the 60-inch at Berkeley. Further studies confirmed that reactor-bred plutonium contained too much Pu-240, an isotope with a high rate of spontaneous fission, to be usable in a gun-type bomb. Upon firing, a plutonium gun would "preinitiate" and fizzle—spewing molten radioactive metal in all directions.[101] Oppenheimer ordered work on Thin Man, the plutonium gun, abandoned.

The so-called implosion crisis forced a reorganization of the laboratory that August. Oppenheimer gave Bacher and Kistiakowsky the job of making the spherical implosion design—Fat Man—a success, creating two new divisions at the lab for the purpose.[102] Calculations carried out earlier by Teller and John von Neumann, a Princeton mathematician brought to the lab as a consultant, had shown how the compression attainable in the implosion design made it potentially far more efficient than the gun. Henceforth, the emphasis at the lab would be upon "fast" implosion and Fat Man.[103]

Despite his previous work on the subject, Teller lost interest in the implosion problem as Oppenheimer brought in more of his colleagues to solve it. (Teller's heart remained with the purely theoretical. A visit to Y-12 earlier in the year had confirmed his belief that the atomic bomb was an engineering, not a physics, challenge. Although he pronounced Y-12 "Super-colossal," he wrote, "[it is] wonderful that I do not have to live there.")[104] With the hydride having hit a dead end, Teller returned to his first pet project: the Super.

Since the fall, Teller had been urging that the level of effort on the superbomb be increased at the lab—citing recent reports that the Germans were experimenting with heavy water, and calculations which indicated that less deuterium might be required than originally anticipated.[105] Preoccupied with the gadget, Oppenheimer and the lab's governing board had denied Teller's request. But Oppie encouraged Edward to continue exploring the possibility of a superbomb with a small group in the Theoretical Division.

One of the key unanswered question from the 1942 Berkeley seminar that was of relevance to the Super concerned what happened to the radiation created in an atomic bomb. Resolving the issue of the superbomb's feasibility awaited discovery of whether its internal components permitted or impeded the transfer of energy in the form of radiation. Teller and Konopinski had yet to do the calculations on the phenomenon known as opacity that they had promised to do at Berkeley.[106] On a visit to New York, Teller persuaded a friend and confidante, Columbia University physicist Maria Göppert Mayer, to carry out the laborious work that might answer the question. Teller had known Mayer since the mid-1930s, describing her as his "Dutch aunt," to whom he confessed both professional and personal problems. ("Slender and blond, she had a natural delicacy and grace as well as considerable strength of mind," Teller later wrote of Mayer. Maria was married to a chemist, and the couple had two small children.)[107]

Oppenheimer gave Teller permission to hire Mayer for the opacity calculations, but forbade him from disclosing the intended application. (Teller later recalled their conversation: "I had to tell her it is uranium, and I had to tell her at what temperature. . . . There was a clear intake of breath. And no more questions.")[108]

But even Teller acknowledged that his own most recent calculations on the Super showed the need for more tritium. The loss of energy due to radiation seemed greater than he had predicted two years earlier. Accordingly, Edward conceded that development of the superbomb "may require longer than was originally anticipated."[109] Oppenheimer agreed to let Teller continue his work, so long as it did not jeopardize the timetable for the fission gadget.*[110]

During the early summer of 1944, amid the crisis over Thin Man, Teller had twice refused a request from T Division's leader, Bethe, to help with calculations on the hydrodynamics of fast implosion. That June, with Bethe's patience at an end, Oppenheimer transferred Teller out of the Theoretical Division, allowing him to work on the Super on his own.[111] Teller also continued to discuss his ideas with Oppenheimer alone for an hour a week. Work on implosion theory was given instead to Rudolf Peierls and members of the British mission at the lab, among whom was Klaus Fuchs.[112]

Fuchs had come to the United States the previous December and began passing secrets to the Russians almost immediately. Shortly before he left England, *Rest* had been asked by his Soviet control what he knew about the electromagnetic method of separating uranium. The question had surprised Fuchs, who, at the time, knew nothing of Lawrence's Calutrons. *Rest* concluded that the Russians must also have a spy at Berkeley.[113]

On February 5, 1944, Fuchs met with his new espionage contact, New York chemist Harry Gold *(Gus)*, on the corner of Fifty-ninth Street and Lexington Avenue. There *Rest* told *Gus* about "the process for the separation of isotopes of *Enormous*," according to a coded cable that Kvasnikov sent to Fitin in Moscow a few days later.[114] The other information received from Fuchs included details on "the electron method developed by Lawrence," and the fact that U-235 obtained by gaseous diffusion was

* An utterance attributed to Oppie—"God protect us from the enemy without and the Hungarians within"—surely had Teller in mind. Ironically, the two men were competitive even in "death": Oppenheimer played the part of the first corpse and Edward the second in the lab's production of *Arsenic and Old Lace*.

to be further enriched by "the electron method for final separation"—the Beta Calutrons, which would not begin operating at Y-12 for another three months.[115]

In Moscow, Kurchatov was in possession of a list of nearly 300 secret technical reports on the Manhattan Project. Many if not most of the papers came from agents in British laboratories, which continued to receive classified reports from the United States.[116] Kurchatov's memos to Pervukhin indicated that the Russians now knew fission cross sections as well as the critical mass of uranium and plutonium. But there were still important gaps in his knowledge, Kurchatov complained. Missing, for example, were the results of experiments at Berkeley on the fissioning of plutonium under fast neutron bombardment. Kurchatov drew the attention of Pervukhin to this lacunae with his blue pencil: "Information on the results of this work by Seaborg and Segrè is therefore of particular importance to us."[117]

On August 12, 1943, the Rad Lab itself had figured in a coded telegram that Pavel Mikhailov (code name *Molière*), the GRU *rezident* at the Soviets' New York consulate, sent to Fitin in Moscow: "In Sacramento, California, in the Radiation Laboratories, large-scale experimental work is being conducted for the War Department. Working there is a progressive professor (blank), whom one can approach through the *Korporant*."[118]

Mikhailov's message identified the *Korporant*—GRU's term for a member of the Communist Party—as Paul Pinsky, the FAECT organizer whom Oppenheimer had helped to give the union a foothold in the Bay Area.[119]

From San Francisco, Kheifets continued to send messages to Moscow via diplomatic pouch and encrypted cables.[120] Most of *Kharon*'s coded telegrams reflected the mundane concerns of a regional consulate; he reported on fleet movements as well as efforts to locate Soviet sailors who had jumped ship and asked for political asylum.*[121] But *Kharon* also passed along secrets received, via a sub-*rezidentura* at the consulate in Los Angeles *(Caen)*, from agents planted in southern California's wartime aviation industries.[122]

Kheifets's sources in the Bay Area included old-time party operatives likes "Pops" Folkoff *(Uncle)*, as well as several new, younger converts.[123] Among the latter was Louise Bransten—code-named *Map*—"the Bernstein

* A particularly chilling set of *Venona* messages concerns the fate of Elizaveta Kuznetsova, a crew member who jumped ship in San Francisco. Despite going into hiding, marrying a cab driver in the city, and finally fleeing to Portland, Oregon, the hapless Kuznetsova was eventually hunted down by the relentless *Kharon*. Kheifets's successor sent this message to Moscow late in 1944: "On 4 November this year the traitor to the fatherland Kuznetsova was shipped to Vladivostok on the tanker *Belgorod*."

woman" whom Steve Nelson had bragged to Zubilin about bringing into the fold, and journalist Anna Louise Strong, code-named *Lyre.*[124] Kheifets was also seeking Fitin's permission to recruit a "talkative" new agent: James Walter Miller *(Vague),* a naturalized citizen of Russian birth who worked as a clerk and translator in the Office of Postal Censorship in San Francisco. If Moscow did not approve his plan to "sign on *Vague,*" Kheifets cabled, he intended to make use of Miller in any case: "*Uncle* will arrange the details with the *Fellow Countrymen* [CPUSA members]. According to this plan *Vague* will pass his information to *Map.* Under a plan of this kind *Vague* will have no inkling that the information is coming to us."[125]

In most cases, ideology rather than monetary reward was the spur to cooperation. The NKVD depended on the romanticism of American Communists. (*Lyre*'s Soviet control identified himself to her with the recognition phrase, "Greetings from Charlotte Corday.")[126]

By early 1944, Bransten/*Map* was in New York, on what the FBI believed to be an espionage mission, in the company of another would-be spy: Haakon Chevalier.

Just five days after Oppenheimer had identified Chevalier as the mysterious go-between in the meeting with Groves, Hoover's agents had begun shadowing the French literature professor through the streets of the city.[127] Chevalier was staying at a nondescript hotel on Fifth Avenue, a few blocks from the apartment where Bransten had taken up temporary residence. Bureau agents obtained access to Chevalier's diary from a cooperative chambermaid. Additionally, an FBI mail cover tracked Chevalier's frustrations in his search for a position with Washington's intelligence services. The job at OWI or OSS was "still hanging fire, so to speak, for reasons that you know," Chevalier wrote Oppenheimer in early December 1943.[128]

Despite Oppie's telling Groves that he had given Chevalier his "comeuppance" for trying to recruit Frank, Oppenheimer's return letters seemed solicitous of his friend's welfare—while simultaneously warning Chevalier not to reveal too much in his reply: "There are some things doubtless that you would not want to write to us here for no certain privacy is assured the mail, but why are you in New York and how long since, and to what end," Oppie inquired.[129]

A few days before Christmas 1943, the FBI followed Chevalier to a rendezvous with Bransten at her apartment. "I would like to see you—it is about the same thing—Earl," a bureau agent overheard Chevalier tell Bransten from the call box in the lobby.[130] Previously, agents had tailed

Bransten to meetings with Earl Browder at the Communist leader's house in the city.[131]

On New Year's day 1944 the FBI intercepted a telephone call between Bransten and another friend in New York. Agents heard Bransten say that she had just received encouraging news from someone who had been trying to find her a job. It "was the kind of job she would like," Bransten said, adding that "every time she thought of it, she got excited, and it made her feel dangerous."[132]

7

BREAK, BLOW, BURN

Back in San Francisco by the spring to host a benefit for Russian war relief, Louise Bransten introduced Gregori Kheifets to another prospective new recruit: Martin Kamen.[1]

For the past year, Kamen had been commuting between Berkeley and Y-12. At both places, the voluble chemist had a reputation as a ready and reliable source of information on what was happening in the project. Kamen had already been reprimanded once by Cooksey for indiscreet comments made at Berkeley's Faculty Club.[2]

At the party, Kheifets asked for Kamen's help in obtaining radiophosphorous treatments for a member of the Soviets' Portland consulate who was suffering from leukemia. Kamen passed the request along to John Lawrence and did not hear from Kheifets again until late June, when the diplomat called to invite him to a farewell dinner.[3] The meal was to thank Kamen for his help and to introduce him to Kheifets's successor at the consulate, Gregori Kasparov.[4] CIC agents monitoring the telephone call heard Kamen agree to meet the Russians two nights hence at Bernstein's Fish Grotto in San Francisco.

On July 1, the morning of the meeting, an army agent in the guise of an electrician repairing a light in Kamen's office saw the chemist pick up a scientific equipment catalog and a handful of unclassified reports on the medical use of radioisotopes before heading out the door to the rendezvous.[5] Other undercover agents shadowed Kamen on the Key System train across the Bay Bridge, where the chemist and the two Russians caught a cab to the restaurant, located near the cable car turntable on Powell Street. The army agents were surprised to find Hoover's men already waiting outside, their surveillance equipment—disguised as hearing aids—at the ready. ("It looked like a convention of the deaf," recalled one gumshoe.)[6]

Following a hurried conference, the army agents took a table in the middle of the room while the bureau's men—equipped with more sensitive technology—were seated in a booth adjoining that occupied by Kamen, Kheifets, and Kasparov.[7] Amid the noise and bustle of the restaurant, the agents overheard only fragments of the conversation, including Kamen's mention of "Lawrence," "radiation," and "military boys."[8]

Following the meal, while his hosts accompanied Kamen to the nearby train station, another army agent snapped a picture of the three men from the upstairs window of a recruiting office across the street. In the photograph, Kasparov is seen clutching the thick sheath of papers that Kamen brought with him. A few days later, FBI agents tailed Kheifets to the docks, where he boarded a ship bound for Russia.[9]

Apprised of the incident, Groves ordered Kamen fired immediately. The unpleasant task fell to Cooksey, who wordlessly handed the stunned chemist his termination notice. The reason given was Kamen's earlier loquaciousness at the Faculty Club. Kamen's frantic telephone calls to Lawrence went unanswered; Fidler had already informed Ernest that since Groves himself had ordered the firing there could be no appeal.[10] The chemist's tearful farewells to Fidler and other well-wishers at the Rad Lab were recorded by army investigators.[11]

With the help of a friend, Kamen got a job a few weeks later as an inspector at Kaiser's Richmond shipyards. His neighbors—seeing young, dark-suited men in late-model cars parked at the curb with their engines running—reported the license numbers to the local police, the selective service, and the gasoline rationing board.

Having finally given up on trying to get a government job in New York or Washington, Haakon Chevalier, too, was back in the Bay Area by late spring 1944.[12] Moving, with Barbara, into a guest cottage at Stinson Beach owned by his wife's parents, Chevalier set about remodeling the house and attempting to repair his marriage. Commuting to Berkeley to teach part-time, he also began work on his long-deferred novel.

For almost a year, the army's wiretaps and mail cover on Frank Oppenheimer's East Bay home had revealed only the usual parenting problems of a mother left alone with two small children. Jackie's dislike of the deep South had made her reluctant to join Frank in Tennessee. Agents reading their letters learned of routine social engagements, the apricots in Jackie's victory garden, and the final illness to afflict Pushkin, the couple's German shepherd.[13]

When Robert Oppenheimer returned to Berkeley that fall, army undercover agents followed him, driving a borrowed roadster, through the winding streets of Kensington to Eagle Hill.[14] Oppie next picked up his brother and the two drove down Telegraph Avenue, where they met David Bohm in front of the Carlton Hotel. Following five minutes of conversation—Frank stood apart and did not participate, the agents noted—Robert and his brother drove across the bridge to Scoma's, a seafood restaurant on Fisherman's Wharf. While the Oppenheimers were eating, the agents searched Robert's overcoat and luggage found in the car. (The items found included a bottle of antidiarrhea medicine, a mostly empty fifth of Black Bear Gin, a full pint of twenty-seven-year-old brandy, and underwear.)[15]

Leaving the restaurant an hour later, the brothers "walked around the block three times during which time they were engaged in earnest conversation, both gestulating [sic] frequently." Frank then drove Robert to the railroad station in Oakland, where Oppie boarded the streamliner for Los Alamos.[16]

By mid-1944, even the army seemed willing to concede that its counterintelligence operation in the Bay Area might have reached the point of diminishing returns. Several months earlier, a devastating critique of the CIC's operations and methods by the army inspector general had resulted in Lansdale's nameless box-within-a-box becoming part of the Manhattan Project's security apparatus. Lansdale and staff moved from the Pentagon to an office next to Groves's at the New War Department building on Twenty-first Street and Virginia Avenue.

Except for the information passed by "Joe" to Steve Nelson, the results obtained by Soviet espionage at Berkeley amounted to little, in retrospect. Yet the "California trouble" had become an early and main focus of the counterintelligence campaign by Groves and Lansdale for one simple reason: Oppenheimer.

In April, Jim Murray, Pash's top counterspy, was transferred to Chicago, where the FBI and Groves had recently uncovered an espionage ring passing Met Lab secrets to Moscow through the Soviets' New York consulate.[17]

That May, Lansdale made preparations to shut down the listening post on Forest Avenue and likewise close the army's dummy storefront office in San Francisco.[18] To save money, the remaining agents and their recording equipment were moved to a new headquarters in Oakland and given a different cover name: the "Universal Adjustment Company." (One hapless visitor, seeking an insurance adjuster, was politely run off by Murray's replacement.)[19]

In the fall, Lyall Johnson would be put in charge of security at Hanford, which soon began regularly shipping plutonium to Los Alamos in converted army ambulances.

Still unaware that the story Oppenheimer had told Pash was a fabrication, army agents continued their dogged search for the three Berkeley scientists whom Chevalier had supposedly asked to pass secrets to the Russians. Oppie himself had meanwhile done nothing to let the agents know that they were following a false trail. Instead, during a trip to Santa Fe with de Silva in early 1944, Oppenheimer had given the Los Alamos security officer the name of another possible suspect: Rad Lab physicist Bernard Peters.[20]

Lansdale was confident that he had meanwhile neutralized the threat represented by the four grad students originally suspected of spying. After trailing Lomanitz and his girlfriend across the country to Oklahoma and back, the army had assigned an agent in uniform to accompany Rossi through basic training. Lomanitz's shadow followed him to a billet at Fort Lewis, Washington, and ultimately to the Pacific without observing any effort on Rossi's part at surreptitious contact.[21] Bohm, like Weinberg, was still teaching physics in Berkeley.[22] Following a succession of failed efforts to find work, Max Friedman had finally returned to being a student, enrolling in graduate physics classes at the University of Puerto Rico.

Lansdale himself had recently shifted his attention to more pressing concerns—including the need to provide security for the growing tide of men and equipment being sent to the Pacific to drop the atomic bomb.[23]

Notably, Groves had raised no objection when Robert Oppenheimer brought his brother to Los Alamos in spring 1945.[24] (Army monitoring remained in place, however. When Teller griped once more about security strictures at the lab, Oppie snapped: "What are you complaining about? I can't even talk to my own brother.") Robert put Frank in charge of security at the desolate desert site where the bomb was to be tested.[25]

A few months earlier, Frank had shared a Pullman compartment on the way to Y-12 with Lawrence. Ernest repeated for Frank's benefit the advice he had given Oppie at the start of the war—that the best way to serve humanity was not by becoming involved in politics but by doing science.[26]

At Los Alamos—where project officials were still innocent of the fact that the nation's real atomic secrets were being driven out the front gate in Klaus Fuchs's blue Buick—de Silva was handed another assignment by

Lansdale: investigating Kitty Oppenheimer's complaint that the army was opening the letters she received from her parents.*[27]

At Y-12 that summer, Lawrence was trying to rush the atomic bomb to completion by drastically increasing the number of Calutrons. "The primary fact now is that the element of gamble in the over-all picture no longer exists," he had written to Conant in May.[28] Ernest asked Groves to approve construction of two more Alpha II racetracks, even though the first of the new machines had barely begun operating.[29]

Novel ways were also being found to improve efficiencies elsewhere. Unable to account for a discrepancy between the Calutrons' calculated rate of production and the amount of enriched uranium actually being shipped to New Mexico, Lawrence had ordered the chemical processing plant at Oak Ridge taken down and the pipes in its labyrinth sawn in half. The missing uranium was found, and the facility was quickly rebuilt to a new design.[30] In late June 1944, Los Alamos received the first shipment of highly enriched U-235 from the Beta machines.[31]

As the production of uranium gradually picked up at Y-12, so, too, did Groves's mood. In July, Groves gave Lawrence the go-ahead to begin work on a revolutionary new thirty-beam Calutron—even though Ernest admitted that the machine could not begin producing weapons-grade uranium until mid-1945 at the earliest.

In August, Groves reported to the Top Policy Group that the scientists at Los Alamos were sufficiently confident of the uranium gun working that they advised it could be used in combat without a prior test. (Thin Man, the original high-velocity plutonium gun, had meanwhile been replaced by a shorter, low-velocity uranium gun, dubbed "Little Boy.")[32] The success of the Fat Man plutonium implosion weapon, on the other hand, remained problematic; a test was scheduled for the following year.

Groves believed that the first atomic bomb might be ready to drop on the enemy as early as the end of March 1945. He estimated that between the spring and the summer Los Alamos would be able to produce from five to eleven implosion gadgets.[33]

By November 1944, all nine Alpha racetracks were running at full capacity—daily feeding more than 100 grams of U-235 into two Beta

* Near the end of the war, because of Fuchs and other spies at Los Alamos, the Russians had a precise description of the component parts of Fat Man, including such engineering details as the makeup and design of the explosive lenses used to compress the plutonium core, and the exact dimensions of the bomb's polonium initiator. The device that the Soviets exploded in their first nuclear test, in August 1949, was essentially a copy of Fat Man.

tracks.[34] Low-grade uranium from gaseous and thermal diffusion plants was also being sent through the Alpha and Beta Calutrons.[35] Weekly shipments of enriched uranium to Los Alamos had begun. Army officers dressed in civilian clothes and carrying concealed sidearms accompanied the special suitcases containing the precious metal as it was transported by ambulance and train to New Mexico.[36]

Just before Thanksgiving, Lawrence telephoned Groves from Oak Ridge to exult that "things are really booming down here." The production of U-235 in November equaled all previous months combined.[37] In December came another new record: nearly 200 grams of uranium, 80-percent pure U-235, were left in the receivers following a single day's run. All nine Alpha tracks and three Beta tracks were in continuous operation for the first time. Spending Christmas on the job, Lawrence gave a holiday pep talk to the workers at Dogpatch. He promised even better news to celebrate "in the not far distant future."[38]

Even as he chided Lawrence for overoptimism, Groves, too, had begun thinking beyond the war's end. As early as spring 1944, he had asked Princeton physicist Henry Smyth to begin writing a technical history of the Manhattan Project that could be publicly distributed after the war. Smyth's report was intended, in part, to be a vindication of the project's cost and effort; as such, it was really Groves's valedictory. But the report was also a tidy and convenient way of dividing what scientists could talk about from what had to remain officially secret.

In August, Bush picked Richard Tolman to head a panel that would make recommendations on postwar atomic research, including its applications to industry.[39]

Two weeks later, Tolman's Committee on Postwar Policy interviewed almost fifty Manhattan Project scientists in Chicago, New York, and Washington, D.C.[40] In a written response, sent from Los Alamos, Oppenheimer focused on the hydrogen superbomb and a hybrid fission-fusion device, the "Booster," which Teller had proposed at the lab late in 1943. But Oppie thought it likely that both the Super and the Booster would remain essentially unexplored at war's end: "I should like, therefore, to put in writing at an early date the recommendation that the subject of initiating violent thermo-nuclear reactions be pursued with vigor and diligence, and promptly."[41]

Lawrence planned a different path: he looked to the government as the engine that would drive and even accelerate postwar scientific research at Berkeley. But he also envisioned an improved, fully automated, peacetime Y-12 producing enriched uranium at five times the wartime rate.[42]

Meeting with Tolman's committee on Wednesday morning, November 8, 1944, at the National Academy of Sciences in Washington, Lawrence spoke of a ten-fold increase in output from the latest version of his Calutron, the Alpha III. Ernest envisioned each future racetrack churning out not only U-235 but also low-grade uranium fuel for the atomic reactors that would generate the electricity to run the plant, in what amounted to a kind of self-sustaining perpetual motion machine. "There must be a postwar policy and program on a very large scale," he declared. "It can't be piddling."[43]

When Oppenheimer appeared before Tolman's committee that afternoon, a more reflective mood prevailed. Oppie declared that wartime secrecy was antithetical to maintaining the country's "technical hegemony" in peacetime. "If we try to work in secret after the war, we will fall behind other countries better able to work in secret," he warned.[44]

Characteristically, Lawrence had already begun laying the groundwork for his postwar plan. Before returning to California, he and Cooksey stopped off at Groves's Washington office to plead for construction of a new electromagnetic separation plant after the war.[45] Lawrence wanted the army to look at abandoned smelters near Las Vegas, Nevada, and in Washington State as possible sites for a reborn Y-12.[46] Another facility was urgently necessary, Ernest argued, because existing equipment was obsolete and the machinery breaking down: the copper liners of the Alpha Calutrons were already wearing out.[47]

To Lawrence's great disappointment, Tolman's report—given to Groves just after Christmas—failed to make a case for the new Calutrons.[48] But even more disturbing to Ernest was a rumor that Oppenheimer had been one of those to speak out against his plans.[49] When Lawrence had last raised the issue of plant expansion with his old friend, Oppie had seemed supportive.[50]

By February 1945, Lawrence was still anxiously awaiting a final decision by Groves on the fate of his proposal. In a telephone call at the end of the month, the verdict was relayed by Fidler: the Calutrons had served their purpose; the army would pay for no more following the conclusion of the war.[51]

A few days earlier, the design of Little Boy had been frozen at Los Alamos. The uranium gun was expected to be ready for combat use by July.[52] Groves tentatively scheduled a test of the implosion bomb for Independence Day, in the New Mexican desert near Alamogordo, 200 miles south of Los Alamos.[53]

For reasons that Oppenheimer decided to keep obscure, he had named the test site *Trinity*—a secret tribute to Jean Tatlock, who had committed suicide at her San Francisco apartment the previous January.*[54]

At Oak Ridge, meanwhile, the gaseous diffusion plant known as K-25 was producing enriched uranium at nearly bomb-grade concentrations, making further processing by the Alpha Calutrons unnecessary. The end product from the cascades was now fed directly into the Beta machines. Because of these additional sources, another milestone was reached that spring: the output of U-235 in March again exceeded production for all previous months combined.[55]

The gathering momentum at both Y-12 and Los Alamos meant that Germany's surrender in early May had little impact upon the Manhattan Project. Despite Robert Wilson's attempt to raise the question of whether their efforts should continue, only one scientist at the lab—a member of the British delegation—elected to quit before the Japanese enemy was defeated. The thrumming of Lawrence's Calutrons continued uninterrupted. As Pash's *Alsos* mission had found that spring, the country where fission was discovered never came close to harnessing it for a bomb.

In another subtle sign that the drama was approaching its climax, Groves lifted the ban that had grounded laboratory directors. The army informed Tennessee Eastman of pending reductions in the workforce at Oak Ridge, while Lawrence was told to trim nonresearch personnel at the Rad Lab by 20 percent.[56] The previous summer, Underhill had advised Oppenheimer that the university was preparing to "taper off" its commitment to run Los Alamos and hoped to be out of the bomb business altogether by the end of the war.[57]

As the Manhattan Project picked up speed, so, too, did Soviet efforts to steal its secrets. Like the U-235 being churned out by the Calutrons, the copious flow of purloined information to Moscow threatened, at times, to swamp the receivers.[58] Kurchatov's April 1945 cables to Pervukhin reflected almost an embarrassment of riches. The bomb secrets coming in were of such "vast importance" and so far outstripped Soviet knowledge, wrote Kurchatov with his blue pencil, that it was *"impossible to formulate pertinent questions that would require additional information."*[59]

In his messages to Pervukhin, Kurchatov also reflected that the greatest contribution of Soviet spies was "enabling us to bypass many labor-

* From a sonnet by John Donne:

> Batter my heart, three-person'd God, for you
> As yet but knock, breathe, shine, and seek to mend;
> That I may rise and stand, o'erthrow me, and bend
> Your force to break, blow, burn, and make me new.

consuming stages of the problem's development." Indeed, Russia's Manhattan Project had already learned through espionage something that it had taken Los Alamos more than a year to find out: that Teller's favored hydride bomb probably would not work.[60]

In San Francisco, *Kharon*'s successor, Kasparov, had meanwhile been transferred to the embassy in Mexico City. His replacement was thirty-five-year-old Stepan Apresyan, code-named *May (Maj)*. Apresyan had served for less than a year as NKVD *rezident* at the New York consulate, his first overseas posting, and was plainly a rising star in the Soviet intelligence service.[61] Word that the inaugural session of the United Nations would take place in San Francisco that spring had given the Bay Area consulate suddenly increased importance.

However, *May*'s youth and inexperience, coupled with Kasparov's rapid departure, made for a rocky transition.

On April 3, 1945, *May* cabled Moscow in a near panic, requesting *Map*'s surname as well as *Uncle*'s "distinguishing features since there is no photograph here and there may be a misunderstanding owing to the rather unfortunate password."[62] He had a meeting with *Uncle* just three days hence, Apresyan explained.*[63]

Two weeks later, however, Apresyan had found his bearings. On April 16, *May* cabled Moscow to say that he had turned over to *Map* the task that Kheifets had originally assigned to Eltenton: luring prospective recruits with honorary membership in the Soviet Academy of Sciences.[64] Shortly thereafter, *Uncle* relayed word from the local head of the Communist Party that Apresyan had a new agent to run: Harry Dexter White, code-named *Richard*. White was in San Francisco as the Treasury Department's representative at the UN conference; he would report sensitive discussions within the U.S. delegation to Moscow.[65]

Also at the United Nations conference was Haakon Chevalier, who found temporary employment as a translator for the French delegation. Although Pieper by that spring had a total of eight agents shadowing Chevalier—five stationed outside the house at Stinson Beach, with three more listening in on a telephone tap—except for a single suspicious incident, the FBI was unable to find any evidence that the former professor was still involved in espionage.[66] Similarly, the bug that the bureau had implanted near Bransten's dining room was picking up only dinnertime

---

* Apresyan had become the New York *rezident* after Zubilin was recalled to Moscow. *Maj*'s brother had been shot during the Stalinist purges, and Apresyan himself had spent time at the NKVD's infamous Lubyanka prison. A colleague wrote of him: "Our *Rezident* had been so deeply traumatized by his own experience as a prisoner that the secret meetings with the agents he handled were absolute torture for him. Several days before a rendezvous he would turn into a withdrawn bundle of nerves, barely listening to what was being said and incapable of making any decisions."

conversations and bickering between *Map* and Chevalier over the wisdom of the party line.[67]

On June 4, 1945, Bransten and *May* cohosted a reception at the Soviet consulate that was organized and sponsored by the American-Russian Institute. The occasion was advertised as an opportunity to introduce American scientists to their Soviet counterparts at the UN conference. As FBI agents noted, both Ernest Lawrence and Frank Oppenheimer attended the reception.[68]

Soviet espionage had been very much on Groves's mind when he and Secretary of War Stimson briefed the new president, Harry Truman, on the atomic bomb a few weeks earlier. (In office less than two weeks, Truman probably found jarring Groves's forecast for the future: "Atomic energy, if controlled by the major peace-loving nations, should insure the peace of the world for decades to come. If misused it can lead our civilization to annihilation.")

"A great deal of emphasis was placed on foreign relations and the Russian situation," Groves wrote in notes of the meeting.[69] Shortly thereafter, in a similar briefing to Secretary of State–designate James Byrnes, Groves chose to focus upon the Soviet spy ring at the University of California.[70]

But Groves also made it plain that he did not intend to make the Russians' job any easier. When Lawrence, at the end of May, asked the general's permission to attend an upcoming celebration in Moscow of the 220th anniversary of the Russian Academy of Sciences, Groves ordered him to decline. Reluctantly, Ernest sent his regrets.[71]

Since the atomic bomb now seemed almost certain to be ready in time to be used in the war, Washington directed that further consideration be given to the circumstances of its use, including how the weapon might be employed, and against what sort of targets—issues that had been deliberately held in abeyance, awaiting assurances that the bomb would work.

In early May 1945, Stimson created a seven-man committee to consider these questions as well as the bomb's postwar role. The secretary of war put himself at the head of what he called the Interim Committee; Truman picked Byrnes as his personal representative. On May 9, the group held its first meeting, in Stimson's office.[72]

At Conant's urging, a Scientific Panel—consisting of Oppenheimer, Lawrence, Fermi, and Arthur Compton—was appointed to advise the committee on technical issues. Conant decided to introduce the panel to its subject with a memorandum that he and Bush had written the previous fall on the international implications of atomic energy.[73]

The Scientific Panel did not join the discussions until the committee's fourth meeting, on the morning of May 31.[74]

Compton had just begun the meeting, summarizing the steps leading to the atomic bomb's development, when Conant—mindful of what was lurking in the wings—interrupted to steer the discussion around to the Super. Under Conant's prodding, Oppenheimer said that he now believed the superbomb would require a minimum of three more years to reach production. To the uninitiated, like Byrnes, the figures that Oppie cited—"an explosive force equal to 10,000,000–100,000,000 tons of TNT"—doubtless came as a stunning surprise.[75]

After a brief diversion onto the subject of postwar research—where Lawrence, predictably, made a pitch for "vigorously pursuing the necessary plant expansion" and "adequate government support," while Oppenheimer advocated returning to a "leisurely and a more normal research situation"—the discussion turned to the Russians.[76]

Oppenheimer thought America's moral position would be greatly strengthened if the nation were to release information on atomic energy's peacetime applications, particularly before the bomb was used.[77] Army chief of staff George Marshall went even further, suggesting that the United States invite a pair of prominent Russian scientists to the upcoming test of the gadget in New Mexico. Byrnes, however, quickly scotched that idea. Compton intervened hurriedly—and unsuccessfully—in an effort to find some common ground, but the morning ended tensely.

At lunch, the committee and its panel spread out among four tables. Lawrence, Oppenheimer, and Compton sat together with Byrnes, Stimson, and Groves. Prompted by Byrnes, Lawrence spoke up on an issue that had been left off the agenda, but that he had raised briefly during the morning's discussion: how the bomb might be used against Japan. Lawrence proposed that the weapon be demonstrated to the Japanese "in some innocuous but striking manner, before it should be used in such a way as to kill many people."[78]

The idea of a so-called demonstration of the bomb had been discussed earlier, at both Los Alamos and Washington.[79] But Lawrence's suggestion was the first time that it had been discussed at such a high level—or with such seriousness.[80]

Numerous practical objections to the scheme were immediately raised by others at the table. Stimson—who was suffering increasing anguish, his personal diary showed, from the daily destruction of Japan's cities—doubted that casualties from the atomic bomb would be any worse than the masses of people killed by conventional bombing, including the recent B-29 fire raids upon Tokyo. Oppenheimer and Groves expressed similar skepticism that a demonstration could be "sufficiently spectacular" to compel Japan's surrender.[81] Byrnes himself worried that the Japanese, if warned of an impending atomic attack on their home islands, might move American prisoners of war into the target area. Cowed by this resistance,

Lawrence did not argue the point. The entire lunchtime discussion had taken perhaps ten minutes.

Assembling afterward in Stimson's office, the Interim Committee officially took up the question of the bomb's use. Notes by Stimson aide Gordon Arneson left little doubt that, in Stimson's mind at least, the issue was settled by meeting's end:

> After much discussion concerning various types of targets and the effects to be produced, the Secretary expressed the conclusion, on which there was general agreement, that we could not give the Japanese any warning; that we could not concentrate on a civilian area; but that we should seek to make a profound psychological impression on as many of the inhabitants as possible. At the suggestion of Dr. Conant the Secretary agreed that the most desirable target would be a vital war plant employing a large number of workers and closely surrounded by workers' houses.[82]

At Los Alamos that spring, Oppenheimer was becoming anxious to leave the lab. In a report to Groves on May 7, Oppie described the wartime laboratory as "singularly unsuited for peacetime perpetuation," requiring a great change "in the way in which the Laboratory is set up and very probably an actual shift in its physical location."[83] Oppenheimer also let Groves know that he should start looking for a replacement: "In particular, the Director himself would very much like to know when he will be able to escape from these duties for which he is so ill qualified and which he has accepted only in an effort to serve the country during the war."

The Scientific Panel gathered once again, at Los Alamos, on June 16. In the waning minutes of the last Interim Committee meeting, Stimson had asked the scientists to draft a memorandum on the future prospects for atomic research. The panel's deliberations had just begun, however, when they were cut short by an urgent phone call from Stimson aide George Harrison, who asked for the scientists' views on a more pressing issue: the use of the bomb against Japan.

Behind Harrison's inquiry was a document that Compton and Chicago physicist James Franck had tried, unsuccessfully, to deliver to Stimson a few days before. The Franck report was a thirteen-page plea by Met Lab scientists for international control of the atomic bomb. Among its earnest recommendations was one which was highlighted, urging "*a demonstration of the new weapon . . . before the eyes of representatives of all the United Nations, on the desert or a barren island.*"[84] Before Stimson responded to the Franck report, Harrison explained, he wanted the panel's opinion. Hoping to do his own lobbying for the report within the panel, Compton had brought copies along with him on the train from Chicago.[85]

Lawrence led the reopened discussion of the demonstration. Although Fermi had remained mute on the subject before the Interim Committee, he evidently sided with Lawrence in this new debate.[86] Ironically, Compton now spoke out against the demonstration—arguing that use of the bomb against a military target would result in a "probable net savings of lives." Were the bomb not used, Compton asserted, "the world would have no adequate warning as to what was to be expected if war should break out again."[87] When Lawrence persisted, Compton hinted that Ernest's views on the subject were unduly influenced by the latter's fond memories of Japanese physics students at Berkeley.[88]

But it was Oppenheimer who made the final, telling argument against the demonstration. His objections were a reprise of the points he had raised at the meeting on May 31: The bomb was not certain to work, and a dud might even be used against us by the enemy; Japanese defenses would be alerted by a warning, and POWs possibly moved onto the target. Most important, no conceivable demonstration of the bomb could be as compelling as its actual combat use against what Groves and the army were calling "built-up areas"—that is, cities.[89]

This time, Lawrence appears to have remained resolute, refusing to back down.[90] Thus the memorandum that Oppenheimer sent to Stimson from Los Alamos acknowledged that the views of the scientists on the use of the bomb were "not unanimous: they range from the proposal of a purely technical demonstration to that of the military application best designed to induce surrender."[91] On the question of the demonstration, Oppie used an artful word—*closer*—to bridge what seems to have been an unresolved difference of opinion: "We find ourselves closer to these latter views; we can propose no technical demonstration likely to bring an end to the war; we see no acceptable alternative to direct military use."[92]

Although he was not part of the Scientific Panel, Edward Teller, too, was looking ahead to the future after the war.[93] At Chicago, Teller's friend and colleague Leo Szilard, recognizing that the Franck report had failed to make a dent upon the mind of official Washington, decided upon making his own last-minute appeal: a petition, addressed to the president, which urged that the atomic bomb not be used without warning against Japan.[94] Szilard circulated his petition at the Met Lab and also sent copies to Oak Ridge and Los Alamos, where Teller brought the document to Oppenheimer's attention. Oppie's immediate response, Teller recalled, was that it was not the job of scientists to decide how the weapon was used.[95]

In a letter he wrote to Szilard, setting out his reasons for not signing the petition, Teller failed to mention Oppie's argument, but instead implied that the efforts of his fellow Hungarian were too little, too late:

> The things we are working on are so terrible that no amount of protesting or fiddling with politics will save our souls. . . . I should like to have the advice of all of you whether you think it is a crime to continue to work. But I feel that I should do the wrong thing if I tried to say how to tie the little toe of the ghost to the bottle from which we just helped it escape.[96]

As Teller alluded in his letter to Szilard, he was already at work on an even more fearsome weapon than the atomic bomb—the Super. For almost a year, Edward had been importuning Oppie and others to promise that they would remain at the lab until the feasibility of the hydrogen bomb had been decided, one way or the other. Teller himself had postponed a decision on whether to return to academe until he was sure of Oppenheimer's answer.

In May, Teller had once more pestered the army to allow Maria Mayer to visit Los Alamos so that she might report in person on the progress of her opacity calculations. But Lansdale had denied the request.[97] Oppenheimer finally brokered a compromise: Mayer could come to Los Alamos, but Teller had to keep her in the dark regarding opacity's application to the Super.[98]

At Y-12, Lawrence's boys were tipped off to the approaching end of the war by an urgent order from Washington, instructing them to shut down the Calutrons and ship all the uranium that could be collected from the receivers and the innards of the machines to Los Alamos.[99] For the first time, the precious cargo was flown from Knoxville, Tennessee, to the tiny airport at Santa Fe. By then, every gram of the U-235 that would go into Little Boy had gone through Lawrence's Calutrons at least once.[100]

A similar edict to Hanford signaled the impending test of the Fat Man device. Operators of the DuPont reactors at Hanford were also instructed to send the next shipment of "product" by air rather than overland.[101] To Groves's disappointment, problems with the molds for the explosive lenses had made it necessary to postpone the test of the implosion bomb; mid-July was now the expected date.[102]

Having finally embarked on a long-deferred vacation, Robert Underhill and his wife were just checking into Yosemite's Awahnee Hotel when he received a priority telephone call at the reception desk from the army. The regents' representative was on a train to Los Angeles the following day to sign a two-word amendment to Contract 36, approving the shipment of men "and *materiel*" to the Pacific. The change allowed the first bomb to be sent to Tinian, the island that would be the launching point for the atomic raids against Japan.[103]

In Berkeley on July 6, Lawrence received a cable from Oppenheimer at *Clear Creek*, the code name for telegrams originating in Los Alamos:

> Any time after the 15th would be a good time for our fishing trip. Because we are not certain of the weather we may be delayed several days. As we do not have enough sleeping bags to go around we ask you please not to bring any friends with you. Let us know where in Albuquerque you can be reached.[104]

Groves, Bush, and Conant flew west in the general's C-47 five days later, for a last inspection of the laboratories and facilities that manufactured components of the bomb.[105] The delegation arrived in Berkeley on the late afternoon of July 13, whereupon Lawrence took his guests out to dinner at Trader Vic's. (The group ordered Ernest's favorites: barbequed spareribs, fried rice, and several rounds of Mai Tais. Ernest paid the bill—$65.15—from the Loomis fund.)[106]

Later that evening, Ernest handed Groves a four-page letter that the general had requested at their previous meeting. It outlined Ernest's postwar plans for the Rad Lab.[107]

From Oakland, Groves, Lawrence, and the rest of the entourage flew south to the Naval Ordnance Station at Inyokern in the California desert—where the explosive lenses for Fat Man were tested—and then on to Los Angeles, where the group visited Caltech. Arriving in Albuquerque on Sunday afternoon, July 15, Groves worried that spies might notice the number of world-renowned scientists gathering in the lobby of the Hilton hotel, and so ordered them dispersed to other lodgings.

Following dinner with Alvarez, in the early morning hours of Monday, July 16, Lawrence, Monsanto executive Charles Thomas, and *New York Times* reporter William Laurence crowded into an olive-drab Plymouth for the three-hour drive to *Trinity* site. Groves had made Laurence a kind of semiofficial chronicler of the bomb's development.[108]

At *Trinity*, Ernest joined a clump of scientists gathering on Compania Hill, the VIP viewpoint located twenty miles northwest of the bomb on its tower. The group included McMillan, Teller, Serber, and British physicist James Chadwick. Gusty winds and driving rain that had lashed the desert all night finally abated.[109] Standing next to Lawrence, Teller unnerved onlookers by smearing suntan lotion on his face, donning heavy gloves and welder's glasses as the countdown approached zero.[110] ("He scared the hell out of me," admitted physicist Willie Higinbotham.)[111] Ernest hopped nervously in and out of the Plymouth's front seat, figuring that the car's windshield would filter out the bomb's ultraviolet rays.

Lawrence was bent down, just getting out of the car, when the bomb exploded. "I was enveloped with a warm brilliant yellow-white light—from darkness to brilliant sunshine in an instant, and as I remember I momentarily was stunned by the surprise," he later wrote in the report that Groves demanded of eyewitnesses.[112]

Teller had just begun to lift the heavy goggles from his eyes to get a better look when he realized that the light outside was as bright as the sun at midday and the heat from the bomb palpable.

Against all advice, Serber had been looking directly at the bomb with unshielded eyes when it exploded; he was momentarily blinded.[113] Alvarez's was a unique perspective: kneeling between the pilot and copilot in the cockpit of a B-29 some twenty miles from ground zero, he saw the bomb as a brilliant light diffused through thick cloud cover. In an artist's pad balanced on his knees, Luis sketched the bulbous top of the roiling mushroom cloud pushing through the undercast.[114]

Lying facedown next to his brother outside the control bunker 10,000 yards south of the tower, Robert Oppenheimer waited for the deep, low rumbling sound of the bomb to subside before he stood up. Oppie then turned to Frank with a smile that mixed pride with relief and said, simply, "It worked."[115]

Later, Bush and Conant walked down to the road that led to the control bunker and waited. As an army car drove by trailing a cloud of dust, Groves and Oppenheimer visible in the backseat, the two men theatrically snapped to attention and, grinning, doffed their hats.[116]

8

A STONE'S THROW FROM DESPAIR

THE MOOD IN GROVES'S plane on the flight back to Washington was triumphant. In the euphoria that followed *Trinity,* all talk of a demonstration was forgotten.[1] From Washington, Lawrence traveled on to Oak Ridge, where U-235 was already being scraped from the Calutrons for a second uranium bomb.[2] From New Mexico, Serber and Alvarez headed west across the Pacific to Tinian Island, where B-29s would launch the atomic raids against Japan.

Oppenheimer returned to Los Alamos to find the latest report concerning the Super on his desk. The most recent calculations suggested that a thermonuclear reaction in tritium and deuterium could indeed be triggered by an atomic bomb.[3] Having just had a glimpse into the abyss, Oppie now saw before him the yawning chasm.

On July 27, 1945, Groves felt it proper to warn Stimson and Marshall where the future could be headed. It might be possible to create a weapon far more powerful than that just tested in New Mexico, Groves reported, using a Little Boy–type bomb as the detonator, a few hundred grams of tritium as a booster, and 1 cubic meter of liquid deuterium as the fuel. The specter that Teller had raised at Berkeley three years earlier returned to haunt those pondering the Super anew: "Such a bomb might introduce the possibility of world destruction if the theories of some scientists are correct that the explosion could ignite the entire world's atmosphere. Further study of this possibility would have to be made."[4]

⚛

But the immediate focus, of course, was upon Japan. Sitting out a vigil, Groves got word of the atomic attack on Hiroshima shortly before midnight on August 5 at his Washington office. News of the bombing came to Los Alamos in the stilted, staccato language of a telegram that was garbled in transmission. Manley passed the word along to Oppenheimer, who, if not yet knowing of the bomb's effects, at least understood its significance.[5]

As an observer in a B-29 that accompanied the *Enola Gay* over the Japanese city, Alvarez had been the closest witness to the lab's handiwork. Luie was onboard to monitor the performance of parachute-rigged detectors he had designed for measuring the explosive force of the atomic bombs.[6] After dropping the detectors, the chase plane had climbed and turned sharply to escape the shock wave from Little Boy. Alvarez missed seeing the actual explosion but, peering out a porthole a moment later, witnessed the aftermath: "I looked out and all I could see was a black, roiling cloud over what looked like a forest. My first thought to myself was that Ernest Lawrence would be furious when he learned that they had wasted all his uranium on a forest. I didn't see any sign of a city."[7]

Teller did not learn of the destruction of Hiroshima until midmorning, while he was walking to work. "One down!"—the greeting shouted out by the driver of a speeding jeep—remained incomprehensible until Edward joined his colleagues at the Tech Area.[8]

In Berkeley, Lawrence heard the news of the bombing at home over the radio. After predicting to Molly that the war would soon be over, Ernest looked to the future. "Now we will have no more war and the most backward countries will be able to start catching up," he told his wife.[9]

On campus later in the day, Lawrence roamed the laboratories, shops, and offices of the Rad Lab, shaking hands and receiving congratulations. Groves telephoned Ernest shortly after noon to thank him and the Rad Lab for their role in the project.[10]

But doubts, second-guesses, and even regrets were not long in coming. Berkeley astronomer Donald Shane, the head of scientific personnel at Los Alamos, remembered Oppenheimer as "excited and elated" during dinner the night after Hiroshima was bombed.[11] Yet as details of that attack and of the second atomic raid—on Nagasaki, three days later—drifted back to the lab, the confident mood and "high-noon strut" that Rabi recalled of Oppie just after the *Trinity* test gradually faded, to be replaced by signs of obvious emotional distress.[12] An FBI report on August 9 described Oppie as a "nervous wreck." A bureau informant who saw the physicist on the *City of San Francisco* a few days later reported that "Oppenheimer kept looking under the table and all around."[13]

When Lawrence flew to Los Alamos for a meeting of the Scientific

Panel on August 10, he found Oppenheimer anxious, distracted, and depressed by the casualty reports from Nagasaki.[14] Discussions that were supposed to take place on the subject of postwar research were side-tracked by the news, and by Lawrence's insistence that Oppenheimer make up his mind whether he was going to return to Berkeley.[15] Repeated entreaties from Birge had gone unanswered, Ernest chided, and plans had to be made for classes that fall.

Instead, Oppenheimer complained bitterly to Lawrence about how he had been treated by Underhill and the University of California. Rival offers, Oppie said, had come from Columbia University, Harvard, and the Institute for Advanced Study at Princeton.[16]

As the discussion turned to the bomb casualties in Japan, Lawrence pointed out, perhaps unkindly, that it was he who had championed the demonstration and Oppie who had opposed it. Stung, in turn, by Oppenheimer's claim that he respected only those who were victorious in life—generals, rich businessmen, and the like—Ernest observed, somewhat plaintively, that both he *and* Oppie had achieved great success. Oppenheimer hinted that Lawrence was jealous of his achievements and eager to make him a mere subordinate once more at the Rad Lab.

Like the spat over Oppenheimer's leftwandering before the war, this fight between friends ended without resolution. Ernest returned home angry and embittered at Oppie, who, in a final gesture of defiance, had refused to say whether he would return to Berkeley.

Two weeks later, when tempers had cooled, Oppenheimer wrote Lawrence a long letter. Although meant as an attempt at reconciliation, it actually showed how much their differences and simmering resentments remained.

> I have very mixed and sad feelings about our discussions on Berkeley. I meant them in a far more friendly, tentative and considerate spirit than they appeared to you; and was aware and tried to make you aware at the time that fatigue and confusion gave them a false emphasis and color. It may seem odd and wrong to you that the lack of sympathy between us at Y and the California administration over the operation of the project could make me consider not coming back: I think it would not have seemed so odd if you had lived through the history as we did, nor so hard to understand if you remembered how much more of an underdogger I have always been than you. That is a part of me that is unlikely to change, for I am not ashamed of it; it is responsible for such difference as we have had in the past, I think; I should have thought that after the long years it would not be new to you.[17]

Oppenheimer, in his letter to Lawrence, confessed to feeling "a profound grief, and a profound perplexity about the course we should be following." Oppie's mixed mood was attributable, in part, to his anxiety over what would be done with the bomb after the war. Stimson's Interim Committee had focused on the military problems at hand and offered little or no guidance for the future.

Japan's surrender in mid-August was announced just as Oppenheimer arrived in Washington to deliver to Stimson a two-page memorandum that the Scientific Panel had drafted at Los Alamos. Oppie had persuaded the panel that its recommendations on postwar research should be postponed pending completion of a more urgent task: a plea for the international control of atomic energy. As his memo noted, the opportunity for international control might soon disappear—particularly given "the quite favorable technical prospects of the realization of the super bomb."[18]

As with the demonstration, members of the Scientific Panel had disagreed over what should go into the memo to Stimson.[19] Lawrence wanted a statement that would acknowledge the need to "stockpile and continue intensive development of atomic weapons" for several years. But he had finally deferred to Oppenheimer, who included this impassioned appeal in the final version:

> We believe that the safety of this nation—as opposed to its ability to inflict damage on an enemy power—cannot lie wholly or even primarily in its scientific or technical prowess. It can be based only on making future wars impossible. It is our unanimous and urgent recommendation to you that . . . all steps be taken, all necessary international arrangements be made, to this one end.[20]

Unable to deliver the document to Stimson—who was on a long-deterred vacation in the Adirondacks, having returned exhausted from the Potsdam summit—Oppenheimer instead briefed Vannevar Bush and George Harrison on its contents.[21] Harrison, who showed the memo to James Byrnes the following day, recorded the latter's reaction: "Secretary Byrnes felt so strongly about all of this that he requested me to tell Dr. Oppenheimer for the time being his proposal about an international agreement was not practical and that he and the rest of the gang should pursue their work full force."[22]

Harrison relayed Byrnes's message to Oppenheimer, who was at his hotel packing for the return to Los Alamos. Oppie had heard that things had gone badly at Potsdam, and so believed the prospects "gloomy" for approaching the Russians on any kind of collaborative control of the bomb.[23] Harrison's news further darkened the physicist's mood.

Retreating a few days later to the sanctuary of Perro Caliente, Oppenheimer wrote to a friend that his feelings about the future were "only a stone's throw from despair."[24] Oppie's letter to Chevalier seemed an attempt to persuade himself that what he wrote was true: "The thing had to be done, Haakon. It had to be brought to an open public fruition at a time when all over the world men craved peace as never before, were committed as never before both to technology as a way of life and thought and to the idea that no man is an island."[25]

By the end of the month that saw the destruction of two cities by nuclear weapons, the future that Oppenheimer despaired of was already taking shape. A week after Japan's surrender, Groves apprised Marshall of the postwar production schedule for atomic bombs. The head of the Manhattan Project anticipated that by year's end there would be twenty Fat Man plutonium bombs in the nation's nuclear arsenal.[26]

Groves's colleagues in the Army Air Force had already identified new targets for America's nascent nuclear stockpile. Less than two weeks after Japan's surrender, the AAF sent Groves its draft of a plan for a possible future war with the Soviet Union. The plan identified fifteen cities—including Moscow and Leningrad—as aiming points for atomic weapons.[27]

For Teller, too, the future seemed full of foreboding—but for reasons altogether different from Oppenheimer's. Having decided, upon Oppie's urging, not to sign Szilard's petition, Edward appeared eager to distance himself from the consequences in a letter he wrote to Maria Mayer: "The week in which we waited whether we have to drop a third baby and go on with this nasty business was horrible. Now I am very happy (even having had little to do with all this). But the confusion is still as great as it ever was."[28]

Teller urged Mayer to continue her work on opacity until the army contract lapsed at the end of the year. But he also warned her not to share the results with anyone: "I think you should not show it to the boys. It is better not to disturb them while there are no decisions."[29]

For Teller, as for Groves and Oppenheimer, a great unknown was the Soviet Union. A childhood spent in Hungary, in part under the short-lived regime of Béla Kun, had left Edward with a profound distrust of communism—an impression reinforced by the experiences of his Russian physicist friends. (During his first few weeks at Los Alamos, Teller had read Arthur Koestler's antiauthoritarian novel, *Darkness at Noon.* "That really settled my mind.")[30]

Barely a week after Japan's surrender, a friend from Princeton, physicist John Wheeler, wrote to Teller from Hanford with a grim inquiry: now that Japan was defeated, should they not begin preparing for a war with the new enemy, the Soviet Union?[31]

His own plans, Teller informed Wheeler, depended largely upon the still-unresolved question of whether Oppenheimer and Los Alamos would decide to pursue the Super. Edward hoped to convince Wheeler to come to the lab to work on the new bomb, and likewise to persuade Hans Bethe to stay at Los Alamos.[32] Bethe was surprised at Teller's dark vision of the future—and particularly the latter's "terribly anticommunist, terribly anti-Russian" views.[33]

But Edward's recruiting efforts had met with little success; most of his colleagues were simply eager to return home.[34] Concerning Oppie's plans for the future, the Los Alamos director had thus far remained silent in Teller's presence.[35]

For Lawrence, on the other hand, the postwar world seemed suddenly bright with possibilities.[36] The only dark cloud on the horizon that he forecast—in an impromptu speech to the regents on the morning after V-J day—was competition from Berkeley's archrival, the University of Chicago.[37] To preempt that threat, he asked Sproul for faculty salary increases across the board in the physics and chemistry departments, as well as a $250,000 boost in the annual Rad Lab budget.[38]

But Lawrence's plans also hinged importantly upon Oppenheimer, which was why he had been so upset at Oppie's vacillating. "Above all," Lawrence had written Groves, "we are looking forward to the return of Professor Oppenheimer to resume direction of research and teaching in the theoretical physics, and it goes without saying that I am counting on him to share with me direction of the Laboratory program."[39]

The army and Groves were, of course, likewise an indispensable part of Lawrence's postwar plans. Two days after Japan's surrender, Nichols notified Underhill that the army wished to extend its contracts with the university for another six months.[40] With the end of the war, Underhill and Sproul had been expecting to transfer the administration of Los Alamos to the government. Behind the scenes, however, Lawrence was already working to ensure that his highly lucrative partnership with the army continued.

Ernest's secret ally in this battle was sixty-year-old John Francis Neylan, chairman of the university regents. Neylan was a former newspaper reporter, born in New Jersey, who had come to California in 1909 to cover Hiram Johnson's bid for governor. Neylan had stayed to manage Upton Sinclair's unsuccessful gubernatorial campaign on the socialist ticket a generation later. Earning a law degree at night school, Neylan had become one of the most successful lawyers in the state—as well as the personal counsel and confidant of conservative publisher William Randolph Hearst.[41] In the course of his rise to power, the young Neylan's progressivism had gradually given way to a strident, even fanatical, anticommunism.[42]

Neylan had met Lawrence early in the latter's career and was immediately enthralled by his knowledge as well as his naive enthusiasm. The head regent soon became Lawrence's biggest promoter on campus, as well as his unofficial political adviser.

On August 24, 1945, Neylan departed from the agenda of an emergency meeting of the regents—he had called the session to discuss the problem of overcrowding in Berkeley's dormitories—to urge creation of a "Special Committee on the Los Alamos Project."[43] Although the committee's ostensible purpose would be to safeguard the university's rights in patent matters, its charter was actually open-ended. In fact, Neylan and Lawrence intended the committee to become the university's instrument for running postwar Los Alamos.

After the measure was quickly approved with little discussion, Neylan appointed himself the special committee's chairman. Sproul and two other regents, to be picked by the president and serve on a rotating basis, were its other members.

Long after the victory parades had ended and life had begun to return to routine at Berkeley, another kind of war silently raged on, in Washington and across the Bay. Five days after the Japanese surrender, Fidler cabled Lansdale that the FBI was seeking the army's help in putting together a legal case against Joe Weinberg and Martin Kamen. The charge would be conspiracy to commit espionage.[44]

The bureau's plans had hit a snag. In Weinberg's case, Fidler wrote, "no written evidence was available and other evidence [was] difficult to obtain"—a veiled reference to the fact that the information gathered by the bureau's bugs and wiretaps might not be admissible in court.[45]

Fidler informed the FBI that there was another potential complication in the Weinberg case—namely, the army's policy of avoiding embarrassment to high project officials: "Since testimony establishing fact that (Weinberg) was working on [Manhattan Project] problems for Rad Lab would probably best be given by JRO or EOL . . . it is recommended that FBI in Washington be requested to withhold action since involving either of these men at this time might not be desirable."[46]

Temporarily stymied in prosecuting those he suspected of being Soviet spies, Hoover sent to the White House that fall the FBI's dossier on Robert Oppenheimer and gave Truman's attorney general the bureau's recently completed "Report on Soviet Espionage in the United States"—a single-spaced, fifty-one-page document that amounted to a historical compendium of Russian spying since the Bolshevik revolution.[47] The report gave the names and backgrounds of dozens of Soviet and American citizens whom the bureau believed to be agents. Weinberg, Kamen, Bransten, and Chevalier were among them.[48]

Yet Hoover also had a backup plan, should legal obstacles frustrate the hoped-for prosecutions: he sent a second copy of the bureau's massive spy report to the House Un-American Activities Committee (HUAC), which Congress had made a permanent body earlier in the year.[49]

Across San Francisco Bay, the Russians, too, were busy tying up loose ends at their consulate, although their efforts had little to do with the return of peace.[50]

A mid-November 1945 cable from San Francisco to Moscow confirmed that Apresyan was still following the movements of local atomic scientists—including Lawrence and both Oppenheimer brothers—even as he warned the NKVD that "scholars who have taken part in these pursuits are under the surveillance of the American counterintelligence."*[51]

Indeed, an assessment of the Smyth report that the consulate sent Fitin two weeks later included a surprisingly cocky assurance on Apresyan's part that he could get whatever secrets Moscow needed. While the published report contained "no information about the quantity of uranium being (processed)," *May* telegraphed, a scientist and agent he identified as "D." had learned the essential details from those involved in the work and could "turn it over to us at any time."[52]

Apresyan's cable showed not only that the Bay Area espionage ring remained active in peacetime, but that—despite the end of hostilities—the war between spy and counterspy continued unabated.

By that spring, one major combatant, the army's Military Intelligence Division, was no longer in the fight. By February, Lansdale's once massive counterintelligence operation in the Bay Area had dwindled to just two agents in Oakland.[53] Harold Marsh and Rufus Shivers received orders from Washington to close the Universal Adjustment Company and send its secret files to the FBI. After driving a borrowed truck containing the

* Apresyan had other pressing, if mundane, concerns. He complained to Moscow in September that he had been unable to meet with two of his agents in Los Angeles *(Caen)* during a recent visit because he lacked a car. *May*'s lament would have struck a sympathetic chord with many Angelenos: "In a town like *Caen* I should be simply walked off my feet." Nonetheless, his request was denied.

files to San Francisco, Marsh handed the documents over to Branigan, the bureau's CINRAD expert.[54]

The last act fell to Shivers, who had earlier tried, unsuccessfully, to persuade the local head of G-2 to take the one remaining car that army agents had used in their surveillance: a beige 1939 Plymouth, registered to a fictitious owner. Given strict orders by Marsh to lose the car, Shivers returned to the Presidio late one night and left the Plymouth in the Officers Club parking lot with the keys in the ignition. After removing the license plates, he took a trolley home to pack his bags.

Without fanfare, cyclotroneers who spent the war years in secret exile at Oak Ridge and Los Alamos had begun returning to the Rad Lab. Luis Alvarez, arriving in mid-September 1945 from Tinian, was surprised to find his Berkeley colleagues fretting over the moral implications of the bomb.[55]

While still in the Pacific, Alvarez had worked out the design for a novel type of linear accelerator. Luie and Ernest were already talking to Alfred Loomis about obtaining financial backing for the new atom-smasher, and Groves had meanwhile promised a freight-trainful of surplus radar vacuum tubes for the machine that Alvarez called the "Linac."[56]

Ed McMillan had similarly ambitious plans. While still at Los Alamos, lying in bed one sleepless night shortly before the *Trinity* test, Lawrence's brother-in-law had hit upon a clever way to synchronize the movement of particles in a cyclotron. McMillan's invention of "phase stability" promised not only to get around the relativistic limits predicted for machines the size of the 184-inch, but also to boost the energies obtainable to 1 billion electron volts or more. Lawrence and McMillan dubbed the new machine the "Synchrotron."[57]

Insulted when Birge offered him only a lowly assistant professorship at Berkeley, Emilio Segrè coyly sought offers from other universities.[58] At archrival Chicago, Seaborg pursued a similar tack. (Sproul eventually caved in—promising Seaborg a new laboratory and the chemistry department "higher salaries and subsequent expansion.")[59] But Segrè did not return to campus until spring 1946, partly to repay Birge for his snub. Even then, he elected to work in the physics department rather than the Rab Lab—having decided that "although an excellent Maecenas, Lawrence was too demanding a boss."[60]

After assessing the damage at Hiroshima and Nagasaki, Serber had come home in late December. Birge assigned him to teach Oppenheimer's quantum mechanics class, while Oppie dithered about returning to Berkeley.[61] Serber's wife, Charlotte, who had been in charge of the classified reports library at wartime Los Alamos, applied for the job of Rad Lab librarian; Oppie wrote her a glowing letter of recommendation.[62]

Frank Oppenheimer wasted no time before becoming once more involved in the kind of political activity that his brother and Lawrence had repeatedly warned him against.[63] That October, he protested the Rad Lab's dismissal of a graduate student, Ted Finkelstein, for repeated security violations.[64] In November and December, Frank spoke to Berkeley's Democratic Forum and the state's CIO convention about the *Trinity* test, ending both lectures with an appeal for the international control of the bomb.[65]

Frank also agreed to teach a night class—"The Social Implications of Modern Scientific Development"—the following spring at the California Labor School, which shared quarters with Communist Party headquarters on Haight Street.[66] During the day, Oppie's brother worked with Serber on Alvarez's Linac.[67]

Lawrence's own plans focused upon completing the long-deferred great cyclotron. For the interim, however, he enjoyed playing the role of conquering hero. Intent upon ensuring that the record of Berkeley's contribution to the war effort would not be eclipsed by Chicago's, Neylan commissioned an official history of the Rad Lab, paid for by the regents.[68] Following suit, Sproul solicited private funds for an official portrait of Lawrence—a project inspired by Ernest himself. A bronze bust by Alfred Loomis's wife, Manette, would soon follow.[69]

But, beyond the trappings of empire, Lawrence's postwar fame and the promise of more money from Groves and Sproul meant that a whole new generation of "boys" had joined the Rad Lab's veterans in the days just after the war.[70] Among the recent additions was Wolfgang Panofsky, a twenty-six-year-old German émigré physicist who had worked with Alvarez at Los Alamos and was nicknamed "Pief." Since the diminutive Panofsky was the only researcher small enough to fit comfortably between the poles of the 184-inch magnet, Pief spent his first days at the lab doing measurements for Duane Sewell.[71]

Herbert York, a twenty-three-year-old experimentalist from Rochester University, whom Ernest had sent to Y-12 to improve the performance of the Beta Calutrons, returned to Berkeley after the war to finish his graduate degree. Lawrence put York to work on the graveyard shift running the 60-inch, which was once again being used to make medical radioisotopes.[72] The peacetime Rad Lab, Ernest had recently written Groves, "should be devoted primarily to the problems of pure science."[73]

Lawrence even revived the Journal Club, whose meetings had been suspended for the duration. In a move symbolizing the return to the status quo antebellum, his red leather chair was restored to its original place of honor in LeConte Hall.

Unwilling to wait until funding for his new projects had been approved, Lawrence ordered that the Rad Lab's cavernous Building 10, home of the prototype Calutron, be made ready for Alvarez's Linac.[74] Ed Lofgren joined Bernard Peters in converting the 37-inch to a scale-model Synchrotron, to be used in a test of McMillan's phase stability concept. Sewell and Panofsky supervised the dismantling of the old 184-inch, in preparation for its conversion to a phase-stabilized cyclotron.

That October, at a convocation in the open-air Greek theater on campus, Groves conferred the army-navy "E"—for "Excellence"—award upon Sproul. But, tellingly, the general had already signaled who would call the shots in the renewed army-university partnership. Groves had chosen Oppenheimer's replacement without consulting either Sproul or Underhill.

Norris Bradbury was a Berkeley-trained physicist and reserve navy commander whose duties at the wartime lab had included supervising the assembly of both the *Trinity* gadget and the Fat Man bomb. Although Bradbury had received Oppenheimer's endorsement, Underhill balked at what he took to be yet another infringement upon the university's prerogatives.[75] Nonetheless, a few weeks later, the regent's representative was once again on his way to New York, to negotiate another six-month extension of the army contracts with Nichols.[76]

Lawrence, for his part, remained unperturbed by the cost of empire. He had already let Groves know that the postwar Rad Lab would look to the army for at least $1 million annually.[77] In the months between the Calutrons' success and the *Trinity* test, Ernest's estimated yearly budget for the peacetime lab had ballooned a hundredfold; it climbed higher still following V-J day.[78]

With peace also came the return of familiar customs. On December 7, 1945, Lawrence hosted a cocktail party for the Rad Lab's returnees at Berkeley's elegant Claremont Hotel, followed by dinner at Trader Vic's. (Ernest's favorite restauranteur invented a new drink for the occasion—a lurid, smoking concoction of rum, blue Curacao, and dry ice dubbed the "A-bomb cocktail." "It was ghastly," Molly remembered.)[79]

The day before departing for a New Year's vacation in Palm Springs, Lawrence received the long-awaited word from Groves: the army agreed to provide the money necessary to complete the 184-inch and authorized the start of construction on McMillan's scale-model Synchrotron. But Groves wanted more details on the cost of Alvarez's Linac. The general agreed to send Nichols out to Berkeley to discuss the $1.6-million appropriation that Ernest had requested for the Rad Lab in 1946.

Where Oppenheimer fit into all these plans remained mysterious. The previous September, when Sproul had hosted a strategy session with Ernest and Birge on how to lure Oppie back to Berkeley, all three men agreed that the physicist was "disaffected."[80] Lawrence even candidly admitted that he was probably one of the reasons why Oppenheimer was playing the part of the reluctant bride.[81]

Ernest seconded Birge's suggestion that they begin by doubling Oppie's salary—rationalizing, unsentimentally, that "how much we pay Professor Oppenheimer really means nothing because the Government will place such large sums at our disposal if Oppenheimer is here, that his salary will be insignificant."[82] When Sproul hesitated, Ernest promised to go out and raise the money himself.[83] The university president finally agreed to make the offer to Oppenheimer in person, at the "E"-award ceremony scheduled for Los Alamos on October 16.

Sitting next to the grim-faced physicist on the bunting-covered dais, Sproul was surprised by Oppie's icy reserve. Oppenheimer had officially resigned as director just that morning; Bradbury had been acting head of the lab since the first of the month. Between the set speeches, Oppenheimer complained that a letter he had recently received from Birge was "cold," whereas telephone conversations with Lawrence had left the impression that Ernest did not want him back in the physics department.[84] Oppie said that he understood the president himself was reluctant to have him back on campus, "because of his difficult temperament and poor judgment"—a charge that Sproul vehemently denied.

Oppenheimer's mood was reflected as well in the remarks he made that morning, in an address that seemed more jeremiad-like than valedictory. Using language that would later come back to haunt him, Oppenheimer taunted: "If atomic bombs are to be added as new weapons to the arsenals of a warring world, or to the arsenals of nations preparing for war, then the time will come when mankind will curse the names of Los Alamos and Hiroshima."[85]

Almost as an afterthought, Oppenheimer told Sproul that he had already accepted an offer from Caltech. But Oppie nevertheless asked that his leave of absence from the university be extended for another year—thus keeping alive the hope that he might someday return to the campus.[86]

Back at Berkeley, stung by this rejection, Lawrence and Birge urged Sproul not to honor Oppenheimer's request; both men offered names for a replacement.[87] But Sproul, overruling them, decided to yield to Oppenheimer's wishes. With more good grace than he felt, Ernest telephoned Oppie with assurances that his office in LeConte was still waiting—"your old hat is on the rack, your desk hasn't been cleaned out."[88]

Another reason for Oppenheimer's bitterness was the news he had received in Washington, where the bomb was already caught in the grip of larger events. In the few months that he had been president, Truman had given little indication of what his postwar policy would be toward either nuclear weapons or the Soviet Union. But press accounts of his tense meeting with Stalin at Potsdam, and rumors of a looming showdown with the Russians over the Soviet occupation of Poland, made it plain that the wartime grand alliance was in tatters. Moreover, newspaper columnists and editorial writers across the country were quick to point out the obvious: America's atomic monopoly would soon be the only counterweight to the massive Red Army, given the country's rapid demobilization.

Despite Byrnes's early rebuff of his overture for international control, Oppie had returned to the capital in late September to proselytize on behalf of his newfound cause. In a series of whirlwind meetings with senior government officials—including Under Secretary of State Dean Acheson and Stimson's successor as secretary of war, Robert Patterson—Oppenheimer's efforts had met with decidedly mixed results.[89]

At the State Department, Oppenheimer told Acheson that the atomic scientists as a group opposed doing any more work on weapons—"not merely a super bomb but any bomb"—as being "against the dictates of their hearts and spirits."[90] Meeting with Truman a day or two later, Oppie badly misjudged his audience. The thin, haunted-looking physicist had shocked the plain-speaking president by declaiming, melodramatically, that he had "blood on his hands." Truman replied that any blood spilt was on *his* hands. In the awkward silence that followed, the president reassured Oppenheimer that, in any event, he would be raising the issue of postwar control with the British in just a few weeks.[91]

While still in Washington, Oppenheimer had also called the Scientific Panel together again to complete the report on future research that Stimson had requested.[92] More than 100 pages long, the study drew upon the work of dozens of scientists and covered topics ranging from biomedical research using radioactive isotopes to possible countermeasures against atomic bombs. A section some 5 pages in length, written mostly by Fermi, dealt with the Super.[93]

Oppenheimer delivered the highly classified report to the Interim Committee at the end of the month. In his executive summary, he chose to focus upon the hydrogen bomb. Noting that successful development of superbombs was not assured, he gauged the task of determining the Super's feasibility as comparable in difficulty to building the atomic bomb: "It is our recommendation that no such effort should be invested in this problem at the present time, but that the existence of the possibility should not be forgotten, and that interest in the fundamental questions should be maintained."[94]

This was a dramatic turnabout from the view that Oppenheimer had expressed to the Tolman Committee just a year earlier—when he had said that the Super should be "pursued with vigor and diligence, and promptly"—and was no doubt, in part, a reflection of the psychological impact of Hiroshima and Nagasaki.[95]

But, as Oppenheimer also realized, the Scientific Panel's report had already been overtaken by events in any case. By the time that the document was presented to the Interim Committee, the seventy-eight-year-old Stimson was already gone from the administration, having made a last—and unsuccessful—appeal of his own for international control as his final act in government. The committee's acting head, George Harrison, recommended that the panel's report be held "in escrow," until such time as Congress could take up the twin issues of domestic legislation and cooperative control.[96]

Oppenheimer and Compton—perhaps anticipating this possibility—had already secretly conspired to move discussion of the Super to a higher level.

On September 27, 1945, Compton sent Commerce Secretary Henry Wallace his own brief summary of the Scientific Panel's report. Acknowledging that there was a "reasonable chance" that a superbomb could be built, Compton wrote that he and his colleagues had nonetheless decided to recommend against proceeding with the weapon. Unlike the lukewarm position that the panel had taken on thermonuclear research in its formal report, Compton's letter to Wallace left no doubt where the panel stood on the Super: "We feel that this development should *not* be undertaken, primarily because we should prefer defeat in war to a victory obtained at the expense of the enormous human disaster that would be caused by its determined use."[97]

It was as though Compton and Oppenheimer had turned the clock back to their lakeside walk in Michigan three years earlier and, glimpsing the future more clearly this time, had chosen a different path.

As a courtesy, Compton sent copies of the letter to Groves, Harrison, and Bush, admonishing each to treat its contents—and especially the paragraph concerning the Super—as "highly secret."[98] Compton obviously hoped that enlisting Wallace's support might help to kill the superbomb, just as Wallace's endorsement had been crucial—in Compton's eyes, at least—to ultimate development of the atomic bomb.

But by the time that the letter reached him, Wallace was hardly in a position to advocate any such controversial stand with Truman. A week earlier, public outcry had followed press accounts of the cabinet meeting where Stimson urged a more cooperative "direct approach" to Russia. What Stimson had proposed was only a symbolic sharing of basic information about atomic energy, as a gesture of good faith. Opponents of the idea in the cabinet, not wanting to attack the venerable Stimson, had focused their scorn instead upon Wallace, who valiantly came to the idea's defense.[99]

Portrayed in newspapers as a scheme to "give the atomic secret to Russia," the so-called Wallace Plan was doomed from the outset.[100] The commerce secretary was forced to write a public apology to Truman, defending himself for even raising the idea.[101] Not surprisingly, Wallace made no mention of Compton's initiative in his letter to the president.[102]

Nor would the Scientific Panel's report, with its more qualified reservations about the Super, have an impact upon official Washington—where Truman, in early October, pointedly described the U.S. atomic monopoly as a "sacred trust." In November, Patterson ordered all copies of the report recalled, pending creation of a permanent commission on atomic energy to replace the Interim Committee. A few weeks later, the Interim Committee itself was dissolved; along with it, the Scientific Panel likewise disappeared.

The panel's lengthy report, as well as Compton's letter to Wallace, passed into dusty filing cabinets fitted with combination locks, and thence into oblivion.[103]

The harsh winter that followed the war froze water pipes at Los Alamos, persuading several more scientists and their families to leave the mesa and return to academe. Included in the general exodus were the Bethes, who went back to Cornell after Rose grew tired of using water trucked from a nearby creek to wash the family's laundry.[104]

The normally stoic Bradbury protested to Groves that it was becoming increasingly difficult to hold people at the lab without a commitment from the army that the work of Los Alamos would continue.[105] Not knowing how long his alliance with the University of California would last, however, Groves gave no assurances. In December, he told Bradbury he could guarantee salaries at the lab for only another six months.[106]

To be on the safe side, Teller had already sounded out his friend Robert Mulliken, chairman of Chicago's physics department, about the possibility of joining Fermi on the faculty there.[107] But Edward postponed making further plans until he knew whether Los Alamos would continue work on the Super.

While awaiting that word, Teller had begun teaching classes in elementary quantum mechanics at "Los Alamos University"—the impromptu classroom that wartime veterans had established to train new recruits and to keep their own minds sharp.[108] Perhaps because he regretted bending to Oppenheimer's will in the matter of Szilard's petition, Edward had also become a political activist of sorts—joining the Association of Los Alamos

Scientists (ALAS) and helping Robert Wilson, one of the group's founders, draft a statement calling for the international control of atomic energy.*[109]

At a subsequent meeting of ALAS, Teller led a discussion on the role of scientists in influencing public opinion. (He urged that they present the facts only, without interjecting their own political views.)[110] That fall, perhaps more out of boredom than conviction, Edward and metallurgist Cyril Smith lectured a rather bewildered assembly of Indians at Taos Pueblo on the prospects for the peaceful atom.[111]

Oppenheimer's speech at the "E"-award ceremony had finally removed any doubt about where he stood on the question of the lab's future. It would be many years before anyone could improve upon the job done at wartime Los Alamos, Oppie told Teller. When Edward asked that Oppenheimer intercede with Bradbury and urge that superbomb research continue, Oppie flatly refused.[112] Teller told friends, in hushed tones of horror, that Oppenheimer spoke of giving the mesa back to the Indians.

On a rainy night in early November 1945, more than 500 scientists and their spouses crowded into the auditorium at the lab to hear Oppenheimer speak about the implications of what they, collectively, had wrought. Even after he had stepped down as director, Oppie remained a dominant presence at Los Alamos. Speaking softly and earnestly for more than an hour, without notes, Oppenheimer argued that the threat of the bomb had created a common interest among humanity—one "which might almost be regarded as a pilot plant for a new type of international collaboration."[113]

The following morning, Oppie, Kitty, and Peter drove down off the mesa in the family Cadillac, bound for Pasadena.

In his inaugural speech as director, Bradbury talked guardedly of the future—defining the principal task of the postwar lab as that of improving the Fat Man bomb. On the topic of superweapons, Bradbury spoke only of possibilities: "This does not mean we will build a Super. It couldn't happen in our time in any event. But someday, someone must know the answer: Is it feasible?"[114]

Unwilling to remain at Los Alamos on the strength of such an equivocal promise, Teller gave the new director an ultimatum: he would stay at the lab only if Bradbury launched an intensive program to develop either

* Oppenheimer carried Wilson's petition to Washington, where it eventually made its way to Stimson and onto Truman's desk. Ironically, the Russians may have seen it first. In a rendezvous outside Santa Fe on September 19, 1945, Klaus Fuchs gave Harry Gold a copy. A summary, which arrived in Moscow on October 29, noted that the scientists' "feelings of distrust toward the government are very strong."

the Super or Teller's other wartime obsession, the hydride bomb.[115] As part of this crash effort, Teller also wanted Bradbury to commit to carrying out at least a dozen *Trinity*-type nuclear tests a year.

Bradbury had already offered to make Teller head of the Theoretical Division, replacing Bethe. But there was neither enthusiasm nor money in Washington for what Edward wanted, Norris patiently explained.[116] Late in October, Teller notified Bradbury that he planned to leave the lab at year's end. Norris obligingly agreed to transfer the contract for opacity research to Chicago, where Mayer had agreed to join Teller and Fermi.[117]

For Teller, the decision to leave Los Alamos was wrenching. "I have started to feel homesick for this place before I have even left it," he wrote to Mayer that fall.[118] But he also began taking steps to ensure that his work on the superbomb survived at the lab as a kind of legacy.

On October 5, 1945, Los Alamos published the "Super Handbook," a top-secret compendium of everything that was known to date about the H-bomb. Teller was its principal author. Three days later, Edward completed the "Super-Gadget Program," a summary report on the thermonuclear research that he had done in cooperation with Fermi and Konopinski. It recommended the production of superbombs in quantity once the feasibility of the weapon was determined.

Teller's work on the Super and related projects continued almost to the day of his departure. In mid-December, shortly after arranging the shipment to Chicago of his piano—a small concert grand with a cracked sounding board which Mici had dubbed "the Monster"—Edward filed a classified patent on the Booster, the fission bomb whose yield would be increased by burning tritium and deuterium at its core.[119]

Teller likewise did what he could before leaving to promote his ideas in the political world. That winter, he flew to Washington to testify before Congress on behalf of a bill that promised to free scientific research from military interference.[120] Tipped off by Fermi that the Scientific Panel had taken a dim view of superbombs in its report on postwar research, Teller prepared a lengthy rebuttal. Presented as the answers to a series of hypothetical questions, Teller's letter was, in essence, his case for the Super.[121]

Teller's letter argued that the first American superbomb could be ready in as little as two years if it were made the focus of a concerted, crash effort, though five years was "a conservative estimate."[122] Since the Super itself did not require any hard-to-obtain materials like enriched uranium or plutonium, Edward posited that a Soviet H-bomb might follow closely the Russians' first fission weapon. As to whether ethical qualms should figure in the decision whether to proceed with the Super, Teller dismissed the question as simply irrelevant: "If the development is possible, it is out of our powers to prevent it."

Exhorting that work on the H-bomb be transferred to "a capable and strong group of men," Teller sent the letter to Fermi on October 31, 1945. A few days later, as promised, Fermi forwarded the document to its real and intended audience, Secretary of War Patterson.

When Teller's move to Chicago was delayed for several more weeks that January, he used the postponement to teach a final class at the lab's impromptu university. In the days before the move, Teller's mood had shifted, and he had even begun looking forward to leaving Los Alamos. Bradbury's decision not to pursue the Super had removed a great burden from him, Edward confided to Maria Mayer. A friend at the lab accused Teller of "behaving like a pious man should when his mother-in-law dies."[123]

On February 1, 1946, Edward, Mici, and Paul drove down from the mesa and headed east.

Those who stayed at Los Alamos regarded the news coming out of Washington about the bomb with emotions that ranged from bemused detachment to speechless outrage.[124]

A much-quoted after-dinner address that Groves gave in September to a group of International Business Machine executives at the Waldorf-Astoria sparked a firestorm at the lab.[125] Groves had spoken of keeping the bomb "under the control of the United States until all of the other nations of the world are as anxious for peace as we are. . . . I mean they must be anxious for peace in their hearts, and not merely by speech or by signature to a treaty they do not intend to honor."[126]

"Did it really add anything to the expression of your opinion to say, 'and the more they talk the shorter the time seems to get'?" John Manley wrote to Groves in exasperation.[127] Groves apologized to Bradbury for the controversy that the speech provoked—but not for its message.[128]

More controversial still was Groves's attempt to railroad through Congress legislation that originated in the War Department, and that would have given the military a dominant voice in the domestic control of the atom. The May-Johnson bill proposed to create a part-time, nine-member commission responsible for the military as well as the civilian applications of atomic energy. Because the commission's four uniformed members would have had veto power over the majority's decisions, however, the bill was derided by civilian-control advocates, including the newly formed Federation of Atomic Scientists.[129]

Surprisingly, Groves's ally in this uphill battle was Robert Oppenheimer. Whether out of conviction, innate pessimism, or residual feelings of gratitude, Oppie joined Groves in championing the "War Department bill," despite opposition from baffled colleagues.[130]

Addressing a meeting of ALAS that fall, Oppenheimer had counseled the lab's scientists against taking precipitous action to get their views before Washington.[131] Yet Oppie's visit to Truman had already shown that he believed in speaking the truth to power—starting at the top. Indeed, the question of how best to influence nuclear policy had been the subject of long and frequent arguments between Oppie and his brother, who favored public education over direct government action. (Robert felt "the path of public education was too slow," Frank later recalled.)[132]

At Groves's request, Oppie even rounded up the signatures of two of his three Scientific Panel colleagues in a telegram of support for May-Johnson.[133] Only Compton, wary, had declined.

But when Lawrence and Fermi joined Oppenheimer in a press conference at the Pentagon, it became embarrassingly evident just how little they knew of the legislation they had endorsed. As Ernest was sheepishly forced to admit to reporters, he had never actually read the May-Johnson bill—and was unaware, for example, that it mandated ten years of prison and a $10,000 fine for the kind of inadvertent security slips that he had repeatedly committed during the war.[134]

Lawrence promptly withdrew his support from May-Johnson. Asked by Wilson and Higinbotham to testify before Congress on behalf of a rival bill, which guaranteed control over the atom to civilians, Lawrence sought the counsel of Neylan.[135]

Acting as the trial attorney he had once been, Neylan asked Lawrence to sit for a mock cross-examination. Within minutes, the lawyer had Ernest sputtering, caught up in contradictory statements about simple matters of fact. Lawrence turned down Wilson and Higinbotham's request.[136] Henceforth, Ernest vowed, he would only wield his influence as Neylan directed—in secret and behind the scenes.

PART THREE

SCIENTISTS IN GRAY FLANNEL SUITS

E. O. Lawrence, Louis Alvarez, Edward Teller—Madison Avenue–type scientists. Scientists in gray flannel suits.

—David Lilienthal,
journal, March 1958

9

A WORLD IN WHICH WAR WILL NOT OCCUR

As the momentum behind the May-Johnson bill slowed to a crawl in the Senate, an ambitious freshman Democrat from Connecticut—Brien McMahon—rose to take advantage of the stalemate. Forty-two-years-old, dapper, and florid-faced, with a trademark diamond stickpin in his lapel, McMahon had a reputation as a crusading prosecutor. While an assistant attorney general, he had brought the Harlan Country Coal Operators to justice.[1] McMahon had been in Congress barely a year.

After creating a special committee on atomic energy in December 1945, and making himself chairman, McMahon introduced legislation that called for a full-time, wholly civilian Atomic Energy Commission. Learning from Groves's debacle, McMahon wisely enlisted the support of atomic scientists and key Republicans beforehand.[2]

But the progress of the McMahon bill through Congress abruptly stalled in mid-February 1946, with disclosure of an espionage ring operating out of the Soviet embassy in Ottawa, Canada. Twenty-two suspected spies were arrested. In testimony before McMahon's Senate committee, Groves used the spy scandal to cast doubt upon the wisdom of giving sole control over atomic energy to civilians.[*3]

* Part of the fallout of the so-called Gouzenko spy case was that Moscow Center ordered its agents to temporarily suspend contact with their sources in the West. The subsequent defection of another spy, Elizabeth Bentley, virtually put an end to the existing network of Soviet agents in the United States.

Two weeks later, when a British veteran of the Manhattan Project who had worked in Canada, physicist Alan Nunn May, confessed to giving samples of enriched uranium to the Russians, the entire community of atomic scientists suddenly came under suspicion.[4]

Not surprisingly, those who had been the subject of previous security investigations became the focus of renewed attention. On May 8, 1946, the wiretap on Robert Oppenheimer's home in Berkeley—deactivated shortly after the war by the army—was reinstalled by the FBI, upon the order of bureau director Hoover.[5] FBI agents once again dogged Oppenheimer's steps on visits to Washington and Los Alamos.[6]

The bureau's wiretapping of Oppenheimer had been approved by Tom Clark, Truman's attorney general, after Hoover presented Clark with what appeared to be incriminating evidence of Oppie's continued association with Communists.

Returning to the Bay Area after the war, Oppie and his family had spent several weeks at his brother's house in nearby Albany, where the FBI had also installed a bug. During a New Year's Day party at Frank's, the bureau's bug picked up a conversation between Oppie and FAECT organizers Paul Pinsky and David Adelson. Afterward, a joking comment by Pinsky to Adelson about Oppenheimer—"shall we claim him as a member?"—was interpreted by bureau agents as confirmation that Oppie was still affiliated with the Communist Party.[7]

As the FBI was also aware, Oppenheimer had remained in touch with other known and suspected Communists since his return from Los Alamos. That spring, Oppie spent a weekend with Haakon Chevalier at the latter's Stinson Beach house. Chevalier was now working full-time on his novel, *For Us the Living,* having been denied tenure by Berkeley the previous fall.[8]

Hoover had once again taken a personal interest in the Oppenheimer investigation—and was becoming increasingly frustrated at Groves's lack of cooperation in the case.[9] Asked to provide details about Oppenheimer's wartime association with Eltenton, Groves flatly refused, claiming that Oppie had given him the information in "the strictest of confidence."[10] The head of the Manhattan Project was similarly closed-mouthed about the results of his December 1943 meeting with Oppenheimer, which the bureau already knew about from Lansdale, however.[11]

That summer, Hoover pressed Groves once more for the truth about the Chevalier incident, but the general again refused to talk. Even after the FBI director put his request in writing, Groves declined to cooperate—defending his unwillingness to provide "details concerning the information reported to me by Oppenheimer" on the grounds that it "would endanger our relationship which must, in the best interest of the United States, be continued in its present state."[12]

"Bearing in mind General Groves' thoroughly uncooperative attitude in this situation," the FBI's Lish Whitson urged his boss to interview Oppenheimer anyway, despite Groves's objections.[13] Hoover, whose memory in such matters was long, neither forgot not forgave Groves's obstinacy.

His patience finally at an end, the FBI director ordered both Chevalier and Eltenton interviewed. On June 26, 1946, a pair of agents picked up Chevalier at his beach house and drove him to bureau headquarters in San Francisco. That same afternoon, agents Branigan and Cassidy went to Eltenton's office at Shell Development, later taking him to a room in the Post Office building in Oakland. During both interrogations, behind the scenes, the agents stayed in touch by telephone, the better to exploit contradictions in the stories of the two men.

Chevalier told the FBI that he had approached only one individual—Robert Oppenheimer—at Eltenton's instigation, and that he had been immediately rebuffed. When one of the agents bragged that he possessed signed affidavits from three scientists whom Chevalier had contacted to spy for the Russians, Haakon asked for the scientists' names. The FBI man remained silent.[14]

Eltenton's account essentially corroborated Chevalier's version. "It is my impression that Haakon Chevalier did not contact any other persons connected with the Radiation Laboratory other than Dr. J. R. Oppenheimer," Eltenton wrote in an unsigned statement.[15] But Eltenton also provided additional details—the use of microfilm, the involvement of the Soviets' San Francisco consulate—leaving the impression that the approach had been part of an elaborate espionage plot, and not the innocent inquiry that Chevalier described.

A few days afterward, on the occasion of a cocktail party at Eagle Hill, Chevalier informed Oppenheimer of the FBI's visit. He later recalled how Oppie's face darkened when he was told how the agents had asked repeatedly about three unnamed scientists. Chevalier said he had been puzzled by the G-men's questions, but Oppenheimer made no reply. Instead, leading Chevalier to a wooded spot at the back of the yard, far away from the house and any hidden microphones, Oppenheimer quizzed him at length. Chevalier remembered his friend seemed "extremely nervous and tense." Oppie rudely snapped at Kitty when she interrupted to remind him that other guests were arriving.[16]

Almost three months would pass before Branigan and Cassidy talked to Oppenheimer, who now freely admitted that the original story he had told Pash in 1943 was a "fabrication."[17] Oppie said that he had been the only person approached by Chevalier and that he had quickly dismissed the idea as "treason" or "close to treason."[18] Nothing more had come of it, he claimed.

But Oppie declared that he "would be reluctant to appear as a witness in any hearing involving Chevalier," and also that he "ha[d] never personally disclosed to Chevalier that he had mentioned his name in connection with the incident under investigation." In their report, Branigan and Cassidy noted that they had to ask the same questions several times during the interview, since Oppenheimer's answers were "indirect or oblique." Neither Oppenheimer—nor Chevalier—had made any mention of Frank.

Evidently forgetting what he had said to Lansdale back in 1943, Oppenheimer expressed surprise upon being told by the agents that Joseph Weinberg was a Communist. Oppie also said that he had never been asked for information about the bomb project by Steve Nelson—a claim that Nelson's recorded conversation with "Joe" flatly contradicted.[19]

Across the Bay, Weinberg, too, was getting the third degree that afternoon. He denied meeting with Steve Nelson at the latter's home or even knowing Nelson.[20]

In the early fall, Hoover sent copies of the interviews to the Justice Department. The FBI director obviously hoped and expected that the attorney general would issue indictments under the espionage statues of all those involved in the Chevalier incident, which was mentioned for the first time in Hoover's report.[21] Instead, a few weeks later, Clark informed Hoover "that after consideration of all the facts presently available, it has been decided that no prosecution will be authorized."[22]

For a few brief weeks early in 1946, Oppenheimer's pessimism had lifted when he believed that the bomb might actually be removed as a threat to humanity's future.

In January, Under Secretary of State Dean Acheson was appointed head of a special committee to study the prospects for the international control of atomic energy.[23] Although Truman had committed the nation, at least temporarily, to maintaining its atomic monopoly, the president also promised to strive for the bomb's cooperative control.[24]

Joining Acheson and the inevitable Bush, Conant, and Groves on the committee was a former Stimson aide and investment banker, John McCloy. Acheson himself chose the five members of a so-called Board of Consultants, which would offer technical advice and draft the actual plan for international control. He made an experienced administrator—former TVA director David Lilienthal—the group's chairman and appointed Robert

Oppenheimer its chief scientist. The other members of the board were all from industry: Monsanto vice president Charles Thomas, who had stood alongside Lawrence on Compania Hill; Chester Barnard, president of New Jersey Bell; and Harry Winne, a vice president at General Electric.

Acheson's first impression of Oppenheimer was that of a smart but hopeless idealist. Following drinks with the physicist at the Shoreham hotel, Lilienthal wrote of Oppie in his journal: "I left liking him, greatly impressed with his flash of mind, but rather disturbed by the flow of words."[25]

Acheson's committee and its technical experts met for the first time in late January at the American Trucking Associations' building in Washington, former OSRD headquarters. Standing once again at a blackboard with chalk in hand, Oppenheimer gave the Board of Consultants a two-day tutorial on atomic theory and nuclear physics. So absorbed was the group that, as night fell, they sent out for sandwiches and shooed away a persistent cleaning lady. (Lilienthal thought it "a soul-stirring experience" to have "the terrible facts of nature's ultimate forces cooly laid before [one] as on an operating table, almost feeling them warm and stirring under one's probing fingers.")[26]

A familiarization tour of Manhattan Project facilities followed—including the gaseous diffusion plant at Oak Ridge and the nuclear weapons vault outside Albuquerque—to introduce the previously uninitiated to the bomb.[27]

Oppenheimer also used the primer to expound on his own ideas about international control. The scheme that he described over the next several weeks was, in fact, the so-called pilot plant for international collaboration that he had spoken of in his speech to ALAS the previous November. The ultimate aim, he had told the scientists then, should be "a world that is united, and a world in which war will not occur."

Oppenheimer had a draft plan prepared by early February, circulating it for discussion by the board.[28] Originally, Lilienthal had thought to offer Acheson's committee a series of possible alternatives, with varying degrees of government interference. Oppie, however, persuaded the group to submit just a single option, the one he had outlined. Once again, force of personality and sheer power of intellect had made Oppenheimer the dominant figure in a group.

The central feature of Oppenheimer's plan was a provision that vested control over all aspects of atomic energy—isotopes, civilian reactors, and bombs—in an international Atomic Development Authority. From the mining of atomic raw materials to the final disposal of the radioactive waste products, the ADA would have suzerainty over the so-called harmless as well as the dangerous aspects of the atom. As such, it came perilously close to being—as Oppenheimer fully realized—a kind of world government.

Another key part of Oppenheimer's plan was the idea of "denaturing": deliberately adding contaminants to weapons-grade uranium and plutonium in order to render them useless for making bombs. Fissionable materials that had been denatured by the ADA, the plan argued, could be returned to national hands and used in peaceful applications, such as power reactors.[29]

The problem with denaturing was that fissionable materials could be all too easily "renatured."[30] Outside scientists on whom Oppie tried the idea out were openly skeptical. (Rabi later remembered a Christmas Day conversation at his apartment, where the two men stood at the window, looking out at the Hudson River. "We were watching the ice drift down the river in the sunset, turning pink. Oppie ruined the mood by bringing up the idea of poisoning uranium.")[31] Fermi was even more blunt than Rabi—telling Oppenheimer that his idea was a "distortion."[32]

"Oppie wanted it to work," explained Rabi.[33]

On March 7, 1946, Acheson's committee and the Board of Consultants assembled at Georgetown's Dumbarton Oaks to vote on Oppie's plan. In a room dominated by an El Greco painting, medieval tapestries, and an alabaster cat from Byzantium, the plan received almost unanimous support.[34] The single prominent naysayer was Groves. (The general had protested against appointing a Board of Consultants in the first place—on the grounds that he, Bush, and Conant already knew more about atomic energy "than any panel that could be assembled.")[35] Groves objected that denaturing would not work and that the ADA would be unable to enforce an effective monopoly of the world's atomic raw materials.[36]

In meetings that lasted till midmonth, other critics surfaced. Bush and Conant complained that implementation of the plan lacked specific stages. Oppenheimer revised the report to include them—the first stage being a comprehensive, worldwide survey of raw materials. A suggestion from McCloy that the survey also be used to spy on the Soviets was politely rebuffed by the board.[37]

Mindful of the danger that their grand vision might be nibbled to death by endless revision, Lilienthal and Acheson gave the committee an ultimatum on March 17: accept the plan as revised, or they would forward it to the secretary of state without a recommendation. To Lilienthal's surprise, the committee unanimously approved the report and sent it on to Byrnes that same day.[38]

The response of atomic scientists to the so-called Acheson-Lilienthal report bordered on ecstatic. Returning to California for a brief vacation, Oppie boasted to Frank that the report was the best thing the U.S. government had ever done.[39] Writing in the *Bulletin of the Atomic Scientists,* Edward Teller hailed it as "the first ray of hope that the problem of international control can, actually, be solved."*[40] The Federation of Atomic Scientists—no longer battling the army over civilian control—suddenly had a new cause to champion. "We clasped the new Bible in our hands and went out to ring doorbells," FAS president Willie Higinbotham later recalled.[41]

In fact, the fate of Oppenheimer's plan was already sealed. The day before Byrnes received the report, he and Truman had picked Bernard Baruch, a seventy-five-year-old financier and self-described presidential adviser, to present the plan to the Russians at the United Nations.

Truman as well as Byrnes soon came to regret their choice. ("[Baruch] wants to run the world, the moon and maybe Jupiter—but we'll see," the president wrote in his journal that night.)[42] To the Board of Consultants, the mistake was clear. "When I read this news last night, I was quite sick," Lilienthal confided to his diary.[43] "We're lost," Oppie had told Higinbotham the day that Baruch was appointed.[44]

Oppenheimer's worst fears were realized when Baruch appointed a coterie of conservative businessmen and longtime cronies to help him "fine-tune" the Acheson-Lilienthal report. "It is the old crowd," Lilienthal lamented. "Wall-Streeters," sniffed Bush.

Barely a week after taking the job, the temperamental Baruch was already threatening to resign, after a description of the Acheson-Lilienthal report appeared in the press.[45]

Over the next fortnight, Baruch and his associates transformed Oppenheimer's vision into something that the Board of Consultants had resolutely rejected from the outset: an updated version of the age-old call for the outlawry of war. Behind the public relations facade of the Baruch plan, moreover, were signs of a more sinister agenda. "They talk about preparing the American people for a refusal by Russia," wrote Lilienthal.[46]

Oppenheimer and the Board of Consultants had deliberately avoided specifying the type of sanctions that violators would encounter—believing it a matter best left up to the United Nations and the ADA. Baruch and his cronies, on the other hand, spoke vaguely but ominously of "condign punishment" for transgressors.[47] (Asked their opinion of the plan, the Joint Chiefs of Staff politely observed that the bases where Baruch was proposing to stockpile atomic bombs to use against would-be aggressors were "all too obviously pointed at the U.S.S.R.")[48]

* In 1950, a congressional aide spoke with Teller about international control of the bomb and summarized Edward's views in a memo: "[Teller] thinks it is foolish to hope for international control while Russia remains under present regime. On the other hand, he does concede that it is important we make all the right moves in the search for international agreement so that we do not lose out to the Russians in the battle for world opinion."

Baruch's principal ally in rewriting Oppenheimer's plan was Groves, whom the septuagenarian had appointed his "interpreter of military policy."[49] Believing that he was wanted merely for window dressing, Oppenheimer twice turned down Baruch's offer to make him the delegation's science adviser. Bush and Lawrence likewise refused. Finally, at Groves's urging, Robert Bacher agreed to become a part-time consultant, and Caltech physicist Richard Tolman joined Baruch and his team in New York—against Oppie's advice.[50]

In talks that he gave on college campuses, Oppenheimer was careful to temper his public criticism of the Baruch plan.[51] But any doubt about Oppie's personal views ended in late May, when Hoover sent to Baruch and to Byrnes—"as of possible interest"—the transcript of a recent telephone conversation between Oppenheimer and an unidentified physicist.[52] The wiretap was revealing not only of Oppie's attitude toward Baruch but of the lengths to which the physicist was prepared to go to counter the new plan.

> I just want to watch this side of it and see if anything can be done. I think that if the price of it is that I have to live with the old man and his people, it may be too high. . . . I don't want anything from them and if I can work on his conscience, that is the best angle I have. . . . It is very hard for me to tell if there is harm, little good, or some good, in my getting in touch with those European scientists.

A few days later, Hoover passed to Baruch the transcript of another wiretapped call, in which Oppie spoke of mobilizing public opinion against the plan, in "an attempt to box the old guy in."[53]

On June 14, 1946, Oppenheimer, Bacher, and Arthur Compton sat silent and glum in the gymnasium of Hunter College, temporary headquarters of the United Nations, in the Bronx, New York, as the Baruch plan was introduced to the world.[54] "We are here to make a choice between the quick and the dead," Baruch began, in a melodramatic flourish suggested by one of his aides, a public relations consultant. The Soviets rejected the plan without qualification or ceremony five days later.

Back in Washington by late July, Lilienthal and Oppenheimer stayed up until the early hours talking in Oppie's hotel room about the opportunity that had been missed. Lilienthal thought the physicist transformed from the self-confident, even ebullient figure of the previous spring.

> He is really a tragic figure; with all his great attractiveness, brilliance of mind. As I left him he looked so sad: "I am ready to go anywhere and do anything, but I am bankrupt of further ideas.

> And I find that physics and the teaching of physics, which is my life, now seems irrelevant." It was this last that really wrung my heart.[55]

Lawrence was conspicuously absent from the ranks of atomic scientists who had trooped up Capitol Hill the previous fall to lobby for international control. Since the chastening experience of Neylan's mock cross-examination, Ernest had refused all appeals for public appearances and political endorsements.[56] "In fact, my own feeling is that this political activity of many of our atomic scientists is unfortunate in many ways," he told a reporter.[57]

The fame that had come to Oppenheimer for his work on the atomic bomb translated for Lawrence into financial opportunity, as well as closer association with those whom Ernest most envied and admired.

By mid-1946, Lawrence was a paid consultant to several corporations, including General Electric, Eastman Kodak, and American Cyanamid—which, in addition to a monthly retainer, provided an annual $10,000 supplement to Loomis's research fund.[58] One unadvertised perquisite of serving on the Board of Directors of the Yosemite Camp and Curry Company was the opportunity to obtain a new Cadillac at cost. Ernest could now afford to replace his favorite baby blue convertible almost annually, selling the car back to the dealer for what he had paid the year before.[59]

With his consultancy fees and the money he received in fall 1945 for the Wheeler award—given annually to "Berkeley's most useful citizen"—Ernest and Molly bought a small beach house on Balboa Island, near Los Angeles, as a summer retreat. Lawrence also purchased a bigger boat, a 30-foot cabin cruiser, to replace the vessel built by Alvarez's uncle.

That summer, Neylan arranged a personal visit to San Simeon, the castlelike villa that William Randolph Hearst built between San Francisco and Los Angeles on the California coast. The experience of meeting Hearst "turned out to be even more fabulous than expected," Ernest gushed in a thank-you note.[60]

Among those used to the penurious academic life, Lawrence's social climbing inspired no small amount of envy. William Knowland, editor of the *Oakland Tribune,* was among the prominent Californians attending a reception and dinner that Neylan hosted for Ernest at the exclusive Pacific Union Club. Following a long weekend spent with the Lawrences at Del Monte Lodge, Neylan and Loomis arranged for a mutual friend and fellow Bohemian Grove campmate—San Francisco attorney Rowan Gaither—to become Ernest's investment counselor.[61]

After Neylan and the regents approved purchase of the Wilson Tract, the land above the giant cyclotron that Lawrence had tried but failed to acquire during the war, Ernest's empire also had more room to grow.

By spring 1946, Lawrence's earlier $1-million-a-year budget for the Rad Lab had doubled and now included funds for, among other things, a new radiochemistry lab on campus for Seaborg and a medical physics clinic for John and his physician colleagues at University Hospital.[62]

Even so, the future was not entirely unclouded, for either Lawrence or his laboratory. Early in the year, a Pentagon advisory committee had recommended that university laboratories focus on unclassified research and fundamental science, leaving secret military research to government-run national labs.[63] Although the report considered Lawrence's Berkeley an exception—"a special type of national laboratory"—it left the future of army funding for the Rad Lab in some doubt.[64] One longtime rationale for the accelerators at Berkeley—the production of radioisotopes for medical research—had already been reassigned to DuPont's reactors after the war. Most of the $75 million that Groves had approved for annual postwar "nucleonics" research was earmarked for two new federal laboratories, potential rivals to Berkeley: one at Argonne, outside Chicago, and the other at a site in the Northeast yet to be determined.[65]

That April, the army promised Lawrence the full $2 million he requested. But Groves—fearful of plutonium spills in populated Berkeley—balked at Seaborg's "hot lab" and at John's medical physics program, which the army saw as having only a tenuous connection to defense. Groves was also still dragging his feet on Alvarez's Linac, pending a fuller accounting of costs. Yet Lawrence was confident that these funds, too, would ultimately be approved. As Cooksey reassured Loomis at the end of the month, "we can see nothing to hold us back."[66]

Indeed, the only real obstacle was the university. As Lawrence was keenly aware, future army funding was contingent upon the relationship between the university and the government continuing. Sproul, however, remained eager to relieve himself of the wartime burden. Nichols had warned Groves that the intercession of Secretary of War Patterson might be needed to persuade the university president to renew the two army contracts.[67]

Underhill, anxious to avoid another fait accompli like Groves's choice of Bradbury, had begun insisting upon personally approving all personnel appointments at Los Alamos.[68] With the June 30, 1946, termination date looming, Underhill urged Sproul to call Lawrence, Groves, and others together for a "roundup and showdown on the New Mexico project."[69]

Instead, the deadline passed uneventfully. Groves once again persuaded the university to extend the contract on a temporary basis.[70] Meeting with the finance committee that fall, Sproul observed in frustration: "If we get rid of bomb making, plutonium, and New Mexico, I would be very happy."[71]

The logjam over the McMahon bill had finally broken that summer, following an amendment that created the Military Liaison Committee to serve as Pentagon watchdog over the civilian Atomic Energy Commission. The MLC disarmed those critics who objected to the exclusion of a military voice in matters pertaining to the bomb.[72]

As well, McMahon's Senate committee had meanwhile expanded to include nine members from the House.[73] Like the Military Liaison Committee, the Joint Committee on Atomic Energy constituted another set of eyes—and interests—to keep watch over the civilian commission. In late July, the day before signing the McMahon bill into law, Truman picked the first of five commissioners for the AEC.

Lewis Strauss, fifty, was a self-made millionaire—a former shoe salesman turned investment banker. Strauss had also been a personal aide to President Herbert Hoover. Commissioned a rear admiral in the Bureau of Ordnance during the Second World War, he worked on procurement and served as an assistant to the navy secretary.[74]

Early on, Strauss had a special stake in atomic energy. The loss of both parents to cancer awakened an early interest on his part in the therapeutic uses of radiation.

Truman's interest in Strauss—a Jew and a lifelong Republican—stemmed from the president's need to appear nonpartisan as well as ecumenical in his appointments to the commission. Overlooked in the choice was Strauss's personality, which combined extraordinary vanity and stubbornness with a vindictive streak.[75] (Oppie, not yet aware of the latter trait, observed of Strauss in a wiretapped conversation with another physicist: "He is not greatly cultivated but will not obstruct things." It was a rare and fateful misjudgment on Oppenheimer's part.)[76]

The lone scientist to be picked to serve on the commission was Los Alamos veteran Robert Bacher.[77] Truman chose David Lilienthal to chair the AEC after James Conant and Karl Compton each turned down the post. (Lilienthal confided to his journal that he feared only "frustrations, neurotic scientists, and insensitive Trumanites.")[78]

The acolytes had a quick familiarization tour. In November, the group visited Manhattan Project sites in a commandeered army C-47 which Lilienthal dubbed "the Flying Neutron," accompanied by an armed guard and a coffin-sized box of top-secret documents.[79] After Los Alamos, where Teller was predictably sanguine about prospects for the Super, Lilienthal saw—for a second time—the room-sized vault where the nation's atomic arsenal was stored. In Berkeley two days later, following drinks and dinner at Trader Vic's, Lawrence enthused about the commercial possibilities of civilian atomic power reactors.

The only sour note on this grand tour was sounded by Groves, whom Patterson would soon appoint to the Military Liaison Committee. (He felt like a mother hen seeing strangers take her chicks away, Groves remarked plaintively to the entourage.)[80] The general made it plain that he considered himself, not Lilienthal, the one best suited to watch over the nation's interests with regard to nuclear energy.

Rather than surrender the Manhattan Project's laboriously compiled personnel security records to the AEC and Lilienthal, Groves that summer had given some of the files to Hoover and the FBI.[81] But the so-called investigation files that Groves had kept in his own personal safe during the war—on the Oppenheimer brothers, Weinberg, Nelson, and others—he took with him to the Armed Forces Special Weapons Project, where he became the director in early 1947. ("General Groves' instructions were that these files were to be wrapped and sealed, and that no person other than himself was to open them," wrote his secretary in a note appended to the files after the war.)[82]

Under the provisions of the McMahon Act, responsibility for atomic energy passed to the civilian AEC at midnight on December 31, 1946. In March 1947, Lilienthal and the commission moved into their new headquarters, the art-deco Public Health Building across Constitution Avenue from the Reflecting Pool.

One unintended consequence of the McMahon Act had been to return Robert Oppenheimer to a position of influence in Washington. The legislation that created the AEC had also established the General Advisory Committee, appointed by the president, to assist the commissioners on technical and scientific matters. There was never any question but that Oppie would be a member of what the press called the AEC's "atomic brain trust." Conant, Fermi, Rabi, and Seaborg also served on the GAC. By the time that Oppenheimer, delayed by a snowstorm, arrived in Washington on January 8, 1947, a day late to the committee's inaugural meeting, he had already been unanimously elected chairman.[83]

The GAC was almost immediately embroiled in controversy. Shortly after assuming office, Lilienthal and the other commissioners had been amazed to discover that America's vaunted atomic arsenal consisted of only a few weapons.[84] Not one of the plutonium pits or uranium cores in the vault at Kirtland Air Force Base was currently usable as a bomb, Bacher reported; it might take as long as two weeks to assemble a single weapon.[85]

Given such a dire situation, the army was exasperated at the lack of enthusiasm shown by the GAC for radiological warfare, a concept once again in vogue with that service, which was promoting "rad war" as a more humane alternative to Hiroshima-sized nuclear weapons.[86] The navy, for its part, objected to recently published remarks by Oppenheimer concerning the obsolescence of its big ships—an issue that had come to the fore during Operation *Crossroads,* the atomic tests at Bikini atoll in summer 1946.[87] (Oppenheimer had expressed "misgivings" about the navy-sponsored tests in a personal letter to Truman, requesting that he be dropped from a panel of scientists asked to analyze the results.)[88] Oppie and Conant would even offend the newest service—the U.S. Air Force—by deprecating the technical feasibility and military worth of a favorite blue-suit project: the nuclear-powered bomber.[89]

But easily the most controversial advice to come from Oppenheimer and his colleagues concerned the Super.

At their second meeting, in February, members of the GAC discussed progress toward the superbomb. They urged the AEC to "assign a higher urgency to this work," in part "as a stimulation to improvement" of atomic bombs by Los Alamos.[90] At that same meeting, however, committee members recommended that reactors rather than superbombs be given priority at the lab. Since "rapid progress was not anticipated" on the Super, wrote Oppenheimer that April, he and his colleagues recommended that Los Alamos simply make regular progress reports on the most promising designs.

Such halfhearted affirmation evoked scorn on the part of Edward Teller. In April 1946, Teller had presided over a classified three-day "Conference on the Super" at Los Alamos. Oppenheimer and Bethe had passed up Teller's invitation in order to attend the annual meeting of the National Academy of Sciences.[91] But among the nearly three dozen scientists in the audience at the lab was Klaus Fuchs.

On the conference's opening day, Fuchs and John von Neumann told Teller and Serber about a new idea they had for using an exploding atomic bomb to compress and ignite the Super's thermonuclear fuel by implosion. A few weeks later, shortly before Fuchs returned to England, he and von Neumann jointly filed a classified patent on their invention.*[92]

In preparation for the conference, Teller and a half dozen of his lab

* Sometime in 1946, Fuchs passed along to the Soviets nine typed pages of notes on a series of lectures that Fermi had given at Los Alamos University on the Super. The notes included detailed calculations on the amount of energy that would be released by the burning of a specific quantity of tritium and deuterium, as initiated by an exploding fission bomb. The problem that had stymied Teller at the Berkeley seminar—the loss of energy through radiation—was noted, along with the importance of shielding the thermonuclear fuel from the intense radiation created by the atomic trigger. "So far all schemes for initiation of the super are rather vague," the notes concluded. But a simple sketch at the bottom of the last page showed one possible solution.

colleagues had written a report—LA-551, "*Prima Facie* Proof of the Feasibility of the Super." Prefaced by sixty pages of classified calculations and drawings, LA-551 concluded that a superbomb fueled by deuterium was indeed feasible. But the report's recommendation—that "a large-scale theoretical and experimental program" be undertaken immediately to develop the weapon—amounted to Teller's special pleading. Edward also urged, as the next logical step, a prompt start on making the tritium necessary for mass production of the Super.

The focus of the Los Alamos conference was upon one specific design, the so-called runaway Super that Teller had first proposed at the 1942 Berkeley summer seminar. His bomb consisted of a cubic meter of uncompressed liquid deuterium at the end of a cylinder attached to one or more high-yield, gun-type fission bombs. The design relied upon the energy from the detonation wave of the atomic explosion to trigger the thermonuclear reaction. A small amount of tritium gas was injected halfway down the tube, between the deuterium and atomic bombs, to start the deuterium burning. Theoretically, there was almost no limit to the power of the device; increasing the yield was simply a matter of adding more deuterium.

The question that dominated the second and third days of the conference—whether the thermonuclear flame would spread or simply go out—was the same problem that had bedeviled the summer meeting at Berkeley. The physics conundrum, which had almost caused the Super to be abandoned at wartime Los Alamos, returned to haunt Teller anew at the 1946 conference: as the energy from the exploding atomic bomb heated the mass of hydrogen fuel, energy was lost through radiation.[93]

Various schemes and fixes were proposed to get around this obstacle. But like a dog chasing its tale, the discussion went round and round; no solution was in sight.[94]

Serber claimed that Teller ultimately "solved" the problem by ignoring it. (Serber was at the meeting under protest; his Urbana colleague, physicist Phillip Morrison, had persuaded him to come, having predicted—correctly—that Teller would use the conference as a springboard to lobby for the Super.)[95] Calculations done by von Neumann's ENIAC computer at Princeton had deliberately left out the radiative cooling effect, since the complex hydrodynamics of thermonuclear burning were beyond the capabilities of the machine. Similarly, optimistic estimates were substituted for hard numbers in the critical opacity calculations, which remained unfinished by Mayer at Chicago.[96]

Teller summarized the results of the conference in a draft report, written that May. It conceded that definitive proof of the Super's feasibility required the actual test of a finished device. He also acknowledged that a crash effort to develop the superbomb would necessarily draw away "a considerable fraction" of the resources needed to build a stockpile of atomic bombs in the coming years. Tritium, for example, could only be produced by Hanford's reactors, which were already engaged full-time in making plutonium for the nuclear arsenal. Accordingly, a decision on whether to proceed with the Super had to be "part of the highest national policy," Edward argued.

Shown the draft report by Teller, Serber thought it "incredibly optimistic," protesting that the runaway Super was not a workable scheme, nor was a solution evident—much less "simple," as Teller argued. Serber sat down with Teller later that month to write a revised version that was more realistic.[97]

Back in Chicago, Edward completed the final "Report of Conference on the Super," LA-575, and sent it to Los Alamos. Two days later, on June 14, 1946, Fuchs left the New Mexico lab to return to England.[98] Checking Teller's report out of the Rad Lab library in Berkeley, Serber was upset to discover it essentially unchanged from the original version.[99]

Teller was back at Los Alamos a few weeks later with his family, following the end of classes at Chicago. Boasting that he had arrived at the lab "in the proper (or rather not proper but usual) crusader spirit," Teller posed a rhetorical question to confidante Mayer: "Do you think there is any chance that I shall be somewhat less foolish than I have been?"[100]

In August, 1946, Teller proposed a new design for a hydrogen bomb, which he christened the "Alarm Clock" to distinguish it from the Super.[101] (*His* Alarm Clock, Teller boasted, would wake up the world.) This device would use an atomic trigger to ignite alternating layers of enriched uranium and a mixture of deuterium and tritium arranged in concentric shells. Although more powerful than a conventional fission bomb, the Alarm Clock, unlike the runaway Super, could not be of unlimited yield. But Teller and the new leader of the lab's Theoretical Division, Robert Richtmyer, hoped that it might be a practical alternative to the Super.[102]

By that fall, calculations by two of their colleagues at the lab—mathematicians Stanislaw Ulam and Nicholas Metropolis—showed that major unresolved problems remained with both the Super and the Alarm Clock. Despite the fact that these obstacles had yet to be surmounted, Teller urged Bradbury to begin scheduling tests of prototype thermonuclear weapons for the coming year.[103]

Bradbury simply ignored him.[104] A seven-page letter that the lab director sent to the army in November, concerning various projects at Los Alamos, neglected even to mention the Super.[105]

It was not only Bradbury but Oppenheimer whom Teller now blamed for raising barriers to his pet project. Through his friendship with Fermi, Teller was aware of the reservations that the GAC had expressed about the superbomb in Washington. On a visit to Stanford that summer, Teller had driven across the Bay to see Oppie, later writing to Mayer of the visit: "We have been extremely friendly. He is a clever man. If he would really like me he would not have acted very differently. But mistakes are not corrected easily."[106]

Oppenheimer had briefly returned to teaching on the Berkeley campus in fall 1946, having already spent much of the year commuting between committee assignments in Washington and his other job at Caltech. ("I did actually give a course, but it is obscure to me how I gave it now.")[107] The experience was less than the triumphant homecoming he may have expected. Because Oppie's affiliation this time was with the Radiation Laboratory rather than the physics department, he suffered the humiliation of having to report to Lawrence. Once, when Ernest uttered a good-natured if insensitive remark about clipping Oppenheimer's wings, Oppie asked sarcastically whether he now needed Lawrence's permission to order office supplies.[108]

Oppenheimer also found it difficult to return to academic life for another reason. Shortly after arriving back in Berkeley, Oppie confided to Birge that he already missed Washington's corridors of power.[109] Offered the directorship of Princeton's Institute for Advanced Study in early 1947, Oppie welcomed the chance to return to the East.[110] The offer came from Lewis Strauss, who served on the institute's board of directors.

Kitty was likewise delighted to be leaving Berkeley. When a salesman called about renewing their automobile club membership, the FBI agent monitoring the call heard her say that they "would not be gone long—only 15 or 20 years."[111] After dithering for several more weeks about whether to leave California, Oppie finally accepted the institute job that April. At a special meeting of the Berkeley physics department, a tearful Birge described Oppenheimer's leaving as "the greatest failure of my life."[112]

Lawrence learned of Oppenheimer's decision from a radio news broadcast. To Rabi, Oppenheimer's leaving Berkeley a second time amounted, in Ernest's eyes, to a kind of treason.

At the Rad Lab, the 184-inch Synchrotron finally sparked to life just after midnight on November 1, 1946. In its first week of operation, Lawrence's machine produced a beam of 200-million-volt deuterons, twice the energy that he had set as the goal for the great cyclotron back in 1939.[113]

Despite such successes, Lawrence was worried anew about how the Rad Lab would fare in the transition from the army to the AEC. The cozy personal relationship that he had built up with Groves over the years did not guarantee good relations with Lilienthal, who remained an unknown quantity to Ernest. That winter, Lawrence submitted a last budget request to the army, asking almost $8 million for the coming year.[114]

Lawrence bid adieu to Groves at a farewell party in Washington on January 17, 1947, amid talk that these were already warning flags flying for the Rad Lab at the AEC.[115] The commission had recently balked at funding John's biomedical clinic and had approved money for only half of Alvarez's Linac.[116]

Yet there were other, worse shocks to come. Most worrisome to Ernest was the news that James Fisk, the AEC's recently appointed director of research, opposed using government funds to support further work on particle accelerators.[117] The utility of his machines was "indefinite," Lawrence bristled in a letter to Fisk, and "the value of such information to be obtained does not require justification."[118]

Adding to Ernest's anxiety was his uncertainty whether Oppie would be an ally or a foe in the coming struggle. When consulted about the Rad Lab budget, the GAC chairman had candidly said that he thought Lawrence's figure too high. Recently, Oppenheimer had also surprised Ernest—and the AEC—by throwing cold water on the commission's exaggerated claims concerning the future of civilian atomic power.[119] At the same time, what had previously been Lawrence's trump card—the university's close ties to the army—was about to be taken out of his hand. Both Contract 36 and Contract 48 were finally scheduled to expire that summer.[120]

The university's much-delayed "roundup and showdown" with the AEC occurred in mid-August, at a meeting of laboratory directors.[121] Hoping to undercut commission bureaucrats, Lawrence had invited Lilienthal out to California a week before the meeting for several days of hiking in Yosemite. Lilienthal was facing his own problems at home: his confirmation was still being held up by Senate Republicans, who had attacked his stewardship of the TVA as pro-labor and even "communistic."[122] ("I am so glad to get away. A change of scene should help," Lilienthal wrote in his journal on the way out west.)[123]

From the mountains, the pair drove to the Bohemian Grove, where Lawrence had moved the lab directors' meeting from Berkeley. Loomis and Gaither had volunteered their respective camps at the Grove for Ernest's guests.[124] (In a letter, Cooksey assured Loomis that the cabins were stocked with "Bourbon, Scotch, vermouth, and gin"—as well as "plenty of red meat.")[125]

The AEC commissioners stayed at Gaither's "Friends of the Forest" camp. Lawrence, Underhill, and the Berkeley contingent bunked at "The Sons of Toil"—Loomis's camp. The remaining lab directors slept in a clubhouse alongside the Russian River. Tellingly, Oppenheimer deserted his former Berkeley colleagues to join his new friends in the AEC.

No formal agenda had been set for the meeting, nor were minutes kept. Informally, however, Fisk had made it clear that the future of government support for the national labs—Lawrence's lab in particular—was at stake.

On August 19, 1947, Alvarez and McMillan began the meeting with presentations on the Linac and Synchrotron. In discussions that occupied the morning, Oppenheimer sided with Lawrence, who argued forcefully that the commission should continue the tradition of support for basic research set by Groves and the army.[126] A protest by Strauss—who accused the university of "running out of the duty it owed"—was countered by Neylan, who claimed that the AEC contracts put too great a strain on Lawrence.[127]

In the course of a walk amid the redwoods with Underhill and Lawrence that afternoon, Neylan sketched the outlines of a deal. Sitting down on a log beside the path, he announced that he planned to introduce a resolution to the regents that would extend the contracts for Los Alamos and the Rad Lab—something Neylan had promised Underhill just weeks earlier he would not do—on the sole condition that Lawrence not bear responsibility for overseeing the agreements but merely serve as a consultant to the government. The long-suffering Underhill could do nothing but silently assent.[128]

The details were subsequently sorted out in telegrams and telephone calls between Neylan and Lilienthal.[129] In the revitalized alliance between the government and the university, Fisk's reservations were simply swept away. Observed a university attorney who witnessed the documents signed by Sproul, in wonderment: "This is not a contract. This is a treaty between sovereign powers."[130]

Less than two weeks after the Bohemian Grove meeting, Lawrence received a promise of $15 million from the AEC for his accelerators during the coming year. Even the money for Seaborg's controversial "hot lab" on campus was reinstated, as was funding for John Lawrence's medical physics clinic. Cooksey informed Loomis in a letter at the end of August that the meeting at the Grove had proven to be "of inestimable value to the country in the phase of atomic energy."[131]

10

CHARACTER, ASSOCIATION, AND LOYALTY

FOLLOWING THE BOHEMIAN Grove meeting, Robert Oppenheimer and Lewis Strauss flew back to Washington together. Part of their conversation en route focused on the charges, newly resurfaced, that Oppie was a security risk. Cooksey wrote to Loomis that Oppenheimer and Strauss had "come to a mutual understanding of each other's problems."[1] But Cooksey's conclusion was premature; and his sense that Oppenheimer's troubles were in the past, wholly mistaken.

Under the McMahon Act, all AEC employees who had received wartime clearances from the army's Manhattan Project had to be reinvestigated by the FBI. The security checks assumed a new urgency in the wake of the Canadian spy scandal. Prominent among the individuals whose cases needed to be reviewed was Oppenheimer. From the outset, Lilienthal realized that Oppie's past was likely to set off alarm bells with the commission's security officials.[2]

The previous November, Groves had dumped the problem of what to do about Oppenheimer's clearance in Lilienthal's lap. When Lilienthal tried to duck the issue, Groves persisted. In a letter that December, the general suggested that the AEC chairman-designate resolve the matter by simply firing the scientist, removing him from the GAC.[3]

At the FBI, the order to reinvestigate Oppenheimer presented Hoover with another opportunity—"since we don't have to be discreet or cautious in the inquiries that we make when we are conducting an open investigation," an aide reminded the bureau's director.[4]

During February 1947, FBI agents interviewed almost two dozen of Oppenheimer's friends and associates. Agents also talked to Willie Higinbotham and Robert Bacher in Washington and Enrico Fermi in Chicago.[5] On the Berkeley campus, Sproul, Lawrence, and Kenneth Pitzer were interviewed.

Sproul told the bureau that Oppenheimer "had been a fool about fifteen years ago due to immature judgment" but was "now thoroughly embarrassed by his past indiscretions."[6] Lawrence said much the same about the physicist—"he has had the rash and is now immune with reference to any similar experiences"—adding that Oppenheimer was "a grand person in every way."

On February 28, Hoover sent the latest dossier on both Oppenheimer brothers to Truman's military aide, Harry Vaughan, asking him to pass them along to the president.[7] A few days later, the FBI director called Lilienthal at home to say that he would be forwarding the Oppenheimers' files to the commission. Hoover pointedly asked Lilienthal to give the matter his personal attention.[8]

On Saturday morning, March 8, a courier from the bureau delivered the files to the AEC building.[9] The twelve pages devoted to Robert Oppenheimer were a compilation of previous FBI reports and contained nothing from the previous month's investigation.[10]

Dutifully, however, the AEC chairman assembled the commissioners around a table in his office on Monday morning to consider the case against the man some of them knew as a friend. That afternoon, James Conant and Vannevar Bush appeared before the commission with assurances that they had heard—and dismissed—the FBI's charges as far back as 1942. They also warned that denying Oppenheimer a clearance "would have very serious consequences in the attitude of his fellow scientists toward this project."[11]

Lilienthal had tried to get Groves to appear at the impromptu hearing, to explain why he had chosen Oppenheimer as Los Alamos director in the first place. But the general, returning from a vacation in Florida, could not be reached.[12] Instead, Bush and Conant asked Patterson to write on Oppie's behalf. (Groves's letter arrived in due course, at month's end. The Manhattan Project director noted that, while he had learned many disturbing things about Oppie since 1942, there was "nothing which, if known to me at that time, would have changed my decision." However, Groves urged the commission to "exercise its own independent judgment based on current circumstances.")[13]

The commissioner most surprised and disturbed by the FBI reports was Lewis Strauss. The AEC's deputy counsel, Joseph Volpe, later remembered spending several hours with Strauss discussing the materials in Oppie's FBI file.[14] Strauss recalled that when he had offered Oppenheimer the directorship of Princeton's institute weeks earlier, Oppie had vaguely alluded to "derogatory information" about his past.[15] At the time, Strauss had dismissed such concerns with a wave of his hand. Strauss told Volpe that he now wished that he had paid more heed to the warning.

Lilienthal, on the other hand, found the allegations in the bureau's file vague, unsubstantiated, and—in some instances—downright ridiculous.[16] Little of the information dealt with the period when Oppenheimer was working on the bomb; most of the bureau's anonymous informants had obviously not known Oppie well.

But Lilienthal also recognized that his own reputation as well as that of the fledging AEC might be at stake. He remained the target of partisan attacks by two of the most powerful figures in Congress: J. Parnell Thomas, chairman of the House Un-American Activities Committee, and the new Joint Committee on Atomic Energy chairman, Senator Bourke Hickenlooper.[17] Moreover, Lilienthal had already infuriated Hoover by refusing to share the AEC's security files with the FBI.[18]

On Tuesday, March 11, Lilienthal, Volpe, and Bush went to the White House to inform the president of the latest charges against Oppenheimer—not realizing that Oppie's dossier had preceded them. Finding Truman preoccupied with a crisis in the Mediterranean, the trio met instead with aide Clark Clifford, who suggested having a panel of esteemed jurists, including retired Supreme Court justices, evaluate the evidence. Lilienthal was cheered to find Clifford seemingly untroubled by the Oppenheimer case and supportive of his decision to withhold Oppie's file from Hickenlooper.[19]

Hoping to defuse the Oppenheimer matter with Hoover, Lilienthal met with the FBI director at the end of the month. AEC security officials had meanwhile concluded that the case against Oppie was too thin to deny the physicist a security clearance.[20]

While conceding that Oppenheimer's contribution to the atomic bomb project had been "unique," and that the scientist had "steadily moved away" from former left-wing associates, Hoover insisted—"with some emphasis," an aide noted—that he was still not "completely satisfied in view of J. Robert's failure to report promptly and accurately what must have seemed to him an attempt at espionage at Berkeley."[21] When the discussion turned to Oppie's brother, Hoover warned that he would personally oppose any effort on the commission's part to renew Frank's security clearance.[22]

Since Lilienthal believed that his meeting with Hoover had put the flap over Oppie behind him, he was alarmed to get another letter just two weeks later from the FBI director, who claimed to have new and even more damaging evidence against Oppenheimer.[23]

The commissioners met a final time on Oppenheimer's clearance in late summer.[24] Most found persuasive the testimony of John Lansdale, who "was absolutely certain of the present loyalty of J. Robert Oppenheimer, despite the fact that he doubtless was at one time at least an avid fellow-traveler."[25] Based largely upon the strength of Lansdale's endorsement, the commissioners—including Strauss—voted on August 11, 1947, to grant Oppenheimer a top-secret "Q" clearance.[26] This time Hoover had no choice but to accept the AEC's verdict.[27]

By now aware of the storm flags flying, Oppenheimer had taken steps to distance himself from his past. He had already broken with the Independent Citizens Committee of the Arts, Sciences, and Professions, the radical organization which had once listed him as vice chairman on its letterhead.[28] The FBI knew, from its wiretaps, that Oppie was also refusing entreaties to speak on behalf of controversial causes.

The physicist had even seemingly given up on what Fermi called "Oppie's favorite idea"—the international control of atomic energy. Oppenheimer's disillusionment with the internationalist cause had seemingly been both sudden and complete—the result of the dramatic deterioration of U.S.-Soviet relations that followed the peace and heralded the coming of the Cold War.[29] That spring, Oppenheimer had held an urgent meeting with Baruch's replacement at the UN, Frederick Osborn. Oppie's pressing message—which he had flown out from California to deliver, he told Osborn—was that America should abandon its negotiations with the Russians on the bomb, lest the nation be lured into an unenforceable ban on the weapon.[30]

Stymied in his campaign to oust Oppenheimer from the GAC, Hoover meanwhile turned his attention elsewhere. In January, the FBI director had asked Branigan to expand and update his 1946 CINRAD report. Branigan's latest "memorandum" grew to a document some 400 pages long and included personal details on more than a dozen Berkeley scientists.[31]

That March, Hoover forwarded Branigan's report to the attorney general, along with a request that Clark "furnish the Bureau with a prosecutive opinion on the possible violations of the espionage laws appearing in this summary."[32] Hoover hoped, once again, to prod the Justice Department into indicting those involved in the Bay Area spy ring—in particular, Steve Nelson and Joe Weinberg. But, once again, the attorney general refused to rise to the bait; as Clark pointed out, the evidence behind the charges (gathered mostly by wiretaps and bugs) would likely be inadmissible in any prosecution.[33]

At Berkeley, the FBI's investigation was interfering with Frank's efforts to find a permanent job. Another apprentice at the Rad Lab, Edward Lofgren, had recently gotten a faculty post at the University of Minnesota, where Joseph Weinberg would also soon go. Lawrence sent a glowing letter of recommendation on Frank's behalf to William Buchta, chairman of the physics department at Minnesota.[34] Buchta hired Frank for the spring of 1947.

At Alvarez's request, Oppie's brother agreed to continue as a consultant on the Linac, which remained a classified project at the lab. Before leaving Berkeley, Frank filled out one of the AEC's new personnel security questionnaires. The "PSQ" was part of the expanded security procedures that the commission had recently adopted. Under organizations to which he had once belonged, Frank listed the Bach Society and the American Federation of Teachers, but not his prior membership in the Communist Party.

In early March 1947, Frank, Jackie, and their two children drove out of Berkeley on their way to Minneapolis, stopping off at Death Valley for a brief vacation. The family moved into temporary quarters at St. Paul's Curtis Hotel while Jackie looked for a house. An FBI wiretap followed them cross-country, to the hotel room and eventually to their new home.[35]

Frank's new career as an assistant professor of physics was initially uneventful—despite the occasional presence of FBI agents in the classroom.[36]

But on July 12, 1947, the *Washington Times-Herald* published a front-page story identifying him as "a card-carrying member of the Communist Party." The article, by James Walter, a reporter with ties to the bureau, had obviously come from FBI files, since it included such details as Frank's Communist Party card number and his party alias, Frank Folsom.[37] While the newspaper printed a disclaimer that its story on the younger Oppenheimer "in no way reflects on the loyalty or ability of his brother," Walter noted that Frank, too, had "worked on the Manhattan project and was aware of many secrets of the bomb from the start."[38]

Reached by telephone by Walter in the early morning hours before the story appeared, Frank had emphatically denied ever being a party member. A follow-up story by the Associated Press, which included Frank's denial, ran in newspapers across the country the following day.[39] Wrote Willie Higinbotham to Frank in sympathy: "The sons-o'-bitches are sure going hog wild."[40]

That summer at Berkeley, Lawrence and Birge were still trying to find a replacement for Oppie. Hans Bethe, who was first on Lawrence's list, could not be lured from Cornell. A second candidate, Stanford's Felix Bloch, was uninterested in cyclotrons and hence unacceptable to Ernest. Birge finally offered the job to Gian Carlo Wick, an Italian theorist and former colleague of Fermi's. Until Wick arrived on campus early in 1948, Serber continued to teach Oppenheimer's quantum mechanics class.[41]

As his interview with the FBI showed, Lawrence had managed to temporarily submerge his differences with Oppenheimer—if only out of sheer pragmatism. Oppie's place on the GAC gave the latter a powerful voice on vital questions affecting the Rad Lab, as the Bohemian Grove meeting had shown.[42]

At Lawrence's lab, Oppenheimer's absence had thus far been no impediment to progress, as several projects long in the works finally came to fruition. Just after the stroke of midnight on October 16, 1947, Alvarez's Linac produced its first beam.[43] A few weeks later, Lawrence sent the AEC his outline for the lab's next two years of operation. The plan announced Ernest's next big machine: the "Bevatron," a Synchrotron 120 feet in diameter, theoretically capable of accelerating protons to 6 billion electron volts. Lawrence's ambitious plan left no doubt that he intended Berkeley to remain the dominant power in high-energy physics: the money he requested for the coming year was nearly two-thirds of the total that the AEC had promised to spend on accelerators.[44]

But the commission's tepid response showed that Lawrence and his laboratory still faced significant political obstacles in Washington. Replying to Berkeley's proposal, Fisk spoke ominously of a "modest effort," the need for "paper studies," and of a decision some six months hence.[45]

Ten days later, Lawrence was back in Washington to lobby for his Bevatron. Opposing Berkeley's new machine was a prominent member of the GAC and a former ally of Ernest's: Isidor Rabi. Rabi's interests were no less parochial; he wanted the commission to build a smaller and cheaper accelerator nearer Columbia, at the AEC's new Brookhaven laboratory on Long Island.[46] Underhill, also in Washington, quickly sent Sproul a warning note: "General conversations around one of the eastern institutions is that it is time to break the University of California atomic trust."[47]

But Lawrence knew that his ace in the hole remained the university's contracts with the AEC, which were due to expire by July 1, 1948.

On the morning of December 31, 1947, Lawrence, Sproul, and Underhill assembled in Sproul's office to consider whether to renew Contracts 36 and 48. When Underhill objected that Bradbury's actions showed the Los Alamos director to be still beyond Sproul's control, Lawrence countered that the university gained much more than it lost from its relationship with the commission. Told that AEC support for the Bevatron might be the quid pro quo for renewing the contract, Sproul sided with Lawrence.[48]

Bacher and AEC general manager Carroll Wilson arrived in Berkeley a week later to seal the deal. While what went on at Los Alamos would continue to be determined by the AEC—"exclusively," Wilson emphasized—the commission agreed to "give Mr. Lawrence, if he is chosen by the University to be its scientific representative, a free run of the place."[49] In a concession to Underhill, Wilson let the university pick the lab's next director, subject to the commission's approval.

It was a wary and guarded partnership at best. Wrote Sproul in his office diary: "My final word was, 'we are now engaged, but the banns are not to be published until each party has had an opportunity to investigate the background and intentions of the other more thoroughly.'"

At the end of January 1948, the regents voted to extend the Los Alamos contract for four more years.[50] Sproul agreed to a faculty appointment at Berkeley for Bradbury, who was about to be dropped from his teaching post at Stanford, having been away from the campus for the past seven years.[51] Bowing to the inevitable, Underhill finally took the step he had long resisted and bought a business license for the University of California in the state of New Mexico.[52]

As part of the vows exchanged in Sproul's office, Lawrence got his Bevatron. But the machine had been scaled down to one-quarter of its original size to make it more palatable to Fisk and the AEC's auditors. In another compromise, Brookhaven received funding for its own, nearly identical accelerator. Designed by Stanley Livingston, Ernest's long-ago collaborator—and now his rival—Brookhaven's machine was dubbed the "Cosmotron."[53]

As Lawrence had hoped, Oppie's help proved to be key in the battle over the accelerators. Fisk had finally left the decision of which of the competing machines to fund up to the General Advisory Committee. At a climactic moment, when Rabi appeared to have swayed the GAC in favor of Brookhaven, Oppie saved the day by arguing that "discouragement of the Berkeley group would result in the loss of something valuable to the national scientific health."[54] Oppenheimer's Solomonic decision had kept the West Coast atomic trust intact, while giving the new East Coast lab a promising start.

Ernest celebrated his good fortune by purchasing a new Cadillac convertible, using money from the Loomis fund.*[55] When mesons—the

* Sproul, however, was growing tired of "such arrangements, as they are purely personal and have nothing to do, except very remotely, with University business." The following year, when Lawrence let it be known that he wished to buy another new car, Sproul urged Berkeley's comptroller to approve the purchase but thereafter to "have nothing further to do with the transaction."

long-sought binding force of the nucleus, previously seen only in cosmic radiation—were observed on the Rad Lab cyclotron later that month, even Lawrence's critics seemed won over.

"Isn't physics wonderful?" cabled Rabi from Columbia.[56]

His close call over the Bevatron convinced Lawrence anew of the importance of having powerful allies in Washington. A Joint Committee survey of the Rad Lab the previous year had noted that even the AEC found it "difficult to know what goes on in the project."[57] Since then, Ernest had taken steps to improve communications. Among those whom Lawrence courted during his visits to the capital was California congressman Chet Holifield, a Joint Committee member whose district included Balboa Island, as well as Hickenlooper, who paid a visit to the Rad Lab in February 1948.[58]

Mutual interest had also made unlikely political bedfellows of Neylan and Lilienthal. In gratitude for his help in brokering the Bohemian Grove deal, the ultraconservative Neylan hosted a dinner for the liberal AEC chairman at the Pacific Union Club that April.[59]

The morning after the dinner, Lawrence and Lilienthal attended the inaugural meeting of Neylan's new oversight committee for Los Alamos, in the regent's law office on Montgomery Street in San Francisco.[60] Afterward, Lawrence took Lilienthal on a leisurely drive down the coast to Balboa Island, where the AEC chairman was a weekend guest at the new beach house. Lawrence used the occasion to lobby Lilienthal on his latest enthusiasm: radiological warfare.

That spring, the AEC and the Pentagon created an ad hoc committee of experts to revisit the subject that had both fascinated and repulsed scientists since the discovery of fission. Lawrence and Alvarez were each asked to join the nine-man panel.[61] Since his proposal to the Interim Committee for a noncombat "demonstration" of the atomic bomb in 1945, the idea of making modern warfare less lethal, especially to noncombatants, had been of special interest to Lawrence.[62]

But Ernest's advocacy of what he claimed was a humane alternative to atomic bombs failed to find an echo with Lilienthal, who listened politely but later wrote in his journal:

> Brimming full of enthusiasm, [Lawrence] said his discovery was a way to make war painless. . . . The idea was to spread radioactive material in a narrow swath, so that the enemy army just couldn't

> get at you; a cordon *in*sanitaire, or radiotaire. . . . When this [was] first mentioned months ago, it hit me in the pit of the stomach so hard that I was almost sick.[63]

Subsequently, Lilienthal ordered the AEC's so-called rad war study redirected, so as to make it "somewhat more endurable."[64]

Unable to persuade Lilienthal, Lawrence was surprised to discover even more spirited opposition coming from an old friend.

James Conant had done work for the Army Chemical Corps during the First World War and found the similarities between "RW" and poison gas too depressing. (The AEC, he thought, had "enough urgent problems without attempting to emphasize this one.")[65] At the Committee on Atomic Energy, which he chaired for the Pentagon's Joint Research and Development Board, Conant resolutely beat back a proposal that would have accelerated research on the subject.[66]

Throughout the summer and fall, Lawrence labored to change Conant's mind. During one three-day period in September, Ernest regaled his friend on the humanitarian potential of radiological warfare at the Bohemian Grove, over lunch in Berkeley's Faculty Club, and during dinner at Trader Vic's.[67] But not even Lawrence's celebrated charm could sway the Harvard chemist's resolve.[68]

When Lawrence and Alvarez raised the subject again, on a drive from Berkeley to San Francisco, Conant protested that he was "getting too old and too tired to be an adviser on affairs of this sort."

"I did my job during the war," he said wearily.[69]

Following another summer spent at Los Alamos, Teller's efforts to spark a crash effort on the Super were similarly falling flat. In Washington, his lobbying mostly consisted of briefing Bacher, who had pledged to keep the Joint Committee informed of progress on the hydrogen bomb. (Privately, Teller protested to Maria Mayer that Bacher was "at best a third rate physicist," yet admitted that there was another reason for disliking the AEC commissioner: "To Oppy he was the ideal yes-man. That, of course, is the main reason of my antipathy.")[70]

Concerning the Super, there was, in truth, not much progress to report. Teller had completed another top-secret report on the subject before returning to Chicago. The previous fall, Los Alamos had published LA-643—"On the Development of Thermonuclear Bombs"—which pulled together all the aspects of H-bomb research at the lab to date. Teller's mood, as reflected in the report, had become decidedly more pessimistic in the eighteen months since the superbomb conference. While Edward still thought the classical Super "probably feasible," even he now acknowledged that its complexity put it at least several years away.

Unexpected problems with both the Super and the Alarm Clock had surfaced in recent studies at the lab. The latest calculations showed that the Super would require almost twice the amount of tritium Teller had earlier estimated. The availability of tritium—which could only be made at the cost of sacrificing the production of plutonium for atomic bombs—was likely to be "the determining factor in the early construction of any thermonuclear bomb," LA-643 noted.[71]

While Teller anticipated no "extremely big difficulties" with the Alarm Clock, this design, too, suffered from some of the same problems that plagued the Super. (Unmentioned in the Los Alamos report was a recent calculation that showed it might take a fission explosion equivalent to 1 million tons of TNT—a megaton—to ignite the device.)[72] In an effort to get around these problems, the Alarm Clock had steadily grown to a behemoth weighing between 40 and 100 tons—much too large to be carried by existing aircraft. Teller himself conceded that further work on the design looked unpromising.[73]

Recognizing that any decision taken at this point was almost certainly going to go against him, Teller recommended postponing a choice between the Super and the Alarm Clock until more detailed calculations could be made on von Neumann's new digital computer.

Notwithstanding these technical barriers, Teller judged that the greatest obstacle to the Super lay in the realm of politics, not physics. Next to Bradbury, he regarded Oppie and the General Advisory Committee as his most serious adversary. While pronouncing LA-643 "admirable," the GAC had failed to endorse either increased tritium production or the thermonuclear tests that Teller's report called for.[74]

Instead, in June 1948, the committee recommended accelerating work on the fission Booster—if necessary at the expense of delaying development of the Alarm Clock and Super.[75] Another of Teller's early ideas that had been revived and modified in LA-643—a boosted hydride bomb—received the back of the hand from both Oppenheimer and the Military Liaison Committee, which dismissed it as "not now considered promising."[76]

By that summer, Teller had what he considered yet another example of Oppie's interference.

In early July, Oppenheimer and other scientists met in Berkeley at the request of the Military Liaison Committee to divine the future of atomic warfare. The "Panel on Long-Range Objectives" had been called into being to forecast likely developments over the next decade in the areas of nuclear weaponry, atomic propulsion, and radiological warfare.[77] Under Oppie's direction, the experts actually ranged further afield into such subjects as the world uranium supply and tactical fission weapons. But the panel gave the Super little attention—and no priority.[78]

Whereas LA-643 had judged it "not very probable" that the Soviets might develop an Alarm Clock–type weapon, barely a week after Oppenheimer's latest report Teller forwarded his own new and very different assessment of the future to Bradbury.

Titled "The Russian Atomic Plan," Teller's memo argued that the Soviet Union, in its efforts to catch up with the West, might have taken a "surprising and disquieting" alternate course.[79] Speculating that the Russians had decided not only to construct but to test their first atomic bomb in secret—"in order not to give us premature warning of their strength"—he hypothesized that large-scale, clandestine production of the ingredients for a Soviet Super had already begun at decentralized sites around the USSR. The implications for U.S. security were obvious. "One may feel less certain about our continued superiority in atomic warfare," Teller concluded.*[80]

The question implicit in "The Russian Atomic Plan"—when would the Soviets have the atomic bomb?—had begun to preoccupy others in Washington, Lewis Strauss among them.

There was already a wide disparity of views as to the answer. Confident that he had cornered the world market on atomic raw materials, Groves thought the American nuclear monopoly might endure for as long as a generation. A few scientists, like Arthur Compton, took a more cautious view, believing it would be a decade or more before the West confronted a Soviet atomic bomb.[81] But most of those who had a hand in building the American bomb predicted that the breathing spell would be much shorter, perhaps five to seven years. Only a few jeremiads in the military—members of the Special Study Group in Air Force Intelligence—warned, late in 1947, that the "Russians could conceivably complete the first atomic bomb in summer or fall of 1949."[82]

Strauss proved to be even more of an alarmist, arguing in spring 1947 that a Soviet nuclear test might be imminent.[83] With the zeal of a dishonored

* While the Russian H-bomb was not yet under construction, planning for it had already begun. On March 13, 1948, Klaus Fuchs, meeting his Soviet control in a London pub, had passed along a drawing of an advanced design for the Super, based in part upon the idea that Fuchs and von Neumann had prepared on the eve of the 1946 Los Alamos conference. Five weeks later, Beria asked Kurchatov and two other Russian physicists to submit their own plan for thermonuclear research. In early June 1948—three months before Teller wrote "The Russian Atomic Plan"—the USSR's Council of Ministers approved the scientists' proposal for a top-secret, high-priority project to build a Soviet Super.

prophet, he appealed to Defense Secretary James Forrestal to be on the lookout for a Soviet bomb.[84]

Oppenheimer, on the other hand, remained surprisingly complacent. As late as April 1948, he predicted that a Soviet nuclear threat was still "a long time to come."[85]

What might have seemed, in calmer days, an honest disagreement or a simple case of bureaucratic inertia took on a more sinister cast to Strauss, who took the GAC's lack of anxiety concerning the Soviet bomb to be part of an emerging pattern; one in which Oppenheimer or Oppie's friends were the common element.

In January 1948, Conant's Committee on Atomic Energy had expressed "grave doubts" about the effectiveness of the long-range detection system that Strauss favored, adding that it seemed "highly improbable any foreign country will detonate an atomic bomb within a period of three years."[86] (Strauss, at the same meeting, said that the air force "urgently needed" $1 million to establish an airborne detection program. When the committee failed to act on his plea, Strauss offered to pay part of the sum out of his own pocket.)[87]

Strauss had earlier had a run-in with the GAC and its influential chairman over another, unrelated issue. At the Bohemian Grove meeting, Strauss had been the only commissioner to vote against a policy extending the prewar custom of making isotopes freely available to hospitals and research institutes overseas.[88] The AEC's 4-to-1 vote, the first occasion where the commission was not unanimous on an issue, had particularly disturbed Lilienthal, who lost sleep over the incident.[89]

Nor had Strauss accepted defeat gracefully. Even after Truman announced the new policy, Strauss continued to lobby the State Department and Forrestal in an effort to overturn the decision.

But perhaps most ominous, from Lilienthal's viewpoint, was Strauss's reaction when the AEC chairman had tried to salve the wound. After Lilienthal genially suggested that "you just didn't realize what you were doing," Strauss's quick reply had disabused him, he wrote, of that naive notion: "[Strauss] turned and grinned in what seemed a very genuine way and said, 'No, I'm old enough; I knew exactly what I was doing.'"[90]

What Lilienthal described as "this secrecy incubus" was also creating an increasingly oppressive political atmosphere in Washington by 1948. The previous fall, the loyalty hearings begun by HUAC chairman J. Parnell Thomas had spread to both sides of the country. On October 28, 1947, Thomas had notified Hoover in a telephone call that he intended to expand his current hearings—on Communist infiltration of the motion picture industry—to include "the tie-up between the Oppenheimers and the Soviet embassy."[91] As Hoover subsequently informed Attorney General Clark, the focus of the new inquiry would be Frank Oppenheimer—whom HUAC "apparently intends to attack." Hoover added that Thomas almost certainly had "tap" (that is, transcripts of army or bureau wiretaps) to use as evidence.[92]

On what was to have been the final day of the Hollywood hearings, Thomas produced a surprise witness. Former FBI special agent Louis Russell was a ten-year veteran of the bureau who had recently joined the staff of the House committee. In testimony prompted by HUAC's chief investigator, Robert Stripling, Russell described the Chevalier incident as Robert Oppenheimer had recounted it to bureau agents a year earlier.

The link between Russell's story and the previous testimony seemed tenuous at best. ("Nobody on the staff could explain what it had to do with the committee's inquiry into Communism in Hollywood," wrote the *San Francisco Chronicle*'s baffled reporter.)[93] But word of Oppenheimer's alleged involvement in a spy plot created an immediate sensation in newspapers across the country.[94]

Cornered by reporters at his home in Stinson Beach, Chevalier described Russell's story as "greatly garbled" and denied that he had approached Oppenheimer "in order to obtain information of any kind."[95] Contacted in England, where he had moved from Berkeley just three weeks earlier, Eltenton refused comment.[96] From Princeton, Oppenheimer declared that he would likewise "withhold comment, either confirmation or denial"—an equivocation that both angered and perplexed Chevalier.[97]

Next to jump on the internal security bandwagon was California's "little HUAC"—the Tenney Committee. Even before HUAC's Oppenheimer story broke, Tenney had notified the FBI that he planned to subpoena Haakon Chevalier to appear before his own committee hearings, in Oakland, the following week.[98]

Like Thomas, Tenney had spent the previous year dealing with public ridicule and a hostile press. (His committee's investigation into sex education at Chico High School was interrupted by picketing students holding signs that read: "The Birds and the Bees; Mr. Tenney, please!")[99]

For the past month, Tenney's reclusive chief investigator, attorney Richard Combs, had planned hearings on links between the Communist Party and the CIO-affiliated Marine Cooks and Stewards Union. Combs also intended to expose Communist ties to the California Labor School in San Francisco.[100] Following HUAC's revelations, however, Tenney and Combs hurriedly expanded the Oakland hearings to include charges of Soviet espionage at the Radiation Laboratory.[101]

Tenney's latest investigation opened on November 1, 1947, the day after Thomas's closed. Amid name-calling between government informers and hostile witnesses, the question of wartime spying at Berkeley was largely ignored. Instead, Combs told of his own recent nocturnal visit to the Rad Lab, where, equipped with a flashlight, he had climbed under a security fence and approached the giant cyclotron undetected.[102]

Almost a week passed before Chevalier was finally called to the stand. But the drama quickly turned anticlimactic when Chevalier was dismissed without ever being questioned about his approach to Oppenheimer.[103] Like Thomas's Hollywood hearings, Tenney's investigation ended abruptly and without resolution.

As subsequent events would show, moreover, neither event clouded the aura that surrounded Oppenheimer, who continued to be lionized by the press as well as the public. So well known and admired a figure was Oppie that when the inaugural issue of *Physics Today* appeared the following May, the editors needed only to put a porkpie hat on the cover for their lead article on recent trends in American science. That July, Oppenheimer spoke defiantly about his left-wing past in a cover story for *Time* magazine. "The Thomas Committee doesn't like this, but I'm not ashamed of it," Oppie boasted. "I'm more ashamed of the lateness. . . . If it hadn't been for this late but indispensable education, I couldn't have done the job at Los Alamos at all."[104]

Lilienthal thought it a telling sign of the times that Oppenheimer's security file—now 1 foot high and weighing some 12 pounds—was once again back on his desk at the AEC later that summer. Wrote the AEC chairman of the prevailing mood: "Suspicion, suspicion, suspicion. And what an opportunity to gouge a man you don't like, one who has disagreed with you. Godalmighty!"[105]

With the exception of Tenney's abortive hearings, Lawrence's laboratory had thus far escaped the security mania that seemed to be sweeping the country.

But an early warning sign had been the government's denial of a security clearance for Charlotte Serber. Refused the job of Rad Lab librarian, she was eventually given another post at the lab that did not require a clearance.[106]

Although security at the Berkeley lab had been described as "poor" in a 1946 army report, the only physical changes imposed since then was a new fence around the giant cyclotron—erected at the AEC's insistence following Combs's nighttime raid. Lawrence had successfully resisted the installation of additional barriers as "giving the laboratory area an industrial appearance."[107]

Behind closed doors and out of the headlines, however, another kind of security investigation was about to get under way at Berkeley. Caught between the need to grant hundreds of new Q clearances on the one hand and congressional charges of lax security on the other, the AEC in April 1948 had issued an "Interim Procedure" containing guidelines for the investigation of suspected security risks.[108]

The new rules created regional Personnel Security Boards staffed by locally prominent citizens. Each board was asked to decide whether prospective AEC employees and contractors deserved a security clearance based upon three so-called fields of inquiry: "character, association, and loyalty."[109] Since the PSB was not a court of law, the usual rules of evidence did not apply. Subjects might not even be informed of specific charges against them; nor were they allowed to confront their accusers. There was usually only forty-eight hours' advance notice of a hearing, and no appeal of the board's ruling outside the commission was possible.[110] As the AEC's Joseph Volpe frankly admitted to the Joint Committee, the PSB was "not much more than a kangaroo court."[111]

The University of California's Personnel Security Board held its first hearing that summer. At Lawrence's request, Neylan agreed to head Berkeley's PSB. Its other members were two war heroes: Admiral Chester Nimitz and Major General Kenyon Joyce.[112]

The first person to be investigated by the board was a young Los Alamos chemist who had come to Berkeley to work with Wendell Latimer. A pall of suspicion had fallen over Robert Hurley because he and his Latvian-born wife had opposed U.S. entry into the war while graduate students at the University of Wisconsin.[113]

Summoned to Neylan's law office on August 4, 1948, Hurley faced the board in the company of his sole defender: Latimer.[114] Three hours later, Neylan handed down the verdict in longhand notes written on a yellow legal pad. The board found Hurley "lacking in frankness and, in many instances, evasive in relation to substantive issues." He was declared "not a justifiable risk" and denied a clearance.[115] Fired by the university, he was subsequently rehired by a defiant Latimer, and promptly fired again at Neylan's direct order.[116]

The next scientist to appear before Berkeley's board was Robert Serber, who, like Hurley, found himself in trouble because of his wife's political associations. Unlike the unfortunate Hurley, however, Serber had the active support of Ernest Lawrence, who attended the August 5 hearing to speak on his behalf.[117] Lawrence's endorsement left Neylan's verdict a foregone conclusion. Excusing Serber's failure to publicly criticize the Soviet Union as "consistent with a retiring nature," the board welcomed the physicist back into the fold.[118]

No such reception awaited Frank Oppenheimer. Hoping to spend the summer in California, Frank had written Lawrence from Minnesota, expecting the usual pro forma invitation extended to Rad Lab alumni. Instead, Ernest's reply was quick, brusque, and negative, prompting this wounded response from Oppie's brother:

> Dear Lawrence:
>
> What is going on? Thirty months ago you put your arms around me and wished me well, told me to come back and work whenever I wanted to. Now you say I am no longer welcome.
>
> Who has changed, you or I?[119]

Frank came to Berkeley anyway. Risking Ernest's wrath, Ed and Elsie McMillan invited the outcast to dinner at their home.[120] When Oppie and his wife, visiting from Princeton, encountered Ernest at a faculty cocktail party, an inebriated Kitty loudly scolded him in front of the other guests for banishing Frank from the lab. Oppie simply looked on in silence, bemused at Ernest's discomfort.[121]

Lawrence never gave a reason for his edict banning Frank. But his Scandinavian temper had flared upon learning that Frank lied about not being a member of the Communist Party. Ernest was no less angry at Oppie for hiding the truth about his brother.[122] At the time of the Tenney hearings, when Ernest had quizzed Oppenheimer about the Chevalier affair, Oppie had cavalierly dismissed the question with an impatience that seemed to imply that Lawrence was too thickheaded to understand the answer.

Baited by Hoover, the trail being followed by Red-hunting investigators was leading inexorably closer to Berkeley. In July 1948, Thomas's HUAC began a series of hearings whose star witnesses, Elizabeth Bentley and Whittaker Chambers, promised to expose Communists at top levels of the U.S. government. Almost in passing, Bentley's testimony identified Louise Bransten—a former Vassar classmate—as someone she had encountered at Communist Party meetings in New York during the late 1930s.

Alert reporters got a hint of the direction that HUAC's next inquiry would take when the committee "inadvertently" released an executive session transcript containing testimony by Harold Zindel, one of the army agents who had shadowed Martin Kamen to his wartime rendezvous with Soviet diplomats at Bernstein's Fish Grotto.[123] Both Zindel and a former bureau agent, Larry Kerley, were currently working for HUAC.[124]

Another former army agent, David Teeple, a colleague's of Zindel's, had meanwhile quit his high school principal's job to join Hickenlooper's personal staff. Retired FBI agent Harold Velde, who had been a member of King's expanded "commie squad" in San Francisco during the war, was now a congressman from Illinois and a member of HUAC.

In mid-August, Louis Russell tipped off the bureau that HUAC's next target would be Berkeley and Chicago scientists suspected of stealing wartime atomic secrets.[125]

Thomas's hearings on Soviet espionage at the wartime Rad Lab began a few weeks later in executive session at the House Office Building. Excluded from the hearing room, reporters waited impatiently outside in the hall. First to be called was Kamen, who, up to a few days before, had been living the quiet life of a junior professor of physics at Washington University in St. Louis. Kamen's subpoena had arrived on the same day that his hometown newspaper, the *St. Louis Post-Dispatch,* broke the story of his 1944 dinner with Kheifets and Kasparov.[126]

Brandishing the FBI's still-classified transcript of the recorded conversation, Stripling questioned Kamen for three hours about the rendezvous at Bernstein's Fish Grotto. Throughout, Kamen denied passing any secret information to the Russians.

Steve Nelson was next to testify. HUAC's subpoena had reached him in New York, where he was serving on the Communist Party's National Board. Invoking the Fifth Amendment, Nelson refused to answer any of the committee's questions. Later, outside the hearing room, he branded his interrogators "political pyromaniacs."[127]

Louise Bransten, next in the lineup, also pleaded the Fifth upon the advice of her attorney. Joseph Weinberg, the last witness to be called for the day, denied for a second time ever having met or even talked to Steve Nelson.

More than two dozen other witnesses, including Groves and Lansdale, would testify before the closed hearings concluded in late September. At the end of the month, a twenty-three-page HUAC report on Soviet atomic espionage featured excerpts from Kamen's testimony and urged the "immediate prosecution" of both Nelson and Bransten for espionage and contempt of Congress. Since the committee said it was considering perjury charges against him, Weinberg was identified in the publication only as "Scientist X."[128]

Defying the wishes of his own party, Thomas vowed to resume the spy hearings following the presidential election, little more than a month away.[129]

11

A RATHER PUZZLED HORROR

TRUMAN'S UPSET VICTORY in the 1948 election and Parnell Thomas's removal from Congress—on a conviction for payroll padding—promised a changed setting in Washington for the coming year. HUAC's new chairman, John Wood, a moderate Democrat from Georgia, announced that the committee's spy hunt was temporarily suspended.

But HUAC was no longer the only committee in Congress with an interest in pursuing "atom spies."

Shortly after regaining the helm at the Joint Committee on Atomic Energy, Brien McMahon had appointed a twenty-eight-year-old recent Yale Law School graduate—William Liscum Borden—the committee's executive director. Smart and driven—to the point of obsessiveness—Borden had come to McMahon's attention for placing a newspaper ad that called upon America's leaders to issue a nuclear ultimatum to Russia: "Let Stalin decide: atomic war or atomic peace." Borden and his like-minded conservative friends called the ad their "Incendiary Document."

While still at Yale, Borden had also authored a grim but foresighted book on the possibility of a "nuclear Pearl Harbor," titled *There Will Be No Time.*[1] The young staffer and McMahon dedicated themselves to ensuring that the nation would achieve what Borden called "atomic abundance."[2]

Inevitably, their attention soon turned as well to the Super, and the security of the nation's atomic secrets.[3] One result of the Thomas hearings had been to persuade Lilienthal to open the AEC's personnel security files to the Joint Co'mmittee.[4]

Borden took a personal interest in the dossier on Robert Oppenheimer, about whom he had heard rumors from the day he joined the Joint Committee. The two men met for the first time on April 6, 1949, in the committee's suite of offices at the Capitol. After introducing the GAC to the Joint Committee's new members, Oppenheimer had outlined the scientists' case against proceeding with Project *Lexington,* the air force's proposed nuclear-powered bomber.*[5] He also warned about the danger of accidents at civilian nuclear power plants, which the AEC was busy promoting. ("It is a dangerous engineering undertaking. I was astonished to know that many people were wishing for this proving ground in their state.")[6]

Although McMahon and Borden fervently supported both nuclear power and the air force project, they remained silent at this meeting. Borden's impression of Oppenheimer was that of "a born leader and a manipulator."[7]

Six months after the Thomas hearings, Lawrence had reason to hope that the Rad Lab would avoid being dragged into the morass of Washington politics. In late April, he attended the weeklong Joint Orientation Conference for AEC laboratory directors at the Pentagon. Participants in the conference toured an aircraft carrier at Norfolk, Virginia, watched a flyover of air force jets at Eglin Field in Florida, and witnessed a practice airborne assault by army paratroopers at Fort Benning, Georgia. Lawrence returned to Berkeley sunburned and relaxed, bearing a souvenir photograph of the sailfish he caught in Florida.[8]

Just two days later, on April 22, 1949, HUAC's long-postponed spy hearings resumed. In an executive session at New York's Biltmore Hotel, Chairman Wood, acting as a subcommittee of one, questioned a thirty-two-year-old chemist who had been a technician at the Rad Lab back in 1943. Like many students of the day, Russell Davis had been drawn to the Communist Party as a way of making new friends. (He was disappointed, Davis admitted, to find "mostly girls with thick glasses and empty faces, who looked like psychology students.")[9] Davis and his wife later testified to seeing various Berkeley scientists at party meetings, including Rossi Lomanitz and Max Friedman.

Wood next summoned Lomanitz, who had meanwhile gotten a job

* Manley recalled only one occasion when Oppie's emotions triumphed over his scientific detachment at a GAC meeting. Following a briefing on nuclear-powered submarines by Vice Admiral Hyman Rickover, Oppenheimer went over to the model sub on the dais of the deserted conference room and, putting his hand around the hull, crushed it.

teaching physics at Tennessee's Fisk University. Also called upon to testify were the other three in the picture taken at Sather Gate. David Bohm was then an assistant professor at Princeton. Max Friedman, who had changed his name to Ken Manfred after the war, was back at Berkeley on sabbatical from the University of Puerto Rico when HUAC's subpoena reached him. Lomanitz, Friedman, and Bohm all pled the Fifth in response to Wood's questions. Joe Weinberg—brought face-to-face with Steve Nelson in the hearing room—denied under oath having previously met him.[10]

The dramatic highlight of the three-month hearings occurred on June 7, when Robert Oppenheimer was called before HUAC in executive session. The committee was only asking for the physicist's help in its investigation of the Radiation Laboratory, Wood explained. Indeed, other committee members took pains to point out that Oppie was not the subject of the hearing, since his loyalty had been "vouched for by General Groves."[11]

Asked about the Chevalier incident, Oppenheimer gave the same version of the story he had told the FBI in 1946: he was the sole person who had been approached. It was only when Wood's queries shifted to Frank that Oppie grew evasive, asking HUAC's chairman "not to press these questions about my brother. If they are important to you, you can ask him. I will answer, if asked, but I beg you not to ask me these questions." Wood, unexpectedly, demurred.[12]

Oppie emerged from the hearings unscathed. Before the session was adjourned, HUAC member Richard Nixon even warmly thanked Oppenheimer for his testimony, adding, "I think we all have been tremendously impressed with him and are mighty happy we have him in the position he has in our program." The entire committee descended from the dais to shake the physicist's hand.

Frank Oppenheimer received very different treatment when he and Jackie appeared before HUAC's executive session a week later.[13] After consulting with their lawyer, Clifford Durr, the couple had decided to admit to their own previous membership in the Communist Party but not to answer questions about the political views of others. Following an afternoon break, Wood opened the hearing room to reporters, and Frank's testimony admitting that he had lied about his party membership was released to the press.[14]

Earlier that day, Oppie's brother had testified in detail about his brief and somewhat haphazard career as the Communist known as Frank Folsom. (He had once absentmindedly left his party identification in a shirt he sent to the cleaners. The laundry returned the pale green card in "a little envelope," Frank remembered.) But neither he nor Jackie would identify any others they knew as Communists, despite Wood's insistent prompting. "I cannot talk about my friends," Frank told the committee.

On the question of whether he had been asked to spy during the war, Frank's reply was direct and unequivocal: "I knew of no Communist activity, nobody ever approached me to get information and I gave none, and I worked very hard and I believe made a valuable contribution."[15]

That evening, the headline of the *Oakland Tribune* read, "Ex-U.C. Bomb Worker Reports Early Ties with Communists." Frank learned from reporters that he had been fired by the University of Minnesota while he was still on the witness stand. The school accepted his resignation, which he had submitted beforehand as a pro forma gesture, less than an hour after he admitted to lying about being a Communist.

Oppie's former students met a similar fate. Bohm was suspended from teaching by Princeton while his trial for contempt of Congress wound its way through the courts; his contract would not be renewed when it expired the following year.[16] Lomanitz's contract at Fisk was likewise allowed to lapse even though he, like Bohm, had received enthusiastic praise from colleagues, students, and peers. Bernard Peters—whom Robert Oppenheimer had identified in his HUAC testimony as "quite a Red"—was forced to leave the University of Rochester after portions of Oppie's executive session testimony were leaked to the *Rochester Times-Union*.[17] Oppenheimer's efforts to get the school to renew Peters's contract were unavailing.[18]

But Oppie himself seemed little affected by the ordeal. He and Kitty spent the weekend at the Chevaliers' beach house just a few weeks after the HUAC hearings ended. FBI agents waited in cars on the road outside. Other G-men, monitoring a hidden listening device, strained to hear conversations above the sound of breaking waves.

For Frank and Jackie, the future was more problematic. Having recently sold a van Gogh he had inherited from his father to buy an 800-acre spread in Blanco Basin, near Pagosa Springs, Colorado, Frank looked forward to a new life as a cattle rancher. But the land, at an elevation of nearly 10,000 feet, had only a small cabin made of rough-hewn logs. During the long winter, the neighboring ranchers would move their cattle to land they owned at a lower elevation—an option not open to Frank and Jackie.

In early spring, the couple piled blankets near the door and heated water on a wood stove. Sitting near a window in the darkened house, watching with binoculars the cattle standing in snow-covered fields, they waited for the first calves to be born.[19]

Having survived HUAC's interrogation with both his reputation and his career intact, Robert Oppenheimer was relaxed and confident when he appeared before the Joint Committee barely a week later. Oppie had been called to testify in hearings begun by Hickenlooper, who was engaged in a last-ditch effort to hamstring David Lilienthal. The Iowa senator had charged the AEC chairman with "incredible mismanagement."[20] Unlike HUAC's closed sessions, the Joint Committee hearings took place under klieg lights, with reporters present.[21]

Still hoping to overturn the commission's ruling on the export of isotopes, Strauss volunteered to speak on that issue as an example of Lilienthal's alleged malfeasance. Strauss had already testified twice in executive session about a request for radioactive iron that had come from a group of Norwegian scientists, one of whom was suspected of being a Communist.

Asked about the potential for misuse of such material, Oppenheimer responded with the kind of quick and casual brutality for which he had become infamous among faculty colleagues at Berkeley. His target this time, however, was Strauss. Deadpan, Oppenheimer compared the military significance of isotopes to that of bottled beer, a shovel, or vitamins. As laughter broke out in the hearing room, even some committee members joined in. Volpe, watching from the sidelines, saw the color rise in Strauss's face and the latter's jaw muscles clench.[22] Afterward, when Oppie asked him, "How did I do, Joe?" Volpe, shaking his head, answered: "Too well, Robert, much too well."[23]

The deteriorating international situation had been a factor in Teller's decision at the end of 1948 to return to Los Alamos full-time for a year.[24] Since 1946, he had been shuttling between the lab and Chicago during summers and holiday breaks. The previous spring, a Soviet coup in Czechoslovakia had dragged one more country behind the Iron Curtain. That summer, a war scare ensued after the Russians cut off Allied access to Berlin. In China, as the new year began, Mao's armies were advancing on all fronts. It is "quite clear that I am needed in Los Alamos more than I am needed in Chicago," Teller wrote Maria Mayer, adding, "being necessary is an extremely important thing for me."[25]

Edward planned to devote the coming year to work on the Super and other bombs. Anxious to accommodate the temperamental Hungarian, Bradbury had created the Committee for Weapons Development, on which Teller served, and had also made him an assistant director of the lab.[26] At the committee's first meeting, Teller proposed testing four new devices by mid-1951: an advanced implosion bomb, the hydride, the

Booster, and a prototype fission trigger for the Super that was dubbed "Little Edward" at the lab.[27]

Initially, his return to the New Mexico lab seemed to have the desired tonic effect. "I think I have a right to feel at home and I do," Teller exulted to Mayer.[28] But just a few weeks later the familiar ennui was back. "The amount of physics I am *not* doing here is considerable," Edward wrote.[29]

What Teller complained was his "hibernation" at Los Alamos was a reflection of the frustrations he was encountering at the lab. His colleagues remained, as ever, unenthusiastic about Teller's original hobbyhorse—the hydride bomb, which the GAC had recently voted to deemphasize—while the Super seemed as far from realization as ever.[30]

So morose had he become about the future, Teller wrote Mayer, that he proposed sending a rocket to Mars loaded with algae and bacteria as "insurance in case an atomic war terminates life on Earth."[31]

American setbacks in the Cold War had also given new importance to the question of when the Russians would get the bomb. Ironically, as time passed without producing evidence of Soviet progress toward a weapon, complacency grew.[32] In July 1948, the Central Intelligence Agency had estimated mid-1950 as "the earliest date by which it is remotely possible that the USSR may have completed its first atomic bomb." The agency believed mid-1953 to be "the "most probable date."[33] A year later, CIA analysts still held to 1953 as the most likely year but added a curious hedge: they now predicted the Russians' first bomb "cannot be completed before mid-1951."[34]

By spring 1949, the United States was flying specially equipped B-29s along the periphery of the Soviet Union, part of a long-range detection system operated by an air force detachment known as AFOAT-1.[35] On the same day in June that Oppenheimer testified before HUAC, Conant's Committee on Atomic Energy recommended cutting research and development funding for airborne detection. Conant's intent was to channel more money and effort into seismic detection, which both he and Oppenheimer believed had a better chance of reliably discovering clandestine nuclear explosions.[36]

For Strauss, however, this interference by a second committee on which Oppenheimer served seemed another example of obstructionism bordering on sabotage. Following a briefing in early August 1949 on the Long-Range Detection Program, Strauss wrote the director of AFOAT-1 with a warning that any "failure to detect the first Russian detonation might be fatal."[37]

The specter of a Soviet bomb had likewise begun to haunt McMahon and Borden, who wrote to the AEC a week later, asking that they be notified immediately when the commission had evidence of an atomic explosion in the Soviet Union. Borden's letter was prompted by recent reports in a Paris newspaper of a major seismic disturbance near the Afghan border.[38] Picked up by the Associated Press, the story had been reprinted in American papers. "The article is inaccurate in most particulars," Sumner Pike, the acting AEC chairman, reassured Borden on August 31, 1949.[39]

At the time Pike wrote his letter, the nuclear arms race between the United States and the Soviet Union was already some forty-eight hours old.

Word of the Russian bomb reached Washington at the start of the busy Labor Day weekend. By the early morning hours of September 7, AFOAT-1 analysts had identified an air sample obtained from a B-29 flying between Alaska and Japan as consistent with debris from a fission explosion. When further analysis confirmed this finding, the air force alerted the Truman administration on September 9.[40]

Official Washington remained skeptical of the news nonetheless.[41] The new defense secretary, Louis Johnson, was one of the doubters. Truman's national security adviser, Admiral Sidney Souers, likewise expressed hope that the radiation had come from a Soviet reactor accident rather than an actual weapon. Even the president himself apparently remained unconvinced that the Russians had the bomb.[42]

Realizing that there was at least a political need for more proof, the air force hastily assembled a covey of experts to make the case that the atomic monopoly had indeed ended.

The first call went out to Vannevar Bush, who was surprised to be the one picked to head the effort. ("But wouldn't it be more reasonable for Dr. Oppenheimer to be chairman?" Bush innocently asked. The reply, he later remembered, was "that they prefer it the way it was.") To Bush, it was the first subtle hint of the trouble to come for Oppenheimer.[43]

Bush nevertheless decided to include Oppie on the top-secret panel, which met for five hours on September 19 before concluding unanimously that the evidence pointed to a Soviet atomic bomb, subsequently dubbed "Joe-1."[44]

The Russian bomb caught many unawares. Oppenheimer had just returned to his Princeton home, Olden Manor, from a week at Perro Caliente when the telephone rang with the summons from Bush.[45] On vacation in Martha's Vineyard, Lilienthal and his wife had been driving back from a dinner in Edgartown when they were startled to see an AEC official suddenly materialize out of the fog, standing by the side of the road. Huddled around a kerosene lamp at Lilienthal's summer home, drinking beer from an icebox, the two men discussed the Soviet bomb and "the whole box of trouble it portended," the AEC chairman wrote in his journal. After a night of little sleep, Lilienthal flew back to Washington early the next morning.

Even for those who had long predicted it, the Russian bomb came as something of a shock. Stopped at a traffic light on his way to Yosemite, Lawrence saw a banner newspaper headline heralding the monopoly's end. Just back from England, Teller learned at the end of a Pentagon briefing on tactical nuclear weapons what everyone else in the room already knew. Acting on impulse, he immediately telephoned Oppenheimer with a desperate query: "What should we do now?" Edward later remembered Oppie's sharp, almost scolding reply: "Keep your shirt on."[46]

But Teller's question was nonetheless the one that preoccupied most Americans—Oppenheimer included—in the days to come. Back in Washington, Lilienthal found Oppie "frantic, drawn" and Bacher "deeply worried" not only about the Russian bomb but by the American reaction.[47] Oppenheimer's hope that Truman might use the news to announce an end to "the miasma of secrecy" that enshrouded the subject of atomic energy had been quickly disappointed.[48]

Others looked to the president to take more tangible—and decisive—action.

Just a few weeks earlier, after much agonizing, Teller had finally decided to accept a teaching offer from UCLA.[49] The Soviet bomb now caused him to reconsider his plans. At a recent meeting on new weapons to be developed at Los Alamos, Teller had put the Super at the end of his list—a reluctant concession to the roadblocks in the device's design, and the persisting stalemate caused by insufficient computing power at the lab.[50] But the sudden end of America's atomic monopoly had him once again actively proselytizing for the Super by that fall.[51]

At Berkeley, chemist Wendell Latimer cornered Ernest Lawrence over lunch at the Faculty Club to talk about the Super. Like Teller, Latimer believed that the hydrogen bomb was the only logical response to Joe-1. Despite his earlier stand against the H-bomb, Lawrence's growing anxiety for the future—as well as a nostalgic remembrance of his role in the Manhattan Project—made him sympathetic to Latimer's appeal. (When, years earlier, Oppie told an MIT audience that physicists had "known sin" because of the atomic bomb, Ernest bristled at the suggestion; there was, he declared, no occasion on which physics had caused *him* to know sin.)[52]

Later that day, Alvarez and Lawrence discussed how they might lobby for the hydrogen bomb at an upcoming conference in Washington on radiological warfare. Receiving further encouragement in a telephone call from Teller, the two left Berkeley a day early in order to stop off at Los Alamos on their way east.

Arriving in the predawn hours of October 7, 1949, the duo received a briefing on the current state of thermonuclear research from Teller, Manley, and two physicist-mathematicians at the lab: George Gamow and Stan Ulam. Energized by Ernest's enthusiasm, Teller followed him and Alvarez back to the Albuquerque Hilton, where the trio talked into the early morning about the newly improved political prospects for the Super. In the room, Lawrence washed one of his new drip-dry shirts in the sink, showing Teller how it could be worn in the morning—a useful trick, he suggested, that would facilitate Edward's forthcoming role of H-bomb lobbyist.[53]

Teller endorsed Lawrence's plan to mobilize support in Washington for the construction of several new heavy-water reactors to produce tritium, since scarcity of that isotope looked to be one of the chief obstacles to the Super. "E.O.L and I said we would get going on that at once," Alvarez wrote in a diary he began keeping of the trip.[54]

At the Capitol, the Soviet bomb had created a mood receptive to the message being borne by Lawrence and Alvarez. In an "emergency" meeting of the Joint Committee on September 23, immediately following Truman's public announcement of Joe-1, Oppenheimer's genial assurance that there was no need for drastic action was simply ignored. Senator Eugene Millikin spoke ominously—if elliptically—of taking "therapeutic measures" against Russia in light of the new development. When Lilienthal faced the gauntlet a few days later, McMahon pointedly rejected what he characterized as the AEC chairman's "doctrine of 'enough bombs.'" "Why not all-out effort for super-weapon, with help of British?" Borden wrote in a note he passed to the senator.[55]

Ironically, those in uniform—to the extent that they knew anything of the H-bomb—remained surprisingly ambivalent about the Super.[56] By contrast, Joint Committee members, pointing to Joe-1 as evidence of America's sudden and glaring military weakness, ascribed near superhuman powers to the Russians. Staffers worried aloud that the Soviets, using captured Nazi scientists, might already have an arsenal of the ultimate weapon that Borden had anticipated in his apocalyptic book: a long-range rocket topped with a nuclear warhead.[57] In the atmosphere of crisis, the Super was presented as a quick way for the United States to recapture its lost hegemony.

During lunch that afternoon with the National Security Council's Souers, Strauss was surprised to learn that Truman evidently knew nothing about the H-bomb. Using Souers as his conduit—the two navy men had become friends during the war—Strauss sent the president a memo he had begun composing shortly after Truman's announcement.[58] It argued that the Soviet Union might already be ahead of the United States in the arms race.[59] Borrowing a term from physics, Strauss urged Truman to leapfrog the Russians with a *quantum jump*—a crash effort for the Super.

Alvarez and Lawrence arrived in Washington on Saturday afternoon, October 8. Not pausing to rest after the flight from New Mexico, the two took a taxi to the AEC building, where they received an encouraging reception from, among others, their former Berkeley colleague Kenneth Pitzer, who had meanwhile replaced Fisk as the commission's head of research. "Told them what we planned to do and got good response," wrote Alvarez in his impromptu diary.[60]

On Monday, the pair had lunch with McMahon and two Californians on the Joint Committee, Carl Hinshaw and William Knowland, who told them of plans to send a scouting party out to Los Alamos and Berkeley later in the month to gauge the prospects for the Super.[61] From Capitol Hill, Lawrence and Alvarez returned to AEC headquarters for a meeting with the commissioners. But the session with Lilienthal went badly. Invoking the "spirit of Groves," Lawrence tried to rally the AEC chairman behind the new reactors and the Super. Instead, Lilienthal wordlessly swiveled his chair and stared silently out the window.[62]

In New York that evening, the two saw Isidor Rabi at Columbia "and found him," Alvarez wrote, "very happy at our plans." Luie found particularly auspicious Rabi's parting comment: "It's certainly good to see the first team back in."[63]

But crowded skies thwarted their plans for enlisting the aid of America's allies. Ernest had hoped to persuade the Canadians to let him use their heavy-water pile at Chalk River to make tritium until Berkeley's new reactors were built. Unable to get seats on a flight to Ottawa, Alvarez returned to Berkeley while Lawrence flew back to Washington. McMahon had scheduled an executive session with the Joint Chiefs of Staff two days hence.

In a meeting the following afternoon with Nichols, who had meanwhile replaced Groves as head of the Armed Forces Special Weapons Project, Ernest added his voice to those urging the joint chiefs to declare a formal military requirement for the Super.[64] Nichols promised to pass Lawrence's message along to the air force's chief of staff and "no. 1 bomber man," General Hoyt Vandenberg. At the Joint Committee meeting on October 14, Vandenberg announced that the air force's view was that the superbomb should be rushed to completion as soon as possible.[65]

In the letter that McMahon sent to Lilienthal and the Pentagon later that month, the speculative thesis that Teller had raised the year before in "The Russian Atomic Plan" suddenly achieved the sober status of accepted fact: "As you know, there is reason to fear that Soviet Russia has assigned top priority to development of a thermo-nuclear super-bomb."[66]

While slow to coalesce, opposition to the superbomb was also forming. During the time that Lawrence and Alvarez had been making their rounds in Washington, Oppenheimer was in Cambridge, attending a meeting of the Harvard Board of Overseers with Conant. In private conversation, the quiet chemist had been surprisingly passionate in his denunciation of the H-bomb.

Back in Princeton on October 21, Oppenheimer received a briefing by Manley and Bradbury on the status of thermonuclear research. That afternoon he put his thoughts on superbombs in a letter to Conant.

Despite the fact that "two experienced promoters have been at work, i.e., Ernest Lawrence and Edward Teller," Oppenheimer wrote, his own view was that the technical problems plaguing the Super seemed no closer to resolution than they had in 1942: "I am not sure the miserable thing will work, nor that it can be gotten to a target except by ox cart." But this was not Oppie's greatest concern: "What does worry me is that this thing appears to have caught the imagination, both of congressional and of military people, as <u>the answer</u> to the problem posed by the Russian advance."[67]

There was little doubt by now where Lilienthal stood on the question of the superbomb. In his journal, the AEC chairman described Alvarez and Lawrence as "drooling with the prospect [of the Super] and 'bloodthirsty.'"[68] But Lilienthal also recognized that the issue required a formal, scientific airing. He and Oppenheimer had agreed to convene a special meeting of the General Advisory Committee shortly after hearing of Joe-1.[69] Lilienthal hoped for a broader inquiry than just whether to proceed with a crash effort for the Super; one that might answer the philosophical query: "Is this all we have to offer?"

Lilienthal also knew that several of those on the commission already agreed with him. In the meeting with Alvarez and Lawrence, only Strauss had spoken out unreservedly for proceeding with the hydrogen bomb. A relatively new commissioner, attorney Gordon Dean—Brien McMahon's former law partner—had seemed pensive and noncommittal. On the other hand, the man who had meanwhile replaced Bacher as the commission's only physicist, Princeton's Henry Smyth, was outraged at the Berkeley scientists' attempt at "short circuiting" the AEC by appealing directly to Congress. "Apart from being an expert in his field and a brilliant scientist," Smyth diplomatically reminded Borden in a note, Lawrence was "also something of a promoter; and that several times in the past he may have overstepped the line in pushing projects which add to his own 'Empire.'"[70]

Engaged at the moment in a frenetic cross-country drive to recruit scientists to work on the Super, Teller was encountering unexpected obstacles. Still hoping to persuade Bethe to join the effort, he had been in the Cornell physicist's office when the telephone rang with a call from Oppenheimer. Arriving at Princeton's Institute for Advanced Study the next day with Bethe in tow, Teller and Oppenheimer eyed each other like rival suitors, while the object of their attention sat silent between them.[71] Teller's indelible memory was of Oppenheimer quoting a phrase by Conant. The Super, Conant had said, would go forward "over my dead body."[72]

For Teller, as troubling as Conant's opposition or Bethe's silence was the uncertain attitude of Enrico Fermi, whose visit to Italy had forced a postponement of the GAC meeting on the Super. Seeing Fermi shortly after his return from Europe, Edward was disappointed to find his former colleague uninterested in talking about superbombs.[73] Unable to change Fermi's mind in the short time remaining—Teller was due back at Los Alamos for the Joint Committee's inspection tour—he telephoned Alvarez, who recorded the mixed results of the recruiting campaign in his diary: "[Teller] said he felt he could count on Bethe. Felt Oppie was lukewarm to our project, and Conant was definitely opposed."[74]

Because of Fermi's European trip, the special meeting of the General Advisory Committee was postponed until late October. Seaborg would not be a participant; not wishing to ruin his own chances for a future Nobel prize, he had refused to turn down an invitation to the awards ceremony in Sweden at month's end. Tipped off by Latimer to the mounting controversy over the Super, Seaborg drafted a letter for Oppenheimer to read to the committee. The missive's tortured syntax reflected its author's reluctance to offend either side in the coming debate.[75]

At Princeton, meanwhile, a steady stream of lobbyists and supplicants had begun arriving at Olden Manor. Upon the heels of Teller and Bethe came James McCormack, head of the AEC's Division of Military Application, various members of the Military Liaison Committee, and Robert LeBaron, the recently appointed Pentagon official responsible for atomic affairs.[76] (A vain and flamboyant figure, LeBaron claimed to trace his ancestry back to the Plymouth colony and boasted that he had studied atomic physics with Madame Curie at the Sorbonne. He had been recommended for the Pentagon post by Strauss.)[77]

But notably absent from the ranks of Oppie's visitors was Lawrence, who had on several occasions been only a short train ride away. Nor was the reason any mystery. Asked years later about the cause of the falling-out between him and Ernest, Oppie answered: "My brother and . . . a rather puzzled horror about the H-bomb were the origin."[78]

Instead, on October 27, Lawrence sent an emissary: Robert Serber.[79] ("Ernest thought I would get a more sympathetic hearing from Oppenheimer than Luie would.")[80] Oppie's shy friend and former student was a logical choice for a proxy, but a poor one. Taking Serber along on the train down to Washington for the meeting, Oppenheimer enumerated the arguments against the Super. Away from Lawrence and the hothouse atmosphere of the Rad Lab, Ernest's would-be advocate joined the ranks of H-bomb skeptics.[81]

Back in Berkeley, Lawrence had meanwhile scouted out a promising location for a half-dozen "Chinese copies" of the Chalk River reactor: Suisun Bay, north of San Francisco, near the little town of Benicia. He told Alvarez that with AEC funding the reactors "could probably be constructed starting immediately."[82] Impulsively, he anointed Luie the future director of the as-yet-unbuilt "Benicia Laboratory." ("I am therefore going on almost full time as director of a nonexistent laboratory on an unauthorized program," wrote the almost-giddy Alvarez.)[83] In anticipation of the move, Luie cleared out his desk at the Rad Lab and transferred his files to Lawrence's office on Cyclotron Hill.

On Friday afternoon, October 28, 1949, Oppenheimer convened the GAC's seventeenth meeting in the wood-paneled conference room on the AEC building's second floor, which looked out onto the Reflecting Pool in front of the Lincoln Memorial. Detained in Cambridge on Harvard business, Conant had sent word that he would not arrive until that evening.[84]

First to speak was George Kennan, the young Soviet expert whose lengthy telegrams from the Moscow embassy had become the intellectual foundation of the Truman administration's "containment" policy. Head of the State Department's policy planning staff, Kennan was in the course of preparing a seventy-nine-page treatise that, when it was finished in January, would cite Shakespeare and the Bible to explain the effect of superbombs upon the nation's relations with Russia.[85] Kennan spoke for almost an hour and was followed by Bethe, who, by contrast, gave a brief, concise, and highly technical account of where research stood on the Super.

Serber spoke next of Lawrence's plans for tritium-producing reactors.

Challenged by Fermi why Berkeley should spearhead the effort—of all the AEC-funded laboratories in the country, the Rad Lab was the only one without experience in reactors—Serber replied that Lawrence saw the need as so great that he was willing to divert the efforts of his boys to meet it. Smyth let it be known that he looked upon this latest evidence of Lawrence's selflessness with a gimlet eye.

Oppenheimer began Saturday morning's session by reading Seaborg's letter.[86] Lilienthal and the commissioners arrived shortly afterward. Worried by reports that the AEC was cool to the idea of the Benicia Laboratory, Alvarez had decided to make an eleventh-hour appearance at AEC headquarters but was able to get no farther than the lobby.[87] He remained there, like an island in the torrent, as the joint chiefs and others summoned by Oppenheimer hurried past.

By acclamation, the committee decided to focus the next two days upon the Super. Disillusioned by the brevity and shallowness of previous GAC meetings, Conant had suggested holding "the equivalent of hearings . . . bringing in as witnesses people as far down the line as we like."[88] Oppenheimer agreed, promising committee members "an opportunity to come to grips with some questions which long have eluded us."[89]

Speaking for the military, the joint chiefs' chairman, General Omar Bradley of the army—"very G.A.R.-ish, countryman's accents," noted Lilienthal—surprised all by arguing that the Super's principal value might be chiefly "psychological."[90] ("A useful thing to have around the house," Lilienthal wrote contemptuously.) General Lauris Norstad, head of air force planning, echoed Bradley's point but had no answer to Lilienthal's question: why not simply increase atomic bomb production instead of building a fearsome new weapon?

Still stuck in the lobby, Alvarez was reduced to searching people's faces for clues to what was going on upstairs. Shortly after noon, he caught Oppenheimer's eye as Oppie and Serber paraded past. During lunch at a nearby restaurant, Alvarez was surprised to hear Oppenheimer argue that the Russians might follow suit if the United States decided not to develop the Super. The last time he could remember discussing the Super with Oppie, in 1943, Oppenheimer had held out the prospect of work on the H-bomb as an inducement to come to Los Alamos.

Realizing that the Benicia Laboratory was doomed if, as it appeared, Oppenheimer and the GAC decided to oppose the Super, Alvarez did not bother to return to his vigil in the lobby but instead booked a flight home. Back in Berkeley, he made a final entry in his diary: "Particularly interesting talk with Oppie. . . . Pretty foggy thinking."

At the AEC conference room on Saturday afternoon, the mood of the meeting subtly began to change.[91] Rabi and Fermi had come to Washington believing that a decision to proceed with the Super was probably foreordained, if only for reasons of domestic politics. But a quiet protest by Hartley Rowe, an engineer who had been at wartime Los Alamos—"We built one Frankenstein," Rowe muttered—sparked a contentious and unexpected debate over the morality of the Super.

When Strauss spoke up to remind the group that the decision on the Super would not be made by popular vote, Conant—"looking almost translucent, so gray," Lilienthal thought—replied that Strauss had missed the point, since "whether it will stick depends on how the country views the moral issue." As for his own views, Conant left no doubt. "This whole discussion makes me feel I was seeing the same film, and a punk one, for a second time," he announced to the meeting.

The intensity of Conant's convictions began to sway the skeptics, Rabi and Fermi included. Although practical objections were also raised—the scientists thought the chances better than even that a successful Super could be built within five years—it was the ethical argument that held sway. When the meeting adjourned that evening, its participants broke into small groups to draft their recommendations. Oppenheimer and Manley agreed to write the overall report. With DuBridge's help, Conant crafted the portion that dealt specifically with the Super. Believing that a recommendation simply not to proceed would be ignored, Rabi and Fermi searched for a more practical approach. Their hope, Fermi said later, was "to outlaw the thing before it was born."[92]

Early on Sunday morning, October 30, Oppenheimer reconvened the GAC and the various drafts were read aloud. Lilienthal, joining the discussion, was surprised to discover that the committee, which he had thought evenly split on the crash effort the night before, now seemed uniformly opposed to the Super. The AEC chairman returned to his office shaken, canceling a previously scheduled trip to the Midwest: "Some terrible and deeply important things to work out in my mind," he wrote in his journal.[93]

Others in the room also noticed the change of mood. Attorney Gordon Dean thought the language used by GAC members surprisingly emotional, evoking "visceral reactions."[94] Even the normally inscrutable Fermi seemed curiously "worked up," Manley recollected.[95] *Genocide,* a relatively new word, appeared twice in the drafts.

After lunch, the committee set about finalizing its report; by three o'clock the task was done. Conant's summary reflected the passion that had flared in the conference room on Saturday afternoon:

> We believe a super bomb should never be produced. Mankind would be far better off not to have a demonstration of the feasibil-

> ity of such a weapon, until the present climate of world opinion changes. . . . In determining not to proceed to develop the super bomb, we see a unique opportunity of providing by example some limitations on the totality of war and thus of limiting the fear and arousing the hopes of mankind.

DuBridge, Rowe, Cyril Smith, and Bell Laboratories president Oliver Buckley added their signatures to what the committee considered its "majority report."

Standing apart from Conant's draft was a single-page letter written by Rabi and Fermi, titled "An Opinion on the Development of the 'super.'" Arguing that any decision on the H-bomb had to be linked to national policy, the two denounced the Super in moral terms even stronger than those used by Conant. "It is clear," they wrote, "that the use of such a weapon cannot be justified on any ethical ground which gives a human being a certain individuality and dignity even if he happens to be a resident of an enemy country."

Going on to describe the hydrogen bomb as "necessarily an evil thing considered in any light," Rabi and Fermi proposed what they hoped would be seen as a workable alternative between a crash program and outright renunciation: a promise not to go ahead with superbombs provided other nations exercised similar restraint. Key to the plan was their faith that the tests necessary to the development of an H-bomb would be detectable "by available physical means"—that is, the same technology that had tipped the United States off to Joe-1. Privately, Lilienthal deemed it a "rather thin proposal."[96]

Before adjourning, Oppenheimer offered each member an opportunity to express a final, personal view. Only then did he thank his colleagues, admitting that he would have felt compelled to resign from the GAC had they not rejected the all-out approach to proceed with the Super.[97] Offering to affix his signature to either Conant's draft or the letter by Rabi and Fermi, Oppie finally signed only the so-called majority report, with its unequivocal rejection of the Super.[98] Evidently forgotten was his earlier admission to Conant that it would be "folly" to oppose the new weapon.

The summary that Oppenheimer and Manley prepared for Lilienthal endorsed the increase in neutron production to the 1-gram-a-day level that Lawrence had sought. But the extra neutrons were to be used to make radiological agents, plutonium for atomic bombs, and the Booster, not tritium for the Super. Almost as an afterthought, the GAC also recommended that any new reactors be built at Argonne, not Berkeley. Thus did Lawrence's dream of the Benicia Laboratory evaporate, as Alvarez had feared.

Late that afternoon, Oppenheimer returned to the AEC building to see Lilienthal once more before catching the train back to Princeton. His concern, Oppie told Manley, was that the AEC chairman no longer had the "drive, stamina and courage left to get enthused about the matter of the super-bomb and carry it through."[99] Although the Hickenlooper hearings had ended two weeks earlier with Lilienthal's exoneration, the effects of the ordeal obviously lingered. Moreover, the showdown over the Super could not be postponed: McMahon was scheduled to meet with the commissioners the following afternoon, Monday, October 31.

For Oppenheimer, the three-day meeting had been a heady time, reminiscent of the optimism that followed the Acheson-Lilienthal report. Back at Princeton, he wrote Niels Bohr: "In fact, it would not seem to me out of the question that great and hopeful changes could occur within the next months."[100]

But Kay Russell, Oppie's secretary at the GAC, had a more realistic view when she handed the majority report back to Oppenheimer for signing. "This will cause you a lot of trouble," she predicted.[101]

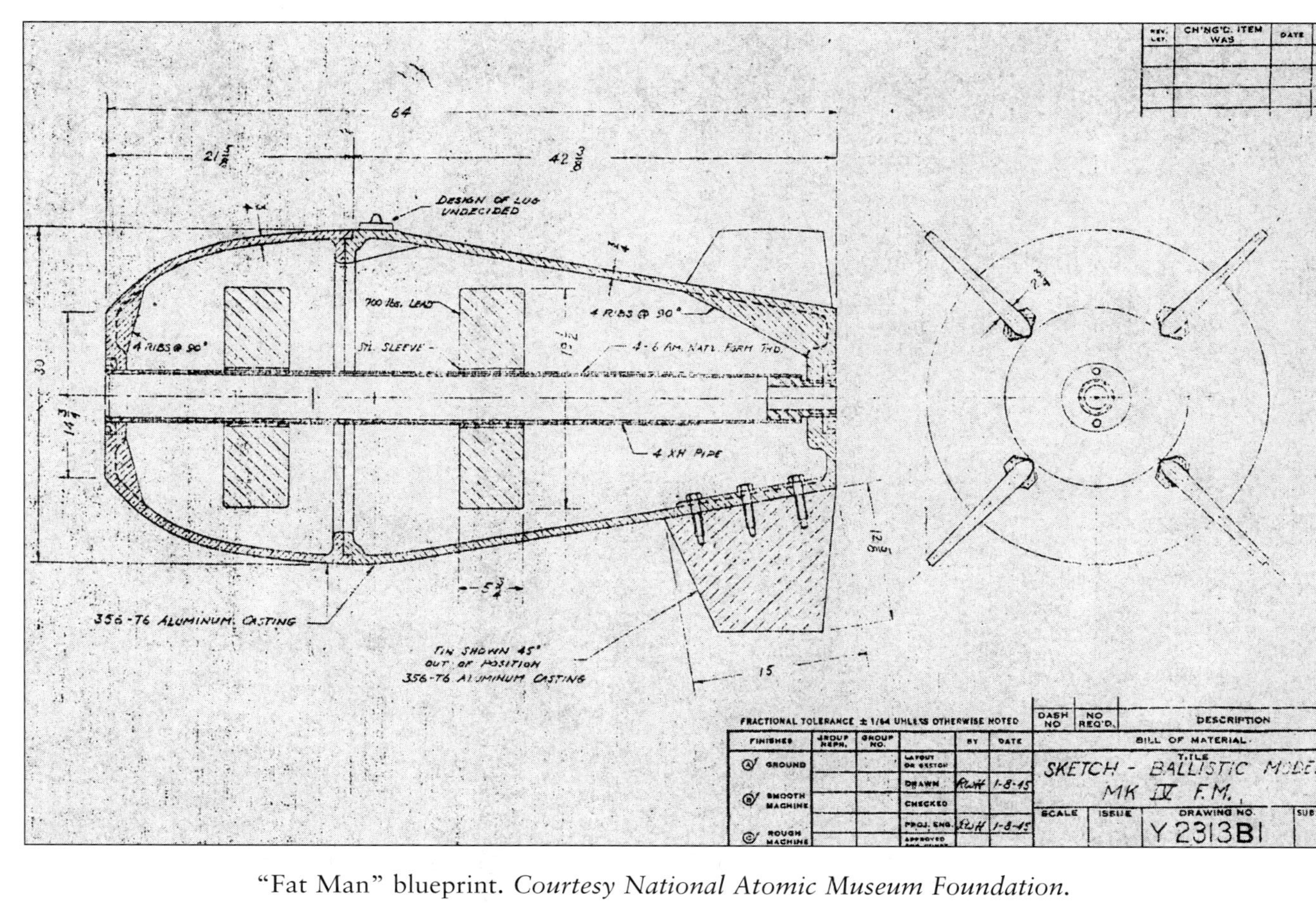

"Fat Man" blueprint. *Courtesy National Atomic Museum Foundation.*

Robert Oppenheimer at twenty-two. An "overgrown choirboy . . . both subtly wise and terribly innocent." *Courtesy Judith Oppenheimer.*

Ernest Orlando Lawrence holding the first cyclotron. By sheer force of personality more than by any power of intellect, Lawrence was a commanding presence at Berkeley by the early 1930s. *Courtesy Lawrence Berkeley National Laboratory.*

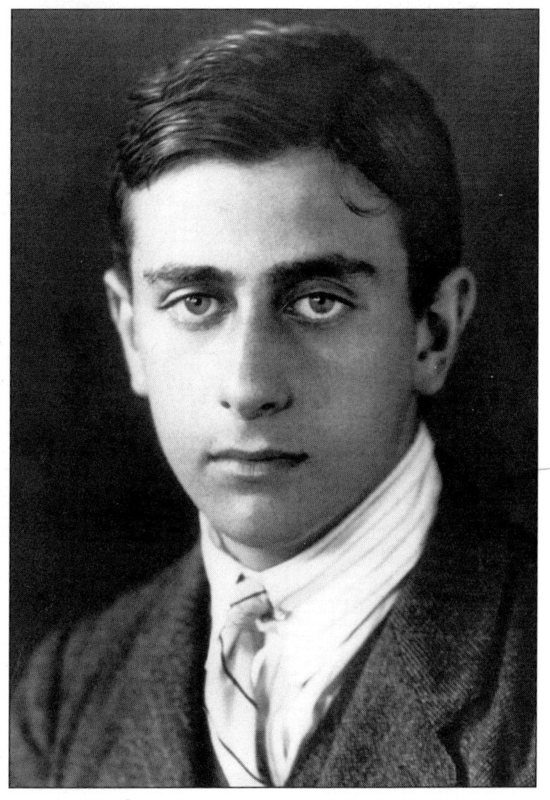

Edward Teller at age seventeen. "I reached adolescence still a serious child with no sense of humor." *Courtesy Edward Teller and Judith Shoolery.*

Robert and Frank Oppenheimer, 1918. Oppie grew unusually protective of his younger brother—"in some ways perhaps part of a father to him." *Courtesy Judith Oppenheimer.*

Richard and Ruth Tolman, 1941. Oppenheimer reportedly first earned Lawrence's disapproval when he seduced the wife of Professor Tolman at Caltech. *Courtesy Judith Oppenheimer.*

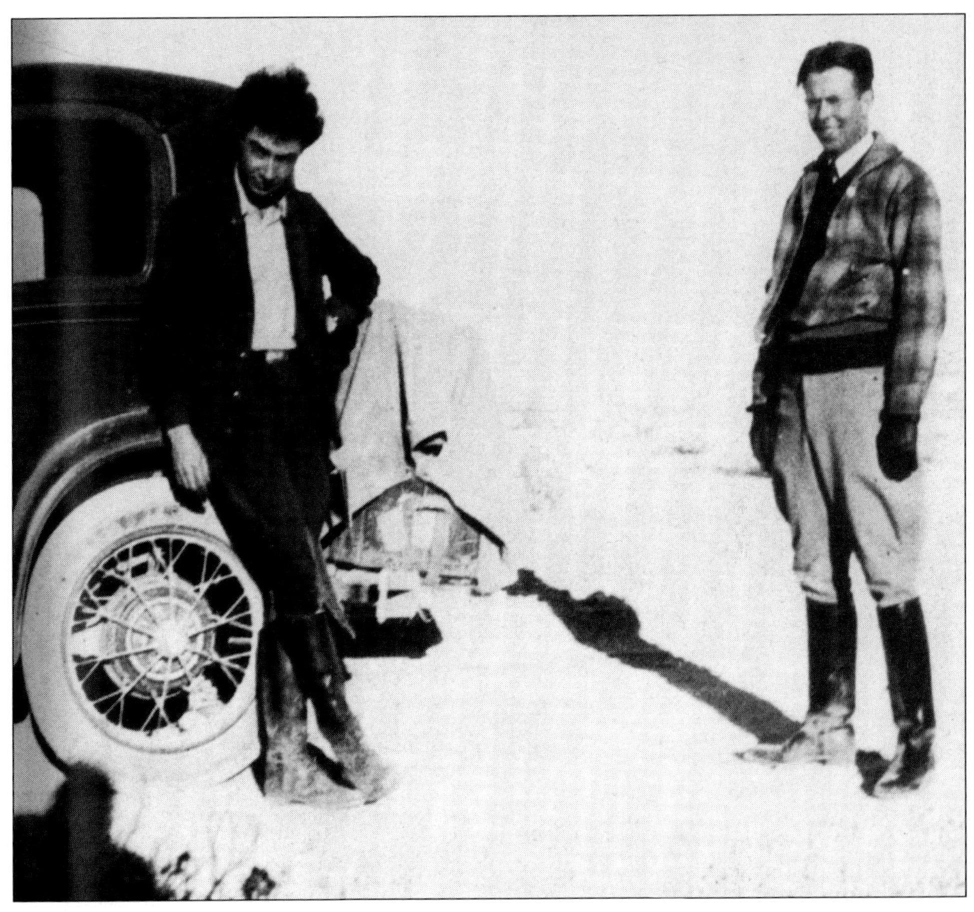

Oppenheimer thought Lawrence's riding outfit a curious affectation—not realizing it was Lawrence's way of distancing himself from his roots. *Courtesy Molly Lawrence.*

Lawrence and the Rad Lab staff with the sixty-inch cyclotron, 1939. *Courtesy Lawrence Berkeley National Laboratory.*

The great cyclotron was to be transformed while still in the womb into a weapon of war. *Courtesy Lawrence Berkeley National Laboratory.*

Lawrence in the control room. Starting the machine was sometimes accompanied by an "ensuing sparking, crash, and blowing out of lights," recalled one cyclotroneer. *Courtesy Lawrence Berkeley National Laboratory.*

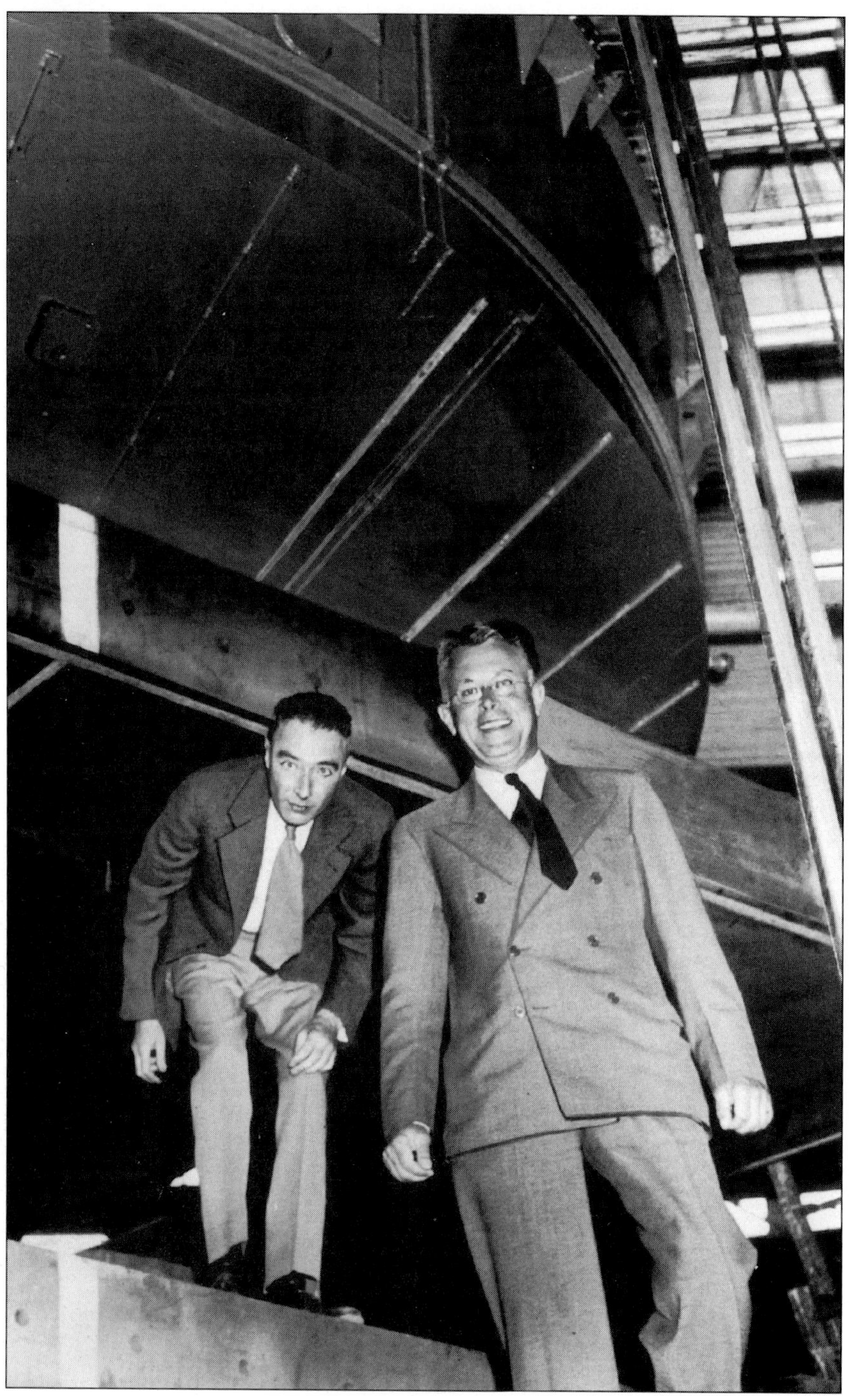

Oppenheimer and Lawrence at the cyclotron. "I can only think that perhaps when they were such really good friends, maybe they never really understood each other," observed one of Lawrence's "boys." *Courtesy Lawrence Livermore National Laboratory.*

Joe Weinberg, Rossi Lomanitz, David Bohm, and Max Friedman on the Berkeley campus, 1943. *Courtesy National Archives.*

Gregori Kasparov, Martin Kamen, and Gregori Kheifets outside Bernstein's Fish Grotto, July 1944. *Courtesy National Archives.*

Haakon Chevalier at Berkeley, 1934. "I certainly don't intend to resign myself to remaining a bystander," he wrote his son, Jacques, during the war. *Courtesy Bancroft Library, University of California.*

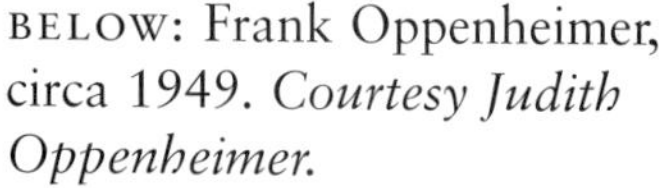

BELOW: Frank Oppenheimer, circa 1949. *Courtesy Judith Oppenheimer.*

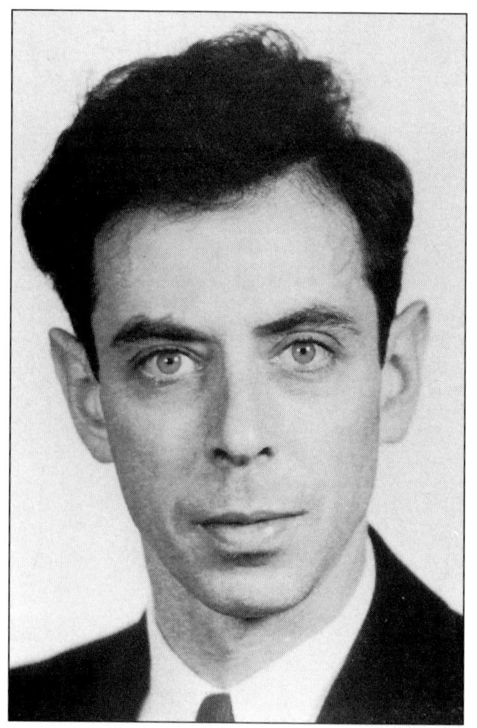

ABOVE: Louise Bransten appearing before HUAC, September 1948. San Francisco's so-called apricot heiress was known as the "Bernstein woman" to Steve Nelson and by the code name "Map" to her Soviet control officer. *Courtesy AP/Wide World Photos.*

ABOVE LEFT: Klaus Fuchs, Los Alamos badge, 1944. At Los Alamos, project officials were still innocent of the fact that the nation's real atomic secrets were being driven out the front gate in Fuchs's blue Buick. *Courtesy Los Alamos National Library.*

ABOVE RIGHT: Wartime army counterintelligence headquarters in Oakland, California. *Courtesy Lyall Johnson.*

BELOW: In March 1948, Klaus Fuchs, meeting with his Soviet control in a London pub, passed along an advanced design for the Super. *Courtesy Joseph Albright and Marcia Kunstel.*

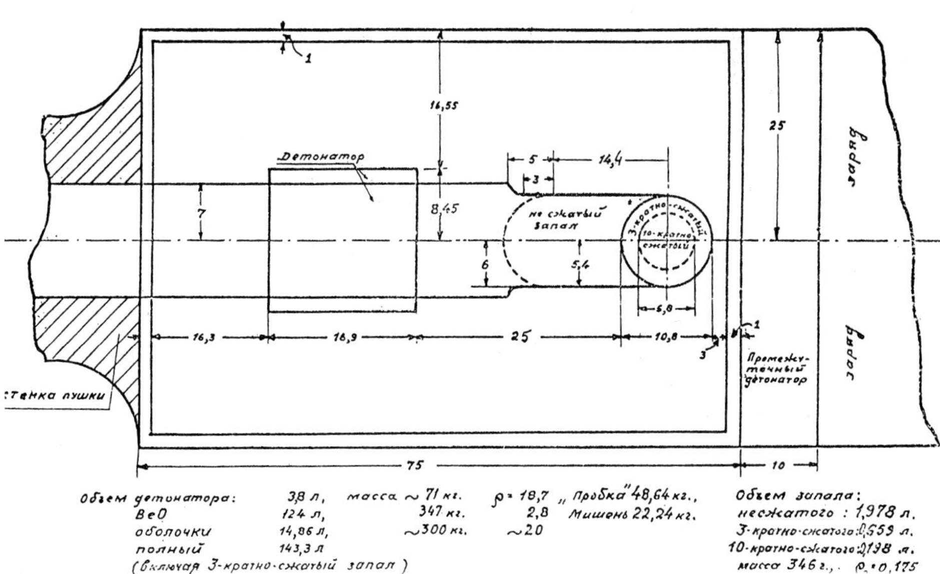

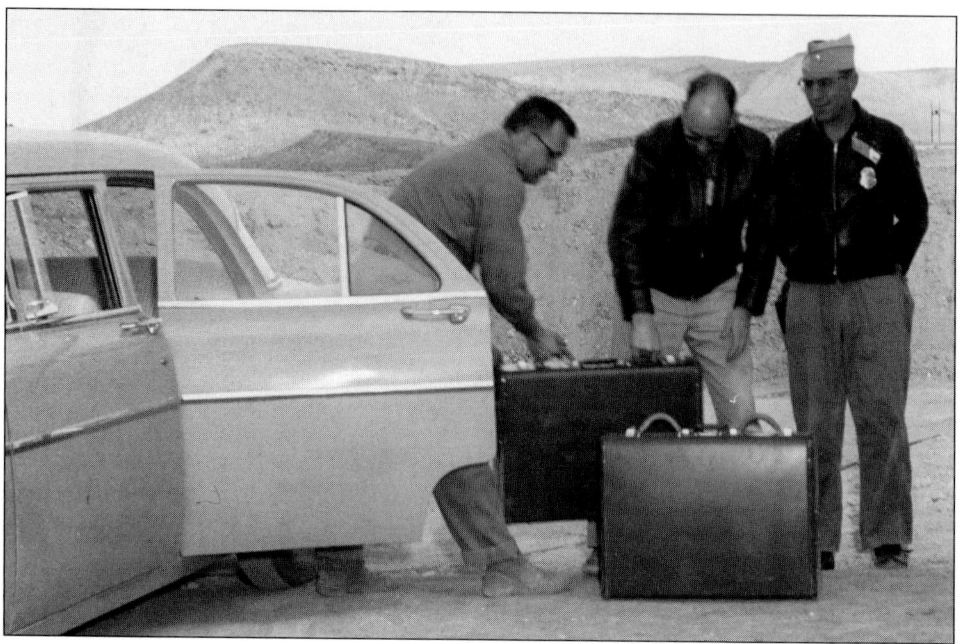

Preparing for "Tesla," 1955. While Los Alamos researchers had traditionally transported their devices on an army flatbed truck, Livermore bomb designers drove to the shot tower in a late-model sedan, their bomb—crammed into a pair of heavily reinforced Samsonite suitcases—sitting in the backseat. *Courtesy Lawrence Livermore National Laboratory.*

Teller at the Pacific test site for "George," May 1951. Eniwetok, he predicted, would not be big enough for his next bomb. *Courtesy Lawrence Livermore National Laboratory.*

Aftermath of "Ruth," Livermore's first nuclear test, 1953. Los Alamos weaponeers suggested that next time their rivals use either a bigger bomb or a smaller tower. *Courtesy Lawrence Livermore National Laboratory.*

Lawrence and the Bevatron, 1957. "His fears that he was being, or might be, undermined in his position were a terror for him," Oppenheimer observed. *Courtesy Lawrence Livermore National Laboratory.*

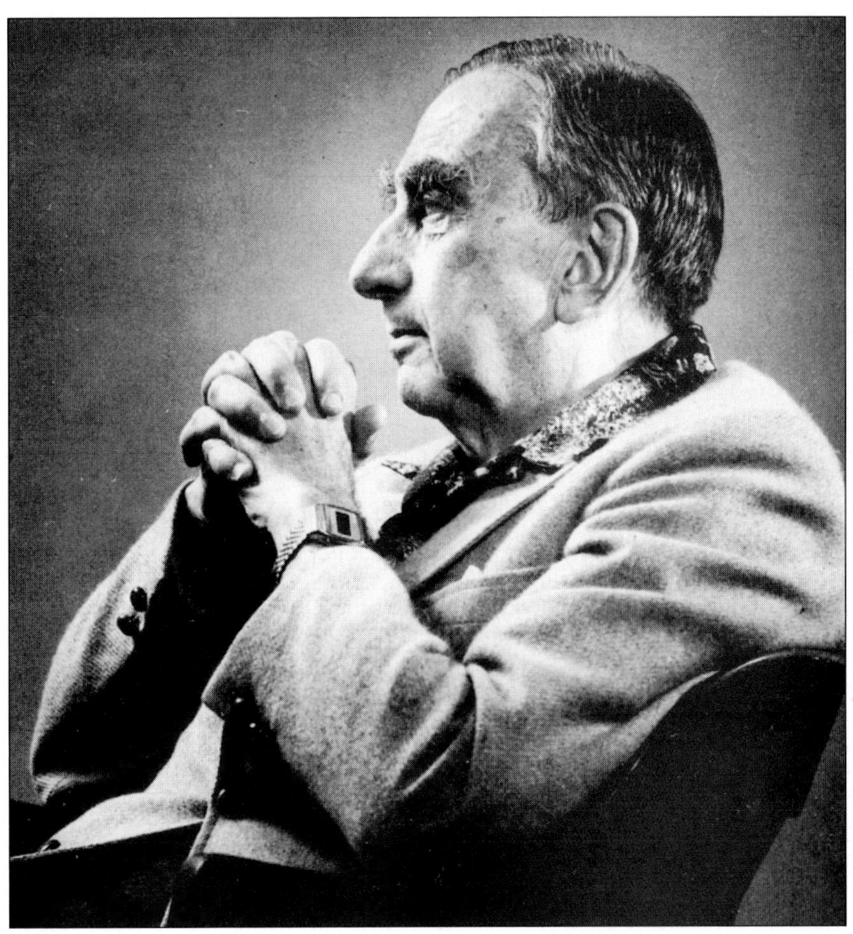

Edward Teller, 1983. He wrote to Bethe: "I would say that physicists have known power." *Courtesy Los Alamos National Laboratory.*

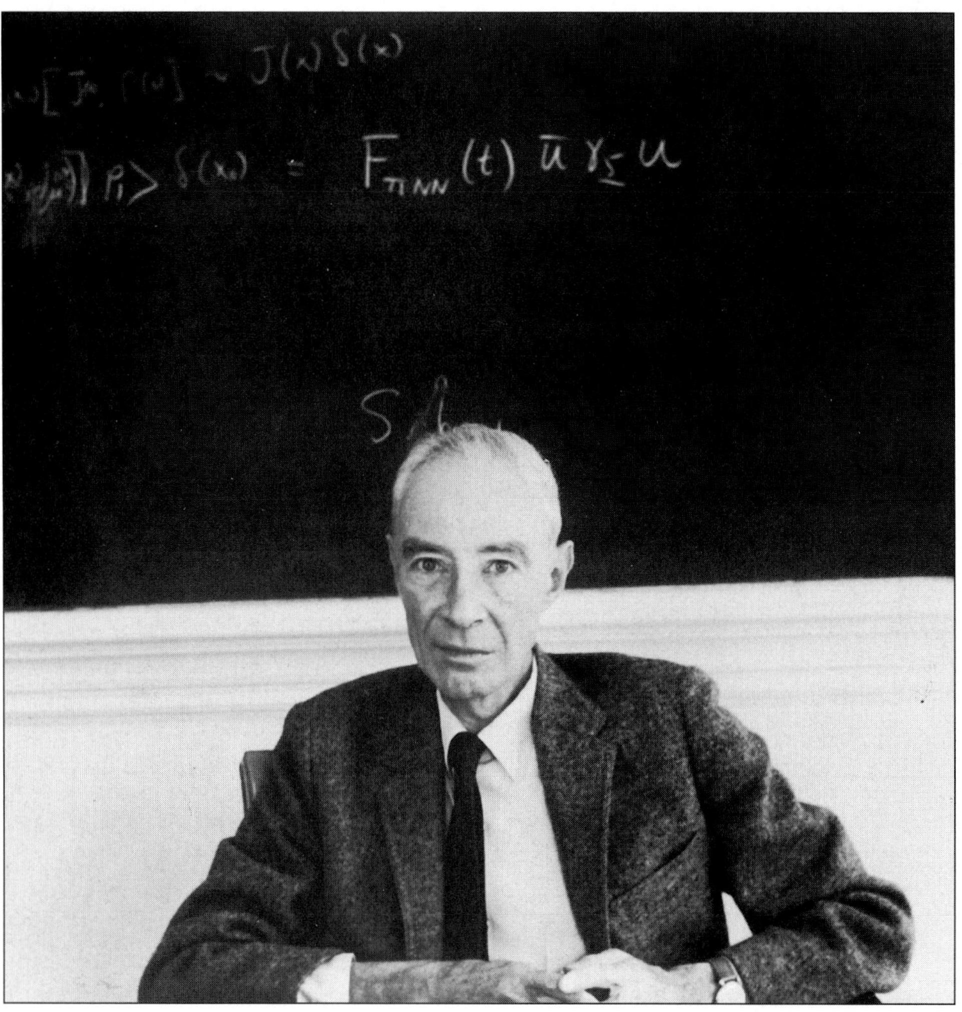

Robert Oppenheimer at Princeton, 1966. "In the forest, in battle, in the midst of arrows, javelins, fire / Out on the great sea, at the precipice's edge in the mountains / In sleep, in delirium, in deep trouble / The good deeds a man has done before defend him." *Courtesy Robert Oppenheimer papers, Library of Congress.*

12

A DESPERATE URGENCY HERE

REACTION TO THE General Advisory Committee's report was not long in coming. Manley recalled a "rather violent discussion" between Lilienthal, the scientists, and McMahon on Monday evening, Halloween. "What [McMahon] is talking is the inevitability of war with the Russians, and what he says adds up to one thing: blow them off the face of the earth, quick, before they do the same to us—and we haven't much time," Lilienthal wrote in his journal afterward.[1] The senator dashed off a letter to Truman the next day, asking for a personal meeting.[2]

On Tuesday morning, November 1, Lilienthal and a somber and reflective Acheson discussed the GAC report on a flight to South Bend, Indiana. When he had first learned of the Super, in 1946, the weapon had seemed but a remote prospect, Acheson said. Now it seemed that the Russians, too, would probably have it in time, unless superweapons were banned.[3] "What a depressing world it is," Acheson reflected.

The secretary of state had asked Lilienthal for the names of people to consult on the Super.[4] But Acheson already had a list in mind. At its top, not surprisingly, was Oppenheimer.

Yet Acheson remained unpersuaded by Oppenheimer's logic when they discussed the GAC report a few days later. "You know, I listened as carefully as I knew how," he told aide Gordon Arneson, "but I don't understand what Oppie was trying to say. How can you persuade a paranoid adversary to disarm 'by example?'"[5]

Teller had headed east from Los Alamos almost immediately after the

GAC meeting. Stopping off in Chicago, he found Fermi unwilling to discuss the report in detail but coyly hinting at its contents. ("You and I and Truman and Stalin would be happy if further great developments were impossible. So, why do we not make an agreement to refrain from such development?" Fermi asked rhetorically.)[6] Edward wrote Maria Mayer that he had been "thoroughly frightened" by what Fermi disclosed, and barely able to control his anger: "Enrico does not know what I think of him. But—unfortunately—he has an inkling."

Going on to Washington, Teller learned more about the GAC report from McMahon. ("It makes me sick," said the senator, succinctly.) "What I saw in Washington makes it quite clear that there are big forces working for compromise and delay," Teller wrote Mayer on the flight back to New Mexico. For the first time, he asked her to burn the letter after she had read it.

Back at the lab, Manley showed Teller the majority report and the letter written by Rabi and Fermi.[7] At first morose and silent—"*very* unusual," Manley noted—Teller offered a bet that he would be a prisoner of the Russians within five years if the United States decided not to proceed with the Super.[8]

Strauss, too, had been uncharacteristically quiet during the long meeting on October 30—interrupting only once to ask, incredulously, whether the scientists actually meant to abandon work on the Super even if the Soviets declared they would not go along. Oppie refused to be baited by Strauss's hypothetical question, answering only that he believed the Russians would not decline.[9]

Back at Berkeley, Serber had naively tried to put a positive face on the GAC's recommendations in his own report to Lawrence. "Oh, Bob, don't be a damn fool!" Ernest erupted impatiently.[10] Alvarez, having meanwhile learned that Oppenheimer had indeed prevailed at the GAC, unceremoniously moved his files back to his old office.[11]

Except for Lilienthal and Strauss, the commissioners seemed unwilling or unable to take a clear stand on the Super. Such indecisiveness was a growing frustration to the AEC chairman, who noted in his journal—with concern—that his own opposition to the weapon "has not proven contagious."[12]

Sumner Pike still waffled at an AEC meeting on November 3. Henry Smyth, while opposed to a crash effort, worried that any decision taken in the current international climate might prove irreversible.[13] Gordon Dean favored a lawyerly approach—a secret diplomatic overture to the Soviets, offering to renounce the Super if the Russians followed suit. Should the Soviets refuse, Dean argued, the road would then be clear for the all-out effort.

Matters were no closer to resolution four days later, when Lilienthal brought the commissioners together with GAC members who were still in town. Conant, Manley wrote admiringly, had not lost the courage of his convictions—"giving it straight from the shoulder to the Commission, not only including his views on the action that they should take but also the remark that if ever there was a point to a civilian commission this was now the one." But Manley feared that the Harvard president's lecture had little impact: "I think that this point that he made was rather lost."[14]

Strauss, on his way to Los Angeles to give a speech, missed the November 7 commission meeting. But the following morning, McMahon—en route between Los Alamos and Hanford, on the Joint Committee's inspection trip—stopped by Strauss's suite at the Beverley Hills Hotel with the welcome news that Dean was wavering on the Super. In a telephone call, the two urged McMahon's former law partner not to yield to pressure from Lilienthal and Oppenheimer.[15]

The H-bomb lobby was becoming a cabal.

For Strauss, opposition to the Super was less a case of mistaken judgment than a crime. Nor was he alone in believing that there was a campaign under way to sabotage the hydrogen bomb. Teller thought it suspicious that a second Los Alamos conference on the superbomb, planned for early November, had been suddenly canceled on October 31 by Bradbury, citing "scheduling complications."[16] The final straw was when Bethe had telephoned to say that he would not be coming to Los Alamos after all.[17]

But Strauss was also privy to a secret that few others in the government knew: the FBI had recent, firm evidence that Soviet agents had penetrated the Manhattan Project.[18]

Some two weeks before the GAC meeting, Strauss had learned from Charles Bates, the FBI agent whom Hoover had assigned as liaison with the AEC, that decrypted Soviet messages revealed the presence of a spy at wartime Los Alamos.[19] Bates informed Strauss and AEC security chief John Gingrich that "Bureau Source 5" pointed to British physicist Klaus Fuchs.[20] Bates added that there was also reason to believe other atomic spies had been operating at the lab, and that secrets of the superbomb had probably been compromised as well.[21]

Without notifying the other commissioners, Strauss had immediately launched his own clandestine campaign to unmask the next spy—or, failing that, to find a scapegoat.

On October 13, 1949, Strauss had telephoned Groves with questions about the British mission at Los Alamos. Following an hour-long meeting with Hoover a few days later, Strauss called Groves again, asking for more details. His queries this time concerned not only British scientists at the lab but some American ones as well—specifically, Frank and Robert Oppenheimer.

Thus alerted that an espionage investigation was under way, Groves wrote a letter to Strauss on November 4 that was an apologia for not having acted on what he knew about the Chevalier incident at the time: "It is true that Robert was very reluctant to disclose the details of the Frank-Haakon situation and I am not sure whether we ever did learn the whole truth about it all. It was finally revealed to me under conditions which made it impossible to do much and it was very difficult to tell just how much Frank was involved and how much Robert was involved."

"Summing it up," Groves wrote, "I believe that it is quite clear that Frank was sponsored, protected and otherwise looked out for by Robert and that this was done knowing full well the background and (at least previous) sympathies of Frank and, particularly of Frank's wife (Jackie)."[22]

Strauss did not tell Groves what he intended to do with the information on the Oppenheimers. But he had already obtained from Nichols a copy of the letter that Oppie's Scientific Panel had sent to Wallace in September 1945—in which panel members had stated that they would rather see the United States defeated in war than victorious at the cost of using superbombs. When Strauss wrote back to Nichols a few weeks later, asking next for a copy of Szilard's petition to Truman, it was clear that the noose was tightening: "Do you suppose your files could locate that document? I would be interested to see who signed it and the nature of the arguments advanced."[23]

Unable to make a unanimous recommendation to the president, the commissioners finally decided to put their separate views in writing. Lilienthal delivered the letters to the White House on November 9. The vote was 3 to 2 against proceeding with the Super. Lilienthal, Pike, and Smyth opposed an H-bomb program, whereas Dean and Strauss were in favor. As all were aware, however, Lilienthal was already a lame duck. Two days earlier, he had announced to Truman that he planned to step down from the chairman's job at year's end but was willing to wait until the question of the superbomb was settled.

Puzzled by the commissioners' conflicting views, the president asked Souers to reconvene a special NSC committee—consisting of Lilienthal, Johnson, and Acheson, its chairman—which had earlier advised him on the production of fissionable material.[24]

Sensing that the tide was beginning to turn in his favor, Teller, ebullient, wrote to Mayer that the current situation reminded him of the earlier debate on whether to proceed with the atomic bomb: "I wonder to how many people it happens that they are set back where they have been before and that they get a second chance. . . . But this time I love the job I am going to do—I shall even love to fight if it must be."[25]

McMahon's resolve, too, had stiffened when he learned from a Los Alamos briefing by Manley that an "orderly, step-by-step" program at the lab might not deliver an H-bomb until 1960. Lawrence had previously told the senator that a crash effort could succeed in as little as two years.[26] Teller, on the other hand, was warning the Joint Committee's Henry Jackson that the Russians might test a Super sometime in the next eighteen months.[27]

Borden spent three days drafting an argument that he and McMahon hoped would prove persuasive to Truman. McMahon sent the result, a letter almost 5,000 words long, to the president on November 21. "The profundity of the atomic crisis which has now overtaken us cannot, in my judgment, be exaggerated," it began. Using language reminiscent of the Incendiary Document and *There Will Be No Time,* the letter's conclusion was suitably apocalyptic: "if we let Russia get the super first, catastrophe becomes all but certain—whereas, if we get it first, there exists a chance of saving ourselves."[28]

Four days later, Strauss sent Truman his own, briefer but still emotional rejoinder to the GAC. "A government of atheists is not likely to be dissuaded from producing the weapon on 'moral' grounds," he argued.[29] Goaded by Nichols and Borden, the joint chiefs, too, had finally weighed in, adding their voices to the growing chorus. The country "would be in an intolerable position if a possible enemy possessed the [Super] and the United States did not," Bradley wrote.[30]

During the next six weeks, McMahon and Borden would send three more letters to the White House—two in one day. Lilienthal had warned the president of a possible 'blitz' on the Super. "I don't blitz easily," Truman replied with a grin.

But the president had not expected this concerted a campaign, and it was also clear that a choice could not be postponed much longer. Following a gaffe by Colorado senator Edwin Johnson, a Joint Committee member—Johnson mentioned in a television interview that the United States was working on a superweapon 1,000 times more powerful than the bomb that had destroyed Hiroshima—McMahon began urging Truman to make his decision soon, and to make it public.[31]

Returning to Washington after the holiday recess, McMahon brought the Joint Committee together on January 9, 1950. Reading the GAC report aloud amid interruptions—"Let me get through this if you don't mind,"

he snapped at one point—McMahon could not refrain from adding his own editorial comments. On the hope that the Russians might renounce the Super, he hooted: "That is certainly a joke. Suppose they did? Who the hell would believe them?"[32]

His meeting with the president had left the impression, McMahon told his colleagues, that "Missouri common sense" would compel Truman to go ahead with the H-bomb. ("Brien, it is not an easy thing to order the development of a weapon that will kill ten million people," the president had told him, McMahon said. His rejoinder had been: "You know damn well that [the Russians] are busy at it right now.")

Strauss, too, was pressing hard for a positive verdict. In a telephone call to Souers, he noted that three months had passed since Acheson's committee had been given its task. "It may be later than we think," Strauss warned.[33]

Since the October GAC meeting, the initiative had plainly passed to the H-bomb's proponents. In a meeting that January between the commission and the Joint Committee, Strauss read his latest letter to Truman amid congratulatory murmurs while Lilienthal sat glum and silent in the background.[34] Not a single commissioner spoke up to defend the scientists' position.[35] Hoping to persuade the Joint Committee to send its own unanimous but unbidden endorsement of the Super to the White House, McMahon scheduled a meeting for January 30 to discuss the issue.

Unexpectedly, Oppenheimer, in town for another GAC meeting, also attended the session. ("I thought it would be cowardly for me not to come up here and let you disagree and raise questions where you thought we had missed the boat," he told the committee.)[36] Asked by a congressman if a war fought with superbombs might make the planet uninhabitable—"Pestiferous, you mean?" Oppie interjected—the physicist said that he was actually more worried about the species's "moral survival."

As Oppenheimer probably realized, his was an effort to sweep back the tide. Just the day before, encountering Teller at a meeting of the American Physical Society in New York, Oppie had conceded that it looked as though his and the GAC's advice would be ignored. When Teller asked if Oppenheimer would then be willing to work on the Super, the answer had been a prompt and unqualified "No."[37]

Acheson—grumbling that he had grown "impatient with obscure argument"—scheduled a final meeting of his NSC committee for January 31.[38] The secretary of state not only held the tie-breaking vote on the committee but also wielded the most influence with Truman. Acheson had at one point toyed with the idea of proposing a two-year "vacation" on the Super—"bilateral if possible, unilateral if necessary"—during which time Washington would make a new effort to ease international tensions. But he had come to the conclusion that such a moratorium would be impossible for domestic politic reasons. He did not see, Acheson had bluntly told Oppenheimer, "how any president could survive a policy of not making the H-bomb."[39]

Frustrations that had welled up for more than a year spilled out at the meeting in Souers's office on the morning of January 31. The Super was "straight gadget-making," Lilienthal objected.[40] But his protest was largely pro forma, as he himself likely recognized. Acheson had already drafted a recommendation for Truman that would direct the AEC "to proceed to determine the technical feasibility of a thermonuclear weapon." Johnson successfully lobbied to have the statement amended to allow the mass production of H-bombs once the weapon's feasibility had been determined. In a desperate rearguard move, Lilienthal argued that any decision should be delayed until after a State Department policy review ordered by Acheson had been completed.[41] But that, too, was rejected. At a little past noon, the three, accompanied by Souers and another presidential aide, trooped across the street to the White House with Acheson's draft in hand.

Lilienthal had barely begun to recite his arguments in the Oval Office when Truman abruptly cut him off, announcing that he intended to go ahead with the Super. Because of the way the Russians were behaving, the president said, he had no other choice. Outside the door, Lilienthal checked his watch; the meeting with Truman had lasted only seven minutes. It was, he wrote later that day in his journal, like saying "'No' to a steamroller."[42]

That afternoon, Lilienthal informed Oppenheimer and the GAC of Truman's choice, and also advised them that they were forbidden from making any public comment on the decision: "It was like a funeral party—especially when I said we were all gagged."[43] Adding to the sense of gloom was the realization that it was now too late to make the personal appeal to the president that Oppie and Lilienthal had once discussed. Bitter talk of a mass resignation was scotched by the AEC chairman, who himself only had a few weeks left in the government.

The president's decision made the Joint Committee's meeting late that day "somewhat academic," McMahon conceded. Asked his opinion of what the next step should be on the Super, Strauss was quick to answer: "I would give it the maximum expedition, Senator."[44]

Truman's radio address that evening brought an end to what Oppenheimer would later call "our large and ill-managed bout with the Super." But doubts lingered—even among those who supported the president's decision.[45] "You know, we make these weapons so that we may never use them," Gordon Arneson remembered a "very solemn" Acheson telling him. Yet Arneson sensed a note of uncertainty in the secretary of state's voice.[46]

For Strauss, on the other hand, Truman's decision was a long-sought-for vindication. Since the AEC's creation, the commissioners had failed to reach unanimity only a dozen times. On each of those occasions, Strauss had been the lone dissenter. A few weeks earlier, he had told Truman that he intended to follow Lilienthal into retirement by early spring.

By coincidence, the party at the Shoreham Hotel that Strauss scheduled for January 31—his fifty-fourth birthday—also became a victory celebration for champions of the Super. Having accepted Strauss's invitation weeks before, Oppenheimer and the GAC felt compelled to attend. Reporters at the party found Oppie alternately distraught and defiant. To one uncomprehending newsman, the physicist compared the superbomb decision to "the plague of Thebes." Long remembered by the host of the event, however, was an unforgivable snub: when Strauss had walked over to introduce his son and daughter-in-law to Oppenheimer at the party, the physicist, not bothering to speak or turn around, had simply proffered a hand thrust over his shoulder.[47]

The following day, February 1, 1950, Hoover telephoned Strauss to announce a second triumph: Fuchs had confessed to espionage in London. The spy's confession was tangible proof of Strauss's long-derided contention that there were traitors in the nation's midst. Moreover, FBI evidence indicated that other spies might still be at large. ("We have got to put more bolts and locks on what we discover from this time forward, and give a very thorough screening," Strauss had told the Joint Committee.)[48] Later that day, Strauss wrote Truman that the Fuchs case "only fortifies the wisdom" of the president's decision, since the "individual in question had worked on the super-bomb at Los Alamos."

The H-bomb decision and Fuchs's arrest heralded a subtle but significant shift in the constellation of power in Washington. Instructed by Hoover to tell only his fellow commissioners about the damage caused by the British spy, Strauss opened an AEC meeting on February 2 by instructing Carroll Wilson to leave the room. After announcing the news about Fuchs, Strauss asked his stunned colleagues to approve an investigation of the commission's general manager for allowing the British into the building.[49]

The news of Fuchs's arrest—announced in the United States on February 3—was bound to make American scientists henceforth more circumspect about what they said in public, Strauss had told Hoover.[50] Lilienthal's assessment was no less blunt. Following his own farewell party at the AEC a few days earlier, he foresaw "witch-hunts" and "anti-scientists orgies." Truman, too, worried about the political fallout from the spy scandal—telling Souers to "tie on your hat."[51]

The storm broke less than a week later. On February 9, Senator Joseph McCarthy announced that he had a list of more than 200 Communists who had infiltrated the State Department. The recent perjury conviction of Alger Hiss in January had already propelled espionage into the headlines.

The Joint Committee spent the first week of February in executive session, trying to gauge the harm done by Fuchs. In separate appearances, Groves and Hoover blamed the debacle upon laxness by the British and the AEC.[52] As if confirming this judgment, Carroll Wilson sent McMahon a list of thirty-two top-secret documents that the commission could not account for.[53]

In one of his last acts as AEC chairman, Lilienthal grimly reported on the results of a quick "damage assessment" carried out by Bethe, Oppenheimer, and others.[54] The report reaffirmed that the spy knew the details of the Booster, the Alarm Clock, and the Super up to the time he left Los Alamos.[55] ("That man knew everything," Conant moaned.)[56]

Oppenheimer, however, discounted the value of what Fuchs might have told the Soviets. Believing the spy's knowledge of the U.S. atomic stockpile dated, and Teller's concept of the Super unworkable—for the Russians, as well as for Teller—Oppie told Pentagon and State Department officials that the Soviets "were marvelous indeed" if they had made any advances based on the secrets obtained from Fuchs.[57]

A week or so later, in early March, Oppenheimer would give the Joint Committee a guarded account of his own, previous leftist leanings. His apologia ended with the proclamation that he was now "a resolute anti-Communist, whose earlier sympathies for Communist causes would give immunity against further infection." Still, Hoover's almost casual mention of the Chevalier incident in his testimony was the first that many in the committee had heard of the affair, and rekindled doubts about Oppie.[58] In his lecture on Soviet espionage, Hoover had spent more time talking about Oppenheimer than Fuchs.[59]

Casting about for ways to speed up work on the Super, the Military Liaison Committee met with the commission early in the month.[60] A testy exchange between Pike and LeBaron, the Pentagon's most outspoken advocate for haste, made the commissioners defensive. Who, Pike inquired skeptically, was suggesting that the H-bomb program could proceed more expeditiously?

"Lawrence," LeBaron replied.[61]

Since the scuttling of his dreams for the Benicia reactors, Ernest had hit upon another way to make the tritium that the superbomb required. His inspiration, in fact, had come just a few days before Alvarez returned to Berkeley carrying the bad news from the GAC.

While briefing a visiting delegation of Joint Committee staffers, Lawrence had made the "somewhat startling suggestion" that the necessary tritium could be created by a gigantic new type of particle accelerator; one modeled after Alvarez's Linac but many times its power and size. ("A cross between a note of hysteria and a tremendous enthusiasm seemed to underline this part of the discussion," the staffers reported to Borden.)[62]

The beauty of what he called his "neutron foundry," Ernest pointed out, was that it made something out of nothing: using spent uranium to create plutonium, making tritium out of deuterium, and turning other, nonstrategic elements into radiological warfare agents.

Hoping to confound Russian spies, Lawrence called his new machine the Materials Testing Accelerator, or MTA.[63]

On New Year's Day, 1950, Lawrence had sent Pitzer plans for a 25-million-electron-volt MTA costing $7 million. Before the week was out, Ernest was already talking about a 350-MeV production version, dubbed the Mark II. More than a quarter-mile long and costing perhaps $150 million, the bigger machine would be able to turn dross into the precious tritium.

The commission approved the more modest version of Lawrence's MTA on February 8, before he had even told the university of his plans. ("I am being informed at a rather late date," grumbled Sproul.) Berkeley's comptroller learned of the project only when Ernest advised him that another half-million-dollar building was needed on campus. But under Neylan's prodding the university once again acceded to Lawrence's wishes. "I made my recommendation, surrounded it with an aura of mystery, and secured the necessary approval," Sproul wearily advised Underhill.[64]

Before construction of the first MTA could be started, however, Lawrence was distracted by a growing political controversy at Berkeley.

Fearful that the Tenney Committee was about to impose a loyalty oath upon state employees, Sproul had decided to preempt the move by voluntarily adopting a watered-down version of the oath at the university.[65] The president assumed that the measure would be uncontroversial and so was stunned when the faculty rebelled. At protest rallies on campus and in late-night faculty meetings, owlish professors likened themselves to the maquis of the French Resistance. The oath's foremost defender among the regents, Neylan, became a particular target of the "nonsigners'" ire.[66]

At the Rad Lab, Lawrence was quickly disabused of the notion that his trademark pep talks might defuse the issue. That winter, a former Rad Lab employee, David Fox—one of the grad students whom Oppie had hired during the war to work on the bomb—became a lighting rod for the debate. Called before HUAC, Fox took the Fifth when asked if he had ever been a Communist. Although Fox subsequently admitted his early membership in the party and even signed the loyalty oath, he was fired from his teaching position in the physics department nonetheless, upon Neylan's order.[67]

Using Fox's firing as a rallying point, three tenured professors at the Rad Lab joined the ranks of the nonsigners.[68] Two were theoretical physicists closely identified with Oppenheimer—including the man who had been hired to replace him, Gian Carlo Wick.[69] During a tense confrontation in Lawrence's office, Ernest had demanded that Wick surrender his security pass to campus guards.[70] Shortly afterward, Wick's teaching assistant was fired following a similar contretemps with Alvarez.[71]

To Lawrence, no less ominous than the loss of Berkeley's theorists was the prospect that Teller, too, was about to be driven away by the oath controversy. Still agonizing over whether to take the job he had been offered at UCLA, Edward wrote to his confidante that the university's recent decision to fire thirty-one professors because of the oath made him "perversely happy. If they are such s.o.b.s I do not have to go there and I might come back to Chicago." Teller had already inquired of the department chairman at Chicago whether his resignation letter might be withdrawn.[72]

The turning point had come when Neylan bragged to faculty members that Teller's appointment was proof the oath was not driving good people away. As Teller wrote Mayer, a last-minute effort to talk him out of withdrawing from the UCLA job backfired:

> You know that I planned to see President Sproul and a few others before resigning and so I went out to California. I did this mostly for the purpose which, in another connection, you had recommended to leave with good feelings. By and large I succeeded. There was one exception: Ernest Orlando Lawrence. Since the days of the Nazis I have seen no such thing. I had talked sufficiently gently and generally so that Lawrence did not attack me personally. But he did use threats and he was quite unwilling to listen to any point of view except to the one of Nylan [sic]. I felt somewhat sick when I left his office.[73]

Although Lawrence was quick to offer an apology, Teller informed Sproul that he intended to return to Chicago.[74] "I am extremely unhappy about the discharge of three theoretical physicists from the University,"

Edward wrote to McMillan. "I feel embarrassed to be in a position where I am, in effect, taking their place."[75]

Birge, however, reassured the university president that there was ultimately more of expediency than principle behind Teller's decision. The oath, he told Sproul, was "not the real reason for [Teller's] resignation but simply a polite way of getting out of a situation which had not turned out as he thought it would."[76]

In Washington, the anxiety over atom spies had meanwhile climbed to a fever pitch.[77] Following the disclosure of Fuchs's treason, the assumptions that had guided U.S. policy in the time of monopoly were turned on their head. What had hitherto been considered a major weakness for the Soviets—their lack of access to high-grade uranium ore—had actually turned out to be an advantage, a memo from the Military Liaison Committee argued, since it had forced the Russians to adopt more efficient production methods and had even pushed them early on to investigate the Super. Accordingly, Russia's atomic stockpile might already be "equal or actually superior to our own," the Pentagon speculated, while a Soviet Super "may be in actual production."[78]

At first reluctant to endorse Nichols's plea for the hydrogen bomb, by month's end the joint chiefs, too, were calling for an "all-out" effort on the Super—even if it meant a slowdown in the production of atomic bombs.

Shown the MLC memo and the chiefs' recommendation by Johnson, Truman issued a secret executive order on March 10, 1950, declaring the superbomb project "a matter of the highest urgency," and approving production of up to ten H-bombs a year.[79]

At Los Alamos, there remained some doubt the weapon that the president had just ordered into production could ever be built. One theoretical physicist working on the hydrogen bomb characterized it as "pure fantasy from the design standpoint, as well as a very difficult delivery problem."[80] The hypothetical Super under consideration was some 30 feet long and a stunning 162 feet wide; the fission trigger alone weighed 30,000 pounds.[81] Another problem facing air force planners was how any aircraft dropping the bomb could escape the shock wave from the mammoth 1,000-megaton explosion. LeBaron was looking into flying drones as well as robot-guided ships and submarines.[82]

To Teller, the most troublesome unknown concerned the amount of scarce and expensive tritium that a superbomb would require. His "best guesses" in 1946 had ranged between 300 and 600 grams. The neutrons necessary to create that much tritium could make the plutonium for up to twenty fission bombs—a point that the GAC had tried, in vain, to bring to the attention of decision makers.[83]

But the "Daddy Pocketbook," a top-secret précis of Teller's lectures on the Super, published in early January before the president's H-bomb decision, predicted that a successful Super would use no more than 100 grams of tritium and could be shrunk to 5,000 pounds—small and light enough to be carried on the nose of prospective long-range rockets. Truman's approval of the crash effort had been based on the imaginary bomb envisioned in Teller's "Pocketbook."[84]

Hoping to narrow these varying estimates, the Weapons Development Committee at Los Alamos had begun calculating the burning of tritium and deuterium in a theoretical Super that winter. The effort was frustrated by the quirks and dubious reliability of the lab's digital computer, designed by von Neumann and dubbed the MANIAC. (Technicians sometimes resorted to whacking the machine with a rubber mallet, to see if it gave the same result on a second run.) Frustrated by the delays, Ulam and a mathematician colleague at the lab, Cornelius Everett, undertook the same task using slide rules, mechanical calculators, and paper and pencil.[85]

Ulam and Everett discovered that the prospects for success were "miserable"—unless considerably more tritium were added.[86] They calculated that the necessary tritium ranged from 3 to 5 *kilograms*. Even so, Ulam reported that the "result of the calculations seems to be that the model considered is a fizzle."[87] Assuming a thermonuclear fire could be lit in the tritium, Ulam and Everett found, the flame failed to spread down the deuterium and tritium-filled tube. Princeton's computer confirmed their findings a few weeks later.[88] "Icicles are forming," von Neumann telephoned Ulam dejectedly.[89]

Teller's response to this news, Ulam recalled, was to turn "pale with fury." (Oppenheimer, on the other hand, seemed "rather glad to learn of the difficulties," Ulam noted.)[90]

Hoping in part to placate Teller, Bradbury in early March put the lab on a six-day workweek, making Edward head of a new group of two dozen scientists at the lab. The so-called Family Committee got its name from the various nicknames—"Sonny," "Little Edward," "Uncle" assigned superbombs of competing design. Teller's so-called tetraton Super, 100 cubic meters of uncompressed liquid deuterium, was known as "the daddy of them all."[91]

Stymied on the Super, the Family Committee turned its attention back to the Alarm Clock. Acknowledging that seemingly insurmountable barriers still blocked that path as well, Teller reluctantly recommended that a choice between the two designs be postponed once again.[92]

With a GAC review of the superbomb program planned for the fall, Teller and the Family Committee that summer approved an experiment meant to show that the lab was making tangible progress toward its goal: a test of "thermonuclear reagents" at the Pacific Proving Ground in the spring of 1951, as part of Operation *Greenhouse.* The test, code-named *George,* would use a large and specially designed atomic bomb of enormous yield to ignite a few grams of tritium and deuterium in an adjoining capsule. The shape of the capsule gave the device its nickname: "the Cylinder."

First proposed back in the summer of 1948, *George* was described by some at the lab as akin to using a blast furnace to light a match. Even proponents of the test conceded that it would do nothing to remove the current roadblock to the Super: the failure of the fusion flame to propagate in deuterium. Skeptics recognized that *George* was largely a symbolic step. Yet without it, Teller feared, the superbomb program might be canceled outright.[93]

After freezing the design of the device at a meeting in October 1950, without any clear idea of where to go next, the Family Committee agreed to disband.[94]

In another setback, Teller's effort to bring other scientists to the lab was still stalled. To help with the task, he had recently persuaded a twenty-five-year-old acolyte, Vienna-born theorist Frederic de Hoffmann, to abandon a Paris sabbatical and return to the lab. Regularly commuting between Washington and Los Alamos, de Hoffmann assumed the role of Edward's alter ego and general factotum.[95]

But even after enlisting the aid of the Joint Committee, few of those on the list that Teller and de Hoffmann had drawn up answered the call. Among those who agreed to come were Princeton's John Wheeler and Edward's former colleague, Emil Konopinski.[96] Most scientists simply refused Teller's summons, not sharing his sense of urgency or preferring academic research.[97] Some, siding with the GAC, refused to work on the Super on moral grounds.[98]

Despairing, Teller had even turned for help to his old nemesis. Writing to Oppenheimer that February, he adopted an almost pleading tone—"things have advanced to a desperate urgency here and I should be most anxious indeed if you could come and help us."[99] But Oppenheimer remained unmoved. While refusing to return to the lab himself, Oppie nonetheless extended leave to a physicist at the institute whom Teller had requested.[100]

Privately, Teller hinted to the Joint Committee that there might be sinister motives behind the paucity of his results. "A man like Conant or Oppenheimer can do a great deal in an informal manner which will hurt or further our efforts," he wrote Borden in April 1950.[101] A few weeks later, Teller remarked to a committee staffer that Robert's relationship with Frank seemed "unusually close." Frank, Teller said, would never have joined the party without his brother's tacit approval. Moreover, Oppie had been the one responsible for bringing Frank to the wartime lab, Edward pointed out.

"Teller," wrote the staffer in a summary sent to McMahon,

> was careful to explain that he did not himself have any idea that Robert was disloyal or intended to injure the best interests of the country according to his lights, however, he did say, that were Robert, by any chance found to be disloyal (in the sense of transmitting information) he could of course do more damage to the program than any other single individual in the country.[102]

PART FOUR

SORCERER'S APPRENTICE

Sir, my dismay is great!
Those spirits that I called,
I now cannot control.

—Goethe,
"The Sorcerer's Apprentice"

13

NUCLEAR PLENTY

THE NUMBER OF Oppenheimer's friends in Washington was steadily dwindling by the spring and summer of 1950. John Manley resigned as secretary to the General Advisory Committee and returned to Los Alamos. ("We've run away," Manley and his wife joked in a vacation postcard they sent to Oppie from Mexico.) Carroll Wilson, one of Oppenheimer's few allies on the Atomic Energy Commission, quit his post as general manager in early August, shortly after Gordon Dean was appointed AEC chairman.[1] "I regret that all of this will add to your troubles," Wilson wrote to Oppie apologetically. Even James Conant, so outspoken on the H-bomb the previous October, would miss several GAC meetings on the Super that year because of illness.[2]

Another old friend of Oppie's, visiting from Berkeley, was himself needy of help. Unemployed, his marriage in ruins, Haakon Chevalier was hoping to move to France but had been unable to obtain an American passport.[3] Oppenheimer genially gave Haakon the name of a lawyer in New York. While a houseguest at Olden Manor, Chevalier had several "long heart-to-heart talks" with the physicist on the big lawn behind the mansion—away from hidden microphones. "I gathered," Chevalier later wrote, "that [Oppenheimer] wanted to maintain a certain fiction regarding some important aspects of our past, that whole areas of our experience were to be considered as never having existed."[4]

After his last appeal was denied by the State Department, Chevalier invoked his dual citizenship and obtained a French passport. That fall, he boarded an airliner bound for Paris. To the FBI, Chevalier's actions looked suspiciously like flight to avoid prosecution.[5]

Oppie was in need of friends because of new charges against him that surfaced in May 1950. Testifying as a friendly witness before the Tenney Committee, Paul Crouch, a former Communist Party organizer in the Bay Area, claimed to have seen Oppenheimer as well as Joseph Weinberg at a secret meeting of the party's professional section in the summer of 1941.[6] Crouch claimed that the gathering had taken place at a house in Berkeley, during late July or early August, shortly after the Nazi invasion of Russia, and that Oppie had hosted the meeting.[7]

The previous month, Crouch had been driven around the Berkeley hills by Combs, Tenney's chief investigator, and campus police until he identified a house that looked familiar—10 Kenilworth Court, where Oppie and Kitty had lived before moving to nearby Eagle Hill.[8] Standing outside the residence, Crouch accurately described the interior and gave investigators details of the alleged 1941 meeting. Crouch's wife, Sylvia, who also claimed to have been at the meeting, backed up her husband's story.[9]

However, in FBI interviews and later, with a press release, Oppenheimer claimed to have no memory of the Crouches, and flatly denied ever having attended any secret meetings of the party.[10] Evidence to the contrary would be proof, Oppie conceded, that he had once been a dedicated Communist.

Oppenheimer told bureau agents that he and Kitty had been in New Mexico, at Perro Caliente, during the time that the Crouches claimed the Berkeley meeting took place. Their son Peter, barely six weeks old, had been left with a nurse in the care of the Chevaliers.

While the investigation of the so-called Kenilworth Court incident continued, Oppie received an unsolicited offer of assistance. "If at any time you should feel that it were wise, I would be pleased to have you make a statement of the general tenor of that which follows," Leslie Groves wrote from his office at Remington Rand, where the general had gone following his retirement from the army. The letter continued:

> General Groves has informed me that shortly after he took over the responsibility for the development of the atomic bomb, he reviewed personally the entire file and all known information concerning me and immediately ordered that I be cleared for all atomic information in order that I might participate in the development of the atomic bomb. General Groves has also informed me that he personally went over all information concerning me which came to light during the course of operations of the atomic project and that at no time did he regret his decision.

"I don't believe that you will find any need to make use of any such statement, but you might," Groves advised. "You might wish to show it to some individual for his use in handling unpleasant situations, if they arise."[11]

The occasion did not arise. Unable to shake Oppenheimer's story, and considering Paul Crouch a somewhat unreliable witness, the FBI decided against pressing the case.[12]

Once more for Oppenheimer, salvation had come from a most unlikely place. Campaigning in California, HUAC congressman Richard Nixon expressed "complete confidence in Dr. Oppenheimer's loyalty" the day following Sylvia Crouch's testimony. While the truth behind the Kenilworth Court incident remained a mystery, the story quickly faded from the headlines.*[13]

To Oppie, nonetheless, the effects lingered. "I took it all very badly and feel now like a man slowly convalescing from a serious illness," he wrote Robert Bacher.[14]

Because of the controversy that continued to dog him, Oppenheimer briefly considered resigning the chairmanship of the General Advisory Committee that fall, shortly after the GAC's new members were announced. Gordon Dean had elected to replace the committee members whose terms were expiring—Seaborg, Fermi, and Hartley Rowe—with three scientists who, in Borden's words, "strongly believe in the necessity of the H program."[15] Ironically, one of those who had urged Oppenheimer not to step down from the GAC was Dean.[16]

Oppie's brother was in far more serious trouble. Although no longer on the FBI's Key Figure list, Frank was still being periodically harassed by bureau agents, who asked local ranchers why their neighbor seemed to have so few cattle. ("It seems such a waste of God's talent to make a good

---

*Despite an exhaustive investigation, bureau agents may have overlooked one hole in Oppenheimer's alibi. While at the ranch that summer, he and Kitty were negotiating to buy the house at Eagle Hill from its absentee owner, Bertha Damon, who lived in Massachusetts. Complicating the purchase was the fact that the house contained three sets of furniture: Mrs. Damon's, a previous renter's, and the current tenant's. Rather than buy new furniture, the Oppenheimers wished to select pieces that Damon offered for sale. On Tuesday, July 21, 1941, Damon sent this cable to Oppie's real estate agent: "Accepted. Please request Oppenheimers meet me Saturday Sunday dispose furniture." When Mrs. Damon later attempted to contact the Oppenheimers directly, the real estate agent informed her that the couple was "traveling."

Between Friday morning, July 25, when Oppie—who had been kicked by a horse the day before—was x-rayed at a Santa Fe hospital, and late Monday afternoon, July 28, when the couple's Packard (with Kitty at the wheel) collided with a New Mexico Fish and Game truck on the road leading to Pecos, the Oppenheimers' whereabouts are unaccounted for. Interviewed by the FBI in 1952, Mrs. Damon recalled meeting with the Oppenheimers to discuss the furniture about a week after she accepted their terms.

Whether—and how—the Oppenheimers made the 2,200-mile round-trip journey in less than eighty hours remains a matter of speculation, however.

physicist into a mediocre rancher," wrote a former colleague.) Since his firing by Minnesota, he had been unable to find another job in academe. Despite Robert's personal lobbying on Frank's behalf, he was turned down for teaching positions at Chicago, Cornell, and MIT—where some faculty members were "overly impressed by 'the great lie' Frank told," Oppie was confidentially informed. A visit by the younger Oppenheimer to Caltech that summer was "painful," Bacher wrote Oppie.[17]

The fact that Robert Oppenheimer remained at the helm of the GAC and continued to serve on several other influential committees in Washington was a cause of increasing dismay to Borden, Strauss, and others in the capital.

On November 20, 1950, Borden requested Oppenheimer's FBI file from Hoover. The staffer's particular interest was the Chevalier affair and the alleged Kenilworth Court meeting. Bryan LaPlante, an AEC security official, borrowed the dossier the following day.[18]

Despite having new, more conservative members, the GAC had done nothing since the H-bomb decision to make it more popular with its critics, who were growing in both number and boldness. Among them was Ernest Lawrence, whom Acheson had recently appointed to a State Department panel advising on nuclear weapons policy. Distinguishing between "working scientists" like himself and "talkers," Lawrence observed disdainfully that "those who once thought the atomic bomb was a terrible thing now have no such scruples about it but have transferred their sense of horror to the H-bomb."[19]

Lawrence's specific complaint was with the GAC's lack of enthusiasm for his proposed giant accelerator. Oppie was not the first to find in Ernest's latest project a hint of déjà vu. Like the original Calutrons, Lawrence's MTA would use a stunning amount of outsized machinery to produce, by brute force, an almost infinitesimal yield—perhaps 1 gram of tritium a day. Expressing concern "over possible excessive cost from too ambitious a program," the GAC had concluded that the project "should not be bulled through, irrespective of cost"—a clear and unmistakable reference to Lawrence and his methods.[20]

In subsequent meetings, too, Oppenheimer and his colleagues had urged the commission to go slow on the MTA. The AEC likewise favored a more economical approach to achieving what Borden and McMahon were calling "a situation of nuclear plenty"—by increasing the incentives for uranium mining in the American Southwest, for example, and by building more Savannah River–type reactors.[21] Pointing out the obvious at one commission meeting, Smyth noted that if Teller's H-bomb did not work, as seemed the case, there was no need for tritium and no justification for Lawrence's huge machine.[22]

That summer, Oppenheimer and the GAC struck at another target close to Teller's heart. Noting their misgivings "as to the value and relevance" of the upcoming *George* test, committee members feared that the thermonuclear experiment might interfere with research at Los Alamos into making smaller and more efficient fission weapons. In summary reports to Dean, Oppenheimer argued that the H-bomb model under consideration would likely fizzle and used far too much tritium to be practical, at the same time leaving the "paramount uncertainties" surrounding the Super no closer to resolution.[23]

Oppenheimer had likewise continued to irritate and embarrass the air force by his advice. Asked by LeBaron to update the 1948 study on long-range military objectives, Oppie's new panel described the superbomb as "more uncertain and much more difficult of development" than originally believed and, pointedly, a "long range undertaking."[24] The report also put more emphasis upon small, tactical fission weapons—whose development was being hindered by the attention given the Super, Oppie argued.[25] Enraged by what he saw as a covert war against the air force's weapon of choice, Chief of Staff Hoyt Vandenberg ordered Oppenheimer barred from participating in a planned study of strategic targeting.[26]

Upon the GAC's recommendation, the commission decided to withhold funds for Lawrence's production accelerator, the Mark II, until the prototype machine had been shown to work. Ernest had meanwhile found a site for his Mark I MTA at an abandoned Naval Air Station in Livermore, a verdant valley of farms and vineyards some 40 miles southeast of Berkeley. An Olympic-size swimming pool, once used to train naval aviators in ditching techniques, would provide cooling water for the big machine. High-tension lines that crisscrossed the sere hills, carrying power generated by melting Sierra snows, supplied the electricity. Leftover barracks were pressed into service as offices for scientists and engineers.[27]

Lawrence had put Alvarez in charge of the MTA. Embracing the project as a surrogate for the ill-fated Benicia Laboratory, Luie imbued it with an enthusiasm that was given added urgency by the Korean invasion. "Anyone who now takes the time to work on mesons is little less than a traitor," Alvarez reportedly lectured his Rad Lab colleagues.[28]

Ernest appointed Pief Panofsky the head designer of the machine.[29] Lawrence assigned two Rad Lab veterans, Robert Serber and Herbert York, and a relative newcomer—physicist Harold Brown—the task of calculating how many neutrons the MTA would produce.[30]

But the lab's focus upon the MTA came at a price: construction of the Bevatron at Berkeley was put on hold. Desks for those assigned to the Livermore project were moved into the building that housed the partially finished machine. Pitzer informed the AEC that, for the foreseeable future, half the Rad Lab's effort would be devoted to the MTA.[31]

Like the Calutrons, Lawrence's latest machine operated at the far edge of the attainable. The Mark I's cylindrical tank—nearly 90 feet long, 60 feet wide—was the largest vacuum chamber built thus far. Standard-gauge railroad tracks were laid down its middle to move the MTA's eighteen massive oscillator tubes, the largest of which weighed 40 tons. The electrical power they required would supply a town of 20,000.[32]

But the Mark I was lilliputian compared to the planned production machine. The Mark II would require concrete walls some 80 feet high and 20 feet thick for radiation shielding alone, and its appetite for water as well as power far outstripped what was available at Livermore.[33] Ernest had scouted out a promising site for the Mark II on the banks of the Missouri River, not far from St. Louis. By late August, he was talking about building up to ten of the mammoth machines in the Midwest. When he encountered resistance to his plans at the AEC, Ernest turned to the Joint Committee.[34] His enthusiasm had found a match in Borden's ambition.

Under pressure from McMahon, the commission gave tentative approval for construction of a single Mark II in September 1950, while the prototype machine was still being built at Livermore.[35]

But only days after the Mark I was completed that fall, it became clear that the MTA project was already in trouble. The most vexing problem was sparking, caused by dust particles in the cavernous vacuum tank and imperfections in its copper lining.[36] Moving cots into the barracks, Alvarez and a colleague began working eighteen-hour shifts: Luie polished the shiny lining while his coworker, crawling out onto a wooden latticework some 30 feet in the air, looked for electrical shorts in the oscillator tubes. Retreating afterward to the control room, the two men held their breath while Alvarez gradually increased the power settings.[37]

Every spark was accompanied by a bright flash of light from portholes in the side of the vacuum tank and a resounding report. Since the sparking pitted the copper, each discharge made the problem worse. In the ensuing silence and stink of ozone came the dawning realization that the tedious process of polishing and testing had to begin anew.[38]

Throughout the fall and into the winter, brilliant flashes of artificial lightning lit up Alvarez's control room while crackling thunder rolled across the former navy base.

Those whom Lawrence had counted upon in the past to fix the problems with his big machines—the theoretical physicists—were gone; the victims, direct or indirect, of the loyalty oath.

Complaining to Sproul of the "almost complete cessation of scientific work of high quality" as a result of the controversy, Panofsky left Berkeley for Stanford that spring. A last-minute effort by Lawrence and Alvarez to change his mind—they arranged a luncheon at Neylan's Woodside estate, where the regent proceeded to lecture the diminutive physicist on patriotism—only hastened Panofsky's departure. Seaborg thought the loss "catastrophic" for the physics department.[39]

Serber was next to go. Berkeley's remaining theorist told Lawrence he was leaving for "family reasons" only because the truth was too painful to tell. ("It was whether loyalty to Oppenheimer or loyalty to Ernest Lawrence would prevail," he said, years later.) "Birge, as you can imagine, is quite broken up at the thought of what is happening to his department—telling him was the hardest part," the shy physicist wrote to Oppenheimer at Princeton.[40]

Another Berkeley veteran, Emilio Segrè, had already taken a job at Urbana. Segrè's complaint was not only the oath, he told Sproul, but the "high-handed position" of Alvarez—who "thinks that all the time of the Department should be spent on war work."[41]

Before leaving Berkeley, Segrè had tried to tell Lawrence what Serber and others had been hinting at for months: that the MTA's sparking problem was essentially unsolvable, given the enormous electrical potential and high vacuum that the MTA required. But Ernest, Segrè later remembered, "reacted with great vehemence, accusing me of being unpatriotic, lazy, selfish, and God knows what more."[42]

In a kind of belated victory for the nonsigners, the California courts declared the university's loyalty oath unconstitutional in April 1951, ordering those who had been fired reinstated. Following Neylan's resignation as chairman of the Board of Regents that fall, the oath requirement was officially rescinded.[43] But the damage had already been done.

Across the Bay, in Livermore, Alvarez soldiered on amid the fearsome thunder of the Mark I. His partner in the control room was relieved to learn that he was being reassigned to another new project at the Rad Lab: preparing the diagnostic measurements for *George*.[44]

At Los Alamos, the war news from Korea had become an almost daily reminder that progress on the Super remained stalled. "The third world war has started and I do not know whether I care to survive it," Teller wrote to his confidante that winter. Physicist Marshall Holloway, whom

Bradbury had made head of the Weapons Division at Los Alamos, had no plans for large-scale thermonuclear tests beyond *George*. The success or failure of the Cylinder would determine whether future tests along the same line would be worthwhile. But Teller, who was once again back at Los Alamos, on leave from Chicago, wanted Bradbury and Holloway to commit in advance to an ambitious series of tests aimed at producing a superbomb.

As 1951 began, Ulam had been toying with a new idea for what he called "a bomb in a box"—confining an exploding atomic bomb for a fraction of a second in a vessel of dense material, so as to compress the thermonuclear fuel at the other end.[45] Key to Ulam's idea was the notion of focusing the energy from the fission trigger, the "primary," upon the fusion fuel, the "secondary," to implode it, thereby dramatically increasing the efficiency of the thermonuclear reaction. In principle, the concept was not unlike the use of high-explosive lenses to implode Fat Man's plutonium core.

Ulam showed a sketch of his so-called staged bomb to Theoretical Division leader Carson Mark and Bradbury one morning in late January. Mark, preoccupied with last-minute preparations for nuclear tests in Nevada, regarded it as just another candidate for the lab's thermonuclear "zoo." Bradbury was only slightly more encouraging.[46] But Ulam's idea received a more welcoming reception from Teller the following day.[47]

While working on the design of the Cylinder, Teller had been wrestling for months with the question of how radiation flowed from the atomic bomb to the adjoining capsule of tritium and deuterium. Ulam's sketch inspired Teller to think of another, better way to compress the fusion fuel without heating it—by using radiation from the exploding fission trigger, traveling at the speed of light.[48]

Heretofore, radiation from the H-bomb's fission trigger had been the principal problem with the Super; it was what had made Teller's design appear unworkable. Now it was the solution. Maria Mayer's work on opacity had finally borne fruit.

Teller had used the words *cylindrical implosion* to describe what happened in *George*. A new term—*radiation implosion*—was coined to describe the phenomenon at work in the Teller-Ulam invention.[49]

Teller modified and refined the concept over the next several weeks. In early March, he informed Hans Bethe, von Neumann, and Oppenheimer of the modified bomb-in-the-box idea during a meeting at Princeton. All immediately recognized the possibilities. "There are some new thoughts which may be important for you to know," Oppie wrote Conant in June.[50]

But Ulam was not nearly as sanguine as Teller that the revolutionary potential of the staged bomb could be exploited anytime soon. The day following the Princeton meeting, Ulam told division leaders at Los Alamos that it might be several years before the lab could incorporate radiation implosion into its weapons. "Edward is full of enthusiasm about these possibilities; this is perhaps an indication they will not work," Ulam puckishly wrote von Neumann.

Teller, on the other hand, had already begun lobbying for a full-scale test of the concept as soon as possible. Just a few weeks before, citing the lack of progress on the Super, Bradbury had pushed the earliest date for the next series of Pacific tests back another six months.[51]

Teller's resentment of Ulam's role in discrediting the original Super also had not abated.[52] On March 9, 1951, Edward published the paper that contained the critical ideas behind the new superbomb: LA-1225, "On Heterocatalytic Detonations I: Hydrodynamic Lenses and Radiation Mirrors." Although Ulam's name was on the cover sheet, Teller later would dismiss his coinventor's contribution as insignificant.[53]

By the time preparations for *George* were under way, Teller was convinced that what he called the "big forces" opposing the superbomb would endeavor to cancel the program if the test of the Cylinder was anything less than a complete success. Lawrence shared his concern.

On May 8, 1951, Ernest rendezvoused with Teller on Eniwetok following the twenty-hour flight from California. Ferried by Piper Cub to the VIP barracks on nearby Parry Island, the two men went swimming in the warm surf that ringed the island. Colleagues whom Edward told of the idea for the staged bomb were surprised to find themselves with goose bumps in the tropic heat.

The next morning, after a delay to allow the weather to clear, Lawrence and Teller joined the admirals, generals, and other VIPs in front of the corrugated tin barracks, where deck chairs had been set up. As at *Trinity,* Edward had brought suntan lotion as protection from the bomb's ultraviolet rays. He and Lawrence slipped dark goggles over their eyes when a green flare signaled the five-minute warning.

At 9:30 the Cylinder exploded on Eleleron Island, 16 miles away. In eerie silence, a brilliant white light shone through the gray overcast, spreading quickly across the horizon. From within the familiar mushroom-shaped cloud, the blue-violet light of ionizing radiation shone.

Despite *George*'s impressive display, the leaden skies made it impossible to know whether the test had been the requisite success. Suspense grew after heavy rains forced the cancellation of the morning's air-sampling mission. By afternoon, Edward was depressed and anxious, awaiting the results from diagnostic instruments and cameras scattered across the atoll. To ease the tension, Lawrence suggested another swim and offered Teller a wager. Morosely, Edward bet that *George* had failed.[54]

The first helicopter did not return until nearly dusk. That evening, Teller nervously paced up and down the beach while the photographic plates were developed.

Early the next morning, Teller received the news while brushing his teeth in the barracks bathroom. A few minutes later, peering at a tiny strip of film through a microscope in the island's makeshift lab, he saw proof that, for a mere glimmer of a second, a thermonuclear flame had burned on Earth. Teller turned and hurried out the door. Hopping on a jeep that was headed to the nearby landing strip, Edward flagged down the Piper Cub that had been preparing for takeoff.[55] As the little airplane taxied up to him, Teller wordlessly thrust a five-dollar bill through the cockpit window into Lawrence's open hand.[56]

Eniwetok, Edward had promised Gordon Dean, would not be big enough for his *next* bomb.

14

A BAD BUSINESS NOW THREATENING

OPPENHEIMER AND THE General Advisory Committee received word of *George* while in a meeting called to discuss the future of Lawrence's Materials Testing Accelerator. "The interesting mixture certainly reacted well," read the terse telegram sent by a Los Alamos physicist. Oppie announced the news, but the GAC minutes remain silent on the response, if any. Despite Alvarez's expressions of "optimism," the committee subsequently voted not to award any money for the Mark II MTA until the Mark I was working. The prototype could still only run for a few seconds before it was shut down by sparking.[1]

Although the success of *George* had been widely predicted, the staged-bomb proposal of Teller and Ulam cast the significance of the experiment in a whole new light. Dean called a meeting for mid-June at Princeton's institute to consider whether to proceed with a full-scale test of the radiation-implosion design, which Teller favored.[2]

Smyth hoped that Princeton might also be a "meeting of the minds between Teller and Oppenheimer."[3] But, as the gathering approached, the two protagonists were instead seen to be jockeying for position. Oppenheimer encouraged Bacher, Conant, and other early H-bomb opponents to attend. Afraid of being outnumbered by Oppie's partisans, Teller made sure that his own allies—including Wheeler and Willard Libby, the Berkeley-trained chemist who had meanwhile replaced Seaborg on the GAC—would be in the audience. Believing that Teller would not wish to be identified as a spokesman for Los Alamos, Bradbury deliberately left him off the agenda at Princeton.

Rather than recognizing this as a polite nod to his independence, however, Teller took Bradbury's gesture as a deliberate snub—and even an effort to silence him.

Barely had the first session begun on June 16, 1951, before Edward became visibly impatient, chafing at progress reports on projects that had long been under way at Los Alamos. His agitation grew when Oppenheimer, the session's chairman, recognized first Bradbury and then Dean, and neither man mentioned the recent discovery by Teller and Ulam. As he had at Berkeley almost a decade earlier, when he had interrupted Serber's primer on the atomic bomb, Teller stood up and demanded to be heard.

At the end of his impromptu presentation, even those who had previously opposed the H-bomb—including Fermi and Oppenheimer—seemed "enthusiastic" about the prospects for the new Super, Dean noted. Bethe joined with Wheeler in rejecting further half-steps: the next test in the Pacific, part of Operation *Ivy*, should be of a prototype superbomb, code-named *Mike*.[4]

Wrote Teller to Smyth in triumph: "It is now my conviction that the thermonuclear program is past its ignition point."[5] "The bickering was gone," confirmed Dean in his diary.

Yet, late that summer, de Hoffmann notified the AEC chairman that Teller was once again talking about leaving Los Alamos. (Dean had grown inured to such tactics. He had come to the conclusion, he wrote in his diary, "that Teller would never be completely happy."[6] A Joint Committee staffer reported from Los Alamos that scientists there had likewise learned to take Teller's resignation threats "in stride.")[7]

Bradbury's appointment of Marshall Holloway to head the lab's accelerated H-bomb project had prompted the crisis. As leader of the Theoretical Megaton Group—the Family Committee's successor, created to spearhead the development of the radiation-implosion bomb at Los Alamos—Holloway refused to agree to Teller's date of July 1, 1952, for the test of *Mike*.[8] Holloway and Bradbury both believed that the earliest the revolutionary new weapon could be built and tested was late in the year.[9] To Teller, the choice of Holloway had been "like waving a red flag before a bull," de Hoffmann told Dean.

A few days later, Teller sent Bradbury his resignation letter. Edward made preparations to move his piano and his family, once more, to Chicago.[10]

Anxious to persuade Dean that he was not "walking out" on the H-bomb project, Teller had told the AEC chairman that were he to stay at the lab, his role there would be minor—merely approving engineering drawings. Teller wrote Strauss that he enjoyed being back at Chicago. But there was another reason, he conceded, why he had decided to make the break.[11] Severing his ties with Los Alamos would free him to campaign without hindrance for a second nuclear weapons laboratory, a rival to "Oppie's lab."[12]

Teller had quietly began recruiting scientists for a second lab as early as May 1950.[13] The notion of a "separate institute" dedicated to building the H-bomb had been raised by the Joint Committee the following month. ("The profits which might be gained by moving out of Los Alamos now might be more top scientists in the project, faster progress on weapons research projects, and financial economies which would free dollars for bombs instead of water wells and golf courses for Los Alamos," a staffer had written then.)[14] More recently, LeBaron had warned the committee that if civilians did not act soon to move the H-bomb and other projects along, the military was "ready to take the driver's seat."[15]

The idea of a "new establishment" likewise appealed to Strauss, who, feeling bored and unappreciated as a financial adviser to the Rockefeller Foundation, had welcomed a recent invitation from Truman to serve on a blue-ribbon panel overseeing procurement for the Korean War.[16] Although no longer formally affiliated with the AEC, Strauss used his new position in Washington to lobby his former colleagues or their recent replacements at the commission.[17]

Strauss's fear was that Oppenheimer would continue to use his behind-the-scenes influence to thwart progress on the new Super. Meeting with Dean the previous winter, Strauss had shown the AEC chairman the draft of a long memorandum, titled "The Russians May Be Ahead of Us." In his memo, Strauss blamed Oppenheimer for delaying the H-bomb program and likened the GAC chairman "to a commander who did not want to fight."[18] When Dean requested that he leave the draft memo and accompanying notes behind, Strauss instead made a show of burning the documents in the fireplace. A few days later, Dean learned that Strauss had originally intended the memo for Truman.

Except for Libby, the scientists of the GAC had thus far expressed little enthusiasm for a "second Los Alamos," which the majority rejected as "neither necessary nor in any real sense feasible."[19] The idea had yet to find any supporters on the commission, either. Early in 1951, however, that situation had begun to change.

Thomas E. Murray was a New York industrialist whom Truman had named in March 1950 to serve out the remainder of Lilienthal's term. Murray, trained at Yale as an engineer, was the holder of more than 200 patents and had been in charge of New York City's subway system during the Second World War. His interest in nuclear power had been awakened by the prediction of a physicist visitor to his office in 1940 that the subways of the future would run on atoms rather than coal.[20]

But perhaps the most crucial fact about the 59-year-old Murray was not on his *résumé:* a prominent Catholic layman, the brother of a Jesuit priest, Murray considered religious faith more important than politics or ideology. Before accepting the post at the AEC, he had consulted several prominent theologians on the question whether the use of nuclear weapons was morally justified in time of war. Taking an almost Manichaean view of the Soviet Union, his tentative conclusion—that waging nuclear war was not only "something we are morally permitted to do; it may be something we are morally obliged to do"—was an issue that Murray continued to wrestle with privately, in frequent visits to the holy shrine at Fatima, Portugal.[21]

At his first GAC meeting, in September 1950, Murray had been surprised that there was not more eagerness to push the H-bomb program. The new commissioner told the stunned scientists that the situation with the Super reminded him of the fate that had befallen one of his father's inventions—which he said an industrial rival had bought the rights to and then simply put "on the shelf."[22]

The GAC meeting was not the first time that Murray had heard of the H-bomb. The superbomb project was being deliberately "sidetracked" at Los Alamos, Strauss had warned him early in his tenure, suggesting that Murray see Teller for the details.

In February 1951, Murray met with Teller, who promptly "left no doubt as to the fact that he would prefer a separate director, a separate group and conditions preventing continual interference with the work."[23] Teller also singled out "Robert Oppenheimer and Associates" for impeding the nation's military buildup.

Three days after the Princeton conference, Murray wrote to Dean, urging immediate creation of a new laboratory, independent of Los Alamos and dedicated to building the new superbomb.[24] Dean had agreed to study the question. When the verdict that autumn turned out to be negative, Murray assumed Strauss's role of the iconoclast in commission meetings. His was consistently the sole vote in favor of a second lab.[25]

On Capitol Hill, McMahon and Borden were also busily promoting the argument that Los Alamos would benefit from competition. The Connecticut Democrat had recently announced his own presidential bid, under the slogan "McMahon's the Man," and had seized upon what he hoped would be a potent issue for his campaign: the need for speeding up work on the Super.[26] Borden had written recently of using super-bombs to "cauterize Soviet global aggression."[27]

Thus far, however, neither McMahon nor Murray had been able to enlist the military in their crusade. Despite prodding from both men, the joint chiefs' poker-faced chairman, Omar Bradley, steadfastly refused to set a military requirement for a specific number of superbombs or to endorse the call for a second lab.[28]

But pressure was building. On September 28, 1951, the AEC's director of intelligence informed Dean that the Soviets had tested a second atomic bomb. Although he was initially reassured by the fact that Joe-2 received smaller headlines than the World Series playoff game, Dean's sense of relief proved short-lived. In late October, the Russians exploded a third bomb; this one, dropped from an airplane, had twice the yield of Fat Man.[29]

The Soviets' feats inspired renewed calls for a speedup in the H-bomb program, as well as increased pressure for a second lab. Murray raised both issues that fall with Truman, who remained noncommittal, however.[30] Dean was likewise resisting the importunings of his former law partner and McMahon's zealous staffer. In a letter to Borden, the AEC chairman expressed serious reservations about another "across-the-board weapons research lab."[31]

Visiting Princeton that fall, Teller persuaded Oppenheimer to let him make the case for the second lab in person at the next meeting of the General Advisory Committee. On December 13, 1951, Oppie presided over an unusually tense meeting of the GAC in Washington, with Murray present. Reading from a six-page statement, Teller outlined a surprisingly modest effort. The lab he proposed would employ no more than 300 scientists, who would work on a diverse arsenal of weapons that included the H-bomb and the hydride. At the end of two hours of sometimes impassioned pleading, Edward believed that he had convinced the GAC of the soundness of his views.[32]

But the only consensus once Teller left the room was against his plan. Rabi predicted that the effort would require a work force of 1,500, not 300. All but Libby expressed fears that Los Alamos would be "pirated" to staff the second laboratory. In a compromise that they suggested—but thought best not to put in writing—Oppenheimer and Rabi volunteered to go to Los Alamos in hopes of persuading Bradbury to organize a new group at the lab, possibly headed by Bethe, but including Teller.[33]

Exasperated, Murray complained afterward that the GAC was simply "trying to juggle personalities." He had already decided to talk to Lawrence, Murray told Libby, about an altogether different approach.[34]

Ernest was in Washington to testify before the Joint Committee on behalf of the MTA. He was still hopeful of seeing a phalanx of Mark II accelerators rise on the banks of the Missouri—even though the prototype at Livermore was still beset by broken welds, persistent sparking, and vacuum leaks. (The cost of fixing the latter was becoming "fantastic," engineers warned. Lawrence assigned everyone at the lab—physicists, engineers, and technicians—to plugging the leaks.)[35] Although he told the Joint Committee that the Rad Lab "approached the accelerator project with increasing confidence and enthusiasm," in fact, both patience and optimism were waning.[36]

Not only were Ernest's grandiose plans being openly sniped at by his old-time foes, but the MTA had become the butt of unkind humor even among former friends. In "discussing the accelerator [Oppenheimer] did not hide his feelings under a bushel," Joint Committee staffer Ken Mansfield reported from Princeton. Rabi observed, puckishly, that although enough money made it possible to do almost anything in science for a while, eventually the laws of physics prevailed.[37]

Told by Murray of the GAC's opposition to a second lab, Lawrence thought "childish and silly" their objection that not enough qualified scientists could be found to staff another Los Alamos. Warming to the topic, Lawrence told Murray that he considered a second lab essential, but that it should start out on a small scale: "He, along with Dr. Teller and a few others, could form the nucleus for such an effort. It could gradually and eventually take over."[38]

On December 14, 1951, Neylan's special Committee on Atomic Energy Projects gathered on the UCLA campus to review an "exceedingly urgent" request from the AEC, received just the day before. The commission was asking the university to approve three subcontracts, totaling $11 million, to "provide for special equipment and material necessary in connection with the primary purposes of Project 36."[39] No other information was forthcoming, nor was any requested. ("The chief function of our committee was to know nothing," Neylan would later boast.)[40]

Assured by Underhill that the university was obligated to carry out the AEC's bidding, the six men approved the request pro forma. With little discussion, and even less understanding, Sproul and the regents of the University of California had unanimously—and unknowingly—authorized construction of the world's first hydrogen bomb.[41]

At the Rad Lab's traditional party that New Year's Eve, Lawrence asked the question that Murray had posed to him—"Do we need a second laboratory?"—of a young protégé. Thirty years old, Herbert York had been Lawrence's graduate student when the war broke out. Sent to Oak Ridge,

York returned to Berkeley after V-J day to finish his degree; later, he had supervised the lab's diagnostic measurements of *George* in the Pacific.

At his mentor's suggestion, York promptly set out on a monthlong, cross-country trip aimed at finding an answer to the question that Lawrence had posed. On one of his first stops—in Chicago, to see Teller—the young physicist discovered that sides on the question were already clearly drawn, and that Teller, not Lawrence, was the real "prime mover" behind the second lab. He was, York later admitted, "readily persuaded to Teller's point of view."[42]

On stationary from his Chicago hotel, York drafted a detailed, twenty-three-page outline of the kind of work that might be done at the new lab. His plan, complete with an organization chart and a list of prospective recruits, left no doubt that the future laboratory would be principally dedicated to building bombs: four different types of H-bombs were listed, including a radiation-implosion Alarm Clock and Teller's classical Super. Ignoring Ernest's parting admonition—"no big names and no big plans"—York also hoped to draw upon the cream of the nation's scientific talent. He anticipated ground breaking as early as May.[43]

On February 2, 1952, Teller visited Berkeley at Lawrence's invitation to discuss the second lab. The duo drove out to Livermore, where Ernest showed off the Mark I in its big corrugated steel building, visible in the flat valley for miles around, and spoke enthusiastically of Livermore as a home for the new laboratory. Later, over Mai Tais and dinner at Trader Vic's, Lawrence asked if Teller would come to Livermore, should it be the site for the second lab. Edward insisted on one condition—that the work at the lab be specifically on thermonuclear weapons.

No promises were made, and few details were discussed.[44] Lawrence's final, avuncular advice was that Teller talk to Murray about how to lobby effectively for the second lab. A few days later, meeting at the AEC with Murray, the evangelical commissioner counseled patience.[45]

By that winter, the GAC had considered—and rejected—the second lab no fewer than three times.[46] Even the AEC's Division of Military Application had come out against the idea, believing it would disrupt the H-bomb program already under way at Los Alamos.[47] Anguished appeals from McMahon and Murray received the usual genial response from Dean but no action.[48] Bradley, too, continued to reject the senator's pleas to join the flagging crusade.[49] Borden had begun toying with a plan to raise private funds for the project.[50] He reported to McMahon that Teller was close to despair.

But Borden also had some good news to report: the Joint Committee had a new, powerful—and secret—ally in its campaign for the second lab.

David Griggs was a Harvard-educated geophysicist who had taught at Caltech and worked for the RAND Corporation. The previous September, Griggs had been appointed the air force's chief scientist.[51] Smart, conservative, and energetic to the point of fanaticism, Griggs combined a bulldoglike tenacity with unorthodox thinking. (In 1952, Griggs proposed overflying the Iron Curtain with an ultralight spy plane powered by radioactive polonium. The idea advanced far in RAND and air force circles until it was pointed out that a crash would make a large area almost permanently uninhabitable, and that one-third of the nation's reactor capacity would be required to make the plane's fuel.)[52]

A quick and early convert to the campaign for a second lab, Griggs volunteered to keep the Joint Committee surreptitiously informed of developments at the Pentagon. Since Griggs's relationship with the civilian committee was illicit, Borden identified him as "Mr. X" in memos to McMahon.[53]

Within days of Griggs's arrival at the Pentagon, Strauss had brought the young scientist and Teller together.[54] When Edward agreed to join the air force's Science Advisory Board, Griggs introduced him to its most senior member, General James "Jimmy" Doolittle, hero of the famed thirty-second raid on Tokyo. After spending only a few hours with Teller during an advisory board meeting in Florida, Doolittle, too, had become an active partisan for the second lab.[55]

That spring, Doolittle and Griggs arranged for Teller to brief top officials in the Pentagon. Except for members of the Military Liaison Committee, most of those in uniform had thus far remained silent on the question of the second lab. The air force's civilian secretary, Thomas Finletter, had yet to enter the fray. Defense Secretary Robert Lovett, on the other hand, wrote McMahon in March that he thought taking H-bomb research away from Los Alamos was a "move in the wrong direction."[56]

A few days earlier, Teller had given Finletter an hour-long briefing on the new Super. Assisted by RAND physicist Ernie Plesset and a collection of colored charts, Teller spoke of the blast and radiation effects of hypothetical 5-megaton and 25-megaton hydrogen bombs.[57] At first silent and seemingly distracted, Finletter grew animated as Teller explained how such weapons could be used to wipe out an entire enemy army group and stop a Soviet invasion of western Europe.[58] A more detailed presentation by Teller and Plesset got an even more enthusiastic reception from the Air Council five days later. At Finletter's suggestion, Teller briefed Lovett and the service secretaries on March 19, 1952.[59]

The impact of Teller's whirlwind briefings was prompt and decisive. Lovett and the service chiefs urged that the question of the second lab be brought before the National Security Council as soon as possible.[60]

Alerted to this sudden change of fortune by a telephone call from Arneson at the State Department, Gordon Dean reacted less with anger than bemusement.[61] Dean promised Arneson that he would expose Teller's next audience "to a few facts of life."[62]

Instead, the AEC chairman sat silent and grim-faced in a Pentagon office on April 1 while Teller recounted a brief and one-sided history of the H-bomb project which emphasized delays, missteps, losses due to espionage, and ended with a frank plea for the second lab. After Teller had left the room, Dean urged Acheson and Deputy Defense Secretary William Foster to withhold judgment until they had heard "the other side of the question."[63]

Ironically, Finletter and Foster had recently gone to Los Alamos and done just that. But Bradbury's ill-advised effort to exclude Plesset from the meeting and an unusually laconic briefing on H-bomb progress by Theoretical Division leader Carson Mark had instead made the visitors determined converts to the second lab.[64] Warned by Acheson that Teller's next audience was likely to be the president, Dean yielded. He promised to explore the possibility of a second lab with Lawrence.[65]

Thus far, not even the lobbyists for the second lab agreed on its location or its scale. Griggs and the air force favored the University of Chicago's Midway Laboratory, where the Pentagon already had a classified project under way.[66] But Teller was still sensitive to Fermi's moral qualms about the H-bomb.[67] For his part, Libby feared that Berkeley bore the taint of the loyalty oath controversy, which would make recruiting for Livermore difficult. Teller told LeBaron that he worried more about Lawrence than Livermore. "If EOL project is started, things will go in grand style but with little understanding," LeBaron wrote in his diary following a meeting with Edward.[68]

After a visit to the Rad Lab in early March, however, Murray had come away persuaded that Livermore was the location and Lawrence the man to lead the effort.[69] Only a few weeks earlier, during a meeting at the Bohemian Club, the regents had unanimously approved a five-year extension of the university's contracts with the AEC. With the war in Korea still raging, the issue had occasioned little debate.[70]

Murray telephoned Lawrence in early April to report "the first break in the long battle."[71] Ernest hoped that a decision by the AEC to put the new lab at Livermore might also rescue his embattled MTA. He promised Murray that, if needed, he would return to Washington "at a moment's notice."[72]

Back in Washington by mid-April to give his now well-practiced H-bomb briefing to the State Department and the NSC, Teller stopped off at the AEC building to see Dean. No longer feeling obliged to be conciliatory, Teller told him he had rejected any possibility of "piecemeal" solutions in his discussions with the Joint Committee, where he had insisted upon the "most vigorous sort of competitive and unified second laboratory."[73] Were the committee to now ask the Pentagon brass whether they wanted a second laboratory, Edward boasted, "the answer would be entirely different."[74]

The second-lab issue had "suddenly come to a boil," Borden notified McMahon. The military, he wrote, "bought Teller hook, line and sinker."[75]

Emboldened by his debut at the Pentagon, Teller wanted the new lab not merely to build bombs but to explode them—at the newly established Nevada Test Site, a domain hitherto exclusive to Los Alamos. (Teller's escalating demands troubled even his allies, among them the deputy director of the AEC's Division of Military Application, Admiral John "Chick" Hayward. Hayward wrote in his diary of a futile attempt to rein in Edward's enthusiasm during a recent visit to Livermore: "Much heat but little light. Long arguments with Dr. Teller. . . . Many martinis and then on to Trader Vics.")[76]

In late April 1952, the juggernaut that Teller's briefings had set in motion collided with a familiar obstacle: Oppenheimer's GAC. Protesting that "a fairly technical decision was being forced by high pressure methods," Oppie acknowledged that the AEC would probably have to yield to the pressure for a second lab. Privately, however, Oppenheimer told his colleagues that it was still "not clear" whether a second laboratory was inevitable.[77]

Dean, too, was suddenly "backtracking" on the second lab, Murray complained to his fellow commissioners.[78] Yet it was not the AEC chairman whom Murray blamed for "roadblocks," but Oppenheimer.[79] During a dinner at the Brookings Institution on May 19, Strauss confided to Murray that he "had very good information to the effect that the 2nd laboratory was being sabotaged. He thought that if some aggressive action was not taken the 2nd laboratory would never be built."[80]

In one of his clandestine meetings with the Joint Committee, Griggs had bluntly asked "what [they] were doing to get Oppenheimer off the GAC."[81] The terms of the GAC's three charter members—Oppenheimer, Conant, and DuBridge—would expire that summer, unless the men were reappointed by Truman. ("Three men—one soul" was how Teller described the trio.) Griggs had told the Joint Committee that the air force considered Oppenheimer's removal from the GAC "an urgent and immediate necessity."[82]

For allies in their campaign to oust Oppenheimer from the GAC, Murray, Griggs, and the Joint Committee turned to Berkeley. During Murray's visit to the Rad Lab that spring, Lawrence had recounted the story of how he had gradually become disillusioned with Oppie, Frank, and mutual associates like Serber. He opposed Oppie's continuing on the GAC, Ernest told Murray.[83]

In March, just weeks after giving up his post at the AEC, Pitzer had made a speech to the American Chemical Society that blamed delays in the H-bomb project on the GAC. Following the speech, Pitzer had lunch with Borden, who urged the chemist to share his views with the FBI. Pitzer told bureau agents the following week that, contrary to his earlier opinion, he was "now doubtful as to the loyalty of Dr. Oppenheimer." Pitzer suggested that Edward Teller could provide the names of those whom Oppie had dissuaded to work on the Super, "if Teller decides to talk."[84]

Teller, too, subsequently unburdened himself to bureau agents, at their request. Claiming that Oppenheimer had always swayed opinions against the Super, he said he was satisfied with Oppie's loyalty but was reluctant to be quoted—lest he be subjected "to considerable cross-examination on this point." Should his views become public, Teller cautioned, his position in the H-bomb project might well become untenable.[85]

Alvarez had already been to the FBI about Oppenheimer—on the same day, in fact, that the GAC had recommended against proceeding with the Mark II. Prior to his interview with bureau agents, Luie had met in the Pentagon with Finletter, Griggs, and LeBaron, for whom Alvarez described how he had originally been lured to wartime Los Alamos by Oppenheimer with a promise to work on the Super. "Although Dr. Alvarez was agitated, he apparently added nothing to the FBI file," a disappointed aide informed Borden.[86]

At the annual meeting of the American Physical Society that spring, Oppenheimer's friends were perplexed and upset by the "vitriolic talk" directed against the physicist—"notably from some of the University of California contingent."[87] Until then, Oppenheimer, like Dean, had tended to dismiss such ad hominem attacks as simply part of "the rather tense atmosphere that still prevail[ed] at Berkeley."

In late May, Hoover couriered the bureau's recent interviews with Pitzer, Libby, and Teller to the White House, the Justice Department, and the AEC's Division of Security.[88] Included in the thick dossier was Teller's admission to the FBI that "he would do most anything to see [Oppenheimer] separated from General Advisory Committee because of his poor advice and policies regarding national preparedness and because of his delaying of the development of H-bomb."[89] Strauss had already talked privately with Truman, asking that the president not reappoint Oppenheimer.[90]

McMahon decided against sending Truman an "eyes only" letter, which Borden had drafted, pleading that Oppenheimer not be reappointed.[91] The senator also canceled a long-planned personal meeting with the president. Neither McMahon nor Strauss wanted Oppenheimer's departure from the GAC to seem forced, lest it become a cause célèbre in the nation's scientific community.[92]

Thus far, among those who knew Oppenheimer, only Pitzer had gone so far as to actually question the physicist's loyalty.[93] While Griggs ominously ascribed delays in the H-bomb program to "almost literally criminal negligence," he had refrained from identifying Oppie as the suspect. Strauss and Borden, too, had been cautious in their efforts to end Oppenheimer's influence in Washington. While both men thought the Crouches' story of a secret Communist meeting at Oppie's house "inherently believable," they confessed to a mutual "feeling of utter frustration about the possibility of any definite conclusion." Strauss told Borden that he thought it impossible "to confirm or deny these fears through the use of any intelligence methods," since "the 'barber'"—Oppenheimer's friend, AEC attorney Joseph Volpe—was in a position to warn Oppie about possible telephone taps.*[94]

But those who had become the target of this attack could no longer be heedless of the danger. "Some of the 'boys' have their axe out for three of us on the GAC of AEC," wrote Conant in his diary on May 9, 1952, following a dispirited lunch at the Cosmos Club with Oppenheimer and DuBridge.[95] "Claim we have 'dragged our heels' on H bomb. Dark words about Oppie!"[96]

A week later, the Weinberg case provided an unexpected opportunity for those hoping to rid themselves of Oppenheimer. On May 16, Dean telephoned Oppenheimer at Princeton to warn that the Kenilworth Court incident "was going to pop again." Government prosecutors were plan-

*Strauss's interest in wiretaps and black-bag operations dated from a bizarre, Watergate-like incident in 1930. Believing Democratic Party officials were in possession of damaging information about his administration, President Herbert Hoover requested that Strauss, formerly his private secretary, secretly retrieve the file, authorizing him "to utilize the services of any one of our various government secret services." Strauss, in turn, approached Paul Foster, the head of the Office of Naval Intelligence in New York City, who assigned an agent to the task. While no incriminating documents were found, Strauss was evidently impressed with the potential of such clandestine—and illegal—operations.

ning a perjury indictment of Weinberg, who had continued to deny under oath any association with Steve Nelson. Dean had learned that the Crouches' story was also to be included in the indictment. Oppenheimer would probably be called to testify at Weinberg's trial and might even be indicted for perjury himself, if the prosecution believed the Crouches.[97]

Dean summoned Oppenheimer and Volpe to his office three days later. Oppenheimer, steadfastly denying that the Kenilworth Court meeting had ever taken place, reaffirmed that he had never been a member of the Communist Party.[98] Following a telephone conversation later that day between Dean and the head of the Justice Department's criminal division, the government's lawyer agreed to temporarily drop the Kenilworth Court incident from the Weinberg indictment.[99] On May 23, 1952, the indictment handed down in Washington's district court made no mention of Oppenheimer or the incident.

Although he had escaped being dragged into the Weinberg trial, Oppenheimer realized that he might yet be called to testify in the case. For Oppie, this latest sword hanging over his head may have been sufficient reason to take the step that he had been contemplating anyway. On June 12, Oppenheimer informed Dean that he intended to resign from the GAC before the question of his reappointment came before the president.[100]

Conant and DuBridge were also stepping down. Conant's ebullient diary entry of June 14, following his last GAC meeting, clearly showed his relief: "Lee DuBridge and I are through as members of the GAC!! 10½ years of almost continuous official conversations with a bad business now threatening to become really bad!!"[101]

Oppenheimer's own feelings were more bittersweet. In July, Oppie wrote to Frank that he hoped someday to return to his first love: "Physics is complicated and wondersome, and much too hard for me except as a spectator; it will have to get easy again one of these days, but perhaps not soon."[102]

15

DESCENT INTO THE MAELSTROM

Even after forcing him off the GAC and blacklisting him with the air force, Oppenheimer's foes discovered that they were still not rid of the physicist. On June 27, 1952, just before trooping over to the White House with Oppie to deliver what the physicist was calling his and Conant's "swan song" to the president, Dean approved a contract extending Oppenheimer's top-secret Q clearance. Oppie was to remain a consultant to the commission for another year.[1]

Oppenheimer also continued to advise the army and the navy on military matters. It was in that capacity that two old friends, Robert Bacher and Lee DuBridge, called upon him to settle a dispute that had arisen in a Pentagon-funded Caltech study known as Project *Vista*.[2] *Vista*'s blue-ribbon panel of scientists had disagreed over the role that tactical nuclear weapons might play in countering a Soviet invasion of western Europe. The task of writing that portion of the top-secret report fell to Oppenheimer.

Griggs's fear that *Vista* would downplay the importance of the Strategic Air Command and the H-bomb was confirmed in preliminary briefings by the Caltech panel.[3] ("We have found no great new weapons—and we believe we can get along with those we have," read the controversial chapter, written by Oppenheimer.)[4] Griggs's anxiety had risen to near-panic in December 1951, when Oppenheimer and DuBridge eluded an air force ban and gave a briefing on *Vista* to General Dwight Eisenhower, NATO's supreme commander in Europe.[5] In desperation, Finletter ordered all copies of the *Vista* report returned to his office and destroyed, on the pretext that it contained security violations.[6]

What was supposed to have been a fence-mending meeting between Griggs and Oppenheimer, subsequently arranged by Rabi, ended instead in mutual recrimination: Oppie accused Griggs of setting Vandenberg and Finletter against him; Griggs charged Oppenheimer with spreading a libelous tale—that Finletter had boasted of using the H-bomb to rule the world. An attempted rapprochement with the air force secretary, over lunch in Finletter's private dining room in the Pentagon, ended just as badly. Oppie sat stone-faced throughout the meal, virtually ignoring Finletter and his aides—who afterward told the Joint Committee that they thought it a legitimate question "whether [Oppenheimer] was a subversive."[7]

Whereas *Vista* had further poisoned Oppenheimer's relations with the air force, Griggs believed that the physicist was behind a far more nefarious plot: a campaign to stop the *Mike* test.

For Oppie's foes, the first sign of trouble had been Acheson's appointment of Oppenheimer to the State Department's Panel of Consultants on Disarmament in late April 1952.[8] Inevitably, Oppie was promptly elected the panel's chairman. Oppenheimer, in turn, persuaded a reluctant Vannevar Bush, since returned to Washington's Carnegie Institution, to join the group.

At their inaugural meeting, in mid-May, Bush had spoken vaguely but earnestly—and with "some urgency," the note taker recorded—of a "test case" that would determine, once and for all, whether the United States and the Russians were serious about reining in the thermonuclear genie.[9] In sessions to come, Bush outlined a radical proposal: a joint Soviet-American ban on thermonuclear tests. Similar to the idea that Rabi and Fermi had put forward almost three years earlier, Bush's proposal likewise required no inspection, since any violation would be quickly detected by the same methods that had ferreted out Joe-1. Without an actual test, Bush argued, neither side could be assured that its H-bomb would work. Bush dubbed his plan a nuclear "standstill."[10]

The disarmament panel honed the standstill idea over the summer, in discussions at Princeton, Harvard, and the Cosmos Club. Not least of the arguments in favor of postponing *Mike* was the fact that Soviet scientists, too, were likely to find valuable data in fallout from the test—including details about the design of the radiation-implosion device. Testing Teller's bomb, ironically, would give its secret away.[11]

The standstill idea also received support, initially, from Acheson and the State Department. Gordon Arneson reminded the secretary of state that *Mike* "may well represent a point of no return," as the last opportunity to "avert the descent into the Maelstrom."[12] In early September, the panel submitted their case to the State Department.[13]

Still bitter about the fate of *Vista,* Oppenheimer had deliberately avoided becoming too closely identified with the standstill.[14] But he had discussed the details with Bush during the train ride down to Princeton for the panel's first meeting and had later inquired of Bradbury whether a postponement of *Mike* would seriously interrupt Operation *Ivy.* In his diary, Dean expressed concern at Oppenheimer's "undue interest in postponement of that operation."[15]

Bush had also discussed the standstill idea with Conant. But the Harvard chemist, with less than a week to serve on the GAC, had evidently had enough of lost causes.[16] Rabi, who was about to replace Oppenheimer as chairman of the General Advisory Committee, was similarly cautious.

There was no such ambivalence at the Pentagon, however—where Arneson reported "very strong feelings" against the standstill.[17] Lovett even urged the panel to destroy Bush's memo and all its supporting documents, lest the group become the next target of Senator Joseph McCarthy.

Even as the standstill idea was being debated in Washington, the question of creating a rival to Los Alamos still hung in the balance. That spring, fate had intervened to remove two of the project's most vocal supporters from the scene. In March, McMahon had been diagnosed with terminal cancer.[18] Although the senator and Borden tried to keep his illness a secret, the disease kept McMahon bedridden during a critical time. In early May, Lawrence was hospitalized with ulcerative colitis, a debilitating disease exacerbated by stress. Once out of the hospital, he was off to Balboa and Yosemite for two weeks of rest, canceling a planned visit to Washington.[19]

Fearful that the air force on its own was about to establish a second Los Alamos at Chicago, Dean on June 9, 1952, decided to preempt that possibility by asking the regents of the University of California to approve a new laboratory at Livermore.[20] But the AEC chairman had defiantly rejected Teller's plea for a written charter spelling out that Livermore's first and principal job would be building bombs.[21]

In Lawrence's absence, York had continued his delicate balancing act. When describing the new lab to Bradbury, he emphasized diagnostic experiments.[22] Two weeks later, however, York told the Rad Lab's business manager that Livermore's "primary objective" would be developing thermonuclear weapons.[23]

Ernest returned to Berkeley long enough to have York brief him and the AEC's head of military application on the real mission of Livermore. Lawrence was stunned at York's matter-of-fact description of an ambitious, independent laboratory that would begin designing nuclear weapons from its first day.[24] Just a few weeks earlier, an aide had reported to Borden that Lawrence remained reluctant "to get fully into the weapons field" and seemed interested, instead, "in instrumentation, research, and [fusion energy.]"[25] Understandably confused about Livermore's real reason-for-being, Dean ordered a showdown meeting in Berkeley to settle both the second-lab question and the fate of the MTA.

On the morning of July 17, Lawrence confronted the issue of Livermore with Bradbury, York, and Teller in his Rad Lab office. Ernest emphasized that the second lab "was to be additive to the Los Alamos effort and that it was the furtherance of the over-all program that was the objective."[26] When he asked if anyone disagreed, Teller instantly spoke up. His fear, Edward said, was that Livermore would become "nothing but a service organization," unless the new lab's charter specifically allowed it not only to design and build nuclear weapons but to test them in Nevada and the Pacific.[27]

The impasse continued into the evening with a cocktail party at Berkeley's posh Claremont Hotel, where the group was joined by Dean. At the bar overlooking the tennis courts, Teller—with a "lugubrious face," York later recalled—announced loudly that he had changed his mind and was not coming to Livermore after all. "Let him go, we'll be better off without him," Lawrence told York in disgust.

Following dinner, however, a peacemaker—Admiral Hayward—intervened. Persuading Dean to return to Lawrence's office, Hayward had drafted a letter that would, he hoped, break the stalemate. An exasperated Dean agreed to sign the letter but insisted upon addressing it to Lawrence, not Teller. The key phrase spoke of "an additional and broad effort" at Livermore.[28]

While Haywood's letter fell short of an explicit charter for the lab, the compromise proved acceptable to both Lawrence and Teller.[29] The following morning, Ernest, suffering another colitis attack, returned to Balboa, leaving the details of organizing the work at Livermore up to York and Teller. In a telephone call, Lawrence passed the good tidings along to Murray, who rejoiced that "the race was on, not only on an international scale, but within the boundaries of the United States as well—and between the best in the scientific fraternity."[30]

Teller's joy was more modulated. He had already asked for and received a year's leave of absence from Chicago and had recently informed the Joint Committee that—"either rightly or wrongly"—he was going to Livermore.[31] (Fermi and von Neumann had each urged him not to take the job.) But an ironic comment may have reflected a dawning realization on Edward's part of the price he would have to pay for his victory: "I have quit the appeasers and joined the fascists," he glumly told a friend of Rabi's.[32]

Almost as an afterthought, Dean and the commission voted to cancel the Mark II shortly after the Claremont meeting. At the Rad Lab, Alvarez greeted the decision with something close to relief.[33] Luie—who had once boasted to the Joint Committee that the MTA would produce a half-ton of plutonium annually—had long since come to view the giant machine as an albatross around his neck. The trouble-plagued Mark I had finally achieved a sustained beam in late May. But, tellingly, the occasion was celebrated without Lawrence, who remained bedridden by his illness. Altogether, the AEC had spent some $45 million on the MTA project since its inception.

There were other, less tangible costs. The day following Livermore's muted celebration, Brookhaven's Cosmotron began operating, generating the world's first 1-billion-electron-volt beam. By contrast, Berkeley's Bevatron remained unfinished.[34] Alvarez calculated that work on the machine had been delayed by at least a year because of the focus upon the Mark I and the disruption caused by the loyalty oath.

Alvarez likewise blamed the MTA and the oath controversy for the fact that he was no longer "in the front lines" of physics.[35] Feeling isolated intellectually and socially, he avoided the Rad Lab table at the Faculty Club, eating his meals instead with grad students and technicians half his age.

Across the Pacific, last-minute changes were still being made to *Mike,* the result of belatedly discovered design flaws, even as discussions continued in Washington about postponing the test.[36] But mounting resistance to the standstill had put an end to Bush's hope that his plan might give Truman's successor the option of reversing course and canceling the Super.[37]

From Georgetown Hospital, Brien McMahon sent word to the White House that he would start impeachment proceedings against Truman if *Mike* was not detonated on schedule. Dean received a telephone call from Strauss, "greatly disturbed—he only calls me when he is disturbed," wrote the long-suffering AEC chairman in his diary—who complained about Oppenheimer's continuing interference with the H-bomb.[38]

Only a few days before the test, Dean dispatched AEC commissioner Eugene Zuckert to Eniwetok to see if *Mike* might still be postponed.[39] But Zuckert found that neither he nor the president could stop the juggernaut that had been set in motion. Reached by telephone at the Chicago hotel where he was making a campaign stop, Truman told Dean that he would not jeopardize the schedule for Operation *Ivy* by calling a halt to *Mike*.[40]

The test that Borden called the "thermonuclear *Trinity*" took place, as scheduled, on November 1, 1952, three days before the U. S. presidential election. In a few millionths of a seconds, the device that Los Alamos dubbed "the Sausage" vaporized the tiny coral island of Elugelab, digging out of the seabed a crater some 200 feet deep and 1½ miles wide. *Mike* was half again as powerful as its creators had predicted—more than 10 megatons.[41] A passenger, with LeBaron, in an air force plane some 60 miles away, Thomas Murray likened the spectacle to "gazing into eternity, or into the gates of hell."[42]

Ironically, neither Teller nor Lawrence was on hand to witness the test. Lawrence, suffering from another colitis attack, was back home. At Griggs's suggestion, Teller was in the basement of the geology building on the Berkeley campus, staring at a seismograph. Because of the bad blood caused by the battle over the second lab, Edward felt unwelcome at the Pacific test site. Alerted by a telephone call from York when the firing signal for *Mike* was given, Teller watched as, minutes later, the instrument's needle moved almost imperceptibly, registering the bomb's shock wave as it passed through the Earth's crust. Lawrence was the first to offer congratulations.[43]

For Borden, too, the moment was one of triumph and vindication. Unwilling to trust the news about *Mike* to the telephone, Dean invited the Joint Committee staffer to the AEC building to hear the details in person.

But for one prominent veteran of the H-bomb lobby, *Mike* came too late. McMahon had died some three months before, the superbomb and a vastly expanded U.S. atomic arsenal his legacy.

At Princeton, where Oppenheimer and nine other scientist-advisers to the Pentagon were meeting at the institute's guest house, the atmosphere was subdued, even grim, a week after the test. Oppie and the members of the Science Advisory Committee to the Office of Defense Mobilization were debating whether to resign en masse. *Mike* had been only the latest and most spectacular example of how the Truman administration had ignored its experts.[44] But the scientists finally decided against such a drastic step, hoping that the next occupant of the White House—President-elect Dwight Eisenhower—might be more receptive to their advice.

Another reason for the gloom that hung over those gathered at the house on Battle Road was a "distasteful" rumor that one scientist said was circulating at MIT: the air force, he understood, was lobbying hard to get Oppenheimer's AEC security clearance revoked.[45]

Since *Vista,* the air force's "total passion" had been oriented toward ending Oppenheimer's influence in Washington, an aide reported to Borden.[46] For the past several months, the Joint Committee's executive director had been diligently preparing his own case against Oppenheimer.[47]

It had long been obvious to Borden that he could not accomplish that task alone. The previous June, he had brought a friend and former classmate down from New York to serve as the committee's counsel. Like Borden, John Walker was a top graduate of Yale Law School.[48] Borden had also hired another staffer, a former FBI agent who had been assigned to Los Alamos after the war. Frank Cotter's assignment was to spearhead an independent investigation of Oppenheimer.

The first job that Borden assigned Walker had been to craft a forty-page-long "Atomic Program Chronology," meant to provide evidence for Borden's claim that delays in the country's nuclear weapons program could be traced to what was, at best, stunning negligence and at worse deliberate sabotage.[49]

But, as Dean would note, the real purpose of Walker's chronology was "to show that the Joint Committee has always been right."[50] Its implicit argument—that the Soviets had drawn abreast, or even moved ahead, of the United States in nuclear research because of Fuchs's treason—had likewise been a major emphasis in Teller's Pentagon briefings and was one reason for their extraordinary impact there.

Dean had initially thought to counter Teller's claim by a careful reading of the British spy's confession—"what [Fuchs] did say and what he didn't say"—but finally abandoned the effort as fruitless.[51] Instead, the AEC chairman had encouraged Bethe to write a refutation of Teller—one which prompted, in reply, a "rather violent" rebuttal from Edward.[52]

Borden and Walker likewise remained haunted by the belief that there was another spy still at large in the U.S. nuclear weapons program.[53] Thus the similarities that the CIA observed between Russian reactors and those at Hanford had persuaded the Joint Committee that the "Soviets must have had agents who are as yet undiscovered."[54]

Believing that Oppenheimer was the prime candidate for this "second Fuchs," Borden next gave Walker the task of reviewing Oppie's classified correspondence going back to the war, as well as the minutes of every GAC meeting.[55]

But McMahon's death had meanwhile removed Borden's sponsor and protector, while the results of the 1952 election had returned the Senate to the Republicans. McMahon's successor, New York congressman Sterling Cole, let Borden know that he should begin looking for a new job.

Borden intended his own legacy to be an even lengthier "H-bomb Chronology," also written by Walker, who had begun working late into the evening and weekends in order to finish the ninety-one-page document in time for Eisenhower's inauguration.[56]

For Walker, there was still a nagging question that the committee's documents had been unable to answer: how much had the Russians actually learned about the American H-bomb from Fuchs? Although the British spy had attended the 1946 Los Alamos conference on the H-bomb, the focus there had been upon Teller's original Super—since thought to be unworkable. If the Russians had followed Teller's lead, as Oppenheimer and Bethe believed, they might still be traveling down the wrong path.

But Teller claimed that radiation implosion—the key concept behind *Mike*—had also been discussed at the Los Alamos meeting. Bethe disagreed, and the question remained unresolved.[57] Walker had summed up the conundrum neatly in a memo to Borden: "Our entire H-bomb program rests, viz-a-viz the Russians, on a gigantic assumption—that we have a short cut and that they are blindly following the 1946 information given them by Fuchs. . . . Under the circumstances, the only point missing is radiation-implosion."[58]

Hoping to shed light on the mystery, Borden had asked Hoover for a copy of the bureau's interview with Fuchs, but the request was denied.[59] Finding the AEC similarly uncooperative, Walker finally turned for help to Princeton's John Wheeler, who had been the committee's ally on the H-bomb and in the second-lab debates. Walker sent Wheeler four pages of his draft chronology, plus two pages taken from a classified Los Alamos history.[60] The six-page sheaf of top-secret documents contained references to the 1946 superbomb conference, details of the design of the *Mike* device, and a précis of the two dueling chronologies prepared by Bethe and Teller.[61]

On the evening of January 6, 1953, Wheeler and a colleague set out from Princeton by overnight train for a meeting with Walker in Washington. When the physicist arrived at the Capitol early the following morning, he telephoned Borden in a panic to announce that he had lost the document on the train en route, presumably during a trip to the lavatory. After dismantling Wheeler's briefcase with a pocketknife on the committee's conference table, without results, Borden notified the FBI. The bureau ordered the Pullman car in which Wheeler had been riding put on a separate siding and minutely examined, while other agents walked the tracks all the way back to Trenton, New Jersey, and interviewed the car's passengers. But no trace of the lost document was found.[62]

Informed of the incident, Eisenhower immediately suspected an "inside job" and wondered aloud whether Borden might actually have been colluding with Fuchs all along.[63] Incredulous that so much sensitive information could be treated so carelessly, Ike summoned the AEC commissioners—

"like errant schoolboys," one said—before him in the Oval Office. The Joint Committee was next to feel what one member called the "unshirted hell" of the president's ire.[64]

Nor was the irony of the situation lost upon Borden. With chagrin he learned that the "Wheeler incident," as he thought of it, was regarded as the "Borden incident" by the commission and the White House.[65] Rather than drawing attention, as Borden had intended, to Oppenheimer and the AEC's supposed malfeasance in the matter of the Super, the H-bomb chronology had inadvertently identified Borden himself as a security risk. Called on the carpet by Cole and the Joint Committee in executive session, the staffer miserably volunteered, "Shoot me or fire me."[66]

Livermore had formally opened for business on September 2, 1952, the day after Labor Day. Early that morning, a gaggle of a half-dozen scientists—dubbed "Teller's Flying Circus" by the guards—arrived at the gate, eager to begin work. But Edward was "miffed" that Lawrence had named Herbert York, not him, to head the new lab.[67]

The x-ray room of the dispensary was pressed into service as York's office. In keeping with the hurried atmosphere of the place, workmen simply covered the black, lead-lined walls with white paint and laid new linoleum. The bathroom, the only place with running water, was transformed into a makeshift chemistry lab; drums of corrosive chemicals, to be used in the analysis of airborne debris from nuclear tests, were stored in shower stalls. The base morgue was converted into a classified documents vault. The old drill hall, the only building large enough to accommodate all 123 of the lab's scientists and engineers, doubled as an auditorium and makeshift machine shop.[68]

The laboratory was afflicted with the usual problems common to any new enterprise, as well as some that were unique. Scientists complained of an inadequate number of desk lamps and telephones, and no mail service. Two physicists shared a single office in a shower. Draftsmen in the un-air-conditioned barracks were sent home when 100-degree temperatures caused sweat to smear the drawings. Especially sensitive discussions were held in an automobile parked at the end of the runway. Engineers hunting rabbits with bows and arrows at lunchtime posed an occasional hazard.

But there was no longer any doubt about the real purpose of Livermore when Lawrence, Teller, and York met with commission members at AEC headquarters on September 8. While Lawrence spoke vaguely of pursuing "promising new concepts," Teller outlined for the commission—in detail and with prepared sketches—his idea for a radically different type of H-bomb, called "Ramrod."[69] Ramrod was to be a thermonuclear trigger for an even larger bomb of uncompressed deuterium. Behind the device lay Teller's still-unabandoned dream of the Super.

The only new structures to be erected at the site were both devoted to Project *Whitney*, the weapons program at Livermore.[70] The dimensions of the cinder-block Fabrication and Assembly Building had been dictated by the requirements of the 21-ton radiation-implosion Alarm Clock, the first device that York planned to build at the lab. A second building was reserved for Livermore's Univac computer, to be used in designing the new Alarm Clock and other weapons.[71]

As part of Livermore's unwritten promise not to compete with or draw resources from Los Alamos, the emphasis at the new lab was upon daring innovation and "bolder" designs.[72] (York joked that a Livermore-designed primary could be any shape but Fat Man–round.)[73] In a compromise meant to placate Teller, York appointed the mercurial physicist to the lab's six-member Steering Committee and gave him sole veto power over its decisions on laboratory programs. That the Ramrod was now the first priority of Project *Whitney* was one result. Another was the fact that a modernized version of the hydride would be the first atomic weapon designed and tested by the lab.

In a jury-rigged blockhouse built within the drill hall, no more than 100 yards from York's office, a two-man team of scientists worked late into the night, mixing uranium with deuterated polyethylene and compressing the mixture in the breech of a 16-inch artillery piece.[74] Teller's hydride bomb was to be tested in the Nevada desert that spring.

Except for unannounced weekly visits, Lawrence was a curiously missing presence at the lab he had helped to create. Early in 1953, Ernest and Molly, their daughter, Margaret, and the family's doctor sailed as passengers onboard a Standard Oil tanker to the Middle East and Europe, for a ten-week tour brokered by Neylan. Like the landscape painting that Lawrence had also recently taken up, at Molly's urging, the cruise was a welcome and needed distraction. John Lawrence hoped it might be a cure for his brother's worsening bouts of colitis.

But Ernest had meanwhile found another diversion—an invention—which put new demands on his time. For almost a year, Lawrence had been working on a new type of picture tube for color television, a technology then in its infancy.[75] Ernest hoped that his invention, conceived in spare moments spent on the beach at Balboa, might also make him rich, the equal of those wealthy businessmen he admired. Rowan Gaither and Alfred Loomis bankrolled the founding of a new corporation, which Lawrence christened "Chromatics." A dilapidated Oakland warehouse was readied as an assembly line for the day when the picture tube was perfected.[76]

Meanwhile, turning the garage of a vacation home that he bought on the slopes of Mt. Diablo, near Livermore, into a makeshift workshop, Lawrence brought Alvarez and others from Berkeley to tinker with the device on nights and weekends. Suffused with the sickly-sweet smell of melted solder, the tiny, crowded garage recaptured for Ernest some of the innocent camaraderie of the early Rad Lab.

On Monday, March 30, 1953, carpenters at the Nevada Test Site put the final touches on a 300-foot wooden tower—three times the height of *Trinity*'s—for Teller's uranium-hydride bomb. On the eve of the test, code-named *Ruth,* Los Alamos veterans had come to regard the confident young upstarts from the rival weapons laboratory with a mixture of curiosity and disdain. (Los Alamos scientists transported their bombs to the test site in custom-made containers of finely machined metal, painted army olive-drab. By contrast, the boxes that contained Livermore's bomb were made of silver-painted plywood. "Ours looked like it came from a garage," said one California physicist enviously.)[77]

Early Tuesday morning, the countdown for *Ruth* began. It ended a short time later with a pregnant pause and what one Livermore weaponeer described as a "sickeningly small" explosion. When the dust and smoke cleared, most of the tower remained standing; only the top portion had disappeared, remnants of it hanging down at weird angles. The ensuing silence was finally broken by hoots of derisive laughter from Los Alamos physicists; one of whom observed, sotto voce, that next time Livermore should build either a bigger bomb or a smaller tower.

In Washington that spring, President Eisenhower was still becoming accustomed to the world that *Mike* had made. Briefed by Dean even before the inauguration on the results of the H-bomb test, Ike had visibly paled when the island of Elugelab was described as "missing" following the explosion.[78]

Thomas Murray was another whose thinking had been fundamentally changed by the superbomb. After he witnessed *Mike,* Murray's memos to the president on the subject of nuclear weapons assumed even more of a religious fervor. In a draft letter that he asked Truman to give to Eisenhower, Murray urged the president-elect to make a new overture at international control—offering "the Russians a last clear chance to avoid a likely doomsday."[79]

In the wake of Dean's briefing, Ike proved surprisingly receptive to Murray's message. Whereas Acheson had counseled that the 1952 disarmament panel's report should be withheld from the public as too disturbing, Eisenhower wholeheartedly agreed with the report's conclusion; namely, that there was an urgent "need for candor about the arms race." Inviting Oppenheimer and Bush to personally make the case for greater openness before the National Security Council that May, Ike afterward told his secretary of state, John Foster Dulles, that one of his administration's goals would be to inform the public about the growing destructiveness of nuclear weapons and, specifically, about the dangers of an unrestricted arms race.[80]

The fact that Oppenheimer was once again advising a president infuriated and depressed Borden, who learned that Oppie had even scheduled a personal meeting with Ike—"on an urgent matter that he would reveal to no one but [Eisenhower]"—for the end of May; coincidentally, Borden's last day on the Joint Committee.[81] In frustration, Borden turned to Strauss, who had provided some of the material for Borden's ill-fated H-bomb chronology from his own personal files.[82]

Eisenhower, worried that he might come under attack for security lapses following the lost-document fiasco, had made Strauss his special assistant for atomic energy a few weeks earlier.[83] (One of Strauss's early actions in that role was to head off Oppenheimer's planned meeting with Ike.) Strauss had welcomed Borden to his office in the old Executive Office Building in late April, where the two men almost certainly discussed Oppie.[84]

Strauss had also been one of the sources for an attack upon Oppenheimer that appeared in the May 1953 issue of *Fortune* magazine. *Fortune* editor Charles Murphy, the anonymous author of "The Hidden Struggle for the H-Bomb," was a reserve air force officer and personal friend of Finletter's.[85] Strauss and Murphy would likewise collaborate on a subsequent *Fortune* article, designed to counteract an essay by Oppenheimer in the July 1953 issue of *Foreign Affairs*. Approved in advance by the president, Oppie's article praised Ike's new policy of candor about the arms race.[86]

As Borden and Strauss were now forced to admit, not only had their campaign against the physicist been ineffective, but the tide of events seemed to be running strongly in Oppie's favor. The Weinberg trial, which Borden originally hoped would implicate both Oppenheimer and his former grad student in espionage, had instead made the mysterious "Scientist X" something of a folk hero.

In March 1953, Weinberg had been found not guilty of lying under oath four years earlier, when he had denied to HUAC ever belonging to the Communist Party. The government had been unwilling to reveal the wiretap evidence that gave proof of Weinberg's meeting with Steve Nelson and Weinberg's party membership. Likewise, the Justice Department had been too fearful of the Crouches' vulnerability as witnesses to even raise the Kenilworth Court episode during the trial.[87] Although the presiding judge voiced his dismay at the jury's verdict, Weinberg went free.[88]

With the aid of Vice Admiral Hyman Rickover—the driving force behind the navy's nuclear submarine program, and a long-time Joint Committee ally—Borden had meanwhile lined up a job as special assistant to the vice president of Westinghouse's reactor division in Pittsburgh.[89] Before leaving the government, however, Borden had also arranged though his successor on the Joint Committee—Corbin Allardice, a former AEC public relations man—a consultancy contract as well as a security clearance for another year.[90]

On May 14, 1953, Borden checked out Oppie's security file one last time from the AEC document vault.[91] Retreating to the family's vacation home on the banks of the St. Lawrence River, Borden would spend the next three months brooding over Oppenheimer's voluminous dossier.[92]

On his last day at the Joint Committee, Borden had handed Allardice a short memo on unfinished business. Among his suggestions—"members should contribute money to a fund for coffee served during Committee meetings," and "re-interviewing Fuchs"—was an attached list that contained thirty-eight questions regarding Oppenheimer.[93]

"In the 1940–1942 period, did Dr. Oppenheimer have any close friends who were *not* identified with Communism?" Borden wondered.[94]

16

NOT MUCH MORE THAN A KANGAROO COURT

IN EARLY JUNE 1953, Strauss told Hoover that he intended to accept the post of AEC chairman, which Eisenhower had offered him three months earlier. Strauss had originally demurred, in part because he suspected those around the president of being too liberal or at least too sympathetic to Oppenheimer. He was particularly suspicious of Ike's national security adviser, Robert Cutler, who still served with Oppie on the board of the Harvard Corporation. In accepting the job, Strauss had warned Ike that he was going to approach Cutler and "'lay the cards on the table' concerning Oppenheimer."[1]

The only "bright part in his taking over these new difficult duties," Strauss told the FBI's Charles Bates, "was the fact that the FBI had been most cooperative with him and he felt he could rely on the Director and the Bureau in matters of mutual interest." Indeed, later that day Strauss requested and received Oppenheimer's security file from Hoover.[2]

Less than a week after being sworn in as AEC chairman, Strauss ordered the classified documents library at Princeton's Institute for Advanced Study eliminated and replaced with a facility under the commission's control.[3] But Strauss discovered that he was one day too late to cut Oppenheimer off entirely from atomic secrets. In one of his last acts as chairman, Dean had renewed Oppenheimer's consultancy contract for another year—to June 30, 1954—on the grounds that Oppie needed a Q clearance to help implement the recommendations of the disarmament panel.[4]

Strauss was also doing what he could to block the administration's push for greater "candor." Early on, he had proposed that all official statements on the hydrogen bomb be cleared first with his office—a form of censorship that Eisenhower resisted. By that fall, when Ike proposed an ambitious plan of his own to share civilian atomic power with the world, Strauss effectively hijacked the administration's "Operation Candor," transforming it—during breakfast meetings at the Metropolitan Club with presidential adviser and speech writer C. D. Jackson—into what Jackson called "Operation Wheaties." What had begun as a sincere effort to inform the public about the dangers of nuclear war was being transformed into a cynical public relations campaign.[5]

As AEC chairman, Strauss showed an almost paranoid obsession with Oppenheimer: passing along to Hoover, for example, the gossip that Earl Browder's son had secured a position at the institute because of Oppie, and claiming that Oppenheimer was cheating on his AEC expense accounts. ("Admiral Strauss stated that while this was a small matter in itself, he thought it did indicate an interesting sidelight upon the character of Dr. Oppenheimer.")[6]

That fall, Strauss hired David Teeple, one of the former army CIC agents who had shadowed Martin Kamen to the rendezvous with Soviet diplomats at Bernstein's Fish Grotto, and later worked for Hickenlooper. Teeple's job was to dig up derogatory information on Oppenheimer.[7] Strauss also put McKay Donkin, an investigator in the AEC's Office of Security, on "special assignment" to assist Teeple. The AEC chairman even personally helped line up interviews for FBI agents investigating the physicist.[8] Increasingly, Strauss treated the commission's security office and the bureau itself as his own private detective agency.[9]

Nor did Strauss hesitate to use his new office to settle old scores.[10] More than three years after Carroll Wilson had left the commission, Strauss interceded to deny the former AEC general manager a clearance when Wilson took a new job at the Metals and Control Corporation. Wilson had finally turned for help to Vannevar Bush and Henry Smyth.[11] When Gordon Arneson, the State Department's atomic energy expert, ran afoul of the man he derisively called "the Tugboat Admiral," Strauss had Arneson declared a security risk and fired.[12]

The Russians' failure to fulfill his worst fears by testing a hydrogen bomb was disturbing his sleep that summer, the AEC chairman told friends.[13] The suspense ended in late August, with the test of Joe-4. But AFOAT-1's analysis of the debris from the bomb actually showed that it was the United States, and not the Soviet Union, which held the thermonuclear advantage. The Soviet device had been similar to Teller's original Alarm Clock, with a yield of 400 kilotons, far less than the multimegaton

Mike.[14] The CIA believed that the radiation-implosion secret of the new Super remained unfamiliar to—or was at least as yet undemonstrated by—America's adversary.

While the advent of a Soviet H-bomb was not unexpected, it had the effect of strengthening Strauss's hand. That autumn, Eisenhower quietly acceded to the AEC chairman's request that all official statements concerning H-bombs be cleared first with him. That step marked the end of "Operation Candor." As Ike announced in a press statement—drafted by Strauss—his administration henceforth did not intend to disclose details "of our strength in atomic weapons of any sort."[15]

By that fall, Borden's original list of 38 questions concerning Oppenheimer had swelled to 500.[16] "All his spare time seems to be devoted to brooding about your business," Ken Mansfield told Teller in early November.[17]

Also worrying Borden was the fact that those who were left behind on the Joint Committee did not seem to share his obsession with Oppie.[18] That included Frank Cotter, who had just completed his months-long review of the case against Oppenheimer. Cotter concluded that legal action against the scientist was problematic at best, since much of the evidence was based upon illegal wiretaps. Moreover, the former FBI agent thought an actual trial both unnecessary and unwise, as likely to alienate the nation's scientists. "I believe that in the future he will become a weaker voice and hope that he will never become a voice speaking for martyrdom," Cotter advised the Joint Committee. He recommended that they merely "continue to follow the case."[19] Allardice, Borden's successor, agreed.[20]

As Borden was well aware, the letter that he had drafted for McMahon to give to Truman, warning about Oppenheimer, had never been delivered. A similar letter, written for Cole's signature and intended for Eisenhower, likewise remained unsent.[21] Meanwhile, Borden's few remaining allies on the committee were fast dwindling: Walker had already returned to his law practice in New York.

The final straw may have been a memo that Cole and Allardice wrote in early November, intending to send to Hoover. Although they appended a partial list of Borden's questions, the two noted that "[they had] not reached any definite conclusion on Dr. Oppenheimer."[22] Borden feared, with reason, that Cole and Allardice were preparing to wash their hands of the case.[23]

The prospect that Oppenheimer might get away with conduct that Borden considered treasonous finally compelled the ex-staffer to act. On November 7, 1953, Borden mailed from Pittsburgh's main post office a three-and-a-half-page, single-spaced letter that he had been mentally writing for more than six months. Addressing the letter to Hoover, Borden recapitulated Oppenheimer's extraordinary influence as a government adviser, listing twenty-one "factors"—most linked to events before 1943—that led him to his "own exhaustively considered opinion . . . that more probably than not J. Robert Oppenheimer is an agent of the Soviet Union."[24]

Hoover's immediate suspicion was that Borden's letter might be a plot to embarrass Eisenhower, in retribution for the humiliation of the Wheeler incident.[25] But he also recognized, Hoover told aides, that he "might later be confronted with the question of what the FBI did about it."[26] While little or nothing in Borden's letter was new to Hoover, the FBI director ordered his agents to interview the ex-staffer.

What else to do about the letter was a dilemma inadvertently solved for Hoover a few days later during a visit from Thomas Murray. The commissioner had come to the bureau to complain about Strauss's hiring of Teeple, but also to inquire whether the FBI had anything new on Oppenheimer.[27] Hoover told Murray about the letter, complaining that Borden had decided "to dump [it] into the lap of the FBI."

At Murray's request, Hoover sent him a copy of the letter a week later. The FBI director also sent a copy to Herbert Brownell, Eisenhower's attorney general. Strauss found a copy of the letter—along with a brief note from Hoover and Oppenheimer's latest FBI file—on his desk when he arrived for work at the commission on Monday morning, November 30.[28]

On Tuesday evening, Strauss received a distraught telephone call from Defense Secretary Charles Wilson, who confessed that Borden's letter had come as "something of a shock." Wilson wondered whether Oppenheimer had not also been involved in the Wheeler incident.[29] "I do not know that he is a Communist," Strauss told Wilson, "but I do know that he is a liar."[30]

The next day, Eisenhower learned about Borden's letter from Wilson. ("Worse one so far," the defense secretary told the president.)[31] Ike recalled that early in his administration someone—he thought it was Strauss—had warned him that Oppenheimer was not to be trusted.[32] Having recently come under attack by McCarthy for laxness in confronting communism, Eisenhower summoned Wilson, Strauss, and Brownell to the White House to discuss what to do about Oppenheimer. The president also ordered a meeting of top officials in the Oval Office for early the following morning.[33]

On Thursday, December 3, Eisenhower ordered that a "blank wall" be put between Oppenheimer and atomic secrets, instructing Brownell to investigate the possibility of "further action, prosecutive or otherwise." Hoover and Strauss feared that Oppenheimer—then traveling in Europe—might decide, upon hearing the news, either to defect to the Soviet Union or to return home and publicly challenge the president's order. Accordingly, they decided to keep the suspension of Oppie's Q clearance a secret. The White House meeting adjourned without agreement on what other steps to take against the physicist.[34]

Indeed, Strauss and Hoover were themselves uncertain about how to proceed. Six months earlier, when McCarthy and his chief counsel had broached with Hoover the possibility of a Senate inquiry focusing on Oppenheimer, the FBI director had discouraged such a step, cautioning that any such hearing would require "a great deal of preliminary spade work."[35] While Strauss told Hoover that he "felt that an inquiry into Oppenheimer's activities might be well worthwhile," he, too, "hoped it would not be done prematurely or by a group that did not thoroughly prepare itself for the investigation."[36] Strauss subsequently wrote Senator Robert Taft, a longtime friend and political ally, "[McCarthy's committee] is not the place for such an investigation, and the present is not the time."[37] Nothing came of McCarthy's threat.

But Borden's letter had suddenly resurrected the possibility of an investigation of Oppenheimer. One option that had been raised at the White House meeting was convening, under AEC auspices, a Personnel Security Board hearing. Heretofore only applied on a regional basis, and in cases much less notorious than Oppenheimer's, a PSB investigation of Oppenheimer's "character, associations, and loyalty" promised to avoid the klieglight publicity of an open congressional hearing. The fact that it would be conducted in secret and was not bound by the usual legal rules of evidence—indeed, was "not much more than a kangaroo court," as former AEC attorney Volpe had observed—made it all the more attractive to Strauss.[38]

Hoover, however, had his own reasons for wanting to avoid a loyalty hearing. His real worry, the FBI director confided to Brownell, was that an investigation of Oppenheimer might reveal "a lot of information which could not be publicly disclosed"—i.e., the bureau's illicit wiretaps. Hoover told Strauss that he had "grave doubts as to the wisdom of a hearing."[39]

As expected, the FBI's interview of Borden had yielded no dramatic new evidence to buttress the charges raised in his letter. (Agents found the ex-staffer "quite intelligent, extremely verbose and inclined toward generalities."[40] Borden, for his part, dismissed the interrogation as "a rather futile and diffuse discussion.")[41] An FBI analysis of Borden's letter, done for Hoover, concluded that it went beyond the evidence in claiming Oppenheimer was a spy.[42]

Another who opposed a hearing was the AEC's new general manager, Kenneth Nichols. Strauss had appointed Groves's former aide to the post just two weeks after becoming chairman.[43] Nichols feared that an Oppenheimer hearing might backfire, damaging the nation's nuclear program by creating dissension within the scientific ranks and making Oppie into a martyr. He proposed that Strauss simply turn Oppenheimer's files over to McCarthy instead.[44]

Strauss, too, worried that alienating the nation's scientists might be too high a price to pay for destroying Oppenheimer's influence. During a visit to Strauss's office on the afternoon of December 3, Teller found the AEC chairman anxious and preoccupied with the case—"predicting disastrous consequences should Oppenheimer's clearance be called into question."[45]

But a long-suppressed secret, finally come to light, would promptly change this calculation. While Strauss was still at the White House on the morning of December 3, Allardice was at FBI headquarters, meeting with Hoover aide Louis Nichols. Allardice had learned from Cole about Borden's infamous letter and wished to be helpful in the bureau's investigation. (An apprentice fingerprint classifier at the FBI before the war, Allardice had subsequently tried, but failed, to join the ranks of special agents.) As Nichols wrote, in a rather breathless summary of the meeting:

> Allardice told me in confidence he had been informed by a source whom he believed to be extremely reliable that J. Robert Oppenheimer had stated that his contact in the Eltenton–Haakon Chevalier espionage apparatus had been his own brother, Frank Oppenheimer, and that J. Robert had admitted that his brother, Frank, had approached him prior to the time the Bureau had ever interviewed J. Robert and that it was his, Allardice's, opinion that J. Robert Oppenheimer did not want the Bureau to have this information, but he had also been led to believe the information had been furnished to the Bureau.[46]

Allardice had further noted that this particular version of events was not in the FBI files held at the Joint Committee, and volunteered that John Lansdale, Groves's former chief of security, would be "one of the best sources of information about the case."[47]

The following week, Hoover ordered the bureau's Cleveland office to interview Lansdale, who since the war had returned to his private law practice.[48] Allardice meanwhile reported that he had also contacted both Groves and William Consodine, Groves's wartime lawyer, to obtain further details of the story.

Evidently alarmed that the secret was about to come out, Groves telephoned AEC headquarters on the morning of December 10 to assure Strauss and the commission's head of security, Bryan LaPlante, that he was "checking further" into Allardice's story.[49] Strauss duly informed the FBI that Groves had contacted him and also that Consodine had identified Frank Oppenheimer, not Oppie, as the real "go-between."[50]

On December 15, FBI agents interviewed Consodine; a day later it was Lansdale's turn. While Lansdale's recollection was "hazy," he and Consodine independently described the meeting that had taken place ten years earlier in Groves's office, where the general had admitted being duped by Oppenheimer into participating in a criminal conspiracy to withhold the truth from the FBI.[51]

On his own, Groves came to FBI headquarters on December 17. There he asked Hoover aide Alan Belmont for access to MED records in the bureau's custody, in order "to refresh his memory."[52] Groves had actually wanted to see Hoover but was told by Belmont that the FBI director was out of town. "It was apparent that General Groves realized the current interest in Oppenheimer and is examining his personal position in so far as Oppenheimer is concerned in the event he is called on to testify at some hearing," Belmont wrote in a memo to his boss.[53]

From FBI headquarters, Groves hurried over to the AEC, where he told LaPlante of his concern "that the agent who interviewed him was not familiar enough with the incident or the subject matter and therefore could not properly evaluate historical data that he (Groves) would give to him."[54]

Groves agreed to be interviewed a second time by the FBI, on December 21, at his home in Darien, Connecticut. Recent conversations with Consodine, as well as a letter from Lansdale and his own review of Manhattan Project documents, had "'clarified' his recollection," Groves told the bureau's agent, Edward Burke.[55] Groves admitted that when he had ordered Oppenheimer in 1943 to give up the names of those contacted by Chevalier he had promised "to put it bluntly that it would not get to the FBI."

Groves told Burke that he had prepared a statement to give to the press in the event that the truth became public. The agent noted that the general still felt some residual loyalty to his onetime friend: "Groves stated that he desired it made a matter of record that even at this time he is not breaching his promise to Oppenheimer and if friends of Oppenheimer should someday see this record it will appear that he only discussed the matter because the facts are already known."

The following day, Hoover sent Brownell and Strauss a detailed summary of the information that had been given the FBI thus far by Lansdale, Consodine, and Groves. Hoover hardly needed to point out that the testimony of all three implicated not only Oppenheimer but Groves in more than one felony offense—withholding vital information about an espionage contact during wartime and lying to a federal official.*[56]

The last person to be interviewed in this round of interrogations was Frank Oppenheimer. Because of snowstorms blocking the mountain passes, the Denver FBI agent assigned to the task was not able to reach the

*Section 80, Title 18 of the U.S. Code specified that any individual who "knowingly or willfully falsifie[d] or conceal[ed] . . . a material fact . . . in any matter within the jurisdiction or agency of the United States" was guilty of a felony. In 1943, Groves had lied to Nichols by repeating Oppenheimer's original story that Chevalier had approached three scientists.

ranch at Blanco Basin until December 29. Once there, he got right to the point. "Were you ever approached by Haakon Chevalier or anyone else for information on the Manhattan Project?" the agent asked Oppie's brother. Frank's reply was an unequivocal "No." Frank went on to volunteer that he and his brother had never discussed being approached by Chevalier "or anyone else concerning MED projects." However, he declined the agent's request to sign a statement to that effect—lest "'a false witness' subsequently appear to contradict it."[57]

As Strauss realized, this latest twist on the Chevalier incident cast the Oppenheimer investigation into a new and altogether different light. Lacking any firm evidence that Oppie had been a member of the Communist Party, Strauss believed that the decade-old approach by Chevalier would be key to any legal case that might be made against Oppenheimer. When he first learned of Borden's letter, Strauss had gone to Bates to ask how long Oppenheimer had waited before reporting the Chevalier incident to Groves.[58]

As recently as December 8, when he returned with Eisenhower from a summit meeting in Bermuda, Strauss had seemed to be looking for an alternative to a loyalty hearing. LaPlante had suggested resolving the imbroglio by unilaterally canceling Oppenheimer's consultancy contract—a simple solution favored, as well, by Murray and Cutler.[59] Others had proposed empowering a special presidential commission to decide Oppie's fate.[60] At a tense AEC meeting on Thursday, December 10, only one commissioner—Joseph Campbell, a New York accounting executive whom Strauss had appointed to the post the previous summer— supported the idea of convening a Personnel Security Board investigation.[61]

Yet that same day, following his telephone conversation with Groves, Strauss took the first step toward a loyalty hearing by instructing William Mitchell, the AEC's general counsel, to draw up a statement of charges against Oppenheimer over the weekend.[62]

By Monday, Harold Green, a young attorney in Mitchell's office, had prepared a draft of the document, based upon Oppenheimer's AEC security file and Borden's letter.[63] At the last minute, Green decided on his own to add seven more charges to the original thirty-one, all having to do with Borden's accusations that Oppie had deliberately sabotaged the H-bomb effort. Green based the new charges upon the FBI's 1952 interviews with Teller and Pitzer.[64]

Strauss had promised Hoover that the latter could personally vet the letter of charges before it was shown to Oppenheimer, in order to ensure that the bureau's informants and wiretaps were not compromised.[65] Hoover proposed only minor changes—among them, that Frank's name be added to the charge dealing with the Chevalier incident.[66]

Elsewhere in the government, doubts about the wisdom of a hearing lingered. Strauss told Bates on December 14 that Brownell was complaining "'our ducks are not in a row' regarding Oppenheimer."[67]

For those preparing the case against the physicist, however, the long, lingering memory of setbacks and slights suffered at Oppie's hand finally overcame hesitation. To Strauss, putting his nemesis on trial—whatever the outcome—was likely to forever tarnish Oppenheimer's reputation in Washington. With the nation's political climate conditioned by war overseas and an undiminished hunt for "atom spies" at home, there was likely to be little forgiveness for those shown to be careless with secrets about the bomb. Not incidentally, an investigation of Oppenheimer also offered the prospect of sweet revenge for the humiliation that Strauss had suffered over the isotopes fiasco.

For Hoover, a PSB hearing—provided it did not divulge the FBI's secrets—promised the outcome that the attorney general, HUAC, and the Joint Committee had thus far been unwilling, or unable, to deliver, without implicating the bureau in the process.

Moreover, Groves's self-incriminating telephone call four days earlier had evidently steeled Strauss's resolve—as did a visit on December 17 to the AEC by Hoover's emissary, Belmont, who relayed the story of Groves's tortured admission concerning the Chevalier incident. Strauss told Belmont that Groves had likewise given him a new version of the story. The possibility of a perjury indictment of Oppenheimer was discussed openly by the two men. "I told Adm. Strauss that the information furnished us at least shows different stories furnished at different times by Oppenheimer," Belmont reported to Hoover.[68]

Oppenheimer returned to the United States from Paris on December 13, oblivious to the storm that was about to break.[69] During the past few months, the physicist had done little to counter the rumors and suspicions that once again were growing up around him. In April, just weeks after Weinberg's acquittal on the charge of perjury, Oppie had written a letter of recommendation for his former graduate student, attesting to Weinberg's "loyalty, integrity, veracity."*[70]

---

*Having meanwhile abandoned his original vocation for another branch of physics—optics—Weinberg was seeking a job at Spero's House of Vision in New York.

The political climate had another of Oppenheimer's former students in more desperate straits. Late in December 1953, the personal director of an oil company in Ponca City, Oklahoma, informed Oppie that Rossi Lomanitz had given his name as a job reference: "Quite frankly, we could use a man having his technical background; but because of his past public record, I find it hard to believe that his loyalty is all that it should be. . . . For your information, he has been living in a hovel on the edge of a swamp for the past three years. He has worked as a day laborer since Jan. 1950."

Invited to England to give the BBC's prestigious Reith lectures that fall, Oppenheimer and Kitty afterward paid a visit to Haakon Chevalier and his new wife, Carol, in Paris. While there, Oppie offered to help his friend with a passport problem. Hoping to visit the United States as a translator for UNESCO, Chevalier was uncertain whether to renounce his American citizenship and travel on his French passport or to seek a visa. Oppenheimer paid a social call on Jefferies Wyman, the science attaché at the American embassy in Paris and Oppie's former classmate at both Harvard and Cambridge. Oppenheimer advised Wyman that an unnamed friend might soon be contacting him for advice.[71]

Oppenheimer's visit to Chevalier did not go unnoticed by American authorities. The London embassy's legal attaché coordinated surveillance of the Oppenheimers while they were in England and the CIA took up the trail once the couple crossed the Channel. Alerted to Oppie's imminent return to the United States, Bates assured Strauss that the "FBI will take care of him in their own way."[72] Bureau agents shadowed the couple from the airport to their home in Princeton.

On December 14, Oppie telephoned Strauss at Brandy Rock Farm, the AEC chairman's retreat in the Virginia horse country, to schedule a visit two days hence. Oppenheimer wished to discuss the appointment of a Swedish scientist to the institute as well as candidates for the Einstein award. Strauss, who recorded the call, informed Bates that Oppenheimer suspected nothing.[73]

Originally, Strauss had hoped to confront Oppenheimer with the statement of charges at Brandy Rock on December 16. But Hoover's delay in vetting the letter thwarted this plan.

Instead, the showdown with Oppenheimer occurred in Strauss's AEC office on the afternoon of December 21. Nichols was also present. ("I had agreed with Strauss that he should do most of the talking.")[74] In a meeting that lasted half an hour, Strauss and Nichols showed Oppenheimer the letter of charges but refused to give him a copy. Having been warned by Mitchell not to offer the physicist any advice, the two demurred when Oppenheimer asked if they thought he should resign.

Obviously shaken by the charges against him, Oppenheimer told Nichols and Strauss that, while he was inclined toward resignation, rumors of a pending Senate investigation of the Kenilworth Court incident had convinced him that such an action "might not be too good from a public relations point of view."[75] Told by Nichols that he had only one day to make a decision on how to respond, Oppenheimer left to consult with the lawyers he had retained in the Weinberg case, Joe Volpe and Herbert Marks. When Oppie called Nichols at home that night to ask once more whether he should resign, Nichols, fearful that Oppenheimer was recording the call, again declined to give an opinion.[76]

Goaded by Strauss, Nichols telephoned Oppenheimer at Princeton the next afternoon to demand a decision. Persuading Nichols instead to grant him an extension, Oppie returned to Washington and talked to Volpe, who counseled his friend to fight the charges.

Even before Oppenheimer had notified Nichols of his response, however, Strauss had taken the first step toward collecting evidence for what would be, to all intents and purposes, a trial. On December 21, immediately following his meeting with Oppenheimer, the AEC chairman asked Hoover to install wiretaps on the telephones in Oppie's home and office at Princeton.[77]

PART FIVE

ALL THE EVIL OF THE TIMES

[Oppenheimer] does not believe the case will come to a quiet end as all the evil of the times is wrapped in this situation.

—"Summary for May 7, 1954,"
FBI wiretap

17

THE GOOD DEEDS A MAN HAS DONE BEFORE

BOTH SIDES SPENT the next two months preparing their case. After Volpe bowed out as Oppenheimer's counsel, citing a conflict of interest with the AEC, Herbert Marks suggested the physicist retain Lloyd Garrison, a New York trial lawyer and descendant of the famous abolitionist. Garrison was well known for defending civil liberty cases.[1]

In late January 1954, Strauss and Nichols chose Roger Robb, a former prosecutor with a reputation for combativeness, to present the evidence against Oppenheimer. As an assistant U.S. attorney, Robb had sat in on the Weinberg case. Earlier, Robb had successfully defended Earl Browder, as the court-appointed lawyer in the U.S. Communist leader's contempt-of-Congress trial.[2]

From the beginning, Strauss and Nichols had the advantage of knowing their adversaries' moves in advance, thanks to the FBI wiretaps, which had been put in place on New Year's Day.[3]

The taps had been operative less than a week, however, when the agent in charge of the bureau's Newark, New Jersey, office threatened to pull the plug, on ethical grounds. He "wanted to be sure that the Bureau desired the technical surveillance continued in view of the fact that it might disclose attorney-client relations," the conscientious G-man notified Hoover. The FBI director—after first checking with Strauss—replied that the wiretaps were "warranted."[4]

The monitoring of Oppie's conversations with his lawyers revealed, as Strauss had predicted, that Garrison intended to summon a parade of notables in Oppenheimer's defense. All could be expected to attest to Oppenheimer's selfless government service and sterling personal qualities. Manhattan Project veterans Rabi, Bacher, Conant, and Bush were among those whom Garrison had lined up as witnesses.[5]

But both sides surely recognized that the most important witness for the defense was almost certain to be Groves, who had always steadfastly defended his pick of Oppie to run Los Alamos. With his case against Oppenheimer well under way, Strauss began making a case against Groves.

Strauss had not bothered to hide his contempt for the former Manhattan Project director in a 1951 conversation with Borden, to whom he confided: "Groves is and always has been stupid. . . . [Strauss] added that whereas once it might have been worthwhile to consult General Groves, that time is long since past."[6]

Already aware that Groves had belatedly admitted lying to the FBI, Strauss had recently located another piece of incriminating evidence to use against the general. The letter that Groves wrote Oppenheimer in May 1950, when the physicist feared being called before HUAC, had been discovered in mid-January by an AEC security man sent to retrieve classified files from Princeton. LaPlante duly gave the letter to Bates, who passed it along to Strauss and Hoover.[7] Groves's unbidden testimonial—"that at no time did he regret his decision"—had been intended as ammunition for Oppenheimer to use against the Crouches. Strauss now planned to use it as ammunition against Groves.

Strauss and Groves probably talked about the letter as well as the upcoming hearing during a train ride together on January 21 to Groton, Connecticut, for the launching of the nuclear submarine USS *Nautilus*. Shortly afterward, therefore, Strauss told Belmont that "Groves might now be sorry that he had sent such a letter to Oppenheimer."[8]

For Hoover, too, the evidence that linked Frank to the Chevalier incident and implicated Groves in the cover-up was a welcome weapon to use against the man who had been his wartime nemesis.[9] ("From the above it is readily apparent that Groves has attempted to withhold and conceal important information concerning an espionage conspiracy violation from the FBI," Belmont wrote his boss. "Even now Groves is behaving with a certain amount of coyness in his dealings and admissions to the Bureau.")[10]

Groves himself was all too aware of how his recent admission to the FBI made his position in the case tenuous. The general also knew—or at least suspected—that Oppenheimer's calls were being monitored. On January 22, when Oppie telephoned to ask Groves if they could have lunch together the following week in New York, FBI agents recorded that Groves was "courteous [to JRO] but has indicated that he knows nothing about the case except some gossip."[11]

With the trap thus set, Strauss judged the time right to spring it. On February 19, 1954, Groves met with the AEC chairman in Washington, at Strauss's request. Asked whether he would clear Oppie now, Groves answered no. Asked, "Do you think Oppenheimer is a security risk?" Groves responded in the affirmative. Afterward, Strauss informed Robb of the results of his interrogation, reminding the lawyer to "be sure to ask these questions of Groves at the hearing."[12] Later that afternoon, Nichols took Groves to see Robb and Arthur Rolander, the AEC security man who was assisting the prosecution.[13]

Confident that the most important defense witness was now solidly in the prosecution's camp, Strauss saw no need to compromise. When Rabi proposed a deal whereby Oppenheimer would agree to resign his AEC contract in exchange for Nichols withdrawing the statement of charges, Strauss promptly rejected the offer as "out of the question." In early March, Garrison, too, told Strauss that he and Oppenheimer would "fight."[14]

With the hearing only weeks away, each side had a new appreciation of the stakes involved. Strauss told Mitchell that the "importance of the Oppenheimer case could not be stressed too much," while a defeat for the AEC would be "another 'Pearl Harbor' as far as atomic energy is concerned."[15] Brownell predicted that the hearing "would be bigger than the Alger Hiss case" and might result in a criminal indictment of Oppenheimer.[16] Strauss and Nichols—who had begun meeting daily on the case in the chairman's office by February—knew they had a vital but unseen ally in Hoover.[17] Robb and Strauss had already assured the FBI director that nothing in the bureau's files would be shared with Oppenheimer's lawyers.[18]

Under Robb's direction, Rolander began collecting documents and conducting interviews on Projects *Vista* and *Lexington,* the air force's ill-fated nuclear bomber, and AFOAT-1, which Strauss claimed Oppenheimer had tried to kill at its birth.[19]

Strauss and Nichols also did what they could to put obstacles in the path of Oppenheimer's defense. When Garrison, having had a preview of the opposition's tactics, began to rethink his early decision not to obtain a security clearance to try the case, Strauss and Nichols rejected his request on the grounds that Garrison's associate, Herbert Marks—a former AEC general counsel—was a security risk.[20] Although Garrison realized that without a clearance the defense would be at a disadvantage when it came to allegations that Oppenheimer had impeded progress on the hydrogen bomb, in deference to Marks, he decided not to press the issue.[21]

The FBI wiretaps revealed tantalizing details not only of Garrison's strategy but of the problems being encountered by the defense.

On February 6, 1954, Oppenheimer telephoned his brother in Colorado, telling Frank that he was in "considerable trouble."[22] The bureau's transcript suggests that Oppie realized not only that his phone was tapped but that his mail was being read: "J. Robert Oppenheimer also indicated that he hoped to see Frank for a talk at the first opportunity as he cannot adequately discuss the problem in a letter."

But the hoped-for visit did not take place. More than a month later, FBI agents picked up mention of Frank's name again in a telephone call from Oppie to Garrison: "Subject feels it necessary that someone contact his brother to discuss his phase of involvement."[23]

Since Garrison could not afford to take time out for the trip—the hearing was now less than two weeks away—he sent an associate in the firm, Samuel Silverman, to see Frank. Silverman arranged a rendezvous in early April at Dorothy McKibben's old Manhattan Project office in Santa Fe.

Told by Garrison simply to "go talk to Frank Oppenheimer and see what he can tell you," Silverman chatted amiably with Oppie's brother in the tiny room on East Palace Avenue.[24] Eventually, Frank invited Silverman to the ranch at Blanco Basin, a few hours' drive over the mountains. The lawyer later reported to Garrison that he and Frank had sat together on the porch overlooking the snow-covered peaks, while Frank spoke of the difficulty of running a cattle ranch.[25] Silverman drove his rental car back to Albuquerque and flew home to New York, little enlightened.

Alerted by the wiretaps to the impressive array of character witnesses that Garrison had lined up for Oppenheimer, Robb and Rolander traveled to Berkeley in early March, seeking witnesses for the prosecution. Strauss's lawyer had already decided that he and Rolander would only interview those the FBI had not already talked to, with one exception: Oppie's former colleagues at Berkeley. (As Pitzer had earlier confided to bureau agents, "We *know* this man.")[26]

The two lawyers arrived in California armed with a lengthy list of questions, based in part upon the Joint Committee's 1950 interview with Teller, which Cole and Allardice had helpfully provided.[27] Additionally, Bates had given Robb transcripts of the bureau's spring 1952 interviews with Teller and Pitzer.[28]

After talking to Pitzer and Latimer, Rolander and Robb interviewed

Lawrence in his office on campus.[29] Ernest spoke with some heat of how his colleagues had been "taken in" by Oppie, but—"giving him the benefit of doubt"—he believed that "everything [Oppenheimer] did can be attributed to bad judgment."[30] Lawrence also told Robb, emphatically, that his former friend "should never again have anything to do with the forming of policy."

Robb and Rolander interviewed Alvarez twice, at Berkeley and Livermore, probably because he was not as circumspect about Oppenheimer's motives. Blaming Oppie for the termination of the Benicia reactor project and the MTA—as well as for the fact that both Livermore and the Rad Lab were now "on the black list" with scientists—Luie hinted that there was more behind Oppenheimer's opposition to the superbomb than moral qualms. "Alvarez said that if a star basketball player suddenly started to miss shots as Oppenheimer did in this instance, everybody would think there was something wrong," Rolander wrote in notes of the interview. The head of British intelligence had once told him, Luie confided, that "Oppenheimer was a Russian agent, worse than Fuchs."*[31]

Teller had since had a charge of heart about being an anonymous informant and told Rolander and Robb that he wanted to be identified as the source for any information of his that might be used in the hearing. Robb's questions to Teller focused upon Oppie's role vis-à-vis the hydrogen bomb: "[Teller] said there is no question that Oppenheimer tried to impede the H-bomb program." As to the reason for this interference, however, Edward seemed ambivalent.

> Teller stated that he did not know what motivated Oppenheimer, nor could he prove that he had not acted in good faith. . . . He said that Oppenheimer has given a great deal of bad advice in the matter of the H-bomb, and that in the future his advice should not be taken and he should never have any more influence. . . . He said he hoped Oppenheimer's clearance would not be lifted for a mere mistake of judgment.[32]

By the time that he returned to Washington in late March, Robb was confident of victory.[33] (Warned that Oppenheimer was too "fast" and "slippery"

*Ironically, the focus of Joint Committee investigators upon Oppenheimer as the "second Fuchs" caused them to miss another real spy at Los Alamos: Harvard-trained physicist Ted Hall. In September 1954, security officials at the lab told Frank Cotter that Hall—who left the lab in spring 1946—was probably the Soviets' other source for secret documents obtained from Los Alamos.

to be caught in a cross-examination, the former prosecutor replied: "Maybe so, but then he's not been cross-examined by me before.")[34]

Strauss, too, no longer feared that the hearing might be more an embarrassment for the commission than for Oppenheimer. Hoover had sent the AEC chairman a copy of Frank Oppenheimer's FBI interview in early January.[35] For weeks, Strauss had known that both Oppenheimer brothers as well as Groves were ensnared in a tangled web of deception over the Chevalier incident: Oppie by having told Pash and Groves two different and conflicting versions of what happened, and then a third to the FBI; Groves by his failure to report Oppenheimer's admission concerning Frank to the FBI at the time; and Frank by denying to bureau agents any involvement whatsoever.

Wherever the truth lay, Strauss and Robb realized that Oppie would either have to admit to lying about the incident or else implicate his brother in the plot, whereas Groves's own complicity ensured his silence in Oppenheimer's defense. Moreover, Robb's recent interview with Lawrence meant that the prosecution would be able to counter Garrison's big guns with witnesses of equal caliber, especially on such highly technical questions as whether Oppenheimer had tried to sabotage the superbomb.

Still, Strauss was taking no chances. Smyth and Rabi had urged that Eisenhower be the one to pick the three-member Personnel Security Board that would sit in judgment of Oppenheimer. Instead, Mitchell had already chosen two members of the board, a scientist and an industrialist. Ward Evans was a chemistry professor at Chicago's Loyola University who had previously served on the AEC's regional board, almost always voting to deny clearance. Thomas Morgan had been president of Sperry Gyroscope before being appointed by Truman to a presidential commission on defense preparedness.

But the most important member of the board—its chairman—was Strauss's choice. Gordon Gray, the president of the University of North Carolina, was an attorney who, following a brief career in Democratic state politics, had been appointed secretary of the army by Truman. Perhaps the most salient of Gray's qualifications from Strauss's point of view, however, was his public defection from Adlai Stevenson's camp in the 1952 campaign. Then, as later, Gray had attacked Stevenson for being too liberal.[36]

In early March 1954, before the Gray board met for the first time, Strauss was compelled to travel to Bikini atoll, where the latest round of U.S. nuclear tests—Operation *Castle*—was taking place. The first test, code-named *Bravo,* was of a "dry" thermonuclear device, a crucial step toward development of an H-bomb small enough for a missile warhead.[37]

Like *Mike, Bravo* turned out to be far more powerful than its designers expected—exploding with a force more than twice the predicted 7 megatons. But while the fallout from *Mike* had dissipated over miles of trackless ocean, the 2 million tons of sand and coral vaporized by *Bravo* were carried by prevailing winds well outside the designated danger zone, passing over inhabited atolls of the Marshall Islands as well as the twenty-three-man crew of the Japanese fishing boat *Fukuryu Maru* (*Lucky Dragon*).[38]

By the time that Strauss returned to Washington in midmonth, one of the boat's crewmen was critically ill and most others were suffering from radiation sickness. The incident had drawn headlines in Japan, prompting criticism of U.S. nuclear testing from around the world. An impromptu remark by Eisenhower later in the month—that the test "must have surprised and astonished the scientists"—inadvertently added fuel to the furor, as did Strauss's subsequent admission to the press that a *Bravo*-sized bomb could destroy any city, including New York. ("I wouldn't have answered that one that way, Lewis," Ike gently admonished.)[39]

Bravo also literally overshadowed the preparations for the test of Livermore's first H-bomb: the Ramrod device proposed by Teller.[40] The unexpected power of the Los Alamos–designed *Bravo* had blown the roof off the corrugated tin hut that housed Livermore's superbomb, while radiation from the test had forced the Livermore firing party off a nearby atoll and out to sea. Lawrence, who had been on hand to witness *Bravo,* was forced by a recurrence of his illness to return to California before the Livermore test, code-named *Koon.*[41]

In the early morning hours of Wednesday, April 7, 1954, the countdown for *Koon* wound down to zero.[42] From the deck of the USS *Curtis,* Duane Sewell and his Livermore colleagues peered into the fog and low overcast as a dim glow briefly penetrated the murk. The contrast with *Bravo* was instantly apparent. ("Did it go off?" asked Sewell anxiously.) Whereas lab pessimists had scaled back early estimates of a *Bravo*-like yield to a single megaton, the actual explosion was only a tenth that magnitude, almost all of it accounted for by *Koon*'s Los Alamos–supplied fission primary.[43]

The fizzle produced a mood of near desperation among the lab's weaponeers. Following the disappointing results of the twin hydride tests, the California lab now had an unbroken record of failure. Eager to get at least one score on the tally board before the end of the series, some urged that the only other Livermore-designed bomb scheduled for *Castle*—a cryogenically cooled, "wet" version of Ramrod, in a test code-named *Echo*—be moved to a barge and exploded as soon as possible, even though any diagnostic data from the shot would be lost. Instead, Herb York and Harold Brown decided to cancel the test. Commission experts agreed with Teller's colleagues that the next bomb, too, was likely to fizzle, given its similarity to the ill-fated *Koon.*[44]

Beyond embarrassment at Livermore's failure, York and Teller had another, deeper concern. In the wake of the lab's disastrous debut in Nevada and the Pacific, they expected that questions would again be raised concerning the need for a second weapons laboratory. Predictably, the loudest criticisms came from a familiar quarter. Just weeks after *Koon,* Norris Bradbury wrote to the AEC questioning whether Livermore needed or deserved an independent test program. Bradbury's memo likewise branded the rival lab for pursuing weapons of dubious design and only "problematic interest."[45]

On Monday, April 12, 1954, five days after Teller's H-bomb had fizzled in the Pacific, the Oppenheimer hearings began in Room 2022 of Building T-3, across Constitution Avenue from AEC headquarters. The barracks-like temporary structure had been erected in the early days of the Second World War, on the empty sward of land between the Washington Monument and the Lincoln Memorial.

Members of the Personnel Security Board—Gray, Evans, and Thomas—sat at a long baize-covered table at the room's east end. The opposing lawyers, Garrison and Robb, and their staffs faced each other across two mahogany tables fitted together and attached like the stem of a *T.* At the base, standing apart, was a single wooden chair for witness testimony; behind it, a nondescript leather sofa, usually occupied by Oppenheimer, sitting alone.[46]

Nichols had forbidden Garrison from making an opening statement, so much of the first morning was taken up by Gray's reading of the statement of charges and Oppenheimer's fourteen-page reply, recounting his life and career. After lunch, Garrison entered into the record wartime letters from Groves and FDR, praising the physicist for his work on the atomic bomb.

Across the street at the AEC that afternoon, there were already signs that Oppenheimer was in trouble. Groves telephoned Nichols with word that, while Garrison still wanted him to testify, Oppie's lawyer was disturbed by the fact that Groves's recollection of the Chevalier incident did not jibe with Oppenheimer's.[47]

Most of the next two days was taken up by Garrison's direct examination of Oppenheimer. On Wednesday morning, April 14, when the subject turned to Frank, it was Oppie who prompted Garrison's question.[48] The lawyer asked, "Was your brother connected with this approach by Chevalier to you?" Oppenheimer's reply had the sound of an answer prepared well in advance: "I am very clear on this. I have a vivid and I think certainly not fallible memory. He had nothing whatever to do with it."

Following the precepts of his youth and the training of the Ethical Culture School, Oppenheimer had elected to do "the noble thing."

Robb's cross-examination later that day focused upon Oppie's graduate students who had worked on the Manhattan Project: Lomanitz, Weinberg, Bohm, and Friedman. In the afternoon, the prosecution turned to the Chevalier incident. Some weeks earlier, Bates had located in bureau files the Presto disk of Pash's interview with Oppenheimer. At the FBI, Nichols, Robb, and Rolander had listened transfixed to the decade-old recording of Oppenheimer telling Pash about three colleagues being contacted by an unnamed intermediary to spy for the Russians.[49]

Prodded by Robb to "begin at the beginning and tell us exactly what happened" with Chevalier, Oppenheimer told the version he had given the FBI in 1946—that he had been the only one approached by the French literature professor.*[50] Surprised to learn that his long-ago interview with Pash had been recorded, Oppenheimer quickly volunteered that what he had told the army security man was a "cock-and-bull story."

"Hunched over, wringing his hands, white as a sheet," Robb later recalled—Oppie, having admitted that he lied, waited almost helplessly for the trap to be sprung.[51]

"Why did you do that, Doctor?" Robb asked.

"Because I was an idiot," Oppenheimer replied.[52]

The physicist went on to venture a further explanation—that he had invented the tale of three contacts in order to protect Chevalier. But Robb pointed out that this new story made no sense, since an approach to others showed his friend to be even more "deeply involved" in espionage. Robb also forced Oppenheimer to admit to having paid a friendly visit to Chevalier—the man he had just implicated as a wartime spy—only months earlier in Paris.[53]

Finally, producing the telegram that Groves had sent Nichols in December 1943, Robb challenged Oppenheimer to account for its reference to three contacts: "You think General Groves did tell Colonel Nichols and Colonel Lansdale your story was cock and bull?"[54]

"I find that hard to believe," conceded Oppenheimer in a quiet voice.

"So do I," Robb shot back.[55]

---

*At one point in this testimony, Oppenheimer seemed about to tell the story of Groves's December 1943 visit, but Robb quickly intervened to get the questioning back on track:

> ROBB: "Then you were interviewed in 1946; is that right?"
> OPPENHEIMER: "In between I think came Groves."
> ROBB: "Yes. But you were interviewed in 1946; is that right?"

That evening, at the AEC building, Groves was coached by Robb and Rolander on the testimony he would give the following day.[56] In the witness chair on April 15, Groves made no mention of his December 1943 meeting at Los Alamos with Oppie. Instead, Robb's questions—and Groves's answers—were what the general and Strauss had gone over nearly two months before.[57]

Although Lansdale, in his own later testimony, vaguely remembered telling the FBI that Frank was the actual contact, he told Robb that he could no longer recall how he came by that information: "My memory is a complete blank."[58] Nor did Robb decide to call any of those who might have shed light on the Chevalier incident—Consodine, Frank Oppenheimer, or Chevalier himself, who denied, the following day in the *International Herald-Tribune,* ever approaching Oppie for secrets of any kind.[59]

Robb chose not to pursue the gaps and inconsistencies in Groves's story.[60] He and Strauss saw little advantage to having Oppenheimer portrayed as a hero for sacrificing himself to save his brother.

Following Oppie's admission of lying and the hand-washing testimony of Groves, Garrison's strategy of relying upon notables to make a proxy case for the physicist went up in smoke—a fact as evident to the prosecution as it was to the defense.

A day after Oppenheimer's ordeal on the stand, Strauss, exultant, wrote Eisenhower: "The counsel who have been in attendance feel that an extremely bad impression toward Oppenheimer has already developed in the minds of the board."[61] Bates informed Hoover that Strauss was "most happy with the way that the Oppenheimer hearing was going."[62]

But a reminder from Rabi of the effect that a protracted hearing was likely to have upon the morale of the nation's scientists prompted Strauss to direct Robb "to make every effort to speed up the hearing."[63] Ever since an article about the supposedly secret proceedings had appeared in the *New York Times* on April 13, Strauss recognized the danger that the hearings might spin out of control.[64] Strauss also worried that Congress might "try to get into the act."[65]

The hearings continued, nonetheless, into a second and then a third week. FBI agents stationed outside the Georgetown house where the Oppenheimers were staying—the home of Garrison's law partner—reported that the physicist was up late into the night, pacing the floor. At the AEC and the FBI, Hoover, Strauss, and Robb were still looking for the final piece of evidence that would unequivocally seal Oppenheimer's fate: convincing proof that Oppie, contrary to his repeated assurances, had once secretly belonged to the Communist Party.

Bureau agents spent countless hours pouring over airline and railroad timetables to see if the Oppenheimers could have returned to Kenilworth Court from Perro Caliente in time to host the clandestine party meeting alleged by the Crouches.[66] The results were inconclusive.[67]

Hoover and Strauss became personally involved in the hunt for new leads and the tying up of loose ends. The FBI director ordered his agents to interview for a second time a former Army private who had been on garbage duty at wartime Los Alamos and remembered seeing copies of the *Daily Worker* and *New Masses* in Oppenheimer's trash.[68] Strauss asked Nichols to ascertain whether the consular official who had tipped the FBI off to Oppenheimer's visit to the Paris embassy would testify that Oppie had tried to help Chevalier reenter the United States (He would not.)[69] When the propriety of wiretapping Oppenheimer's conversations with Garrison once more came under question at the FBI, Hoover ordered the taps continued, again at Strauss's request.[70]

Nor was the dragnet only out for Oppenheimer. Following testimony on April 22 by physicists Norman Ramsey and Isidor Rabi, Nichols asked the FBI for any derogatory information it might have on others whom Garrison intended to call to the stand in Oppie's defense—"in order that AEC can use the information against the potential witness if desired." Included on the list of two dozen names that Nichols gave the bureau were both of Strauss's predecessors at the AEC: Lilienthal and Dean.[71]

Yet it was becoming clear that a drawn-out hearing might be a mistake for the prosecution. Vannevar Bush's testimony on Friday, April 23, was particularly strong. (He had warned Strauss in advance, Bush wrote Conant, "that I was going to sail into him and I proceeded to do so.")[72] Unintimidated by Robb, Bush vigorously defended his attempt to postpone *Mike*—"I still think we made a grave error in conducting that test at that time, and not attempting to make that type of simple agreement with Russia"—and attacked the board for "placing a man on trial because he held opinions."*[73]

Conant, too, proved a surprisingly outspoken witness for the defense. The former Harvard president, now high commissioner to Germany, had defied the wishes of Secretary of State Dulles in order to appear at the hearing; afterward, Conant spoke to Eisenhower about the case.[74]

*Shortly before the *Trinity* test, Oppenheimer recited a passage from Hindu scripture, which had so impressed Bush that he wrote it down on a slip of paper and kept it in his wallet throughout the war: "In the forest, in battle, in the midst of arrows, javelins, fire / Out on the great sea, at the precipice's edge in the mountains / In sleep, in delirium, in deep trouble / The good deeds a man has done before defend him."

Garrison's tack since Groves's testimony—to argue that Oppenheimer's service to the nation outweighed any personal shortcomings—even seemed to be gaining ground with the judges.

Fear that the tide might be turning against him drove Strauss to increasingly desperate measures. While Bush was still on the witness stand, FBI agents acting on an anonymous tip were interviewing an Office of Naval Research employee who had once been Oppenheimer's graduate student. The bureau questioned Harvey Hall about an alleged homosexual affair between Hall and his mentor. Hall denied it.[75]

Even Hoover and his aides were becoming tired of Strauss's ceaseless demands—and worried by their ally's growing recklessness. Informed that Strauss and Teeple wanted Ike's national security adviser put under FBI surveillance—Cutler had last met with Oppenheimer at a gathering of Harvard overseers in March—Belmont finally drew the line: "No. I see nothing to be gained. We have given them all we have. They are making a mountain out of nothing."[76]

Gray, too, was becoming uncomfortable with the direction the hearing was taking. The head of the Personnel Security Board asked Robb, anxiously, whether the proceedings could be speeded up. They could not, the lawyer replied. The most powerful witnesses for the prosecution had yet to be heard.

As if anticipating Robb's next move, the board inquired on Friday, April 23, when it would hear from Oppenheimer's former colleagues at Berkeley.[77] Strauss and Robb already knew from FBI wiretaps that Oppie considered Lawrence and McMillan "encamped against him."[78]

That same day, Nichols telephoned four of those previously interviewed by Rolander and Robb—Lawrence, Alvarez, Pitzer, and Latimer—to confirm that each would be in Washington to testify during the coming week.[79] On Saturday, Nichols reached Teller in Berkeley. "He said he would be glad to testify," wrote Nichols in his diary.[80]

Lawrence had also recently spoken with Teller, having summoned him to his Rad Lab office on April 14 to discuss what the two would say at the hearing. As they talked, Lawrence grew more animated and angry at Oppie—a generation's worth of personal slights and suspicions coming to the fore.*[81] Lawrence accused Oppenheimer of trying to shut down Los

*There was also a new and personal element to Lawrence's animosity. A week or so earlier, at a cocktail party in Balboa, he learned from a friend of the Tolmans that Oppenheimer had carried on an affair with Ruth while her husband, Richard, was still alive. Molly remembered her husband returning to their house in a rage. Ernest evidently passed the story along to Strauss, who would write to Teller, years after the hearing: "Did Ernest Lawrence ever tell you what [Oppenheimer] did in the Tolman household?"

Alamos and Oak Ridge at the end of the war, and of later attempting to sabotage the hydrogen bomb, the long-range detection program, and Livermore.

However, stopping off in Oak Ridge on April 24 to attend a weekend meeting of laboratory directors on his way to Washington, Lawrence began to rethink the promise he had made to Strauss and Nichols. Angrily confronted at the meeting by Rabi, who asked what he would say about Oppenheimer, Ernest began to get an inkling of the high emotion that surrounded the case. (In his own testimony a week earlier, Rabi, growing frustrated at Robb's assault upon Oppie, had finally blurted out: "We have an A-bomb and a whole series of it. . . . what more do you want, mermaids?")[82]

Beyond the cost to his own reputation, Lawrence worried about the price that Livermore and the Rad Lab might have to pay for his testimony. Rabi and Smyth—"barely civil" to him at Oak Ridge—held the decisive votes on whether a new AEC-funded particle accelerator would be built at Berkeley.[83] The Oppenheimer hearing also dominated discussions at the annual meeting of the American Physical Society in Washington, D.C., earlier that week, where Oppenheimer, celebrating his fiftieth birthday, had sat silent at the speaker's table, an honored guest.[84]

Lawrence nonetheless called Nichols on Monday morning, April 26, to say that he would be arriving in Washington the following evening.[85] That night, Ernest suffered his most severe colitis attack yet. Telephoning Strauss early Tuesday morning, Lawrence told the AEC chairman that he was returning home at his brother's orders and would not be testifying after all.

Strauss was apoplectic. Failing at length to change Lawrence's mind, he abruptly ended the call by branding him a coward.[86] (Fearing that others might accuse him of malingering, Ernest summoned another physicist at the Oak Ridge meeting into the bathroom to witness the blood in the toilet bowl.)[87] Before leaving for the airport, Lawrence telephoned Alvarez and implored Luie not to testify either, for the sake of the Rad Lab.

But Alvarez's ambition, and his eagerness to settle scores with Oppenheimer, proved even stronger than his long allegiance to Lawrence. Hectored by Strauss in another late-night telephone call—"Lewis's emotional intensity increased as he ran out of arguments," Alvarez later remembered—Luie agreed to ignore Ernest's order and boarded the next flight to Washington.[88]

Latimer had already testified, as scheduled, that afternoon. Speaking in a low and barely audible voice, he told of how Oppenheimer's "astounding" and "extraordinary" influence with other scientists had persuaded them not to work on the hydrogen bomb.[89]

Pitzer testified to much the same effect on Wednesday, April 28. But with Lawrence hors de combat, there was no scientist of Oppenheimer's stature to speak about the physicist—save Teller. Until almost the eve of Edward's testimony, moreover, there was no certainty as to what he would say about the man that he had known for more than twenty years.

Ironically, Oppenheimer had originally thought of asking Teller to testify as a witness for the defense. Encountering Edward at a scientific conference in Rochester, New York, earlier in the year, Oppie had asked him if he believed that Oppenheimer had ever done anything "sinister."[90] When Teller averred that he did not, Oppenheimer suggested he speak with Garrison about testifying. But Teller's meeting with the defense lawyers proved unproductive.[91]

Despite his obvious dislike of Oppenheimer, Teller also had reservations about Strauss which he had earlier expressed to Thomas Murray. "[Strauss] has one blind spot and that is security," Edward had confided to Murray the previous January, citing the flap over Oppenheimer as "a case . . . in point."[92]

Indeed, only a few days before his scheduled testimony—on April 22, when Teller was interviewed by Charter Heslep, a speechwriter for Strauss—Edward's views had seemed to change once more. Heslep had come to Livermore to sound Teller out on the AEC's Atoms for Peace program but found him "interested only in discussing the Oppenheimer case."[93] Believing that Teller was—"consciously or otherwise"—rehearsing what he planned to say at the hearings, Heslep wrote Strauss that Edward had spoken with intensity of the "Oppie machine," lamenting, "Oppie is so powerful 'politically' in scientific circles that it will be hard to 'unfrock him in his own church.'" (The phrase was Heslep's, but Teller agreed it was "apt.")

When Nichols telephoned Teller on April 24 to confirm the date for his testimony, Teller had clearly made up his mind about what he was going to say: "He said he would be very glad to repeat the statement he had given earlier to Rolander and Robb if I thought it would be of any use," wrote Nichols in his diary.[94]

On Tuesday morning, April 27, Teller spent another forty-five minutes in Nichols's office discussing his testimony and the hearing. Teller also met with Murray in the afternoon and that evening with Robb, who showed him the portion of the transcript containing Oppenheimer's abject reply to Robb's question about the Chevalier incident. Teller told Robb—"with some heat," the lawyer later recalled—that Oppenheimer had lied to him as well. ("He felt that by leaving out important and relevant facts in his statement to Dr. Teller about his past associations, Dr. Oppenheimer had deceived and misled Dr. Teller," Robb later wrote to Strauss.)[95]

Possibly with Robb's prompting, Teller agreed to make one important change to his planned testimony. Whereas in past interviews with the FBI he had always dismissed the idea that Oppenheimer might be a security risk, Teller told Robb that, in light of Oppie's recent admission of lying, he felt he could no longer give such an assurance. For Teller, as for Alvarez, the prospect of finally "unfrocking" Oppenheimer proved too tempting to resist.[96]

On Wednesday afternoon, April 28, Teller was sworn in and had barely given the board some brief details of his career when Robb asked him, "Do you or do you not believe Dr. Oppenheimer is a security risk?

Teller's carefully worded reply was a subtle variation on what he had told Robb and Rolander in Berkeley six weeks earlier, when he had expressed concern that Oppie's clearance might be "lifted for a mere mistake of judgment":

> In a great number of cases I have seen Dr. Oppenheimer act—I understand that Dr. Oppenheimer acted—in a way which for me was exceedingly hard to understand. I thoroughly disagreed with him in numerous issues and his actions frankly appeared to me confused and complicated. To this extent I feel that I would like to see the vital interests of this country in hands which I understand better, and therefore trust more.[97]

Lest there be any doubt about what Teller meant, Gray repeated Robb's question in the cross-examination, to which Teller replied, "If it is a question of wisdom and judgment, as demonstrated by actions since 1945, then I would say one would be wiser not to grant clearance."*[98]

Earlier in the day, Robb had announced at the hearing that Lawrence would not appear after all, because of illness.[99] Alvarez's testimony on Thursday afternoon, April 29, continued into Friday morning, as Robb and the board quizzed Luie about the diary he had kept during the H-bomb debate. But neither Alvarez's testimony nor the brief, notarized affidavit that Lawrence submitted to the board a few days later would affect the outcome.[100]

On May 3, Rolander informed Bates that the prosecution was finished with its witnesses. Robb said he hoped to wrap things up in another two

---

*In his memoirs, published in 2001, Teller claimed that his reservations concerning Oppenheimer's "judgment" referred not to the latter's advice on the H-bomb but to a proposal Oppie had supposedly made to Eisenhower, shortly after the *Mike* test, urging that consideration be given to using the H-bomb in Korea. While no corroborating evidence could be found for Teller's claim, Rabi did confirm, during the Oppenheimer hearings, that his friend had at one time in the early 1950s entertained the notion of preventive war.

days.[101] On May 6, following a three-hour summation by Garrison, the hearings finally ended. Oppie and Kitty returned home to Princeton that evening.

Four days later, the agent in charge of the FBI's Newark office once more asked for permission to discontinue the Oppenheimer wiretaps.[102] Strauss again requested that they be kept in place, since further testimony might be given when the board reconvened in Washington on May 18. There was, moreover, Hoover wrote the conscience-stricken Newark agent, another reason to continue the wiretaps on the physicist: "Since his testimony under oath, investigation may now be directed with a view toward possible prosecution provided legally admissible evidence can be developed to corroborate the [Crouches'] allegations."[103]

18

LIKE GOING TO A NEW COUNTRY

BELIEVING THAT THE Gray board would take from four to six weeks to reach a decision, Garrison and Oppenheimer began work almost immediately on a rebuttal, should the AEC declare Oppie a security risk. The FBI's bugs picked up their efforts. Hoover reported to Strauss that two problems were bothering the defense. One—a question that had been "pressed at the hearing," and which Oppenheimer considered "wholly messy"—was presumably the Chevalier affair. The other was the disarmament panel's discussion in 1952 about the possible postponement of *Mike*. Rolander requested the panel's minutes from the State Department so that he might be able to counter Garrison's arguments in advance.[1]

Garrison's summation on May 6, 1954, had focused in some detail on Oppenheimer's contradictory versions of the Chevalier incident—only to conclude, somewhat weakly, that "Dr. Oppenheimer has surely learned from this experience."[2] Gray himself had tried to finally get at the truth of the matter when he asked Oppie, during the physicist's last day on the stand, why he had told a complicated lie to Pash if his motive was to protect Chevalier. But Oppenheimer once again dodged the question. It was, averred the physicist, "most difficult to explain."[3]

Strauss's concern grew after a week passed without a verdict. His particular concern was Ward Evans. The chemistry professor had startled the other members of the board by making disparaging and even anti-Semitic remarks about Oppenheimer at a dinner early in the proceedings. Gray and Morgan had told Rolander that they feared Evans was so outspoken he might prejudice the case.[4]

On May 20, no longer able to contain his anxiety, Strauss telephoned Belmont, asking that Hoover intervene personally with the board: "[Strauss] said that the Oppenheimer Hearing Board is in the last stages of its considerations and that things are 'touch and go.' He said a slight tip of the balance could cause the Board to commit a serious error." Protesting that "it would be highly improper" for him to do what Strauss suggested, Hoover declined.[5]

The suspense ended three days later, when the board, in a 2-to-1 vote, declared Oppenheimer a security risk and recommended that his clearance not be renewed.

As Nichols had predicted, the Gray board's verdict was largely based upon the issue of Oppenheimer's veracity as reflected by the Chevalier incident. While the board found that the account given by Oppenheimer to the FBI was "substantially true," it therefore concluded that Oppie's earlier admission of lying showed he recognized that the contact by Chevalier was not just an innocent conversation but, rather, "that it was a criminal conspiracy."

"Loyalty to one's friends is one of the noblest of qualities," wrote Gray in the majority decision. "Being loyal to one's friends above reasonable obligations to the country and to the security system, however, is not clearly consistent with the interests of security."[6]

Ironically, the single dissenting vote had been Evans's, who argued, in a minority opinion, that Oppenheimer's clearance should be reinstated. Gray and Morgan noticed that Evans had seemed "morose" during the hearing's last days and concluded that he was "probably ill."[7] During the recess the chemist had gone home to Chicago. When he returned to Washington, his attitude toward Oppenheimer seemed at such a variance with his earlier views that Robb and Rolander believed "someone had 'gotten to' Evans." Like Lawrence, the professor had likely learned from academic colleagues what the personal cost might be of pillorying Oppenheimer.[8]

Robb learned of the verdict on May 23 and immediately notified Strauss. Bates informed the FBI that both the AEC chairman and his lawyer were "very happy" with the results.[9]

Not surprisingly, the scene at Princeton was altogether different, as captured by the bureau's wiretaps: "[Oppenheimer] reported to be very depressed at the present time and has been ill-tempered with his wife."[10] At Mitchell's order, Oppie's secretary at the institute had returned the last of the AEC's classified documents a few days earlier.[11]

Anticipating a long-deferred vacation in the Caribbean with his family, Oppenheimer felt obliged to send Hoover a registered letter telling of his plans, lest the bureau fear that he was about to flee the country.[12] Hoover notified Strauss, Brownell, and the CIA, nonetheless, that Oppie might be preparing to defect to Russia via submarine.[13]

On June 29, 1954, the Atomic Energy Commission handed down its verdict on Oppenheimer. By a vote of 4 to 1—Smyth was the only holdout—the commission upheld the Gray board's decision to strip Oppenheimer of his clearance, just one day before it was due to expire.[14] In separate opinions appended to the majority report, Zuckert gave a lengthy and torturous justification for his decision to vote with the majority. Murray's statement, reportedly coauthored with a Jesuit priest, was most notable for its moralistic fervor.[15] Curiously, while the religion-minded commissioner thought Oppenheimer's opposition to the hydrogen bomb defensible on ethical grounds, he still declared the scientist "disloyal."[16]

Garrison had not been allowed to make his case in person before the commissioners; nor was he permitted to see the letter that Robb and Nichols wrote in support of the board's decision, which emphasized the Chevalier incident. (Oppie's "misrepresentation and falsification constitutes criminal . . . dishonest . . . conduct," Nichols intoned.)[17] The AEC's majority report, drafted by Strauss, found Oppenheimer guilty of "fundamental defects of character," echoing Nichols in its emphasis upon Oppenheimer's questionable "associations."[18]

On the same day that he filed the majority report, Strauss paid a personal visit to the FBI, thanking Bates and the bureau's director effusively for their assistance. For Hoover, however, the Oppenheimer case did not end officially until two weeks later, when the Justice Department ruled that Oppie could not be prosecuted for lies told in 1943 or at the hearing.[19]

On July 20, Hoover advised Strauss that so far as he and the bureau were concerned, the Oppenheimer case was closed.[20]

At Princeton, the Oppenheimers prepared for a life of academic exile. Although Oppie was still very much in demand as a speaker on campuses and at academic conferences, the familiar summonses from Washington had abruptly ceased.[21] In an irony that perhaps only he was able to appreciate, the AEC's verdict had made Oppenheimer himself one of the institute's "solipsistic luminaries—shining in separate and helpless desolation" that he had disdained in a letter to Frank almost twenty years earlier.[22]

Finding more time to spend with the children—Peter, now fourteen, and Toni, eleven—Oppie and Kitty revived a favorite ritual: the family would search for four-leaf clovers on the New Jersey campus or wherever they might be visiting; the finder would Scotch-tape the little plant to an index card and present it, inscribed, to another family member—a gift of luck.

Elsewhere, the repercussions of the Oppenheimer case were just beginning to be felt. On June 9, 1954, journalist Drew Pearson reported in his syndicated column that Strauss had secretly recorded AEC meetings and tapped the telephones of individual commissioners. Strauss's prompt denial was also an outright lie: "No tapping of Commissioners' telephones or any other telephones has ever been made on my behalf by security officers or by anyone else," he assured the president, Sterling Cole, and Pearson.[23] Attacks upon Strauss for his role in the Oppenheimer case would continue throughout the coming weeks—including, most notably, in a series of articles by political columnists Joseph and Stewart Alsop.[24]

Teller was also much affected by the controversy. "The people here are quite worked up about the whole thing," Rabi wrote DuBridge in late June from a meeting at Los Alamos, where physicists stood in line to read the transcript of the hearing.[25] Rabi thought the testimony "much worse than [he] thought possible"—including "some horrifying passages" from Alvarez—but Teller's remarks, he felt, were the nadir: "It does take quite a lot of nerve for him to show up at this time."

Edward, indeed, would have reason to regret his appearance at a picnic outside Fuller Lodge later that day. Approaching Robert Christy, a wartime colleague with whom he had once shared a house in Chicago, Teller was devastated when Christy wordlessly turned on his heel and walked away. "I won't shake your hand either, Edward," Rabi told him.[26] Teller and Mici quickly retreated to their hotel room and made plans to leave.[27] Alvarez was so alarmed by Teller's psychological state that he telephoned Strauss to warn that their mutual friend might be suicidal.[28] Thus alerted, the AEC chairman canceled his planned visit to the lab.[29]

For Teller, it was the beginning of his third and final exile. Having fled the Communists in Hungary and then the Nazis in Germany, he suddenly found himself shunned by friends, like Bethe, who had been his companions in the European diaspora. Ironically, Edward was no less isolated than Oppie, but with fewer sympathizers.*

More than just mental anguish, the hearings also took a physical toll—and Teller was not the only victim. For almost a year, Teller and Lawrence

*Several weeks after the hearings, William Borden wrote Teller a confidential letter containing words of encouragement. In it, Borden offered this explanation for why he had sent his famous missive to Hoover: "In weighing the danger of having a probable subversive continue to orient our national policies against the danger of 'alienating our scientists,' it struck me that someone had to take the first unequivocal step toward belling this cat and that I was the logical nominee, not only because I knew more about the cat than others . . . but because I am outside the scientific fraternity."

had been seeing the same specialist for treatment of ulcerative colitis. In July, following a brief remission, Ernest's attacks returned.[30] Bradbury later recalled an emotional Lawrence unburdening himself on the subject of Oppenheimer at a Bohemian Grove encampment that August.[31] Physicist James Brady, a former Rad Lab colleague, likewise remembered Ernest being "bitter, very bitter" that Oppie had lied to wartime security officials. ("I got Oppenheimer that job in the first place," Lawrence had complained to Brady. "Of course, we've got a better man around here now." "Who's that?" Brady asked. "Teller," Lawrence replied.)[32]

Barely two months after the Oppenheimer hearings, Lawrence was approached by another former colleague—Martin Kamen—with a request that he testify in Kamen's libel suit against the *Washington Times-Herald* and the *Chicago Tribune*. David Teeple was compelled to admit at the trial that he had given the newspapers the picture of Kamen arm-in-arm with Soviet diplomats outside Bernstein's Fish Grotto.[33] The papers had reported that Kamen was a spy.

Lawrence agreed to testify only if Kamen guaranteed that he would not be subject to cross-examination—plainly, an impossible condition in a trial. Instead, Cooksey wrote a deposition on Kamen's behalf. After he won a settlement from the newspapers the following spring, Kamen thanked Cooksey for rising above "the failures of men of fatal timidity."[34]

As a result of the hearings, both Teller and Lawrence wound up on a kind of scientists' blacklist. Even though Oppie himself subsequently nominated Ernest to the editorial board of the *Bulletin of the Atomic Scientists,* Lawrence's name was quietly scratched from the list after Bethe objected that his views might "lead to a watering down of the contents of the *Bulletin.*"[35]

But Strauss need not have feared that the hearings would result in the wholesale refusal of the American scientific community to carry out defense work. Although Los Alamos scientists fired off their weapon of choice—a petition with 288 signatures, which they sent to the AEC, condemning the verdict—the National Academy of Sciences pointedly refused to issue a strong statement in support of Oppenheimer.[36] As Strauss wrote to Neylan in July, "[I am] very contented with the attitude of the scientists with whom I talked. Their position has been very much misrepresented to the public by a few prejudiced columnists."[37]

Spurred, in part, by Lawrence and Enrico Fermi—who, dying of cancer, made his request a kind of last wish—Teller that fall agreed to try to heal the rift created by his testimony, and, in the process, rehabilitate his own reputation.[38] In "The Work of Many People," an article published in

February 1955 by *Science* magazine, Teller gave Ulam credit for the "imaginative suggestion" that led to the radiation-implosion breakthrough on the H-bomb.[39]

In time, Teller's own health slowly began to improve. Old friends lost over the Oppenheimer imbroglio were replaced with new ones found at Livermore. That winter, Edward exulted to Maria Mayer: "Going to California was like going to a new country. . . . I never worked as hard as now and, incidentally, I am establishing a reputation that I never fight and am always pleasant . . . a thoroughly new existence."[40]

Livermore itself, however, remained in serious trouble, the legacy of its back-to-back failures in Nevada and the Pacific. In late September 1954, Bradbury had sent a top-secret memo to the AEC's Division of Military Application suggesting that the second lab be made subordinate to Los Alamos. As Bradbury hardly needed to remind the commission, "The brilliant new ideas have not appeared."[41]

The General Advisory Committee, now under Rabi's leadership, was also raising questions about the future of Livermore. At a GAC meeting shortly after the Oppenheimer verdict was announced, Rabi described the effort there as "amateurish," adding, ominously, that Teller's lab did not have responsibility for any "necessary" part of the weapons program.[42] After *Koon*'s failure, the AEC had canceled its order for Ramrod, to Teller's chagrin.[43] (Stung by the move, Teller told the GAC that he had plans for a 10,000-megaton bomb—something that Rabi and colleagues dismissed as "an advertising stunt.")[44]

That winter, York began experiencing sudden, inexplicable fevers that caused him to be absent from the lab for long periods. By December, Rabi was wondering aloud at GAC meetings whether Livermore would ever "really be an important laboratory."[45]

Despite the failure of the hydride bomb and *Koon,* Teller remained a dominant presence at Livermore. Lawrence had recently arranged for Edward's promotion to full professor at Berkeley, where he remained one of the few theorists left in the physics department.

But Livermore had also acquired a new group of young and ambitious physicists, and their efforts were beginning to have an impact.[46] At twenty-four, Harold Brown was already a three-year veteran of the Rad Lab as head of A Division, which designed thermonuclear weapons. The leader of B Division, John Foster, was a thirty-two-year-old physicist whose Canadian father, a longtime friend of Lawrence, had built the first cyclotron at McGill University. The junior Foster rode a motorcycle to the lab, where he and a half dozen others designed small atomic bombs and the fission primaries for Brown's still hypothetical, multimegaton H-bombs.[47]

One of Foster's first projects at Livermore was an innovative approach to an admittedly old idea: linear implosion, which promised smaller and more efficient atomic bombs. While experiments with nonspherical designs dated from the early days of Los Alamos—the canyons of the wartime lab had once echoed with Seth Neddermeyer's failed efforts to perfect the art—Foster's counterpart at the New Mexico lab questioned whether the phenomenon still had any practical application.[48] Grudgingly, Rabi and the GAC urged the commission to approve only one of a pair of linear-implosion tests that Livermore proposed for the upcoming *Teapot* series in Nevada.[49] A decision to proceed with the second test would depend on the results of *Teapot/Tesla,* scheduled for spring 1955.

Livermore scientists prepared for *Tesla* with their customary bravado. Whereas Los Alamos had traditionally transported their devices to the test site on an army flatbed truck with a military escort, Foster and his colleagues jauntily drove to the shot tower in a late-model sedan, their bomb—crammed into a pair of heavily reinforced Samsonite suitcases—sitting in the backseat.[50]

The hush countdown for *Tesla* began in the early morning hours of March 1, 1955, and ended at dawn's light with a 7-kiloton explosion—more than three times what Foster had predicted.[51] To the relief of Livermore scientists, the blast this time also completely obliterated the bomb's 300-foot tower. The AEC promptly gave approval to Livermore's second test. Six days later, *Turk*—another small-diameter, boosted device—yielded the hoped-for 40 kilotons.[52]

For Lawrence, who flew out from Berkeley to witness *Turk,* the occasion was one for celebration. On March 8, he telephoned Thomas Murray to congratulate the man he called "the 'founder'" of the second lab.[53] Among the scientists gathered in York's office, joy was unrestrained. "We're still in business, we're still in business!" shouted Livermore's business manager as he ran down the hall.[54]

Hoping to forestall any further talk of closing the lab, Lawrence had formally made York the director of Livermore the previous fall.[55] A subsequent contract from the army for an atomic bomb small enough to be fired from a cannon gave York the justification he needed for dramatic new expansion: the lab's scientific staff swelled to 500, following a $6-million increase in budget. By spring 1955, Livermore had outgrown its parent, Berkeley's Rad Lab, in both staff and budget.[56] But perhaps most important, symbolically, was the fact that for the first time Livermore had taken a weapons project away from Los Alamos.[57]

The California lab's belated successes had also removed a great burden from Teller, who informed Strauss in mid-April that he and his colleagues were "proud and happy and grateful that . . . [their] work needed no further elaborate justification."[58] Wrote Edward to Maria Mayer that same day: "Livermore is now running fine. In fact, it's running so fast, it's running away with us."[59]

In Washington, however, York and Teller were appalled to learn that the rug might be yanked out from under Livermore just as it was finally getting on its feet.

The possibility of a ban on nuclear testing had been raised as early as January 1954 by Murray, who had argued to his fellow commissioners that "some control over testing offers an avenue of approach to atomic disarmament which should not be overlooked."[60] Ignored by Strauss, the crusading commissioner had next approached Eisenhower with a plea for an international moratorium on tests, which might "prevent the future development of much larger yield weapons."[61] Ike's reply, drafted by Strauss, had curtly dismissed the idea.

The public outcry over *Bravo* a few weeks later encouraged Murray to try again. His particular interest was in stopping the testing of multimegaton hydrogen bombs—what he called "big cheap bombs"—replacing them with an arsenal of less powerful fission bombs, more useful against enemy troops than enemy cities.[62] As always, there was an element of fervent religious conviction behind Murray's appeal: he objected not only to the radioactive fallout caused by peacetime H-bomb tests like *Bravo,* but to the fact that city-destroying superbombs violated the Christian doctrine of proportionality.[63] (That Murray saw no conflict between his religious views and his duties as an AEC commissioner was evident in a letter he once wrote to Truman. Just before leaving on another visit to Fatima, he informed the president that he was "going to Portugal first of all to pray to the Blessed Virgin and second to try to increase Portugal uranium production.")[64]

Privately, Ike found Murray's notion of an end to testing attractive—if only for public relations reasons. "Everybody seems to think that we're skunks, saber-rattlers and warmongers," the president had complained that spring.[65] After *Castle* was completed, the president told Secretary of State John Foster Dulles, he was "willing to have a moratorium on all further experimentation whether with H-bomb or A-bombs."[66]

Strauss and Teller grew alarmed as the moratorium idea gained momentum, inside as well as outside the White House.[67] That spring, responding to his constituents' concerns, Joint Committee chairman Sterling Cole endorsed "a halt to a search for more destructive bombs" in a letter to Eisenhower.[68] Even the redoubtable Dulles, architect of the administration's controversial "massive retaliation" military doctrine, thought the moratorium "an area where we have a chance to get a big propaganda advantage—and perhaps results."[69]

But the handwritten note that Eisenhower slipped Dulles at an NSC meeting, called in early April to study the test ban, probably foreordained the outcome. "Ask Strauss to study," Ike instructed.[70]

Strauss reported back that the development of promising new weapons—including the small, low-yield bombs that Murray favored—would be seriously hampered by such a ban. More to the point, Strauss and Defense Secretary Charles Wilson argued, was the fact that the Russians could cheat by testing secretly, in such remote regions as Antarctica. Reluctantly, Eisenhower and Dulles conceded that the time was not yet ripe for a test ban.[71]

A year later, the public's rising fear of radiation threatened to bring about an end to nuclear testing anyway, at least within the continental United States. Hoping to dampen the furor over tests in Nevada, Teller proposed using northern Alaska as an alternate site.[72] The air force, taking a different tack, recommended that the AEC henceforth describe U.S. tests as "friendly blasts."[73]

In September 1954, the Defense Department had asked both Los Alamos and Livermore to explore the possibility of designing a new type of H-bomb—one in which the effects of radioactive contamination could be either diminished or enhanced.[74]

There was little enthusiasm at the nuclear labs—or anywhere else—for the so-called dirty bomb, where large areas of enemy territory could be made almost permanently uninhabitable by jacketing the weapon with a common element, like cobalt, which produced long-lived fission products. Conversely, there were few advocates among the military for the reduced-radiation, or "clean," bomb, at a time when U.S. war plans regarded enemy casualties caused by fallout as "bonus effect."[75]

Recognizing that the future of all nuclear testing might well depend on their ability to reduce fallout, however, Livermore scientists responded to the Pentagon order with alacrity. In December, York reported that his lab was working on two different and promising approaches to the clean bomb. The Defense Department awarded the Livermore program "urgent" status, asking the lab to make clean weapons a major effort.[76]

Murray was another enthusiast for what the religion-minded commissioner called "the 'pure' bomb." "Our objective should be to test a weapon of this type at the earliest possible date," he had written Strauss that fall.[77] In a meeting just two days after *Tesla,* Teller informed Murray that the lab's recent success had "opened up a completely new field" for small bombs as well as large ones. He looked forward to the time when "the 'pure' weapon idea could take on added impetus," Murray told Teller.[78]

One reason for Murray's avid interest in the clean bomb was the fact that his campaign to ban large H-bomb tests had reached a dead end with the administration. (His latest meeting, this time with Dulles, lasted only five minutes. "I thanked Mr. Murray for his ideas," the secretary of state wrote in a memo of their conversation.)[79] Undaunted, Murray had written once more to the president in mid-March 1955, this time proposing a so-called threshold test ban, which would eliminate thermonuclear tests in the megaton range—tests that the GAC claimed would be easily detectable.[80] Strauss, however, advised Eisenhower against any such agreement with "a cynical and treacherous enemy."[81]

Ike, in fact, already had another approach in mind. Unwilling to abandon the test ban as an eventual goal, the president on March 18 appointed Harold Stassen his special assistant for disarmament.[82]

The thirty-one-year-old former "boy governor" of Minnesota had made a career disguising his considerable ambition behind a facade of midwestern blandness. Three years earlier, Stassen's maneuvering had guaranteed Eisenhower a first-ballot nomination at the Republican convention. As Stassen was well aware, Ike owed him a political debt.

But what Stassen intended to be his first step—a comprehensive review of American foreign policy and strategy—was preempted by the Soviets, who, in early May, themselves called for a ban on nuclear testing. Although the Russian proposal was quickly rejected by the American side, since it had no provisions for inspection or enforcement, the fact that the Soviets had been first to propose a test ban infuriated Eisenhower.[83] Following the failure of the Geneva summit that June, the president encouraged Stassen to wrest the diplomatic initiative from the Russians.[84]

In July, Stassen announced the creation of eight blue-ribbon panels to study different aspects of disarmament, including a test ban.[85] Hoping to placate conservative critics, the Minnesotan put well-known and respected figures at the head of each group. (Jimmy Doolittle was chairman of one panel; Walt Disney and Charles Lindbergh were among Stassen's candidates for "disarmament consultant.")[86] To lead the all-important Task Force on Nuclear Inspection, Stassen chose Lawrence. Stassen also asked the various agencies involved—the Pentagon, the AEC, and State Department—to provide "experienced men with brilliant analytical minds" to assist the experts.[87]

Deeply skeptical of Stassen's enterprise—as he was, indeed, of any initiative to the Russians—Strauss volunteered McKay Donkin, the "special assistant" he had earlier used to dig up dirt on Oppenheimer, to serve as the commission's liaison with Lawrence's task force.[88] But Donkin's real job was to spy on the inspection panel. At Strauss's urging, Teller and Griggs were also added to Lawrence's task force, which comprised a dozen scientists, most drawn from RAND and Livermore.[89]

Stassen had assigned Lawrence's panel responsibility for devising an effective inspection system to uncover clandestine nuclear explosions, the fatal weakness of every test-ban proposal put forward thus far. Eisenhower hoped to make Lawrence's scheme the centerpiece of his diplomatic overture to the Russians at the next summit.

Using the cover name Project *Alpine,* the group met for the first time that fall in Washington, where they received briefings from the CIA, the AEC, and the air force on Russian nuclear capabilities.[90] While opinion among the panel's experts varied as to the feasibility—and desirability—of a test ban, one task force member, York, remembered another, Teller, as being "unabashedly hostile to the whole idea."[91]

Lawrence, on the other hand, seemed at least willing to maintain an open mind.[92] Stassen scheduled a meeting of all the groups for late October 1955 at the Quantico Marine Base in Virginia, where task force leaders would report on progress.[93]

Plainly concerned that Lawrence, whether out of sympathy or enthusiasm, might be about to embrace Stassen's vision of a disarmed world, Strauss advised caution: "All that the man in the street will realize is that a great scientist, inventor of the cyclotron, has accepted this assignment and, because of the stature of his scientific ability, is a magician and will pull the rabbit out of the hat."[94]

Strauss need not have worried. As Donkin assured the AEC chairman, Lawrence's report to the Quantico conference would be direly pessimistic about the prospects for a test ban. Indeed, Ernest told his peers that a moratorium on testing could be "dangerous" for the United States, since the nation's technological edge might be lost. His task force had concluded that the Russians would be able not only to test but to produce and stockpile nuclear weapons clandestinely. Unwilling to grant Russian inspectors access to Los Alamos or Livermore, Lawrence's experts were nonetheless proposing to send tens of thousands of U.S. and UN inspectors to comb the Soviet Union for hidden bombs.[95]

The plan encountered immediate resistance when it was submitted to Eisenhower and the NSC that December. State Department representatives protested that Lawrence's task force had an "exaggerated idea" of what was required to verify a test ban. An internal AEC study had recently concluded that 7,500 inspectors—not the 20,000 to 30,000 proposed in Lawrence's report—would be required for the job. (The authors of the AEC report lamented, ironically, that no one from "the Oppenheimer camp" had been on Lawrence's panel to counter the anti-ban sentiment there.)[96]

Dulles's response to the plan was even less diplomatic. The secretary of state told Stassen that Lawrence's "all-or-nothing proposition," with its divisions of inspectors and armadas of aircraft and helicopters, "would make the United States a laughing stock" at Geneva.[97] Disheartened, Dulles and Eisenhower urged Stassen and Lawrence to "refine" their inspection plan.

In rejecting Lawrence's plan, the president observed that there had been "too much talk about too little."[98] Temperamentally at least, Ernest seemed inclined to agree. Moreover, on at least one subject—the Russians—he had begun to split from Strauss.

During an Atoms for Peace conference in Geneva the previous summer, Lawrence and another *Alpine* recruit, Glenn Seaborg, had invited Soviet physicist V. I. Veksler to dinner at Perle du Lac, a French restaurant near the Palais des Nations.[99] Veksler was in Geneva to announce that Russia would soon complete a particle accelerator with twice the power of Berkeley's Bevatron.[100] Ernest and the Russians had gotten on so well that Lawrence urged Veksler to make a long-deferred visit to the Rad Lab.[101]

Lawrence also surprised colleagues by not lobbying the AEC for an accelerator at Berkeley to match or exceed the Russians'. But age, and illness, had muted Lawrence's enthusiasm for empire.[102] Because of the MTA fiasco, moreover, Brookhaven's Cosmotron was already more powerful, better funded, and hence more likely to yield the next big discoveries in particle physics.[103] Sitting together at a café on the shore of Lake Geneva, drinking beer, Lawrence and his erstwhile collaborator-turned-rival, Stan Livingston, reminisced fondly about times long past.[104]

Strauss, by contrast, was feeling besieged. Early in 1956, the AEC chairman found himself under attack by the press, the public, and Congress. "For the first time in my life, I have enemies," he confided to a friend.[105]

The midterm election victory that had returned control of Congress to the Democrats had also made Clinton Anderson, a senator hostile to Strauss, the new chairman of the Joint Committee on Atomic Energy. Anderson was openly critical of Strauss for favoring private industry in awarding AEC contracts for nuclear power plants. For Anderson, moreover, there was an even more important issue literally closer to home:

radioactive fallout. The New Mexico senator believed that Strauss had shown a cavalier disregard for scientists' warnings about the harmful effects of nuclear testing in the American Southwest.[106]

The AEC's spokesman in the fallout debate was chemist Willard Libby, whom Strauss had picked to replace Smyth on the commission the previous year. Despite Libby's repeated assurances that radiation from U.S. nuclear tests presented "no basis for concern," his claims were so often contradicted by other scientists—and, occasionally, by the AEC's own press releases—that Libby quickly lost effectiveness in the role.[107]

Even more worrisome to Strauss than his critics outside the commission was the man he viewed as the enemy within: Thomas Murray. The long-simmering tension between the crusading commissioner and the AEC chairman had come to a boil over the same conflict-of-interest issue that irked Anderson: the awarding of AEC contracts. Murray considered the so-called Dixon-Yates deal—in which the commission agreed to buy power in the Southeast from two private utility companies rather than the TVA—another instance where Strauss had exceeded his authority as chairman.[108] Verbal exchanges between Murray and Strauss at AEC meetings had become so heated that the secretary sometimes felt compelled to clear others from the room.[109]

Murray's latest enthusiasm was an "Atomic Summit," which he hoped might awaken world leaders to the as-yet-unappreciated consequences of a global thermonuclear war. Murray had urged Eisenhower to invite "an audience representative of all the peoples of the world" to Eniwetok for the next series of U.S. tests, so that they might witness, as he had, the effects of a large H-bomb detonation close up. Libby and Strauss opposed Murray's demonstration idea as likely to give the Russians vital clues as to the design of America's weapons.[110]

After Strauss and Libby beat back Murray's efforts to amend a blanket AEC pronouncement that testing was safe, the maverick commissioner made the case for his H-bomb test ban before a closed session of Anderson's Joint Committee.[111] Six weeks later, Murray went public with his appeal in open testimony before the Senate Foreign Relations Committee. Basing his argument unabashedly upon ethics rather than strategy, he claimed that the targeting of Russian cities and civilians was morally unjustifiable.[112]

Murray's testimony infuriated Strauss, particularly when Adlai Stevenson, Eisenhower's likely opponent in the upcoming presidential election, adopted the test-ban issue as his own less than two weeks later.[113] Stevenson echoed Murray's call for a unilateral end to multimegaton H-bomb tests.[114] Desperately seeking a way to counter Stevenson's initiative, Eisenhower announced a few days later that the next series of U.S. nuclear explosions in the Pacific—Operation *Redwing*—would include tests aimed at perfecting the clean bomb.

Like a Wild West shoot-out, *Redwing* would also determine which of the two nuclear labs would get the assignment to develop the warhead for the country's first intercontinental-range ballistic missile, the Atlas. Strategists were already calling the hypersonic, H-bomb-tipped ICBM the "ultimate weapon."[115]

Bradbury showed little heart for the coming contest. The previous fall the Los Alamos director had given the AEC notice that, in his view, the art of nuclear weapons design had already entered a rococo phase. Indeed, Bradbury thought the future of the bomb looked "unrewarding."[116]

Livermore, on the other hand, anticipated *Redwing* with unbridled enthusiasm. Ignoring Eisenhower's injunction that the United States would never again have a nuclear test as powerful as *Bravo,* York talked of exploding a 20-megaton device somewhere over Alaska's Brooks Range. (York abandoned the plan after being informed that the airplane dropping the bomb might not be able to escape the explosion.)[117] At the request of hawkish members of the Joint Committee, Livermore's director also promised to look into the feasibility of "atomic grenades." (They would be "too heavy to throw," York subsequently reported.)[118]

Boasting that it bred racehorses—compared to Los Alamos's workhorses—Livermore particularly looked forward to the debut of its candidate for the clean bomb, a test code-named *Zuni.*

Zuni was detonated in the predawn hours of May 28, 1956. The bomb gouged a half-mile-wide crater out of Bikini atoll's Eninman Island and cast some 3 million cubic yards of vaporized rock and coral into the stratosphere. Although the test was considered successful—more than 80 percent of the bomb's yield came from fusion—*Zuni* still rained radiation over a broad expanse of ocean. In what at first seemed likely to be a repeat of the *Lucky Dragon* incident, another Japanese vessel, the freighter *Mizuho Maru,* and its crew were downwind of the explosion and received a dusting of fallout.[119]

Hoping to make political capital from the clean bomb test, Strauss announced in a press release that *Redwing* had produced "much of importance not only from a military point of view but from a humanitarian aspect."[120] To the AEC chairman's dismay, his comment created its own firestorm. Murray cited it as further evidence that Strauss intended to ignore the opinions of the other commissioners.[121] Test-ban supporters publicly ridiculed the notion of "humanitarian H-bombs."[122]

Eisenhower, too, was becoming increasingly disenchanted with the man whom Stevenson had identified as Ike's "chief atomic energy adviser."[123] Pressed by his Democratic rival again on the test ban that fall, Eisenhower scolded Strauss for not coming up with new ideas: "We've just got to get going here. And you haven't done much."[124]

But Strauss remained secure in the knowledge that there seemed little alternative to the status quo. Stassen's ill-timed support of a "dump Nixon" movement had alienated Eisenhower as well as the vice president. Testifying before Congress that spring, the AEC chairman had stubbornly refused even to discuss what inspection measures might be necessary for a test ban, citing security as his reason.[125]

While Lawrence and his experts had meanwhile made some progress, reducing the number of on-site inspectors to a fraction of their original estimate—6,890 to be exact—it was still too large a force to likely be accepted by the Russians.[126] The day after *Zuni,* Lawrence and other members of his task force met with Stassen in Washington to discuss the upcoming strategy for Geneva.

Flanked by Teller and Mark Mills, an associate director at Livermore, Lawrence informed Stassen without preamble that the task force "had not changed its views at all" and still opposed setting any limits to testing.[127] Teller reminded the group of Livermore's continuing work on the clean bomb. Although he challenged Teller's assumption that any limitations on testing would necessarily benefit the Russians, Stassen reluctantly agreed not to raise the test ban as a separate issue with the Soviets at Geneva.

It was Stevenson who made the test ban an unavoidable issue in the presidential campaign a few weeks later. In a speech to the American Legion's annual convention, the Democratic nominee cited Murray in support of his claim that the United States could already detect H-bomb tests "anywhere."[128]

Anxious to counter Stevenson, who had already received endorsements from Smyth and other prominent scientists, Strauss issued a press release claiming that the fallout threat was "vague, unproven," and in any case secondary to "the more immediate and infinitely greater dangers of defeat and perhaps obliteration" at the hands of the Russians."[129]

Conceding that voters might find a response by experts more persuasive, Strauss and Cutler enlisted the aid of a dozen scientists, led by Libby, who met with Eisenhower in late October. The group subsequently issued their own press release, lamenting "the injection into a political campaign of statements and conclusions which extend beyond . . . existing scientific evidence."[130]

But Strauss was not content to stop there.[131] Mindful of the merciless moot-court grilling he had undergone from Neylan years earlier, Lawrence had hitherto refused to make any public statements on the test ban or the fallout debate, although his own views on radiation had hardly changed in that time. (Ernest continued to shun routine dental and medical x-rays. Molly, who shared his concerns, had recently led a successful campaign to ban the portable x-ray machines that were popular with children in Bay Area shoe stores.)[132]

But Lawrence may also have felt a residual debt to Strauss, particularly in light of his last-minute failure to testify in the Oppenheimer case.

On the evening of November 4, 1956, Lawrence summoned the head of the university's press office, Dan Wilkes, to his Berkeley home. Wilkes was surprised to encounter another visitor, Teller. Ernest—who was "feeling no pain," Wilkes later recalled—asked the former newspaperman to draft a press release in response to Stevenson. Teller's version, Wilkes and Lawrence both agreed, was "too long and said too much."[133]

Lawrence and Teller finally signed a brief statement which Wilkes wrote and telephoned to the wire services that night. It appeared in newspapers around the country the following morning, election day. In three numbered points, the statement proclaimed that there were "no sure methods of detecting nuclear weapons tests," that continued testing was necessary to maintain the country's arsenal, and that the radioactivity produced by nuclear testing was "insignificant."[134]

19

A CROSS OF ATOMS

TWO WEEKS AFTER his victory in the 1956 election, Eisenhower endorsed a new initiative by Stassen to separate the test-ban negotiations from the seemingly interminable disarmament talks.[1] With Stevenson's defeat, the most outspoken advocate in Washington of a ban on the testing of big bombs remained Thomas Murray.

In his latest crusade, the evangelical commissioner sought to amend the AEC's *Weapons Effects Handbook,* the most recent version of which described the explosion of a hypothetical 100-megaton superbomb. Murray hoped to discourage even consideration of such a weapon by limiting the descriptions to only such weapons as were already planned for the U.S. arsenal.[2]

But Murray's Jesuitical distinctions concerning what he called "rational nuclear armament" were little understood by the public, and completely unappreciated by Strauss and the president. "He ought to be locked up. I think he is off his rocker," a furious Ike told Strauss following Murray's appearance before the Joint Committee early in 1957. After Strauss blocked a study—proposed by Murray—of the effects of an all-out nuclear war, the Democrat persuaded his allies on the committee to hold open hearings on the subject.[3] Having tried—but failed—to have Murray's security clearance revoked, Strauss told Eisenhower that he, too, was patiently marking the days on his calendar until June 30, 1957, when Murray's term on the commission would expire.[4]

Murray, however, was determined to go down fighting. He had begun writing, in secret, what was intended to be a kind of political last testament. It was also, and no less, his parting shot at Strauss. Having arranged for the article to appear in *Life* magazine, Murray negotiated last-minute editorial changes from a pay telephone a block away from the AEC building—lest Strauss learn of the project via a bug in Murray's office. (As Murray pointed out to an aide, *Life* publisher Henry Luce was a friend of Strauss, and the AEC chairman also served on the Board of Directors for a distillery that was a major advertiser in the magazine.)[5]

Appearing in the May 6, 1957, issue, "Reliance on H-bomb and Its Dangers" was a final warning against the allure of "the big cheap bomb." Haunting the article was an apocalyptic vision of an all-out nuclear exchange between the United States and the Soviet Union—what Murray called "the three-hour war."[6]

At Livermore, the test ban was likewise a growing concern, but for altogether different reasons. Despite the lab's successes in *Redwing,* its future was still far from assured. The previous summer, the contract for the Atlas warhead had gone to Los Alamos. Although the clean bomb was still a priority at the lab, there was as yet no formal military requirement for the innovative designs coming out of Brown's A Division.[7] Livermore's big bombs had yet to find a patron.

Teller, Brown, and Foster undoubtedly had this fact in mind when they attended a navy-sponsored scientific conference at Nobska Point, near Woods Hole, Massachusetts, in summer 1956. The meeting had been called to consider a variety of defense projects, but the scientists eventually focused upon a new kind of weapon—one that, not long before, had seemed only on the distant horizon: a submarine-launched ballistic missile.[8]

The rocket under consideration was a behemoth. To carry Los Alamos's 1-megaton warhead, it would have to be almost five stories tall, weighing 80 tons. Too large to fit inside the submarine, a pair of the missiles would be borne in bulky compartments welded to the sub's hull. The navy looked to Nobska's experts for a better solution.

Because of his colleagues' youth and inexperience, Teller spoke for Livermore. At a brainstorming session on July 20, Edward stood up to make a dramatic announcement. The navy, he suggested, had it backward: rather than build a bigger missile, it should make a smaller warhead. Teller's remarks drew murmurs of surprise and then incredulity when he promised that Livermore could give the navy a miniature 1-megaton warhead, barely 1 foot across and weighing only 600 pounds, within five years. Teller's bomb would be less than half the size of the smallest and lightest device that the Los Alamos lab had yet produced with comparable yield.

Teller's promise was hardly a surprise to Brown and Foster, who had originated the recent ideas at Livermore for shrinking the size of superbombs.[9] But a multitude of experiments in Nevada and the Pacific would be necessary just to prove the feasibility of the lilliputian H-bomb. A ban on nuclear testing at such a critical juncture, on the other hand, would stop Livermore in its tracks.

By early 1957, the clean bomb, still Livermore's first priority, had become the AEC's chief argument for continued testing.[10] At the same time, recent developments at the Kremlin had given Eisenhower renewed hope for progress on the test ban. The consolidation of power in the hands of a relatively young and reform-minded leader, Nikita Khrushchev, was followed in mid-June by a Soviet proposal for a moratorium on nuclear testing lasting two to three years. Khrushchev had also accepted—"in principle"—on-site inspection of a test ban.[11] On Wednesday, June 19, 1957, Eisenhower announced that he would be "perfectly delighted" to see an end to nuclear testing.[12]

The following day, Lawrence, Teller, and Mark Mills, the head of Livermore's theoretical division, appeared before a subcommittee chaired by the Joint Committee's Senator Henry Jackson. Jackson had called the session to discuss increasing plutonium production at Hanford. Within the first few minutes, however, Teller steered the discussion around to the clean bomb. Experiments then under way in Nevada, Edward claimed, would prove the feasibility of building small, highly efficient weapons. But bombs that were virtually fallout-free awaited further tests in the Pacific. At Jackson's prompting, the trio agreed to make their case for the clean bomb before the full Joint Committee the following day.[13]

In the wake of Teller's briefing, Republicans on the committee wondered aloud whether Eisenhower and Stassen knew of the various ways that the Russians might secretly violate a moratorium. While Lawrence remained mum about *Alpine,* Teller replied that the administration was probably unfamiliar with the latest thinking on how the Soviets could cheat. In a telephone call to the White House, Sterling Cole arranged a meeting with the president for Monday. Lawrence, Teller, and Mills spent the weekend at a Washington hotel, being prepped by Strauss.[14]

Accompanied by the AEC chairman, the physicists were ushered into the Oval Office on the afternoon of June 24. Lawrence—"all tight and excited," Teller later recalled—was literally tongue-tied in the presence of Eisenhower. ("This awe was something I just could not imagine. Ernest's ease with authority had always been assumed; the Regents to him were like close friends.")[15] Seizing the opportunity, Teller told the president that additional testing would dramatically reduce the radiation caused by multimegaton weapons and might even eliminate fallout altogether. The resulting bombs could then be used for peaceful purposes: to excavate harbors, modify the weather, or liberate oil and gas trapped deep underground.[16]

Finding his voice at last, Lawrence chimed in with a suggestion: Eisenhower might wish to invite UN observers to a future clean bomb test in the Pacific, so that the world could see the progress that was being made.[17]

While no one could disagree with the technical points they had made, Ike told the group, opposition to testing at home and abroad was gathering momentum. He feared that the country risked being "crucified on a cross of atoms."[18]

The impact of the physicists' visit was evident in a telephone call that Eisenhower made to Dulles the next morning. Complaining that Teller had make "it look like a crime to ban tests," Ike said he had been persuaded that the "real peaceful use of atomic science" depended upon clean bombs.[19] Later that day, Dulles sent an "eyes only" cable to Stassen, in London for the latest disarmament talks, apprising him of the changed situation in Washington: "You should know that this conversation made deep impression on President and that since then he has had serious mental reservations as to the correctness of our proposal to suspend testing."[20]

Teller and Strauss had once complained that whenever they opened a door in Washington they found Oppenheimer behind it. Wrote Lilienthal in his diary that fall: "Teller's is now the featured face (instead of Oppenheimer's) in the role of Scientific Statesman."[21]

Jubilant that "everything has worked out as we had hoped it would," Strauss sent a letter congratulating the Livermore scientists for their "performance."[22] Strauss's aide, navy captain Jack Morse, echoed this praise in his own personal note to Teller and Lawrence: "The situation called for over-selling rather than under-selling, particularly when a simple statement could not possibly cover all the complexities involved."[23]

That the trio had oversold the clean bomb was hardly subject to doubt. Memos that York had been sending to the AEC for months indicated that a typical reduced-radiation weapon would have only half the yield of a standard H-bomb but would weigh considerably more.[24] Lawrence, Teller, and Mills had neglected to inform Eisenhower of a dirty little secret behind the clean bomb: its increased size and decreased yield made it no better suited for tactical use on the battlefield—the very role that promoters like Murray envisioned—than old-fashioned fission bombs.[25]

Likewise worried that the Livermore physicists had exaggerated the clean bomb's potential, the head of the AEC's Division of Military Application, Army General Alfred Starbird, interrogated York for several hours on the subject immediately following the June 24 meeting. "He is the man who must develop the weapon and is a man who is generally most optimistic," Starbird subsequently wrote Strauss in a secret report.[26] But even York had warned that a tactical clean bomb was still several years away—and "this would be based on very lucky breaks."

There was a "great danger," Starbird cautioned Strauss, that the public "will get mistaken ideas as to how soon we shall have clean weapons and in what types."[27]

But Strauss was no longer the only one to whom Ike could turn for advice on the bomb. After stepping down from the General Advisory Committee, Rabi had become chairman of the Science Advisory Committee of the Office of Defense Mobilization when DuBridge resigned that post the previous year. Once almost moribund, its members on the verge of resigning, the committee had experienced a resurgence of influence under Rabi's leadership.[28] While president of Columbia University, Ike had learned to rely upon the street-smart Rabi to mediate disputes between the administration and the faculty.[29]

Moreover, that fall an unexpected event caused the stock of the fifty-nine-year-old Rabi and his committee to soar.

The Soviets' launch of the first Earth-orbiting artificial satellite on October 4, 1957, caught most of official Washington flat-footed.[30] Informed by a young AEC aide that the Russians had a new satellite, Strauss initially thought that the Soviets had added another country to their empire. "Where?" he asked, ashen-faced. "There," replied the aide cheerily, pointing skyward.[31]

Belated and clumsy efforts by the administration to dismiss the Soviet achievement as a "neat technical trick" and a "silly bauble" only heightened public concern. Asked at a congressional hearing what he expected to find on the Moon, Teller replied with sullen insolence: "Russians."[32]

Official disclaimers aside, however, *Sputnik* had provoked a surprisingly prompt and decisive response from Eisenhower. Following an Oval Office meeting in mid-October, the president asked Rabi to draft the charter for a new advisory committee of scientists, one that would report to him directly.[33]

Before he would complete that task, Rabi and Hans Bethe sent Eisenhower an "eyes only" memo on October 28, outlining plans for an impenetrable shield in space against Russian rockets. Rabi's prospective missile shield relied upon a recently discovered vulnerability in Soviet thermonuclear warheads. This fatal flaw had been uncovered in the analysis of debris from the most recent Russian explosions by Bethe, who headed the committee that analyzed foreign nuclear tests for the AEC. If the United States detonated its own nuclear bombs in the path of incoming Soviet missiles at a critical point in their trajectory, Rabi explained in the memo, enemy warheads could be made to explode prematurely, and harmlessly, in space.[34]

Bethe's remarkable discovery justified not only "priority development" of the emergency anti-ICBM system he described, Rabi argued, but also consideration "of securing immediately a world-wide moratorium on nuclear explosions."[35]

Old wounds that had never healed were reopened when Eisenhower summoned Rabi and Strauss to his office the following morning to discuss the proposal. Rabi's space shield was temporarily forgotten as emotions that had lain dormant since the Oppenheimer hearing came to the fore.[36] Ignoring Strauss, Rabi told Eisenhower that "it had been a great mistake for the President to accept the views of Drs. Teller and Lawrence" on the clean bomb, and "a tragedy" that nuclear testing had not been banned before the last Russian series was completed.[37] His own temper rising, Strauss replied that he was "inclined to question some of [Rabi's] assumptions and conclusions"—since "the Soviets can always steal our secrets."

Puzzled by the high feeling in the room, Eisenhower asked whether there was not mutual respect among the atomic scientists. Rabi answered simply that he and Teller had known each other for more than twenty years.

The meeting ended abruptly and inconclusively. While admitting that he was sympathetic to an immediate ban on testing, Eisenhower worried about how such "a complete, sudden reversal in our position" would be greeted by our allies. Ike asked Strauss and Rabi to assemble a blue-ribbon panel of scientists to study the matter further.

"I learned that some of the mutual antagonisms among the scientists are so bitter as to make their working together almost an impossibility," Ike wrote in his private journal that evening. "I was told that Dr. Rabi and some of his group are so antagonistic to Doctors Lawrence and Teller that communication between them is practically nil."[38]

By early 1958, Eisenhower's personal science adviser was ensconced in the old Executive Office Building next to the White House. Soft-spoken, pragmatic, and even "disarmingly pleasant," MIT president James Killian was nonetheless already a Washington insider: Killian had headed the top-secret study that, three years earlier, had recommended both the U-2 spy plane and reconnaissance satellites.

But Killian, too, was surprised to discover how much the ghosts of the past haunted his new office.[39] Invited to lunch by Strauss, Killian was stunned when the AEC chairman asked that he promise not to reopen the question of Oppenheimer's security clearance. ("On matters of this sort, Strauss could become emotional," Killian wrote in his memoirs.)[40]

Killian and the inaugural members of what was now, pointedly, the *President's* Science Advisory Committee, were prompt to recognize their opportunity. For almost a year, the U.S. negotiating position had been in disarray at Geneva. Following a failed bid for the governorship of Pennsylvania, the unpredictable Stassen had launched an ill-fated diplomatic initiative of his own. The overture succeeded only in alienating U.S. allies and, with them, Eisenhower and Dulles. By the start of the new year, with Ike's gentle urging, Stassen was preparing to resign.[41]

At an NSC meeting called on January 6, 1958, to discuss the latest Russian proposal, Killian volunteered PSAC's help with the test ban—noting that his committee had already started to look into the matter on its own. Eisenhower and Dulles seized the offer like a life preserver in heavy seas.[42]

Killian's choice to lead PSAC's study was Bethe, who was instructed to look not only at the wisdom and feasibility of a test ban but also at its potential impact upon the nuclear labs. (Warned by Strauss and the Pentagon that a test ban would turn Los Alamos and Livermore into "ghost towns," Eisenhower had responded acidly that he "thought scientists, like other people, have a strong interest in avoiding nuclear war.")[43]

Bethe did not hesitate to blame the AEC and Livermore for putting obstacles in the way of the test ban. He and Killian had already advised Stassen that U.S. negotiators "had been sold a bill of goods" by Lawrence's task force.[44]

In early April, Bethe and Killian reported to the president and the National Security Council on the results of the PSAC study.[45] What Bethe proposed was a far more modest and less intrusive inspection system than that outlined by Lawrence. Instead of several hundred monitoring stations, manned by thousands of inspectors, Bethe's "practical detection system" called for an even 100 stations worldwide, 70 of which would be behind the Iron Curtain. Augmented by aircraft, orbiting satellites, and a handful of ships, his system, Bethe argued, would make it possible to detect any militarily significant nuclear explosions underground, underwater, or in space.[46]

The next day the Russians, as expected, declared that they were suspending nuclear tests indefinitely and invited the United States to do the same. While Eisenhower felt compelled to publicly dismiss the Soviet overture as "a side issue" and "a gimmick," a few days later he proposed that both sides send technical experts to Geneva, to discuss methods of monitoring a test ban.[47]

While PSAC and Bethe's panel had thus far avoided giving advice on whether a test ban or moratorium was in the nation's interest—believing the question to be more political than technical in nature—Killian argued that Eisenhower deserved the advice of those he called "*his* scientists" on such an important matter. In order to discuss that question away from the pressures of Washington, the science adviser scheduled the next gathering of PSAC at Ramey Air Force Base in Puerto Rico.

On April 17, 1958, following the Ramey meeting, Killian reported to Eisenhower and the NSC that a test ban would be "greatly to the advantage of the United States."[48] While the president's scientists thought it impractical to cancel the next series of U.S. nuclear tests—Operation *Hardtack* was scheduled to begin in just four days—PSAC urged Ike to seek a moratorium on testing immediately upon *Hardtack*'s conclusion.[49]

Voting for the first time on a question before them, PSAC members at Ramey had been all-but-unanimous in endorsing a ban. Only York—de facto the labs' representative on the committee—abstained. After a day of coaxing by other PSAC members, however, York, too, voted for a ban. At Livermore, Teller branded York's turnabout "traitorous."[50]

Rumors that Eisenhower might cancel *Hardtack* before it began sparked a near panic at the California lab.[51] Less than a week after *Sputnik*, the Pentagon had restored funds cut from the budget for Polaris, the navy's new submarine-launched ballistic missile. As the Nobska study had predicted and Polaris proved, a second generation of intercontinental-range missiles—smaller, more concealable, and quicker to fire—was already waiting in the wings.[52]

Work at Livermore on the miniature warhead for the Polaris, the W-47, had likewise been sped up.[53] Development tests of the device dominated the Livermore shots scheduled for *Hardtack* and were anxiously awaited at the lab.[54]

By contrast, the "open shot" of a clean bomb that Lawrence proposed to carry out before a crowd of international observers was regarded with a mixture of disdain and amusement by weaponeers at both labs. ("If you require Japanese lanterns or potted palms as part of the decor please let us know," a sympathetic Los Alamos physicist wrote his counterpart at Livermore.)[55] Bradbury hardly bothered to hide his contempt for what he decried as an empty public relations exercise and a "Roman holiday."[56]

Because of the need to test the W-47's components, *Hardtack* had grown to thirty-five shots—ten more than the number that "appalled" Eisenhower when Strauss had outlined the series the previous summer. Two of the recently added tests were multimegaton, high-altitude explosions that Lawrence had requested to try out new detection techniques for *Alpine*.[57]

Another series of experiments, deemed both vital and urgent, was meant to be the trial of yet another concept for an emergency missile defense, the brainchild of Nick Christofilos—a brilliant but eccentric Livermore physicist whom colleagues described as an "idea factory." Christofilos theorized that enemy missiles might be rendered harmless in flight if hundreds of nuclear weapons were exploded above them, in space, where a temporary cordon sanitaire of high-energy electrons would scramble the missiles' warheads and delicate electronics.[58]

Operation *Argus*—the test of the so-called Christofilos effect—would be carried out in secret, partly as a trial of Teller's hypothesis that nuclear explosions could go undetected in space.[59]

So busy was Livermore with the W-47, the clean-bomb demonstration, and *Argus*, that Starbird worried the workload at the lab might be "approaching criticality."[60] Adding to the stress was the fact that York, virtually on the eve of *Hardtack*, had left the lab to head up a newly created civilian research office at the Pentagon.

York's departure prompted Teller to ask Lawrence for permission to take over leadership of the California lab until *Hardtack* was completed. Lawrence agreed to let Edward take the reins, on the condition that he yield them after a year to Mark Mills, whom Ernest had already picked as York's successor.[61] In early April 1958, Teller officially assumed the role that many believed he had occupied de facto since the start of the lab: director of Livermore.[62]

That spring at Los Alamos, Bradbury was complaining that his laboratory had "lost control of its destiny in the weapon business"—largely because of Livermore.[63] His chief worry, Bradbury advised Starbird, was that unless Los Alamos transformed itself into "a factory-sort of business," it would be judged "less 'enthusiastic'" than Livermore: "We can do the weapons described in the laboratory program, but is it really the right thing for the country? I don't know."

Bradbury's crisis of confidence caused him to take an altogether different view of a temporary ban on testing than Teller and Livermore. For his lab, Bradbury wrote, "the thought of a moratorium, cast in the proper context, is not too painful."

The ennui at Los Alamos found a mirror in Lawrence's situation at Berkeley. Although it had been several months since his last serious bout with colitis, the disease had taken a visible toll. Not quite fifty-seven, Lawrence's shock of blond hair, while still full, had turned gray. Ernest's famous grin, though undiminished, was set in a face going slack and jowly.

Perhaps the most notable change, however, was the fading of Lawrence's legendary energy. Longtime friends were stunned to hear him talk of retirement. (Asked by Ernest and John to scout out some land in northeastern California for a ranch, a friend was struck by its barrenness: "It wouldn't raise three jackrabbits an acre. They only liked it because it reminded them of South Dakota.")[64]

Ernest had also been forced to abandon his dream of riches from his color-TV invention when Paramount sold the Chromatics production facility in Emeryville to Litton, which promptly converted it to making military radars. The venture that had begun with such enthusiasm and the financial support of Loomis and Gaither never produced a commercial product.*[65]

Even at Livermore, Lawrence had begun to seem only a detached spectator—a victim of changing times. As was now evident to all, research that produced weapons was of far more interest to Lawrence's government patrons than the basic science that went on at Berkeley.[66] The man who had long been Ernest's biggest booster on campus—Jack Neylan—had resigned from the regents in 1955, following a final row with Sproul over the handling of a labor dispute at Livermore.[67]

The GAC had meanwhile decreed, pointedly, that machines costing tens of millions of dollars to build and $1 million or more annually to operate were "too large for *single* universities."[68] An AEC-sponsored report on the future of the national labs might have had Lawrence in mind when it warned about the aging of the laboratory directors.[69]

Lawrence's fatigue was reflected as well in his changed attitude toward physics. When a twenty-year veteran of the Rad Lab asked Ernest what he had in mind to supplant the Bevatron, the answer surprised him. The era of big machines was probably over, Lawrence reflected, since the energies employed were already "so far beyond human scale."[70] "I'm in favor of doing the science but you should do it more slowly," Lawrence had told York during a recent visit to Washington.[71]

At the Rad Lab itself, the political passions aroused a decade earlier by the loyalty oath had also long since cooled. All of the nonsigners fired during the controversy had been quietly offered their jobs back—including even David Feldman, the physicist whom Lawrence had once accused

*For Lawrence at least. The Sony corporation would later develop and market the three-gun picture tube under its "Trinitron" trademark.

Oppenheimer of trying to "plant" on him. Like Feldman, not all accepted the invitation.[72]

Ironically, Alvarez, once Lawrence's protégé, had lately become one of his most vocal critics at the lab. Angered when his own experiments did not receive priority on the Bevatron, Luie hinted darkly about reporting his former mentor to the AEC for misappropriating federal funds. Upset as well by what he viewed as Ernest's increasing conservatism in science, Alvarez had formed an alliance instead with Stanford's Pief Panofsky, one of the young physicists who had been driven away by the oath controversy.[73]

Lawrence had even recently informed Sproul that he was thinking about stepping down as Rad Lab director, the position he had held for more than twenty years.[74] To Birge, already retired, Ernest spoke wistfully of someday returning to LeConte, so that he might putter around again in his own small laboratory.

The loss of close friends and longtime associates had also given Lawrence a heightened sense of his own mortality. The premature death, from cancer, of Bernard Rossi, an early operator of the 60-inch, was seen by many at the Rad Lab as an ominous harbinger of tragedies to come. "It appears that time is beginning to catch up with all of us," wrote a Berkeley colleague to Joseph Hamilton on the occasion of Rossi's death.[75] Less than a year later, Hamilton, too, was dead, at age forty-nine the victim of leukemia.[76] Shortly thereafter, Lawrence advised Molly's mother against daily x-ray treatments following cancer surgery.[77]

But the death that affected Lawrence most was that of Mark Mills, the man whom Ernest had chosen to be York's heir apparent. Mills was killed a week later, in a helicopter crash at the Pacific proving grounds. Fearful that any delay might give opponents an excuse to cancel *Hardtack,* he had ignored the regulation forbidding nighttime flights in order to fix a diagnostics problems at an outlying atoll: ground zero for the first *Hardtack* test. The helicopter had run into a sudden squall on the return flight and crashed near a reef. Both pilots and another physicist escaped; Mills, trapped in the craft under twelve feet of water, drowned.[78]

Concerned that word of Mills's death might prompt a recurrence of Lawrence's colitis, Rad Lab colleagues tried, unsuccessfully, to keep the news from him. Shortly after writing John that he felt "fit as a fiddle," Ernest was struck by an attack of severe bleeding that left him weak and pale. He left Berkeley to spend several days recuperating at the house on Balboa Island, returning in time for Mills's funeral.[79]

While there was no outward sign that Lawrence's views on the test ban had changed since he, Teller, and Mills appeared before Eisenhower in the

Oval Office, at the final meeting of the *Alpine* task force, in March 1957, only Lawrence and Stassen had sounded an optimistic note. But Ernest, who said on that occasion that he favored a "reasonable limitation" of testing, had yet to define what that was.[80]

A year later, whatever hopes that Lawrence might have had for putting reasonable limits on testing seemed pinned not on talks in London or Geneva but on personal diplomacy. During the *Alpine* meetings, Lawrence had spoken to Stassen of "disarming personalities" and a "common sense approach" should formal negotiations fail and the Russians reject the U.S. inspection plan. He told Stassen that a broadening of scientific and cultural exchanges between the two countries might even "break down the Iron Curtain."[81]

The possibility that a diplomatic breakthrough could come about from face-to-face contact between American and Soviet physicists was also a subject that Lawrence had discussed with Admiral Chick Hayward, Ernest's host for a trip around Cape Horn onboard the aircraft carrier *Franklin D. Roosevelt* in summer 1956. Hayward thought Lawrence not only enthusiastic about but even obsessed with the idea of meeting his opposite numbers in the Soviet Union.[82]

During subsequent visits to the East Coast, Loomis and Gaither were likewise surprised—and even alarmed—by the intensity of Ernest's expressions of faith that he could get to the Russians through their scientists.[83]

At Berkeley, Lawrence had taken to giving visiting Soviet physicists personal tours of the Rad Lab. When the State Department vetoed a planned dinner for the Russians at Trader Vic's, Ernest barbequed hot dogs at home for his guests. Although Lawrence was forced to turn down a reciprocal invitation from the Soviet Academy of Sciences—to the relief of J. Edgar Hoover—he again played host late in 1957, taking four Russian scientists on a driving tour of the California coast.[84] Another visit, by a Soviet chemist in spring 1958, kept such contacts alive.[85] He found the Russian scientists "very friendly and normal," Ernest had informed Stassen.[86]

Strauss was likewise aware of and disturbed by Lawrence's contacts with the Russians. But the clipped warning that Donkin sent the AEC chairman on the final *Alpine* meeting had undoubtedly been a new cause for alarm: "Lawrence et al unanimously agreed that nuclear tests should be limited at earliest date with or without an armament agreement."[87]

In early May 1958, when Khrushchev accepted his proposal for a conference of experts on the test ban, Eisenhower lost no time, instructing Killian to schedule the talks for that summer in Geneva. (He had "never been too much impressed, or completely convinced by the views expressed by Drs. Teller, Lawrence, and Mills that we must continue testing of nuclear weapons," Ike told his stunned science adviser.)[88] On May 21, while on vacation in Yosemite, Lawrence learned that he was one of those chosen by the president to represent the United States.

Ernest was the compromise candidate.[89] Although Strauss had campaigned strenuously to have Teller at the talks, Edward was plainly anathema to Eisenhower, Dulles, and Killian. The significance of the choice of the other two scientists picked for the American team was also surely not lost upon Strauss. Robert Bacher and James Fisk, the delegation's leader, had both testified strongly in Oppie's defense at the 1954 hearings. Initially disappointed not to be among those chosen for the U.S. delegation—"Adm. Strauss saw to that"—Bethe was nonetheless pleased to be appointed a consultant to the group. Harold Brown was also made a consultant at Geneva, as was Strauss's personal assistant, Jack Morse.

Still, the AEC chairman looked to the forthcoming talks with undisguised dread. "Nothing good has ever come out of Geneva," Strauss told journalist Clare Boothe Luce.[90]

Strauss, too, was now facing an end of sorts. "Just as a ship too long at sea collects barnacles," he told the president, "the hostility of a small but vocal coterie" made it unlikely that he could continue to serve as AEC chairman. Clinton Anderson held an "almost pathological dislike" for him, Strauss admitted to Eisenhower.[91]

Anderson had already made it plain that Strauss would face an uphill confirmation battle should he be reappointed by the president.[92] Strauss told Ike that he planned to step down at the end of June. Eisenhower picked engineer and investment banker John McCone to replace him.[93]

Strauss, however, had not so much yielded the field as simply decided to direct his campaign against the test ban from a different vantage point: behind the scenes. At his request, he was appointed a special consultant to the Atoms for Peace program by Eisenhower, a role that allowed him to attend NSC meetings whenever nuclear matters were discussed.

By that summer, there may also have been a nagging concern in Strauss's mind about where Lawrence's ultimate loyalties lay. With the start of the Geneva talks and the end of his own government service only a week away, he sent Lawrence this "parting thought": "No matter how eminent the Russian scientists are or how persuasive, never let yourself forget that they are the envoys of men who are cold-blooded murderers. Deal with them with reserve."[94]

Although left exhausted by the travel and late-night briefings required as preparation for the technical talks at Geneva, Lawrence ignored the entreaties of Molly and John that he decline the president's summons for reasons of health.[95] Indeed, as the prospect of meeting with his Soviet counterparts neared, Ernest's enthusiasm and vitality actually seemed to return. "I don't think we'll have any trouble with the Russians," he told a Rad Lab colleague before embarking on his last trip to Washington.[96]

Stopping off en route to see Arthur Compton, in a St. Louis hospital recuperating from a heart attack, Lawrence justified his unscientist-like willingness to see limits put on nuclear experiments as the price that had to be paid for control of the arms race.[97] In Washington, Lawrence paid a visit to his boyhood friend, Carnegie Institution physicist Merle Tuve. "We helped start this and have to do what we can about it," he told Tuve.[98] On June 27, 1958, Ernest and Molly boarded a Swissair flight for Geneva.

Hardtack had meanwhile gotten off to an inauspicious start, while preparations for the Geneva conference were still under way.[99] Nearly half of the devices exploded in April and May had given lower-than-expected yields. Two of the prototype clean bombs fired by Los Alamos and Livermore had been outright fizzles.[100]

Reporting on *Hardtack*'s failures to Eisenhower in mid-June, Bethe noted that they "may show that we are close to the limit of what we can attain in 'cleanness' of weapons."[101] He also informed the president of what was surely, for both, a much keener disappointment: the most recent Russian tests had fixed the previous flaw in Soviet ICBM warheads. The opportunity for deploying Rabi and Bethe's missile defense shield had passed.

Hardtack's troubles even extended to *Pinon,* the proposed clean-bomb demonstration. After only five of the fourteen invited countries agreed to send observers, *Pinon* had been postponed to the end of July.[102] In late June, four AEC division heads wrote to the commission's general manager urging that the test be canceled. As they pointed out, the so-called clean bomb would produce many times the fallout of the weapon that had been dropped on Hiroshima. But fallout was not their only—or even their primary—concern:

> The *Pinon* weapon is so large that it clearly will not illustrate the cleanliness of *tactical* defensive weapons, development of which we have stressed in reference to *Hardtack* and in other statements of policy with respect to testing. What *Pinon* will do is to show not

how "clean" is a nuclear weapon, but rather how "dirty" is a high yield thermonuclear weapon.[103]

As the AEC's head of public relations warned Starbird, *Pinon* would "disclose that we have made essentially no progress in our attempts to reduce substantially the size of feasible clean weapons."[104]

At Geneva's Palais de Nations, eleventh-hour demands by the Russians had raised doubts whether the Soviet delegation would even show up. The test-ban negotiations were set to begin in an atmosphere "of no nonsense, no politics, and not much hope," *Time* magazine reported on July 1, 1958. Still travel weary, Lawrence felt well enough by that weekend to attend a reception sponsored by CERN, Europe's nuclear research center.

In the garden of the Hotel du Rhône, Ernest encountered Robert Oppenheimer, in Geneva for the CERN meeting. The unexpected meeting, while brief, was neither strained nor unpleasant for either man, Oppie later remembered: "There was, I would say, a sense of disengagement, but certainly not hostility."[105] It was the last time the two men would see each other.

At Gaither's expense, Lawrence had brought along a Russian-speaking engineer from Berkeley, Leo Tichvinsky. Ernest hoped to use Tichvinsky as a facilitator as well as a translator in his personal meetings with the Russians. Lawrence most looked forward to meeting his opposite number on the Russian side, physical chemist Nikolai Semenov, the sole Nobel prize–winner on the Soviet delegation.[106]

In an effort to persuade the Russians not to walk out of the talks, Lawrence had drafted a so-called break statement—a brief speech to be used in the event that negotiations seemed about to collapse. He planned to address his plea to Semenov, asking the Russian, as a fellow Nobel laureate, not to abandon the negotiations for the sake of both their countries, and the world.[107]

Ernest's appeal turned out to be unnecessary; the Russians stayed. But his attitude was already a concern to Ron Spiers, the foreign service officer whom the State Department had appointed a liaison with the U.S. delegation. Spiers cabled Washington: "Lawrence is like a little boy, indiscriminately enthusiastic. When the Russians handed their agenda across the table, they gave copies to Fisk and Lawrence. The latter quickly glanced over it, nodded his head happily and said 'that's good. Very good.' I shuddered and tried to get a copy."[108]

Although relieved that his prepared speech to Semenov proved unnecessary, Lawrence was disappointed when the latter brushed aside his subsequent attempts at conversation, apologizing that he spoke only Russian. Ernest's invitation to dinner, extended to Semenov and his wife, seemed to offer a second opportunity. But the appearance at the Perle du Lac of an uninvited guest, an English-speaking Soviet foreign ministry official, promptly dashed that hope, too. Semenov remained an "enigma," Tichvinsky reported to Lawrence.[109]

On July 13, only two days after his discouraging démarche with Semenov, Lawrence came down with a severe cold and fever. While Ernest remained bedridden at the Hotel du Rhône, Brown, Bethe, and Tichvinsky reported in relays on the negotiations.

To the surprise of the U.S. negotiators, the talks were making rapid and steady progress. "My summary impression," telegraphed Spiers, "is the Russians really want this conference to produce unanimous agreement."[110]

Lawrence was frustrated at his inability to take part in the talks. His condition worsened, but he continued to resist Molly's pleas that they return home. "I could never live with myself if I left before this conference is over!" Ernest told her.[111]

On July 23, physical examination by a doctor summoned to the hotel confirmed acute ulcerative colitis. A few days later, still feverish and in pain, Lawrence bowed to the inevitable and asked the State Department to book an emergency flight home. Molly and John arranged for Ernest to be admitted to Berkeley's Peralta Hospital immediately upon his arrival.[112]

Half a world away, at Bikini atoll, the Livermore firing party was readying the proof-tests of the Polaris warhead. On July 22, *Juniper,* one candidate for the W-47 primary, exploded with a force of 65 kilotons, exceeding even the lab's highest estimate. The following day, *Olive,* the test of the W-47's fusion secondary, gave almost twice the predicted yield: 200 kilotons.[113] These back-to-back successes ensured that the W-47, and Polaris, stayed on their accelerated schedule.[114]

The irony of Livermore's triumph was not lost on those at the lab. Having failed to build a small clean bomb, Livermore had produced an exceptionally dirty one in the W-47. Moreover, the Polaris warhead, while arguably revolutionary, would be attached to a missile that was, given the inaccuracy of submarine-launched missiles of the time, suited to only one purpose: city-killing.[115]

Two days later, on July 26, *Pinon* was canceled outright by the AEC with little fanfare. Lack of interest, security concerns, and a desire to avoid embarrassing publicity contributed to the decision.

Hoping that Livermore's dramatic results with the W-47 might be enough to turn thinking around on the test ban, Teller telegraphed Starbird, asking that he also pass word of the lab's stunning successes to the Joint Committee.[116]

Accompanied by Bradbury and McCone, Teller was at the White House on August 12 to brief Eisenhower in person on Livermore's *Hardtack* results. The W-47, he told the president, represented an improvement "by a factor of two to five" over existing weapons.[117] Equally dramatic progress might be made if testing could be continued for another year or two. The president, silent throughout Teller's presentation, observed quietly at its end that the worldwide consensus that opposed nuclear testing was even more powerful than thermonuclear weapons. While Ike had recently approved another extension of *Hardtack*—adding several more tests, meant to ensure the safety of existing bombs—this time he made it plain that he intended to go no further.[118]

In desperation, Teller and Libby turned to McCone. Unwilling to confront the president on so important a matter after only a few weeks in office, however, the new AEC chairman instead asked his predecessor to intercede—warning Strauss that he might want to don a bulletproof vest first.[119]

On August 20, Strauss met with Eisenhower in the Oval Office. When Ike began to read a draft announcement he had prepared, welcoming the successful conclusion of the Geneva talks, Strauss interrupted to accuse the president of "surrendering." Eisenhower exploded: the only future that Strauss was able to envision led either to war or to a never-ending arms race; a test ban, on the other hand, might eventually be the way to a stable peace. Stunned by Ike's reaction, Strauss said that he personally thought it impossible to compromise with sin. He and the president had come to a "permanent fundamental disagreement," Strauss wrote that night.

The next morning, the White House received a cable from Fisk in Geneva, announcing that both sides had come to full agreement on an inspection system for a test ban before adjourning. The "Geneva system" would be modeled closely on the plan outlined by Bethe and PSAC: a total of 170 inspection posts on the ground and ten ships would monitor compliance with the moratorium.

On the afternoon of August 22, Eisenhower announced that U.S. nuclear testing would cease with the completion of *Hardtack* at the end of October. While Ike indicated that the moratorium would be reviewed on a year-to-year basis, he invited Khrushchev to begin talks immediately on making the test ban permanent.

The news from Geneva failed to stir a reaction in Lawrence, who had been transferred by ambulance to Stanford Hospital, at John's insistence, a week earlier. Molly's concern had grown when Ernest stopped boasting of making a quick recovery at Balboa.

Finally, reluctantly, Lawrence consented to the colostomy operation he had long refused to consider. Even in extremis, he refused to submit to x-rays.

On August 27, surgeons discovered severe atherosclerosis of the main artery leading to the abdomen in the course of the operation. Not knowing the degree to which Lawrence's circulation was compromised by the blockage, the doctors had already severed many of the vessels that carried blood to the lower trunk during the procedure. Before the five-hour ordeal was over, the patient had gone into circulatory shock. Numerous blood transfusions were of no avail. Ernest's final words to Molly were "I'm ready to give up now."

He died shortly before midnight.

Earlier that day at the White House, Fisk and Bacher, just returned from Geneva, had briefed Eisenhower and the NSC on the successful conclusion of the negotiations.[120] McCone, meeting with Ike in the Oval Office beforehand, had persuaded the president to approve a few last underground tests in Nevada, to be carried out in the waning days before the moratorium went into effect.[121]

Thousands of miles and many time zones away, in the South Atlantic, one test was awaited with particular eagerness. In the early morning hours of August 27, a rocket carrying the first *Argus* experiment lifted off the deck of the navy support ship *Norton Sound*. Rising slowly at first, the missile disappeared through broken clouds. Minutes later, its 2-kiloton warhead detonated, some 100 miles up.

While the final results would not be known for several days, it was immediately evident that the "Christofilos effect" had fallen short of expectations. An orbiting American satellite detected no signs of any new and deadly radiation belt.[122] Like the grin of the Cheshire cat, the prospective shield against attacking missiles had simply and silently faded into space. There would be no magical defense against the nuclear weapons already in U.S. and Soviet arsenals, or those about to be added.[123]

Nine weeks later—following a final, furious volley of tests by both sides—the proving grounds in the Soviet Union, the Pacific, and the American desert fell suddenly silent.

EPILOGUE: "AS STREAMES ARE . . ."

As streames are, Power is; those blest flowers that dwell
At the rough streames calme head, thrive and do well
But having left their roots, and themselves given
To the streame's tyrannous rage, alas are driven
Through mills, and rockes, and woods, and at last, almost
Consum'd in going, in the sea are lost.

—John Donne, *Satyre III*

THE MORATORIUM ON nuclear testing lasted barely 1,000 days. On September 1, 1961, the Soviet Union conducted a low-yield test and the following month set off the biggest bomb in history—a mammoth 58-megaton explosion. Khrushchev strongly defended his action, arguing that the West—that is, the French—had been first to violate the test ban, and that the United States had failed to carry through on promises made at the 1958 conference of experts.[1] Unmentioned by the Soviet leader was the fact that he was also under pressure from his own generals to catch up with the United States, which had pulled further ahead in the arms race with *Hardtack*. Among the weapons tested by the Russians that fall would be the warhead for a Soviet submarine-launched ballistic missile.[2]

The Geneva talks on a permanent test-ban treaty had broken down suddenly in January 1959, after the U.S. delegation announced that some of the assumptions on which the moratorium was based were in error. A new "decoupling theory"—proposed by David Griggs and scientists at

Livermore—of how the Russians might cheat by testing underground, and a subsequent reanalysis of seismic data from the Nevada Test Site, had forced a reappraisal of the U.S. negotiating position.[3] The result was a nearly tenfold increase in the number of inspection stations to be located on Soviet territory.[4]

Although Livermore's theory was later discredited, America's diplomatic *votre-face* produced "the most violent reaction imaginable" from the Russians, the U.S. ambassador in Geneva later remembered, and "spread a pall over the negotiations from which they never completely recovered."[5]

Nearing the end of his presidency, Eisenhower was forced to abandon his goal of putting an end to nuclear testing. Killian's successor as science adviser, George Kistiakowsky, would attribute a little-noticed line in the president's farewell address—which warned about "the unwarranted influence of a scientific-technological elite"—to Ike's fury with Teller and Livermore over the fate of the test ban.[6]

Lewis Strauss had hoped to carry on the fight against communism as Eisenhower's commerce secretary.[7] But Strauss's enemies in the Senate, led by Clinton Anderson, conspired to deny him that post. Like the ghost at the banquet, the Oppenheimer case haunted Strauss's confirmation hearing.[8]

For Oppie's defenders, the humiliation of the so-called Tugboat Admiral was poetic justice. "It's a lovely show—never thought I'd live to see my revenge," telegraphed the wife of a Berkeley physicist to Oppenheimer from the capital. "In unchristianly spirit, enjoy every squirm and anguish of victim. Having *wonderful* time—wish you were here!"[9]

Edward Teller resigned as Livermore director in 1960, the better to oppose without hindrance the test-ban treaty that was soon to be pursued by President John Kennedy. Ironically, Teller's opposition was based on the argument that testing needed to continue in order to develop a defense against ballistic missiles.[10] Stalemated by the same intractable technical disputes which had bedeviled Eisenhower, Kennedy finally settled for a less ambitious goal—one previously dismissed by Killian as a mere "propaganda step": a test-ban treaty that forbade nuclear testing everywhere but underground. While it pushed public concern with fallout from the headlines, the 1963 Limited Test-Ban Treaty had little or no restraining effect upon the nuclear arms race, which continued, and even accelerated, despite the agreement.[11]

In April 1963, Kennedy announced that Robert Oppenheimer would be the next recipient of the Enrico Fermi medal. Edward Teller had received the prize the year before. Subsequent attempts by PSAC scientists to restore Oppie's security clearance were quietly turned back by Kennedy's national security adviser, McGeorge Bundy, who feared rekindling emotions over the case.[12]

Barely a week after the assassination in Dallas, Texas, President Lyndon Johnson hung the Fermi medal around Oppenheimer's neck at a brief ceremony in the cabinet room. During the reception, Teller stepped up to shake Oppenheimer's hand. For David Lilienthal, who was also present, the occasion was "a ceremony of expiation for the sins of hatred and ugliness visited upon Oppenheimer."[13]

But the event reawakened strong emotions nonetheless. From his farm at Brandy Rock, in retirement, Strauss wrote *Life* magazine that the honor visited upon Oppenheimer had "dealt a severe blow to the security system which protects our country . . ."[14] "Justice sometimes moves slowly—but it does move, and sometimes it arrives," wrote Birge to Oppenheimer from Berkeley.[15] Rabi, on the other hand, thought there "too much history for simple rejoicing."[16]

For some, it was too late for either reconciliation or expiation. Lilienthal remembered the time, a few years before, when Oppenheimer had stopped by his house in Princeton to talk. Lilienthal thought it remarkable that his friend expressed no bitterness about his fate, except when Lawrence's name was mentioned—whereupon Oppie offered this "strange sidelight":

> Lawrence died of frustration, Robert as much as said, because of the long strain of over-reaching ambition, culminating in his efforts to torpedo the talks in Geneva concerning the ending of the bomb tests. I said I was surprised; that E.O. Lawrence had always seemed to my observation to be a very picture of the extrovert, the satisfied man, the man of bounce and buoyancy. "No," Robert said, "I have know him longer and closer than you; his fears that he was being, or might be, undermined in his position were a terror for him."[17]

Oppenheimer declined to take part in the national debate over nuclear weapons policy and rarely spoke thereafter of his loyalty hearing.[18] Asked to speculate on what Lawrence might have said had he testified in 1954, Oppie answered: "It would have been hard for Ernest but it would have been good. I know that there were several fatalities in a sense with this business. All sorts of directors and myself."[19] Oppenheimer's voice trailed off in the interview, and he left the sentence unfinished.

When David Bohm wrote to him in December 1966, asking whether he felt any regret over the bombing of Hiroshima, Oppie wrote back: "My own feelings about responsibility and guilt have always had to do with the present, and so far in this life that has been more than enough to occupy me."[20] Oppenheimer died a few weeks later, on February 18, 1967, of throat cancer.

But Oppenheimer lived long enough to see the fulfillment of the prediction he had made in his 1953 *Foreign Affairs* article on candor. When the United States built its 20,000th bomb, in 1960, that weapon did not—"in any deep strategic sense"—offset the Soviet Union's 2,000th bomb, built perhaps the year before.

Instead, for the next thirty years the nuclear arms race would dominate the fears and drain the resources of both superpowers, a competition mirrored, in microcosm, by the unceasing rivalry of Livermore and Los Alamos. By the time that Norris Bradbury retired, in 1970, the laboratory that he had originally agreed to run for six months had designed more than sixty different nuclear weapons, ranging from a subkiloton "backpack" bomb to the 15-megaton *Bravo*.[21]

Over the next twenty years, Livermore would make similarly impressive additions to the U.S. arsenal, among them the so-called enhanced-radiation weapon, or neutron bomb. An ironic and unintended spawn of the lab's clean weapons program, the neutron bomb was designed to kill people while leaving buildings intact. Livermore director Harold Brown puckishly dubbed it "the capitalist bomb."[22]

The technical advances that began with Livermore's W-47 also made it possible, starting in the early 1970s, to place several nuclear warheads on a single missile. Further improvements, subsequently matched in lockstep by the Soviet Union, led to rapidly growing arsenals on both sides and, in response, to a nuclear freeze movement by the early 1980s.

In March 1983, President Ronald Reagan's announcement of a Strategic Defense Initiative—a space-based shield promising to make nuclear weapons "impotent and obsolete"—was inspired in part by Teller's claims for a so-called third generation of bombs being developed at Livermore.[23] The centerpiece of early "Star Wars" planning was a nuclear-pumped x-ray laser heavily promoted by Teller and his allies in Washington. When underground tests in Nevada raised doubts about the performance of the x-ray laser, Teller and a young protégé at the lab proposed *Brilliant Pebbles,* a nonnuclear alternative that became the new focus of SDI.[24]

Four and a half decades of unrelenting Cold War would test the faith of even true believers, leaving some doubting, some confirmed in their beliefs, and some simply transformed.

Although Haakon Chevalier was unwilling to jump off what he called "the socialist 'train'" during the Hungarian uprising in 1956, his faith in communism had been severely shaken. He continued to ask himself, Chevalier wrote in an unpublished memoir, "whether what was wrong was deep rooted and ineradicable or a condition that could and would disappear. . . . The answer that the future gave, in August, 1968, was Czechoslovakia."[25]

Chevalier also informed friends that he was writing "a final book, a short one, on Oppenheimer: I've recently discovered, if I'm not completely off my rocker, something which completely changes the estimate of

Oppenheimer and his integrity."[26] Chevalier's book remained unfinished at the time of his death, on July 4, 1985.[27]

George Eltenton and Frank Oppenheimer had both attended Chevalier's eightieth-birthday celebration in Berkeley a few years earlier.[28] Eltenton's widow, Dorothea, waited until she was ninety-four and living in England to publish *Laughter in Leningrad,* a nostalgic account of the couple's life in Russia during the 1930s.

Steve Nelson lived long enough to witness the collapse of the Soviet Union and the political system to which he had devoted much of his life.[29] Nelson quit the party in 1957, after Khrushchev confirmed Stalin's crimes, but he remained true to the cause at a more local and personal level. Shortly before his death, at ninety, Nelson was active in lobbying on behalf of low-income housing for the community of Truro, Massachusetts, where he lived.

Lloyd Lehmann, the Young Communist League organizer whose 1942 conversation with Nelson had given the Federal Bureau of Investigation its first evidence of spies in the Manhattan Project, was hounded by FBI agents, HUAC investigators, and the Tenney Committee throughout the 1950s. Unable to find a job, Lehmann taught himself carpentry and eventually got a contractor's license. By the late 1990s, he and his family owned several apartment buildings in Oakland, California.[30]

Joseph Weinberg, likewise unable to find work in his chosen field, went on to specialize in a different branch of physics—optics—heading a research laboratory for the Spero House of Vision in Rochester, New York. Among the inventions in which Weinberg reportedly would have a part was the lineless bifocal lense. While neighbors in upstate New York during the 1990s, Joe Weinberg and Rossi Lomanitz attended concerts by the local symphony orchestra, in which Rossi's wife, Josephine, played recorder.[31]

After failing as a rancher and returning to the teaching of physics, Frank Oppenheimer founded the Exploratorium, a pioneering science museum in San Francisco, serving as its director until his death in 1985. Neither Frank nor his brother ever explained the nature or extent of his involvement in the Chevalier incident. Groves, too, took whatever he might have known of that secret to the grave in 1970.

While the breakup of the USSR late in 1991 would fulfill the prophecy of John Foster Dulles—who had forecast, forty years earlier, that the United States would exhaust its adversary if it were simply "able to run the full mile"—only at the end of the nuclear arms race could its material cost be calculated: $5.5 trillion.[32] Whether the competition between the United States and the Soviet Union might have been cheaper, safer, and ended sooner, before some 125,000 nuclear weapons were built by both sides, is a question that will remain forever unanswerable.[33]

After waging a campaign throughout the 1970s and 1980s to remove her husband's name from the Livermore laboratory—on the grounds that Ernest would not want to be remembered for a "bomb factory"—Molly Lawrence abandoned her efforts when the end of the Cold War prompted Livermore to announce that it was shifting its focus away from weapons work.[34]

Although Edward Teller retired from Livermore in 1975, he remained an éminence grise there long afterward. Even in his nineties, Teller was still active, proposing a way to intercept Earth-destroying asteroids and reportedly seeking a solution to the problem of global warming.

Having known both notoriety and influence, what Teller sought was vindication. In the mid-1960s, he had hoped to prove the feasibility of his original H-bomb concept by simulating the explosion of a hypothetical Super, using one of Livermore's early supercomputers.[35] When the Persian Gulf War erupted in 1991, Teller warned Washington that Saddam Hussein might be building a uranium-hydride bomb.[36] Fifty years after the imaginative breakthrough that led to radiation implosion, Teller was again denying Ulam a role in the invention.[37]

But on one subject—Oppenheimer—vindication always eluded Teller.[38] When Oppenheimer died, Oppie's long-time friend, Hans Bethe, assumed the mantle of the scientist of conscience in this country.[39] Like Jefferson and Adams, Teller and Bethe would live on into the new century which they and their colleagues had done so much to shape. They brought with them an old and unresolved conflict.[40]

In 1983, when Teller rose at a White House reception to applaud Reagan's SDI announcement, Bethe was next to stand and denounce Star Wars as folly. In response, Edward subsequently published an "open letter," appealing to scientists to join the missile defense crusade.[41] Although he addressed the letter to Bethe, Teller's message might well have been directed to Oppenheimer's ghost:

> The one regret I have about the atomic bomb is that we missed the opportunity to attempt to end the war by a demonstration of the bomb to the Japanese. . . . Oppenheimer persuaded me on that occasion that it was not the business of a physicist to give advice on such matters of policy. I was too easily persuaded. Later I learned that Oppenheimer gave advice on that very question, recommending that the atomic bomb should indeed be dropped. Not much later, Oppenheimer made his famous statement that "physicists have known sin."

At the end of Edward's letter was a decades-late rejoinder. "I would say," Teller wrote, "that physicists have known power."

NOTES

The notes published here are an abbreviated version of a much longer and more comprehensive set of endnotes, which were edited for reasons of space. Those original notes, containing additional information and citations, may be accessed at the Web site www.brotherhoodofthebomb.com and downloaded without charge. A copy of the original notes—along with copies of most of the documents cited in the notes, as well as transcripts of personal interviews recorded by the author—will also be deposited with the National Security Archive at George Washington University.

Abbreviations Used in the Notes

AEC/NARA	Records of the U.S. Atomic Energy Commission, RG 326, National Archives, College Park, Md.
AECP	Committee on Atomic Energy Commission Projects, University of California archives
Army/NARA	Records of the U.S. Army Chief of Staff, RG 319, National Archives, College Park, Md.
CFBM	Committee on Finance and Budget Management, University of California archives
CIC/DOE	Coordination and Information Center, U.S. Department of Energy, Las Vegas, Nev.
CINRAD	"Communist Infiltration of the Radiation Laboratory, University of California," file no. 100–190625, FBI Reading Room
COMRAP	"Comintern Apparatus," file no. 100–203581, FBI Reading Room
EOL	Ernest Orlando Lawrence papers, Bancroft Library, University of California, Berkeley.
FAECT	Federation of Architects, Engineers, Chemists, and Technicians, file no. 61–7231, FBI Reading Room

FRUS	U.S. Department of State, *Foreign Relations of the United States*
GAC	General Advisory Committee, U.S. Atomic Energy Commission
Groves/NARA	Papers of General Leslie Groves, RG 200, National Archives, College Park, Md.
HUAC	House Un-American Activities Committee
ITMOJRO	U.S. Atomic Energy Commission, *In the Matter of J. Robert Oppenheimer*
JCAE	Joint Congressional Committee on Atomic Energy, RG 128, National Archives, Washington, D.C.
JRO	J. Robert Oppenheimer papers, Library of Congress, Washington, D.C.
JRO/AEC	Records of the Personnel Security Board, AEC Division of Security, RG 326, National Archives, College Park, Md.
JRO/FBI	J. Robert Oppenheimer, file no. 100–17828, FBI Reading Room
LANL	Los Alamos National Laboratory archives, Los Alamos, N. Mex.
LBL	Lawrence Berkeley National Laboratory archives, Berkeley, Calif.
LLNL	Lawrence Livermore National Laboratory archives, Livermore, Calif.
LLS/HHPL	Lewis Strauss papers, Herbert Hoover Presidential Library, West Branch, Iowa
LLS/NARA	Lewis Strauss AEC papers, National Archives, College Park, Md.
MED/NARA	Records of the Manhattan Engineer District, RG 77, National Archives, College Park, Md.
NARA	National Archives, Washington, D.C., and College Park, Md.
OSD/NARA	Records of the Office of the Secretary of Defense, RG 330, National Archives, College Park, Md.
OSRD/NARA	Records of the Office of Scientific Research and Development, RG 227, National Archives, College Park, Md.
PSAC	Records of the President's Science Advisory Committee, RG 359, National Archives, College Park, Md.
SBFRC	Federal Records Center, National Archives, San Bruno, Calif.
TEM	Thomas E. Murray papers, Rockville, Md.
TWPC	U.S. Atomic Energy Commission, Thermonuclear Weapons Program Chronology
UC	Records of the University of California, Oakland, Calif.
USAF/NARA	Records of Headquarters, U.S. Air Force, RG 341, National Archives, College Park, Md.
USDS/NARA	Records of the U.S. Department of State, RG 59, National Archives, College Park, Md.
UCSF	Library Archive, University of California, San Francisco

1: The Cyclotron Republic

1. Lawrence to Sproul, Lawrence folder, box 64, Vannevar Bush papers, Library of Congress, Washington, D.C.

2. A cyclotron is defined as a machine that accelerates charged particles by the influence of a steady magnetic field and a rapidly alternating electrical field. Henry A. Boorse et al., *The Atomic Scientists: A Biographical History* (Wiley, 1989), 358–59.

3. Kitchen-chair cyclotron: Luis Alvarez, "Ernest Orlando Lawrence, 1901–1958," *Biographical Memoirs* (National Academy of Sciences, 1970), 263; J. L. Heilbron and Robert Seidel, *Lawrence and His Laboratory: A History of the Lawrence Berkeley Laboratory* (University of California Press, 1989), vol. 1, 88.

4. Herbert Childs, *An American Genius: The Life of Ernest Orlando Lawrence, Father of the Cyclotron* (Dutton, 1968), 171; Heilbron and Seidel (1989), 84.

5. Childs (1968), 168; J. L. Heilbron, Robert Seidel, and Bruce R. Wheaton, "Lawrence and His Laboratory: Nuclear Science at Berkeley" (Lawrence Berkeley Laboratory, 1981), 12; Heilbron and Seidel (1989), 100.

6. Transcript of interview with Jack Neylan, box 2, Herbert Childs papers, Bancroft Library, University of California, Berkeley, Calif.

7. Transcript of interview with Don Cooksey, box 1, Childs papers; Childs (1968), 89–90.

8. Heilbron and Seidel (1989), 10, 99; Childs (1968), 161.

9. Childs (1968), 169–70.

10. Nuell Pharr Davis, *Lawrence and Oppenheimer* (Simon and Schuster, 1968), 198; author interview with Wolfgang Panofsky, Stanford, Calif., Aug. 3, 1993.

11. Luis W. Alvarez, *Alvarez: Adventures of a Physicist* (Basic Books, 1987), 47–48; Childs (1968), 158; author interview with Eldred Nelson, Brentwood, Calif., Apr. 14, 1999.

12. "Autobiography," series 7, box 1, Henry Smyth papers, American Philosophical Society, Philadelphia, Penn.

13. Author interview with Molly Lawrence, Balboa, Calif., Aug. 11, 1992.

14. Childs (1968), 154–55.

15. Ibid., 253.

16. Early Rad Lab: Alvarez (1987), 40–44; author interview with Kenneth Street, Alamo, Calif., Aug. 6, 1993; transcript of interview with Arthur Hudgins, Lawrence Livermore National Laboratory archives, Livermore, Calif. (LLNL).

17. Kenneth Street interview (1993).

18. Alvarez (1987), 40.

19. Childs (1968), 251.

20. Notes on "How Well We Meant," Isidor Rabi remarks at the fiftieth anniversary of Los Alamos, Mar. 1983.

21. Boorse et al. (1989), 333–40.

22. Heilbron, Seidel, and Wheaton (1981), 18.

23. Richard Rhodes, *Dark Sun: The Making of the Hydrogen Bomb* (Simon and Schuster, 1995), 27.

24. "Atom-Powered World Absurd, Scientists Told," *New York Herald Tribune,* Sept. 12, 1933.

25. Solvay Congress: Heilbron, Seidel, and Wheaton (1981), 18–23; Davis (1968), 58–59.

26. Panofsky interview (1993); Alvarez (1970), 266.

27. Emilio Segrè, *A Mind Always in Motion* (University of California Press, 1993), 134.

28. Author interview with Robert Serber, New York, N.Y., Apr. 4, 1992.

29. Haakon Chevalier, *Oppenheimer: The Story of a Friendship* (Braziller, 1965), 11.

30. Edith Jenkins, *Against a Field Sinister: Memoirs and Stories* (City Lights Books, 1991), 23.

31. Robert Oppenheimer: Richard Rhodes, *The Making of the Atomic Bomb* (Simon and Schuster, 1986), 119–27; Davis (1968), 20–24; Peter Michelmore, *The Swift Years: The Robert Oppenheimer Story* (Dodd, Mead, 1969), 7–9.

32. Transcript of interview with Robert Oppenheimer, box 2, Childs papers.

33. The art was later split between Robert and his brother, Frank, upon their father's death. My thanks to Robert Oppenheimer's son, Peter, for allowing me access to his father's personal papers in his possession.

34. Childs (1968), 143; transcripts of interviews with Paul Horgan, Francis Fergusson, and Jeffries Wyman, Oppenheimer Oral History Collection, MIT archives, Cambridge, Mass.

35. Childs (1968), 510–11.

36. Transcript of interview with John Edsall, Oppenheimer Oral History Collection, MIT.

37. Childs (1968), 144–45.

38. Experimentalists, unlike theorists, apparently did not name their cars.

39. Michelmore (1969), 30; Childs (1968), 127, 144. Oppie's cars: Alice Kimball Smith and Charles Weiner, eds., *Robert Oppenheimer: Letters and Recollections* (Harvard University Press, 1980), 119, 135, 165 fn.; Frank Oppenheimer to Ed McMillan,

n.d., "N.P. Davis" file, series 7, Edwin McMillan papers, RG 434, Federal Records Center, San Bruno, Calif. (SBFRC).

40. S. S. Schweber, *In the Shadow of the Bomb: Oppenheimer, Bethe, and the Moral Responsibility of the Scientist* (Princeton University Press, galley proofs, 2000), 63.

41. S. S. Schweber, "J. Robert Oppenheimer: Proteus Unbound," 7. The author thanks Sam Schweber for a copy of his unpublished manuscript.

42. Smith and Weiner (1980), 144.

43. Lawrence to Oppenheimer, n.d. (fall 1936), folder 9, carton 14, Ernest Orlando Lawrence papers, Bancroft Library, University of California, Berkeley (EOL).

44. Robert to Frank Oppenheimer, n.d., unmarked folder, box 1, Frank Oppenheimer papers, Bancroft Library.

45. Chevalier (1965), 39.

46. Letter to ?, n.d., carton 1, Frank Oppenheimer papers; Smith and Weiner (1980), 165 fn.

47. Perro Caliente: Peter Goodchild, *J. Robert Oppenheimer: Shatterer of Worlds* (BBC, 1980), 27; U.S. Atomic Energy Commission, *In the Matter of J. Robert Oppenheimer* (MIT Press, 1971) (*ITMOJRO*), 101.

48. Interviews: Molly Lawrence (1992) and Elsie McMillan, Bellingham, Wash., Sept. 24, 1992.

49. Smith and Weiner (1980), 159.

50. Michelmore (1969) 53.

51. Smith and Weiner (1980), 171.

52. Childs (1968), 172–73.

53. Lawrence to C. D. Shane, Jan. 28, 1936, folder 9, carton 14, EOL.

54. Schweber (2000), 199.

55. Oppie evidently absorbed Adler's lessons well; he was valedictorian of his class.

56. Schweber (2000), 52.

57. Cited in Oppenheimer to F. Osborn, Feb. 14, 1949, Osborn folder, box 54, Robert Oppenheimer papers, Library of Congress (JRO).

58. Melba Phillips incident: Transcript of Alvarez interview, box 1, Childs papers; Robert Serber, *Peace and War: Reminiscences of a Life on the Frontiers of Science* (University of California Press, 1998), 27.

59. Transcript of interview with Edwin McMillan, 128, Bancroft Library.

60. Author interview with Robert Wilson, July 16, 1996, Ithaca, N.Y.

61. Cottrell: Heilbron and Seidel (1989), 107–8; Davis (1968), 40.

62. Heilbron and Seidel (1989), 127.

63. Ibid., 116–24; transcript of interview with Robert Stone, Oral History Collection, Library Archive, University of California, San Francisco (UCSF).

64. Lawrence to Leuschner, April 12, 1935, folder 13, carton 20, EOL.

65. Joliot-Curies and Fermi: Boorse et al. (1989), 362–65, 340–50.

66. Childs (1968), 190, 215; Alvarez (1970), 266.

67. Childs (1968), 221.

68. Martin Kamen, *Radiant Science, Dark Politics: A Memoir of the Nuclear Age* (University of California Press, 1986), 117.

69. Hamilton and human radiation experiments: "The University of California Case Study," *Report of the Advisory Committee on Human Radiation Experiments*, supplemental vol. 2, *Sources and Documentation* (U.S. Government Printing Office, 1995), 600–30.

70. Childs (1968), 146.

71. Transcript of interview with Robert Stone, Library Archive, UCSF.

72. Childs (1968), 263.

73. Among the brothers' early guinea pigs were Oppie and Joe Hamilton. Alvarez (1987), 63.

74. Molly Lawrence interview (1992).

75. Childs (1968), 249.

76. Ibid., 250.

77. The boat had been built by Luis Alvarez's uncle. Alvarez (1987), 62; Molly Lawrence interview (1992).

78. Gunda Lawrence to Elmer Seubert, n.d. (c. May 1939), folder 39, carton 10, EOL.

79. Alvarez (1970), 270–71; author interview with Patricia Durbin, Berkeley, Calif., Aug. 11, 1994.

80. Childs (1968), 278, 283; Davis (1968), 76–77; transcript of interview with John Lawrence, Bancroft Library.

81. Alvarez (1987), 44.

82. Ibid., transcript of telephone conversation between EOL and C. D. Shane, Nov. 12, 1945, folder 16, carton 1, EOL.

83. Segrè (1993), 112, 118, 215.

84. Ibid., 128–29.

85. Ibid., 135, 138.

86. Ibid., 136, 158; Raymond Birge, "History of the Physics Department, University of California, Berkeley" (unpublished manuscript, in Bancroft Library, n.d.), vol. 5, chap. 18, 4–10.

87. Author interview with Martin Kamen, Santa Barbara, Calif., March 12, 1997.

88. Kamen (1986), 132.

89. Heilbron, Seidel, and Wheaton (1981), 20.

90. Davis (1968), 69; author interview with Edward Lofgren, Berkeley, Calif., Jan. 22, 1998.

91. Childs (1968), 273, 280–81.

92. Alvarez (1987), 74–75.

93. Rhodes (1986), 348.

94. Lawrence to Fermi, Feb. 7, 1939, folder 15, carton 7, EOL.

95. Childs (1968), 297.

96. Heilbron and Seidel (1989), 445–46.

97. Quoted in ibid., 444.

98. Smith and Weiner (1980), 208–9.

2: A Practical Philosopher's Stone

1. Lawrence to parents, Aug. 29, 1939, folder 39, carton 10, EOL.

2. Szilard, Wigner, and Teller already knew each other, having grown up in Budapest, where Edward and Leo attended the Minta (Model) gymnasium. Stanley Blumberg and Gwinn Owens, *Energy and Conflict: The Life and Times of Edward Teller* (Putnam, 1976), 14–15; Rhodes (1986), 14–15.

3. Edward Teller, *Energy from Heaven and Earth* (Freeman, 1979), 145.

4. "Almost eighty years later, I still feel the discouragement of that moment," Teller wrote in his memoirs. Teller: Edward Teller with Judith Shoolery, *Memoirs: A Twentieth-Century Journey in Science and Politics* (Perseus Press, 2001), 32, 65; Edward Teller and Allen Brown, *The Legacy of Hiroshima* (Doubleday, 1962), 7–10; Blumberg and Owens (1976), 42–88; author interviews: Edward Teller, Los Alamos, N. Mex., July 7, 1993, and Milton Plesset, Pasadena, Calif., Mar. 15, 1988.

5. Szilard and Teller: Teller (1979), 141–43; Edward Teller, *Better a Shield Than a Sword: Perspectives on Defense and Technology* (Free Press, 1987), 46–47; William Lanouette, *Genius in the Shadows: A Biography of Leo Szilard, the Man Behind the Bomb* (Scribners, 1992), 182–87.

6. Teller (1987), 48–49.

7. Spencer Weart and Gertrude W. Szilard, eds., *Leo Szilard: His Version of the Facts* (MIT Press, 1978), vol. 2, 84; author interview with I. I. Rabi, New York, N.Y., Oct. 26, 1984.

8. Transcript of interview with Edwin McMillan, Bancroft Library; transcript of interview with Robert Oppenheimer, box 2, Childs papers.

9. Notes by George Harrison, n.d., folder 14, carton 3, EOL; Lawrence to Bush, Oct. 12, 1939, Lawrence folder, box 64, Vannevar Bush papers, Library of Congress.

10. Vannevar Bush: G. Pascal Zachary, *Endless Frontier: Vannevar Bush, Engineer of the American Century* (Free Press, 1997), 23–38; transcript of interview with Vannevar Bush, reel 1, 178, Vannevar Bush papers, MIT.

11. Confidential memo, Sproul to L. A. Nichols, "Radiation Laboratory, EOL" folder, box 39, Robert Sproul papers, Bancroft Library.

12. Lawrence to Bush, Nov. 9, 1939, Lawrence folder, box 64, Bush papers, Library of Congress.

13. Childs (1968), 295–96.

14. Heilbron and Seidel (1989), 488.

15. Childs (1968), 298.

16. Heilbron and Seidel (1989), 478.

17. Childs (1968), 299.

18. Heilbron and Seidel (1989), 480.

19. R. W. Wood to Lawrence, Nov. 13, 1939, folder 37, carton 24, EOL.

20. Transcript of Vannevar Bush interview, reel 6, 366, Bush papers, MIT.

21. Childs (1968), 300–301.

22. Loomis: Alvarez (1987), 78–81; Robert Buderi, *The Invention That Changed the World* (Simon and Schuster, 1996), 38–39; "Alfred Lee Loomis: Amateur of the Sciences," *Fortune,* Mar. 1946, 132–69.

23. The setting was perfect for a murder mystery and in fact became one later that year, in a novel written by James Conant's brother-in-law, who had worked at Loomis's lab. Willard Rich, *Brain Waves and Death* (Scribner, 1940); James Hershberg, *James B. Conant: Harvard to Hiroshima and the Making of the Nuclear Age* (Knopf, 1993), 137–38.

24. Author interview with Eleanor Davisson, Pacific Grove, Calif., Aug. 22, 1992.

25. Childs (1968), 300–301.

26. Serber (1998), 46.

27. Smith and Weiner (1980), 211; San Francisco field report, Sept. 22, 1941, vol. 1, Steve Nelson file, no. 100–16847, FBI Reading Room (FBI).

28. Oppenheimer did not vote in a presidential election until 1936. "Tell me, what has politics to do with truth, goodness and beauty?" he asked one of his students in those days. Smith and Weiner (1980), 195.

29. R. Oppenheimer to F. Oppenheimer, supplemental folder, box 294, JRO.

30. Jenkins, 24; author interview with Phillip Morrison, Cambridge, Mass., Nov. 17, 2000. Informed of Tatlock's suicide in 1994 by an army security agent, Oppenheimer wept. "He then went on at considerable length about the depth of his emotion for Jean, saying there was really no one to whom he could speak." My thanks to Marilyn de Silva for a copy of the outline of her husband's unfinished book about Oppenheimer.

31. Tatlock: Jenkins (1991), 21–23; *ITMOJRO,* 4, 8, 153; Stephen Schwartz, *From West to East: California and the Making of the American Mind* (Free Press, 1998), 378–80; Goodchild (1980), 30–32; Phillip Stern, *The Oppenheimer Case: Security on Trial* (Harper and Row, 1969), 15–16; author interview with Robert Serber (1992).

32. A 1944 FBI report listed Addis as "active in 27 Communist Front organizations in the San Francisco Bay Area during the last ten years." Addis: San Francisco field report, May 17, 1944, sec. 4, FAECT file, no. 61–723, FBI; Herbert Romerstein and Eric Breindel, *The Venona Secrets: Exposing Soviet Espionage and America's Traitors* (Regnery, 2000), 266.

33. "E. told me of O[ppenheimer] having last summer gone East. . . . Is better read than most party members. A phenomenal fellow, quite obviously," Chevalier wrote in his diary in 1937. "Our friendship was initiated by a common wish to participate in an activity that seemed to us to hold out the greatest hope for the future, which is to say the work of the communist party," Chevalier wrote in notes for his unpublished memoir. Entries,

July 20, 1937, and Aug. 31, 1980, Chevalier diary, Haakon Chevalier papers, Valreas, France. The author thanks Karen Chevalier for granting him access to her father's diary and private papers.

34. New York field report, Dec. 29, 1943, sec. 21, Haakon Chevalier file, no. 100–18564, FBI.

35. In a 1964 letter to Oppenheimer, Chevalier wrote that he and Oppie had been members "in the same unit of the CP from 1938 to 1942." Chevalier to Oppenheimer, July 23, 1964, Chevalier folder, box 200, JRO.

36. Haakon Chevalier, *The Man Who Would Be God* (Putnam, 1959), 80. Chevalier intended to call his autobiographical novel *Flight Is Ended.* Dec. 11, 1933, diary entry, Chevalier papers.

37. In Mar. 1940, the FBI listed the house as "one of those to be used as a 'hide-out' by Communist Party members in case of an emergency." Chevalier (1965), 31; undated field report, sec. 1:2a, Chevalier file, FBI.

38. Jenkins (1991), 25; Dec. 24, 1933, and July 13, 1934, entries, Chevalier diary, Chevalier papers.

39. Schwartz (1998), 290.

40. "Subject: Jean Tatlock," June 29, 1943, records of the Personnel Security Board, U.S. AEC Division of Security, box 1, RG 326 (JRO/AEC), National Archives, Washington, D.C.

41. Teachers union: Chevalier (1965), 25; *ITMOJRO,* 8, 156; Goodchild (1980), 32.

42. Through his association with Tatlock and Chevalier, Oppenheimer also met key figures of California's radical political scene, including labor leader Harry Bridges and journalist Lincoln Steffens. Jenkins (1991), 23; Serber (1998), 31; author interview with Richard Criley, Carmel, Calif., Sept. 21, 1998.

43. Serber (1998), 31.

44. Lofgren interview (1998).

45. In a 1973 letter, Chevalier identified those members of "the secret C.P. unit" who had since died. Chevalier to Beeferman, Apr. 25, 1973, "Correspondence, 1972" folder, Chevalier papers.

46. In 1964, Chevalier wrote to member Lou Goldblatt, asking him to confirm that Oppie also belonged to the group: "I had originally planned to reveal the fact that O. had been, from 1937 to 1943, a CP member, which I knew directly. On thinking it over, I decided that I shouldn't, even though the fact is of considerable historical importance." Goldblatt, hinting at his own concern with self-incrimination, sent a noncommittal reply. Possibly because he feared the legal consequences of doing otherwise, Chevalier described it as "a discussion group" in his memoirs. In a letter to Chevalier, Oppenheimer denied ever being a member of the Communist Party. Oppenheimer subsequently sent a copy of his letter and Chevalier's letter to his lawyer. Chevalier to Beeferman, Apr. 25, 1973, "Correspondence, 1972" folder, and Chevalier to Goldblatt, Aug. 25, 1964, "Correspondence, 1964" folder, Chevalier papers; Chevalier to Oppenheimer, July 23, 1964, and reply of Aug. 7, 1964, Chevalier folder, box 200, JRO; Chevalier (1965), 19, 207; draft of "The Bomb," unpublished manuscript, 39, Chevalier papers.

47. The epigram was from the poet's "September 1, 1939": "Hunger allows no choice / To the citizen or the police; / We must love one another or die." W. H. Auden, *Another Time* (Random House, 1940). The first report took the Soviet Union's side in the war against Finland and deplored attacks upon the Communist Party in this country. Copies of both reports were sent to President Sproul's office by concerned administrators on other campuses. My thanks to Bancroft archivist Bill Roberts for locating the two reports in the university archives. William Roberts, Feb. 21, 2000, personal communication.

48. There were evidently earlier broadsides that Oppenheimer had a hand in. Phillip Morrison, Oppie's then-graduate student, remembered arranging the printing of a glossy pamphlet that Oppenheimer wrote and which argued against intervention in the so-called winter war between the Soviet Union and Finland. The publication was prepared in response to a speech by Czech foreign minister Jan Masaryk in Berkeley's Greek Theater on Charter Day, Mar. 23, 1939. As with the subsequent reports, Oppenheimer paid for

the cost of printing and distributing the 1939 broadside. Morrison interview (2000) and personal communication, Dec. 8, 2000.

49. Thomas Powers, *Heisenberg's War: The Secret History of the German Bomb* (Knopf, 1993), 173; author interview with Hans Bethe, Ithaca, N.Y., 1996; Schweber (2000), 108; *ITMOJRO,* 441.

50. "I think we'll go to war—that the Roosevelt faction will win over the Lindbergh. . . . I see no good for a long time: & the only cheerful thing in these parts is the strength & toughness & political growth of organized labor." Smith and Weiner (1980), 217.

51. Transcript of interview with Robert Oppenheimer, box 2, Childs papers.

52. Transcript of interviews with Luis Alvarez and Philip Abelson, box 1, Childs papers.

53. Rhodes (1986), 314–17.

54. Teller (2001), 149; Blumberg and Owens (1976), 100–101; Rhodes (1986), 335–37.

55. Bethe interview (1996).

56. Childs (1968), 299; "Diary Notes of Donald Cooksey," folder 23, carton 4, EOL.

57. "Nobel Prize Awarded to Lawrence for Invention of Cyclotron," *Daily Californian,* Mar. 1, 1940, Bancroft Library.

58. Stassen to Lawrence, Mar. 29, 1940, folder 46, carton 16, EOL.

59. Transcript of telephone conversation, folder 30, carton 15, EOL.

60. Jewett to Compton, June 24, 1940, folder 5, box 139, Karl Compton papers, MIT.

61. "Diary Notes of Donald Cooksey," folder 23, carton 4, EOL; Childs (1968), 302; Alvarez, "Alfred Lee Loomis, "*Biographical Memoirs* (National Academy of Sciences, 1980), vol. 51, 327.

62. Rhodes (1986), 361; Childs (1968), 309; O. Lundberg to F. Stevens, Sept. 23, 1940, folder 18, carton 46, EOL; Lawrence to Compton, July 21, 1940, folder 10, carton 4, EOL.

63. Gray Brechin, *Imperial San Francisco: Urban Power, Earthly Ruin* (University of California Press, 1999), 315–17.

64. Childs (1968), 302–3.

65. Lawrence to K. Compton, May 21, 1940, folder 3, box 133, Compton papers; "Vast Power Source in Atomic Energy Opened by Science," *New York Times,* May 5, 1940.

66. Childs (1968), 301; Heilbron and Seidel (1989), 444–45.

67. Rhodes (1986), 298.

68. Childs (1968), 328; Alvarez and Oppenheimer to Furman, June 5, 1944, Los Alamos National Laboratory archives, Los Alamos, N. Mex. (LANL).

69. Richard Hewlett and Oscar Anderson, Jr., *The New World: A History of the United States Atomic Energy Commission,* vol. 1, 1939–46 (University of California Press, 1990), 33–34; Rhodes (1986), 348–50.

70. "I am puzzled as to what, if anything, ought to be done in this country in connection with [fission]," Bush wrote in May 1940. Zachary (1997), 190.

71. Besides being busy with the great cyclotron, Ernest was helping John build his own empire at Berkeley. "Diary Notes of Donald Cooksey," folder 23, carton 4, EOL.

72. Lawrence to Urey, folder 40, carton 17, EOL.

73. Bush to Lawrence, Aug. 30, 1940, Lawrence folder, box 64, Bush papers, Library of Congress.

74. Childs (1968), 306.

75. Ibid.

76. Draft telegram in pencil, Bush to Lawrence, n.d., Lawrence folder, box 64, Bush papers, Library of Congress.

77. Buderi (1996), 39.

78. Alvarez (1987), 87, 91; transcript of McMillan interview, Bancroft Library.

79. W. B. Reynolds, "Notes on the 184-inch Cyclotron," June 16, 1945, folder 4, carton 29, EOL.

80. Kamen to McMillan, Feb. 1941, folder 10, carton 10, EOL.

81. Kamen (1986), 141, 145.

82. Transcript of interview with Vern Denton, n.d., LLNL.

83. Kamen to McMillan, folder 10, carton 10, EOL.

84. Hewlett and Anderson (1990), 29–32.

85. Childs (1968), 311.

86. Stanley Goldberg, "Inventing a Climate of Opinion: Vannevar Bush and the Decision to Build the Bomb" *ISIS,* 1992, 429–52. Lawrence, "Historical Notes on My Early Activities in Connection with the Tuballoy Project," Mar. 26, 1945, folder 4, carton 29, EOL.

87. Arthur Compton, *Atomic Quest* (Oxford, 1956), 48.

88. Henry DeWolf Smyth, *Atomic Energy for Military Purposes: The Official Report on the Development of the Atomic Bomb Under the Auspices of the United States Government, 1940–1945* (Stanford University Press, 1989), 64–65.

89. Hewlett and Anderson (1990), 41.

90. Transcript of interview with Luis Alvarez, box 1, Childs papers.

91. Lawrence to Bush, July 29, 1941, Lawrence folder, box 64, Bush papers, Library of Congress.

92. Oliphant: Childs (1968), 206, 210; Rhodes (1986), 360.

93. The British were also upset that the Americans continued to publish the results of their work on fission. After the article by McMillan and Abelson appeared in *Physical Review,* the British sent an envoy from their San Francisco consulate to reprimand Lawrence.

94. M.A.U.D. report: Powers (1993), 76–77; Robert Williams and Philip Cantelon, eds., *The American Atom: A Documentary History of Nuclear Policies from the Discovery of Fission to the Present, 1939–1984* (University of Pennsylvania Press, 1984), 19–23.

95. Rhodes (1986), 372.

96. The Australian naturally assumed that Oppenheimer's presence during his discussions with Lawrence meant that Oppie, too, had been initiated into the secrets of the uranium project. Powers (1993), 174; "Diary Notes of Donald Cooksey," folder 23, carton 4, EOL; Compton (1956), 6.

97. Rhodes (1986), 373.

98. Compton (1956), 6.

99. The lecture concluded with the demonstration of a radiosodium tracer. Two Rad Lab alumni, current members of the Chicago faculty, drank the isotope cocktail.

100. Compton (1956), 7.

101. Smyth (1989), 52.

102. Heilbron and Seidel (1989), 523.

103. Ibid., 515.

104. Childs (1968), 317.

105. Hershberg (1993), 149.

106. Compton (1956), 8; Heilbron and Seidel (1989), 523.

107. Wallace was also a friend of Compton's. Hewlett and Anderson (1990), 45.

108. Compton (1956), 55.

109. Childs (1968), 319; Hershberg (1993), 150; Powers (1993), 174; Oliphant to Oppenheimer, Sept. 25, 1941, box 53, JRO.

110. Transcript of Vannevar Bush interview, reel 1, Bush papers, MIT. Members of the Top Policy Group were Henry Wallace, Henry Stimson (secretary of war), and George Marshall (army chief of staff), as well as Bush and Conant.

111. Possibly with Lawrence in mind, Bush reminded committee members that "they [were] asked to report upon the techniques, and that considerations of general policy ha[d] not been turned over to them as a subject." Rhodes (1986), 377–78; Hewlett and Anderson (1990), 45–46.

112. Lawrence later thought his own role, not Compton's, crucial to FDR's decision to proceed with the bomb. "Notes," Nov. 27, 1945, folder 4, carton 29, EOL.

113. Rhodes (1986), 387.

114. Compton (1956), 56; Hershberg (1993), 139, 149.

115. Lawrence to Compton, Oct. 14, 1941, and Lawrence to Compton, Oct. 17, 1941, folder 19, carton 27, EOL.

3: A Useful Adviser

1. Smith and Weiner (1980), 216–17.

2. Even on the eve of the Nazi invasion, Oppenheimer was still evidently promoting the anti-interventionist cause. Author interview with Paul Pinsky, San Francisco, Calif., Sept. 3, 1997, Schwartz (1998), 333–34.

3. Minutes of meeting, Oct. 21, 1941, folder 1, carton 27, EOL.

4. Oppie also spoke of possible countermeasures to the bomb, including using the cyclotron beam as a kind of death ray to defend especially important targets. Minutes of meeting, Oct. 21, 1941, folder 1, carton 27, EOL.

5. Compton (1956), 57.

6. Lawrence to Compton, Oct. 22, 1941, folder 13, carton 22, EOL.

7. Hamilton, "A Report . . . ," Feb. 24, 1941, folder 25, carton 8, EOL.

8. Lawrence, "Historical Notes . . . ," 7, Mar. 26, 1945, folder 4, carton 29, EOL.

9. Hewlett and Anderson (1990), 36.

10. Rhodes (1986), 386.

11. Smyth (1989), 71–72; "Autobiography," series 7, box 1, Smyth papers.

12. Lawrence to A. H. Compton, Nov. 29, 1941, folder 19, carton 27, EOL.

13. Smyth (1989), 188–89.

14. Mass spectrograph: Rhodes (1986), 487–88.

15. Hewlett and Anderson (1990), 44.

16. Smyth (1989), 66; Childs (1968), 320.

17. Hewlett and Anderson (1990), 57.

18. Smyth (1989), 66.

19. Bush to Lawrence, Dec. 13, 1941, folder 18, carton 27, EOL; Vincent Jones, *U.S. Army in World War II, Special Studies, Manhattan: The Army and the Atomic Bomb* (U.S. Government Printing Office, 1985), 34.

20. Chevalier (1965), 49.

21. Davis (1968), 120–21.

22. Kamen (1986), 148.

23. Childs (1968), 326–27; author interview with William Douglass, Orinda, Calif., Dec. 17, 1992.

24. Hewlett and Anderson (1990), 52.

25. Lawrence, "Historical Notes . . ." (1945).

26. Wilson interview (1996).

27. Ibid.

28. Isotron: Smyth (1989), 197–99; James Gleick, *Genius: The Life and Science of Richard Feynman* (Pantheon, 1992), 143–44; "Final Report, Oct. 1943," series 7, box 1, Smyth papers.

29. Wilson interview (1996).

30. Lawrence to Smyth, Dec. 29, 1941, Lawrence folder, box 24, Smyth papers.

31. Compton (1956), 58; Hewlett and Anderson (1990), 54.

32. Lawrence, "Historical Notes. . . ." (1945); Hewlett and Anderson (1990), 57.

33. Lawrence to A. H. Compton, Dec. 24, 1941, folder 19, carton 27, EOL.

34. Lawrence to Smyth and reply, Dec. 24, 1941, folder 24, carton 27, EOL.

35. Lawrence to Smyth, Dec. 29, 1941, no. 209, Bush-Conant file, records of the Office of Scientific Research and Development, RG 227, National Archives (OSRD/NARA).

36. Rhodes (1986), 388.

37. Alvarez (1987), 112–13.

38. Compton (1956), 81.

39. Compton to Lawrence, Aug. 25, 1945, folder 10, carton 4, EOL.

40. Lawrence to Conant, Jan. 24, 1942, folder 20, carton 27, EOL.

41. Alvarez (1970), 263–65.

42. Glenn Seaborg, *Journals* (Lawrence Berkeley Laboratory, 1992), vol. 1, 255–58.

43. Kamen (1986), 148–49; author interview with Kenneth Pitzer, Berkeley, Calif., May 30, 1997.
44. Transcript of Robert Stone oral history interview, Library Archive, UCSF.
45. Childs (1968), 331.
46. Author interview with Owen Chamberlain, Oakland, Calif., Aug. 4, 1993.
47. Hewlett and Anderson (1990), 57–58.
48. Ibid., 60–61.
49. Rhodes (1986), 406.
50. Lawrence to Briggs, Jan. 31, 1942, folder 17, carton 27, EOL.
51. Lawrence to Conant, Feb. 28, 1942, folder 20, carton 27, EOL.
52. Calutrons: Hewlett and Anderson (1990), 91–93, 142–45; Childs (1968), 335.
53. Lawrence to Conant, Mar. 13, 1942, folder 20, carton 27, EOL.
54. Lawrence to Conant, Mar. 26, 1942, folder 20, carton 27, EOL.
55. Lawrence to Conant, Mar. 26, 1942, folder 20, carton 27, EOL.
56. Childs (1968), 309.
57. Chevalier (1965), 31. Another of Oppenheimer's early romantic interests—Ann Hoffman, Haakon Chevalier's sister-in-law—observed of Oppie: "He liked to be fought over." Author interview with Ann Hoffman, Mill Valley, Calif., May 1, 2001.
58. Kitty: Army Military Intelligence Division (MID) report on Katherine Harrison, Oct. 2, 1943, sec. 5, CINRAD file, no. 100–190625, FBI; Rhodes (1995), 122.
59. Schwartz (1998), 360.
60. Stern (1969), 30.
61. Army MID reports, Sept. 2, 1943, and Oct. 28, 1943, sec. 5, CINRAD file, FBI.
62. Tolman: Serber (1998), 35.
63. Serber (1998), 60.
64. Telegram, Nov. 1, 1940, folder 9, carton 14, EOL; Serber (1998), 58–60; Smith and Weiner (1980), 214; Molly Lawrence interview (1992).
65. Chevalier (1965), 38.
66. Frank: Transcript of interview with Frank Oppenheimer, Bancroft Library; summary report, Apr. 22, 1947, COMRAP file, 60–62, FBI.
67. Transcript of 1985 Frank Oppenheimer interview, Caltech archives.
68. *ITMOJRO,* 101. Caltech president Robert Mullikan told the FBI that he considered Frank "an appendage to his brother, not so capable and a close follower of his brother's ideas." Army MID report on Robert Oppenheimer, Aug. 27, 1943, box 1, JRO/AEC.
69. Robert to Frank Oppenheimer, n.d., box 1, Frank Oppenheimer papers.
70. Robert to Frank Oppenheimer, Mar. 12, 1930, box 1, Frank Oppenheimer papers.
71. Smith and Weiner (1980), 158. Interviewed by the FBI, Caltech physicist Charles Lauritsen, a friend of Frank's, described him as "very hard to understand [and] not too prone to accept discipline and leadership by others." Army MID report, Sept. 7, 1943, sec. 5, CINRAD file, FBI.
72. Transcript of Frank Oppenheimer interview, Caltech archives.
73. *ITMOJRO,* 9, 101.
74. Transcript of Frank Oppenheimer interview, Caltech archives. Copies of the couple's party membership cards, later obtained by the House Committee on Un-American Activities, show that they paid dues from 1937 to 1939; Frank claimed that both he and Jackie quit the party in 1941. Romerstein and Breindel (2000), 272–73. Robert told the FBI that he had tried to talk Frank out of joining the party and thought he had succeeded, only to find out that his brother joined a week later. *ITMOJRO,* 184.
75. Iris Chang, *Thread of the Silkworm* (Basic Books, 1995), 80, 159.
76. Smith and Weiner (1980), 195; *ITMOJRO,* 102.
77. Army MID report on Frank Oppenheimer, July 28, 1943, series 8, box 100, records of the Manhattan Engineer District, RG 77, National Archives (MED/NARA); summary report, Jan. 31, 1947, CINRAD file, FBI.
78. *ITMOJRO,* 199.

79. Ibid., 117.

80. "Q: You knew that if it were known that your brother was a member of the Communist Party, he could not get the job, didn't you? A: Yes. My honor was a little bit involved because of my having talked to Lawrence." *ITMOJRO*, 187.

81. Childs (1968), 320.

82. Clifford Durr to Frank Oppenheimer, Dec. 10, 1969, Durr folder, box 1, Frank Oppenheimer papers.

83. Tenney Committee: David Caute, *The Great Fear: The Anti-Communist Purge Under Truman and Eisenhower* (Simon and Schuster, 1978), 77; Edward Barrett, *The Tenney Committee: Legislative Investigation of Subversive Activities in California* (Cornell University Press, 1951); and Ingrid Scobie, *Jack B. Tenney: Molder of Anti-Communist Legislation in California, 1940–49* (University Microfilms, 1970).

84. "I may be out of a job by [April]," Oppenheimer wrote to a friend, "because UC is going to be investigated next week for radicalism and the story is that the committee members are no gentlemen and that they don't like me." Smith and Weiner (1980), 216.

85. After his expulsion, May became the education director of the Communist Party in Alameda County. Ellen Schrecker, *No Ivory Tower: McCarthyism and the Universities* (Oxford University Press, 1986), 74–75, 135; Schwartz (1998), 322.

86. *ITMOJRO*, 156.

87. San Francisco field report, Nov. 18, 1952, 65, sec. 14, JRO/FBI.

88. FAECT file, no. 61–7231, and Marcel Scherer file, no. 100–34665, FBI; Pinsky interview (1997).

89. Pinsky claimed that Oppie joined FAECT in either 1939 or 1940. George Engebretson, *A Man of Vision: The Story of Paul Pinsky* (HICL, 1997), 15; Pinsky interview 1997. David Jenkins, a Bay Area labor leader and Communist, remembered in a 1980 interview that "Oppenheimer had been helpful to [FAECT] in organizing the Shell scientists and technical workers, and, of course, knew Pinsky." Transcript of David Jenkins interview, Bancroft Library.

90. FAECT was interested in replacing the American Association of Scientific Workers, which was also riven by factional fighting, and which Oppenheimer had joined in 1939. Chevalier (1965), 38. The FBI considered FAECT "communist-dominated." AASW and FAECT: Donald Strickland, *Scientists in Politics: The Atomic Scientists Movement, 1945–46* (Purdue University Press, 1968), 82; Peter Kuznick, *Beyond the Laboratory: Scientists as Political Activists in 1930s America* (University of Chicago Press, 1987), 230–31.

91. Kamen (1986), 184–85; transcript of Martin Kamen interview, Bancroft Library. The FBI identified Eltenton as the "ringleader" of Shell's FAECT Local 25. San Francisco field report, Apr. 7, 1943, sec. 3, FAECT file, FBI.

92. Oppenheimer claimed in 1954 that he opposed joining the union, the American Association of Scientific Workers, at this meeting. *ITMOJRO*, 131. Kamen, however, asserted in his memoir that Oppenheimer was a vocal advocate of AASW. Kamen (1986), 183–86. Since Oppenheimer volunteered to hold the meeting in his own home and had previously championed FAECT's cause, Kamen's account seems the more plausible. Kamen interview (1997).

93. Kamen (1986), 185.

94. Kamen made a futile attempt to tell Lawrence his side of the story: "He urged me to 'get out,' whereupon I somewhat hotly asserted that I had never been 'in.'" Kamen (1986), 185.

95. Ibid.; Childs (1968), 319–20.

96. Army records from 1943 indicate that an "investigation of the Subject (Robert Oppenheimer) was made by the administration of the University of California several years ago." Army MID report on Robert Oppenheimer, Aug. 27, 1943, box 1, JRO/AEC.

97. By May 1941, both Oppenheimer and Chevalier were on FBI director J. Edgar Hoover's "preventive detention" list of persons to be rounded up in the event of a national emergency. FBI field report, Mar. 28, 1941, box 1, JRO/AEC; Ellen Schrecker, *Many Are the Crimes: McCarthyism in America* (Little, Brown, 1998), 106; and Barton

Bernstein, "The Oppenheimer Loyalty-Security Case Reconsidered," *Stanford Law Review,* July 1990, 1391.

98. San Francisco field report, May 19, 1941, sec. 1, Haakon Chevalier file, no. 100–18564, FBI.

99. The government would later try, unsuccessfully, to deport Schneiderman. Schrecker (1998), 103; summary report, Dec. 15, 1944, 196, COMRAP file, FBI.

100. Folkoff: Summary memo, Dec. 15, 1944, 85–88, COMRAP file, FBI; author interview with Philip Bowser, San Mateo, Calif. May 21, 1997. Bowser, the FBI's "wire man" in San Francisco, claimed that he found the wiretaps on Schneiderman and Communist Party headquarters already in place when he arrived at the office in early 1941.

101. In May 1940, President Roosevelt overrode the Supreme Court's decision outlawing wiretapping, authorizing the FBI to use wiretaps and bugs in cases of "persons suspected of subversive activities against the Government of the United States." Schrecker (1998), 106. The legal status of the wiretaps—and, specifically, whether they would be considered admissible evidence in a courtroom trial—remained unclear, however. Author interview with Robert King, Eugene, Oreg., Mar. 26, 1997; Branigan to Miller, "Major Intelligence Programs," May 31, 1972, House Un-American Activities Committee file, no. 61–7582, FBI.

102. King and Bowser interviews (1997); "Re: Installation of Microphones and Technical Survelliance," Nov. 24, 1942, vol. 1, Nelson file, FBI.

103. Author interview with Philip Scheidermayer, Washington, D.C., May 8, 1998.

104. King interview (1997).

105. San Francisco field report, May 19, 1941, sec. 1, Chevalier file, FBI.

106. San Francisco field report, Feb. 10, 1943, box 1, JRO/AEC; *ITMOJRO,* 183.

107. Summary report, Jan. 31, 1947, CINRAD file, FBI.

108. San Francisco field report, Apr. 23, 1943, vol. 1, Nelson file, FBI.

109. Steve Nelson: "Report on Soviet Espionage in the United States," Nov. 27, 1945, 30, entry 11, Central Intelligence Agency records, RG 233, National Archives (CIA/NARA); "Memorandum for the file: 'COMRAP,'" Feb. 6, 1948, Robert Louis Benson and Michael Warner, eds., *VENONA: Soviet Espionage and the American Response, 1939–1957* (Central Intelligence Agency, 1996), 105–6; John Earl Haynes and Harvey Klehr, *Venona: Decoding Soviet Espionage in America* (Yale University Press, 1999), 229; Nelson file, vol. 1, and summary report, Dec. 15, 1944, 58–61, COMRAP file, FBI.

110. Nelson and Oppenheimer: San Francisco field report, Sept. 19, 1946, vol. 3, Nelson file, FBI; Stern (1969), 30–31; Steve Nelson, James Barrett, and Rob Ruck, *Steve Nelson: American Radical* (University of Pittsburgh Press, 1969), 240, 268. Nelson and Kitty: *ITMOJRO,* 574–75.

111. Nelson et al. (1969), 251–65.

112. Smith and Weiner (1980), 220.

113. *ITMOJRO,* 9.

114. Pieper to Hoover, Jan. 26, 1942, sec. 1, Chevalier file, FBI.

115. San Francisco field report, May 19, 1942, sec. 1, Chevalier file, FBI.

116. The OSRD questionnaire, dated Apr. 28, 1942, is in box 1, JRO/AEC.

117. Lawrence: "To Whom It May Concern," Jan. 15, 1943, series 8, box 110, MED/NARA.

118. Lansdale diary, Feb.–Mar. 1942, and "John Lansdale, Jr.—Military Service" (unpublished manuscript), 14–22.

119. Lansdale, "Military Service," appendix; author interview with John Lansdale, Galesville, Md., Sept. 6, 1996.

120. Lansdale, "Military Service," 16; Barrett (1951), 11.

121. Segrè (1993), 173.

122. Ernest and John Lawrence, engaged in negotiations with a potential funder for expansion of the Donner Laboratory, were unavailable when Lansdale dressed down the boys.

123. Lawrence to Bush, Apr. 20, 1942, box 46, Lawrence folder, Bush papers, Library of Congress.

124. Seaborg (1992), vol. 3, 51.

125. Lawrence to Conant, May 23, 1942, folder 20, carton 27, EOL.

126. Rhodes (1986), 407.

127. Hewlett and Anderson (1990), 70–71.

128. "Diary Notes of Donald Cooksey," folder 23, carton 4, EOL.

129. E. O. Lawrence to Bush, June 15, 1942, box 46, Lawrence folder, Bush papers, Library of Congress.

130. Seaborg (1992), vol. 1, 77; Jones (1985), 53, 70.

131. Robert Serber, *The Los Alamos Primer: The First Lectures on How to Build An Atomic Bomb* (University of California Press, 1992), xxix.

132. Segrè believed that Oppie's students deliberately walked flat-footed—"an infirmity of their master's"—just as he and others among Fermi's students had unconsciously mimicked Fermi's intonation. Segrè (1993), 138.

133. Author interview with Rossi Lomanitz, Sackett's Harbor, N.Y., July 15–16, 1996; army MID report on Rossi Lomanitz, July 15, 1943, entry 8, box 100, MED/NARA.

134. Author interview with Arthur Rosen, San Luis Obispo, Calif., Mar. 11, 1997; army MID report on Arthur Rosen, Aug. 5, 1943, entry 8, box 100, MED/NARA.

135. Weinberg: San Francisco field report, Aug. 19, 1949, box 6, JRO/AEC; army MID report on Joseph Weinberg, Aug. 2, 1943, Weinberg file, no. 100–190625, FBI; Michaelmore (1969), 51.

136. Bohm: David Bohm file, May 23, 1952, no. 100–17787, FBI; F. David Peat, *Infinite Potential: The Life and Times of David Bohm* (Addison-Wesley, 1997), 39–60.

137. Friedman: Army MID report on Max Bernard Friedman, Aug. 21, 1943, entry 8, box 100, MED/NARA; Lomanitz interview (1996).

138. Peat (1997), 58; transcript of Mar. 29, 1943, wiretap, entry 8, box 100, MED/NARA; Lomanitz interview (1996).

139. Lomanitz interview (1996); Peat (1997), 49–50.

140. Eldred Nelson interview (1999).

141. "Uranium was never mentioned. It didn't need to be." Lomanitz interview (1996).

142. *ITMOJRO*, 126, 275–76; Lomanitz interview (1996).

143. Oppenheimer told the FBI in 1946 that Weinberg "ha[d] an extremely nervous temperament and for this reason, he disapproved his employment at Los Alamos." San Francisco field report, Sept. 19, 1946, vol. 3, Nelson file, FBI.

4: An Adventurous Time

1. Breit: Rhodes (1986), 410; Allan Needell, *Science, Cold War, and the American State: Lloyd V. Berkner and the Balance of Professional Ideals* (Harwood Academic Publishers, 2000), 49.

2. *ITMOJRO*, 11.

3. Serber (1998), 25–27.

4. Ibid., 11–13, 46–47; Teller (2001), 151.

5. Serber (1998), 51.

6. "Peace and War: Berkeley and Los Alamos," transcript of Robert Serber lecture, June 7, 1994, Brookhaven National Laboratory, N.Y.

7. Anne Fitzpatrick, *Igniting the Light Elements: The Los Alamos Thermonuclear Weapons Project, 1942–1952* (University Microfilms, 1998), 57–60.

8. Seaborg (1992), vol. 1, 73.

9. Bethe believed that Teller's personality underwent a change in 1932, when Edward was humiliated by physicist George Placzek while studying in Rome: "Placzek treated Teller very roughly. He made fun of him." Author interview with Hans Bethe, Santa Barbara, Calif., Feb. 12, 1988.

10. Bethe: Schweber (2000), 76–104; Rhodes (1986), 188–90; Blumberg and Owens (1976), 108.

11. Blumberg and Owens (1976), 75–76.

12. Teller to Fermi, July 17, 1942, "Enrico Fermi, 7/17/42–5/17/44" folder, box 74-17, LANL.

13. Berkeley seminar: Fitzpatrick (1998), 58; Eldred Nelson interview (1999).

14. Serber (1998), 68–69; Eldred Nelson interview (1999).

15. Bethe's theories of how the stars produced their energy would win him a Nobel prize the following year.

16. Bethe claimed that he and Teller worked together to restrain Serber, "who was trying to make things too complicated." Bethe interview (1988).

17. Serber interview (1992).

18. Oppenheimer evidently left in such a hurry that the exact purpose of his mission remained unclear to those he left behind. Both the H-bomb and the possibility of setting fire to the atmosphere fit the description of "very disturbing news" that Oppenheimer had hurriedly and cryptically given Compton over the phone.

19. "Better to accept the slavery of the Nazis than to run a chance of drawing the final curtain down on mankind!" was how Compton remembered their thinking in his memoirs. Teller disputes Compton's version. Compton (1956), 128; Teller (2001), 160.

20. Hewlett and Anderson (1990), 102.

21. Serber subsequently described the seminar as "very lively" and even "a lot of fun." Serber (1992), xxxi.

22. Teller had not overlooked the inverse Compton effect but believed that it occurred too slowly to have an impact upon the reaction. Bethe claimed that he proved otherwise. Bethe interview (1988).

23. Hewlett and Anderson (1990), 104, 675 fn.; *ITMOJRO,* 11; Rhodes (1986), 420–21.

24. Rhodes (1986), 421.

25. Oppenheimer evidently belonged to the ranks of the doubters. Jones (1985), 58–59.

26. "The W[ar] D[epartment] has turned thumbs down on O[ppenheimer] by telephone," Compton's secretary informed him. Memorandum of conversation, Aug. 18, 1942, box 1, JRO/AEC.

27. Oppenheimer clearance: "Subject: Oppenheimer, J. Robert," various documents, box 1, JRO/AEC records; "The Counter Intelligence Corps with Special Projects," vol. 8, 62, *History of the Counter Intelligence Corps* (U.S. Army Intelligence Center, Fort Holabird, Md., n.d.), Modern Military Records, National Archives.

28. Oppenheimer to Conant, Oct. 12, 1942, no. 140, Bush-Conant file, OSRD/NARA. Wensel to Lawrence, Sept. 1, 1942, and Lawrence to Wensel, Sept. 9, 1942, no. 140, Bush-Conant file, OSRD/NARA.

29. Oppenheimer to Conant, Oct. 12, 1942, no. 140, Bush-Conant file, OSRD/NARA.

30. "Report of S-1 Meeting," June 25, 1942, no. 120, Bush-Conant file, OSRD/NARA.

31. Aug. 15, 1942, memos, box 39, Sproul papers.

32. Harold Fidler, Jan. 14, 1997, personal communication.

33. "Minutes of Fifth Meeting," Sept. 13–14, 1942, no. 117, Bush-Conant file, OSRD/NARA; Leslie Groves, *Now It Can Be Told: The Story of the Manhattan Project* (Harper, 1962), 18.

34. Heilbron, Seidel, and Wheaton (1981), 32; Hewlett and Anderson (1990), 141–44.

35. Childs (1968), 379, 383–84.

36. "Report on Multiple Mass Spectrograph," Sept. 13, 1942, folder 4, carton 29, EOL; Childs (1968), 336.

37. Smyth (1989), 82–83; Groves (1962), 3–4.

38. K. D. Nichols, *The Road to Trinity: A Personal Account of How America's Nuclear Policies Were Made* (Morrow, 1987), 42–43.

39. Groves (1962), 22.
40. Transcript of interview with Vannevar Bush, reel 7, 422, Bush papers, MIT.
41. Lansdale interview; Lansdale, "Military Service," 23–24.
42. Hewlett and Anderson (1990), 83.
43. Seaborg (1992), vol. 1, 279.
44. Serber (1992), xxxii.
45. *ITMOJRO,* 12.
46. Groves (1962), 61–62; *ITMOJRO,* 166.
47. Davis, 146; transcript of interview with Edwin McMillan, 207, Bancroft Library.
48. Lawrence Badash et al., eds., *Reminiscences of Los Alamos, 1943–1945* (Reidel, 1985), 13.
49. "Report of Special Agent Robert Stepp," Sept. 20, 1942, box 1, JRO/AEC.
50. Alvarez (1987), 78.
51. Groves (1962), 61.
52. Compton (1956), 130; Childs (1968), 337.
53. Goodchild (1980), 66.
54. San Francisco field report, Feb. 10, 1943, file, box 1, JRO/AEC.
55. Oppenheimer to Bethe, Oct. 19, 1942, box 20, JRO.
56. Teller (2001), 163–64.
57. Teller to Oppenheimer, Mar. 6, 1943, Teller file, LANL; Rabi to Oppenheimer, Mar. 8, 1943, box 59, JRO.
58. Telegram, Oppenheimer to Dudley, Nov. 10, 1942, folder 29, carton 8, EOL.
59. Badash et al. (1985), 1–20; Hewlett and Anderson (1990), 229.
60. Badash et al. (1985), 13–20.
61. Jones (1985), 85.
62. Conant to Bush, Nov. 20, 1942, no. 140, Bush-Conant file, OSRD/NARA.
63. Oppenheimer's medical history: Memo to record, Jan. 15, 1943, box 100, series 8, MED/NARA; Harold Fidler, Jan. 14, 1997, personal communication.
64. Smith and Weiner (1980), 247.
65. Oppenheimer to Rabi, box 59, JRO. Bacher agreed to join the lab but promised to quit the day that the army took it over.
66. Hewlett and Anderson (1990), 237.
67. Lillian Hoddeson et al., *Critical Assembly: A Technical History of Los Alamos During the Oppenheimer Years, 1943–1945* (Cambridge University Press, 1993), 57–58; Badash et al. (1985), 21–40.
68. Oppenheimer to Robert Underhill, Mar. 8, 1943, folder 1, box 14, Robert Underhill papers, LANL.
69. Smith and Weiner (1980), 243.
70. Childs (1968), 351.
71. Underhill: Transcript of "Robert Underhill: Contract Negotiations for the University of California," (Underhill interview) box 2, Underhill papers, Bancroft Library; "Transcript of Robert Underhill Memoirs," Underhill papers, LANL.
72. "Transcript of Robert Underhill Memoirs," Underhill papers, LANL.
73 Underhill interview, 18; box 2, Underhill papers, Bancroft Library.
74. Jones (1985), 126; Norton to Groves, Jan. 14, 1943, Organization and Administration file, MED History, U.S. Army Chief of Staff records (Army/NARA), RG 319, National Archives.
75. Sproul to Conant, Jan. 26, 1943, no. 96, Bush-Conant file, OSRD/NARA.
76. Irwin Stewart to Underhill, Jan. 23, 1943, and Sproul to Underhill, Feb. 10, 1943, folder 1, box 14, Underhill papers, LANL.
77. The deal was informally sealed on February 22, 1943. A separate contract was negotiated for Lawrence's Calutrons. Underhill to Stewart, March 15, 1945, folder 4, box 13, Underhill papers, LANL.
78. Hewlett and Anderson (1990), 109.
79. Lawrence to Conant, Nov. 23, 1942, file 201c, series 5, MED/NARA.

80. Victor Bergeron, *Frankly Speaking: Trader Vic's Own Story* (Doubleday, 1973); Harold Fidler, May 28, 1997, personal communication.

81. The DuPont engineer was, nonetheless, impressed by Lawrence: "He could have made any salary that he chose to name as a salesman." Transcript of interview with Crawford Greenewalt, n.d., Hagley Museum, Wilmington, Del. The author thanks Professor David Hounshell for a copy of the Greenewalt interview.

82. Jones (1985), 104–5.

83. Interview with Wallace Reynolds, n.d., Bancroft Library.

84. Minutes of Coordinating Committee, Dec. 23, 1942, book 1, box 27, Lawrence Berkeley Laboratory archives, Berkeley, Calif. (LBL).

85. Jones (1985), 130; Smyth (1989), 201.

86. Nelson et al. (1969), 269.

87. Serber (1998), 73.

88. Chevalier (1965), 49.

89. Ibid., 48.

90. Ibid., 50.

91. Ibid., 46. In his unpublished memoir, Chevalier wrote: "In the spring of 1942, Oppenheimer was called to Chicago—it was the first time, I believe, that an absence of his would coincide with a planned meeting of our 'closed unit'—to discuss the state of work on the projected bomb." Typescript of "The Bomb," 43, Chevalier papers.

92. Haakon Chevalier to "Snipe," Mar. 6, 1943, and Feb. 28, 1943, "Snipe's Diary–1935," Chevalier papers.

5: Enormoz

1. Transcript of Underhill interview, box 2, Underhill papers, Bancroft Library.

2. Marshall to Underhill, Apr. 1, 1943, official file, Contract 48 records, SBFRC.

3. Serber (1992), 3.

4. Serber (1998), 104.

5. Hoddeson et al. (1993), 86.

6. Tolman to Oppenheimer, Mar. 27, 1943, "Design and Testing Bomb" folder, MED history, Army/NARA; Serber (1998), 72.

7. Serber (1998), 104.

8. Serber (1992), 33; Oppenheimer to Groves, June 21, 1943, "Design and Testing Bomb" folder, MED history, Army/NARA.

9. Hoddeson et al. (1993), 65.

10. "Notes on Los Alamos Meeting," Apr. 26–29, 1943, Tolman folder, MED file, OSRD/NARA.

11. Teller (2001), 171, 176; Davis (1968), 177; Michelmore (1969), 79.

12. Compton to Conant, Dec. 8, 1942, box 99, LLNL.

13. "Controlled Hydride Explosion," n.d., LAMS-125; Teller to Lavender, July 17, 1944, LANL. Hydride: Hoddeson et al. (1993), 136; Joseph Albright and Marcia Kunstel, *Bombshell: The Secret Story of America's Unknown Atomic Spy Controversy* (Times Books, 1997), 113–14. Serber claimed that Teller raised the question of the hydride bomb even before the Super at the Berkeley seminar. Serber interview (1992).

14. The plant began operations in Apr. 1944 but was shut down the following Sept., when Long was transferred to work on the gadget. Fitzpatrick (1998), 111.

15. Hoddeson et al. (1993), 75.

16. "Report of Special Reviewing Committee on Los Alamos Project," May 10, 1945, Tolman folder, MED file, OSRD/NARA.

17. Oppenheimer to Groves, June 21, 1943, "Design and Testing Bomb" folder, MED history, Army/NARA.

18. "It would be much more comfortable to like everybody. Before I got to Los Alamos I even managed to do this—at least approximately," Teller wrote to Maria Mayer

in 1946. Teller to Mayer, n.d., box 3, Maria Mayer papers, Special Collections, University of California, San Diego (La Jolla), Calif.

19. Fitzpatrick (1998), 110.

20. Radiological warfare: Smyth (1989), 65; Barton Bernstein, "Radiological Warfare: The Path Not Taken," *The Bulletin of the Atomic Scientists,* Aug. 1985, 44–49.

21. Oppenheimer to Hamilton, May 24, 1943, folder 8, carton 5; and Hamilton, "A Brief Review of the Possible Applications of Fission Products in Offensive Warfare," n.d., folder 25, carton 8, EOL.

22. Oppenheimer to Fermi, May 25, 1943, LANL.

23. Davis (1968), 182.

24. Fitin: Haynes and Klehr (1999), 391–92.

25. Soviet atomic espionage: Benson and Warner (1996), x; Allen Weinstein and Alexander Vassiliev, *The Haunted Wood: Soviet Espionage in America—the Stalin Era* (Random House, 1999), 182–83.

26. Trotskyists, for example, were referred to as *khorki*—"polecats."

27. Silvermaster group: Haynes and Klehr (1999), 131–32, 191–207; Weinstein and Vassiliev (1999), 151–71; Nigel West, *Venona: The Greatest Secret of the Cold War* (HarperCollins, 2000), 289–316; and Nathan G. Silvermaster file, no. 65–56402, pt. 1, FBI.

28. White went on to become director of the International Monetary Fund; he also had the code names *Jurist* and *Lawyer.* Currie was FDR's special representative to China and deputy administrator of the Foreign Economic Administration. Haynes and Klehr (1999), 346, 369.

29. *Crook,* Morris Dickstein, was elected to the U.S. House of Representatives in 1923 and subsequently served eleven terms in Congress. *Liza* was Martha Dodd, who was recruited as an agent in the 1930s. *Ernst* was Noel Field, who was likewise recruited by the Russians in the 1930s. *Frank* was Laurence Duggan, a Latin American expert who also went by the code names *Prince* and *Sherwood. Ales* is believed to be Alger Hiss. Weinstein and Vassiliev (1999), 140–50, 57–60, 18–20, 44–49; Haynes and Klehr (1999), 269–73, 201–4, 167–71.

30. Haynes and Klehr (1999), 196. One OSS agent, Jane Foster (*Slang*), was a friend of Haakon Chevalier's and spied for the so-called Perlo group. *Slang* appears in *Venona* messages from New York to Moscow on June 21, 1943, and May 30, 1944. Foster: Haynes and Klehr (1999), 272–73; Jane Foster, *An UnAmerican Lady* (Sidgwick and Jackson, 1980), 96.

31. A *Venona* cable sent from San Francisco to Moscow in Mar. 1944 showed that the watchers, too, were being watched: "According to information from *Brother-in-Law,* the chief of *Salt* in *Babylon,* Lieutenant Colonel Pash, left for Italy at the end of December." Haynes and Klehr (1999), 447 fn.

32. As early as that summer, *Anton* was passing atomic secrets to Moscow. In June 1943, these included a detailed description of the gaseous diffusion process from a still-unidentified American scientist code-named *Quantum. Venona* decrypts: New York to Moscow, June 22 and 23, 1943.

33. Gore Field: Rhodes (1995), 96–100; George R. Jordan, *From Major Jordan's Diaries* (Harcourt, Brace, 1952).

34 As of this writing, the decrypts are also available on the National Security Agency's Web site, www.nsa.gov.

35. The illegal radios were evidently meant as a backup, should cable traffic be suspended. Both transmitters fell silent in fall 1943, days after a newspaper story reported their existence. "Probe to Bare Reds' Illegal Radios in U.S.," *New York Journal-American,* Oct. 17, 1943. My thanks to Jim David for uncovering the facts about the Soviet radio transmitters.

36. The Soviets' top spy in the United States, Gaik Ovakimyan, had been arrested in May 1941 and deported. Soviet espionage in England: Christopher Andrew and Vasili Mitrokhin, *The Sword and the Shield: The Mitrokhin Archive and the Secret History of the KGB* (Basic Books, 1999); West (1999), 52–94.

37. Gorski's source, John Cairncross, was private secretary to Lord Hankey, a minister in Churchill's War Cabinet and head of the scientific panel that reviewed the work of the M.A.U.D. Committee. David Holloway, *Stalin and the Bomb: The Soviet Union and Atomic Energy, 1939–1956* (Yale University Press, 1994), 82; Rhodes (1995), 52.

38. Fuchs: Robert Williams, *Klaus Fuchs: Atom Spy* (Harvard University Press, 1987), 21–30, 38; Rhodes (1995), 108; Andrew and Mitrokhin (1999), 114–16. Fuchs had begun work at Birmingham in late May 1941. By Aug., he was passing information on atomic research there to his Soviet contacts. Benson and Warner (1996), 201–2.

39. Rhodes (1995), 53–54; Holloway (1994), 84.

40. A translation of Beria's memo to Stalin appears in Pavel Sudoplatov et al., *Special Tasks: The Memoirs of an Unwanted Witness—a Soviet Spymaster* (Little, Brown, 1994), 441.

41. Holloway (1994), 40.

42. The Nazi attack had the effect of shifting research into areas that had a better chance of showing short-term results. Kurchatov and others at Leningrad's institute were put to work at demagnetizing ships to protect them from mines.

43. Sudoplatov, et al. (1994), 448.

44. Holloway (1994), 70.

45. Ibid., 91–94. The translated memos of Mar. 7 and Mar. 22, 1943, are reprinted in Sudoplatov et al. (1994), 446–53.

46. Sudoplatov et al. (1994), 454.

47. Details of Fermi's Dec. 1942 experiment apparently reached Moscow in late Jan. 1943. Albright and Kunstel (1997), 75–76.

48. Holloway (1994), 68.

49. Kurchatov noted that it would be at least another year before the Soviet Union could carry out the kind of research on plutonium that was then under way at Berkeley, since Russia's cyclotrons had been put out of operation by the war.

50. Schwartz (1998), 226–32.

51. Kheifets: Ibid., 338; Sudoplatov et al. (1994), 84–85; "COMRAP" memo, Feb. 6, 1948, Benson and Warner (1996), 105; "Report on Soviet Espionage in the United States," Nov. 27, 1945, entry 11, RG 233 (Dies Committee records), National Archives.

52. Eltenton-Kheifets meeting: Eltenton interviews, June 26 and June 29, 1946, George Eltenton FBI file, no. 100–5113, box 6, JRO/AEC.

53. The FBI hoped to find out more about Kheifets from a surreptitious entry of his apartment. But the bureau's "black-bag job" yielded disappointing results. King interview (1997).

54. Ivanov: Haynes and Klehr (1999), 325. "Finding new recruits for a Soviet intelligence service within either the open section of a national Communist Party or within its secret cells or study groups is one of the duties of the Party liaison agent himself, but he may also have trusted Party members scattered throughout the Party organization who help him with this work," noted a CIA memo on "talent spotting." "Exploitation of the International Communist Movement by the Soviet Intelligence Services," July 1954, file 13, box 78, RG 263 (Central Intelligence Agency records), National Archives.

55. Eltenton and Kheifets: Interviews, June 26 and June 29, 1946, Eltenton FBI file, box 6, JRO/AEC.

56. Eltentons: Eltenton interview, June 26, 1946, 11–12, Eltenton file, FBI; Dorothea Eltenton, *Laughter in Leningrad: An English Family in Russia, 1933–1938* (privately published, 1998); summary report, Dec. 15, 1944, 39–40, COMRAP file, no. 100–17879, FBI. The author thanks Priscilla McMillan for bringing Dolly's book to his attention.

57. The credulous Ms. Eltenton remained a true believer even after a close friend—her children's nanny—was arrested and disappeared into the Soviet gulag.

58. Eltenton FBI interviews.

59. FBI agents witnessed several meetings in 1942 between Eltenton and Ivanov, who was on the bureau's active "watch" list. Haynes and Klehr (1999), 329.

60. Conroy to Hoover, Aug. 14, 1943, sec. 6, COMRAP file, FBI. The following Nov., Lawrence, Gilbert, and Cannon served as honorary chairmen of a science panel at the Congress of American-Soviet Friendship in New York. Kuznick (1987), 266.

61. Eltenton FBI interview, June 26, 1946.

62. Ibid. Other evidence suggesting that either Eltenton or Chevalier attempted to recruit Oppie comes from a report that NKVD agents in the United States sent to Moscow in February 1944. The report noted that Oppenheimer "ha[d] been cultivated by the 'neighbors' [GRU] since June 1942." Weinstein and Vassiliev (1999), 184.

63. Eltenton FBI interview, June 29, 1946.

64. Louise Bransten: "Rich Woman Balks at Reply on Spying," *New York Times*, Sept. 20, 1948; "Apricot Heiress," *New York Mirror*, Nov. 8, 1948; "Biography," n.d., and "Statement of Louise R. Berman to Committee on Un-American Activities," Sept. 20, 1948, Louise Berman papers, State Historical Society of Wisconsin, Madison, Wis. Louise married Lionel Berman in 1947 and changed her name.

65. Richard Bransten was heir to the MJB coffee-importing business founded by Morris J. Brandenstein. Bransten later became a successful Hollywood scriptwriter, providing financial backing to the magazine *New Masses*. Bransten had been the subject of an FBI investigation since 1941. Summary report, n.d., 444–45, pt. 6, Silvermaster file, FBI.

66. Louise Bransten and Silvermaster: Summary report, Dec. 15, 1944, no. 100–17879, COMRAP file, FBI; Weinberg and Vassiliev (1999), 158. In Nov. 1945, the FBI obtained a copy of a lengthy autobiography that Bransten had prepared for Mikhail Vavilov, then the Soviet consul in San Francisco. Preparation of such an autobiography was one of the final steps in the recruitment of an agent. Summary report, Apr. 22, 1947, COMRAP file, FBI.

67. San Francisco field report, May 31, 1944, sec. 44, COMRAP file, FBI.

68. Bransten's Rosenberg Foundation also bankrolled the publication and distribution to Bay Area schools of a children's book that Dolly had written while in Russia, *The Boy from Leningrad*.

69. Transcript of Louis Goldblatt interview, 1980, "Working Class Leader in the ILWU, 1935–1977," vol. 2, 959–60, Bancroft Library.

70. Louise Bransten was the subject of two lengthy COMRAP reports, in 1944 and 1947. Summary report, Dec. 15, 1944, and Apr. 22, 1947, COMRAP file, FBI.

71. Interviews: King and Bowser (1997). A May 1943 FBI report, noting the "illicit relationships" between Bransten and Kheifets, concluded, "These possibilities will be borne in mind in future investigations." San Francisco field report, May 7, 1943, vol. 1, Nelson file, FBI.

72. Jerrold and Leona Schecter, *Sacred Secrets: How Soviet Intelligence Operations Changed American History* (Brassey's, 2002), uncorrected page proofs, 47–50, 315–16. In their previous book, written in collaboration with Soviet spymaster Pavel Sudaplatov, the authors had claimed that Oppenheimer also informed Kheifets that American atomic scientists "were planning to move from Berkeley, California, to a new site to conduct research in nuclear weapons." In Dec. 1941, of course, neither the Met Lab at Chicago nor the laboratory at Los Alamos could have been discussed by Oppenheimer or anyone else. Sudaplatov et al. (1994), 174–75.

73. In the winter of 1942–43, the Chevaliers hosted another party for Russian war relief which Robert and Kitty Oppenheimer attended. "And of course the Soviet consulate was represented." Chevalier (1965), 51.

74. San Francisco field report, n.d. sec. 5, Chevalier file, FBI.

75. Oct. 13, 1942, entry, "Snipe's Diary," Chevalier papers.

76. Chevalier to "Snipe," Apr. 4, 1943, "Snipe's Diary—1935," Chevalier papers. Chevalier was hoping to get a posting in North Africa, which, Schwartz writes, was "then a major target of the KGB, as revealed in the *Venona* traffic." Chevalier (1965), 55; Schwartz (1998), 410.

77. George Eltenton told the FBI that he had arranged Chevalier's meeting with Lattimore. Eltenton interview, June 26, 1946, Eltenton FBI file, box 6, JRO/AEC. Lattimore:

"Statement Before Foreign Relations Committee," Senate Hearings folder, box 33; and Ladd to Hoover, Oct. 25, 1949, correspondence, April 1944–June 1952 folder, box 28, Owen Lattimore papers, Library of Congress; Owen Lattimore file, no. 100–24628, FBI; Schrecker (1998), 248–50.

78. King interview (1997).

79. Harold Fidler, Feb. 20, 1997, personal communication.

80. Pash: "Biography" folder, box 1, and "Colonel Boris T. Pash—Teacher, Soldier, Dedicated Worker for the Orthodox Church," *Russian Orthodox Journal,* Feb. 1971, 6–11, photo box, Boris Pash papers, Hoover Institution Library, Stanford, Calif.

81. Pash to "Coney," June 9, 1942, correspondence folder, box 3, Pash papers.

82. After the war, Pash went to work for the CIA's Directorate of Plans.

83. Robert King, Feb. 6, 1997, personal communication.

84. San Francisco field report, Feb. 10, 1943, JRO/FBI. Oppenheimer investigation of 1942–43: Burton to Ladd, Mar. 18, 1943, JRO/FBI; Hoover to Strong, Mar. 10, 1943, and Strong to Hoover, Mar. 18, 1943, box 1, JRO/AEC; "Re: Dr. J. Robert Oppenheimer," Apr. 16, 1954, JRO/FBI.

85. Hoover to Strong, Mar. 10, 1943, box 1, JRO/AEC.

86. Jones (1985), 256.

87. Hoover to Strong, Mar. 10, 1943, box 1, JRO/AEC.

88. Hoover to Pieper, Mar. 22, 1943, JRO/FBI; Pieper to Hoover, Dec. 2, 1943, JRO/FBI.

89. The transcript of the Nelson-"Joe" conversation, without date or title, was kept by Groves in his personal safe during the war. Transcript, entry 8, box 100, MED/NARA. Excerpts are also in a memo of Aug. 19, 1949, Joseph Weinberg FBI file, box 6, JRO/AEC.

90. Doyle was the organizational secretary of the Communist Party in Alameda County. She and Nelson had met with Joe the previous Thursday, Mar. 25. Glavin to Tolson, Sept. 29, 1948, 50, HUAC file, FBI.

91. Transcript, entry 8, box 100, MED/NARA. "Joe dictated and Steve wrote down at this point approximately 150 to 200 words, largely indistinguishable, but believed to be from the conversation a basic formula of some type," Branigan noted. The "magnetic spectrograph" was Lawrence's Calutron. The "velocity selector" referred either to the Isotron or to an apparatus used by Nelson and Frankel in measuring uranium cross sections. A 5-centimeter sphere may have referred to the critical-mass calculations performed by Nelson and Frankel; the plutonium core of the first atomic bomb would have made a solid sphere approximately 5.5 centimeters in diameter. The mention of deuterium suggests that "Joe" might also have passed along information about the 1942 summer seminar that discussed the Super, since deuterium plays no role in electromagnetic separation. David Hawkins, *Project Y: The Los Alamos Story* (Tomash Publishers, 1983), pt. 1, 99–100; transcript, entry 8, box 100, MED/NARA; personal communications: Herbert York, Nov. 5, 1997; Eldred Nelson, Jan. 25, 1998.

92. Ironically, Nelson told Joe that he and his friends "should never talk in a house but only when they were outside." Nelson-"Joe" transcript, 26.

93. King interview (1997).

94. Coincidentally, Nelson's meeting with "Joe" occurred just a week after the FBI and the FCC discovered the secret radio transmitter at San Francisco's Soviet consulate. See note 35.

95. Pieper to Hoover, Mar. 31, 1943, sec. 1, CINRAD file, FBI.

96. San Francisco field report, May 7, 1943, sec. 1, CINRAD file, and Glavin to Tolson, Sept. 29, 1948, HUAC file, FBI.

97. Zubilin's real name was Zarubin, his code name *Maxim;* both he and his wife, Elizabeth (code names *Vardo* and *Helen*), were senior NKVD agents. Zubilins: Haynes and Klehr (1999), 394; Robert Louis Benson, *Venona Historical Monograph,* no. 2 (U.S. National Security Agency, 1996), 4–6; Benson and Warner (1996), 51–54.

98. A 1952 publication by the House Committee on Un-American Activities contained a slightly different version of this conversation. U.S. Congress, *The Shameful Years: Thirty Years of Soviet Espionage in the United States* (U.S. Government Printing

Office, 1952), 31. The version here is taken from verbatim transcripts contained in two contemporaneous FBI reports on Nelson. Ladd to Hoover, Apr. 16, 1943, 1–9, vol. 2; and San Francisco field report, May 7, 1943, 10–22, vol. 1, Nelson file, FBI.

99. Nelson has been suggested as a candidate for a still-unidentified West Coast Soviet operative who appears in *Venona* messages, code-named *Butcher.* Nelson's real name, Mesarosh, means "meat-cutter" in Hungarian. Haynes and Klehr (1999), 428 fn.

100. Although "Bernstein" is deleted from the transcript in most of the FBI's report, a subsequent analysis of the Nelson-Zubilin conversation by the bureau notes a reference by Nelson to "the Bernstein woman," whom the bureau concluded was Louise Bransten. San Francisco field report, May 7, 1943, 30, vol. 1, Nelson file, FBI.

101. Tamm to Hoover, Apr. 6, 1943, sec. 1, CINRAD file, FBI; Groves (1962), 138.

102. Ladd to Hoover, Apr. 7, 1943, sec. 1, CINRAD file, FBI.

103. "Under no circumstances should this matter be discussed at conferences with representatives of G-2 and ONI [Office of Naval Intelligence]," the FBI director instructed. Hoover to SACs, Apr. 9, 1943, sec. 1, CINRAD file, FBI.

104. The Hoover-Hopkins memo is cited in Benson and Warner (1996), 49–50. It is unclear whether Hopkins ever responded to Hoover's warning. However, Robert King remembered Pieper telling him that the reaction from the White House had been simply, "Do nothing to embarrass our ally." King interview (1997).

105. Lansdale to Strong, Apr. 5, 1943, "DSM Project" folder, box 2, Pash papers.

106. Lyall Johnson, July 19, 1996, personal communication.

107. Author interview with Lyall Johnson, Washington, D.C., Sept. 12, 1996.

108. House on Forest Avenue: John Titus to Groves, Feb. 20, 1946, file 132.2, entry 5, MED/NARA; Lyall Johnson interview (1996).

109. Stanley Goldberg, Aug. 13, 1994, personal communication; Jones (1985), 125; author interview with Harold Fidler, Oakland, Calif., Dec. 16, 1992.

110. Goodchild (1980), 87.

111. DeSilva: Davis (1968), 188–89; Hoddeson et al. (1993), 96. Pash and de Silva found the instructions puzzling; Lansdale seemed to be suggesting that they not scrutinize Oppenheimer too closely. Lansdale to Pash, Mar. 13, 1943, box 1, JRO/AEC.

112. Hoover's Mar. 1943 letter to General Strong wrongly asserted that Lomanitz had been present in the meeting with Nelson and volunteered to commit espionage.

113. Lomanitz interview (1996).

114. De Silva to Lansdale, June 12, 1943, box 3, JRO/AEC.

115. Weinberg to "Opje," Apr. 12, 1943, box 77, JRO. Technically, Weinberg's conversation with Nelson in late March may not have violated the security act, since Weinberg filled out the OSRD's personnel security questionnaire on Apr. 14, 1943, and was put on the Rad Lab payroll on Apr. 27. Marshall to Groves, July 24, 1943, entry 8, box 100, MED/NARA. When Nelson asked whether any experiments had yet been conducted, Joe's answer indicates that his friends were still being tight-lipped: "Joe stated that he did not know, that he had asked his friends the results of the tests but that they had refused to say, these friends feeling that possession of the knowledge was extremely dangerous." Transcript, entry 8, box 100, MED/NARA.

116. Eldred Nelson interview (1997).

117. Hoover to Strong, June 22, 1943, sec. 4, CINRAD file, FBI.

118. They were, observed one reader of the transcripts, "the most boring conversations imaginable." Weinberg folder, CINRAD file, FBI. My thanks to Stan Norris for copies of CINRAD documents on the investigation of Weinberg and his family.

119. Weinberg's Rad Lab personnel file contained this notation by a security agent, quoting Birge: "Oppenheimer knows all about this man. If he wants W. it is his decision." Marshall to Groves, July 24, 1943, entry 8, box 100, MED/NARA.

120. Lansdale to Strong, June 12, 1943, entry 8, box 100, MED/NARA.

121. *ITMOJRO,* 197.

122. Ibid., 116.

123. Hawkins: Hawkins MID file, Sept. 20, 1943, entry 8, box 100, MED/NARA; "Subject: David Hawkins," June 29, 1943, box 1, JRO/AEC.

124. Serber interview (1992).
125. Murray to "Officer in Charge," July 14, 1943, and Pash to Lansdale, June 29, 1943, box 1, JRO/AEC.
126. Calvert to Pash, July 6, 1943, box 1, JRO/AEC.
127. Ladd to Hoover, Apr. 24, 1943, and Pieper to Hoover, June 30, 1943, sec. 4, CINRAD file, FBI.
128. Lansdale to Groves, July 6, 1943, entry 8, box 99, MED/NARA. On plans to replace Oppenheimer, see also Pieper to Hoover, June 30, 1943, sec. 4, CINRAD file, FBI.
129. Welch to Ladd, July 28, 1943, sec. 4, CINRAD file, FBI.
130. Groves to "District Engineer," July 20, 1943, entry 8, box 99, MED/NARA.

6: A Question of Divided Loyalties

1. Lansdale to Groves, Aug. 12, 1943, box 9, AEC/JRO.
2. Lansdale, "Military Service," 35; author interview with John Lansdale, Washington, D.C., Sept. 28, 1993.
3. Welch to Ladd, July 28, 1943, sec. 4, CINRAD file, FBI.
4. Jones (1985), 128.
5. Beta Calutrons: Hewlett and Anderson (1990), 295.
6. Y-12: Jones (1985), 130; Hewlett and Anderson (1990), 129.
7. Jones (1985), 132; Childs (1968), 343; Anthony Cave Brown and Charles MacDonald, eds., *The Secret History of the Atomic Bomb* (Delta Books, 1977), 159.
8. Brown and MacDonald (1977), 169.
9. Minutes of Feb.–Apr. 1943 Coordinating Committee, book 1, box 27, LBL; Jones (1985), 142.
10. Transcript of Aug. 16, 1943, telephone conversation, book 1, box 1, records of the Radiation Laboratory (Rad Lab records), Bancroft Library.
11. Minutes of Sept. 2, 1943, Coordinating Committee, book 2, box 27, LBL.
12. Minutes of Nov. 4, 1943, Coordinating Committee, book 3, box 27, LBL.
13. Welch to Ladd, Apr. 12, 1943, sec. 1, CINRAD file, FBI.
14. Hoover to Strong, June 22, 1943, sec. 4, CINRAD file, FBI.
15. Pieper to Hoover, July 23, 1943, sec. 4, CINRAD file, FBI.
16. Welch to Ladd, July 23, 1943, sec. 5, CINRAD file, FBI.
17. Weinberg folder, CINRAD file, FBI.
18. Interviews: King and Bowser (1997).
19. Groves to Wallace, Stimson, and Marshall, Aug. 21, 1943, no. 61, Harrison-Bundy file, MED/NARA.
20. Groves to Bundy, Aug. 17, 1943, no. 61, Harrison-Bundy file, MED/NARA.
21. Stimson to FDR, Sept. 9, 1943, no. 61, Harrison-Bundy file, MED/NARA.
22. Stimson to Roosevelt, Oct. 20, 1943, no. 61, Harrison-Bundy file, MED/NARA.
23. Roosevelt to Stimson, Oct. 26, 1943, no. 61, Harrison-Bundy file, MED/NARA.
24. Anna Marie Rosenberg to Roosevelt, Nov. 2, 1943, no. 61, Harrison-Bundy file, MED/NARA.
25. Author interview with Lyall Johnson, Washington, D.C., Feb. 11, 1993.
26. Oppenheimer-Lomanitz meeting: *ITMOJRO,* 128, 136, 208.
27. Oppenheimer-Weinberg/Bohm meeting: Ibid., 208–9, 277.
28. Tipped off to a meeting of the four suspects with Steve Nelson and Bernadette Doyle at Weinberg's flat, army CIC agents crowded onto the landing of an adjoining building on the evening of Aug. 17, 1943.
29. Weinberg to Oppenheimer, Apr. 12, 1943, box 77, JRO.
30. Summary report, Dec. 15, 1944, COMRAP file, FBI.
31. Lyall Johnson, May 1, 2000, personal communication.
32. Oppenheimer-Pash interview: *ITMOJRO,* 845–63; Lyall Johnson, Apr. 4, 1997, personal communication.

33. Ironically, Oppenheimer suggested that Pash find out the names on his own by planting a spy in FAECT.

34. King interview (1997).

35. The Aug. 7 letter was probably written by Lieutenant Colonel Mironov of the NKVD, an aide to Zubilin. Mironov was subsequently recalled and confined to a mental institution in the Soviet Union. Weinstein and Vassiliev (1999), 274–75. The anonymous letter is reprinted in Benson and Warner (1996), 51–54.

36. King interview (1997); *ITMOJRO,* 813; Lansdale to Hoover and Whitson, Aug. 27, 1943, USSR file, no. 47C, U.S. Army Chief of Staff records (Army/NARA), RG 319, National Archives.

37. Murray to "Officer in Charge," Sept. 6, 1943, Weinberg folder, CINRAD file, FBI.

38. Pieper-Hoover, Sept. 8, 1943, sec. 6, CINRAD file, FBI.

39. Lansdale to Strong, Sept. 18, 1943, sec. 10, CINRAD file, FBI.

40. Herbert York, *Making Weapons, Talking Peace: A Physicist's Odyssey from Hiroshima to Geneva* (Basic Books, 1987), 33.

41. Peat (1997), 84; San Francisco field report, May 23, 1952, Bohm file, FBI.

42. Weinberg FBI file, Aug. 19, 1949, box 1, AEC/JRO; U.S. Congress, HUAC, *Report on Atomic Espionage (Nelson-Weinberg and Hiskey-Adams Cases).* 81st Congress, 2nd sess., Sept. 29, 1949, 8–9.

43. California Legislature, "*Third Report: Un-American Activities in California, 1947*" (Sacramento, Calif., 1947) (Tenney hearings, 1947), 212.

44. Beyond not wanting to tip its hand, the government had no clearly admissible evidence to use against Weinberg. Lansdale to Hoover, Aug. 2, 1943, Weinberg folder, CINRAD file, FBI. Since Weinberg was the only part-time scientist at the lab, the army issued an edict firing all part-time workers. Lyall Johnson interview (1993).

45. L. Johnson to Fidler, Sept. 20, 1943, and Friedman to Oppenheimer, Sept. 25, 1943, no. 8, box 100, MED/NARA.

46. Friedman to Oppenheimer, Sept. 25, 1943, no. 8, box 100, MED/NARA.

47. *ITMOJRO,* 119; Peat (1997), 5.

48. Bohm would later be assigned to work with the Rad Lab's British contingent on theoretical calculations related to the Calutrons. Peat (1997), 64–65.

49. Lansdale to Groves, Aug. 2, 1943, no. 8, box 100, MED/NARA.

50. Army MID report on Lomanitz, July 15, 1943, Weinberg folder, CINRAD file, FBI. Lansdale arranged for Lomanitz to be assigned to a signals unit of the Forty-fourth Infantry Division, which was training in Washington State.

51. Lansdale to Groves, July 19, 1943, and Lansdale to Groves, July 31, 1943, no. 8, box 100, MED/NARA.

52. Goodchild (1980), 91; Stern (1969), 52.

53. Murray to "Officer in Charge," Sept. 22, 1943, box 1, AEC/JRO.

54. Groves may have wanted to draft Lomanitz so that Rossi could later be court-martialed. When the general raised the idea with aide Joseph Volpe, however, Volpe, a lawyer, pointed out that Lomanitz could call his own counsel to challenge the charges. Groves dropped the idea. Joseph Volpe, Mar. 9, 2001, personal communication.

55. Friedman to Oppenheimer, Sept. 25, 1943, no. 8, box 100, MED/NARA.

56. Murray to "Officer in Charge," Sept. 22, 1943, box 1, AEC/JRO.

57. When Lomanitz telephoned Los Alamos from his home in Oklahoma, where he had gone on furlough before basic training, Oppie refused to take the call. Oppenheimer to Lansdale, Sept. 29, 1943, no. 8, box 100, MED/NARA.

58. *ITMOJRO,* 815.

59. Ibid., 816.

60. Ibid., 186, 277–78.

61. Oppenheimer-Lansdale interview: Ibid., 871–86.

62. Summary report, Apr. 18, 1952, 19, Robert Oppenheimer file, FBI/JRO.

63. Among those Lansdale suspected of being the contacts were Robert and Charlotte Serber and Phillip Morrison, another of Oppie's grad students. Morrison interview (2000).

64. A list of candidates that Jim Murray sent Pash included not only Weinberg but Birge. Murray to Pash, Nov. 22, 1943, box 1, AEC/JRO.

65. A few days before going overseas, Pash sent Lansdale a list of nine individuals he considered likely candidates for Eltenton's go-between; the list was drawn from the physics and chemistry faculty at Berkeley.

66. *Alsos:* Groves (1962), 191–92.

67. Minutes of Nov. 1943 Coordinating Committee, book 3, box 27, LBL; Jones (1985), 135.

68. Transcript of Nov. 10, 1943, telephone conversation, book 1, box 1, Rad Lab records.

69. Transcript of Nov. 25, 1943, telephone conversation, book 1, box 1, Rad Lab records; minutes of Nov. 1943 Coordinating Committee, book 3, box 27, LBL.

70. Transcript of Nov. 26, 1943, telephone conversation, book 1, box 1, Rad Lab records.

71. Transcripts of Dec. 1943 telephone conversations, book 1, box 1, Rad Lab records.

72. Childs (1968), 348–49.

73. Groves arrived at Y-12 on Dec. 14 to find things little improved. Transcript of Dec. 28, 1943, telephone conversations, book 1, box 1, Rad Lab records; Jones (1985), 136.

74. Minutes of Dec. 1943 Coordinating Committee, book 3, box 27, LBL; Jones (1985), 136–38.

75. Interview with Duane Sewell, July 30, 1993, Lawrence Livermore National Laboratory archives, Livermore, Calif. (LLNL).

76. Transcript of Dec. 31, 1943, telephone conversation, book 1, box 1, Rad Lab records; Lawrence to Conklin, Jan. 5, 1944, book 3, box 27, LBL.

77. This account is taken from FBI interviews done in late 1953 and early 1954 with Groves, Lansdale, and William Consodine. Frank Oppenheimer, also interviewed at this time, denied ever being approached by Chevalier. Interviews, box 1, AEC/JRO. In spring 1946, Chevalier would tell the FBI that he had approached only Oppie, while the two men were mixing drinks in the kitchen of the Eagle Hill home, at a dinner party shortly before Oppenheimer and his family moved to Los Alamos. By that time, however, the two had gotten together socially and would have been able to coordinate their stories, as Chevalier himself acknowledged. Chevalier (1965), 68–69.

78. Consodine reasoned, as he later told the FBI, that Oppie was "more inclined to protect a blood relative than a friend." Newark field report, Jan. 5, 1954, box 1, AEC/JRO.

79. Joseph Volpe, Mar. 9, 2001, personal communication.

80. It was not the first time that Groves sought an extralegal solution to a security problem in the project. Earlier in the war, Groves had wanted to intern physicist Leo Szilard for the duration as an enemy alien. Stimson to Attorney General, Oct. 1943, no. 61, Harrison-Bundy file, MED/NARA; Lanouette (1992), 240; Stern (1969), 70.

81. The available record does not indicate whether Groves knew of and tacitly approved this plan, or Consodine and Lansdale arrived at it independently.

82. Pash was already in Europe and did not learn that Oppenheimer had identified Chevalier as the go-between until much later. *ITMOJRO,* 817, 153.

83. Lansdale, however, did notify Hoover in writing on Dec. 13 that Oppenheimer had identified the professor as Chevalier. Lansdale to Hoover, USSR file, no. 47C, Army/NARA.

84. There is no indication in Nichols's memoir, published in 1987, that Groves told his second-in-command what Oppenheimer had said about Frank's role. Lansdale confirmed his late-night visit to Tamm and Whitson during the 1954 Oppenheimer hearings and, previously, in a private letter to Groves. *ITMOJRO,* 262–63; Lansdale to Groves, Dec. 16, 1953, box 5, RG 200 (Groves/NARA), National Archives.

85. Author interview with Duane Sewell, Livermore, Calif., July 30, 1993; transcript of Jan. 1, 1944, telephone conversation, book 2, box 1, Rad Lab records.

86. Seaborg (1992), vol. 4, 117.

87. One particularly enterprising worker used a screwdriver to adjust the gauge. Sewell interview (1993).

88. Kamen soon made the unpleasant discovery that chemical processes that worked in the lab failed to give the same results when tried on an industrial scale. Transcript of Jan. 8, 1944, telephone conversation, book 2, box 1, Rad Lab records.

89. Jones (1985), 144. Cyclotroneers made a distinction between water-soluble "gunk" and insoluble "crud," which had to be laboriously scraped from the machine. Lofgren interview (1998).

90. Transcript of Jan. 22, 1944, telephone conversation, book 2, box 1, Rad Lab records.

91. Transcript of Jan. 18, 1944, telephone conversation, book 2, box 1, Rad Lab records; Dobbs to "Officer in Charge," Aug. 31, 1943, and attachments, no. 8, box 100, MED; army MID report on Fox, Sept. 13, 1943, box 99, AEC/JRO.

92. Hewlett and Anderson (1990), 164.

93. Brown and MacDonald (1977), 170–71.

94. Segrè (1993), 186–95.

95. Alvarez (1987), 130–35; Badash et al. (1985), 55.

96. Badash et al. (1985), 16–18.

97. R. Oppenheimer to Groves, Mar. 25, 1944, no. 4, pt. 2, series 1, MED/NARA.

98. Oppenheimer to Groves, Jan. 1, 1944, "Design and Testing Bomb" file, Army/NARA.

99. Hoddeson et al. (1993), 137, 181; Hawkins (1983), 118; J. Askin, R. Ehrlich, R. P. Feynman, Jan. 31, 1944, "First Report on the Hydride," LAMS-45, LANL.

100. Hoddeson et al. (1993), 137, 181.

101. Implosion crisis: Ibid., 1–3; Hewlett and Anderson (1990), 252–53; Rhodes (1986), 548.

102. Hewlett and Anderson (1990), 311; Hoddeson et al. (1993), 245–48.

103. "Fast" implosion: Hoddeson et al. (1993), 130, 159–60; Rhodes (1986), 545.

104. Teller to Mayer, n.d. (early 1944), box 3, Mayer papers.

105. Hoddeson et al. (1993), 203; Fitzpatrick (1998), 108.

106. Opacity: Serber (1995), xxi; Teller to Urey, May 18, 1944, LANL.

107. Teller (2001), 127; Teller to Mayer, n.d. (May–June 1944), box 3, Mayer papers.

108. Teller interview (1993).

109. Hoddeson et al. (1993), 204; Fitzpatrick (1998), 110; Rhodes (1986), 546; Hewlett and Anderson (1990), 240.

110. Teller (2001), 180, 220; R. Oppenheimer to Groves, Mar. 25, 1944, no. 4, pt. 2, series 1, MED/NARA.

111. Fitzpatrick (1998), 112; Hoddeson et al. (1993), 157–60; Teller (2001), 177.

112. Fuchs was subsequently one of the authors of a top-secret, five-volume series of reports on implosion theory. Teller told his biographers that he had no memory of refusing Bethe's requests, but acknowledged that he balked at doing the calculations. Rhodes (1986), 545–46; Hoddeson et al. (1993), 162; Blumberg and Owens (1976), 131.

113. Williams (1987), 189.

114. New York to Moscow, Feb. 9, 1944, *Venona* decrypts. Fuchs-Gold meeting: Rhodes (1995), 107–8; Albright and Kunstel (1997), 78.

115. Independent of *Rest,* the Russians had other sources of information on Oak Ridge and Los Alamos. Just two days after *Anton* forwarded Fuchs's information, Fitin received another encrypted cable from New York, relaying a report by *Vogel* that dealt with construction of the facility at Oak Ridge to make heavy water. New York to Moscow, Feb 11, 1944, *Venona* decrypts. Eleven days later, Kurchatov wrote an assessment of new "materials" derived from espionage that may have included *Vogel*'s information, since it dealt with heavy-water production in the United States.

116. One of the Soviets' sources in England was *Hola,* a secretary in Britain's Non-Ferrous Metals Association, who was later identified as Melita Norwood. Another British spy, *Eric,* remains unidentified as of this writing. Andrew and Mitrokhin (1999), 115–16; Weinstein and Vassiliev (1999), 181–83.

117. Kurchatov to Pervukhin, July 3, 1943, reprinted in Sudoplatov, et al. (1994), 455.

118. New York to Moscow, Aug. 12, 1943, *Venona* decrypts. The name of the "progressive professor"—redacted by the censors when they declassified *Venona*—was reportedly "Lawrence." If so, *Moliere*'s political intuition was no better than his grasp of California geography. Mikhailov sent his cable the same day that Ernest was formally inducted into the Soviet Academy of Sciences. See chapter 5. The author thanks Nigel West for these insights.

119. Late in 1941, Pinsky left FAECT to become research director for the CIO in California. Pinsky interview (1997).

120. San Francisco to Moscow, Mar. 9, 1944; San Francisco to Moscow, Dec. 11, 1943, *Venona* decrypts.

121. San Francisco to Moscow, Nov. 2, 1943, *Venona* decrypts.

122. Benson, *Venona Historical Monographs,* nos. 4 and 5.

123. San Francisco to Moscow, Feb. 8, 1944, and Jan. 14, 1944, *Venona* decrypts.

124. Strong: Tracy Strong and Helene Keyssar, *Right in Her Soul: The Life of Anna Louise Strong* (Random House, 1983), 206–8; Haynes and Klehr (1999), 367; Philip Scheidermayer, Jan. 14, 1998, personal communication.

125. Miller: San Francisco to Moscow, Nov. 1, 1943, *Venona* decrypts; San Francisco field reports, Feb. 25, 1944, May 31, 1944, and Apr. 22, 1947, COMRAP file, FBI; Haynes and Klehr (1999), 358.

126. San Francisco to Moscow, Nov. 1, 1943, and June 22, 1944, *Venona* decrypts. Corday was Marat's assassin in the French Revolution; she was guillotined for the murder.

127. The previous day, Pieper had put Chevalier back on the FBI's watch list. Pieper to Hoover, Dec. 17, 1943, sec. 1, Chevalier file, and "Haakon Chevalier," n.d., sec. 30, COMRAP file, FBI.

128. Chevalier to Oppenheimer, n.d., and Dec. 3, 1943, Chevalier folder, JRO.

129. "Haakon Chevalier," n.d., sec. 30, COMRAP file, FBI.

130. Summary report, Apr. 22, 1947, 37–38, COMRAP file, FBI.

131. Summary report, Dec. 15, 1944, 222–24, COMRAP file, FBI.

132. The following day, Bransten and Chevalier went to Washington, D.C., where they met with Silvermaster. Summary report, Apr. 22, 1947, 37–38, COMRAP file, and summary report, Mar. 6, 1946, CINRAD file, FBI.

7: Break, Blow, Burn

1. Kamen (1986), 164–65.

2. Lansdale to Osborne, July 17, 1944, Tolman papers, OSRD/NARA; Lyall Johnson interview (1996).

3. San Francisco field report, May 7, 1956, John Hundale Lawrence file, no. 77–32400, FBI.

4. Kamen incident: U.S. Congress, *Excerpts from Hearings Regarding Investigation of Communist Activities in Connection with the Atom Bomb,* (1948 HUAC hearings), Sept. 9, 14, and 16, 1948 (U.S. Government Printing Office, 1948), 11–49; Sudoplatov et al. (1994), 214, 298; Weinstein and Vassiliev (1999), 334.

5. Lyall Johnson interview (1996).

6. Fred "Dusty" Rhodes, Apr. 12, 2001, personal communication.

7. Philip Scheidermayer, May 8, 1998, personal communication.

8. "Summary: Russian Situation," n.d., "Recently Declassified Extracts," MED/NARA; Glavin to Tolson, Sept. 29, 1948, 56–57, HUAC file, FBI; Kamen interview (1997).

9. "Summary: Russian Situation," n.d., "Recently Declassified Extracts," MED/NARA.

10. Fidler to Lawrence, July 11, 1944, folder 10, carton 10, EOL.

11. Fidler interview (1992).

12. "I still want to do something about the war besides having a son in it . . . but so far nobody will have me." Chevalier to Edouard, Feb. 20, 1945, "Correspondence, 1944–45," Chevalier papers.

13. The wartime personal correspondence of Jackie and Frank Oppenheimer is in an unmarked folder in the Frank Oppenheimer papers, Bancroft Library.

14. Perhaps the best evidence that Oppie was not a spy surfaced in 1999: in a February 1944 cable reportedly sent to Moscow Center from New York, the NKVD was still evidently hopeful of recruiting Oppenheimer, possibly with the assistance of his brother. The message also identified Robert Oppenheimer as a "secret member of the Compatriot organization," or Communist Party. However, there is no independent collaboration of the authenticity of this cable as of this writing. Weinstein and Vassiliev (1999), 183–84.

15. An electronic device found in Oppie's overcoat occasioned some excitement until the G-men realized that it was a dry-cell battery.

16. During his Berkeley visit, Oppie had discussed with Lawrence whether Bernard Peters should be dismissed from the Rad Lab staff. Stern (1969), 43.

17. Jones (1985) 265; U.S. Congress, HUAC, *Testimony of James Sterling Murray and Edward Tiers Manning* (1949 HUAC hearings), 81st Congress, 1st sess., Aug. 14 and Oct. 5, 1949, 877–78.

18. Titus to Groves, Feb. 20, 1946, file 132.2, entry 5, MED/NARA.

19. Lyall Johnson interview (1996).

20. Peters was a German-born Communist and anti-Nazi activist who had escaped from Dachau and come to America in 1934, later becoming a naturalized citizen. His wife, Hannah—another German refugee and a friend of Oppie's and Jean Tatlock's—was a physician at a San Francisco hospital and a party member close to Steve Nelson. Oppenheimer was probably aware that the army and FBI were already investigating the couple, since Bernard was prominent in FAECT. Bernard Peters's name had been on a list of four that DeSilva showed to Oppenheimer; the list also included Weinberg's name. DeSilva to Calvert, Jan. 6, 1944, box 1, AEC/JRO. Peters: Childs (1968), 353; *ITMOJRO,* 120–21, 150–51; Bernard Peters MID file, Aug. 6, 1943, entry 8, box 100, MED/NARA.

21. In Jan. 1944, army agents monitoring the bug in Weinberg's home overheard Joe tell his wife about Lomanitz: "They would not have sprung a trap on [Rossi] if they did not have reason to believe that something was wrong with [Rossi's?] activities. They're wrong but they have reason to believe." Weinberg also said that he and Bohm were in "complete cahoots." Summary report, Jan. 31, 1947, 19–21, CINRAD file, FBI.

22. Summary report, Apr. 22, 1947, 57, COMRAP file, FBI; Albright and Kunstel (1997), 104–5.

23. Lansdale, "Military Service," 44–45.

24. Rhodes (1986), 654.

25. Frank's meager responsibilities at the lab included drafting a list of safety "dos and don'ts" for the upcoming bomb test. "Safety Precautions," n.d., no. 90339, Coordination and Information Center, U.S. Department of Energy, Las Vegas, Nev. (CIC/DOE).

26. Frank Oppenheimer interview, box 2, Child papers; Childs (1968), 354.

27. Lansdale to R. Oppenheimer, n.d., Lansdale folder, JRO. Soviet atomic espionage: "Issues in the History of the Science and Technology" (translation of Russian title), 3/1992, St. Petersburg, Russia, 128; Holloway (1994), 222–23; Rhodes (1995), 244–46. A copy of the journal article, withdrawn from Russian libraries shortly after publication, was obtained from the Hoover Library at Stanford.

28. Lawrence to Conant, May 31, 1944, OSRD/NARA; Oppenheimer to Lawrence, May 24, 1944, Los Alamos file, box 7, Underhill papers, LANL; Hewlett and Anderson (1990), 166.

29. The first hybrid racetrack—using the magnet and vacuum tanks of the Alpha I but Alpha II's higher voltage four-beam source—began its inaugural run on June 3, 1944. Hopes for the improved Calutron faded immediately, however, when insulators broke down under the greater load and the new machine sputtered to a halt. Improved heat shielding and better insulators solved the problem. Brown and MacDonald (1977), 170; Hewlett and Anderson (1990), 155.

30. Author interview with Herbert York, La Jolla, Calif., Mar. 14, 1997; Jones (1985), 145.

31. Jones (1985), 143.
32. Serber (1998), 104.
33. Conant, "Report on Visit to Los Alamos," Aug. 17, 1944, no. 86, Bush-Conant file, OSRD/NARA.
34. Brown and MacDonald (1977), 171; Rhodes (1986), 600.
35. Hewlett and Anderson (1990), 168–73.
36. Ibid., 300.
37. Nov. 13, 1944, Groves diary, Groves/NARA.
38. Childs (1968), 357.
39. Tolman's committee: Groves to Tolman, Aug. 29, 1944, file 334, series 5, MED/NARA; Hewlett and Anderson (1990), 324–25; Jones (1985), 556–58.
40. Tolman to Lawrence, Sept. 16, 1944, file 334, series 5, MED/NARA.
41. Oppenheimer to Tolman, Sept. 20, 1944, file 334, series 5, MED/NARA; Rhodes (1986), 563.
42. Untitled memo, Oct. 1944, folder 37, carton 29, EOL.
43. Notes, Nov. 8, 1944, box 9, Tolman file, OSRD/NARA.
44. *ITMOJRO*, 956.
45. Nov. 8 and Nov. 23, 1944, Groves diary, Groves/NARA; transcript of telephone conversation, Jan. 19, 1945, book 6, box 1, Rad Lab records.
46. Nonetheless, Lawrence telegraphed Groves on January 6 to badger him again for "a continuing construction program to the end of the war."
47. Dec. 27, 1944, Groves diary, Groves/NARA.
48. "Report of Committee on Postwar Policy," Dec. 28, 1944, file 3, pt. 2, series 1, MED/NARA.
49. Ernest was still not willing to admit defeat. Lawrence to Groves, Jan. 6, 1945, folder 37, carton 28, EOL.
50. Transcript of telephone conversation, Jan. 19, 1945, book 6, box 1, Rad Lab records; Jan. 20, 1945, Groves diary, Groves/NARA.
51. Transcript of telephone conversation, Feb. 27, 1945, book 6, box 1, Rad Lab records; Feb. 27, 1945, Groves diary, Groves/NARA.
52. Jones (1985), 510.
53. Hoddeson et al. (1993), 335–49.
54. Tatlock's death: Jenkins (1991), 24–25; Schwartz (1998), 378–79.
55. Brown and MacDonald (1977), 171; Jones (1985), 148.
56. Workforce reductions at Y-12 and Rad Lab: Entries for Apr.–May 1945, Cooksey diary, folder 23, carton 4, EOL; transcripts of telephone conversations, book 7, box 1, Rad Lab records; May 3, 1945, Groves diary, Groves/NARA.
57. Oppenheimer continued to foil Underhill's efforts to find out about the project. Transcript of interview, box 2, Underhill papers, Bancroft Library.
58. In addition to Fuchs, David Greenglass, and Ted Hall—an idealistic nineteen-year-old Harvard physics graduate, who had arrived at Los Alamos the following Jan. and began to spy shortly thereafter—there were reportedly other Soviet spies, as yet unrevealed, at the New Mexico lab. Sudoplatov et al. (1994), 172–219; Albright and Kunstel (1997), 100–109.
59. Kurchatov to Pervukhin, Apr. 7, 1945, reprinted in Sudoplatov et al. (1994), 460–61.
60. Kurchatov to Pervukhin, Mar. 7, 1945, reprinted in Sudoplatov et al. (1994), 446.
61. San Francisco to Moscow, Jan. 10, 1945, *Venona* decrypts; Benson, *Venona Historical Monograph,* no. 3, 3.
62. San Francisco to Moscow, Apr. 3, 1945, *Venona* decrypts.
63. San Francisco to Moscow, Apr. 6, 1945, *Venona* decrypts; Alexander Feklisov, *The Man Behind the Rosenbergs* (Enigma Books, 2001), 53.
64. Earlier, Apresyan informed Moscow that he had "already established official contact with [*Map*'s] institution," presumably the American-Russian Institute in San Francisco. San Francisco to Moscow, Apr. 3, 1945, *Venona* decrypts.

65. San Francisco to Moscow, May 4, 1945, *Venona* decrypts. White and the UN: Romerstein and Breindel (2000), 48–49; Weinstein and Vassiliev (1999), 168 fn.

66. The previous summer, when Kheifets was about to return to Moscow, Chevalier had given him a letter of introduction to the daughter of the Mexican ambassador in Moscow. Chevalier to Jane Quintanilla, June 29, 1944, "Correspondence, 1944–45," Chevalier papers.

67. While Bransten defended Moscow resolutely, Chevalier was more critical of communist dogma. San Francisco field report, Jan. 26, 1945, sec. 3, Chevalier file, FBI.

68. It was evidently at this reception that Ernest joined the American-Russian Institute, a step that would later get him into trouble with the FBI, which obtained ARI membership rolls in a black-bag operation. Unidentified agent to Whitson, Oct. 6, 1949, and San Francisco field report, Feb. 20, 1951, Ernest Lawrence file, no. 116–10798, FBI.

69. "Report of Meeting with the President," Apr. 25, 1945, file 24, series 1, part 1, MED/NARA.

70. "Summary Russian Situation," n.d., "Recently Declassified Extracts," MED/NARA. Groves estimated it would take the Russians twenty years or more to produce a bomb. Transcript of telephone conversation, May 21, 1945, file 12, series 1, pt. 1, MED/NARA.

71. Entry, May 28, 1945, Groves diary, Groves/NARA. The Soviets hoped to use the occasion to forge personal links with several U.S. atomic scientists. Moscow to New York, Apr. 3, 1945, *Venona* decrypts; Weinstein and Vassiliev (1999), 209–10.

72. Interim Committee: Martin Sherwin, *A World Destroyed: The Atomic Bomb and the Grand Alliance* (Vintage, 1987), 169–70.

73. Scientific Panel: "Notes of an Informal Meeting," May 9, 1945, file 100, MED/NARA; Hewlett and Anderson (1990), 344–45; Sherwin (1987), 169; May 10, 1945, Groves diary, Groves/NARA.

74. "Memorandum for the Secretary," May 30, 1945, and "Memorandum for Mr. Schott," May 30, 1945, file 100, MED/NARA.

75. "Notes of the Interim Committee Meeting," May 31, 1945, file 100, MED/NARA; James Byrnes, *All in One Lifetime* (Harper, 1958), 283.

76. "He felt that research had to go on unceasingly. . . . He thought it might be possible one day to secure our energy from terrestrial sources rather than from the sun."

77. Oppenheimer suggested that "we might open up this subject with them in a tentative fashion and in the most general terms without giving them any details of our productive effort."

78. The quotation is from Lawrence's subsequent account of the meeting in a letter to a friend, Karl Darrow, a historian of science. Darrow to Lawrence, Aug. 9, 1945, and Lawrence to Darrow, Aug. 17, 1945, folder 20, carton 28, EOL; Compton (1956), 238.

79. Bush and Conant, for example, had raised the possibility of a demonstration—of the bomb or possibly radiological poisons—in a Sept. 30, 1944, memo to Stimson. Sherwin (1975), 286–88. The demonstration was also discussed on at least two occasions at Los Alamos, in meetings of Mar. 1943 and late 1944 that Robert Wilson helped to organize. Oppenheimer spoke against the demonstration at the 1944 meeting, Wilson later recalled. Author interview with Robert Wilson, Los Alamos, N. Mex., Apr. 15, 1983.

80. No notes were taken of this lunchtime discussion, and two conflicting versions exist. Herbert Childs interview with Arthur Compton, n.d., Childs papers.

81. The phrase is from Lawrence's letter to Darrow, Aug. 17, 1945, folder 20, carton 28, EOL.

82. Sherwin (1987), 302.

83. Oppenheimer to Groves, May 7, 1945, "Bomb Design and Testing" folder, Army/NARA.

84. Franck report: Sherwin (1987), 210–15; Alice Kimball Smith, *A Peril and a Hope: The Scientists' Movement in America, 1945–47* (MIT Press, 1971), 371–83.

85. The demonstration had been resurrected as well by Glenn Seaborg, one of the contributors to the Franck report, in a letter that Lawrence received just before leaving for Los Alamos. Seaborg to Lawrence, June 13, 1945, folder 22, carton 30, EOL.

86. Peter Wyden, *Day One: Before Hiroshima and After* (Simon and Schuster, 1984), 170–71. Teller claimed that Fermi asked his opinion on how the bomb should be used about this time, and that his answer was "noncommittal"—not realizing that Fermi was on a panel advising on the weapon's use. "Had I known, I would have said that it should be tested and then shown, but not used." Edward Teller, Feb. 26, 1999, personal communication.

87. Although Compton had commissioned the Franck report, he did not agree with its conclusion about the demonstration. Compton's arguments against the demonstration were in a dissent that he disguised as a cover memo to Stimson's copy of the Franck report. Compton (1956), 238–41; Sherwin (1987), 213.

88. Childs (1968), 363.

89. Robert Serber claimed that Oppenheimer took the demonstration option seriously enough to explore it with high-ranking representatives of the army's air force; but the latter were, Serber later remembered, "adamantly opposed." Author interview with Robert Serber, New York, N.Y., Oct. 26, 1984.

90. "There was not sufficient agreement among the members of the panel to unite upon a statement as to how or under what conditions such use [of the bomb] was to be made," Compton later wrote. Compton (1956), 240; Wyden (1984), 171; Oppenheimer to Secretary of War, June 16, 1945, no. 76, Harrison-Bundy file, MED/NARA.

91. Oppenheimer to Secretary of War, June 16, 1945, no. 76, Harrison-Bundy file MED/NARA. The recommendation on the immediate use of the bomb is reprinted in Sherwin (1987), 304–5.

92. Scientists at Los Alamos later remarked upon Ernest's "obvious distress that weekend though they did not know the cause." Wyden (1984), 170; "Memorandum for the Secretary of War," June 26, 1945, no. 77, Harrison-Bundy file, MED/NARA.

93. In an earlier letter to Maria Mayer, Teller noted that he had asked Harold Urey "to talk with the Boy-scout about postwar plans." It is unclear whether the "Boy-scout" in this case was Lawrence or Groves. Teller to Mayer, n.d., box 3, Mayer papers.

94. Szilard's petition urged that the bomb not be dropped until the surrender terms had been made public in detail and the Japanese, knowing those terms, had still refused to surrender. Lanouette (1992), 269–75.

95. Oppenheimer's report to Stimson on the views of the Scientific Panel noted: "With regard to these general aspects of the use of atomic energy, it is clear that we, as scientific men, have no proprietary rights." The report is reprinted in Sherwin (1987), 304–5.

96. In a 1993 interview, Teller claimed that Oppenheimer had argued that scientists should not take sides for or against the use of the bomb. When he later discovered that the Scientific Panel had done just that, Teller said he felt betrayed. Teller did not mention Oppenheimer's opposition to the petition in his letter to Szilard since he knew that Oppie would see the letter before it was sent. Teller to Oppenheimer, and Teller to Szilard, July 2, 1945, LANL; Edward Teller, Feb. 26, 1999, personal communication. Teller's letter to Szilard is reprinted in Blumberg and Owens (1976), 156–57.

97. Tolman to Lansdale, June 19, 1944, file 400.112, series 5, MED/NARA.

98. May 5 and May 8, 1945, Groves diary, Groves/NARA.

99. York interview (1997).

100. Rhodes (1986), 601.

101. Lyall Johnson interview (1996).

102. Oppenheimer told Groves that the probable date for the test was July 18 and that Fat Man's plutonium core weighed 6.2 kilograms. "Notes Taken at Meeting at Y," June 27, 1945, file 20, MED/NARA.

103. Another two words—*or without*—were placed before "the Continental United States" in the description of where the work of the contract would take place. Underhill interview, n.d., Underhill papers, LANL.

104. Oppenheimer to Lawrence, July 5, 1945, folder 15, carton 29, EOL.

105. Groves (1962), 290; July 13, 1945, Cooksey diary, EOL.

106. Unmarked folder, carton 48, EOL. The talk at dinner was mostly about Lawrence's plans for the postwar Rad Lab. Fidler interview (1992).

107. Lawrence requested an annual postwar budget of $1 million—more than thirty times what the Rad Lab had received from private sources before the war. Lawrence to Groves, July 13, 1945, folder 38, carton 29, EOL.

108. July 11, 1945, Groves diary, Groves/NARA.

109. Teller and Brown (1962), 16–17.

110. "A hundred-to-one it's not needed, but what do we know?," observed Teller, according to Joe Kennedy, who was also standing nearby. Seaborg (1992), vol. 4, 4.

111. Author interview with Willie Higinbotham, Los Alamos, N. Mex., June 9, 1993.

112. "O.E. [sic] Lawrence's thoughts," July 16, 1945, file 4, series 1, part 1, MED/NARA. Eyewitness accounts by McMillan, Serber, Alvarez, and others are in the *Trinity* file, Tolman papers, OSRD/NARA.

113. Serber (1998), 91–93. The intensity of the light was so unexpectedly great that the following day some Los Alamos scientists suggested using it as a weapon. Bradbury et al. to Parsons, "Proposal for a Modified Tactical Use of the Gadget," box 29–9, LANL.

114. Alvarez (1987), 141–42.

115. Frank Oppenheimer interview (1983). Oppie's much more famous formulation from the *Gita*—"Now I am become Death, the Destroyer of Worlds"—evidently came later.

116. Vannevar Bush interview, reel 7, 422, MIT.

8: A Stone's Throw from Despair

1. A passenger on the plane, Admiral John "Chick" Hayward, recalled that there was even talk of recalling the cruiser *Indianapolis*—already on its way to Tinian with the uranium rings for the Hiroshima bomb—and substituting the more powerful and efficient implosion gadget. Interview with John "Chick" Hayward, Jacksonville Beach, Fla., Mar. 6, 1996; telex, Oppenheimer to Groves, July 19, 1945, and Groves to Oppenheimer, July 19, 1945, Oppenheimer folder, LANL.

2. Two days after *Trinity,* Lawrence met with George Harrison at the Pentagon to urge that Groves be promoted. Lawrence to Harrison, July 18, 1945, Harrison-Bundy file, MED/NARA.

3. "Development of Atomic Weapons," Jan. 30, 1950, no. 1447, RG 128, Records of the Joint Committee on Atomic Energy (JCAE), National Archives; *ITMOJRO,* 32.

4. Groves to Secretary of War, July 27, 1945, box 6, MED history, Army/NARA.

5. Telegram, n.d., John Manley papers, folder 3, box 7, LANL.

6. Alvarez (1987), 144–45.

7. Author interview with Luis Alvarez, Los Alamos, N. Mex., Apr. 14, 1983.

8. Teller and Brown (1962), 18.

9. Molly Lawrence interview (1992).

10. Lawrence, "To Radiation Laboratory Employees," Aug. 9, 1945, folder 23, carton 30, EOL; transcript of telephone conversations, Aug. 6, 1945, book 7, box 1, Rad Lab records.

11. Shane, "Autobiography," chap. 7, p. 31, Donald Shane papers, Lick Observatory archives, University of California, Santa Cruz, Calif.

12. Author interview with I. I. Rabi, New Haven, Conn., Sept. 21, 1982.

13. Field report, Apr. 18, 1952, 11, sec. 12, Robert Oppenheimer file, FBI.

14. Oppenheimer to Lawrence, Aug. 30, 1945, folder 30, carton 29, EOL; Childs (1968), 366, 372.

15. Harrison to Oppenheimer, July 20, 1945, Harrison-Bundy file, MED/NARA.

16. Conant was hoping to recruit Oppenheimer to Harvard. Conant to Oppenheimer, Aug. 24, 1945, and Oppenheimer to Conant, Sept. 25, 1945, Conant folder, JRO.

17. Oppenheimer to Lawrence, Aug. 30, 1945, folder 30, carton 29, EOL. The letter is also reprinted in Smith and Weiner (1980), 300–302.

18. Oppenheimer to Stimson, Aug. 17, 1945, reprinted in Smith and Weiner (1980), 293–94.

19. The telegrams exchanged between panel members are in folders 15 and 30, carton 29, EOL.

20. Oppenheimer to Secretary of War, Aug. 17, 1945, no. 77, Harrison-Bundy file, MED/NARA.

21. Oppenheimer to Lawrence, Aug. 30, 1945, folder 30, carton 29, EOL; Hewlett and Anderson (1990), 417.

22. "Memorandum for the Record," Aug. 18, 1945, no. 77, Harrison-Bundy file, MED/NARA.

23. Oppenheimer to Lawrence, Aug. 30, 1945, folder 30, carton 29, EOL.

24. Oppenheimer to Herbert Smith, Aug. 26, 1945, reprinted in Smith and Weiner (1980), 297.

25. Oppenheimer to Chevalier, Aug. 27, 1945, supplemental files, Jon Else, *The Day After Trinity: J. Robert Oppenheimer and the Atomic Bomb* (Voyager CD, 1999).

26. Groves to Chief of Staff, Aug. 23, 1945, "Postwar Bomb Production," MED history, Army/NARA.

27. Early postwar U.S. war plans: Rhodes (1995), 23–24; Gregg Herken, *The Winning Weapon; The Atomic Bomb in the Cold War* (Knopf, 1980), 195–218.

28. Teller to Maria Mayer, n.d. (Aug.–Sept. 1945), box 3, Mayer papers.

29. Teller to Mulliken, Sept. 22, 1945; and Teller to Mayer, Sept. 25, 1945, LANL.

30. Teller (2001), 105; Blumberg and Owens (1976), 13–20; Teller interview (1993).

31. Wheeler to Teller, Aug. 12, 1945, Teller file, LANL.

32. John Wheeler and Kenneth Ford, *Geons, Black Holes and Quantum Foam: A Life in Physics* (Norton, 1998), 190.

33. Blumberg and Owens (1976), 185. Teller's anti-Russian views and his pessimism about the future were also reflected in other correspondence at this time. Teller to Stephen Brunauer, Dec. 29, 1945, Teller file, LANL.

34. Chemist George Kistiakowsky recalled Teller coming to him in late 1944 or early 1945 with a request that he and his division work on the Super. Kistiakowsky said his refusal cooled his subsequent relations with Teller. Carl Sagan interview with George Kistiakowsky, Feb. 1982, 137. My thanks to Steven Soter for a copy of the Sagan interview.

35. Teller wrote to his usual confidante that he was conflicted about whether to stay at the lab or go to Chicago. Teller to Mayer, n.d. (Mar. 1945), box 3, Mayer papers.

36. Lawrence to Lewis Akeley, Aug. 16, 1945, folder 12, carton 1; transcript, "The Atomic Bomb Project," Aug. 17, 1945, folder 27, carton 40, EOL.

37. "The Atomic Bomb Project," Aug. 17, 1945, folder 27, carton 40, EOL.

38. Minutes, Committee on Finance and Business Management (CFBM), Sept. 4, 1945, records of the University of California, Oakland, Calif. (UC).

39. Lawrence to Groves, July 13, 1945, folder 38, carton 29, EOL.

40. Oppenheimer to Deutsch, Aug. 24, 1945, reprinted in Smith and Weiner (1980), 295; telegram, Stewart to Underhill, Aug. 17, 1945, and Nichols to Underhill, Aug. 20, 1945, folder 5, box 5, Underhill papers, LANL.

41. Neylan: Biographical sketch, n.d., John Neylan papers, Bancroft Library. The author would like to thank the president and regents of the University of California for allowing him access to these restricted papers.

42. The previous May, Neylan had vigorously protested Sproul's plan to award an honorary degree to Soviet foreign minister Molotov at Berkeley's 1945 commencement. Neylan to Sproul, May 1, 1945, folder 12, box 157, Neylan papers.

43. Minutes of regents meeting, Aug. 24, 1945, and Underhill to Neylan, Aug. 24, 1945, folder 1, box 171, Neylan papers.

44. Fidler to Washington Liaison Office, Aug. 20, 1945, box 3, AEC/JRO.

45. Ibid.

46. Fidler to Washington Liaison Office, Aug. 11, 1945, box 3, AEC/JRO.

47. Bernstein (1990), 1396.

48. "Report on Soviet Espionage in the United States," Nov. 27, 1945, entry 11, RG 233 (Dies Committee records), National Archives.

49. Hoover to Attorney General, Dec. 4, 1945, and July 11, 1946, sec. 3, Eltenton file, FBI.

50. That October, the NKVD learned about the FBI's electronic surveillance in documents obtained from a source in the Justice Department. The woman who spied on the bureau—Judith Coplon, code-named *Sima*—provided Moscow with a copy of a May 1943 FBI memo concerning phone conversations between Robert Oppenheimer, Chevalier, and Thomas Addis. Following the twin defections of Elizabeth Bentley, a longtime courier in Washington, and Igor Gouzenko, a code clerk at the Soviet embassy in Ottowa that fall, Moscow instructed its control officers in the United States to break off contact with their active agents. Weinstein and Vassiliev (1999), 216, 276, 286.

51. San Francisco to Moscow, Nov. 13, 1945; San Francisco to Moscow, Sept. 13, 1945, *Venona* decrypts.

52. San Francisco to Moscow, Nov. 27, 1945, *Venona* decrypts.

53. John Titus to Groves, Feb. 20, 1946, entry 5, file 132.2, MED/NARA.

54. Lyall Johnson interview (1996); Harold Marsh, Mar. 31, 1997, personal communication.

55. Sept. 13, 1945, Cooksey diary, box 4, folder 23, EOL; Alvarez interview (1983); Alvarez (1987), 155.

56. Linac: Alvarez to Lawrence, Apr. 9, 1945, folder 16, carton 1, EOL; transcripts of telephone conversations, Apr. 14 and May 9, 1945, book 7, box 1, Rad Lab records. The surplus tubes, however, proved unusable for the Linac and remained in the warehouse. Childs (1968), 375; Alvarez (1987), 153–54.

57. McMillan and Synchrotron: Alvarez (1987), 154, 160; McMillan interview, Bancroft Library; McMillan, "Value of the Synchrotron as a Source of High-energy Electrons," Nov. 29, 1945, folder 31, carton 12, EOL; Edward Lofgren, "The Principle of Phase Stability and the Accelerator Program at Berkeley, 1945–1954," 1994, LBL. The phase stability principle was independently discovered at about the same time by Russian physicist V. I. Veksler.

58. Segrè (1993), 208–9.

59. Seaborg (1992), vol. 4, 99, 174.

60. Segrè (1993), 210–11.

61. Transcript of Serber lecture, "War: Tinian and Japan," June 7, 1994, Brookhaven National Laboratory, N. Y.

62. Smith and Weiner (1980), 313.

63. Telegram, F. Oppenheimer to Lawrence, Aug. 18, 1945, folder 5, carton 29, and Lawrence to F. Oppenheimer, Jan. 31, 1945, folder 11, carton 46, EOL.

64. Fidler interview (1992).

65. Transcript of speech, Nov. 27, 1945, unmarked folder, carton 1, Frank Oppenheimer papers; summary report, July 23, 1947, and San Francisco field report, Frank Oppenheimer file, FBI. According to FBI documents, Frank's speeches had been cleared in advance by army censors.

66. *ITMOJRO*, 4. Frank never gave the class; the head of the school, David Jenkins, thought the topic too technical.

67. Frank Oppenheimer to Alvarez, "Magnet Design for Linac," Oct. 9, 1946, "Linear Accelerator—Correspondence" folder, box 1, Alvarez papers, SBFRC.

68. "History of the University of California Radiation Laboratory," undated, box 171, folder 1, Neylan papers.

69. Sproul thought the results "good not great." Notes of telephone conversation, Oct. 3, 1945, memos, Sproul papers; minutes, Jan. 4, 1946, Committee on Finance and Budget Management, University of California archives (CFMB); Lawrence to Loomis, June 15, 1946, folder 8, carton 46, EOL.

70. However, the cross-country recruiting drive that Lawrence and Cooksey began near war's end would mean an overall increase in the research staff.

71. Lofgren interview (1998); Panofsky interview (1993).

72. York (1987), 31; York interview (1997).

73. "Recommended Program for the Radiation Laboratory at Berkeley," Sept. 15, 1945, folder 37, carton 29, EOL.

74. Alvarez planned a machine that would be almost half a mile long and achieve energies five times that of the great cyclotron. "Some accelerator!" Lawrence observed. Alvarez (1987), 156–57; Panofsky interview (1993); Lawrence to Alvarez, Apr. 9, 1945, folder 16, carton 1, EOL.

75. Entry, Sept. 20, 1945, Groves diary, Groves/NARA; Underhill to Sproul, Sept. 26, 1945, Underhill papers, LANL.

76. Underhill to Bradbury, Sept. 26, 1945, Underhill papers, LANL.

77. "Proposed Post-War Program of Dr. E.O. Lawrence," Captain J. A. King to General Groves, Sept. 20, 1945, and Groves to Lawrence, Oct. 15, 1945, series 5, MED/NARA; "Gen. Groves' talk," Oct. 21, 1945, box 171, folder 1, Neylan papers; Oct. 1, 1945, Groves diary, Groves/NARA.

78. In 1944, Lawrence had projected an annual postwar budget of $85,000 for the Rad Lab. Heilbron, Seidel, and Wheaton (1981), 46–47.

79. Molly Lawrence interview (1992).

80. Oppenheimer was more embittered than they knew. Smith and Weiner (1980), 307.

81. Sept. 28, 1945, memos, Sproul papers.

82. Oct. 11, 1945, memos, Sproul papers.

83. Birge, vol. 5, xvii–9.

84. Oct. 16, 1945, memos, Sproul papers.

85. Smith and Weiner (1980), 310–11.

86. Birge, vol. 5, xxii–6.

87. Oct. 26, 1945, memos, Sproul papers.

88. Childs (1968), 375–76. Oppenheimer's request "places the University of California in a very difficult position," Birge wrote, since the physics department could not recruit a replacement for Oppie while he remained on leave. Birge to Sproul, Oct. 29, 1945, folder 42, box 16, Sproul papers.

89. Oppenheimer also met with Charles Kramer, an aide to Senator Harley Kilgore, the sponsor of one of many bills then before Congress for the domestic control of atomic energy. Unknown to Oppie, Kramer was an NKVD informant code-named *Mole,* who subsequently reported to the Soviet *rezident* that Oppenheimer believed technical information on the bomb should be shared "only when there is political cooperation among the countries." Weinstein and Vassiliev (1999), 184–85.

90. Harrison, "Memorandum for the Files," Sept. 25, 1945, no. 77, Harrison-Bundy file, MED/NARA.

91. Truman-Oppenheimer meeting: *ITMOJRO,* 35; Davis (1968), 258; Michelmore (1969), 121–22; David Lilienthal, *The Journals of David E. Lilienthal,* vol. 2, (1964), 118. *The Atomic Energy Years, 1945–1950* (Harper and Row, 1964). It was this visit that inspired Truman's later characterization of Oppenheimer as a "cry-baby scientist." Herken (1980), 401 fn.

92. Groves's diary indicates that the Scientific Panel met in Washington from Sept. 19 to Sept. 22, 1945.

93. Groves to Harrison, Aug. 29, 1945, series 1, pt. 2, file 3, MED/NARA.

94. "Proposals for Research and Development in the Field of Atomic Energy," box 20, tabs 1 and 2, MED/NARA.

95. Asked in 1954 "at what time did your strong moral convictions develop with respect to the hydrogen bomb?" Oppenheimer answered: "When it became clear to me that we would tend to use any weapon we had." *ITMOJRO,* 250.

96. Harrison to Karl Compton, Oct. 8, 1945, no. 69, Harrison-Bundy file, MED/NARA.

97. Compton to Wallace, series 5, file 312.1, box 48, Harrison-Bundy file, MED/NARA. Compton evidently drafted his letter after the panel's meeting in Washington but

was careful to confirm that he had the others' assent. From New York, Lawrence wrote Compton on October 8: "It is a fine statement and, as you already know, I am in complete agreement." "Memorandum to the panel," n.d., folder 15, carton 29, EOL; Bernstein (1990), 1396. The author thanks Barton Bernstein for a copy of Lawrence's letter to Compton.

98. In a footnote, Compton indicated that the paragraph containing the panel's emphatic recommendation against the Super was particularly sensitive.

99. Wallace had irritated Acheson at the meeting by telling, at length, a story about his visit years earlier to a Mongolian animal disease laboratory. Dean Acheson, *Present at the Creation: My Years in the State Department* (Norton, 1969), 124–25.

100. "Plea to Give Soviet Atom Secret Stirs Debate in Cabinet; Wallace Plan to Share Bomb Data as Peace Insurance," *New York Times,* Sept. 22, 1945; Herken (1980), 31–32.

101. A month later, Wallace would launch his own ill-fated secret diplomatic initiative on the bomb—one that resembled Stimson's plan—in a meeting with the new NKVD *rezident* in Washington, Anatoly Gorski. Weinstein and Vassiliev (1999), 284.

102. Wallace letter: Wallace to Truman, Sept. 24, 1945, Henry Wallace papers, University of Iowa, Iowa City; John Morton Blum, ed., *The Price of Vision: The Diary of Henry A. Wallace* (Little, Brown, 1973), 485.

103. Patterson to Bush, Nov. 12, 1945, and Patterson to Oppenheimer, Dec. 4, 1945, no. 69, Harrison-Bundy file, MED/NARA. Compton's letter would later figure into the AEC's investigation of Oppenheimer. *ITMOJRO,* 70.

104. Hawkins (1983), 305; Blumberg and Owens (1976), 185; Bethe interview (1988).

105. Badash et al. (1985), 162; Bradbury to Stewart, Nov. 14, 1945, Underhill papers, LANL.

106. J. A. Derry to Groves, Dec. 14, 1945, series 5, file 600.12, MED/NARA.

107. Teller to Mulliken, Sept. 22, 1945, Teller file, LANL.

108. "Catalogue of Los Alamos University Courses and Student Enrollment," Sept. 17, 1945, reprinted in Edith Truslow and Ralph Carlisle Smith, *Project Y: The Los Alamos Story,* vol. 2, *Beyond Trinity* (Tomash, 1983), 377.

109. Weinstein and Vassiliev (1999), 215–16.

110. Smith (1971), 115.

111. Ibid., 288; Teller to Mayer, n.d. (fall 1945), box 3, Mayer papers.

112. "I neither can nor will do so" was Oppenheimer's response, according to Teller. Teller and Brown (1962), 23.

113. Smith and Weiner (1980), 320; "A Speech Given by J. R. Oppenheimer at a Meeting of the Association of Los Alamos Scientists," Nov. 2, 1945, no. 125509, CIC/DOE.

114. "Notes on Talk Given by Comdr. N. E. Bradbury at Coordinating Council," Oct. 1, 1945, CIC/DOE.

115. Teller and Brown (1962), 22.

116. Bradbury to Division and Group Leaders, Nov. 14, 1945, no. 120953, CIC/DOE; Hawkins (1983), 307; Teller and Brown (1962), 22–23. "I was very much tempted to take [Bethe's job]. At last it would have meant some activity." Teller to Mayer, n.d. (Aug.–Sept. 1945), box 3, Mayer papers.

117. Bradbury to Groves, Oct. 30, 1945, series 5, file 400.112, MED/NARA.

118. "Partly it is just sad to see the place disintegrating and partly I am sorry for all the things I could have done and did not do." Teller to Mayer, n.d. (late 1945), box 3, Mayer papers.

119. Los Alamos reports and patent: "Policy and Progress in the H-bomb Program" (H-bomb Chronology), Jan. 1, 1953, no. DLXXXIV, 11, JCAE.

120. Teller to Ball, Dec. 29, 1945, and Teller to McMahon, Jan. 28, 1946, Teller file, LANL.

121. Fermi to Patterson, Nov. 3, 1945, no. 76, Harrison-Bundy file, MED/NARA.

122. Teller to Fermi, Oct. 31, 1945, no. 76, Harrison-Bundy file, MED/NARA. Oppenheimer later testified that Bethe and Teller had boasted to him in fall 1943, regard-

ing the Super: "If we had the material now, we could have a bomb in 3 weeks." *ITMOJRO,* 84.

123. "By now even [Oppenheimer] is pessimistic about the political situation," Teller wrote. Teller to Mayer, n.d. (late 1945), box 3, Mayer papers.

124. Having gone to the first postwar meeting of foreign ministers in London that fall with "the bomb in his pocket," Byrnes returned convinced that the atomic monopoly had been more a liability than an asset to American diplomacy there. Herken (1980), 43–91.

125. The outcry began anew six weeks later, when army occupation troops in Japan, following an order attributed to Groves, destroyed five cyclotrons at research institutes in Toyko, Osaka, and Kyoto. Groves (1962), 367–72.

126. Telegram, Groves to Bradbury, Sept. 27, 1945, Bradbury folder, JRO. The text of Groves's speech is in the *New York Times,* Sept. 22, 1945.

127. Manley to Groves, Sept. 26, 1945, Groves folder, box 36, JRO.

128. Groves wrote Bradbury. Groves to Bradbury, Sept. 28, 1945, Groves folder, JRO.

129. May-Johnson bill: Hewlett and Anderson (1990), 431–48; Smith (1971), 128–73; Herken (1980), 116–25.

130. Groves to Patterson; Patterson to Byrnes, Nov. 23, 1945, series 1, pt. 1, file 13, MED/NARA.

131. Smith (1971), 150–59.

132. Frank Oppenheimer to Editor, *New York Review of Books,* Jan. 28, 1969, unmarked folder, box 1, Frank Oppenheimer papers. As a result of Frank's refusal to publicly criticize the May-Johnson bill, the Communist Party rescinded an invitation to lecture on nuclear policy.

133. Harrison to file, Oct. 17, 1945, no. 98, Harrison-Bundy file, MED/NARA; Smith (1971), 142–48.

134. Hewlett and Anderson (1990), 432. The following day, Lawrence telegraphed Patterson, notifying him: "I do not favor certain provisions relating to control and security." Lawrence to Patterson, Oct. 12, 1945, folder 31, carton 30, EOL.

135. Lawrence sent Neylan copies of all three bills then before Congress with the request: "I would be very grateful if you would have a look at them and give me the benefit of your thoughts." Lawrence to Neylan, Feb. 5, 1946, folder 1, box 171, Neylan papers.

136. Serber interview (1992); Smith (1971), 311. Lawrence also politely declined a personal appeal from the sponsor of a rival bill, Senator Brien McMahon, that he testify before Congress. Lawrence to Neylan, Feb. 5, 1946, and Lawrence to McMahon, Feb. 13, 1946, folder 1, box 171, Neylan papers.

9: A World in Which War Will Not Occur

1. "Biography," n.d., Brien McMahon papers, Special Collections, Georgetown University Library, Washington, D.C.

2. McMahon bill: Hewlett and Anderson (1990), 454–55.

3. Weinstein and Vassiliev (1999), 104–5. Groves may have been the source of the leak to a Washington columnist, who reported that the Russians were after atomic secrets. Herken (1980), 130–33.

4. Higinbotham interview (1993); Hewlett and Anderson (1990), 485; Strickland (1968), 89.

5. Bernstein (1990), 1397; summary report, Apr. 16, 1954, JRO/FBI.

6. An FBI informant was in the audience when Oppie admonished ALAS members not to become involved in politics.

7. *ITMOJRO,* 10–11; summary report, Apr. 22, 1947, 136, COMRAP file, FBI.

8. "I expressed my opinion that Chevalier will never be a great scholar, and it would be better if he went somewhere else," Sproul wrote in his office diary. Chevalier's novel, published in 1949, was panned by critics and made little money for the now-struggling writer. Oct. 1, 1945, memos, Sproul papers.

9. "Re: Communist Infiltration of the Radiation Laboratory, University of California, Berkeley, California," Mar. 5, 1946, CINRAD file, FBI.

10. Ladd to Tamm, June 17, 1946, sec. 30, Eltenton file, FBI.

11. Ladd noted that a "confidential informant"—almost certainly Lansdale—had already told the bureau about Groves's December 1943 meeting with Oppenheimer. Ladd to Tamm, June 17, 1946; Ladd to Hoover, July 10, 1946; Hoover to Attorney General, July 19, 1946, sec. 3, Eltenton file, FBI.

12. Hoover to Groves, June 13, 1946; Groves to Hoover, June 21, 1946, box 99, series 8, MED/NARA.

13. Strickland to Ladd, Aug. 13, 1946, sec. 3, Eltenton file, FBI.

14. San Francisco field report, Mar. 27, 1947, sec. 4, Chevalier file, and June 28, 1946, sec. 3, Eltenton file, FBI; Chevalier (1965), 61–68.

15. San Francisco field report, July 3, 1946, sec. 3, Eltenton file, FBI.

16. Chevalier (1965), 69–70.

17. As Whitson pointed out, "Chevalier has been in contact with Oppenheimer since immediately after Chevalier interview." Strickland to Ladd, Aug. 13, 1946, and San Francisco field report, Sept. 18, 1946, sec. 3, Eltenton file, FBI.

18. Like Chevalier and Eltenton, Oppenheimer and Weinberg were interviewed separately but on the same day. San Francisco field report, Sept. 18, 1946, box 1, JRO/AEC.

19. Summary report, Apr. 18, 1952, JRO/FBI; Rhodes (1995), 309.

20. San Francisco field report, Aug. 19, 1949, Weinberg file, FBI.

21. The bureau was informed of the Justice Department's decision on November 19, 1946. San Francisco field report, Mar. 27, 1947, sec. 4, Chevalier file, FBI; Bernstein (1990), 1397.

22. Hoover to Lilienthal, Mar. 8, 1947, 11, JRO/FBI. Tamm reminded Hoover that the evidence on the Chevalier incident was "presented to the [Justice] Department and prosecution was declined." Hoover evidently wrote to Clark again about the case shortly thereafter. Schrecker (1998), 235.

23. Secretary of State's Committee: Hewlett and Anderson (1990), 531–32; Herken (1980), 97–98.

24. Herken (1980), 35–39.

25. Lilienthal (1964), 13.

26. Ibid., 17.

27. Board of Consultants: Daniel Lang, "Seven Men on a Problem," *New Yorker*, Aug. 17, 1946, 49–60.

28. *ITMOJRO*, 37–38.

29. Rabi interview (1982).

30. Baffled by Oppenheimer's explanation of denaturing at a Joint Committee briefing, the congressmen expressed regret that there was not a simpler way to safeguard the peace.

31. Rabi interview (1982).

32. Oppenheimer to Freeman Dyson, Oct. 9, 1960, Fermi folder, box 31, JRO.

33. Rabi interview (1982). Denaturing was perhaps the weakest element of the plan—as Oppie himself would later acknowledge. Oppenheimer et al., "Notes on Denaturing," n.d., file 319.1, series 5, MED/NARA.

34. Lilienthal (1964), 29.

35. Groves (1962), 411.

36. Lilienthal (1964), 27; Hewlett and Anderson (1990), 540–51.

37. Hewlett and Anderson (1990), 549–51.

38. Ibid., 551–54; Lilienthal (1964), 29–30.

39. Transcript of interview for "The Day after Trinity," box 3, Frank Oppenheimer papers.

40. Teller (2001), 234; "HB" to Borden, Apr. 29, 1950, no. 1497, JCAE.

41. Smith (1971), 335.

42. James Chace, *Acheson: The Secretary of State Who Created the American World* (Simon and Schuster, 1998), 125.

43. Lilienthal (1964), 30.

44. Higinbotham interview (1993).

45. Groves (1962), 412; Acheson (1969), 154.

46. Lilienthal (1964), 43.

47. Baruch plan: Herken (1980), 158–65.

48. Herken (1980), 166.

49. Groves to Secretary of War, Mar. 27, 1946, file 10, series 1, pt. 1, MED/NARA.

50. Baruch told Bush why he had decided to drop the scientists: "because as I told them, I knew all I wanted to know. It went boom and it killed millions of people." Herken (1980), 161, 168.

51. *ITMOJRO*, 40; Acheson (1969), 155.

52. Herken (1980), 162.

53. Truman and Byrnes yielded when Baruch threatened to quit unless his revisions of the Acheson-Lilienthal report were approved.

54. Hewlett and Anderson (1990), 576–77.

55. Oppenheimer's prediction of what would happen if the UN negotiations failed would later seem prophetic, but Lilienthal attributed his friend's pessimism to "nerves." Lilienthal (1964), 70.

56. Alfred Loomis reinforced Neylan's message. Childs (1968), 379.

57. Ibid., 378.

58. Ibid., 374. "He says that these will mean considerable income to him, and that, moreover, he is practically being ordered by his present federal superiors to accept," Sproul wrote in his office diary. Oct. 1, 1945, memos, Sproul papers.

59. York (1987), 37.

60. Lawrence to Neylan, Aug. 13, 1946, folder 85, box 155, Neylan papers.

61. Childs (1968), 379.

62. "Program for the Radiation Laboratory," Apr. 1, 1946, administrative files, box 1, LBL; Lawrence to Groves, Feb. 15, 1946, file 600.12, series 5, MED/NARA.

63. Nichols to Groves, Jan. 22, 1946, file 334, series 5, MED/NARA.

64. "Meeting of the Advisory Committee on Research and Development," Mar. 8–9, 1946, file 334, series 5, MED/NARA.

65. Hewlett and Anderson (1990), 633–35.

66. Cooksey to Loomis, Apr. 23, 1946, folder 8, carton 46, EOL.

67. Nichols to Groves, Mar. 14, 1946, file 600.12, series 5, MED/NARA.

68. Teletype, Bradbury to Douglas, Jan. 11, 1946, and Nichols to Regents, Jan. 14, 1946, Underhill papers, LANL.

69. Mar. 12, 1946, memos, Sproul papers.

70. Nichols to Underhill, Apr. 3, 1946, and Underhill to Regents, "Re: New Mexico Project," Sept. 18, 1946, Underhill papers, LANL.

71. "I want to keep Lawrence as close to atomic energy as I can," Sproul told the regents. Minutes of the Finance Committee, Sept. 27, 1946, Underhill papers, LANL.

72. Military Liaison Committee and Joint Committee: Hewlett and Anderson (1990), 434–35, 504–13.

73. Ironically, McMahon was no longer the committee's leader. Iowa senator Bourke Hickenlooper became chairman of the Joint Committee on Atomic Energy when the Republicans captured control of Congress in the 1946 election.

74. Strauss met Lawrence in fall 1939, when Ernest was looking to fund the 184-inch. Strauss had known Teller since 1938, when Edward spoke at Temple Emanu-El in New York, where Strauss was president of the congregation. Virginia Walker to Teller, May 5, 1959, Teller folder, Lewis Strauss papers, Herbert Hoover Presidential Library, West Branch, Iowa (LLS/HHPL); Lawrence to Strauss, Apr. 4, 1940, folder 52, carton 16, EOL; Richard Pfau (1984), *No Sacrifice Too Great: The Life of Lewis L. Strauss* (University of Virginia Press, 1984), 55.

75. Strauss insisted that his name be pronounced "Straws." His inflexible self-righteousness more than once cost Strauss friends and delayed his promotion in the navy. Pfau (1984), 49, 75.

76. San Francisco field report, Oct. 24, 1946, sec. 3, JRO/FBI.

77. Hewlett and Anderson (1990), 640; Lewis Strauss, *Men and Decisions* (Doubleday, 1962), 213.

78. Lilienthal (1964), 95; Hewlett and Anderson (1990), 621.

79. Lilienthal (1964), 107.

80. Ibid., 109; Hewlett and Anderson (1990), 642.

81. In late spring or early summer 1946, Groves ordered the Military Intelligence Division's files consolidated at Oak Ridge and shipped to the FBI in Washington. However, these evidently did not include his own "investigation files," on Oppenheimer and others. Rhodes to Groves, Jan. 16, 1947, file 313.3, entry 5, MED/NARA; and Fred Rhodes interview (1998). As late as 1948, the army's wartime investigative files had to be "borrowed" from the FBI by the AEC. Gingrich to Lilienthal, Nov. 9, 1948, series 1, "Div. of Security" file, AEC/NARA.

82. Groves later passed these files along to his successor at AFSWP, Kenneth Nichols, when he stepped down in 1948. J. Dossett to Colonel Lampert, Oct. 7, 1948, and Groves to Nichols, Feb. 29, 1948, MED investigative files, Defense Nuclear Agency records, RG 374, Army Corps of Engineers archive, Ft. Belvoir, Va.

83. GAC: Hewlett and Anderson (1990), 648; Richard Hewlett and Francis Duncan, *Atomic Shield: A History of the United States Atomic Energy Commission,* vol. 2, 1947–1952 (University of California Press, 1990), 15–17.

84. McMahon later claimed that "when the Commission took over, there were exactly two bombs in the locker." The size of the U.S. nuclear arsenal had also been a shock to Lilienthal: "Actually, we had one [bomb] that was probably operable when I first went off to Los Alamos; one that had a good chance of being operable." Borden to files, July 5, 1951, no. 2365, JCAE; Herken (1980), 196–97. Early U.S. atomic arsenal: Rhodes (1995), 282–83; David Alan Rosenberg, "U.S. Nuclear Stockpile, 1945 to 1950," *Bulletin of the Atomic Scientists,* May 1982, 25–30.

85. Bacher had just returned from personally inventorying the atomic stockpile at Kirtland Air Force Base. Transcript of Bacher interview, n.d., 108, Robert Bacher papers, Caltech archives, Pasadena, Calif.; "Draft Minutes of the General Advisory Committee," Feb. 2–3, 1947, no. 79441, CIC/DOE.

86. McCormack to Wilson, Apr. 16, 1947, Radiological Warfare folder, box 1223, AEC/NARA.

87. Oppenheimer's comments were widely reported in the press. *Chicago Tribune,* Dec. 6, 1945.

88. Oppenheimer to Truman, May 3, 1946, box 73, JRO. *Crossroads:* Jonathan Weisgall, *Operation Crossroads: The Atomic Tests at Bikini Atoll* (Naval Institute Press, 1994).

89. The project was finally canceled by President Kennedy in 1961. Nuclear-powered bomber: Hewlett and Duncan (1990), 106–7.

90. "The H-bomb Chronology," 17, no. DLXXXIV, JCAE; minutes, GAC no. 2, Feb. 2–3, 1947, no. 79441, CIC/DOE; and Oppenheimer to Lilienthal, Apr. 3, 1947, GAC no. 3, LANL.

91. Bethe to Frankel and Richtmyer, Apr. 5, 1946, folder 11, box 11, Hans Bethe papers, Special Collections, Cornell University archives, Ithaca, N.Y.

92. A Joint Committee memo noted that Fermi's H-bomb lectures occurred shortly after the *Trinity* test and "were attended by almost everyone in the laboratory." Walker to file, Jan. 13, 1953, no. 3344, JCAE. Fuchs–von Neumann patent: Anderson to Borden, June 30, 1952, no. 2910, JCAE. The secret patent—S-5292X, "Improvements in Methods and Means for Utilizing Nuclear Energy"—was signed by Fuchs on June 5, 1946, just nine days before he returned to England. Four years later, interviewed in prison by FBI agent Robert Lamphere, Fuchs was asked whether he or von Neumann had suggested using implosion to ignite the Super: "[Fuchs] stated laughingly that this was his, Fuchs', suggestion, and that he did not furnish information concerning the ignition of the super bomb by the implosion process." Lamphere to Hoover, June 6, 1950, serial 1412, Klaus Fuchs file, no. 65–58805, FBI. The author would like to thank Joe Albright and Marcia Kunstel for a copy of the document that Fuchs gave to the Russians, and Jennifer DeCapua for locating the Lamphere interview in FBI files.

93. Rhodes (1995), 254; Chuck Hansen, "The Apr. 1946 Super Conference" (unpublished manuscript, 2001). My thanks to Chuck Hansen for a copy of his unpublished chapter on the superbomb meeting.

94. Ironically, Teller himself admitted in a 1993 interview that he was the one responsible for initially discouraging the idea of compressing the thermonuclear fuel. Teller interview (1993).

95. Morrison to Serber, Mar. 26, 1946, correspondence, Bethe papers.

96. Carson Mark, "A Short Account of Los Alamos Theoretical Work on Thermonuclear Weapons, 1946–1950," LA-5647-MS, (LANL, 1974); Rhodes (1995), 254.

97. "We agreed on a text." Serber interview (1992).

98. Fuchs did not leave Los Alamos, however, until after he had read Teller's report on the superbomb conference. Rhodes (1995), 259.

99. "Edward went back to the original report. He just forgot about all the changes we had agreed on." Serber interview (1992); Serber (1998), 150–51.

100. The April conference also revived interest in whether a fusion bomb might ignite Earth's atmosphere. Teller left the calculations up to his colleague Emil Konopinski. Their joint report concluded that "no self-propagating chain of nuclear reactions is likely to be started." The same phenomenon that stood in the way of realizing the Super—the loss of heat through radiation—likewise protected the planet from accidental incineration by overreaching scientists. E. J. Konopinski, C. Marvin, and E. Teller, "Ignition of the Atmosphere with Nuclear Bombs," LA-602 (LANL, 1946).

101. Alarm Clock: Rhodes (1995), 305–6; Mark (1974), 3–5; Hansen (1988), 45–46. Teller noted that the Alarm Clock was born on the same day as his daughter Wendy: Aug. 31, 1946. Walker to file, Jan. 13, 1953, JCAE.

102. Rhodes (1995), 307; Mark (1974), 5.

103. Teller, "Proposed Outline of Laboratory Program," Oct. 1, 1946, no. 125647, CIC/DOE.

104. Bradbury to AEC, Nov. 14, 1946, no. 125518, CIC/DOE.

105. Bradbury to Nichols, Nov. 16, 1946, no. 71787, CIC/DOE.

106. Teller to Mayer, n.d. [fall 1946], box 3, Mayer papers.

107. *ITMOJRO,* 35. Oppenheimer spent part of the third week of each month teaching at Caltech. Oppenheimer to Dubridge, Sept. 3, 1946, box 111.3, DuBridge papers, Caltech.

108. Childs (1968), 376.

109. Birge, vol. 5, xvii–11.

110. Oppie had described the institute as a "madhouse"—"its luminaries shining in separate and helpless isolation"—in a 1935 letter to Frank. Smith and Weiner (1980), 327; Childs (1968), 393; Rhodes (1995), 308.

111. San Francisco field report, May 9, 1947, JRO/FBI.

112. Birge, vol. 5, xvii–11.

113. Public announcement of the feat was followed in midmonth by a private reunion of those who had endorsed Lawrence's original appeal to the Rockefeller Foundation. As before, Loomis picked up the bill.

114. Between January and Apr. 1947, the Rad Lab budget for the coming year had increased by almost $1 million, to $8.85 million. An earlier version had been pegged at $10 million, but Oppenheimer urged restraint. Priestly to Lawrence, Dec. 9, 1946, folder 37, carton 21, EOL; and Peterson to Williams, Apr. 3, 1947, file 121.4, Central Correspondence series, AEC/NARA.

115. Ernest's encounter with the AEC caused him to miss Groves. Kelly to Lawrence, Mar. 10, 1947, Contract 48 files, SBFRC.

116. "The University of California Case Study," *Report of the Advisory Committee on Human Radiation Experiments,* supplemental vol. 2, *Sources and Documentation* (U.S. Government Printing Office, 1995), 600–630.

117. Fisk postponed a decision on support for the Rad Lab, pending determination of the "extent to which the University of California will continue its functions as somewhat of a national laboratory."

118. Peterson to Fields, Jan. 20, 1947, file 121.4, Central Correspondence series, AEC/NARA.

119. Hewlett and Duncan (1990), 98.

120. Army-university negotiations: Underhill to Nichols, Sept. 20, 1946, series 5, MED/NARA; Underhill to Bradbury, June 24, 1947, Underhill papers, LANL.

121. Originally, the meeting was to have been held at Berkeley. But more pressing concerns—including the still-uncertain status of Los Alamos, and bottlenecks in the production of atomic bombs—forced a postponement.

122. Lilienthal confirmation: Hewlett and Duncan (1990), 48–53.

123. Lilienthal (1964), 234.

124. Lawrence to AEC commissioners et al., June 19, 1947, folder 28, carton 30, EOL.

125. The first night at the Grove was spent developing "a mutual understanding of each other's problems," Cooksey wrote. Cooksey to Loomis, Aug. 25, 1947, folder 28, carton 30, EOL.

126. Bohemian Grove meeting: Hewlett and Duncan (1990), 108–9. My thanks to Richard Rhodes for a copy of the AEC's unofficial minutes of the meeting.

127. "We've given our notice and that's that. It stands," Neylan claimed he told Strauss. Notes of interview with Neylan, May 6, 1960, box 2, Childs papers.

128. Childs interview with Neylan, box 2, Childs papers.

129. Underhill to file, Sept. 10, 1947, Underhill papers, LANL.

130. Transcript of interview with Arthur Hudgins, n.d., LLNL.

131. Cooksey to Loomis, Aug. 25, 1947, folder 28, carton 30, EOL.

10: Character, Association, and Loyalty

1. Cooksey to Strauss, and Cooksey to Loomis, Aug. 25, 1947, folder 28, carton 30, EOL.

2. Joseph Volpe, Aug. 31, 1998, personal communication; Stern, (1969), 105; "Re: Dr. J. Robert Oppenheimer," Apr. 16, 1954, Robert Oppenheimer file, FBI.

3. Groves to Lilienthal, Nov. 14, 1946; Lilienthal to Groves, Dec. 4, 1946; Groves to Lilienthal, Dec. 19, 1946; Rolander to Ford, Sept. 2, 1948, box 2, JRO/AEC; Groves (1962), 397.

4. Bernstein (1990), 1398.

5. Washington, D.C., field report, Apr. 7, 1947, Robert Oppenheimer FBI file, box 2, JRO/AEC.

6. San Francisco field report, Apr. 5, 1947, and Riley to files, July 17, 1947, Robert Oppenheimer FBI file, box 2, JRO/AEC.

7. Hoover to Vaughan, Feb. 28, 1947, president's secretary's files, Harry Truman papers, Truman Library, Independence, Mo. Hoover had first sent Robert Oppenheimer's file to Vaughan in November 1945 and forwarded Frank's file a few months later. Bernstein (1990), 1396; Hoover to attorney general, Mar. 18, 1946, box 3, JRO/AEC.

8. Stern (1969), 101; Lilienthal (1964), 157.

9. Hoover to Lilienthal, Mar. 8, 1947, and Rolander to Mitchell, Feb. 18, 1954, box 2, JRO/AEC.

10. Both files are in box 2, JRO/AEC; Lilienthal (1964), 157. Neither report made any mention of Chevalier approaching Frank for information to pass to the Soviets.

11. Wilson to file, Mar. 11, 1947, box 2, JRO/AEC; Conant to Lilienthal, Mar. 29, 1947, file 1193/4/2, general administrative files, MED/NARA.

12. Davis (1993), 273; Lansdale to Davis, Oct. 18, 1968, box 5, Groves/NARA. My thanks to Stan Norris for a copy of Lansdale's letter.

13. Groves to Lilienthal, Mar. 24, 1947, box 3, JRO/AEC. Patterson wrote that he

had "confidence in [Oppenheimer's] character and loyalty to the United States." *ITMO-JRO,* 375–77.

14. Author interview with Joseph Volpe, Washington, D.C., May 30, 1996. In other cases, Strauss showed himself to be the AEC commissioner most concerned with security. Hewlett and Duncan (1990), 101.

15. Stern (1969), 104.

16. One bureau informant turned out to be a twelve-year-old boy. Los Angeles field report, Apr. 4, 1947, Robert Oppenheimer FBI file, box 2, JRO/AEC.

17. Relations between Lilienthal and Hickenlooper had been strained from the start. In one of his first acts as JCAE chairman, the senator had asked the commission for both Robert and Frank Oppenheimer's files; Lilienthal refused.

18. Lilienthal objected to the fact that the bureau refused to identify the source of the allegations contained in its reports. Volpe interview (1996).

19. Wilson to file, Mar. 12, 1947, box 3, JRO/AEC; *ITMOJRO,* 379. Starting in Apr. 1948, the AEC provided its personnel security files to the Joint Committee. Lilienthal to Clark, June 19, 1949, Justice Department file, series 11, AEC/NARA.

20. Menke to file, Mar. 12, 1947, and Menke, "Analysis of Report on J. Robert Oppenheimer," Mar. 14, 1947, box 2, JRO/AEC.

21. T. O. Jones to file, Mar. 27, 1947, file 1143/4/2, general administrative files, MED/NARA.

22. Davis (1993), 275.

23. Hoover to Lilienthal, Apr. 12, 1947, box 3, JRO/AEC; Rhodes to Hickenlooper, July 18, 1947, no. 201, JCAE; Riley to file, July 17, 1947, box 3, JRO/AEC.

24. Jones to Belsley, July 18, 1947, box 3, JRO/AEC.

25. Jones to file, July 14, 1947, box 2, JRO/AEC.

26. Jones to Uanna, Aug. 11, 1947; and Uanna to AEC, Aug. 14, 1947, box 2, JRO/AEC.

27. Hoover sent Attorney General Clark the results of the 1947 investigation of Oppenheimer on Aug. 25, 1948. "Re: Dr. J. Robert Oppenheimer," Apr. 16, 1954, Robert Oppenheimer file, FBI.

28. The disillusionment may have been mutual. The ICCASP had withdrawn an invitation to Oppenheimer to speak on its behalf because of Oppie's support of the May-Johnson bill.

29. That February, in a speech at the University of Denver, Oppenheimer described Soviet communism as "deeply abhorrent." The following month, a speech that Oppenheimer wrote in response to the Russians' latest attack on the Baruch plan reportedly had to be toned down before it could be delivered by the U.S. representative to the UN. Stern (1969), 100; New York field report, Apr. 7, 1947, Robert Oppenheimer FBI file, box 2, JRO/AEC. Fermi's comment is in a Chicago FBI field report of Apr. 3, 1947, in the same folder.

30. *ITMOJRO,* 41, 344.

31. Branigan to Hoover with memo, Jan. 31, 1947, CINRAD file, FBI.

32. Glavin to Tolson, Sept. 29, 1948, HUAC file, no. 54, FBI.

33. The FBI noted that no prosecution "was instituted in regard to Nelson or Weinberg, apparently because the only information obtained indicating their espionage activities was obtained from a combination microphone-technical surveillance on the residence of Steve Nelson." HUAC file, 54, FBI.

34. Lawrence to Buchta, Oct. 16, 1946, folder 11, carton 46, EOL.

35. Field report, Mar. 15, 1947, Frank Oppenheimer file, FBI.

36. Bureau agents were asking Buchta about Frank even before he got to campus. "They went there just to make him leary [sic] of me before I arrived," Frank wrote. "The Tail that Wags the Dog," unpublished manuscript, unmarked folder, Frank Oppenheimer papers.

37. Lilienthal suspected that Groves was behind these and other recent leaks. Lilienthal (1964), 224; Stern (1969), 109.

38. "U.S. Atom Scientist's Brother Exposed as Communist Who Worked on A-Bomb," *Washington Times-Herald,* July 12, 1947.

39. "Oppenheimer Hits Red Tag," *Oakland Tribune,* July 13, 1947; F. Oppenheimer to Dean T. R. McDonnell, materials re HUAC, 1945–50, box 4, Frank Oppenheimer papers.

40. Higinbotham to F. Oppenheimer, July 14, 1947, materials re HUAC, 1945–50, Box 4, Frank Oppenheimer papers.

41. June 9, 1947, and Oct. 21, 1947, memos, Sproul papers; Birge, vol. 5, xix–20.

42. Lawrence to Oppenheimer, Oct. 21, 1947, box 45, JRO.

43. Alvarez (1987), 158.

44. Bevatron: Robert Seidel, "Accelerators and National Security: The Evolution of Science Policy for High-Energy Physics, 1947–1967," *History and Technology* 2 (1994), 394–95.

45. Fisk to Lawrence, Dec. 1, 1947, folder 25, carton 32, EOL.

46. Hewlett and Duncan (1990), 117.

47. Underhill to Sproul, Dec. 15, 1947, Underhill papers, LANL; Dec. 31, 1947, memos, Sproul papers. Brookhaven-Berkeley rivalry: Robert Seidel, "Accelerating Science: The Postwar Transformation of the Lawrence Berkeley Laboratory," *Historical Studies in the Physical and Biological Sciences,* 14, no. 2 (1983), 394.

48. Dec. 31, 1947, memos, Sproul papers; Underhill to Sproul, Dec. 29, 1947, and Dec. 31, 1947, Underhill papers, LANL.

49. Jan. 9, 1948, memos, Sproul papers.

50. Sproul to Wilson, Jan. 24, 1948, Underhill papers, LANL.

51. Bradbury's induction into the University of California faculty took place in Sproul's office. Feb. 26, 1948, memos, Sproul papers.

52. Minutes, CFBM, Feb. 24, 1948, UC; Underhill to Bradbury, Mar. 11, 1948, Underhill papers, LANL.

53. Bevatron: Hewlett and Duncan (1990), 249–51; Seidel (1983), 394–97.

54. Minutes, Apr. 23–25, 1948, GAC no. 9, CIC/DOE; Seidel (1983), 394.

55. Cooksey to Loomis, Mar. 24, 1948, folder 10, carton 46, EOL.

56. Childs (1968), 401.

57. Report, May 9–26, 1947, no. 356, JCAE.

58. Hickenlooper to Lawrence, Feb. 21, 1948, and Lawrence to Hickenlooper, Feb. 25, 1948, folder 26, carton 32, EOL.

59. Lilienthal (1964), 332.

60. Minutes, Apr. 27, 1948, folder 6, box 172, Neylan papers; Apr. 27, 1948, memos, Sproul papers.

61. Alvarez was an alternate on the panel. Interest in RW: Hamilton to Nichols, "Radioactive Warfare," Dec. 31, 1946, folder 19, carton 32, EOL.

62. A few weeks earlier, Lawrence had presented his ideas to the service secretaries at the Pentagon and Secretary of Defense James Forrestal. Walter Millis, ed., *The Forrestal Diaries* (Putnam, 1952), 399.

63. David Lilienthal, *The Journals of David E. Lilienthal,* vol. 4, *The Road to Change, 1955–1959* (Harper and Row, 1969), 205; Lilienthal (1964), 349.

64. Lilienthal (1964), 349.

65. Minutes, Feb. 6–8, 1948, GAC no. 8, CIC/DOE; Hershberg (1993), 333.

66. Hershberg, 356.

67. Entries for Sept. 8–10, 1947, Lawrence day books, carton 11, EOL.

68. "Meeting Notes on Radiological Warfare Conferences," June 26, 1948, no. 70749, CIC/DOE.

69. *ITMOJRO,* 805.

70. Teller to Mayer, n.d. [fall 1946], folder 5, box 3, Mayer papers.

71. LA-643: H-bomb Chronology, Jan. 1, 1953, no. DLXXXIV, 15–16, JCAE; Rhodes (1995), 305–7; Mark (1974), 8–9.

72. Fitzpatrick (1998), 128.

73. The only encouraging sign on the horizon was the possibility that a solid compound—lithium deuteride—might substitute for the cryogenically cooled liquid deuterium, which seemed impractical for use in a weapon.

74. Minutes, Oct. 10, 1947, GAC no. 6, CIC/DOE.

75. Oppenheimer to Lilienthal, June 6, 1948, GAC no. 10, CIC/DOE. Booster: Minutes, July 28–29, 1947, GAC no. 5, no. 30337, CIC/DOE.

76. Webster to AEC, Dec. 2, 1948, no. 71763, CIC/DOE.

77. Long-range objectives panel: Oppenheimer to Parsons, June 18, 1948, and Carpenter to Greenewalt, June 9, 1948, file 184, RG 330, records of the Office of the Secretary of Defense (OSD/NARA), National Archives; Nichols (1987), 264.

78. Oppenheimer sent the report to Nichols that Aug. H-bomb Chronology, no. DLXXXIV, 16–17, JCAE.

79. Bradbury to McCormack, Sept. 7, 1948, and Teller to Bradbury, "The Russian Atomic Plan," Sept. 3, 1948, no. 125268, CIC/DOE.

80. Fuchs's new Soviet control officer, Alexander Feklisov, would confirm in his memoirs that Fuchs at these meetings gave him some ninety secret documents—including "the diagram of the principle behind the hydrogen bomb." Alexander Feklisov, *The Man Behind the Rosenbergs* (Enigma Books, 2001), 219. The bomb that Fuchs outlined was considerably more sophisticated than the device based on Fermi's lectures that the spy had given Harry Gold a year and a half earlier. While the new design still employed a gun-type primary, three different stages of thermonuclear burning—involving sequentially increasing amounts of tritium and deuterium—were represented in the drawing. The effect of compression in increasing the efficiency of the thermonuclear reaction was also noted for the first time in the documents that Fuchs gave the Russians. Soviet Super: Albright and Kunstel (1997), 346 fn.; "Construction of the DTB," June [?] 1948, in possession of the author. The author would like to thank Joe Albright and Marcia Kunstel for a copy of the Fuchs-Feklisov document, Herb York for comments on its significance, and Cole Goldberg for a translation of the document. Soviet H-bomb: German Goncharov, "Thermonuclear Milestones: Beginnings of the Soviet H-Bomb Program," *Physics Today* 49, no. 11 (1996), 50–54; Albright and Kunstel (1997), 187–88; Holloway (1994), 294–319.

81. Estimates of Soviet atomic bomb: Borden to Walker, May 20, 1952, no. 2814, JCAE; Herken (1980), 112; Charles Ziegler, "Intelligence Assessments of Soviet Atomic Capability, 1945–1949: Myths, Monopolies, and *Maskirovka,*" *Intelligence and National Security* 12, no. 4, (1997), 1–24.

82. Cabell to Chief of Staff, Dec. 12, 1947, box 4, series 337, Headquarters records, U.S. Air Force, R.G. 341, National Archives (USAF/NARA).

83. Strauss (1962), 201–2; Strauss to Secretary of Defense, Mar. 17, 1948, no. 69943, CIC/DOE.

84. Long-range detection: Charles Ziegler and David Jacobson, *Spying Without Spies: Origins of America's Secret Nuclear Surveillance System* (Praeger, 1995), 63–70.

85. *ITMOJRO*, 47.

86. Minutes, AEC-MLC meeting, Jan. 7, 1948, "Agendas and Minutes" folder, series 1, AEC/NARA.

87. The AEC later obligated the amount. Strauss (1962), 204.

88. The GAC "heartily concurred" with the prewar policy, urging that it be further liberalized. Hewlett and Duncan (1990), 81; Stern (1969), 115.

89. "I don't think, actually, [Strauss] sensed at all that this was no way to treat his brother Commissioners." Lilienthal (1964), 234.

90. Ibid., 240.

91. Hoover to Tolson, Tamm, et al., Oct. 30, 1947, sec. 2, Frank Oppenheimer file, FBI; "Ex-FBI Man Testifies Russ Tried to Get Atom Data from Oppenheimer in 1942," *San Francisco Chronicle,* Oct. 31, 1945; U.S. Congress, HUAC, *Hearings Regarding the Communist Infiltration of the Motion Picture Industry* (1947 HUAC hearings), 80th Congress, 1st sess., Oct. 1947, 514–22.

92. HUAC's efforts to expose a Soviet spy ring in the film industry had been "a complete flop," Hoover advised Clark. Hoover to Tolson, Tamm, et al., Oct. 30, 1947, Frank Oppenheimer file, FBI. Hoover's memo also coyly put pressure once again on Clark to hand down indictments in the CINRAD investigation.

93. A HUAC staffer told the Associated Press that the bureau had approved release of Russell's story about the Chevalier incident "ahead of time." *San Francisco Chronicle,* Oct. 31, 1947.

94. In a letter to Consodine, Groves thought "Oppie's remarks regarding the treasonable acts was especially interesting. I would appreciate hearing from you as to your reaction and recollections if any on the *whole* affair." Groves to Consodine, Nov. 5, 1947, series 5, MED/NARA.

95. "Oakland Inquiry into Communism Opens Monday," San Francisco *Chronicle,* Nov. 1, 1947.

96. Schwartz (1998), 410.

97. Stern (1969), 111.

98. Kimball to Hoover, Oct. 30, 1947, sec. 4, Chevalier file, FBI.

99. Barrett (1951), 31; Scobie (1970), 201.

100. So secretive a figure was Combs that journalists routinely misspelled his name. However, it was Combs who organized the Tenney Committee hearings, wrote the questions asked of witnesses, drafted the final reports, and even served subpoenas. "Tenney Hearing: Subpoena Servers Arrive—Witness Sought Hurt in Fall," *San Francisco Chronicle,* Nov. 2, 1947.

101. Like HUAC's Thomas, Tenney relied heavily on information contained in FBI files, including the wartime records of army counterintelligence. California Legislature, *Third Report: Un-American Activities in California, 1947* (Sacramento, Calif., 1947), 201–19.

102. "Investigator Reports on Atomic Laboratory," San Francisco *Chronicle,* Nov. 7, 1947.

103. "Ex-U.C. Professor Isn't Asked Details of FBI Man's Story," *San Francisco Chronicle,* Nov. 7, 1947.

104. Stern (1969), 112.

105. Lilienthal (1964), 377–78.

106. Everson to Kelly, Jan. 8, 1947, folder 16, carton 16, EOL.

107. Lilienthal (1964), 361–62; "Survey of Berkeley Area," Aug. 15, 1947, no. 380.01, Central Correspondence series, AEC/NARA.

108. "Interim Procedure," Apr. 15, 1948, folder 9, box 175, Neylan papers.

109. Wilson to J. Stewart, June 19, 1948, folder 9, box 175, Neylan papers.

110. In a letter to the AEC, Neylan defended Berkeley's PSB. Neylan to Flaherty, Aug. 28, 1948, folder 2, box 171, Neylan papers.

111. Minutes, Aug. 25, 1949, no. 1203, JCAE.

112. Berkeley PSB: folder 9, box 175, Neylan papers.

113. Mrs. Hurley also came under suspicion for buying "folk song albums" at a Washington, D.C., book store reportedly owned by Communists. Pollman to Hurley, June 24, 1948, folder 9, box 175, Neylan papers.

114. Following the Hurley hearing, Latimer himself became a target of suspicion, in a letter by Neylan to the AEC. Latimer to Lilienthal, Aug. 10, 1948, and Neylan to Lilienthal, Aug. 12, 1948, folder 9, box 175, Neylan papers.

115. Neylan, "Findings in the Matter of Carl Robert Hurley," n.d., folder 9, box 175. Ironically, the AEC wrote back to Neylan, asking for more details on why Berkeley's PSB was denying Hurley a clearance—since the transcript of the hearing "tends to build up the employee's case." Tammaro to Neylan, Aug. 30, 1948, folder 9, box 175, Neylan papers.

116. Childs (1968), 406.

117. "Proceedings Before the Personnel Security Board of the Atomic Energy Commission, United States of America, in the Matter of Robert Serber," n.d. The author thanks Robert Serber for a copy of the transcript of his PSB hearing.

118. "Findings in the Matter of Robert Serber," n.d., folder 9, box 175, Neylan papers.

119. F. Oppenheimer to Lawrence, Oct. 25, 1948, carton 1, Frank Oppenheimer papers.

120. Elsie McMillan interview (1992).

121. "I don't think Ernest minded that, but, as often the case, my wife said something sharper, and I think maybe he minded that." Interview with Robert Oppenheimer, n.d., box 2, Childs papers.

122. Nuell Pharr Davis speculated that Lawrence learned the truth about Frank's party membership from Hoover. Davis (1993), 275. But Ernest may also have had Fisk look into the matter. Fisk to Lawrence, Aug. 18, 1948, folder 25, carton 32, EOL; Fisk to Oppenheimer, July 28, 1948, box 33, JRO.

123. Ibid.

124. Ibid. Velde: Walter Goodman, *The Committee: The Extraordinary Career of the House Committee on Un-American Activities* (Farrar, Straus and Giroux, 1968), 279–81. Although Truman issued a "freeze order," forbidding members of the executive branch and the military from cooperating with the House committee, the order actually had little effect upon HUAC, which was seemingly already in possession of a comprehensive set of MED and FBI espionage files.

125. Stripling described HUAC's strategy in a Sept. 7, 1948, telephone call to Hoover aide Louis Nichols. H. B. Fletcher to Ladd, Aug. 19, 1948, HUAC file, FBI.

126. "Martin D. Kamen Fired from Army Project at California U. After Talking to Reds," *St. Louis Post-Dispatch,* Sept. 2, 1948; Kamen to Oppenheimer, Jan. 26, 1949, box 43, JRO; Kamen, 222.

127. Nelson et al. (1969), 291–95; Goodman (1968), 241.

128. U.S. Congress, HUAC, *Report on Soviet Espionage Activities in Connection with the Atom Bomb,* 80th Congress, 2nd sess., Sept. 28, 1948.

129. HUAC's report left some doubt as to whether the committee's real target was Soviet spies or the Truman administration, and specifically, Tom Clark. L. Day to Slavin, Sept. 23, 1948, HUAC file, FBI.

11: A Rather Puzzled Horror

1 Borden: Allardice to Westinghouse Security, July 3, 1953, and undated memo, Borden folder, box 105, JCAE; Gregg Herken, *Counsels of War* (Knopf, 1985), 10–14; author interview with William Borden, Washington, D.C., Nov. 30, 1981.

2. Stockpile: Hewlett and Anderson (1990), 450–51; Rosenberg (1982), 26; Hewlett and Duncan (1990), 178–79; Rhodes (1995), 361.

3. H-bomb Chronology, 23, JCAE.

4. Lilienthal to Clark, Sept. 28, 1948, Justice Department file, series 11, AEC/NARA.

5. Transcript of John Manley interview, box 1, Robert Oppenheimer Oral History Collection, MIT.

6. Minutes, Apr. 6, 1949, no. 1059, JCAE.

7. Borden interview (1981); Borden to Oppenheimer, Apr. 11, 1949, box 22, JRO.

8. Letters, folder 10, carton 6, EOL.

9. U.S. Congress, HUAC, *Hearings Regarding Communist Infiltration of Radiation Laboratory and Atomic Bomb Project at the University of California, Berkeley, Calif.* (1949 Rad Lab hearings), 81st Congress, 2nd sess., April–June 1949, vol. 1, 282.

10. U.S. Congress, HUAC, *Hearings Regarding Steve Nelson,* June 8, 1949, 128–53, and U.S. Congress, HUAC, *Report on Atomic Espionage (Nelson-Weinberg and Hiskey-Adams Cases),* 7; Nelson et al. (1969), 295.

11. Lomanitz interview (1996); Stern (1969), 120–24.

12. Wood's deference may have had its roots in an earlier deal between HUAC and the Joint Committee. Author interview with Fred "Dusty" Rhodes, Washington, D.C., Nov. 2, 1998.

13. R. Oppenheimer to F. Oppenheimer, Sept. 18, 1948, unmarked folder, box 1, Frank Oppenheimer papers.

14. HUAC, 1949 Rad Lab hearings, vol. 1, 362.

15. Ibid., 373.

16. Bohm and Lomanitz: Peat (1997), 90–103.

17. Stern (1969), 124–29.

18. Ibid., 126.

19. Author interview with Judith Oppenheimer, San Jose, Calif., Apr. 30, 2001.

20. Lilienthal (1964), 488, 528. By summer 1947, there were no fewer than six bills before Congress to return control of atomic energy to the army. Hewlett and Duncan (1990), 91.

21. Joint Committee on Atomic Energy, "Investigation into the U.S. Atomic Energy Project," pt. 5, June 8, 1949, 224–27; AEC press release, June 13, 1949, no. 140804, CIC/DOE.

22. Volpe had earlier experienced Strauss's vindictiveness. Volpe interview (1996).

23. Ibid.

24. Teller (2001), 259. "I keep wishing for someone to whom I could talk about physics, about politics or about any other subject," Teller complained to Mayer that fall. Teller to Mayer, n.d. (late Oct. 1948), box 3, Mayer papers.

25. Teller to Mayer, n.d. (Aug. 1948), box 3, Mayer papers.

26. Bradbury to Sproul, July 29, 1948, Underhill papers, LANL. "It is clear that I must not mix in politics again—wherever I am—not, for some time to come," Teller vowed upon his return to the lab. Teller to Mayer, n.d. (Dec. 1948–Jan. 1949), box 3, Mayer papers.

27. Fitzpatrick (1998), 140.

28. However, Teller's return to Los Alamos signaled no change in his point of view, as indicated by a letter to Mayer: "It is very dangerous not to believe in anything. It is very dangerous not to be clear about one's beliefs. It is very dangerous to believe in anything half-heartedly, to try to believe in something that one knows (in some other way) not to be quite true."

29. "Even my lethargy is counted here as praiseworthy industry." Teller to Mayer, Jan. 20, 1949, box 3, Mayer papers.

30. In a 1974 interview for an authorized biography, Teller claimed that he "had no intention of working on the super" when he returned to Los Alamos in 1948. But Teller's efforts at the lab indicate otherwise. Blumberg and Owens (1976), 201.

31. Teller to Mayer, n.d. [Jan. 1949], box 3, Mayer papers.

32. Bacher to commissioners, May 26, 1947, series 17, AEC/NARA.

33. The CIA predicted that the maximum number of weapons in the Soviet's nuclear stockpile by 1955 would be twenty to fifty. Hillenkoetter to Hickenlooper, July 1, 1948, file CD11–1–2, series 199, OSD/NARA. In Jan. 1949, the agency raised this figure. Hillenkoetter to Hickenlooper, Dec. 18, 1948, no. CXXIX, JCAE.

34. Rhodes (1995), 363.

35. Strauss showed a personal interest in the long-range detection program. Minutes, AEC-MLC meeting, Nov. 24, 1948, no. 71764, CIC/DOE; Strauss, 200–207; Pfau (1984), 95–97; Ziegler and Jacobson (1995), 176–78.

36. Oppenheimer and the committee believed that the Russians might evade detection of their first bomb by testing it underground. Zielger and Jacobson (1995), 135.

37. Finney to McCormack, Aug. 2, 1949, no. 28483, CIC/DOE.

38. McMahon to Secretary of Defense, Aug. 9, 1949, no. XLVII, JCAE.

39. Pike to McMahon, Aug. 31, 1949, no. 1196, JCAE.

40. More than three weeks after the Russians' first nuclear test, a CIA estimate pegged mid-1950 as "the earliest possible date" for a Soviet bomb. Michael Warner, ed., *The CIA Under Harry Truman* (CIA Center for the Study of Intelligence, 1994), 319–20; Doyle Northrup and Donald Rock, "The Detection of Joe 1," *Studies in Intelligence* 10 (fall 1966), 23–33, box 14, CIA/NARA; Ziegler and Jacobson (1995), 199–224.

41. The Soviets exploded their bomb on Aug. 29, 1949, over the steppes of Kazakhstan, in a test code-named *First Lightning*. Joe-1 was a virtual copy of the Fat Man device, based upon blueprints stolen by Russian spies. Holloway (1994), 213–19.

42. Ziegler and Jacobson (1995), 208; Gordon Arneson, "The H-bomb Decision," *Foreign Service Journal,* May 1969, 28. As late as 1953, Truman questioned whether the Russians had actually exploded an atomic bomb in 1949. Robert Oppenheimer, *The Open Mind* (Simon and Schuster, 1955), 70.

43. *ITMOJRO,* 910; Zachary (1997), 349.

44. Truman decided to wait another four days to make the news of Joe-1 public, and then pointedly announced only that there had been "an atomic explosion" in Russia, refusing to concede that it was, in fact, a bomb.

45. *ITMOJRO,* 75.

46. Childs (1968), 413; Teller and Brown (1962), 33.

47. Lilienthal (1964), 570.

48. Lilienthal to Oppenheimer, Sept. 23, 1949, box 46, JRO.

49. "[Teller] said that these talks would be just a courtesy inasmuch as he has made up his mind to leave Chicago and come to us." May 25, 1949, memos, Sproul papers.

50. Peter Galison and Barton Bernstein, "In any light: Scientists and the decision to build the Superbomb, 1942–1954," *Historical Studies in the Physical and Biological Sciences,* 19, no. 2 (1989), 283; Teller to von Neumann, Aug. 23, 1949, AEC/NARA.

51. Teller to Mayer, n.d., box 3, Mayer papers.

52. Childs (1968), 405.

53. Teller (2001), 282.

54. Oct. 7, 1949, diary, box 3, Alvarez papers, SBFRC.

55. Minutes, Sept. 23, 1949, no. CXXIII, and "Reaction to Russian Atomic Development," Sept. 28, 1949, no. LXXXVI, and "Questions for Meeting," Sept. 23, 1949, no. LIII, JCAE.

56. Nichols, 272–73; Donnelly to Schlatter and Kennedy, Oct. 3, 1949, file 471.6, entry 197, USAF/NARA.

57. Bergman to Borden, Oct. 19, 1949, no. LXVIII, JCAE.

58. Hewlett and Duncan (1990), 373; Pfau (1984), 113.

59. Hewlett and Duncan (1990), 374; Strauss (1962), 217.

60. While Alvarez remained pessimistic about the future of radiological warfare—"Program approved but probably nothing will happen"—he was cheered that the RW panel's recommendation for expanded neutron production "tie[d] in well with our program."

61. Borden to files, Oct. 10, 1949, no. LXVI, JCAE; Oct. 10, 1949, diary, box 3, Alvarez papers.

62. In his diary, Alvarez described Lilienthal's response as "lukewarm." Borden to files, July 5, 1951, no. 2365, JCAE.

63. Alvarez (1987), 171.

64. Nichols (1987), 273–74; *ITMOJRO,* 682.

65. Minutes, Oct. 14, 1949, no. LXIV, JCAE.

66. Strauss to Lilienthal, Oct. 17, 1949, no. LXIII, JCAE.

67. Oppenheimer to Conant, Oct. 21, 1949, Oppenheimer file, entry 60, box 11, AEC/NARA.

68. Lilienthal (1964), 577, 582.

69. Lilienthal to Oppenheimer, Oct. 11, 1949, box 46, JRO.

70. A Joint Committee staffer warned Borden of the "peculiar situation" at the Rad Lab—namely, Lawrence's propensity for empire building. Borden to files, Oct. 20, 1949, no. LXVII, and Brobeck to Borden, Oct. 20, 1949, no. 1266, JCAE.

71. Teller believed that Bethe had agreed to go to Los Alamos. "The Development of Atomic Weapons," Jan. 30, 1950, no. 1447, JCAE; *ITMOJRO,* 715.

72. Blumberg and Owens (1976), 210.

73. Hewlett and Duncan (1990), 380.

74. Oct. 24, 1949, diary, Alvarez papers; H-bomb Chronology, 29–30, JCAE.

75. "I would have to hear some good arguments before I could take on sufficient courage to recommend not going toward such a program," Seaborg wrote. Seaborg to Oppenheimer, Oct. 14, 1949, AEC/NARA.

76. Another visitor was Oppie's former Berkeley colleague, Kenneth Pitzer. Pitzer was surprised to learn of Conant's opposition and disturbed that Oppenheimer seemed to share Conant's view. Pitzer interview (1997).

77. LeBaron: "Robert LeBaron—Man of Many Talents," n.d., folder 4, box 1, Robert LeBaron papers, Hoover Institution Library, Stanford University; author interview with Gerard Smith, Ratcliffe Manor, Md., Sept. 15, 1992.

78. Oppenheimer was gradually severing his ties with Berkeley. In early Nov., he informed Birge that, for the first time since the war, he would not be back on campus in the summer to teach Physics 221A. Interview with Robert Oppenheimer, n.d., box 2, Childs papers.

79. Oppenheimer to Birge, Nov. 9, 1949, box 20, JRO.

80. Serber interview (1992).

81. "I had no idea that people like Conant and Oppenheimer would harbor such ideas. At Berkeley they would have been unthinkable." Serber (1998), 169.

82. Hamilton to files, Nov. 8, 1949, no. LXXVI, JCAE.

83. Oct. 18, 1949, diary, box 3, Alvarez papers.

84. Tomei to Conant, Oct. 18, 1949, box 27, JRO.

85. Kennan report: U.S. Department of State, *Foreign Relations of the United States: (FRUS), 1950* (U.S. Government Printing Office, 1977), vol. 1, 22 fn. Kennan later wrote a draft press statement for Truman to announce that he had decided against proceeding with the Super as "not in the national interest." Untitled draft, Nov. 18, 1949, box 43, JRO.

86. Although Oppenheimer was later unable to remember whether he acquainted the committee with Seaborg's waffling letter—a point that would assume some importance in his 1954 security hearing—Smyth recalled following the text over the chairman's shoulder while Oppie read aloud.

87. Hewlett and Duncan (1990), 379–81.

88. The previous spring, Conant had threatened to quit the committee. Conant to Oppenheimer, Mar. 7, 1949, box 27, JRO.

89. JRO to DuBridge, Oct. 8, 1949, box 33, JRO.

90. Lilienthal (1964), 581.

91. John Manley, "A Fateful Decision," unpublished manuscript, Manley papers, LANL.

92. *ITMOJRO*, 395.

93. Lilienthal (1964), 582.

94. Roger Anders, ed., *Forging the Atomic Shield: Excerpts from the Office Diary of Gordon E. Dean* (University of North Carolina Press, 1987), 59.

95. Davis (1968), 314.

96. Rabi agreed that what he and Fermi proposed—in effect, a verifiable thermonuclear test ban—should have been more clearly spelled out. "It should have been many pages." Rabi interview (1984).

97. Stern (1969), 145–46.

98. Rabi interview (1984). Oppenheimer decided to sign the majority report because he thought that the letter by Rabi and Fermi, in proposing a diplomatic initiative to Russia, presumed too much upon the State Department's prerogatives. "Development of Atomic Super Weapons," Jan. 30, 1950, no. 1447, JCAE.

99. Manley diary, Oct. 31, 1949, Manley papers, LANL.

100. Oppenheimer to Bohr, Nov. 2, 1949, box 21, JRO.

101. Hewlett and Duncan (1990), 385–86; Michelmore (1969), 173.

12: A Desperate Urgency Here

1. Manley diary, Manley papers, LANL; Lilienthal (1964), 584–85.
2. McMahon to Truman, Nov. 1, 1949, no. LXXII, JCAE.
3. Lilienthal (1964), 584.
4. Manley diary, Manley papers, LANL.
5. Arneson (1969), 29; Acheson (1969), 346.
6. Teller to Mayer, n.d. [Nov. 1949], box 3, Mayer papers.
7. *ITMOJRO*, 91.
8. Manley, "Recollections and Memories," 5; Manley diary, 13–14; and "A Fateful Decision," 5, Manley papers, LANL. Los Alamos colleague Stanislaw Ulam bet that Teller would not be quiet for long. Ulam to von Neumann, Nov. 15, 1949, box 2229, von Neumann collection, AEC/NARA.
9. Pfau (1984), 116.
10. Serber interview (1992).
11. Alvarez to Teller, Nov. 10, 1949, Teller folder, box 3, Alvarez papers, SBFRC.
12. Lilienthal (1964), 591.
13. Hewlett and Duncan (1990), 386–87.
14. Manley diary, 13, Manley papers, LANL.
15. Hewlett and Duncan (1990), 391.
16. Bradbury to Oppenheimer, Oct. 27, 1949, and Oct. 31, 1949, Bradbury folder, box 22, JRO. Teller to Alvarez, Teller folder, box 3, Alvarez papers. Teller accused Manley of trying to prevent him from meeting with McMahon. "Recollections and Memories," and Manley diary, 6–8, Manley papers, LANL archives; Teller and Brown (1962), 44.
17. Although Bethe explained that he had changed his mind after talking with two physicist friends—Victor Weisskopf and George Placzek—Teller blamed Oppenheimer. Rhodes (1995), 393; Bethe interview (1996).
18. "November was as early as I heard a name mentioned, and then only informally and under seal," Strauss later told the Joint Committee. But other evidence suggests that Strauss learned about Fuchs earlier. Minutes, Mar. 10, 1950, no. CXXXVIII, JCAE. Strauss knowledge of spying: Pfau (1984), 114–15; Williams (1987), 115–16.
19. The bureau became suspicious of Fuchs in Aug. 1949, when it learned that the Soviets were in possession of a top-secret Manhattan Project document on gaseous diffusion, written by Fuchs. On Oct. 21, 1949, Hoover formally informed the AEC that Fuchs was the subject of its investigation. Dean had been advised in Sept. that the German-born physicist was a suspect. Minutes, Mar. 10, 1950, no. CXXXVIII, and Hoover to McMahon, Apr. 21, 1950, no. CXL, JCAE.
20. "Bureau Source 5" was probably the *Venona* decrypts. See chap. 5. Robert Lamphere, Oct. 22, 1997, personal communication.
21. Robert Bacher recalled that before he went to England in Sept., AEC security officials instructed him to ask John Cockcroft whether the British had any reservations about Klaus Fuchs. Transcript of Bacher interview, Caltech archives.
22. Groves to Strauss, Nov. 4, 1949, Strauss folder, Groves/NARA.
23. Strauss to Nichols, Dec. 3, 1949, Harrison-Bundy file, MED/NARA.
24. The committee's first meeting dissolved almost immediately into rancor when Johnson brusquely declared that the military services were unanimous on proceeding with the Super as the "minimum" next step. Hewlett and Duncan (1990), 398–99, 643 fn; Acheson (1969), 348.
25. Teller to Mayer, n.d. [Dec. 1949–Jan. 1950], box 3, Mayer papers.
26. Los Alamos briefings: Hamilton to files, Nov. 8, 1949, no. LXXVI, and Hamilton to files, Nov. 10, 1949, box 6; and minutes, Jan. 9, 1950, no. CXXV, JCAE.
27. Minutes, Jan. 9, 1950, no. CXIII, JCAE.
28. McMahon to Truman, Nov. 21, 1949, in "Thermonuclear Weapons Program Chronology" (TWPC), n.d., 53–59, AEC/NARA.
29. Strauss (1962), 220; Borden to file, Nov. 28, 1949, no. LXXXI, JCAE.

30. Bradley to Truman, Jan. 13, 1950, 78–86, TWPC, AEC/NARA; Borden, "Questions for the Joint Chiefs of Staff," Jan. 10, 1950, no. CVIII, JCAE.

31. Hewlett and Duncan (1990), 394.

32. Minutes, Jan. 9, 1950, no. CXXV, JCAE.

33. Pfau (1984), 121.

34. "You can't expect morals from immoral people?" ventured Texas Congressman Paul Kilday. "This is the point, sir!" responded Strauss. Minutes, Jan. 27, 1950, no. CXVIII, JCAE.

35. Hewlett and Duncan (1990), 405.

36. Oppenheimer defended the GAC report: "We thought the beginning of wisdom was to stop, look and listen about weapons of mass destruction, and this was the place to do it." Minutes, Jan. 30, 1950, no. 1447, JCAE.

37. Teller and Brown (1962), 46.

38. Acheson (1969), 347; Rhodes (1995), 405.

39. U.S. Department of State, *FRUS: 1949* (U.S. Government Printing Office, 1976), vol. 1, 573–76; transcript of Warner Schilling interview, box 65, JRO.

40. Lilienthal (1964), 582; Arneson (1969), 25.

41. Jan. 31 meeting: Acheson (1969), 348–49; Lilienthal (1964), 623–32.

42. Lilienthal (1964), 632. Earlier, on Jan. 19, Souers had told Acheson that Truman thought the joint chiefs' memo "made a lot of sense and he was inclined to think that was what we should do." H-bomb decision: *FRUS: 1950,* vol. 1, 511; Herken (1980), 319–21.

43. Lilienthal (1964), 633.

44. Minutes, Jan. 31, 1950, no. CXXVI.

45. Davis, 316.

46. Author interview with Gordon Arneson, Washington, D.C., Oct. 19, 1979.

47. Pfau (1984), 123.

48. Minutes, Mar. 10, 1950, no. CXXXVIII, JCAE.

49. Pfau (1984), 124. Wilson had agreed to allow British members of the Anglo-American Combined Development Trust to have an office in AEC headquarters, where they could roam unescorted. One—Donald Maclean—was later found to have been passing secrets to the Soviets.

50. Cited in Galison and Bernstein, p. 311; "Hydrogen Bomb Secret Feared Given Russians," *Washington Post,* Feb. 3, 1950.

51. Lilienthal (1964), 635.

52. Minutes, Feb. 4, 1950, no. 1371, and minutes, Feb. 6, 1950, no. 1376, JCAE. Hoover later passed MI-5's interview with Fuchs along to the Joint Committee to prove his point. Minutes, Mar. 10, 1950, no. CXXXVIII, JCAE.

53. Wilson to McMahon, Mar. 14, 1950, series 10, AEC/NARA.

54. Lilienthal to McMahon, Feb. 7, 1950, series 10, AEC/NARA.

55. The damage report was not completed until late Apr. 1950. Boyer to Borden, Oct. 3, 1951, no. 2390, JCAE.

56. Minutes, Feb. 3, 1950, no. CXXXI, and Lilienthal to McMahon, Feb. 7, 1950, no. CXXII, JCAE.

57. Minutes, Feb. 27, 1950, *FRUS: 1950,* vol. 1, 173. In response to a Joint Committee inquiry as to when he thought the Russians might have an H-bomb, Oppenheimer wrote that it was his "conviction that what Fuchs may have told the Russians about thermonuclear weapons would prove substantially misleading." Oppenheimer to Borden, December 1, 1952, no. 7807, JCAE.

58. Cited in Bernstein (1990), 1408.

59. Borden to Chairman, Nov. 3, 1952, no. DCXXXV, JCAE.

60. "I mean, it was pretty laconic," Bradbury conceded of Carson Mark's presentation. "Carson didn't put himself out in the best Air Force briefer style." Transcript of Bradbury interview, Bancroft Library.

61. Hewlett and Duncan (1990), 411–12.

62. Minutes, Nov. 8, 1949, no. LXXVI, JCAE.

63. Pike to LeBaron, Mar. 2, 1950, series 1, MLC folder, and Pike to McMahon, Mar. 2, 1950, series 4, "Classified Reading" file, AEC/NARA. MTA: Heilbron et al. (1981), 64–65; Hewlett and Duncan (1990), 425; Pitzer to Tammaro, Feb. 10, 1950, LBL.

64. Entries of Jan. 20, May 12, and Sept. 12, 1950, memos, Sproul papers; Sproul to Bradbury, May 2, 1950, Contract 48 file, LBL.

65. Ironically, all thirteen of the bills that Tenney proposed to the California legislature, requiring the oath, died in committee.

66. Oath controversy: George Stewart, *The Year of the Oath: The Fight for Academic Freedom at the University of California* (Da Capo, 1971); Sproul to Cooksey, Aug. 18, 1949, folder 14, carton 33, EOL. Neylan regularly received reports of closed meetings of the Academic Senate from the Rad Lab's assistant personnel director. Documents in black binders, boxes 187–88, Neylan papers.

67. Fox decided to admit his Communist past after talking with Sproul, who reportedly assured him "that everything would be all right if he just told the truth." David Fox, June 11, 1998, personal communication. Fox controversy: Stewart (1971), 42–46; Birge, vol. 5, XIX, 20–21, 44–45.

68. "[Birge] tells me that the physics department is sharply divided between two factions, one of which is led by the Rad. group (Alvarez, Lawrence, et al.), and the other by the more academic physicists (Segrè, Brode, et al.)." Jan. 2, 1950, memos, Sproul papers.

69. In Sept. 1950, Oppenheimer signed a statement condemning the regents' stand on the oath. Oppenheimer et al., "UC-Group for Academic Freedom" folder, box 25, JRO.

70. Wick firing: Segrè (1993), 235; Reynolds to Everson, Sept. 28, 1950, "Loyalty Oath" file, box 7, LBL.

71. Birge, vol. 5, XIX, 53; Reynolds to file, Aug. 1, 1950, "Loyalty Oath" file, box 7, LBL. Observed Segrè of the oath's effect upon Berkeley's physics department: "For theory, it was a body blow; for experiment, something a bit less." Segrè (1993), 235.

72. Teller's letters to Mayer showed a range of conflicting feelings about whether to stay at Los Alamos, return to Chicago, or go to UCLA. Teller to Mayer, various letters, n.d. [Jan.–Oct. 1950], box 3, Mayer papers.

73. Teller to Mayer, n.d. [late Nov. 1950], box 3, Mayer papers.

74. Lawrence to Teller, Dec. 1, 1950; Teller to Lawrence, Dec. 5, 1950, folder 9, carton 17, EOL.

75. "You know that I did not mind signing the Oath—by now I have signed it four different times." Teller to McMillan, Nov. 16, 1950, Teller file, series 4, McMillan papers, SBFRC.

76. Dec. 29, 1952, memos, Sproul papers.

77. Strauss had recently shown Defense Secretary Johnson four top-secret documents from the commission's vault. All pertained to the hydrogen bomb and had been compromised by Fuchs, Strauss claimed. Ironically, one was apparently the 1946 Fuchs–von Neumann patent. Strauss refused to show the documents to his fellow commissioners.

78. "Basis for Estimating Maximum Soviet Capabilities for Atomic Warfare," Feb. 16, 1950, "NSC Atomic Energy—Russia folder," box 201, president's secretary's files, Harry Truman papers, Truman Library.

79. Rhodes (1995), 420–21.

80. Teller and de Hoffmann to Bradbury, Dec. 5, 1949, AEC/NARA. Wrote Teller to Bradbury in Dec. 1949: "It must be kept in mind that it is by no means certain that a super can be made at all." Cited in Fitzpatrick (1998), 261.

81. The bomb was plainly too big and heavy to be carried by existing bombers. Lee Bowen, U.S. Air Force Historical Division, *A History of the Air Force Atomic Energy Program, 1943–1953* (USAF history)(U.S. Air Force History office, n.d.), vol. 4, 188; Rhodes (1995), 379.

82. Wilson to Schlatter, Oct. 20, 1949, entry 197, and Feb. 3, 1950, series 26, USAF/NARA; USAF history, vol. 4, 187, 206.

83. Smyth to McMahon, Jan. 25, 1950, no. CXIV, JCAE; Fitzpatrick (1998), 122. LeBaron admitted to Johnson that it was "becoming clearer that the program will cost us a sizeable number of fission atomic weapons." LeBaron to Johnson, Mar. 1, 1950, series 184, OSD/NARA. In May 1950, Bethe testified before the Joint Committee that the neutrons necessary to make 1 gram of tritium could make 100 grams of plutonium. Minutes, May 3, 1950, no. CXLIV, JCAE.

84. "Daddy Pocketbook": Appendix E, Sept. 12, 1952, no. DLXIII, JCAE; Fitzpatrick (1998), 261–62; Rhodes (1995), 414, 424.

85. Norman Macrae, *John von Neumann: The Scientific Genius Who Pioneered the Modern Computer, Game Theory, Nuclear Deterrence, and Much More* (Pantheon, 1992), 312–14; Wheeler, (1998), 221–22.

86. "The expense of such a large amount of tritium would make the design wholly impractical," Teller admitted. Teller (2001), 302–3; appendix E, Sept. 12, 1952, no. DLXIII, JCAE.

87. Oppenheimer to Dean, no. 104150, CIC/DOE; Rhodes (1995), 424.

88. Von Neumann to Teller, May 18, 1950, LANL; Hewlett and Duncan (1990), 439–40; Rhodes (1995), 423–24; S. M. Ulam, *Adventures of a Mathematician* (University of California Press, 1991), 212–16; Ulam to Manley, Aug. 10, 1988, Manley papers, LANL. "Together, the two pieces of work appeared to sound the death knell for the super: it would neither light nor burn." Peter Galison, *Image and Logic: A Material Culture of Microphysics* (University of Chicago Press, 1997), 723.

89. Ulam (1991), 217.

90. H-bomb Chronology, 54; Wheeler (1998), 200; Ulam (1991), 217.

91. Family Committee: Fitzpatrick (1998), 222; Hewlett and Duncan (1990), 536; Bradbury to Teller, Mar. 3, 1950, no. 125511, CIC/DOE.

92. Rhodes (1995), 419.

93. *George* test: Fitzpatrick (1998), 141–42; Rhodes (1995), 456–57.

94. Teller to Bradbury, July 28, 1950, no. 1452, CIC/DOE; Wheeler (1998), 206–7.

95. De Hoffmann: Ulam (1991), 211; Wheeler (1998), 191; Fitzpatrick (1998), 148–49.

96. Borden to file, Mar. 2, 1950; Teller to Borden, Mar. 8, 1950; Teller to Borden, Mar. 15, 1950, series 2, Oppenheimer file, JCAE.

97. Edward Teller, "Back to the Laboratories," *Scientific American,* Mar. 1950. Teller told Borden he was "shocked at the icyness [sic]" with which young physicists rejected his appeal. Fitzpatrick (1998), 273.

98. "I can not in good conscience work on this weapon," Bethe informed Bradbury. However, Bethe changed his mind following the Communist invasion of South Korea that June; like Fermi, he would spend summers at the lab. Bethe to Bradbury, Feb. 14, 1950, no. 125241, CIC/DOE.

99. Telegram, Teller to JRO, Feb. 17, 1950, box 71, JRO.

100. Blumberg and Owens (1976), 239. Teller reportedly rejected suggestions coming from scientists at the lab whom he considered pro-Oppenheimer, fearing sabotage. Borden to files, Feb. 9, 1951, no. CCLXXXIII, JCAE; Blumberg and Owens (1976), 257.

101. Teller to Borden, Apr. 13, 1950, no. 7201, JCAE.

102. Bergman to Borden, May 7, 1950, no. 1531, JCAE.

13: Nuclear Plenty

1. Hewlett and Duncan (1990), 443.

2. Manleys to Oppenheimer, box 50; and Conant to Oppenheimer, July 25, 1950, box 27, and Wilson to Oppenheimer, box 77, JRO; Anders (1987), 75–76. Isidor Rabi suspected that Conant's absences at the GAC were not all on account of illness: "He saw which side was stronger." Rabi interview (1984).

3. Oppenheimer was not the only one eager to cover up his past. "Before the State Department . . . ," n.d., Chevalier papers.

4. "I still had my theory about him that I had conceived several years before, and this fiction that he was putting forward was presumably necessary for his protection in the carrying out of an ideal purpose which I had no doubt he was pursuing." Chevalier (1965), 84.

5. Ibid. The FBI continued to track Chevalier's movements in Paris, evidently through his calls to Barbara at Stinson Beach. San Francisco field report, Oct. 5, 1953, Chevalier FBI file, box 1, JRO/AEC.

6. Crouch had testified before HUAC about the alleged meeting the previous year but did not mention Oppenheimer on that occasion. U.S. Congress, HUAC, *Hearings Regarding Clarence Hiskey Including Testimony of Paul Crouch,* 81st Congress, 2nd sess., May 24, 1949, 399–408.

7. The purpose of the alleged meeting was to brief professional section members on the change in the party line since the German invasion.

8. Combs's search was not random; he took Crouch to homes whose owners had subscribed to the *Daily Worker* during the 1940s. San Francisco field report, Nov. 18, 1952, sec. 14, JRO/FBI; Paul Crouch, "Broken Chains," chap. 20, unpublished memoir, box 17, Paul Crouch papers, Hoover Institution Library, Stanford, Calif.

9. "Woman Witness Says She Saw Nuclear Expert at Session," *Oakland Tribune,* May 9, 1950.

10. Newark field report, May 5, 1950, sec. 8, JRO/FBI; "Statement by J. Robert Oppenheimer," May 9, 1950, "Weinberg Perjury Trial, 1953" folder, box 237, JRO; Bernstein (1990), 1411–13.

11. Groves to Oppenheimer, May 18, 1950, box 36, JRO. Groves was evidently unaware of the role that Oppenheimer had played in ousting him from his posts on the Air Force Special Weapons Project and the Military Liaison Committee, leading to his retirement from the army. Hershberg (1993), 357.

12. Crouch had spent two years in Alcatraz in the mid-1920s for trying to recruit party members while in the army. Crouch, "Broken Chains," chap. 27, Crouch papers.

13. Kenilworth Court incident: Letter and telegrams, "Financial: Real Estate" folder, box 232, JRO; Albuquerque field report, July 10, 1952, sec. 13; and San Francisco field report, Nov. 18, 1952, JRO/FBI.

14. Bacher to Oppenheimer, May 25, 1950, and Oppenheimer to Bacher, May 23, 1950, box 18, and Groves to Oppenheimer, May 18, 1950, box 36, and Conant to Oppenheimer, May 15, 1950, box 27, JRO.

15. Oppenheimer's candidates for replacements on the GAC included von Neumann, Bethe, and Bacher. Borden to McMahon, May 11, 1950, no. 1516, JCAE; Hewlett and Duncan (1990), 486.

16. *ITMOJRO,* 83. FBI director Hoover had reportedly been assured by the White House in July that Oppie would not be reappointed GAC chairman. Bernstein (1990), 1421.

17. S. Allison to Oppenheimer, various letters, box 15, and Wilson to Oppenheimer, n.d., box 77, JRO.

18. Waters to Strauss, May 12, 1954, miscellaneous correspondence, 1953–54, AEC/NARA.

19. Acheson had summoned Lawrence, among others, to advise on the review of U.S. nuclear policy occasioned by the H-bomb decision. *FRUS: 1950,* vol. 1, 200–201.

20. Minutes, GAC no. 20, Apr. 1, 1950, no. 30335, CIC/DOE.

21. Oppenheimer to Dean, May 11, 1951, no. 2098, JCAE.

22. Minutes, AEC meeting no. 471, Sept. 20, 1950, AEC/NARA.

23. Oppenheimer to Dean, Sept. 13, 1950, AEC/NARA; Oppenheimer to Dean, Nov. 1, 1950, no. 1757, JCAE; Bradbury to Tyler, Nov. 17, 1950, no. 71710, CIC/DOE.

24. "Military Objectives in the Use of Atomic Energy," Dec. 29, 1950, attached to Lovett to McMahon, June 28, 1951, no. CCCLV, JCAE.

25. Ibid.

26. Ivan Getting, *All in a Lifetime: Science in the Defense of Democracy* (Vantage Press, 1989), 238–39; *ITMOJRO,* 57–8, 684; Ridenour to Saville, Mar. 6, 1951, no. 360.8, series 10, USAF/NARA.

27. MTA and Livermore: Pike to F. Matthews, Mar. 14, 1950, series 11, AEC/NARA; transcript of Larry Crooks interview, LLNL; "Site Selection Report MTA Project," Mar. 15, 1950, Box 48–1, Contract 48 records, SBFRC.

28. Mansfield to files, June 15, 1951, no. 2141, JCAE.

29. Lawrence's choice prompted Panofsky to write a poem about Livermore, inspired by Poe's "The Raven." Wolfgang Panofsky, Aug. 3, 1993, personal communication.

30. Choice of Livermore: Herbert York, *The Advisors: Oppenheimer, Teller, and the Superbomb* (Freeman, 1976), 121–26; Childs (1968), 418.

31. Minutes, June 3, 1950, GAC no. 21, AEC/NARA.

32. MTA: Heilbron, Seidel, and Wheaton (1981), 64–69.

33. Two-thirds of the MTA's annual operating budget of $14 million would go to pay for electricity. Lawrence to Pitzer, Aug. 24, 1950, and "Reports—MTA Mark III," box 12, LBL.

34. In executive session, Ernest told the Joint Committee that the MTA could be used to produce radiological agents in the event of a wartime emergency. "Production Particle Accelerators," Apr. 11, 1950, no. 2041, JCAE.

35. John Derry, Mar. 15, 1999, personal communication; Cook to Derry, May 1, 1951, AEC general correspondence, 1951 folder, general administrative files, LBL.

36. Mark I: Various documents, folder 11, carton 33, EOL; Hamilton and Mansfield to Borden, July 26, 1950, no. CLXXXXI, JCAE.

37. Author interview with Hugh Bradner, La Jolla, Calif., Aug. 10, 1992; Alvarez (1987), 173–75.

38. Undeterred, Ernest had already proposed a Mark III to the commission. Lawrence to Pitzer, Nov. 20, 1950; Reynolds to Pitzer, Nov. 22, 1950, "Proposal for MTA Mark III" folder, box 8, LBL.

39. Panofsky: Nov. 2, 1950, memos, Sproul papers; Panofsky interview (1993).

40. Serber to Oppenheimer, Feb. 21, 1950, box 66, JRO.

41. Dec. 22, 1950, memos, Sproul papers.

42. Segrè, (1993), 237.

43. "Case History of a Failure: What the Loyalty Oath Did to the University of California," *Look,* Jan. 29, 1952; "Loyalty Oaths and Academic Freedom: Address of John Francis Neylan before the Commonwealth Club, San Francisco," Nov. 23, 1951, folder 44a, carton 13, EOL.

44. Bradner interview (1992).

45. Ulam later explained his idea in a Mar. 16, 1962, letter to Seaborg, which is attached to Bradbury to Anderson, Mar. 22, 1962, no. 125261, CIC/DOE.

46. Wheeler (1998), 211; author interview with Carson Mark, Los Alamos, N. Mex., May 30, 1991.

47. F. Ulam to Manley, Aug. 10, 1988, folder 6, box 15, Manley papers, LANL.

48. Rhodes (1995), 462–67.

49. Teller-Ulam idea: According to Fitzpatrick, the term *radiation implosion* was first used by Teller in Family Committee meetings on the design of *George*. Fitzpatrick (1998), 161–62. Teller confirmed in a 1993 interview that he discouraged talk of compression until Ulam's invention, not believing the compression obtained by mechanical shock alone would be enough to make a difference. Teller interview (1993).

50. Oppenheimer to Conant, June 8, 1951, box 27, JRO.

51. H-bomb Chronology, 62, JCAE.

52. Galison (1997), 726.

53. Teller suggested a further improvement in the H-bomb—a fission "sparkplug" inside the thermonuclear fuel—a few weeks later. Rhodes (1995), 472–73. Comparing the relative contributions of Teller and Ulam, Bethe thought Teller deserved "90 percent" of the credit for invention of the superbomb. Bethe interview (1988). As recently as 2001, Teller disputed the importance of Ulam's contribution. "Who Built the H-Bomb?: Debate Revives," *New York Times,* Apr. 24, 2001; Teller (2001), 316.

54. *George* test: U.S. Defense Nuclear Agency, "Operation Greenhouse, 1951" (U.S. Government Printing office, 1983); Hansen (1988), 46–54; Teller and Brown (1962), 49–52; personal communications: Edward Teller, Feb. 26, 1999, and Louis Rosen, Mar. 3, 1999.

55. Louis Rosen, Mar. 3, 1999, personal communication. My thanks to Professor Rosen for a copy of his personal account of *George*.

56. Teller's memory is that Lawrence was in the jeep; Rosen believes the rendezvous was at the airstrip. Teller (2001), 323–24.

14: A Bad Business Now Threatening

1. Minutes, May 10, 1951, GAC no. 26, no. 79443, CIC/DOE.

2. Princeton meeting: Anders (1987), 143–44; Hewlett and Duncan (1990), 542; *ITMOJRO,* 84; H-bomb Chronology, 65, JCAE; Teller (2001), 325–26.

3. May 31, 1951, Dean diary, Gordon Dean papers, National Archives, College Park, Maryland.

4. *Mike* was meant to be a proof-of-principle test of radiation implosion and not a deliverable bomb. Housed in a six-story building, it weighed more than 80 tons. *Mike:* Hansen (1988), 54–55; Rhodes (1995), 490–96.

5. Hewlett and Duncan (1990), 542; *ITMOJRO,* 305; Rhodes (1995), 477.

6. DeHoffmann called back a few days later to say that Teller was rethinking his decision. Anders (1987), 161.

7. Mansfield to file, "Los Alamos Opinions of Dr. Edward Teller," Aug. 29, 1951, no. 2330, JCAE.

8. Theoretical Megaton Group: Fitzpatrick (1998), 313; Rhodes (1995), 482–87.

9. "H-bomb Status Report," Sept. 28, 1951, no. CDXVIII, and Walker to file, Nov. 13, 1951, no. CDXXXI, JCAE; "Who Built the H-Bomb? Debate Revives," *New York Times,* Apr. 24, 2001.

10. Teller (2001), 327; Bradbury to McCormack, Mar. 31, 1951, no. 71793, CIC/DOE.

11. "It was a painful decision for me to leave Los Alamos," Teller later wrote Strauss. "One of the most powerful reasons why I did so was the conviction that I could not decently argue for a second laboratory while staying at Los Alamos." Teller to Strauss, Mar. 5, 1956, Teller folder, LLS/HHPL.

12. Walker to file, Oct. 3, 1951, no. 2398, JCAE; Hewlett and Duncan (1990), 556; Mansfield to file, Oct. 2, 1951, no. 2389, JCAE.

13. "Hal" to "Bill," May 9, 1950, no. 1532, JCAE.

14. Hamilton to files, June 29, 1950, no. 1572, JCAE.

15. Borden to file, Mar. 10, 1950, no. 1429, and Hamilton to file, June 29, 1950, no. 1572, and Borden to file, Nov. 28, 1950, no. CCXLI, JCAE.

16. Pfau (1984), 129.

17. Entry, Aug. 6, 1950, Glennan diary, Keith Glennan papers, AEC/NARA.

18. Bernstein (1990), 1414 fn; Anders (1987), 117–18.

19. Oppenheimer to Dean, Oct. 13, 1951, no. 74703; minutes, GAC no. 27, Oct. 13, 1951, no. 74703, CIC/DOE.

20. Thomas Murray: Hewlett and Duncan (1990), 466; Thomas E. Murray, *Nuclear Policy for War and Peace* (World Publishing, 1960), 15–17, and *The Predicament of Our Age: The Impact of the Atom on the Relationship Between Man and the World in which He Lives* (n.p., 1955). The author thanks Bradley Murray for a copy of his father's privately published book of speeches, and Jack Crawford for access to Thomas Murray's personal papers.

21. Teller and Brown (1962), 53.

22. "From the looks of the faces around me, one would think I had exploded such a device in the conference room," Murray wrote in his diary. Diary of Thomas E. Murray (TEM diary), vol. 2, pt. 1, 4, Thomas Murray papers, Rockville, Md. (private collection).

23. Ibid., vol. 2, pt. 2, 7–8.

24. Murray to Dean, June 21, 1951, AEC/NARA; TEM diary, vol. 2, pt. 2, 12.

25. Smyth et al. to Dean, Aug. 15, 1951, no. 74410, and Dean to Snapp, Aug. 28, 1951, no. 74407, and "Status Report," n.d., no. 74402, CIC/DOE; TEM diary, vol. 2, pt. 2, 23–24.

26. That fall, McMahon shepherded through the Senate a nonbinding resolution to "go all-out in atomic development and production." "Biography," McMahon papers; Dean to Lawrence, Sept. 19, 1951, folder 32, carton 30, EOL.

27. "The Deterrent Value of Atoms," May 20, 1952, no. 2812, JCAE.

28. TEM diary, vol. 2, pt. 1, 8.

29. Joe-2 was the first indigenous Soviet design and was similar to the Mark IV implosion bomb exploded by the United States in the 1948 *Sandstone* tests. Joe-3 was the Russians' first composite core—utilizing enriched uranium and plutonium—and had twice the yield of the Nagasaki bomb. "H-bomb Status Report," Sept. 28, 1951, no. CDXVIII, JCAE. Joe-2 and Joe-3: Rhodes (1995), 482 fn.; Holloway (1994), 219; "Preliminary Analysis . . . ," Nov. 27, 1951, series 26, USAF/NARA.

30. McMahon to Dean, Oct. 5, 1951, no. 2392, JCAE; TEM diary, vol. 2, pt. 2, 27; "Meeting with the President," Oct. 5, 1951, Murray papers.

31. Anders (1987), 176.

32. Minutes, Dec. 14, 1951, GAC no. 28, no. 73278, CIC/DOE; Teller and Brown (1962), 59.

33. TEM diary, vol. 2, pt. 2, 41–43. Oppenheimer's summary of the meeting neglected even to mention the second lab discussion. Oppenheimer to Dean, Dec. 14, 1952, no. 74702, CIC/DOE.

34. TEM diary, vol. 2, pt. 2, 43–44.

35. Minutes of meeting, June 30, 1951, folder 15, carton 33, EOL; transcript of interview with Cliff Bacigalupi, LLNL.

36. Walker to files, Nov. 19, 1951, no. 2472, JCAE.

37. Mansfield to files, June 15, 1951, no. 2141, JCAE.

38. Asked if he would be willing to personally lead the effort for six months to a year, Lawrence "offered no strenuous objection." TEM diary, vol. 2, pt. 2, 45.

39. Minutes, Dec. 14, 1951, folder 3, box 171, Neylan papers.

40. Neylan interview, May 6, 1960, box 2, Childs papers.

41. Oppenheimer once compared the university's administering of a weapons laboratory to the monastic orders that made a profit from the manufacture of liqueurs. Daniel Kevles, "Cold War and Hot Physics: Science, Security, and the American State, 1945–56," *Historical Studies in the Physical and Biological Sciences* 20, no. 2 (1990), 243.

42. Herbert York, "The Origins of the Lawrence Livermore Laboratory," 17, May 1975, unpublished manuscript, Herbert York papers, Special Collections, University of California, San Diego (La Jolla), Calif.; York (1987), 62–64.

43. York added research on fusion as a source of energy—an area which many physicists, including Teller, regarded as promising—to his list as a recruiting tactic. Untitled document, n.d., "Herb York: Personnel Notes on Establishing LLNL" folder, box 184, LLNL; Childs (1968), 443.

44. Teller (2001), 337. Lawrence told Duane Sewell that the laboratory he envisioned would not be building bombs. Hewlett and Duncan (1990), 582; interviews: Fidler (1992), Sewell (1993), and Teller (July 30, 1993).

45. Teller to Lawrence, Feb. 7, 1952, folder 9, carton 17, EOL; Teller to Murray, Feb. 7, 1952, Murray papers.

46. TEM diary, vol. 2, pt. 2, 52.

47. Minutes, AEC no. 639, Dec. 19, 1951, AEC/NARA.

48. TEM diary, vol. 2, pt. 2, 47–53; H-bomb Chronology, 74, and "Status of Hydrogen Project," Feb. 21, 1952, no. CDLXIX, with attachments, JCAE.

49. H-bomb Chronology, 71–72, JCAE.

50. Walker to Borden, Feb. 21, 1952, no. 2665, JCAE.

51. Griggs: Ivan Getting and John Christie, "David Tressel Griggs, 1911–1974" (National Academy Press, 1994); author interview with Ivan Getting, La Jolla, Calif., Mar. 13, 1997.

52. Polonium airplane: Walker to file, May 28, 1952, no. DXIII, and June 19, 1952, no. 2890, JCAE.

53. "Mr. X loses his job if the fact of the interview . . . becomes known," Borden cautioned McMahon. Walker and Borden to McMahon, Apr. 4, 1952, no. CDXCIX, JCAE.

54. Griggs notes, n.d., file 360.11, series 10, USAF/NARA.

55. Teller (2001), 336–37; Teller and Brown (1962), 59; Walkowicz to Assistant Chief of Staff, Aug. 3, 1951, file 334.5, series 10, USAF/NARA.

56. Lovett to McMahon, Mar. 9, 1952, no. CDLXII, JCAE.

57. Teller briefing: Mansfield to file, Feb. 12, 1953, no. DXCIII, JCAE; Griggs notes, n.d., file 360.11, series 10, USAF/NARA; RAND R-237, "Implications of Large-Yield Nuclear Weapons," July 10, 1952, 1952 file, box 3, Fred Kaplan donation, National Security Archives, George Washington University, Washington, D.C.

58. RAND R-237, Kaplan donation, National Security Archives; Teller and Brown (1962), 60–61.

59. "Memorandum for the Record," Mar. 11, 1952, folder 3, series 18; and Griggs's notes, n.d., file 360.11, series 10, USAF/NARA.

60. Lovett's memo was drafted by Griggs. Alexander et al. to Lovett, Mar. 27, 1952; and Foster to Acheson, Mar. 28, 1952, Thermonuclear Weapons Program file, series 184, OSD/NARA.

61. Dean wrote in his diary: "Teller has end-runned it again. He is taking the occasion to go off on the second lab question again. These poor guys topside . . . don't know what it is all about. I live with it every day and I think I do know." Anders (1987), 204.

62. Ibid., 204.

63. Ibid., 206–9.

64. Author interview with Ernie Plesset, Woodside, Calif., May 14, 1988; Hewlett and Duncan (1990), 582.

65. Anders (1987), 210.

66. Griggs to Finletter, n.d. [Mar., 1952], file 360.11, series 10, USAF/NARA.

67. It was also unclear whether the air force had the legal authority to establish a nuclear weapons lab. Griggs asked Pentagon lawyers to look into the matter. T. R. Hogness to Griggs, Mar. 26, 1952, and "Summary," n.d., file 360.11, series 10, USAF/NARA.

68. Griggs's notes, Mar. 20, 1952, file 360.11, series 10, USAF/NARA; Borden to Sheehy, Feb. 9, 1952, no. 2622, JCAE.

69. TEM diary, vol. 2, pt. 2, 55–56; "Meeting with Dr. E. O. Lawrence," Mar. 4, 1952, TEM papers.

70. The proposed extension had been for four years; Lawrence, however, urged that it be for five. Minutes of meeting, Jan. 24, 1952, folder 6, box 172, Neylan papers.

71. Libby had recently informed Ernest that the commission wished to wait another six months before making a decision on whether to fund the Mark II.

72. TEM diary, vol. 2, pt. 2, 62.

73. Ibid., 64–65; Walker to file, Apr. 17, 1952, no. 2753, JCAE.

74. Teller was "somewhat discouraged," the staffer wrote, "because he stressed that he had been trying to keep out of people's way, and that he was following the course of merely obeying orders and not taking the initiative in anything." Walker to Borden, Apr. 3, 1952, no. 2739, JCAE.

75. Walker and Borden to McMahon, Apr. 4, 1952, no. CDXCIX, JCAE.

76. Hayward interview (1996).

77. Minutes, GAC no. 30, Apr. 30, 1952, no. 74700, CIC/DOE; TEM diary, vol. 2, pt. 2, 69.

78. Murray's battle with Dean had become increasingly personal. Borden to files, Mar. 12, 1952, no. 2688, JCAE; TEM diary, vol. 2, pt. 2, 57.

79. *ITMOJRO*, 755.

80. TEM diary, vol. 2, pt. 2, 72.

81. "The hint was pointedly dropped that Admiral Strauss would be a most useful man in this struggle," the staffer wrote. Walker to Borden, Apr. 7, 1952, no. 2738, JCAE.

82. Walker and Borden to McMahon, Apr. 4, 1952, no. CDXCIX, JCAE.

83. "Meeting with Dr. E. O. Lawrence," Mar. 4, 1952, Murray papers.

84. DuBridge to Pitzer, Mar. 18, 1952, box 168.3, DuBridge papers; Borden to file, Mar. 22, 1952, no. 2704, JCAE; San Francisco special agent-in-charge to Hoover, Apr. 5, 1952, JRO/FBI.

85. Albuquerque special agent-in-charge to Hoover, May 27, 1952; and Branigan to Belmont, June 10, 1952, JRO/FBI.

86. Walker to file, Oct. 3, 1952, no. 3049, JCAE.

87. May 19, 1952, Dean diary, Dean papers.

88. Hoover sent this latest file to Truman's second attorney general, Howard McGrath, possibly in the hope that McGrath might do what Tom Clark would not: indict Oppenheimer for violation of the espionage laws. Hoover to Souers, May 19, 1952, JRO/FBI.

89. McCabe to Hoover, June 12, 1952, JRO/FBI.

90. Walker to file, May 28, 1952, no. DXIII, JCAE.

91. McMahon asked Truman to burn the letter after reading it, since he had "to live with" the atomic scientists. McMahon to Truman, May 21, 1952, J. K. Mansfield papers, Washington, D.C. The author thanks Jane Mansfield for access to her late husband's papers.

92. McMahon was "fearful of the influence this might have on other scientists in the event there is an open rupture," an aide informed Hoover. Nichols to Tolman, May 19, 1952, JRO/FBI.

93. David Teeple, the former army CIC agent who worked for Hickenlooper, told the FBI early in 1952 that he feared Oppie might defect to Russia, taking atomic secrets with him. Bernstein (1990), 1417.

94. Jeffery Dorwart, *Conflict of Duty: The U.S. Navy's Intelligence Dilemma, 1919–1945* (Naval Institute Press, 1983), 3–6. Because of Strauss's experience with wiretaps and bugs, he and Borden routinely used code names in telephone conversations and correspondence. Borden's code name for Strauss was *Luigi*. Borden to file, Aug. 13, 1951, no. 3464, JCAE; Ken Mansfield, Oct. 22, 1997, personal communication.

95. Two years earlier, Conant had been a target of both Latimer and Pitzer, who helped block his nomination as president of the National Academy of Sciences. Hershberg (1993), 485–86.

96. May 9, 1952, Conant diary, box 11, James Conant papers, Pusey Library, Harvard University, Cambridge, Mass.

97. Waters to Boyer, May 15, 1952, box 2, JRO/AEC; Bernstein (1990), 1425. "Oppenheimer is going to have to be a witness in this, and we may well turn out to be the defendant in the public eye," Dean wrote in his diary that fall. Nov. 24, 1952, Dean diary, Dean papers.

98. "Did Oppie answer the '64 dollar question' as to whether he was ever a Commie?" Dean said he asked the AEC's head of security. Marks to Oppenheimer, Dec. 2, 1952, "Weinberg Perjury Trial" folder, box 237, JRO; San Francisco FBI field report, Nov. 18, 1952, box 2, JRO/AEC.

99. Nichols to Tolson, May 29, 1952, JRO/FBI.

100. There is some suggestion of a tie-in between Oppenheimer's leaving the GAC and the Weinberg indictment. Assistant Attorney General James McInerney—whom Dean had gotten to know during the Rosenberg trial—promised he would withhold a decision on whether to mention the Kenilworth Court incident until after he had talked to Brien McMahon and Paul Crouch. On May 29, 1952, McMahon told FBI agent Louis Nichols that he had "worked out a plan whereby Oppenheimer would take the initiative and decline to serve another term [on the GAC] by an exchange of letters and everybody will be happy." June 13, 1952, Dean diary; and Dean to Oppenheimer, June 14, 1952, Dean papers. Murray, too, would later take credit for getting Oppenheimer off the GAC.

101. June 14, 1952, Conant diary, box 11, Conant papers.

102. R. Oppenheimer to F. Oppenheimer, July 12, 1952, "Weinberg Perjury Trial, 1953" folder, box 237, JRO.

15: Descent into the Maelstrom

1. June 27, 1952, Dean diary, Dean papers.

2. The project was carried out at Pasadena's Vista del Arroyo Hotel during the spring and summer of 1951; DuBridge was the group's chairman. Project *Vista:* David Elliot, "Project *Vista* and Nuclear Weapons in Europe," *International Security,* summer 1986, 163–83.

3. G. Norton to Finletter, July 1, 1952, entry 63, box 4, AEC/NARA; G. Norton to Burden, Nov. 15, 1951, general (TS) file, entry 4, records of the secretary of the air force, RG 340, National Archives.

4. Transmittal letter, "Project *Vista:* A Study of Ground and Air Tactical Warfare," Feb. 4, 1952. The author thanks David Elliott for a copy of the *Vista* report.

5. Oppenheimer and *Vista:* DuBridge to Eisenhower, Dec. 21, 1952, box 32, JRO; *ITMOJRO,* 757; "Notes of Conference," Jan. 19, 1954, box 202, JRO. The author thanks Carrie Allen for a copy of the notes found in the Oppenheimer papers.

6. By the time that DuBridge briefed the Pentagon on *Vista,* many of the report's most controversial recommendations had been amended or deleted altogether. Walker to file, n.d. [Dec. 1952], no. DLXXXVII, JCAE.

7. Walker to file, July 2, 1952, no. 2925; and Walker to file, n.d. [Dec. 1952], no. DLXXXVII, JCAE; Stern (1969), 190–91.

8. Walker to file, May 28, 1952, no. DXIII, and Borden to McMahon, May 28, 1952, no. 3831, JCAE; Rabi to Lauritsen, n.d. [May–June 1951], folder 14, box 3, Charles Lauritsen papers, Caltech archives.

9. Minutes, "Panel of Consultants on Arms and Policy," May 16–18, 1952, "Disarmament Panel, Misc." folder, box 191, JRO.

10. Standstill: Minutes, "Disarmament Panel, Misc." folder, box 191, JRO; Walker to file, n.d. [Dec. 1951], no. DLXXXVII, JCAE.

11. *FRUS: 1952–54,* vol. 2, pt. 2, 1001; *ITMOJRO,* 248.

12. Arneson to Acheson, Sept. 29, 1952, *FRUS: 1952–54,* vol. 2, pt. 2, 1017–25.

13. *FRUS: 1952–54,* vol. 2, pt. 2, 994–1008; Barton Bernstein, "Crossing the Rubicon: A Missed Opportunity to Stop the H-bomb?" *International Security,* fall 1989, 143.

14. "I did nothing whatever about it," Oppenheimer would later testify. *ITMOJRO,* 247.

15. GAC swan song: Anders (1987), 224; Walker and Hamilton to file, July 1, 1952, no. 2914, JCAE; Oppenheimer to Truman, June 14, 1952, no. 74674, CIC/DOE.

16. Hershberg (1993), 603.

17. LeBaron had heard that the panel would urge "that all U.S. thermonuclear efforts cease." Walker to file, n.d. [Dec. 1952], no. DLXXXVII, JCAE.

18. McMahon's illness did not extinguish his hopes of becoming his party's vice presidential nominee. He died on July 28, 1952.

19. Cooksey to A. Loomis, May 6 and 10, 1952, folder 10, carton 46, EOL.

20. The AEC approved "early participation of [the Rad Lab] in the diagnostic measurements field, and later along such additional lines as may be determined by the Commission." Dean to Regents, June 9, 1952, AEC/NARA.

21. Dean agreed to add a phrase to his letter to the regents: "the Commission hopes that the group at UCRL will eventually suggest broader programs of thermonuclear research." But Murray complained that the AEC chairman's letter made it "clear that at least in Dean's mind this action with regard to Berkeley did not constitute the establishment of a second laboratory strictly speaking." TEM diary, vol. 1., pt. 1, 18; Jacobvitz to Brinck, Apr. 29, 1954, no. 79166, CIC/DOE.

22. York to Bradbury, June 3, 1952, no. 125187, and Bradbury, "Observations on the Livermore Laboratory Proposal," May 21, 1952, no. 125188, CIC/DOE.

23. Sybil Francis, *Warhead Politics: Livermore and the Competitive System of Nuclear Weapon Design* (University Microfilms, 1996), 58.

24. York interview (1997).

25. Walker to Borden, Apr. 7, 1952, no. 2738, JCAE.

26. Hayward to "all concerned," July 23, 1952, AEC/NARA.

27. LeBaron had evidently tried to reconcile the two warring parties at breakfast that morning, without success: "Gradually, as time passed, Teller, as he had with Bradbury, began to usurp Lawrence's role. No one had ever challenged his authority before. It was not an experience he enjoyed. In his own way, he let Teller feel his displeasure." Transcript of interview by Lin Root, n.d., folder 4, box 1, LeBaron papers.

28. Walker to file, Nov. 10, 1952, no. DCVII, JCAE. Dean to Lawrence, July 17, 1952, folder 18, carton 33, EOL. "Tell Teller he can blow up anything he wants," Dean reportedly told Hayward. Hayward interview (1996).

29. Underhill to Dean, July 1, 1952, AEC no. 425/21, AEC/NARA.

30. TEM diary, vol. 2, pt. 1, 19.

31. Walker and Hamilton to file, July 1, 1952, no. 2914, JCAE.

32. Teller's confidant was journalist Stephen White. Rabi interview (1982). Although Teller subsequently denied making the comment to White, he wrote of his decision to go to Livermore: "I turned away from my original choice—to work on pure science—with my eyes open." Teller (1987), 122.

33. AEC no. 295/60, Oct. 10, 1952, AEC/NARA.

34. Bevatron: Childs (1968), 446; Hewlett and Duncan (1990), 500–501.

35. Alvarez (1987), 176–77.

36. Dean to Lay, Oct. 30, 1952, AEC/NARA. Had the bomb been tested earlier, as Teller had urged, the AEC concluded that a failure was likely. Rhodes (1995), 487.

37. Bethe had written to Dean that fall, urging that the test be delayed until mid-November—"to give the smoke of battle time to dissipate." Bethe to Dean, Sept. 9, 1952, no. 73974, CIC/DOE.

38. Nov. 21, 1952, Dean diary, Dean papers.

39. Anders (1987), 226–27.

40. Dean to AEC directors, Oct. 30, 1952, no. 102137, CIC/DOE; Hewlett and Duncan (1990), 592.

41. *Mike* test: Rhodes (1995), 509; Hansen (1988), 56–57.

42. Murray (1960), 20–21.

43. Teller (2001), 351; York interview (1997); transcript of Bradbury interview, Bancroft Library.

44. The resignation letter, drafted by DuBridge, was never sent. SAC/ODM: Gregg Herken, *Cardinal Choices: Presidential Science Advising from the Atomic Bomb to SDI* (Oxford University Press, 1992), 54–58; draft letter, "Nov. 1952," folder 9, box 186, DuBridge papers.

45. Princeton meeting: Various letters, box 189, JRO; Hershberg (1993), 569.

46. Walker to file, July 2, 1952, no. 2925, JCAE.

47. That fall, Borden sent the Joint Committee chairman a sixty-four page "working paper" that detailed the charges against Oppenheimer. Borden to Cole, Nov. 3, 1952, no. DCXXXV, JCAE.

48. Walker: Author interview with J. K. Mansfield, Washington, D.C., Oct. 27, 1993; transcript of John Walker interview by Jack Holl, June 18, 1976. The author thanks Ken Mansfield for a copy of the Walker interview. Cotter: Frank Cotter, Oct. 21, 1997, personal communication.

49. "The Scale and Scope of Atomic Production: A Chronology of Leading Events" (A-bomb Chronology), Jan. 30, 1952, "Atomic Program Chronology" folder, series 2, JCAE.

50. McMahon to Dean, May 7, 1952, no. DCCIX, JCAE.

51. Anders (1987), 211.

52. Walker to file, Oct. 3, 1952, no. 3049, JCAE; Bethe, "Memorandum on the History of the Thermonuclear Program," May 28, 1952, box 4930, AEC/NARA; Walker to file, June 25, 1952, no. DXXXVI, JCAE.

53. There "may yet be another Fuchs in the project," the committee's intelligence expert warned Borden. JCAE, *Soviet Atomic Espionage,* (U.S. Government Printing office, 1951); Sheehy to Borden, Mar. 20, 1951, no. 2036, JCAE.

54. Mansfield to Borden, May 28, 1951, no. CCCXXXI, JCAE.

55. Second Fuchs: Minutes, Apr. 14, 1953, no. DCLXII, JCAE; Walker to Borden, Apr. 3, 1952, no. 2742; Fields to Borden, May 5, 1952, no. 2773; and Mansfield to file, May 28, 1952, no. DLVI, JCAE.

56. The president was told about the document by the Joint Committee's acting chairman, Congressman Carl Durham, the day following the inauguration; Ike asked to see a copy a few days later. Eisenhower did not acknowledge receipt of the chronology until Feb. 14, 1953. Richard Hewlett and Jack Holl, *Atoms for War and Peace, 1953–1961: Eisenhower and the Atomic Energy Commission* (University of California Press, 1989), 34.

57. Borden and Walker contemptuously dismissed Bethe's counterchronology as a "whitewash"; the Cornell physicist had not even been at the 1946 conference, they pointed out. Walker to files, Oct. 3, 1952, no. 3049, JCAE.

58. Walker to Borden, July 16, 1952, no. 3098, JCAE.

59. Pike to McMahon, June 12, 1950, AEC/NARA; 1950 Fuchs interview: Robert Lamphere to Hoover, June 6, 1950, serial 1412, Klaus Fuchs file, no. 65–58805, FBI.

60. "Committee Business," Feb. 18, 1953, no. 3281, JCAE.

61. Cotter to Borden, Jan. 27, 1953, no. 3217, and Dean to Cole, Apr. 9, 1953, no. DCXV, JCAE; Hewlett and Holl (1989), 38. A subsequent "damage assessment" done for the AEC by Bethe, Teller, and others—based on the documents that Walker sent Wheeler—concluded that it "clearly reveals the *idea* of the radiation implosion" as well as "construction elements" of *Mike.* In his memoirs, Wheeler misremembered what was in the lost document. Wheeler and Ford (1998), 285.

62. Wheeler incident: "Committee Business," Feb. 18, 1953, no. 3281, and Cotter to file, Mar. 25, 1953, no. 3389, JCAE.

63. "Meeting with President Eisenhower and NSC," Feb. 16, 1953, Mansfield papers. The unknown author writes of Ike's reaction: "I never saw anyone more excited and concerned. I remember [Eisenhower] saying that if this had happened in the Army the man would have been shot."

64. Dean diary, Feb. 17, 1953, Dean papers.

65. Borden interview (1981).

66. Borden tried, unsuccessfully, to distract attention from the incident. Borden to Cole, Apr. 15, 1953, no. DCXVII, JCAE.

67. Fidler interview (1998); Hayward interview (1996).

68. Livermore origins: "Resumé of Meeting," Aug. 19, 1952, LBL archives; *Preparing for the 21st Century: 40 Years of Excellence, the Lawrence Livermore National Laboratory* (LLNL, 1998), 5–10; Phil Scheidermayer, "Recollections, Reminiscences, Reflections," UCRL-AR-125101, July 1996, and various interviews, LLNL archives.

69. Even at this late date, Lawrence "said it was not intended that Livermore should become the second major weapons laboratory." Minutes, AEC no. 744, Sept. 8, 1952, AEC/NARA. Ramrod: Livermore interviews. As its name implied, Ramrod showed Teller's belated appreciation of the importance of compression in igniting the Super.

70. Project *Whitney,* named by York, was evidently inspired by Wheeler's Project *Matterhorn* at Princeton. The AEC had originally hoped to keep the weapons work at Livermore a secret. AEC to Cooksey, Feb. 25, 1953, LBL.

71. Responsibility for the new Alarm Clock was transferred from Los Alamos to Livermore that summer. AEC no. 425/24, Aug. 18, 1952, AEC/NARA.

72. Francis (1996), 67.

73. Daring and bold did not always mean practical. Transcript of Arthur Hudgins interview, LLNL archives.

74. Hydride bomb: "Procurement of Deuterated Polyethylene," Oct. 17 and 24, 1952, LBL; author interview with Wallace Decker, Livermore, Calif., June 11, 1997, and Street interview (1997).

75. Chromatics: Various correspondence, folder 3, carton 4, EOL; Childs (1968), 420–26; transcript of interviews with Alvarez and Gaither, box 1, Childs papers; Crawford Cooley, May 29, 1997, personal communication.

76. Neylan intervened with the regents to ensure that Lawrence retained sole patent rights on the tube.

77. "If you guys are going to do this kind of business, you are going to have to learn to put out a better looking product," a Los Alamos physicist scolded his Livermore counterpart. *Ruth* test: Hansen (1988), 39 fn.; transcript of Wallace Decker interview, LLNL archives; Francis (1996), 68.

78. Eisenhower briefing: Hewlett and Holl (1989), 3–5; Anders (1987), 286.

79. Murray to Truman, Jan. 6, 1953, Murray papers.

80. Disarmament panel's report: *FRUS, 1952–1954,* vol. 2, pt. 2, 1106–14, 1169–74.

81. Hewlett and Holl (1989), 51.

82. Ibid., 45.

83. Eisenhower was also reportedly concerned that he might be criticized for having too few Jews in his administration. Pfau (1984), 137.

84. After his meeting with Borden, Strauss spoke by telephone with Lawrence, Alvarez, and Pitzer. All knew of the 1942 Berkeley meeting and had been outspoken in their criticism of Oppie. Telegram, Borden to Lawrence, Dec. 23, 1952, and reply; Borden to Lawrence, Jan. 19, 1953, folder 25, carton 32, EOL.

85. Murphy's principal source for the article had been Teddy Walkowicz, head of the air force's Special Study Group, but Strauss reviewed the draft and evidently suggested changes. Hewlett and Holl (1989), 57; interview with Charles Murphy, June 12, 1954, sec. 42, JRO/FBI.

86. Hewlett and Holl (1989), 57.

87. Belmont to Ladd, May 23, 1952, sec. 12, JRO/FBI. Until a week before the verdict, Oppenheimer had expected to be called to the witness stand. Oppenheimer to Ruth Tolman, Feb. 27, 1953, box 72, JRO; Feb. 25, 1953, Dean diary, Dean papers.

88. "Weinberg Freed," *Kansas City Star,* Mar. 5, 1953. Taking no chances, Weinberg's defense attorney had filed a motion to suppress any evidence gathered by electronic means. Criminal docket, *United States vs. Joseph W. Weinberg,* May–June, 1953, U.S. District Court records, Washington, D.C. My thanks to Jim David for the records of the Weinberg trial.

89. Borden and McMahon had been Rickover's ally in his protracted battles with the navy's "battleship admirals." Norman Polmar and Thomas Allen, *Rickover: Controversy and Genius* (Touchstone, 1982), 198; Pfau (1984), 150.

90. Allardice had been recommended to the Joint Committee by Strauss. Allardice: "Committee Business," May 12, 1953, no. 3470, JCAE.

91. Previously, Borden had gone to the FBI for Oppenheimer's security dossier. He was reluctant to go to the AEC for the file, Borden told the bureau, "as this might stir up some speculation." Tolson to Nichols, Mar. 28, 1952, JRO/FBI. AEC records indicate that Borden returned the file on Aug. 18, 1953; Strauss checked it out the next day. Waters to Strauss, May 12, 1954, Mansfield papers.

92. Borden to Allardice, May 29, 1953, 1953 correspondence, JCAE. Hoover and CIA director Allen Dulles turned down the Joint Committee's request to interview Fuchs. Cole to Hoover, July 14, 1953, no. DCLXXI, and Hoover to Cole, July 16, 1953, no. DCLXXXI, and Dulles to Cole, July 23, 1953, no. DCLXXXIX, JCAE.

93. "Questions raised in my mind by JRO file—WLB," May 29, 1953, no. DCXXXVIII, and Borden to Allardice, June 1, 1953, no. DCXXXIX, JCAE.

94. Borden told the author that he had hoped to be the prosecutor in a trial of Oppenheimer for treason. Borden interview (1981).

16: Not Much More than a Kangaroo Court

1. Belmont to Ladd, June 5, 1953, sec. 14, JRO/FBI.

2. Ibid.

3. Pfau (1984), 145.

4. June 5, 1953, Dean diary, Dean papers; Hewlett and Holl (1989), 53.

5. Hewlett and Holl (1989), 55–62, 71–72; Pfau (1984), 146–48. Although Eisenhower hoped that "Atoms for Peace" might be a spur toward disarmament, Strauss was under no such illusion. *FRUS: 1952–1954,* vol. 2, pt. 2, 1218–20.

6. Ladd to Hoover, May 25, 1953, sec. 14, and Hoover to Attorney General, Apr. 13, 1954, sec. 24, JRO/FBI.

7. Teeple: Kamen (1986), 252–53, 323; "Senator Hickenlooper Aide Is Ordered by Court to Give Testimony in Libel Suit," *Washington Post,* Nov. 19, 1954.

8. Nov. 7, 1942, Dean diary, Dean papers; "Dr. J. Robert Oppenheimer," Dec. 14, 1959, box 3, JRO/AEC.

9. The fact that Oppenheimer never went to the White House on the appointed day convinced Strauss that Oppie was either "a spy or a liar." Oppenheimer's appointment book indicates that he had scheduled a meeting with Cutler for Sept. 1. Bernstein (1990), 1435; Belmont to Ladd, Sept. 2, 1953, sec. 14, JRO/FBI; Pfau (1984), 147.

10. Nearly five years after his humiliation at Oppenheimer's hands over the export of isotopes, Strauss wrote to Rabi claiming that he had evidence vindicating his claim that one of the recipients of isotopes given to Norway was a Communist. Strauss to Rabi, Oct. 20, 1953, Strauss folder, Isidor Rabi papers, Library of Congress.

11. Wilson to Bush, Aug. 25, 1954, box 120, Bush papers, Library of Congress; Smyth to Wilson, Sept. 9, 1954, box 39, Smyth papers; Gordon Arneson, "R. Gordon Arneson: Memories of the State Department's 'Mr. Atom'" (unpublished manuscript, n.d.); Gordon Arneson, Mar. 12, 1992, personal communication.

12. Arneson later discovered that his FBI dossier included the complaint of an irate neighbor. Arneson interview (1979).

13. Strauss (1962), 345–46.

14. Joe-4: Rhodes (1995), 523–24; Holloway (1994), 305–8. Joint Committee chairman Sterling Cole boasted in a letter to Ike: "we are now well ahead of the Soviets—both in fission weapons and in thermonuclear developments." *FRUS: 1952–1954,* vol. 2, pt. 2, 1185–86.

15 Pfau (1984), 148.

16. Allardice to files, Dec. 21, 1953, no. CMXXV, JCAE; unsigned draft memo, Sept. 1, 1953, no. DCXXXIX, JCAE.

17. Mansfield to Teller, Nov. 10, 1953, Teller folder, JCAE.

18. Borden's lengthy brief on Oppenheimer came as something of a shock and a revelation to Allardice. Allardice to file, June 13, 1953, no. DCXLIX, JCAE.

19. Cotter to Allardice, Oct. 22, 1953, no. 3687, JCAE. Allardice wrote at the bottom of Cotter's memo: "I concur."

20. In an assessment for the Joint Committee, Cotter disputed many of the points made by Borden in his letter to Hoover. Cotter to Allardice, Dec. 16, 1953, no. CMXXI, JCAE; Frank Cotter, Oct. 6, 1997, personal communication.

21. Chairman to president, May 21, 1953, no. DCXXXVI, JCAE.

22. Hickenlooper apparently talked Cole out of sending the letter to Hoover. Belmont to Ladd, Nov 27, 1953, sec. 15, pt. 1, JRO/FBI; Cole to Hoover, Nov. 24, 1953, no. CMXXII, JCAE.

23. In Dec. 1953, Allardice told an FBI agent that he and Cotter had "concluded it was best all around not to do anything except continue to watch the case." Allardice to files, Dec. 21, 1953, no. CMXXV, JCAE.

24. One of the things that caused Borden to suspect Oppie of being a spy was Fuchs's conclusion "that the Soviets had acquired an agent at Berkeley who informed them of electromagnetic separation research during 1942 or earlier." Borden to Hoover, Nov. 7, 1953,

Oppenheimer file, JCAE. Borden letter: Allardice to Strauss, Aug. 14, 1953, no. DCXXXV, JCAE; *ITMOJRO,* 839; Pittsburgh field report to Hoover, Dec. 6, 1953, sec. 15, pt. 2, JRO/FBI; Teller (2001), 389.

25. Hoover's suspicions were shared by others. Nichols (1987), 306; Pfau (1984), 150.

26. Hoover to Tolson et al., Dec. 3, 1953, sec. 15, pt. 2, JRO/FBI.

27. Murray had become increasingly distrustful of Strauss. Hoover to Tolson and Ladd, Nov. 25, 1953, sec. 14, JRO/FBI; Pfau (1984), 155.

28. Hoover to Brownell, Dec. 3, 1953, sec. 15, pt. 2, JRO/FBI; Pfau (1984), 148–49.

29. Hoover to Tolson et al., Dec. 2, 1953, sec. 15, pt. 2, JRO/FBI.

30. Pfau (1984), 151.

31. Ibid.

32. Robert Ferrell, ed., *The Eisenhower Diaries* (Norton, 1981), 261–62; Belmont to Ladd, June 5, 1953, sec. 14, JRO/FBI.

33. Hewlett and Holl (1989), 69.

34. Hoover to Tolson et al., Dec. 3, 1953, sec. 15, pt. 2, JRO/FBI; Hewlett and Holl (1989), 69–70.

35. Hoover to Tolson et al., May 19, 1953, sec. 14, JRO/FBI.

36. Hoover to Tolson and Ladd, June 24, 1953, sec. 14, JRO/FBI.

37. Pfau (1984), 141.

38. Minutes, Aug. 25, 1949, no. 1203, JCAE. Volpe's comment had been made in the context of the AEC's reinvestigation of Berkeley's scientists. See chapter 10.

39. Hoover to Tolson et al., Dec. 3, 1953, sec. 15, JRO/FBI.

40. Pittsburgh field report to Hoover, Dec. 4, 1953, sec. 15, pt. 2, JRO/FBI.

41. Borden to Allardice, Dec. 6, 1953, Borden correspondence, JCAE.

42. Bernstein (1990), 1439.

43. Nichols (1987), 297; Strauss to Nichols, May 7, 1952, folder 70, box 4, Kenneth Nichols papers, Army Corps of Engineers archives, Ft. Belvoir, Va.

44. Bernstein (1990), 1448.

45. Teller-Strauss meeting: Teller to Strauss, Nov. 6, 1953 and Dec. 11, 1953, LLS/HHPL; Teller (1987), 63.

46. Nichols to Tolson, Dec. 3, 1953, sec. 15, pt. 2, JRO/FBI.

47. Allardice's original informant was probably William Consodine, Groves's wartime lawyer. The Consodines were longtime friends of Allardice and his wife. Nichols to Tolson, Dec. 14, 1953, sec. 16, JRO/FBI; Joseph Volpe, Aug. 9, 2000, personal communication.

48. Hoover to Cleveland Special Agent-in-Change, Dec. 10, 1953, sec. 16, JRO/FBI.

49. Strauss immediately telephoned Allardice after talking to Groves. Belmont to Ladd, Dec. 14, 1953, sec. 15, pt. 2, JRO/FBI; telephone log, Dec. 1–30, 1953, box 6, LLS/NARA.

50. Belmont to Ladd, Dec. 14, 1953, sec. 15, pt. 2, JRO/FBI.

51. The following day, Lansdale wrote to Groves, at the latter's request, with his recollection of the Dec. 1943 meeting in Groves's office: "You had promised J. Robert that the information would not be given to the F.B.I. and so directed me. I will confess that in this one instance I disobeyed your instructions and orally passed the information along to the F.B.I." Lansdale to Groves, Dec. 16, 1953, box 5, Groves/NARA. My thanks to Stan Norris for a copy of the Lansdale letter.

52. Belmont to Ladd, Dec. 29, 1953, sec. 16, JRO/FBI.

53. Belmont to Ladd, Dec. 17, 1953, sec. 16, JRO/FBI.

54. Groves was not able to see either Strauss or Nichols, so he met with LaPlante. Groves visit to FBI and AEC: Belmont to Ladd, Dec. 17, 1953, sec. 15, pt. 2, JRO/FBI; LaPlante to files, Dec. 17, 1953, AEC/NARA.

55. SAC Newark to Hoover, Dec. 22, 1953, and Hoover to Brownell, Dec. 22, 1953, sec. 16, JRO/FBI.

56. Hoover to Brownell, Dec. 22, 1953, sec. 16, JRO/FBI; Stern (1969), 69.

57. Joseph Learned to Hoover, Dec. 31, 1953, sec. 16, JRO/FBI. Hoover passed along the interview with Frank to Strauss on Jan. 7, 1954. "Dr. J. Robert Oppenheimer," Dec. 14, 1959, box 3, JRO/AEC.

58. Bernstein (1990), 1442; telephone log, Dec. 1–30, 1953, box 5, LLS/NARA.

59. Bernstein (1990), 1447–48. Entry of Dec. 9, 1953, LaPlante diary, AEC/NARA; Murray to Strauss, Dec. 7, 1953, sec. 15, pt. 2, JRO/FBI.

60. Hewlett and Holl (1989), 78.

61. Among the traits that Strauss praised at Campbell's confirmation hearings was the latter's "personal loyalty." Campbell was the only commissioner to whom Strauss revealed Ike's "blank wall" order prior to the Dec. 10 meeting. Hewlett and Holl (1989), 31, 75.

62. According to Strauss's telephone log, Strauss talked to Groves twice on the morning of Dec. 10; Strauss also talked to Allardice in between Groves's calls. While it is likely that the topic of discussion was the story that Allardice had given the FBI a week earlier, no subject is indicated in the log. Telephone log, Dec. 1–30, 1953, box 5, LLS/NARA.

63. Nichols stopped by Green's office twice that weekend to remind the young lawyer to include the Chevalier incident in the list of charges. Nichols (1987), 307.

64. Hewlett and Holl (1989), 75–77; Stern (1969), 228–30.

65. Dec. 10, 1953, LaPlante diary, AEC/NARA.

66. Hoover to Strauss, Dec. 18, 1953, sec. 16, JRO/FBI; Williams and Cantelon (1984), 144–47.

67. Belmont to Ladd, Dec. 14, 1953, sec. 16, JRO/FBI.

68. Belmont to Ladd, Dec. 17, 1953, sec. 16, JRO/FBI.

69. As an indication of his innocence—or his hubris—Oppenheimer asked the trustees of Princeton's Institute for Advanced Study to pay the $12,000 he had spent in legal fees preparing for the Weinberg trial. Strauss informed the FBI that "finally the 'long-haired professors' on the Board went along with him" and rejected Oppie's appeal. Belmont to Ladd, June 19, 1953, sec. 14, JRO/FBI.

70. Oppenheimer to P. Spero, Apr. 29, 1953, Weinberg folder, box 77, and Reynolds to Oppenheimer, Dec. 31, 1953, box 47, JRO.

71. Paris visit: Legal attaché, Paris to FBI, Apr. 19, 1954, sec. 30, and telex, Apr. 26, 1954, sec. 31, JRO/FBI; Stern (1969), 213–15.

72. Belmont to Ladd, Dec. 4, 1953, sec. 15, pt. 2, JRO/FBI; Dec. 12, 1953, Nichols diary, folder 77, box 4, Nichols papers.

73. Belmont to Ladd, Dec. 14, 1953, sec. 15, pt. 2, JRO/FBI; Pfau (1984), 157.

74. Nichols (1987), 308.

75. Oppie had at one time looked to Strauss to defend him against such attacks. Nichols (1987), "Meeting with Dr. J. Robert Oppenheimer . . . ," Dec. 21, 1953, folder 80, box 4, Nichols papers; Hewlett and Holl (1989), 78–80.

76. Nichols (1987), 308.

77. Dec. 22, 1953, Nichols diary, folder 80, box 4, Nichols papers; Hoover to Brownell, Dec. 21, 1953, supplemental releases, JRO/FBI.

17: The Good Deeds a Man Has Done Before

1. Garrison: Stern (1969), 244.

2. Robb: Ibid., 243; Jan. 26, 1954, Nichols diary, Nichols papers.

3. In addition, the bureau tapped at least one of Oppie's lawyers and also had an informant at Princeton's Institute of Advanced Study. Wiretaps: Branigan to Belmont, Apr. 7, 1954, sec. 15, JRO/FBI. Hewlett and Holl (1989), 80; Heinrich to Belmont, June 29, 1954, supplemental releases, JRO/FBI; Bernstein (1990), 1451.

4. Strauss was telling Bates by month's end that the wiretaps "had been most helpful to the AEC in that they were aware before hand of the moves [Oppenheimer] was contemplating." Belmont to Ladd, Jan. 5, 1954, and Jan. 28, 1954, supplemental releases, JRO/FBI.

5. Belmont to Ladd, Feb. 19, 1954, sec. 21, JRO/FBI.

6. Borden to files, Aug. 13, 1951, no. 3464, JCAE.

7. Hoover to Strauss, Jan. 18, 1954, sec. 17, JRO/FBI.

8. Belmont to Ladd, Feb. 25, 1954, sec. 21, JRO/FBI.

9. Hewlett and Holl (1989), 74.

10. "Details," n.d., and Branigan to Belmont, Jan. 22, 1954, sec. 18, JRO/FBI.

11. "Summary for Jan. 22, 1954," sec. 18, JRO/FBI.

12. Belmont to Ladd, Feb. 25, 1954, sec. 21, JRO/FBI.

13. Feb. 19, 1954, Nichols diary, Nichols papers. Groves asked Nichols what he should say in his testimony. The general's former aide responded cheerily: "Tell Oppie to be very truthful about all matters—maybe you and I will learn the truth about the Chevalier matter. Is he protecting Frank?" Nichols (1987), 315.

14. Belmont to Boardman, Mar. 4, 1954, sec. 21, JRO/FBI; Mar. 3, 1954, Nichols diary, Nichols papers.

15. Belmont to Ladd, Jan. 26, 1954, sec. 19, JRO/FBI.

16. Belmont to Boardman, Apr. 11, 1954, sec. 31, JRO/FBI.

17. Admiral Deke Parsons died of a heart attack the day before he was to go to the secretary of the navy to denounce the investigation of Oppenheimer. The FBI obtained Parsons's medical records for Robb, so that he might counter the widow's claim that the attack on Oppie had killed her husband. Parsons: Branigan to Belmont, Mar. 22, 1954, sec. 23, JRO/FBI; Stern (1969), 224.

18. Belmont to Ladd, Feb. 19, 1954, sec. 21, JRO/FBI.

19. Exculpatory evidence, on the other hand, was buried. Rolander to file, Mar. 18 and Apr. 2, 1954; and Branigan to Belmont, Apr. 15, 1954, sec. 25, JRO/FBI.

20. Rolander to Nichols (1987), Jan. 21, 1954, AEC/NARA; Mitchell to file, Feb. 23, 1954, AEC/NARA. On May 4, at the end of the hearing, Nichols wrote in his diary: "I told LaPlante I don't want anything in the files saying we determined Garrison doesn't require clearance." Mar. 29, 1954, and May 4, 1954, Nichols diary, Nichols papers.

21. Nichols (1987), "Memo for Record," Jan. 19, 1954, Nichols papers. Samuel Silverman, Garrison's legal partner, recalled that Marks "was the most opposed to getting a clearance—on principle." Author interview with Samuel Silverman, New York, N.Y., Nov. 14, 2000.

22. Hoover to Strauss, Feb. 18, 1954, sec. 19, JRO/FBI.

23. Newark SAC telex, Mar. 25, 1954, sec. 23, JRO/FBI.

24. "I don't really remember that the Chevalier incident came up at all in my conversation with Frank." Silverman interview (2000).

25. Ibid.

26. Hewlett and Holl (1989), 86.

27. Hoover to Strauss, Jan. 22, 1954, file C, vol. 2, box 2, JRO/AEC. The log of Strauss's telephone calls indicates that he talked to Allardice on Feb. 15, 17, and 18, 1954. Telephone log, Jan.–Mar. 1954, box 6, LLS/NARA.

28. Hewlett and Holl (1989), 86.

29. Rolander to file, Mar. 15, 1954, file C, vol. 2, box 2, JRO/AEC.

30. Ibid. Lawrence also accused Oppenheimer of trying to "plant a man from Princeton on me" who had later been turned down by AEC security. The Princeton physicist—David Feldman—was a former fellow at the institute whom Oppie had recommended that Ernest hire at the Rad Lab in 1950. Rolander to file, Mar. 18, 1954, box 3, AEC/JRO; David Feldman, Aug. 25, 1993, personal communication.

31. Rolander to file, Mar. 15, 1954, file C, vol. 2, box 2, JRO/AEC; Cotter to Allardice, Sept. 7, 1954, no. 4888, JCAE.

32. Rolander to file, Mar. 15, 1954, file C, vol. 2, box 2, JRO/AEC.

33. Pfau (1984), 162.

34. Goodchild (1980), 231.

35. Hoover to Strauss, Jan. 4, 1954, sec. 17, JRO/FBI.

36. Gray: Stern (1969), 241; Hewlett and Holl (1989), 83. Although praised as "a man with no ax to grind," Gray, a week before the hearing began, was already passing derogatory information on Oppenheimer to Robb. Hewlett and Holl (1989), 90.

37. *Bravo:* Hansen (1988), 62–68.

38. *Bravo* and *Lucky Dragon:* Minutes, May 29, 1954, GAC no. 40, no. 73405, CIC/DOE; Rhodes (1995), 542–43; Hansen (1988), 65–66.

39. Strauss told Eisenhower's press secretary that the *Lucky Dragon* was probably a

"Red spy ship" and the crew's injuries faked. At Strauss's request, CIA agents boarded the *Lucky Dragon* while it was in port in Japan. Robert Divine, *Blowing on the Wind: The Nuclear Test Ban Debate, 1954–1960* (Oxford University Press, 1978), 6–9; Stephen Ambrose, *Eisenhower,* vol. 2, *The President* (Simon and Schuster, 1984), 168. Spy ship charge: Mar. 18, 1954, Nichols diary, Nichols papers; Hewlett and Holl (1989), 177; Herken (1992), 80; Pfau (1984), 166.

40. Two Livermore H-bomb tests were scheduled for *Castle.* The device to be tested first was a lithium-fueled, or "dry," version of Ramrod dubbed "Morgenstern" (Morning Star) at the lab. The second device, called "Ramrod," was a "wet," or cryogenically cooled, version of the same device. Interviews.

41. Like *Ruth,* Livermore's second hydride test, *Ray,* on Apr. 11, 1953, had also fizzled. The explosion, however, managed to level the bomb's 100-tower. Hansen (1988), 67–68; interviews: York (1997) and Decker (1997).

42. Beset by last-minute doubts about the design of the radiation case, Livermore physicists surrounded the railroad car–sized Morgenstern with water-filled jerry cans. York interview (1997).

43. Interviews: LLNL (1997).

44. Strauss to LeBaron, Apr. 26, 1954, no. 72323, CIC/DOE. Both the Morgenstern device tested in *Koon* and *Echo*'s Ramrod were based upon Teller's concept of a two-stage thermonuclear trigger for his original Super. Chuck Hansen, "Operation Castle," unpublished manuscript, 57. The author would like to thank Chuck Hansen for a copy of his unpublished update to *U.S. Nuclear Weapons: The Secret History.*

45. Francis (1996), 69.

46. Rhodes (1995), 543; Stern (1969), 260–61.

47. Apr. 12, 1954, Nichols diary, Nichols papers.

48. *ITMOJRO,* 103.

49. Bates found the recording in the boxes of army CIC files that Groves turned over to the FBI at the end of the war. Nichols (1987), 315.

50. As Hoover and Strauss were aware, by sticking to the story that he told the FBI in 1946, Oppenheimer avoided a possible perjury indictment; the statute of limitation had already run out on any lie told to Pash in 1943. Branigan to Belmont, Apr. 19, 1954, sec. 31, JRO/FBI; Pfau (1984), 171.

51. Stern (1969), 280. Nichols told Strauss that he believed the reason Oppenheimer was taken by surprise at the 1954 hearing was that Oppie assumed the commission knew little of his prewar past. Strauss to file, Nov. 12, 1969, LLS/HHPL.

52. *ITMOJRO,* 137.

53. "How can any individual report a treasonable act on the part of another man and then go and stay at his home for several days? It just doesn't make any sense to me," Ike told his press secretary, James Hagerty. Hewlett and Holl (1989), 104.

54. *ITMOJRO,* 153. Wrote Nichols in his memoirs, published in 1987: "I certainly do not believe that Oppenheimer told Groves that it all was a 'cock and bull story' in the autumn of 1943." Nichols (1987), 319.

55. *ITMOJRO,* 153.

56. Apr. 13, 1954, Nichols diary, Nichols papers.

57. *ITMOJRO,* 170–79. Robb did not ask Groves whether he considered Oppenheimer a security risk, but instead—quoting the May 1950 letter that the general had written for the physicist—asked whether "the expressions of confidence in him contained in this letter you wrote hold?" Groves answered, "you can draw your own conclusions as to what I feel today."

58. Ibid., 265.

59. "One extraordinary thing about this case is that, while I seem to occupy such an important role in it, no one has seen fit to ask me to contribute my two-bits worth," Chevalier wrote to Oppie's lawyer after the hearing. Chevalier to Garrison, Aug. 5, 1954, courtesy of Priscilla McMillan.

60. The AEC's historians remarked upon this fact in their account of the Oppenheimer hearing: "Curiously, Robb had been inexplicably gentle when it came to pressing

Oppenheimer, Groves, and Lansdale for the facts concerning Frank Oppenheimer's involvement in the Chevalier affair." Hewlett and Holl (1989), 100. Garrison thought that Oppie was just "a bad liar and he got confused and the story bit by bit crystallized into something he had not intended to portray. . . . I tried to get him to let me argue this way to the Board, but for some reason which I have never quite understood he was reluctant to have me do so." Garrison to Charles Curtis, Aug. 17, 1954, courtesy of Priscilla McMillan.

61. Bernstein (1990), 1463.

62. Belmont to Boardman, Apr. 17, 1954, sec. 26, JRO/FBI.

63. Apr. 16, 1954, Nichols diary, Nichols papers.

64. Hewlett and Holl (1989), 89–90; "Dr. Oppenheimer Suspended by AEC in Security Review," *New York Times,* Apr. 13, 1954.

65. Strauss was attempting to "head off" a Senate investigation of Oppenheimer, David Teeple informed the bureau. Belmont to Boardman, Apr. 22, 1954, sec. 30, JRO/FBI; Hoover to Waters, May 3, 1954, file C, vol. 9, box 3, JRO/AEC; Crouch to Jenner, n.d., sec. 32, JRO/FBI.

66. Boardman to Hoover, Apr. 23, 1954, sec. 32, JRO/FBI; Waters to Hoover, May 1, 1954, box 3, JRO/AEC.

67. In an attempt to prove that Oppenheimer could not have been at the Kenilworth Court meeting, Garrison produced Hans Bethe, who testified that he had been at Perro Caliente with the Oppenheimers in July 1941. As Dorothy McKibben's notebooks confirm, however, Bethe spent only one day at the ranch, departing Friday morning, July 25, when Kitty drove Oppie to St. Vincent Hospital in Santa Fe. My thanks to Nancy Steeper for allowing me access to McKibben's notebooks.

68. Hoover later sent a transcript of the interview to the attorney general. Hoover to Brownell, Apr. 16, 1954, sec. 25, JRO/FBI.

69. Apr. 19, 1954, Nichols diary, Nichols papers. Wyman was on vacation in Italy when the hearing began. The diplomat, when finally located, refused to implicate Oppenheimer in a plot to assist Chevalier. Legal attaché, Paris to FBI, Apr. 17 and 19, 1954, sec. 30, JRO/FBI.

70. The Oppenheimer wiretaps also prompted an internal debate within the FBI, but "Strauss requested that 'tech' be continued for about 2 weeks, till after hearing," Belmont wrote. Branigan to Belmont, Apr. 9, 1954, sec. 25; Branigan to Belmont, Apr. 7, 1954, supplemental releases, and Feb. 2, 1954, memo, sec. 19, JRO/FBI.

71. Belmont to Boardman, Apr. 21, 1954, sec. 28, JRO/FBI.

72. Bush to Conant, June 17, 1954, Conant folder, box 27, Bush papers, MIT.

73. *ITMOJRO,* 562–67. Transcript of Vannevar Bush interview, reel 10, Bush papers, MIT; Oppenheimer to Bush, n.d. [Jan. 1952?], box 23, JRO.

74. Hershberg (1993), 680.

75. Teletype, Apr. 23, 1954, sec. 31, JRO/FBI.

76. Hennrich to Belmont, Apr. 23, 1954, supplemental releases, JRO/FBI.

77. Apr. 23, 1954, Nichols diary, Nichols papers.

78. "Summary for Apr. 6, 1954," sec. 25, JRO/FBI.

79. Apr. 23, 1954, Nichols diary, Nichols papers.

80. Apr. 24, 1954, Nichols diary, Nichols papers.

81. Strauss to Teller, June 6, 1961, folder 3, box 4, Edward Teller papers, Hoover Institutution Library, Stanford, Calif. Lawrence-Teller meeting: Lawrence day books, folder 9a, carton 11, EOL; Teller interview (July 30, 1993). Tolman affair: Molly Lawrence, May 20, 1997, personal communication. In 1957, following a conversation with Lawrence, Strauss wrote that Oppenheimer "first earned [Ernest's] disapproval a number of years ago when he seduced the wife of Prof Tolman at Caltech. According to Dr. Lawrence, it was a notorious affair which lasted for enough time for it to become apparent to Dr. Tolman who died of a broken heart." Strauss to file, Dec. 9, 1957, box 1, LLS/HHPL. Tolman died in Sept. 1948 at age 67, following a stroke.

82. *ITMOJRO,* 468.

83. Author interview with Clarence Larson, Washington, D.C., Nov. 5, 1992, Rabi to Strauss, Aug. 24, 1953, no. 73455, CIC/DOE.

84. Bethe to Oppenheimer, Apr. 22, 1954, box 20, JRO.

85. Apr. 26, 1954, Nichols diary, Nichols papers.

86. Transcript of Alvarez interview, box 1, Childs papers.

87. Larson interview (1992); Childs, (1968), 471.

88. Alvarez (1987), 180; Alvarez to Nichols, Apr. 27, 1954, folder 11, carton 32, EOL.

89. *ITMOJRO,* 662.

90. Teller interview (July 30, 1993); Teller (2001), 373.

91. Teller interview (July 30, 1993).

92. Jan. 31, 1954, TEM diary, Murray papers.

93. Heslep to Strauss, May 3, 1954, LLS/HHPL.

94. Apr. 24, 1954, Nichols diary, Nichols papers.

95. Apr. 27, 1954, Nichols diary, Nichols papers; Teller to Strauss, Dec. 15, 1963, LLS/HHPL; Robb, "Memorandum for the Files," July 24, 1967, folder 80, box 4, Nichols papers.

96. Hans Bethe's hope that he might persuade Teller to speak on Oppenheimer's behalf was promptly shattered that night, when Hans and Rose encountered Teller at the APS meeting, fresh from meeting with Robb. It was, Bethe would later recall, "the most unpleasant conversation of my whole life." Cited in Freeman Dyson, *Disturbing the Universe* (Harper and Row, 1979), 90.

97. *ITMOJRO,* 710.

98. Ibid., 726; Teller (2001), 352–53, 396.

99. *ITMOJRO,* 679.

100. Ibid., 969.

101. Belmont to Boardman, May 3, 1954, sec. 32, JRO/FBI.

102. Belmont to Boardman, May 10, 1954, sec. 33, JRO/FBI.

103. Hoover-SAC Newark, May 12, 1954, sec. 33, JRO/FBI.

18: Like Going to a New Country

1. Hoover to Waters, May 20, 1954, sec. 34, JRO/FBI.

2. *ITMOJRO,* 981.

3. Ibid. 887–88.

4. Stern (1969), 303; Bernstein (1990), 1470.

5. Hennrich to Belmont, May 20, 1954, sec. 40, JRO/FBI.

6. Gray board to Nichols, May 27, 1954, sec. 37, JRO/FBI.

7. Belmont to Boardman, June 2, 1954, sec. 37, JRO/FBI.

8. Evans's draft opinion was so poorly written and was so weak in argument that Gray feared it might discredit the whole proceeding. Accordingly, he asked Robb to rewrite it. Bernstein (1990), 1472–73; Stern (1969), 386–88.

9. Belmont to Boardman, May 24, 1954, sec. 36, JRO/FBI.

10. Transcript, May 12, 1954, sec. 36, JRO/FBI.

11. Mitchell to Garrison, May 17, 1954, box 3, JRO/AEC.

12. Oppenheimer to Hoover, July 17, 1954, Hoover folder, box 201, JRO.

13. Hoover to Brownell, June 18, 1954, sec. 41, JRO/FBI. Ironically, the Russians did apparently consider sending an agent to sound Oppenheimer out about defecting, but nothing came of the plot. Goodchild (1980), 267–68; Weinstein and Vassiliev, 137.

14. "Dissenting Opinion of Henry DeWolf Smyth," June 29, 1954, box 30, Teller papers, Hoover Institution Library; Oppenheimer to Smyth, Jan. 15, 1964, "JRO, introduction of" folder, series 6, box 1, Smyth papers.

15. Joseph Volpe, who observed Murray at many commission meetings, noted that "you never knew what the hell Murray would say." Volpe interview (1996).

16. "Concurring Opinion of Commissioner Thomas E. Murray," June 29, 1954, box 30, Teller papers, Hoover Institution. "Murray felt that Oppenheimer was guilty of disloyalty—not in the sense of treason, but, rather, of not being on the team," said one of his former aides. Gerard Smith, Sept. 12, 1992, personal communication. Strauss may also have "fixed" one or more commissioners' votes. Zuckert worked for Strauss after the hearing, and Murray claimed that Strauss "subsidized" Glennan while the latter served on the commission, before the Oppenheimer hearing. Bernstein (1990), 1477; transcript, "LLS Confirmation" folder, series 3, box 2, Smyth papers; "Meeting with Dr. Smyth, Mr. Zuckert, and Keith Glennan," Apr. 7, 1954, Murray papers.

17. Nichols (1987), 320.

18. Strauss deliberately left out of the AEC statement any mention of Oppenheimer's role in the H-bomb controversy to avoid alienating other scientists. Strauss to Smyth, June 21, 1954, Smyth folder, LLS/HHL.

19. The Justice Department concluded that "prosecution is not possible with regard to either the 1954 or the 1943 statements." Tompkins to Hoover, July 14, 1954, supplemental releases, JRO/FBI.

20. Hoover and the FBI continued to pursue the possibility of prosecuting some of Oppenheimer's defenders. Various memoranda, sec. 35, JRO/FBI file. The FBI disconnected the wiretap on Oppenheimer in early June, but Hoover ordered it reinstalled later in the month, hoping that it might lead to evidence that would allow prosecution of Oppie.

21. Abraham Pais, *A Tale of Two Continents: A Physicist's Life in a Turbulent World* (Princeton University Press, 1997), 330.

22. J. Oppenheimer to F. Oppenheimer, Jan. 1953, Frank Oppenheimer folder, box 294, and undated note, Bush folder, box 32, JRO.

23. Strauss also lied when he claimed that he had tried to obtain a salary increase for Oppenheimer after the hearings. In fact, Strauss tried to get Oppie fired as director of Princeton's institute, but he lacked the votes. "Atomic Gestapo," *Washington Post,* June 9, 1954; Pfau (1984), 180, 184; entry of June 9, 1954, Nichols diary, Nichols papers; "Ex-U.S. Lawyer Says FBI Bugged Talks Between Oppenheimer and His Attorneys," *Los Angeles Times,* Dec. 28, 1975.

24. The Alsops' articles were later published as a book, *We Accuse!* (Simon and Schuster, 1954).

25. Rabi to DuBridge, June 21, 1954, box 111.3, DuBridge papers.

26. Rabi interview (1983).

27. Teller to Mayer, n.d. (summer 1954), box 3, Mayer papers; Teller (2001), 399–400.

28. "Memorandum for Files . . . ," June 23, 1954, Teller folder, LLS/HHTL; Bernice Brode to Oppenheimer, Apr. 14, 1955, box 23, JRO.

29. Surprised by the reaction to his testimony, Teller had second thoughts. But Strauss and Robb dissuaded him from issuing a statement attempting to explain his remarks. Teller to Strauss, July 2, 1954; Strauss to Teller, July 6, 1954; Robb to Teller, July 8, 1954, and Teller to Robb, July 30, 1954, Teller folder, LLS/HHL.

30. Teller (1987), 123. Untitled notes, Sept. 3, 1954, "Lawrence Medical Records" folder, box 3, Childs papers.

31. Childs (1968), 476.

32. James Brady folder, box 1, Childs papers; Molly Lawrence interview (1992).

33. Kamen (1986), 247; "Senator Hickenlooper Aide Is Ordered by Court to Give Testimony in Libel Suit," *Washington Post,* Nov. 19, 1954, and "Ex-Aide of AEC Says He Saw A-Chemist with Red Consuls," *Washington Post,* Dec. 5, 1954.

34. Kamen to Cooksey, Feb. 2, 1954, folder 29, carton 4, EOL. The defamation suit that Kamen brought against the *Washington Times-Herald* and the *Chicago Tribune* in 1952 went to trial in Jan. 1955. Six months later the newspapers paid an undisclosed sum to Kamen. Kamen to Cooksey, Dec. 26, 1954, and Kamen to Cooksey, Feb. 23, 1955, folder 29, carton 4, EOL.

35. Bethe to Oppenheimer, Feb. 9, 1956, box 20, JRO.

36. "I hope I can speak about this interference in the past tense," wrote Teller to Strauss concerning Oppenheimer. Teller to Strauss, May 13, 1954, Teller folder, LLS/HHPL.

37. Strauss to Neylan, July 22, 1954, folder 5, box 171, Neylan papers.

38. Blumberg and Owens (1976), 375–76; Teller interview (July 7, 1993).

39. Teller's article was also meant to be a response to a recent book, which mistakenly gave Livermore credit for the hydrogen bomb. In subsequent versions of the H-bomb story, Teller would discount Ulam's contribution. Teller and Ulam: "Oct. 19, 1954," Murray papers; Stanley Blumberg and Louis Panos, *Edward Teller: Giant of the Golden Age of Physics* (Scribners, 1990), 123–25; Teller (2001), 404; Teller to Strauss, Oct. 7, 1954, Teller folder, LLS/HHPL.

40. Teller to Mayer, n.d. (late 1954), box 3, Mayer papers.

41. Bradbury to Fields, Sept. 22, 1954, no. 125192, CIC/DOE; Hansen (1995), vol. 5, 22–29; Francis (1996), 93.

42. Minutes, July 12–15, 1954, GAC no. 41, no. 73403, CIC/DOE.

43. Francis (1996), 88.

44. Hansen (1995), vol. 5, 60.

45. Francis (1996), 94.

46. Teller claimed that he agreed to the promotion only after those fired during the oath controversy had been offered their jobs back. Teller interview (July 30, 1993).

47. Brown and Foster: York (1987), 71–72.

48. Linear implosion: Hansen (1988), 172–76; Francis, 94–95; Defense Nuclear Agency, *Report on Operation* Teapot, Feb.–Mar. 1955 (U.S. Government Printing Office, 1981), 1.

49. Minutes, Dec. 22, 1954, GAC no. 43, no. 31045, CIC/DOE.

50. Decker interview (1997).

51. *Tesla:* Hansen (1995), vol. 5, 112; AEC press release, Mar. 1, 1955, no. 76635, CIC/DOE.

52. *Tesla/Turk:* Chuck Hansen, Sept. 25, 2000, personal communication; Strauss to Anderson, Mar. 24, 1955, no. 31120, CIC/DOE.

53. Mar. 8, 1955, entry, TEM diary, Murray papers.

54. Transcript of Wally Decker interview (1983), LLNL.

55. Lawrence to Fidler, Sept. 2, 1954, no. 73036, CIC/DOE.

56. Francis (1996), 105.

57. Ibid., 99.

58. Ibid., 96.

59. Teller to Mayer, Apr. 15, 1945, box 3, Mayer papers. The army program, abbreviated AFAP—artillery-fired atomic projectile—was also said to stand for "as far as possible" at the lab. "Teller . . . had a remarkable ability to find convergence between his own interests and those of potential sponsors," Francis writes. AFAP: Francis (1996), 73, 76, 96; Teller to Strauss, May 13, 1954, Teller folder, LLS/HHPT; Gerald Johnson interview (1991); minutes, Oct. 15, 1955, AECP, UC records.

60. Murray (1960), 76. Eisenhower to Strauss and enclosure, Jan. 4, 1954, no. 100815, CIC/DOE.

61. Murray test-ban appeals: Murray (1960), 76; Hewlett and Holl (1989), 222–23.

62. Murray (1960), 48–52; Murray to Strauss, Aug. 30, 1954, no. 72371, CIC/DOE.

63. Hansen (1995), vol. 5, 350.

64. Mar. 15, 1955, TEM diary, Murray papers; Thomas E. Murray, "God *Meant* Us to Find the Atom!," *Better Homes and Gardens,* Apr. 1955.

65. Hewlett and Holl (1989), 274; *FRUS: 1952–1954,* vol. 2, pt. 2, 1426.

66. Ambrose (1984), 170.

67. Mar. 3, 1955, TEM diary, Murray papers.

68. Cole to Teller with enclosure, Apr. 6, 1954, Edward Teller papers, LLNL.

69. *FRUS: 1952–1954,* vol. 2, pt. 2, 1387; May 19, 1954, entry, Nichols diary, Nichols papers.

70. Hewlett and Holl (1989), 223–24, 274–75.

71. Test ban: Ibid., 275–76; Charles Appleby, *Eisenhower and Arms Control, 1953–1961: A Balance of Risks* (University Microfilm, 1987), 162; *FRUS: 1952–1954,* vol. 2, pt. 2, 1465–70. The author thanks Charles Appleby for a copy of his dissertation.

72. Teller to Strauss, June 16, 1954, Teller folder, LLS/HHPL; York to Fields, Nov. 9, 1954, no. 32159, CIC/DOE.

73. Armstrong to Leahay, Aug. 25, 1954, no. 29988, CIC/DOE.

74. Fields to Bradbury, Sept. 29, 1954, no. 125679, Murray to Strauss, Nov. 3, 1954, no. 74380, and Nichols to Quarles, Jan. 7, 1955, no. 71955, CIC/DOE.

75. Clean and dirty bombs: Hansen (1995), vol. 5, 10–27, 88–89, 231; Mansfield to file, Oct. 26, 1954, JCAE; author interview with Gerald Johnson, La Jolla, Calif., June 6, 1991.

76. Hansen (1995), vol. 5, 87–88.

77. Ibid., 88.

78. Nov. 26, 1954, and Mar. 3, 1955, entries, TEM diary, Murray papers.

79. Herken (1992), 83; Gerard Smith, Sept. 12, 1992, personal communication.

80. Murray to Eisenhower, Mar. 14, 1955, *FRUS: 1955–57,* vol. 20, 56–57; Rabi to Strauss, May 29, 1954, no. 73407, CIC/DOE.

81. Appleby (1987), 171–72.

82. *FRUS: 1955–57,* vol. 20, 60; Divine (1978), 60–61.

83. Divine (1978), 11.

84. Open Skies: Appleby (1987), 90–106.

85. Stassen to Matteson, July 13, 1955, records of the U.S. Department of State (USDS/NARA), RG 59, lot file 58D-133, box 20; *FRUS: 1955–57,* vol. 20, 173–75.

86. Larsen to Stassen, July 29, 1955, box 16, USDS/NARA.

87. *FRUS: 1955–57,* vol. 20, 60.

88. This time Ike simply ignored Strauss. Hewlett and Holl (1989), 299.

89. The task force eventually expanded to twenty-one members; nine of the original dozen were from Livermore. Donkin to file, Aug. 19, 1955, and Donkin to Odom, Aug. 31, 1955, box 66, USDS/NARA.

90. Donkin to Larsen, Sept. 6, 1955, box 20, USDS/NARA.

91. There was no circumstance under which a test ban could be in our interest," York later wrote of Teller's views. York (1987), 82.

92. Matteson to Stassen, Sept. 8, 1955, box 16, USDS/NARA; Panofsky interview (1993).

93. "Agenda," Oct. 14, 1955, box 64, USDS/NARA.

94. Strauss did not send his letter to Lawrence. Appleby (1987), 148.

95. Just a month later, the Russians demonstrated that they, too, had the radiation-implosion secret, exploding a 1.6-megaton H-bomb at their test site in Semipalatinsk. Soviet H-bomb: Holloway (1994), 314–15. Lawrence plan: Donkin to Stassen, Oct. 13, 1955, box 64, USDS/NARA; Appleby (1987), 145–48.

96. Strauss was so confident that the Russians would reject on-site inspection that he endorsed the AEC study. Appleby (1987), 146–47; *FRUS: 1955–57,* vol. 20, 229.

97. *FRUS: 1955–57,* vol. 20, 253.

98. Ibid., 317.

99. Veksler dinner: Holloway (1994), 114–15, 352; Childs (1968), 487–88.

100. "Admiral Strauss felt that it was still something of a mystery as to why the Soviets had built it. It could have no military significance and was only useful for developments in the realm of pure basic science." *FRUS: 1955–57,* vol. 20, 213.

101. Childs (1968), 495.

102. "The greatest possibility of practical value of the machine lies in uses not yet discovered," Ernest argued. Lawrence to Johnson, Jan. 12, 1955, MTA folder, LBL.

103. Cosmotron: Research Division to GAC, July 16, 1956, "Research Div. Activities, 1952–57" file, AEC/NARA.

104. Childs (1968), 492–93; Davis (1968), 352.

105. Pfau (1984), 188.

106. Hewlett and Holl (1989), 288–91. Privately, Strauss was more forthright. Minutes, AEC Meeting no. 1062, Feb. 23, 1955, AEC/NARA.

107. Strauss and Libby: Hewlett and Holl (1989), 287–88, 293–95.

108. Dixon-Yates: Pfau (1984), 183–85; Hewlett and Holl (1989), 247–49.

109. Hewlett and Holl (1989), 243.

110. *FRUS: 1955–57,* vol. 20, 119.

111. Ironically, Murray's views on tactical nuclear weapons were nearly identical to Oppenheimer's in *Vista.* Hewlett and Holl (1989), 336–38.

112. Ibid., 338.

113. Ibid., 338–40. After Strauss failed in his efforts to have Murray's Q clearance lifted, he ordered all copies of the commissioner's letters and memos on the test ban recalled at the AEC. Earl Voss, *Nuclear Ambush: The Test-Ban Trap* (Regnery, 1963), 78; Jack Crawford, Aug. 15, 2001, personal communication.

114. Because of the distinctions that Murray made concerning what he called "rational nuclear armament," he and Strauss agreed on the need to continue testing in order to develop the clean bomb.

115. Francis (1996), 107–8. ICBM and von Neumann report: Mansfield to file, Mar. 5, 1955, no. DCCCLXII, JCAE; York (1987), 91; Borden to Jackson, June 27, 1955, folder 37, box 18, Henry Jackson papers, Special Collections, University of Washington, Seattle, Wash.

116. Bradbury wrote: "Everyone will ultimately have all the weapons in all the variety wanted, and the number will probably be more than the world can safely tolerate being used." But he would come to regret his "frankness." Bradbury to Johnson, Nov. 21, 1955, folder 12, carton 32, EOL; Libby to Strauss, Nov. 14, 1955, Murray papers; Bradbury to Strauss, Feb. 7, 1956, no. 125634, CIC/DOE.

117. "Airborne H-bomb Exploded by U.S. over Pacific Isle," *New York Times,* May 21, 1956.

118. York (1987), 75; Francis (1996), 97.

119. *Zuni:* Hansen (1995), vol. 5, 192–95.

120. Hewlett and Holl (1989), 345–47.

121. Murray to Strauss, July 26, 1956, no. 74363, CIC/DOE.

122. "Statement by the President," July 8, 1956, no. 107756; Murray to Strauss, Aug. 3, 1956, no. 74359; Strauss to Murray, Aug. 6, 1956, no. 74358; Murray to Strauss, Sept. 11, 1956, no. 74356, CIC/DOE.

123. Hewlett and Holl (1989), 301, 360.

124. Pfau (1984), 201.

125. Hewlett and Holl (1989), 349; *FRUS: 1955–57,* vol. 20, 419.

126. Task force report: "Disarmament Study," Jan. 1956; "Personnel Requirements for Nuclear Inspection," June 1, 1956; Stassen to Twining, Feb. 2, 1956, box 66, USDS/NARA; Arnold Kramish, personal communication; Starbird to Strauss, Dec. 26, 1956, no. 72441, CIC/DOE.

127. Griggs suggested that inspection stations in Russia could also be used to secretly eavesdrop on Soviet radio communications. "Verbatim Record," 97; Odom to Stassen, May 22, 1956, box 64, USDS/NARA.

128. Hewlett and Holl (1989), 367–69; Divine (1978), 84–104; Ambrose (1984), 349.

129. Divine (1978), 105; "The Nuclear Test Issue," *Washington Post,* Oct. 17, 1956. Lawrence complained to the university's president when two Rad Lab veterans joined Stevenson's campaign. "He seemed to be very much upset by this but not very clear as to what he thought I could do about it," wrote Sproul in his office diary. Nov. 2, 1957, memos, Sproul papers.

130. Divine (1978), 105.

131. "[Strauss] encouraged his friends Edward Teller and Ernest Lawrence to tell the public that 'we are never sure a device will work until it is tested.'" Pfau (1984), 199.

132. Childs (1968), 474.

133. Wilkes subsequently wrote of the incident: "My recollection is that Ernest made it clear that AEC Chairman Strauss encouraged such a statement." Wilkes, "Notes for discussion . . . ," Nov. 9, 1986, Wilkes folder, box 2, John Lawrence papers, LBL; Wilkes to Lawrence, n.d., folder 9, carton 17, EOL; Childs (1968), 498–99.

134. The final version deleted Teller's pitch for the clean bomb and did not mention Ernest's role on Stassen's task force. Press release, Nov. 4, 1956, folder 9, carton 17, EOL; "2 Scientists Back Tests of H-bomb," *New York Times,* Nov. 6, 1956.

19: A Cross of Atoms

1. Hewlett and Holl (1989), 380.

2. Notes on Oct. 10, 1958, memo, Murray papers; Murray to Strauss, Mar. 28, 1957, no. 72358, and McGruder to Strauss, Apr. 3, 1957, no. 108370, CIC/DOE.

3. Clinton Anderson made Murray a special consultant to the Joint Committee. "Dear Mr. President," n.d., Murray papers; Hewlett and Holl (1989), 331, 408; Hansen (1995), vol. 5, 276–77.

4. Appleby (1987), 252; Pfau (1984), 204.

5. Murray feared that Henry Luce might spike the piece, or that Strauss would blackmail the magazine's advertisers into stopping publication. Personal communication, Jack Crawford, Mar. 11, 1993. Three weeks after Murray's article appeared, Luce wrote to Strauss with an apology. Luce to Strauss, May 23, 1957, H. Luce folder, LLS/HHPL.

6. "The civilized tradition has always declared that an unlimited and indiscriminate use of force in warfare is unjust," Murray wrote.

7. Livermore received the contract for a subsequent ICBM, the Titan. Francis (1996), 112–13.

8. Nobska: Ibid., 119–21; *Project Nobska: The Implications of Advanced Design on Undersea Warfare,* final report, Dec. 1, 1956, Committee on Undersea Warfare, "Physical Sciences, 1956" file, National Academy of Sciences, Washington, D.C.

9. Just a few days earlier, York had notified the AEC that Livermore was on the verge of developing a small, lightweight H-bomb, based upon two ideas that had shown promise in the last Nevada tests. Hansen, "Submarine-Launched Ballistic Missile Warheads" (unpublished manuscript); Teller (2001), 421.

10. Murray to Strauss, Dec. 20, 1956, no. 74345, CIC/DOE.

11. Appleby (1987), 248.

12. Hewlett and Holl (1989), 398; Divine (1978), 146.

13. Hewlett and Holl (1989), 399.

14. Bryan to Strauss, June 20, 1957, Cole folder, and Strauss to Lawrence, July 1, 1957, LLS/HHPL; Strauss to Gerard Smith, Sept. 12, 1957, no. 108301, CIC/DOE.

15. Childs (1968), 504.

16. Teller and Strauss had previously talked, for example, of using nuclear explosions to change the dust content of the atmosphere or to clear away Los Angeles's famous smog by blowing a hole in the city's surrounding mountains.

17. Stassen had raised the idea of an "open" test in a previous memo to Lawrence's task force. Stassen to Lawrence, box 66, Arneson file, USDS/NARA.

18. June 24 meeting: Childs (1968), 504; Hewlett and Holl (1989), 400–401; Divine (1978), 148–50; Ambrose (1984), 399–400; Gerard Smith to Stassen, July 1, 1957, box 127, Arneson file, USDS/NARA; *FRUS: 1955–57,* vol. 20, 638–40.

19. After also listening to the scientists' appeal, Dulles had written to Eisenhower, urging the president not to reverse his position on the test ban. Appleby (1987), 212; 249.

20. In their own press conference, immediately following the White House visit, Teller and Lawrence had spoken of weapons that were 96 percent "pure." Transcript of press conference, June 26, 1957, *Public Papers of the Presidents: Dwight Eisenhower, 1957,* 497–501; Dulles to Stassen, July 1, 1957, *FRUS: 1955–57,* vol. 20, 649–50.

21. Lilienthal (1969), 232.

22. Strauss to Mills, July 3, 1957, Mills folder, LLS/HHPL; Hansen (1995), vol. 5, 321.

23. Morse to Teller, July 3, 1957, Morse folder, LLS/HHPL; Hansen (1995), vol. 5, 321.

24. York calculated that the weight of a clean bomb would be three to five times that of a "standard" H-bomb. York to Starbird, Oct. 24, 1956, no. 74348, and York to Starbird, July 11, 1957, no. 103901, CIC/DOE. Clean-bomb limitations: Livermore interviews; Hansen (1995), vol. 5, 89; York to Huston, Apr. 25, 1955, no. 74365, CIC/DOE.

25. Murray to Strauss, May 29, 1957, no. 74336, and Starbird to Fields, June 4, 1957, no. 103903, CIC/DOE.

26. Hansen (1995), vol. 5, 328.

27. Ibid., 274–75.

28. "Conference with the President," Aug. 9, 1957, no. 33078, CIC/DOE; Ambrose (1984), 344.

29. Rabi interview (1983).

30. Rabi's influence upon Eisenhower was already subtly evident. When Strauss urged Ike to approve additional high-yield H-bomb tests, the president replied that a 40-megaton weapon would only cause about half again the damage of a 10-megaton bomb because "the scaling laws apply on a cube route basis."

31. Pfau (1984), 208; Killian, *Sputniks, Scientists, and Eisenhower: A Memoir of the First Special Assistant to the President for Science and Technology* (MIT Press, 1977), 8.

32. *Sputnik* reaction: Killian (1977), 6–12; Pfau (1984), 209.

33. *FRUS: 1955–57,* vol. 20, 607–10.

34. Rabi proposal: Ibid., vol. 19, 615–17, 308–9; Herken (1992), 103.

35. Should the Soviets be allowed to continue testing, Rabi told Ike, they "seem certain to discover the feature that they now lack." Ferrell (1981), 348–49.

36. Gordon Gray—about to replace Cutler as Ike's national security adviser—was a silent witness to the confrontation in the Oval Office.

37. *FRUS: 1955–57,* vol. 20, 755–56; Strauss to file, Nov. 6, 1957, Teller file, LLS/HHPL.

38. Ferrell (1981), 348–49; Teller to Fields, May 29, 1957, no. 137190, CIC/DOE; Teller to Strauss, June 4, 1957, Teller folder, LLS/HHPL; Mark interview (1991).

39. Killian and PSAC: Killian (1977), 20–30; Herken (1992), 104–5; Divine (1978), 171.

40. Killian (1977), 37.

41. Stassen: Hewlett and Holl (1989), 384, 469–71; Ambrose (1984), 447.

42. *FRUS: 1958–60,* vol. 3, 49–51, 567–72.

43. Ibid., 572.

44. Author interview with Hans Bethe, Pasadena, Calif., Jan 1, 1991. *FRUS: 1958–60,* vol. 3, 551–53.

45. Jeremy Bernstein (1981), 109.

46. *FRUS: 1958–60,* vol. 3, 575–89.

47. Hewlett and Holl (1989), 479; *FRUS: 1958–60,* vol. 3, 589–90.

48. *FRUS: 1958–60,* vol. 3, 597–98; 603–4. "Cessation of testing, in the judgment of the group, would leave the United States in a position of technical advantage for a few years, which will otherwise be lost," Killian told Ike.

49. At the Ramey meeting, PSAC concluded that a moratorium before *Hardtack* stood no chance of approval by the AEC and Pentagon. Bethe interview (1991).

50. Teller (2001), 343–44; York (1987), 117–18; York interview (1997).

51. Appleby (1987), 272; Hewlett and Holl (1989), 477.

52. Hewlett and Holl (1989), 302; J. D. Hunley, "Polaris and Minuteman: The Solid-Propellant Breakthrough in Missiles" (unpublished manuscript, 2001).

53. Hansen (1995), "W-47," 8–9; Strauss to Quarles, Jan. 2, 1958, no. 72458, CIC/DOE.

54. Strauss to Eisenhower, Jan. 29, 1958, no. 101731, CIC/DOE.

55. Agnew to Mills, Mar. 28, 1958, no. 123855, CIC/DOE. Open shot: "Demonstration Shot for Operation *Hardtack,*" Oct. 17, 1957, no. 72401, and teletype, Dec. 12, 1957, no. 123862, CIC/DOE; "Description of Devices," n.d., box 99, LLNL.

56. Bradbury to York, Nov. 5, 1957, no. 101852, CIC/DOE.

57. Lawrence was interested in closing a loophole that his task force had identified in the inspection scheme: the possibility that the Russians might hide nuclear tests by exploding their bombs in space. Starbird to Lawrence, July 8, 1956, and Fields to Lawrence, Mar. 7, 1957, box 99, LLNL.

58. Christofilos and *Argus:* York (1987), 128–32; Beckerley to Thornton, Mar. 2, 1953, folder 10, carton 30, EOL; Loper to Chairman, July 3, 1958, no. MCCLXXXIII, JCAE.

59. Fields to Lawrence, Mar. 7, 1957, no. 137176; Strauss to Eisenhower, Nov. 23, 1957, no. 28933, CIC/DOE. Two of the high-altitude detonations, *Teak* and *Orange,* were also weapons-effects tests for a possible antiballistic missile system. Libby to Durham, Apr. 8, 1958, no. 7808, JCAE.

60. Starbird to Bradbury, Feb. 13, 1958, no. 125211, CIC/DOE.

61. Teller interview (July 30, 1993); Teller and Brown (1962), 72; Teller (2001), 434.

62. "The Compelling Need for Nuclear Tests," *Life,* Feb. 10, 1958; Edward Teller and Albert Latter, *Our Nuclear Future: Facts, Dangers, and Opportunities* (Criterion Books, 1958); Hewlett and Holl (1989), 475; author interview with Albert Latter, Los Angeles, Calif., Mar. 11, 1985.

63. "If this goes on we shall just become a factory for making atomic bombs in whatever size or shape the customer wants and will boast, annually like the automobile manufacturers, of our fantastic improvements—although to the jaundiced eye, only the fenders have been changed," Bradbury wrote. Bradbury to Starbird, Jan. 8, 1958, no. 125654, CIC/DOE.

64. Author interview with Edward Huddleson, San Francisco, Calif., Dec. 17, 1992.

65. Transcript of Don Gow interview, box 1, Childs papers; Childs (1968), 500.

66. Early in 1958, Lawrence feared "a severe reduction in the Berkeley program." Lawrence to Tammaro, Jan. 15, 1958, folder 15, carton 30, EOL.

67. Neylan to Regents, July 13, 1954, box 171, Neylan papers.

68. Rabi to Strauss, Dec. 22, 1954, GAC file, AEC/NARA.

69. Dec. 14, 1955, GAC file, AEC/NARA.

70. "He saw no connection between higher energies and useful things, and then his enthusiasm dropped." Lofgren interview (1998).

71. York interview (1997); Davis (1968), 351.

72. Feldman was invited back in 1955 but declined the invitation. David Feldman, Nov. 3, 1993, personal communication.

73. "Luis was telling Lawrence how to run the lab," observed the Rad Lab's amazed business manager. Transcript of Wallace Reynolds interview, 82, Bancroft Library; Alvarez (1987), 189, 205.

74. Dec. 9, 1957, confidential memos, box 4, Sproul papers.

75. Aebersold to Hamilton, Feb. 24, 1956, folder 22, carton 32, EOL.

76. Von Neumann had also died of cancer, ten days earlier.

77. Childs (1968), 516.

78. Teletype, Apr. 7, 1958, folder 1751, box 185, LLNL. Teller persuaded Mills's widow to write to Eisenhower, urging completion of *Hardtack.* Author interview with Polly Plesset, Woodside, Calif., May 14, 1988.

79. Childs (1968), 518.

80. When Teller announced that he was "extremely unhappy about any agreement which starts with the word 'don't,'" Louis Ridenour dryly observed that God and Moses had previously found the formulation convenient. "Discussion on 'Ban the Missile,'" Oct. 21, 1955; and "Task Force Meeting," Mar. 1, 1957, box 64, Arneson file, USDS/NARA.

81. "Verbatim Record . . . ," May 19, 1956, 93, Arneson file, USDS/NARA.

82. "He wasn't interested in a lot of things except the test ban, because he wanted to talk with the Russians." Hayward interview (1996).

83. Author interview with James Gaither, San Francisco, Calif. Dec. 17, 1992. The Loomis fund paid for the Russian scientists' visits to Berkeley.

84. Childs (1968), 511.

85. Waters to Hoover, July 12, 1955, Ernest Lawrence file, no. 116-10798, FBI.

86. "Verbatim Record . . . ," May 29, 1956, 138, Arneson file, USDS/NARA.

87. Donkin to Strauss, Mar. 4, 1957, "McKay Donkin's Top Secret Material," box 8, LLS/NARA.

88. *FRUS: 1958–60,* vol. 3, 604.

89. Voss (1963), 182; Davis (1968), 352; Killian (1977), 158; "Strauss Defeat on Delegates Is Disclosed," *Washington Evening Star,* May 29, 1958; "Dr. Teller's Influence with Ike Wanes After Error on 'Clean Bomb,'" *Buffalo Evening News,* Apr. 12, 1958.

90. Smith interview (1992).

91. Pfau (1984), 215–17.

92. Appearing on a television talk show, Anderson raised doubts about Strauss's veracity concerning the clean bomb. Transcript, *Face the Nation,* May 4, 1958, no. 100116; Kline to Anderson, May 8, 1958, no. 100132; AEC press release, May 4, 1958, no. 74322, CIC/DOE.

93. McCone: Hewlett and Holl (1989), 489–91.

94. Strauss to Lawrence, June 23, 1958, folder 52, carton 15, EOL.

95. Bacher later told Oppenheimer that Lawrence was "extraordinarily devoted" to the U.S. mission. Bethe confirmed that "Lawrence surprised us" with his willingness to accept a ban on testing: "He was entirely in favor of having that meeting with the Russians." Bethe interview (1996); DuBridge to Cooksey, Sept. 23, 1958, folder 17, carton 6, EOL; Childs (1968), 523–24.

96. Davis (1968), 353.

97. Childs (1968), 521.

98. Ibid.

99. Hansen (1988), 77–79.

100. Hansen, "Announced U.S. Nuclear Detonations . . . ," 14–15; Bradbury to Starbird, June 3, 1958, no. 101951, CIC/DOE.

101. *FRUS: 1958–1960,* vol. 3, 612–13.

102. In May, the head of testing in the Pacific wrote to Starbird, "do every thing you can to cancel *Pinon* shot." Ogle to Starbird, May 20, 1958, no. 101882, CIC/DOE.

103. Directors to General Manager, June 24, 1958, no. 101883, CIC/DOE.

104. Salisbury to Starbird et al., June 26, 1958, no. 101884, CIC/DOE. Starbird worried that *Pinon* "might unduly awe rather than mollify the observers." Starbird to General Manager, Feb. 21, 1958, no. 72447, CIC/DOE.

105. Childs (1968), 524.

106. Dolly Eltenton had been Semenov's secretary and George Eltenton his colleague when the Russian directed Leningrad's Institute of Chemical Physics in the 1930s. Holloway (1994), 451.

107. Harold Brown and Hans Bethe confirmed Lawrence's break statement. Observed Brown: "Lawrence in his grand statement to prevent a break appealed to the spirit of science and the fact that there were Nobel prize winners on each side." Author interview with Harold Brown, Washington, D.C., June 28, 1996; Bethe interview (1996).

108. Spiers to "Phil and Vince," July 5, 1958, box 85, Arneson file, USDS/NARA.

109. Tichvinsky, "Impressions . . . ," Aug. 23, 1958, folder 27, carton 17, EOL.

110. "It was most encouraging—Morse is genuinely worried from the point of view of a vigorous opponent of test suspension that there may be an agreement among the experts of the two sides." Farley to Spiers, July 17, 1958, box 85, Arneson file, USDS/NARA.

111. Childs (1968), 527.

112. "U.S. Atomic Aide Ill," *New York Times,* July 30, 1958.

113. Teller described *Juniper* as Livermore's "most radical" *Hardtack* shot and "an entirely new concept in bomb design." Strauss to Eisenhower, Jan. 29, 1958, no. 101731, CIC/DOE.

114. Author interview with Carl Haussmann, Livermore, Calif., July 30, 1993; transcript of transcript, "Dr. Teller's 80th Birthday," LLNL.

115. The radical design of the W-47 also made it particularly susceptible to accidental detonation—a problem that was reportedly not solved before the test moratorium went into effect. The W-47, writes Hansen, was "an explosion in search of an accident." Starbird to Mills et al., Mar. 25, 1958, no. 104003, CIC/DOE; Hansen (1995), "W-47," 19.

116. "Needless to say we are all extremely happy with the results of these two shots." Teller to Starbird, July 23, 1958, no. 102007, CIC/DOE.

117. Hewlett and Holl (1989), 544.

118. *Hardtack-II:* Strauss to Eisenhower, June 12, 1958, no. 72692, CIC/DOE.

119. Hewlett and Holl (1989), 545.

120. *FRUS: 1958–60,* vol. 3, 654–59.

121. Ambrose (1984), 479; AEC press release, Aug. 29, 1958, no. 137262, CIC/DOE.

122. Loper to Durham, Aug. 29, 1958, no. MCCXCVI, JCAE.

123. The fact that the Soviet Union promptly detected the secret *Argus* tests demonstrated the viability of the Geneva agreement, Killian told Eisenhower. Two weeks after an article in *Izvestia* attributed a previously undiscovered band of radiation to an unannounced U.S. nuclear test, the *New York Times* published an account of *Argus. Argus:* York (1987), 128–32; 149–50.

Epilogue: "As Streams Are . . ."

1. The French detonated their first nuclear device in the Sahara on Feb. 13, 1960. The Soviets had never made it clear in the test-ban negotiations whether they would consider a French test a violation of the moratorium. Glenn Seaborg, *Kennedy, Khrushchev, and the Test Ban* (University of California Press, 1992), 21–22; Sergei Khrushchev, *Nikita Khrushchev and the Creation of a Superpower* (Penn State University Press, 2000), 346–48.

2. The Soviets' last test was Nov. 3, 1958. Steven Zaloga, *The Kremlin's Nuclear Sword: The Rise and Fall of Russia's Strategic Nuclear Forces, 1945–2000* (Smithsonian Institution Press, draft manuscript, 2000), 76–78. Resumption of testing: Khrushchev (2000), 295–302, 466–67; William Taubman et al., eds., *Nikita Khrushchev* (Yale University Press, 2000), 262–63.

3. Decoupling theory: Killian (1977), 166; Voss (1963), 272; Latter interview (1985); Teller, "Comments on the Geneva Conference on Nuclear Test Detection," Sept. 13, 1958, Teller folder, LLS/HHPL; Teller (2001), 443.

4. Herken (1992), 115; "Visit with Ed Teller," Oct. 13, 1958, Teller folder, Murray papers. Murray remained Teller's steadfast, if unlikely, ally in opposing the test ban until his death from a heart attack in spring 1961.

5. In his memoirs, Killian described decoupling as "a bizarre concept, contrived as part of a campaign to oppose any test ban." Killian (1977), 166; Herken (1992), 115.

6. Author interview with James Killian, Cambridge, Mass., Jan. 16, 1985; Killian (1977), 168.

7. Pfau (1984), 223.

8. Ibid., 233–35.

9. B. B. to Oppenheimer, May 6, 1959, Robert Brode folder, box 23, JRO.

10. A key test-ban supporter, William Fulbright, described Teller to Kennedy as "John L. Lewis and Billy Sunday all wrapped in one." Blumberg and Owens (1976), 370; "Winning Senate Support for the Nuclear Test Ban Treaty, 1963," belt 26C, Presidential Recording Transcripts, John F. Kennedy Library, Boston, Mass.

11. Teller and David Griggs had originally proposed underground testing in 1956 as a way of avoiding weather delays and calming public fears over fallout. But the success of the first U.S. underground test in Nevada—*Rainier,* on Sept. 19, 1957—awakened Teller, and Livermore, to the possibility of moving all subsequent tests underground. *Rainier:* Teller and Griggs, "Deep Underground Test Shots," Feb. 1956, UCRL-4659, LLNL; AEC press release, Sept. 20, 1957, no. 71470, and York to Starbird, Oct. 4, 1957, no. 74196, CIC/DOE.

12. Herken (1992), 307–8 fn.

13. Lilienthal's diary describes the scene at a National Academy of Sciences' reception which followed the White House ceremony: "Robert Oppenheimer . . . a figure of stone, gray, rigid, almost lifeless, tragic in his intensity. . . . Kitty was a study in joy, in exultation almost." David Lilienthal, *The Journals of David E. Lilienthal,* vol. 5, *The Harvest Years, 1959–63* (Harper and Row, 1971), 529–30.

14. Strauss to Donovan, Dec. 31, 1963, box 78, *Life* magazine folder, LLS/HHPL.

15. Birge to Oppenheimer, Apr. 6, 1963, box 20, JRO.

16. Rabi to Oppenheimer, Apr. 5, 1963, box 59, JRO.

17. Lilienthal (1969), 307.

18. Wrote Lilienthal in his dairy, following a visit to Oppenheimer in early 1961: "The tension in him about the problems we were asked to face sixteen years ago is gone. It shows in his manner, in his face and voice. The reason: 'There is nothing I can do about what is going on; I would be the worst person to speak out about them in any case.'" Lilienthal (1971), 275.

19. Transcript of Childs interview with Oppenheimer, Apr. 27, 1963, Oppenheimer folder, box 1, Childs papers.

20. Bohm to Oppenheimer, Dec. 2, 1966, box 20, JRO.

21. Thomas Cochran et al., *Nuclear Weapons Databoook,* vol. 1, *U.S. Nuclear Forces and Capabilities* (Ballinger, 1984), 7–9.

22. Origins of neutron bomb: Morse to Henry Jackson, July 18, 1961, and Strauss to Morse, July 21, 1961, box 1, John Morse papers, Hoover Institution Library. In an appeal to presidential candidates in 1960, Thomas Murray cited the need to develop "a 'third generation' weapon, as radically different from the H-bomb as the H-bomb was from the Hiroshima-type A-bomb." The next day, Rabi and Bethe were among the first to denounce the neutron bomb. Press release, Nov. 4, 1960; "Four Top Scientists Deny Neutron Bomb Potential," *New York Herald Tribune,* Nov. 5, 1960, folder 24, carton 22, EOL.

23. Origins of SDI: Frances Fitzgerald, *Way Out There in the Blue: Reagan, Star Wars, and the End of the Cold War* (Simon and Schuster, 2000); Herken (1992), 199–216, and "The Earthly Origins of Star Wars," *Bulletin of the Atomic Scientists,* Oct. 1987, 20–28.

24. William Broad, *Teller's War: The Top-Secret Story Behind the Star Wars Deception* (Simon and Schuster, 1992), 245–67; Teller (2001), 535–36.

25. Typed notes for "The Winter of Our Discontent," n.d., Chevalier papers.

26. Chevalier had evidently come to believe that the premise of his 1965 novel, *The Man Who Would Be God,* was what had actually happened in Oppenheimer's case: namely, that Groves used the Chevalier incident to blackmail Oppie into supporting the bombing of Hiroshima. Chevalier's unpublished memoir was tentatively titled "The Bomb." Chevalier to Jon Else, Jan. 6, 1981, Chevalier papers.

27. "Do what we may, by your unfathomable folly, you and I are linked together in a cloudy legend, which nothing, no fact, no explanation, no truth will ever unmake or unravel." Chevalier to Oppenheimer, Dec. 13, 1954, box 200, JRO.

28. The FBI had evidently stopped its physical surveillance of Chevalier by the time he returned to California for his eightieth birthday, on Sept. 10, 1981. Frank attended the party with his new wife, Millie.

29. "Steve Nelson, Ex-Communist Tied to Ruling on Sedition, Dies at 90," *New York Times,* Dec. 14, 1993; Robert Nelson and Josephine Yurck, Feb. 1, 2002, personal communication.

30. Lehman interview (1996).

31. Lomanitz interview (1996).

32. Stephen Schwartz, ed., *Atomic Audit: The Costs and Consequences of U.S. Nuclear Weapons Since 1940* (Brookings, 1998), 3.

33. Cochran et al. (1984), vol. 1, 15; Stan Norris, "Table of USSR/Russian Nuclear Warheads: 1959–70/1971–96" (Natural Resources Defense Council, 1996).

34. Molly's efforts were vigorously opposed by John Lawrence until his death in 1991. Molly Lawrence interview (1992).

35. Broad (1992), 55–56. Accounts differ on the results, which remain classified. Author interview with Robert Budwine, Livermore, Calif., June 5, 1997.

36. Interviews: Mark (1991) and Gerald Johnson (1991).

37. "Who Built the H-Bomb?: Debate Revives," *New York Times,* Apr. 24, 2001.

38. In his memoirs, Edward would argue that he and the others who had first brought the atomic bomb to Einstein's attention—Wigner and Szilard—had "a shared vision of needing the bomb to *deter* Hitler's use of such a weapon," whereas Oppenheimer had not only approved dropping the bomb on the enemy but had even lobbied for its use. Teller (2001), 376, 395–96.

39. Schweber (2000), 107–14. Bethe once made the observation that there are two things that warped Teller—being denied power and attaining it. Bethe interview (1996).

40. The declassification of Bethe's 1954 article on the Super and of Teller's reply revived their decades-old debate over the H-bomb. Bethe, "Comments on the History of the H-bomb," *Los Alamos Science,* fall 1982, 43–53; Broad, "Rewriting the History of the H-bomb, *Science,* Nov. 19, 1982, 769–72; Broad, "Hans Bethe Confronts the Legacy of His Bomb," *New York Times,* June 12, 1984.

41. "National Defense and the Scientists: An Open Letter to Hans Bethe from Edward Teller," *Policy Review,* Mar. 1987.

BIBLIOGRAPHY

Author's Interviews

Alvarez, Luis. Los Alamos, N. Mex., Apr. 14, 1983.
Arneson, Gordon. Washington, D.C., Oct. 19, 1979.
Bacher, Robert. Pasadena, Calif., Mar. 14, 1985.
———. Pasadena, Calif., Apr. 29, 1988.
Bethe, Hans. Santa Barbara, Calif., Feb. 12, 1988.
———. Pasadena, Calif., Jan. 1, 1991.
———. Ithaca, N. Y., July 16, 1996.
Bigelow, William. Berkeley, Calif., Jan. 21, 1998.
Borden, William. Washington, D.C., Nov. 30, 1981.
Bowser, Philip. San Mateo, Calif., May 21, 1997.
Bradbury, Norris. Los Alamos, N. Mex., Oct. 2, 1992.
Bradner, Hugh. La Jolla, Calif., Aug. 10, 1992.
Brown, Harold. Washington, D.C., June 28, 1996.
Budwine, Robert. Livermore, Calif., June 5, 1997.
Carothers, James. Livermore, Calif., May 11, 1988.
Chamberlain, Owen. Oakland, Calif., Aug. 4, 1993.
Chevalier, Barbara. Stinson Beach, Calif., Apr. 13, 1999.
Chew, Geoffrey. Berkeley, Calif., July 26, 1993.
Criley, Richard. Carmel, Calif., Sept. 21, 1998.
Davisson, Eleanor. Pacific Grove, Calif., Aug. 22, 1992.
Decker, Wallace. Livermore, Calif., June 11, 1997.
Douglass, William. Orinda, Calif., Dec. 17, 1992.
Durbin, Patricia. Berkeley, Calif., Aug. 11, 1994.
Fidler, Harold. Oakland, Calif., Dec. 16, 1992.
———. Berkeley, Calif., Jan. 21, 1998.
Gaither, James. San Francisco, Calif., Dec. 17, 1992.
Getting, Ivan. La Jolla, Calif., Mar. 13, 1997.

Gofman, John. San Francisco, Calif., Aug. 5, 1993.
Haussmann, Carl. Livermore, Calif., July 30, 1993.
Hayward, Admiral John "Chick." Jacksonville Beach, Fla., Mar. 6, 1996.
Higinbotham, Willie. Los Alamos, N. Mex., June 9, 1993.
Hoffman, Ann. Mill Valley, Calif., May 1, 2001.
Huddleson, Edward. San Francisco, Calif., Dec. 17, 1992.
Johnson, Gerald. La Jolla, Calif., June 10, 1988.
———. La Jolla, Calif., June 6, 1991.
Johnson, Lyall. Washington, D.C., Feb. 11, 1993.
———. Washington, D.C., Sept. 12, 1996.
Kamen, Martin. Santa Barbara, Calif., Mar. 13, 1997.
King, Robert. Eugene, Oreg., Mar. 26, 1997.
Kramish, Arnold. Livermore, Calif., Feb. 20, 1992.
Lansdale, John. Washington, D.C., Sept. 28, 1993.
———. Galesville, Md., Sept. 6, 1996.
Larson, Clarence. Washington, D.C., Nov. 5, 1992.
Latter, Albert. Los Angeles, Calif., Mar. 11, 1985.
Lawrence, Molly. Balboa, Calif., Aug. 11, 1992.
Lehmann, Lloyd. Aptos, Calif., Dec. 6, 1996.
Leith, Cecil. Livermore, Calif., June 11, 1997.
Lofgren, Edward. Berkeley, Calif., Jan. 22, 1998.
Lomanitz, Rossi. Sackett's Harbor, N. Y., July 15–16, 1996.
Manley, John. Los Alamos, N. Mex., Mar. 29, 1985.
Mansfield, J. K. Washington, D.C., Oct. 27, 1993.
Mark, Carson. Los Alamos, N. Mex., May 30, 1991.
McMillan, Elsie. Bellingham, Wash., Sept. 24, 1992.
Morrison, Phillip. Cambridge, Mass., Nov. 17, 2000.
Nelson, Eldred. Brentwood, Calif., Apr. 14, 1999.
Oppenheimer, Judith. San Jose, Calif., Apr. 30, 2001.
Panofsky, Wolfgang. Stanford, Calif., Aug. 3, 1993.
Pinsky, Paul. San Francisco, Calif., Sept. 3, 1997.
Pitzer, Kenneth. Berkeley, Calif., May 30, 1997.
Plesset, Ernie. Woodside, Calif., May 14, 1988,
Plesset, Milton. Pasadena, Calif., Mar. 15, 1988.
Plesset, Polly. Woodside, Calif., May 14, 1988.
Rabi, I. I. New Haven, Conn., Sept. 21, 1982.
———. New York, N. Y., Apr. 17, 1983.
———. New York, N. Y., Oct. 26, 1984.
Rhodes, Fred "Dusty." Washington, D.C., Nov. 2, 1998.
Rosen, Arthur. San Luis Obispo, Calif., Mar. 11, 1997.
Scheidermayer, Philip. Washington, D.C., May 8, 1998.
Seaborg, Glenn. Berkeley, Calif., Aug. 29, 1993.
Serber, Robert. New York, N. Y., Oct. 26, 1984.
———. New York, N. Y., Apr. 4, 1992.
Sewell, Duane. Livermore, Calif., July 30, 1993.
Silverman, Samuel. New York, N. Y., Nov. 14, 2000.
Smith, Gerard. Ratcliffe Manor, Md., Sept. 15, 1992.
Street, Kenneth. Alamo, Calif., Aug. 6, 1993.
Teller, Edward. Stanford, Calif., Sept. 28, 1981.
———. Los Alamos, N. Mex., July 7, 1993.
———. Livermore, Calif., July 30, 1993.
Volpe, Joseph. Washington, D.C., May 30, 1996.
York, Herbert. La Jolla, Calif., Jan. 9, 1991.

———. La Jolla, Calif., July 9, 1992.
———. La Jolla, Calif., Mar. 14, 1997.
———. Pleasanton, Calif., Jan. 10, 2000.
Wilson, Robert. Los Alamos, N. Mex., Apr. 15, 1983.
———. Ithaca, N. Y., July 16, 1996.

Manuscript Collections

Alvarez, Luis. Papers. Federal Records Center, San Bruno, Calif.
Bacher, Robert. Papers. Caltech archives, Pasadena, Calif.
Bethe, Hans. Papers. Special Collections, Cornell University archives, Ithaca, N. Y.
Bohm, David. Papers. Library, Birkbeck College, London, England.
Bush, Vannevar. Papers. Library of Congress, Washington, D.C.
———. Papers. Special Collections, MIT, Cambridge, Mass.
California, University of
Minutes, Committee on Finance and Budget Matters.
Minutes, Committee on Atomic Energy Commission Projects.
Contract 48 records. Federal Records Center, San Bruno, Calif.
Records of the Lawrence Berkeley National Laboratory. LBL archives, Berkeley, Calif.
Records of the Lawrence Livermore National Laboratory. LLNL archives, Livermore, Calif.
Records of the Los Alamos National Laboratory. LANL archives, Los Alamos, N. Mex.
Records of the Radiation Laboratory. Bancroft Library, Berkeley, Calif.
Chevalier, Haakon. Papers. Valreas, France (private collection).
Childs, Herbert. Papers. Bancroft Library, University of California, Berkeley, Calif.
Compton, Karl. Papers. Special Collections, MIT, Cambridge, Mass.
Conant, James. Papers. Pusey Library, Harvard University, Cambridge, Mass.
Crouch, Paul. Papers. Hoover Institution Library, Stanford, Calif.
Dean, Gordon. Papers. National Archives.
DuBridge, Lee. Papers. Caltech archives, Pasadena, Calif.
Fisk, James. Papers. Special Collections, MIT, Cambridge, Mass.
Jackson, Henry. Papers. Special Collections, University of Washington, Seattle, Wash.
Lattimore, Owen. Papers. Library of Congress, Washington, D.C.
Lauritsen, Charles. Papers. Caltech archives, Pasadena, Calif.
Lawrence, Ernest Orlando. Papers. Bancroft Library, University of California, Berkeley, Calif.
Lawrence, John Hundale. Papers. Lawrence Berkeley Laboratory, Berkeley, Calif.
LeBaron, Robert. Papers. Hoover Institution Library, Stanford, Calif.
Manley, John. Papers. Los Alamos National Laboratory, Los Alamos, N. Mex.
Mansfield, J. K. Papers. Washington, D.C. (private collection).
Mayer, Maria. Papers. Special Collections, University of California, San Diego (La Jolla), Calif.
McMahon, Brian. Papers. Special Collections, Georgetown University Library, Washington, D.C.
McMillan, Edwin. Papers. Federal Records Center, San Bruno, Calif.
Morrison, Phillip. Papers. Special Collections, MIT, Cambridge, Mass.
Morse, John. Papers. Hoover Institution Library, Stanford, Calif.
Murray, Thomas E. Papers. Rockville, Md. (private collection).
Neylan, John. Papers. Bancroft Library, University of California, Berkeley, Calif.
Nichols, Kenneth. Papers, Army Corps of Engineers archive, Ft. Belvoir, Va.
Oppenheimer, Frank. Papers. Bancroft Library, University of California, Berkeley, Calif.

Oppenheimer, Robert. Oral History Collection, Special Collections, MIT, Cambridge, Mass.
———. Papers. Library of Congress, Washington, D.C.
Pash, Boris. Papers. Hoover Institution Library, Stanford, Calif.
Rabi, Isidor. Papers. Library of Congress, Washington, D.C.
Shane, Donald. Papers. Lick Observatory archives, University of California, Santa Cruz, Calif.
Smyth, Henry. Papers. American Philosophical Society, Philadelphia, Penn.
Sproul, Robert. Papers. Bancroft Library, University of California, Berkeley, Calif.
Teller, Edward. Papers. Hoover Institution Library, Stanford, Calif.
———. Papers. Lawrence Livermore National Laboratory, Livermore, Calif.
———. Papers. Los Alamos National Laboratory, Los Alamos, N. Mex.
Tolman, Ruth. Papers. Caltech archives, Pasadena, Calif.
Underhill, Robert. Papers. Bancroft Library, University of California, Berkeley, Calif.
———. Papers. Los Alamos National Laboratory archives, Los Alamos, N. Mex.
U.S. Air Force
Headquarters records. RG 341. National Archives, College Park, Md.
U.S. Army
Chief of Staff files. RG 319. National Archives, College Park, Md.
General Groves files. RG 200. National Archives, College Park, Md.
Manhattan Engineer District files. RG 77. National Archives, College Park, Md.
MED investigative files. Records of the Defense Nuclear Agency. RG 374. Army Corps of Engineers archive, Ft. Belvoir, Va.
U.S. Central Intelligence Agency
RG 263, National Archives, College Park, Md.
U.S. Congress
Records of the Dies Committee. RG 233. National Archives, Washington, D.C.
Records of the Joint Congressional Committee on Atomic Energy. RG 128. National Archives, Washington, D.C.
U.S. Department of Defense
Records of the Office of the Secretary of Defense. RG 330. National Archives, College Park, Md.
U.S. Department of Energy
AEC Secretariat files.
Dean, Gordon. Papers.
Documents on nuclear testing.
Oppenheimer, J. Robert. Personnel Security Board files.
Records of the U.S. Atomic Energy Commission. RG 326. Coordination and Information Center, Las Vegas, Nev.
Records of the U.S. Atomic Energy Commission. RG 326. National Archives, College Park, Md.
Strauss, Lewis. Papers.
U.S. Federal Bureau of Investigation files
Bohm, David. No. 100–17787.
Chevalier, Haakon. No. 100–18564, secs. 1–8.
CINRAD. No. 100–190625, secs. 1–10.
COMRAP. No. 100–203581 secs. 1–93.
Eltenton, George. No. 100–214312, secs. 1–4.
FAECT. No. 61–7231, secs. 1–5.
Fuchs, Klaus. No. 65–58805, serial 1412, pt. 1.
HUAC. No. 61–7582.
Lawrence, Ernest. No. 116–10798.
Lawrence, John Hundale. No. 77–32400.

Nelson, Steve. No. 100–16847, vols. 1–6.
Oppenheimer, Frank. No. 100–237735, secs. 1–2.
Oppenheimer, Robert. No. 100–17828, secs. 1–44 and supplemental releases.
Scherer, Marcel. No. 100–34665, secs. 1–2.
Silvermaster, Nathan G. No. 65–56402, pt. 1.
Weinberg, Joseph. No. 100–190625.
U.S. Office of Scientific Research and Development
Bush-Conant file. RG 227. National Archives, College Park, Md.
Wilson, Carroll. Papers. Special Collections, MIT, Cambridge, Mass.
York, Herbert. Papers. Special Collections, University of California, San Diego (La Jolla), Calif.

Books, Articles, and Unpublished Manuscripts

Acheson, Dean. *Present at the Creation: My Years in the State Department.* Norton, 1969.
Albright, Joseph, and Marcia Kunstel. *Bombshell: The Secret Story of America's Unknown Atomic Spy Conspiracy.* Times Books, 1997.
Alvarez, Luis. "Alfred Lee Loomis." *Biographical Memoirs.* Vol. 51. National Academy of Sciences, 1980.
———. *Alvarez: Adventures of a Physicist.* Basic Books, 1987.
———. "Ernest Orlando Lawrence, 1901–1958," *Biographical Memoirs.* Vol. 41. National Academy of Sciences, 1970.
Ambrose, Stephen. *Eisenhower.* Vol. 2, *The President.* Simon and Schuster, 1984.
Anders, Roger. "The Division of Military Application." U.S. Department of Energy History Office, 1980.
———, ed. *Forging the Atomic Shield: Excerpts from the Office Diary of Gordon E. Dean.* University of North Carolina Press, 1987.
Andrew, Christopher, and Vasili Mitrokhin. *The Sword and the Shield: The Mitrokhin Archive and the Secret History of the KGB.* Basic Books, 1999.
Appleby, Charles. *Eisenhower and Arms Control, 1953–1962: A Balance of Risks.* University Microfilms, 1987.
Arneson, Gordon. "The H-Bomb Decision." *Foreign Service Journal,* May 1969.
Arneson, Gordon, and Nancy Long Arneson. *Memories of the State Department's "Mr. Atom."* Privately published, 1997.
Badash, Lawrence, et al., eds. *Reminiscences of Los Alamos, 1943–1945.* Reidel, 1985.
Barrett, Edward. *The Tenney Committee: Legislative Investigation of Subversive Activities in California.* Cornell University Press, 1951.
Benson, Robert Louis. *Venona Historical Monographs.* Nos. 1–6. National Security Agency, 1995–98.
Benson, Robert Louis, and Michael Warner, eds. *VENONA: Soviet Espionage and the American Response, 1939–1957.* Central Intelligence Agency, 1996.
Bentley, Eric, ed. *Thirty Years of Treason: Excerpts from Hearings Before the House Committee on Un-American Activities, 1938–1968.* Viking Press, 1971.
Bergeron, Victor. *Frankly Speaking: Trader Vic's Own Story.* Doubleday, 1973.
Bernstein, Barton. "Crossing the Rubicon: A Missed Opportunity to Stop the H-bomb?" *International Security,* fall 1989.
———. "Oppenheimer and the Radioactive-Poison Plan." *Technology Review,* May–June 1985.
———. "The Oppenheimer Loyalty-Security Case Reconsidered." *Stanford Law Review,* July 1990.
———. "The Struggle for the Second Laboratory, 1951–54." Unpublished manuscript, 1999.

Bernstein, Jeremy. *Hans Bethe: Prophet of Energy.* Dutton, 1981.

Birge, Raymond. "History of the Physics Department, University of California, Berkeley." Vols. 4–5. Unpublished manuscript, n.d. In collection of Bancroft Library, University of California, Berkeley.

Blumberg, Stanley, and Gwinn Owens. *Energy and Conflict: The Life and Times of Edward Teller.* Putnam, 1976.

Blumberg, Stanley, and Louis Panos. *Edward Teller: Giant of the Golden Age of Physics.* Scribners, 1990.

Boorse, Henry A., et al. *The Atomic Scientists: A Biographical History.* Wiley, 1989.

Brechin, Gray. *Imperial San Francisco: Urban Power, Earthly Ruin.* University of California Press, 1999.

Broad, William. *Teller's War: The Top-Secret Story Behind the Star Wars Deception.* Simon and Schuster, 1992.

Brown, Anthony Cave, and Charles MacDonald, eds. *The Secret History of the Atomic Bomb.* Delta Books, 1977.

Buderi, Robert. *The Invention That Changed the World.* Simon and Schuster, 1996.

California Legislature. *Third Report: Un-American Activities in California, 1947.* Sacramento, Calif., 1947.

———. *Sixth Report of the Senate Fact-Finding Committee on Un-American Activities.* Sacramento, Calif., 1951.

Caute, David. *The Great Fear: The Anti-Communist Purge Under Truman and Eisenhower.* Simon and Schuster, 1978.

Chace, James. *Acheson: The Secretary of State Who Created the American World.* Simon and Schuster, 1998.

Chang, Iris. *Thread of the Silkworm.* Basic Books, 1995.

Chevalier, Haakon. *The Man Who Would Be God.* Putnam, 1959.

———. *Oppenheimer: The Story of a Friendship.* Braziller, 1965.

Childs, Herbert. *An American Genius: The Life of Ernest Orlando Lawrence, Father of the Cyclotron.* Dutton, 1968.

Compton, Arthur. *Atomic Quest.* Oxford University Press, 1956.

Cochran, Thomas, et al. *Nuclear Weapons Databook.* Vol. 1, *U.S. Nuclear Forces and Capabilities.* Ballinger, 1984.

Davis, Nuell Pharr. *Lawrence and Oppenheimer.* Simon and Schuster, 1968.

Divine, Robert. *Blowing on the Wind: The Nuclear Test Ban Debate, 1954–1960.* Oxford University Press, 1978.

Dorwart, Jeffery. *Conflict of Duty: The U.S. Navy's Intelligence Dilemma, 1919–1945.* Naval Institute Press, 1983.

Dyson, Freeman. *Disturbing the Universe.* Harper and Row, 1979.

Elliot, David. "Project *Vista* and Nuclear Weapons in Europe." *International Security,* summer 1986.

Else, Jon. "The Day After Trinity: J. Robert Oppenheimer and the Atomic Bomb." Voyager CD-ROM, 1999.

Eltenton, Dorothea. *Laughter in Leningrad: An English Family in Russia, 1933–1938.* Privately published, 1998.

Engebretson, George. *A Man of Vision: The Story of Paul Pinsky.* Privately published, 1997.

Feklisov, Alexander. *The Man Behind the Rosenbergs.* Enigma Books, 2001.

Ferrell, Robert, ed. *The Eisenhower Diaries.* Norton, 1981.

Fitzpatrick, Anne. *Igniting the Light Elements: The Los Alamos Thermonuclear Weapons Project, 1942–1952.* University Microfilms, 1998.

Foster, Jane. *An UnAmerican Lady.* Sidgwick and Jackson, 1980.

Fowler, Dan. "What the Loyalty Oath Did to the University of California." *Look,* Jan. 29, 1952.

Francis, Sybil. *Warhead Politics: Livermore and the Competitive System of Nuclear Weapons Design.* University Microfilms, 1996.

Friedan, Betty. *Life So Far.* Simon and Schuster, 2000.

Galison, Peter. *Image and Logic: A Material Culture of Microphysics.* University of Chicago Press, 1997.

Galison, Peter, and Barton Bernstein, "In Any Light: Scientists and the Decision to Build the Superbomb, 1942–1954." *Historical Studies in the Physical and Biological Sciences* 19, no. 2, (1989).

Garber, Marjorie, and Rebecca Walkowitz, eds., *Secret Agents: The Rosenberg Case, McCarthyism, and Fifties America.* Routledge, 1995.

Gilpin, Robert. *American Scientists and Nuclear Weapons Policy.* Princeton University Press, 1962.

Getting, Ivan. *All in a Lifetime: Science in the Defense of Democracy.* Vantage Press, 1989.

Gleick, James. *Genius: The Life and Science of Richard Feynman.* Pantheon, 1992.

Goldberg, Stanley. "Groves and Oppenheimer: The Story of a Partnership." *Antioch Review,* fall 1995.

———. "Inventing a Climate of Opinion: Vannevar Bush and the Decision to Build the Bomb." *ISIS,* 1992.

Goncharov, German. "Thermonuclear Milestones," *Physics Today* 49, no. 11 (1996).

Goodchild, Peter. *J. Robert Oppenheimer: Shatterer of Worlds.* BBC, 1980.

Goodman, Walter. *The Committee: The Extraordinary Career of the House Committee on Un-American Activities.* Farrar, Straus and Giroux, 1968.

Gorin, Peter. "Intelligence Services of the USSR and Russia: Selected Historical Aspects." Unpublished manuscript, 1999.

Groves, Leslie. *Now It Can Be Told: The Story of the Manhattan Project.* Harper, 1962.

Hansen, Chuck. *The Swords of Armageddon: U.S. Nuclear Weapons Development Since 1945.* CD-ROM, Chukelea Publications, 1995.

———. *U.S. Nuclear Weapons: The Secret History.* Orion Books, 1988.

Harris, Ruth, and Richard Hewlett. "The Lawrence Livermore National Laboratory: The Evolution of Its Mission, 1952–1988." History Associates 1990.

Hawkins, David. *Project Y: The Los Alamos Story.* Vol. 1, *Toward Trinity.* Tomash, 1983.

Haynes, John Earl, and Harvey Klehr. *Venona: Decoding Soviet Espionage in America.* Yale University Press, 1999.

Heilbron, J. L., and Robert Seidel. *Lawrence and His Laboratory: A History of the Lawrence Berkeley Laboratory.* University of California Press, 1989.

Heilbron, J. L., Robert Seidel, and Bruce R. Wheaton. "Lawrence and His Laboratory: Nuclear Science at Berkeley." Lawrence Berkeley Laboratory, 1981.

Herken, Gregg. *Cardinal Choices: Presidential Science Advising from the Atomic Bomb to SDI.* Oxford University Press, 1992.

———. *Counsels of War.* Knopf, 1985.

———. *The Winning Weapon: The Atomic Bomb in the Cold War.* Knopf, 1980.

Hershberg, James. *James B. Conant: Harvard to Hiroshima and the Making of the Nuclear Age.* Knopf, 1993.

Hevly, Bruce, and John Findlay, eds. *The Atomic West.* University of Washington Press, 1998.

Hewlett, Richard, and Oscar Anderson, Jr. *The New World: A History of the United States Atomic Energy Commission.* Vol. 1, *1939–1946.* University of California Press, 1990.

Hewlett, Richard, and Francis Duncan. *Atomic Shield: A History of the United States Atomic Energy Commission.* Vol. 2, *1947–1952.* University of California Press, 1990.

Hewlett, Richard, and Jack Holl. *Atoms for Peace and War, 1953–1961: Eisenhower and the Atomic Energy Commission.* University of California Press, 1989.

Hoddeson, Lillian, et al. *Critical Assembly: A Technical History of Los Alamos During the Oppenheimer Years, 1943–1945*. Cambridge University Press, 1993.

Holloway, David. *Stalin and the Bomb: The Soviet Union and Atomic Energy, 1939–1956*. Yale University Press, 1994.

Jacobson, Harold Karan, and Eric Stein. *Diplomats, Scientists, and Politicians: The United States and the Nuclear Test Ban Negotiations*. University of Michigan Press, 1966.

Jeffery, Inez Cope. *Inside Russia: The Life and Times of Zoya Zarubina*. Eakin Press, 1999.

Jenkins, Edith. *Against a Field Sinister: Memoirs and Stories*. City Lights Books, 1991.

Jones, Vincent. *U.S. Army in World War II, Special Studies, Manhattan: The Army and the Atomic Bomb*. U.S. Government Printing Office, 1985.

Jordan, George R. *From Major Jordan's Diaries*. Harcourt, Brace, 1952.

Kamen, Martin. *Radiant Science, Dark Politics: A Memoir of the Nuclear Age*. University of California Press, 1986.

Kaplan, Fred. *The Wizards of Armageddon*. Touchstone, 1983.

Kempton, Murray. "The Ambivalence of J. Robert Oppenheimer." *Esquire*, Dec. 1983.

Kevles, Daniel. "Cold War and Hot Physics: Science, Security, and the American State, 1945–1956." *Historical Studies in the Physical and Biological Sciences* 20, no. 2 (1990).

———. *The Physicists: The History of a Scientific Community in Modern America*. Vintage, 1979.

Khariton, Yuli, and Yuri Smirnov. "The Khariton Version." *Bulletin of the Atomic Scientists*, May 1993.

Khrushchev, Sergei. *Nikita Khrushchev and the Creation of a Superpower*. Pennsylvania State University Press, 2000.

Killian, James. *Sputnik, Scientists, and Eisenhower: A Memoir of the First Special Assistant to the President for Science and Technology*. MIT Press, 1977.

Klehr, Harvey, John Earl Haynes, and Fridrikh I. Firsov. *The Secret World of American Communism*. Yale University Press, 1995.

Kramish, Arnold. "The Thermonuclear Paradigm: Remaining Puzzles." Unpublished manuscript, 1999.

Kunetka, James. *Oppenheimer: The Years of Risk*. Prentice-Hall, 1969.

Kuznick, Peter. *Beyond the Laboratory: Scientists as Political Activists in 1930s America*. University of Chicago Press, 1987.

Lamphere, Robert, and Tom Shachtman, *The FBI-KGB War: A Special Agent's Story*. Berkley Books, 1987.

Lang, Daniel. "Seven Men on a Problem." *New Yorker*, Aug. 17, 1946.

Lanouette, William. *Genius in the Shadows: A Biography of Leo Szilard, the Man Behind the Bomb*. Scribners, 1992.

Lansdale, John. "John Lansdale, Jr.—Military Service." Unpublished manuscript, n.d.

Lilienthal, David. *The Journals of David E. Lilienthal*. Vol. 2, *The Atomic Energy Years, 1945–1950*. Harper and Row, 1964.

———. *The Journals of David E. Lilienthal*. Vol. 4, *The Road to Change, 1955–1959*. Harper and Row, 1969.

———. *The Journals of David E. Lilienthal*. Vol. 5, *The Harvest Years, 1959–1963*. Harper and Row, 1971.

Mackenzie, Donald. *Inventing Accuracy: A Historical Sociology of Nuclear Missile Guidance*. MIT Press, 1993.

Mackenzie, Donald, and Graham Spinardi. "The Shaping of Nuclear Weapon System Technology: U.S. Fleet Ballistic Missile Guidance and Navigation: I: From Polaris to Poseidon." *Social Studies of Science* 18 (1988).

Macrae, Norman. *John von Neumann: The Scientific Genius Who Pioneered the Modern Computer, Game Theory, Nuclear Deterrence, and Much More*. Pantheon, 1992.

Magraw, Katherine. "Teller and the 'Clean Bomb' Episode." *Bulletin of the Atomic Scientists,* May 1988.

Mark, Carson. "A Short Account of Los Alamos Theoretical Work on Thermonuclear Weapons, 1946–1950." Los Alamos National Laboratory, 1974.

Mark, Hans, and Lowell Wood. *Energy in Physics, War and Peace: A Festschrift Celebrating Edward Teller's 80th Birthday.* Kluwer Academic Publishers, 1988.

McCullough, David. *Truman.* Simon and Schuster, 1992.

Michelmore, Peter. *The Swift Years: The Robert Oppenheimer Story.* Dodd, Mead, 1969.

Millis, Walter, ed. *The Forrestal Diaries.* Putnam, 1952.

Moynihan, Daniel Patrick. *Secrecy.* Yale University Press, 1998.

Murray, Thomas E. *Nuclear Policy for War and Peace.* World Publishing, 1960.

Needell, Allan. *Science, Cold War, and the American State: Lloyd V. Berkner and the Balance of Professional Ideals.* Harwood Academic Publishers, 2000.

Nelson, Steve, James Barrett, and Rob Ruck. *Steve Nelson: American Radical.* University of Pittsburgh Press, 1969.

Nichols, K. D. *The Road to Trinity: A Personal Account of How America's Nuclear Policies Were Made.* Morrow, 1987.

O'Neill, Dan. *The Firecracker Boys.* St. Martin's Press, 1994.

Pais, Abraham. *A Tale of Two Continents: A Physicist's Life in a Turbulent World.* Princeton University Press, 1997.

Peat, F. David. *Infinite Potential: The Life and Times of David Bohm.* Addison-Wesley, 1997.

Pfau, Richard. *No Sacrifice Too Great: The Life of Lewis L. Strauss.* University of Virginia Press, 1984.

Powers, Thomas. *Heisenberg's War: The Secret History of the German Bomb.* Knopf, 1993.

Rhodes, Richard. *Dark Sun: The Making of the Hydrogen Bomb.* Simon and Schuster, 1995.

———. *The Making of the Atomic Bomb.* Simon and Schuster, 1986.

Rich, Willard. *Brain Waves and Death.* Scribner, 1940.

Romerstein, Herbert, and Eric Breindel. *The Venona Secrets: Exposing Soviet Espionage and America's Traitors.* Regnery, 2000.

Rosenberg, David Alan. "U.S. Nuclear Stockpile, 1945 to 1950." *Bulletin of the Atomic Scientists,* May 1982.

Royal, Denise. *The Story of J. Robert Oppenheimer.* St. Martin's, 1969.

Schecter, Jerrold L., and Leona P. Schecter. *Sacred Secrets: How Soviet Intelligence Operations Changed American History.* Brassey's, 2002.

Schiedermayer, Phil. "Recollections, Reminiscences, Reflections." Lawrence Livermore Radiation Laboratory, 1996.

Schrecker, Ellen. *Many Are the Crimes: McCarthyism in America.* Little, Brown, 1998.

———. *No Ivory Tower: McCarthyism and the Universities.* Oxford University Press, 1986.

Schwartz, Stephen. *From West to East: California and the Making of the American Mind.* Free Press, 1998.

Schweber, S. S. *In the Shadow of the Bomb: Oppenheimer, Bethe, and the Moral Responsibility of the Scientist.* Princeton University Press, 2000.

———. "J. Robert Oppenheimer: Proteus Unbound." Unpublished manuscript, 2001.

Scobie, Ingrid. *Jack B. Tenney: Molder of Anti-Communist Legislation in California, 1940–49.* University Microfilms, 1970.

Seaborg, Glenn. *Journals.* Vols. 1–4, *April 19, 1942–May 19, 1946.* Lawrence Berkeley Laboratory, 1992.

———. *Kennedy, Khrushchev, and the Test Ban.* University of California Press, 1981.

Segrè, Emilio. *A Mind Always in Motion.* University of California Press, 1993.

Seidel, Robert. "Accelerating Science: The Postwar Transformation of the Lawrence Berkeley Laboratory." *Historical Studies in the Physical and Biological Sciences* 14, no. 2 (1983).

———. "Accelerators and National Security: The Evolution of Science Policy for High-Energy Physics, 1947–1967." *History and Technology* 2 (1994).

———. "The DOE Weapons Laboratories." Los Alamos National Laboratory, 1992.

———. "The Origins of the Lawrence Berkeley Laboratory." In Peter Galison and Bruce Hevly, eds., *Big Science: The Growth of Large-Scale Research.* Stanford University Press, 1992.

Serber, Robert. *The Los Alamos Primer: The First Lectures on How to Build an Atomic Bomb.* University of California Press, 1992.

———. *Peace and War: Reminiscences of a Life on the Frontiers of Science.* University of California Press, 1998.

Sherwin, Martin. *A World Destroyed: The Atomic Bomb and the Grand Alliance.* Knopf, 1975.

Smith, Alice Kimball. *A Peril and a Hope: The Scientists' Movement in America, 1945–47.* MIT Press, 1971.

Smith, Alice Kimball, and Charles Weiner, eds. *Robert Oppenheimer: Letters and Recollections.* Harvard University Press, 1980.

Smyth, Henry DeWolf. *Atomic Energy for Military Purposes: The Official Report on the Development of the Atomic Bomb Under the Auspices of the United States Government, 1940–1945.* Stanford University Press, 1989.

Stern, Phillip. *The Oppenheimer Case: Security on Trial.* Harper and Row, 1969.

Stewart, George. *The Year of the Oath: The Fight for Academic Freedom at the University of California.* Da Capo, 1971.

Strauss, Lewis. *Men and Decisions.* Doubleday, 1962.

Strickland, Donald. *Scientists in Politics: The Atomic Scientists Movement, 1945–46.* Purdue University Press, 1968.

Strong, Tracy, and Helene Keyssar. *Right in Her Soul: The Life of Anna Louise Strong.* Random House, 1983.

Sudoplatov, Pavel, et al. *Special Tasks: The Memoirs of an Unwanted Witness—a Soviet Spymaster.* Little, Brown, 1994.

Tanenhaus, Sam. *Whittaker Chambers.* Random House, 1997.

Taubman, William, Sergei Khrushchev, and Abbott Gleason, eds. *Nikita Khrushchev.* Yale University Press, 2000.

Teller, Edward. *Better a Shield than a Sword: Perspectives on Defense and Technology.* Free Press, 1987.

———. *Energy from Heaven and Earth.* Freeman, 1979.

Teller, Edward, and Allen Brown. *The Legacy of Hiroshima.* Doubleday, 1962.

Teller, Edward, and Albert Latter. *Our Nuclear Future: Facts, Dangers, and Opportunities.* Criterion Books, 1958.

Teller, Edward, with Judith Shoolery. *Memoirs: A Twentieth-Century Journey in Science and Politics.* Perseus Press, 2001.

Truslow, Edith, and Ralph Carlisle Smith. *Project Y: The Los Alamos Story.* Vol. 2, *Beyond Trinity.* Tomash, 1983.

Ulam, S. M. *Adventures of a Mathematician.* University of California Press, 1991.

U.S. Air Force Historical Division. *A History of the Air Force Atomic Energy Program, 1943–1953.* Vol. 4, *The Development of Weapons.* U.S. Air Force History Office, n.d.

U.S. Atomic Energy Commission. *In the Matter of J. Robert Oppenheimer.* MIT Press, 1971.

U.S. Congress. House Un-American Activities Committee. *Hearings Regarding Clarence Hiskey Including Testimony of Paul Crouch.* 81st Congress, 2nd Sess., May 24, 1949.

———. House Un-American Activities Committee. *Hearings Regarding Communist*

Infiltration of Radiation Laboratory and Atomic Bomb Project at the University of California, Berkeley, Calif. Vols. 1–3. 81st Congress, 2nd sess., April–June 1949.

———. House Un-American Activities Committee. *Hearings Regarding Steve Nelson.* 81st Congress, 2nd sess., June 8, 1949.

———. House Un-American Activities Committee. *Hearings Regarding the Communist Infiltration of the Motion Picture Industry.* 80th Congress, 1st sess., October 1947.

———. House Un-American Activities Committee. *Report on Atomic Espionage (Nelson-Weinberg and Hiskey-Adams Cases).* 81st Congress, 2nd session, Sept. 29, 1949.

———. House Un-American Activities Committee. *Report on Soviet Espionage Activities in Connection with the Atom Bomb.* 80th Congress, 2nd session, Sept. 28, 1948.

———. House Un-American Activities Committee. *The Shameful Years: Thirty Years of Soviet Espionage in the United States.* U.S. Government Printing Office, 1952.

———. House Un-American Activities Committee. *Testimony of James Sterling Murray and Edward Tiers Manning.* 81st Congress, 1st sess., Aug. 14 and Oct. 5, 1949.

———. Joint Committee on Atomic Energy, 81st Congress, 1st sess., June 6, 1949. *Investigation into the United States Atomic Energy Project.* Pts. 4, 7, and 23. U.S. Government Printing Office, 1949.

———. Senate Committee on the Judiciary, 83rd Congress, 1st sess., October–December 1953. *Interlocking Subversion in Government Departments.* U.S. Government Printing Office, 1953.

———. Senate Select Committee on Intelligence. *Electronic Surveillance Within the United States for Foreign Intelligence Purposes.* 94th Congress, 2nd sess., June–August 1976.

U.S. Department of State. *Foreign Relations of the United States.* Vol. 1, *1949–1950.* U.S. Government Printing Office, 1976–77.

———. *Foreign Relations of the United States.* Vol. 2, pt. 2, *1952–1954.* U.S. Government Printing Office, 1984.

———. *Foreign Relations of the United States.* Vol. 20, *1955–1957.* U.S. Government Printing Office, 1990.

———. *Foreign Relations of the United States.* Vol. 3, *1958–1960.* U.S. Government Printing Office, 1996.

Voss, Earl. *Nuclear Ambush: The Test-Ban Trap.* Regnery, 1963.

Weart, Spencer, and Gertrude W. Szilard, eds. *Leo Szilard: His Version of the Facts.* Vol. 2. MIT Press, 1978.

Weinstein, Allen. *Perjury: The Hiss-Chambers Case.* Random House, 1997.

Weinstein, Allen, and Alexander Vassiliev. *The Haunted Wood: Soviet Espionage in America—the Stalin Era.* Random House, 1999.

Weisgall, Jonathan. *Operation Crossroads: The Atomic Tests at Bikini Atoll.* Naval Institute Press, 1994.

West, Nigel. *Venona: The Greatest Secret of the Cold War.* HarperCollins, 1999.

West, Nigel, and Oleg Tsarev. *The Crown Jewels: The British Secrets at the Heart of the KGB Archives.* HarperCollins, 1998.

Wheeler, John A., and Kenneth Ford. *Geons, Black Holes, and Quantum Foam: A Life in Physics.* Norton, 1998.

Williams, Robert. *Klaus Fuchs: Atom Spy.* Harvard University Press, 1987.

Williams, Robert, and Philip Cantelon, eds. *The American Atom: A Documentary History of Nuclear Policies from the Discovery of Fission to the Present, 1939–1984.* University of Pennsylvania Press, 1984.

Wyden, Peter. *Day One: Before Hiroshima and After.* Simon and Schuster, 1984.

York, Herbert. *The Advisors: Oppenheimer, Teller, and the Superbomb.* Freeman, 1976.

———. *Making Weapons, Talking Peace: A Physicist's Odyssey from Hiroshima to Geneva.* Basic Books, 1987.

———. "The Origins of the Lawrence Livermore Laboratory." Unpublished manuscript, 1975.

Zachary, G. Pascal. *Endless Frontier: Vannevar Bush, Engineer of the American Century.* Free Press, 1997.

Zaloga, Steven. *The Kremlin's Nuclear Sword: The Rise and Fall of Russia's Strategic Nuclear Forces, 1945–2000.* Smithsonian Institution Press, 2001.

Ziegler, Charles, and David Jacobson. "Intelligence Assessments of Soviet Atomic Capability, 1945–1949: Myths, Monopolies, and *Maskirovka.*" *Intelligence and National Security* 12, no. 4 (1997).

———. *Spying Without Spies: Origins of America's Secret Nuclear Surveillance System.* Praeger, 1995.

———. "Waiting for Joe-1: Decisions Leading to the Detection of Russia's First Atomic Bomb Test." *Social Studies of Science* 18 (1988).

ACKNOWLEDGMENTS

THERE IS A decade's worth of gratitude behind the researching and writing of this book. First to acknowledge is the contribution of a Smithsonian colleague, Jim David, who was an early and sustained collaborator on the project. Jim possesses a unique skill as a researcher—combining the mind of a lawyer with the tenacity of a bulldog.

My thanks also go to all who agreed to be interviewed for the book, as well as those who read portions or all of the manuscript—particularly Lyall Johnson, Joe Albright, Eldred Nelson, Stan Norris, Joe Volpe, Richard Rhodes, Herb York, Tom Powers, Robert Seidel, and Spencer Weart. Though they caught errors of omission and commission, those that remain are my own.

Archivist Bill Roberts was of great help at the Bancroft; Martha Demarre at DOE's archive in Las Vegas is a national treasure; Marcia Daniel was a "FOIA angel" at the FBI and deserves all the awards the bureau can possibly give her. Phil Schiedermayer was helpful in opening doors to other former FBI agents; Lou Benson of the National Security Agency helped in the interpretation of *Venona;* Jennifer Decapua hunted down Joint Committee records. Steve Wofford, Jim Carothers, and Beverly Bull, at Livermore, were of more assistance than I was able to appreciate at the time; as was Roger Meade at Los Alamos.

Joe Albright and Marcia Kunstel shared with the author documents that they brought out of the former Soviet Union and that are reprinted, in part, in the text. Bart Bernstein, John Haynes, Harvey Klehr, Chuck Hansen, Stan Norris, Kai Bird, and Priscilla McMillan were likewise generous in sharing the insights and documents that they discovered in their own, related research. Peter and Judy Oppenheimer were kind enough to provide photographs and papers from their respective fathers, Robert and Frank. Jack Crawford made available the private papers of AEC Commissioner Thomas Murray. Karen Chevalier not only gave the author permission to quote from her father's papers in Valreas, France, but also hosted my wife and me during a marvelous week-and-a-half stay in Provence. Many thanks to Marilyn de Silva for a copy of her husband's uncompleted manscript on Oppenheimer.

Smithsonian secretary Bob Adams and several directors of the National Air and Space Museum—Martin Harwit, Bob Hoffman, Donald Engen, and Jack Dailey—deserve thanks for allowing me the time to complete the book. The faculty of the history and politics departments at my undergraduate alma mater, the University of California, Santa Cruz, provided fellowship and a place to work during a sabbatical in 1996–97. My thanks to the MacArthur Foundation for a research and writing grant in 1992.

Dan Guttman and the staff of the President's Advisory Committee on Human Radiation Experiments, my colleagues during 1994–95, not only tolerated my peculiar interest in Lawrence but are responsible for a most intellectually exciting time.

To all those unnamed friends who provided logistical and emotional support over the past decade, an inscribed copy of the book is promised. You have my gratitude now.

Molly Lawrence, who played an early and important part in my research, got to welcome in the new century, as she had hoped. With luck, her other wish will also come to pass.

Finally, I'd like to acknowledge an intellectual debt to a late friend, colleague, and inspiration to all those who have labored in this particular vineyard—Stanley Goldberg. Stan, we still miss you every day.

INDEX

ABOUT THE AUTHOR

GREGG HERKEN is a senior historian and curator at the Smithsonian Institution's National Air and Space Museum and previously taught at Oberlin College, Yale University, and Caltech. He is the author of *The Winning Weapon*, *Counsels of War*, and *Cardinal Choices*. Herken received a MacArthur research and writing grant for *Brotherhood of the Bomb* and in 1984–85 was detailed as a senior research and policy analyst to the President's Advisory Committee on Human Radiation Experiments, as a result of some of the discoveries he made researching this book. He and his family live in Alexandria, Virginia.